S0-AWV-917

THE DICTATOR'S SEDUCTION

AMERICAN ENCOUNTERS/GLOBAL INTERACTIONS

A series edited by Gilbert M. Joseph and Emily S. Rosenberg

This series aims to stimulate critical perspectives and fresh interpretive frameworks for scholarship on the history of the imposing global presence of the United States. Its primary concerns include the deployment and contestation of power, the construction and deconstruction of cultural and political borders, the fluid meanings of intercultural encounters, and the complex interplay between the global and the local. American Encounters seeks to strengthen dialogue and collaboration between historians of U.S. international relations and area studies specialists.

The series encourages scholarship based on multiarchival historical research. At the same time, it supports a recognition of the representational character of all stories about the past and promotes critical inquiry into issues of subjectivity and narrative. In the process, American Encounters strives to understand the context in which meanings related to nations, cultures, and political economy are continually produced, challenged, and reshaped.

THE DICTATOR'S SEDUCTION

*Politics and the Popular Imagination
in the Era of Trujillo*

LAUREN DERBY

Duke University Press
Durham and London
2009

© 2009 Duke University Press

All rights reserved

Printed in the United States of America on acid-free paper ∞

Designed by Heather Hensley

Typeset in Warnock Pro by Keystone Typesetting, Inc.

Library of Congress Cataloging-in-Publication data and republication acknowledgments appear on the last printed pages of this book.

Duke University Press gratefully acknowledges the generous contribution to this book provided by the Department of History, the Latin American Institute, and the Division of Social Sciences at the University of California, Los Angeles.

FOR

L.H.D.
and
R.A.D.

CONTENTS

PREFACE

This study presents a cultural history of the Trujillo regime as seen through the microcosm of Santo Domingo, since this was the official stage for national civic life. Furthermore, public life in the provinces was largely modeled after policies first created for Ciudad Trujillo. The focus on how the regime was experienced has created a different event history or emplotment than that composed by some scholars. The exile invasions and the infamous Mirabal sister assassination—the key crises—are overlooked in favor of incidents people remember as central—the hurricane of San Zenón, the 1955 World's Fair, and denunciation as a political practice and form of terror. Although the violence of the regime has inspired accounts of heroes and villains, this study enters a more murky quotidian terrain where most people lived in a space of ambivalence and complicity, of passive action in the subjunctive mood—what Blanchot has called "equivocal dissimulation."[1] Indeed, when one listens to how individuals narrate the regime, they do so embedded within their respective social "fields of force," to use E. P. Thompson's image—in terms of fellow family, neighbors, and friends—not the regime as an abstraction. Social webs of affinity knitted them to people on either side of the Trujillista divide—those who needed jobs to feed large families, for example, and whose political affinities were more pragmatic than ideological.

The story commences with the prelude to the Trujillo period, the period of U.S. military government of 1916–24. Chapter 1 explores the mass culture of consumption introduced during the 1920s, which threatened traditional modes of distinction and elicited fears of the democratization of social class. I demonstrate how the perceived challenge to national sovereignty and aristocratic identity was countered with a resurgence of cultural nationalism in the form of hispanicism and Catholicism, and fomented the crisis of liberalism which helped set the stage for Trujillo's assumption of power; it also considers how the crisis of liberalism was also a crisis of Dominican manhood.

Chapter 2 treats the hurricane of San Zenón, which in 1930 razed the physical and social space of the capital city of Santo Domingo, rendering social distinctions illegible, and giving Trujillo the perfect opportunity to take control. I explore how the discourse of social disorder came to focus on the itinerant shanty dwelling, and how elites gave Trujillo free reign to eliminate this scourge, a move which entailed a far wider infringement on civil liberties than they had originally intended. In the aftermath, housing policy became a key element of state patronage during the regime. Trujillo's populist agenda championed state efforts to make Dominican peasants into citizens through the creation of new forms of urban space and civic ritual.

In chapter 3, through an exploration of the largest festival of the Trujillo era—the Free World's Fair of Peace and Confraternity in 1955—I examine the hidden class, race, and gendered meanings smuggled into state ritual. I consider how gender operated within official iconography and how the spectacle of women was used to augment the masculinity and aura of the presidential persona of Trujillo as he displayed his daughters and lovers in official rites. Chapter 4 explores official oratory, in particular denunciation and panegyric, and how the political economy of discursive exchange shaped politics within the inner circle. It considers how the officialization of denunciation as a political practice was a form of domination and populism since it deployed a popular practice—gossip—in the political arena.

The following chapters analyze various aspects of state fetishism under the regime. Chapter 5 examines Trujillo's approximation of the popular barrio antihero, the *tíguere* (literally tiger)—an underdog figure with deep roots in Dominican popular culture that embodies a form of upward mobility via the audacious conquest of women of higher status—and how Trujillo and his onetime son-in-law Porfirio Rubirosa came to represent a fantasy of upward mobility with much appeal to many Dominicans. Chapter 6 considers the intersection of the religious and the political in popular narratives of Trujillo's extraordinary power, his *mana*. There is much lore in the Dominican Republic that Trujillo used the services of several *curanderas* or healers for divination and protection.[2] This chapter treats a lesser-known story that he had a personal *muchachito* or guardian angel, which provided him with occult power and thus gave him a kind of omniscience that protected him from his enemies. Chapter 7 examines a popular healing cult, Olivorismo, which emerged in full force in the southwest region of San Juan de la Maguana after Trujillo's death; I argue that this cult represented the complex yet contradictory impact of the Trujillato in popular culture since it reflected and refracted the dense ritualization of public life that was a hallmark of that period, yet simultaneously sought to purge the nation of many attributes of corruption and modernity associated with the dictatorship.

Oral history was an important source for this project, and I collected more than sixty hours of interviews on a range of subjects to get a sense of how policy making, planning, and implementation operated under the regime, as well as how people experienced and understood everyday life over the course of 1992 and early 1993. These interviews were enriched by previous fieldwork funded by a collaborative IIE Fulbright Grant with Richard Turits on the 1937 Haitian massacre, which had initially piqued my interest in the hegemony of the regime, yet most of those testimonies were collected in the frontier provinces. I interviewed architects and engineers who worked for the regime such as Margot Taulé, Jose Ramón Baez López-Peña, and Ramón Vargas Mera, and contemporary architects such as William Reid Cabral, Amparo Chantada, Gustavo Moré, and Erwin Cott. I also spoke with individuals who received houses from the state in the popular barrios built by the Trujillo regime, including Ensanche Luperón, Ensanche Espaillat, María Auxiliadora, and Mejoramiento Social. In addition, I sought out life histories from people in other neighborhoods across the class spectrum—from the Zona Colonial and Gazcue to San Carlos, Villa Duarte, Capotillo, and La Cienaga in Santo Domingo, as well as in San Cristóbal since this was Trujillo's birthplace and residence. I also looked for those who could speak to how politics operated within the civil service, including Arístides Incháustegui, Francisco Elpidio Beras and his family, Julián Pérez, Virgilio Díaz Ordóñez, José Antinoe Fiallo, Max Uribe, Antonio Zaglul, and Jesús Torres Tejeda.

My quest to understand Dominican religiosity launched me into another set of networks and social spaces altogether. For these issues, I interviewed priests such as Santiago Erujo, Fathers Vargas of Bayaguana, Antonio Camilo, and José Luis Saez, as well as scholars of popular religosity such as Fradique Lizardo, Dagoberto Tejeda, June Rosenberg, and Martha Ellen Davis. I visited healers in Santo Domingo and Baní, and followed four in Villa Duarte, Capotillo, La Cienaga, and La Feria. I also attended major national patron saint festivities for the Virgin of Altagracia at Higüey and the Virgin of Las Mercedes at La Vega, as well as regional events hosted by the *hermandad* for the miraculous Christ of Bayaguana and the Cofradía del Espíritu Santo in San Juan de la Maguana and Las Matas de Farfán; ceremonies for Dios Olivorio Mateo at Maguana Arriba and Media Luna at the home of Don León Ventura Rodríguez with Lusitania Martínez; several celebrations for the *misterios* in Villa Mella with Martha Ellen Davis; and a feast for Gran Bwa in the *bateyes* of La Romana with Carlos Andújar. I collected some fifteen hours of interviews at these pilgrimages but talking was only part of the experience; these visits also involved staying up all night, and a lot of walking, watching, standing, drinking, feasting, sleeping in cars, and finally sipping very hot and sweet thumb-sized cupfuls of fragrant ginger tea at dawn. Most of the interviewing was done with Julio César Santana, and the popular religious visits were accompanied by Julio and Andrew Apter.

ACKNOWLEDGMENTS

This book commenced as a dissertation at the University of Chicago ably guided and inspired by John Coatsworth, Friedrich Katz, Bernard Cohen, and Michael Geyer. The research and writing was supported by the Fulbright-Hays program, the Social Science Research Council, the American Council of Learned Societies, and the Charlotte W. Newcombe Foundation; many thanks for their generous support. During my fieldwork in the Dominican Republic, I benefited from the guidance of many individuals who gave amply of their time to orient me and to assist me in securing research materials in an environment in which that is no easy task. Eddy Jaquez of the National Archives of Santo Domingo was tireless and dedicated, locating materials that otherwise I would not have known about. I am grateful to the National Archives directorship for giving me carte blanche to explore controversial and sensitive topics in Dominican history. Very special thanks go to Julio César Santana, whom I met while working at COPADEBA/Ciudad Alternativa, where he helped shantytown dwellers fight for land rights. Julio was an extraordinary research assistant. I owe more than I can express for his assistance, his penetrating insights, and most of all his contagious love of Dominican popular culture. Raymundo González has been a brilliant colleague and dear friend, whose knowledge of many topics touched upon here, from Catholic saints to political thought, deepened my understanding of Dominican history. I am grateful to the many people who took time to talk about life under the Trujillato and helped me locate contacts to interview. The community of Dominican scholars has always been extremely helpful and welcoming, especially Lipe Collado, Mu-Kien Sang, Bernardo Vega, Frank Moya Pons, Emilio Cordero Michel, José Antinoe Fiallo, Roberto Cassá, Ruben Silié, Arístedes Incháustegui, and the late Ciprián Soler. Thanks to the many people who have always made me feel that I have a second home in Santo Domingo, including César Zapata and Geo Ripley. I am especially grateful to Martha Ellen Davis, who has been an extraordinarily generous mentor on matters of popular religiosity and who provided crucial support.

René Fortunato and the always hospitable Francisco Beras and his family gave generously of their time, friendship, and advice. Lusitania Martínez shared her deep knowledge and contacts in the many worlds of Dominican popular religiosity in Santo Domingo and San Juan de la Maguana, as did Carlos Andújar and the late June Rosenberg. I am also grateful to Olivorista friends in Las Matas de Farfán and San Juan de la Maguana, especially the Liborista leaders Ezequiel Lorenzo and Don León, as well as María de Olios, who warmly welcomed me and my research colleagues Julio Santana and Andrew Apter on several occasions. Neici Zeller, Jochy Herrera, and Dennis Hidalgo have been dear friends and interlocutors. Thanks go to Gustavo Moré and Ramón Vargas Mera, who spoke to me at length and provided me with many leads on the history of Santo Domingo. I feel extremely lucky to have enjoyed the *compañerismo*, support, and insights of fellow *dominicanistas* Steven Gregory, Catherine LeGrand, Eric Roorda, Julie Franks, Michiel Baud, Bruce Calder, Rosario Espinal, Fernando Valerio-Holguín, Emelio Betances, Pedro San Miguel, Ginetta Candelario, Ramonina Brea, Barbara Deutsch Lynch, Patricia Pessar, and Richard Turits. Thanks to Renée Hartman for providing some important research materials.

Peter Evans and Tom Fiehrer are responsible early on for generating my interest in the Caribbean and in the state and issues of development. The stimulating environment of the University of Chicago nurtured this project; I am grateful to Ralph Austen, Raymond Smith, John MacAloon, Tom Holt, David Laitin, Michel-Rolph Trouillot, Claudio Lomnitz, Tamar Herzog, Bill Sewell, Danilyn Rutherford, Lisa Wedeen, Jennifer Cole, Kate Bjork, Laura Gotkowitz, Katherine Bliss, Judy Boruchoff, Paul Liffman, Frank Romagosa, Carmen Ramos, Lisa Peréz, Micheal Werner, Deborah Cohen, Peter Guardino, Cristóbal Aljovín, and Michelle Molina for providing thoughtful feedback. The University of California, Los Angeles has provided a unique combination of intellectual rigor and warmth. Special thanks to the Department of History for time and resources that allowed me to complete this project; to Teo Ruiz, Kevin Terraciano, Robert Hill, Don Cosentino, Jessica Wang, Michael Salman, Ellen Dubois, Mark Sawyer, Steve and Amy Aron, Ruth Bloch, José Moya, and an extraordinary group of graduate students for their encouragement and insightful engagement; and to David Sartorius, Micol Siegel, Raul Fernández, and the Latin American Reading Group for being supportive and stimulating intellectual buddies. I would like to thank Randal Johnson, Ned Alpers, the Department of History, the Latin American Institute, and the Division of Social Sciences at UCLA for their support as well.

Thanks to Peter Pels, Birgit Meyer, José Frias, Bill Beezley, Linda Curcio-Nagy, Louis Pérez, Ilán Semo, Howard Wiarda, Lester Langley, Gil Joseph, Ana Alonso, Fernando Coronil, Kathryn Litherland, Reinaldo Román, Lisa Paravisini-Gebert, Karen McCarthy Brown, Nicola Miller, Mark Healey, and Irene Stengs for encouragement and critical feedback on chapters. A visit to the Tepoztlán Institute for the Transnational History of the Americas was stimulating and thought provoking. Brendan Kiley and Mir Yarfitz showed me the wonders of spreadsheets and through their tabulations generated some original insights about the data that I had not considered. Adrián López Denis, Jorge Marturano, Dennis Hidalgo, Diego Ubiera, and Melissa Madera graciously helped with translations. Rob Sierakowski provided a keen editorial eye in the final stages of completion, and carefully read and copyedited the manuscript in its entirety, as did Judith Bettelheim, and Mir Yarvitz; Diana Schwartz provided superb editorial assistance with the citations and thanks to Robert Swanson for a fine index. Hubert Ho, Mark Lewis, Jakobi Williams, Sean Guillory, Alex Lowe, Chris Yuan, and Reza Tavassoli helped solve some seemingly intractable formatting problems. Thanks to Tracy Smith for the map, and to Roberto Cassá, Rafael Bello Camacho, and the staff at the Archivo General de la Nación, as well as René Fortunato, for images. The anonymous readers for Duke Press were able to see beyond a very messy manuscript and provided excellent concrete suggestions on how to clean it up and thus greatly improve it. Valerie Millholland and Miriam Angress have been extraordinarily patient and Pam Morrison was an outstanding editor. My brother Bill Derby has provided encouragement, enthusiasm, and a keenly appreciated sense of humor throughout the writing process. Thanks to Argentina Ramírez and Claudia Medina for keeping the household going during my absences, as well as for their many interesting ruminations about Latin American strongmen, political intrigues, and rumors. I am grateful to Ellie and David Apter for their thoughts on political spectacle and politics, and most of all for always being there.

A very special note of thanks goes to Andrew Apter, who opened up the world of Dominican popular religion to me, and whose unwavering support and enthusiasm have been crucial throughout, especially in the final stages when my energy was waning. His mark is indelibly inscribed in these pages, as are those of Julian, James, and Alec, who have taught me much about the triumphs and tribulations of emerging manhood.

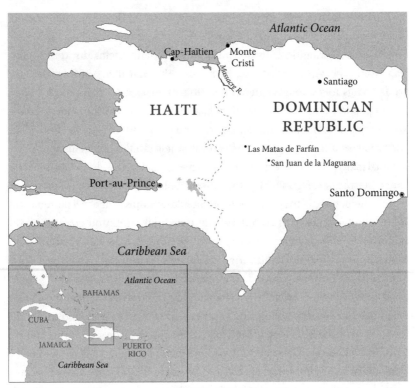

MAP 1 Map of the Dominican Republic and Haiti. CREDIT: TRACY ELLEN SMITH, CREATIVE DESIGN RESOURCES, 2008.

INTRODUCTION POPULISM AS VERNACULAR PRACTICE

A black legend has been created around Trujillo. In order to judge him it is necessary to know what was here when he came to power. This was a very savage, very wild and backward country. We had just emerged from an occupation that had come to pacify and disarm because the country was in constant war—a political catastrophe, which made for poverty because the countryside was full of bandits and no one could work and everyone wanted a political position. Trujillo did away with the political disaster; he did away with the disorder, and put everyone to work. People preferred to sacrifice some of their liberty so that the country could rise above the state of anarchy.

INTERVIEW WITH JULIÁN PÉREZ, 28 JANUARY 1993, SANTO DOMINGO

To know the art of impressing the imagination of crowds is to know at the same time the art of governing them.

GUSTAVE LE BON, *THE CROWD*

Trujillo is the only statesman of this century who has converted dreams into stone.

MANUEL DE JÉSUS GOICO CASTRO

Edward Said has suggested that the essence of Verdi's opera *Aïda* is the way it links power with pleasure. Perhaps no one understood this better than Rafael Leonidas Trujillo Molina, the ruthless dictator who ruled the nation of the Dominican Republic with an iron fist for over three decades (1930–61).[1] Taking full advantage of the authority, opportunities for pillage, and visibility that his position as head of state afforded him, Trujillo was known for his lasciviousness, vanity, and larger-than-life theatricality. This was evidenced in his penchant for grandiose costumes, his immaculate grooming, and the prodigious consumption of food, drink, and women for which he and his inner circle were notorious, and for which he earned the sobriquet "the goat."[2] It may have been this passion for using power in the service of pleasure that drove Trujillo to name two of his children, Ramfis and Rhadamés, after characters in *Aïda*.[3] Or, in characteristic conceit, it may have been the way the opera itself, which was commissioned for the opening of the Suez Canal, dissembled imperial domination as high art. Whatever the case, *Aïda* captures the theater that was central to the exercise of authority under Trujillo's rule, even if it is precisely the dramaturgy of power that has escaped the attention of scholars.

EL GENERALISSIMO

Trujillo established one of the longest and most repressive authoritarian regimes in Latin America, characterized by bouts of extreme carnage interspersed with everyday forms of terror such as random abductions, pervasive surveillance, and institutionalized forms of ridicule. Repression was both systematic, such as the infamous concentration camp at Nigüa and "La Cuarenta" prison, where "vagrants" and political prisoners languished, as well as highly arbitrary, since frequently family members, associates, and even entire townships of those accused of "indifference" (which was taken as opposition) to the regime were tortured and assassinated as well. There were periodic waves of heightened repression until 1957, when Trujillo turned over military intelligence to the ruthless hatchet man Johnny Abbes García, who centralized intelligence gathering and formed several paramilitary organizations, after which the terror was taken to new extremes. In contrast to disappearances in the Southern Cone military regimes, abductions under Trujillo were typically public affairs, as official spies patroling the capital in their black Volkswagen beetles created the sensation that Trujillo was always watching. Indeed, a prominent psychologist who directed a mental hospital during the Trujillo period has even argued that, as a result of the regime, paranoia became a national characteristic.[4]

Forms of terror were often chosen to highlight their theatrical effect. Trujillo expanded the military fifteen-fold, developing a formidable air force and a navy second only to that of Venezuela; he took pride in exhibiting his military power through impressive pageants and parades. He also restructured this instrument of national defense into a tool for internal security.[5] The theater of violence included highly public episodes of grotesque brutality such as the slaughter of twenty thousand Haitian border migrants by machete, a tactic chosen to horrify both Haitian victims and Dominican collaborators compelled to assist.[6] Political opponents met with a quick death that could include chilling spectacles to spread the demonstration effect. For example, the assassination of Sergeant Enrique Blanco, who led the last regional uprising against Trujillo, was fashioned into a macabre ritual when the caudillo's corpse was paraded in a chair throughout the province and his peasant supporters were forced to dance with his remains.[7] These acts of unspeakable cruelty generated a thick fog of fear that permeated the atmosphere.

Formal political repression was thus certainly key to explaining the extraordinary longevity of the regime, as well as its extremely tight and penetrating control over civil society. Indeed, Trujillo's rule has been described by scholars as "totalitarian," since he effectively quashed any form of organized opposition on Dominican soil, establishing a level of iron-clad obedience that has been described as unique in Latin America.[8] Unlike comparable regional strongmen such as Fulgencio Batista of Cuba, whose armed forces lost any modicum of institutional discipline by the end of the regime due to rampant graft, Trujillo maintained strict control of his military and civil service. Systematic torture, espionage, and random arrests made dissent an impossibility on Dominican soil. Trujillo's repressive apparatus even extended overseas, as he repeatedly attempted to assassinate various heads of state, including Fulgencio Batista, Fidel Castro, and Rómulo Betancourt.[9] Indeed, the terror was so appalling that it has been described more readily in literature than in history.[10] In a far smaller population, the death toll probably exceeded that of the chilling military junta in Argentina.[11]

Trujillo established a predatory regime which combined bossism and extensive graft with an ideology of developmentalism and national progress; the implicit logic was that Trujillo represented the very embodiment of the nation, so his personal enrichment somehow aggrandized the republic.[12] He then fashioned all public works, policy formation, and patronage as personal gifts from the dictator to the *pueblo* or people. With his family and a few close friends, Trujillo used the state to develop a system of highly profitable economic monopolies as he gradually took over all core national industries such as meat, milk, sugar, rice, oil, cement, and beer. He then used the law to guarantee their profitability and allocated state contracts to his family and cronies. For example, he prohibited the production of sea salt so that the public would have to purchase salt from the Barahona mines which he controlled. His wife María Martínez was allotted a government bank for cashing state paychecks. Trujillo's sister's husband was given the military pharmaceutical contract, a highly lucrative enterprise given the massive expansion of the armed forces.[13] In this extreme example of prebendelism—the appropriation of the state for private ends—the state became an instrument that guaranteed flows of profit to Trujillo and his circle. Trujillo eventually became one of the wealthiest men in Latin America. Under his regime, there was no effective distinction between the national treasury and the dictator's own purse.[14] He also used the state as a legal screen which shielded the public from the regime's extraordinary lawlessness and corruption. He enabled his own divorce, for example, by altering divorce legislation.

Trujillo eventually "nationalized" even those industries dominated by foreign investment, such as sugar, by buying out foreign investors, as always cloaking his own entrepreneurial designs in patriotic guise. He then spread the wealth by creating a system of kickbacks among subordinates, who were free to collect as long as they did not compete with Trujillo.[15] For example, his control over the rice monopoly was established by prohibiting rice imports, with his campaign in favor of Creole rice couched in nationalist terms.[16] Like the Mafia, the system was informal, cemented by ties of kinship and personal trust, permeated by infighting among minor bosses, and enforced by the threat of violence.[17] Trujillo's deep mistrust of outsiders resulted in efforts to groom his eldest son Ramfis as his successor, as his friend Anastasio Somoza had succeeded in doing with his son.[18]

Trujillo took great pains to create a republican mirage, carefully choreographing elections and even fictive opposition parties, yet this official face camouflaged a personal kleptocracy run by Trujillo and his family. The regime's public face of republicanism is what Rosario Espinal calls "a legal fantasy" (*fantasía del derecho*) or Julio Campillo-Pérez describes as "legalitus."[19] This veil of deception and secrecy also created an intense rumor culture about what truly motivated the hidden recesses of power and a hermeneutics of suspicion owing to the fact that little real information trickled down to the masses.[20] As Trujillo's inner sanctum became a virtual secret society, the veil of invisibility appeared to augment the powers within, as the "milling of the pretense and reputation of secrecy" made the secrets appear to grow in force as well as form.[21] "Secretism" thus generated popular narratives about the occult and even magical powers of the ubiquitous yet invisible inner circle—such as the stories about Trujillo's "animal magnificence," about his never sweating, and about the evil glass eye of his right-hand man, Anselmo Paulino. People knew that Trujillo was up to something, but they did not always know exactly what.[22]

Trujillo's total control over the economy and polity were affirmed through a symbolic apparatus dedicated to el Generalissimo's aggrandizement; one generated by Trujillo's own megalomania in combination with Trujillo's minions' efforts to accumulate symbolic capital as they competed to garner his favor and avoid his ire. Civil servants were both a highly privileged and particularly vulnerable group, since their salaries were relatively high, yet their proximity to Trujillo and access to the secrets of power made them suspect as potential conspirators; as a result, they were forced to sign letters of resignation when hired, enabling frequent bureaucratic turnover. Bureaucratic shuffling also generated gossip about who was to be ousted next.

In La Era de Trujillo, public space became a hall of mirrors all of which refracted Trujillo's greatness in his many costumes: the statesman in jacket and tie, the caudillo on horseback, or the army general in full military brass with his distinctive Napoleonic chapeau. Trujillo's image was eventually inscribed upon virtually every aspect of Dominican life. Parks, mountains, and provinces were renamed in Trujillo's honor, including the capital city itself, Santo Domingo, which became Ciudad Trujillo. Over 1,800 busts of Trujillo were displayed, as was a thirteen-foot statue of his likeness in gold plate, some say the largest statue of its kind ever produced.[23] National time was also reconstructed to highlight the achievements of Trujillo; not only did the dates of his inauguration and birthday become national holidays, but the calendar itself was transformed to date from the first year of the Era of Trujillo. Hundreds of titles, deeds, orders of merit and decorations were invented for and bestowed upon Trujillo in the course of his regime, as well as for his immediate family.[24] The First Son, Ramfis, was appointed honorary army colonel at age four.

Not all of Trujillo's deification, however, was iconic. The "political liturgy" of the regime involved the creation of a new style of mass participation, including mandatory rites of deference and adulation toward the *generalissimo*.[25] Citizens were expected to display photographs of the Benefactor, as well as placards such as "Only Trujillo cures us" and "God and Trujillo are my faith" in their homes and businesses. As we shall see, praise to Trujillo became part of a political economy of discourse, one which enabled minions to garner symbolic credit with the dictator, while satisfying Trujillo's need to accumulate the symbolic capital he lacked due to his ruffian background. Elements of this discursive economy over time trickled down into civil society, as hieratic military epithets such as "Capitán" were adopted as popular male forms of address.[26]

This "theater state" commenced and ended with grandiose state processions.[27] Upon his inauguration, Trujillo led a procession of his entire armed forces throughout the center and northwest of the country on horseback; and months before his assassination in 1961, all able-bodied citizens were asked to march to demonstrate their faith in *La nueva patria dominicana*, Trujillo's era, in a "million man march." These grand militaristic displays which served to remind Dominicans of their subjection were paired with plebeian displays of his generosity, such as the legions of barefoot campesinos invited to the National Palace so that Trujillo could personally attend to their problems and needs. More everyday rituals included *revistas cívicas*, or civic reviews, as well as frequent civic events organized by the Dominican Party to commemorate holidays. Neoclassical economic theory—with its utilitarian logic of investment and returns—cannot explain why Trujillo, the nation's largest employer by the end of the regime, would establish over a hundred new holidays, which, on top of the traditional Catholic calendar of religious events, created a furlough schedule that made a deep dent into productive labor time. Some scholars have dismissed the ideology of "sultanistic" regimes such as the Trujillato as mere "window-dressing" and the culture of adulation as a form of comic opera.[28] In this view, Trujillo was a madman, and the only aspects of his regime worthy of study are its real political and economic effects. Yet to Dominicans, state culture was a very serious matter since failure to comply with the myriad rites of political participation could be met with economic pressure or even death, and nationalism was a powerful political currency which Trujillo deployed very effectively to conjure support for his regime.

Trujillo thrust aside the elite, which saw him as a rogue outsider, and relied upon the military, the United States, and the peasantry to maintain himself in office. These central pillars of his rule have received excellent attention by Valentina Peguero, Eric Roorda, and Richard Turits. Military expansion was crucial to the development of the repressive apparatus of the regime, as well as to the sociology of politics. Trujillo made his army one of the largest in Latin America; in a country of three million, he placed more than thirty thousand men in uniform.[29] He also developed paramilitary organizations within civil institutions such as the university as a means of surveillance. These two aspects of his regime were also central to his populism. He used the armed forces as a system of patronage, giving poor Dominicans a chance at upward mobility by providing them prestige through their "aristocratic" Italian uniforms and establishing them as a privileged status group and the basis of the middle class.[30] And through an extensive policy of land grants, he bought the support of much of the peasantry.[31]

During the Good Neighbor policy when the United States needed a united front during World War II, Trujillo skillfully used the United States as a means of acquiring arms and equipment as well as legitimating his regime at home.[32] He paid U.S. congressmen to disseminate good will about the regime overseas, spending an estimated five to ten million dollars on bribes and public relations in Washington.[33] He then used the appearance of American support to frame the Dominican Republic as a junior partner of the United States, and thus as a modern and powerful country, by scripting the U.S. diplomatic corps into his official pageants. As Roorda has put it, "Trujillo's mimicry of U.S. diplomatic and political projects was not an abdication of independent action; it was an assertion of the sovereign nation's right to choose among options and to put its imprint on the option of its choice."[34] In a small, poor country with a history of United States intervention, this sent a powerful nationalist message. In popular parlance, Trujillo put the Dominican Republic on the map of nations.[35]

This study examines the everyday forms of domination of the Trujillo regime. I explore the political culture of the Trujillato to help explain the cult of excess of the regime, what Achille Mbembe has termed "the aesthetics of vulgarity," and how the combination of patronage and fear created a culture of compliance.[36] In contrast to statist approaches that focus solely on formal political institutions, I consider how the regime extended the state into civil society by fashioning what I term a vernacular politics based upon popular idioms of masculinity, personhood, and fantasies of race and class mobility.[37] I wish to document one of the most pernicious aspects of the terror under Trujillo: the way he adopted popular forms such as gossip, gift exchange, fictive kinship, and witchcraft into the repertoire of domination of the regime, leaving almost no place for Dominicans to hide or resist.

Political scientists often treat the state as an abstraction, favoring structuralist explanations and dismissing personalistic ideologies as without significance since they lack a transcendent message beyond the glorification of the dictator. Yet Latin America has a long tradition of imagining sovereignty through the personal qualities of leaders, one that dates back to the figure of the distant yet divine Spanish monarch who at times became the embodiment of popular expectations and desires; this tendency was reinscribed during the nineteenth century in the era of caudillo rule.[38]

Although I want to focus attention on the cult of the dictator, by no means do I wish to reinstate a "great dictator" theory of history. While Trujillo personally defined policy making under the regime to an extraordinary extent, the literature on Trujillo frequently reduces the regime solely to the man himself, thus buying into the image he wished to project that was so integral to the terror of Trujillo—that he was omniscient and omnipresent. I seek to problematize the role of dictator by rethinking the boundaries of state activity and to consider the president in relation to his inner circle and beyond, and how state practices helped produce the idea that Trujillo was completely in control.

The inner sanctum of the Trujillo regime was constituted as a kind of court society, a mode of authority based on proximity to the dictator in which etiquette was an important idiom of power.[39] Indeed, the monarchical feel of being at Trujillo's beck and call was acknowledged among insiders such as Joaquín Balaguer, who described himself as a "courtier in the era of Trujillo."[40] As Norbert Elias has proposed, a specific social formation develops among the individuals surrounding the king, one bound together by intense competition for status and prestige, and in this case by fear, as well as "envy, ambition and resentment."[41] In Elias's model, the very essence of kingship resides in this new court subculture, the courtesans' distinction from those outside the inner circle becoming the crucial boundary maintaining the social formation. Trujillo, whose favorite drink was Carlos I cognac, extended his royalism into the domain of symbolic politics as well, enforcing strict decorum and flying into a rage if napkins were taken out of turn, or rituals such as baptisms were disturbed.[42] Feudal epithets such as "your Excellency" and "you, Lord of the people" became required forms of address. Trujillo was described as a "slave to etiquette," requiring the use of a jacket at public events regardless of the tropical climate and enforcing proper conduct under threat of denunciation; he pressured his closest associates to move into more luxurious abodes to reflect their status.[43]

Trujillo's pervasive agency was a central myth of state under the regime, and he cultivated it assiduously.[44] The figure of the dictator certainly played a major role in shaping the political arena, yet I wish to suggest that the cult of Trujillo developed at the nexus of a series of exchanges between ruler, ruled, and the class of political brokers who surrounded him. The notion that Trujillo himself was behind every single political move during the regime is itself what Abrams would term an "effect of power."[45] A full understanding of the regime requires bringing both the theater of power and the backstage choreography of politics into the analysis since this was the real scene of politics—the informal practices and deals, and the kingmakers or courtiers who choreographed the state pageants and oratory that framed Trujillo as larger than life and who helped veil the true rationale behind politics during the regime.

Trujillo's charisma—his superhuman aura or *fucú* as it might be termed in popular Dominican parlance—was the product of a complex series of negotiations and symbolic exchanges between leaders, followers, and these interstitial brokers, who played a key role in concealing as well as at times revealing Trujillo's trickery.[46] The massive expansion of the Dominican Party, which as an institution essentially represented Trujillo and extended his persona into civil society through his surrogates, was a crucial factor in producing his overblown image. The party achieved this through organizing and executing the myriad civic rites that reminded citizens of their subjection, while channeling intelligence about loyalty and treachery in remote regions of the country back to the center. In this study, I seek to contribute to a growing literature within Latin American studies that aims to rethink the boundaries of the state and the locus of politics.[47] Trujillo ultimately became a master symbol of Dominican identity, even if it was less a product of deeply held belief than the entanglement of individuals in the transactional web of exchanges of debt and reciprocity, of honor and stigma, that the regime required. Trujillo's charisma made him not as much a divine king but a state fetish, the diabolical product of a conjuring trick.

There are many styles of populism; Trujillo's was based not on love but fear.[48] An important aspect of his regime's hegemony was his recasting of forms of trust such as gossip and gift exchange into forms of terror. While the regime offered no more than a charade of democratic representation, the adoption of popular cultural forms that made it seem "of the people" helped give rise to a kind of political compliance. But compliance here does not connote active support for the regime. The palpable fear that all Dominicans experienced mitigated against this. Yet most Dominicans, I think, lacked the perspective necessary to see the daily rituals and propaganda as "transparently phony" "command performances" owing to the lack of a free press and any available alternatives.[49] And most people developed a highly pragmatic approach to the overblown ideological apparatus of the regime.[50] Yet if most political subjects were not always consciously dissimulating, they were also not actively resisting, since this option was almost patently impossible under the regime.

Notions of political legitimacy must be evaluated in light of local understandings of social identity, of self and person, and how these vary among social classes.[51] The concept of political consent presumes that the person is an active agent free to choose among political alternatives—a freewheeling and transcendental political subject able to act autonomously and with clearly defined rational interests. During the regime, there were no political alternatives to Trujillo. Moreover, most Dominicans lived in conditions of great poverty, operated partially outside the cash nexus of the market economy, and held multiple debts and obligations to family and other immediate kin. This interdependence shaped a political subjectivity of accommodation and consensus since one's personhood or public identity was more socially significant than one's private self because poverty forced reliance on social capital or contacts—people who could help out during times of need. This collective form of identity shaped a form of political subjectivity based on, in Mahmood's words, "proximity and coimbrication, not just opposition or accommodation."[52]

Owing to a scarcity of specie—the Mexican peso, the Haitian gourde, and the U.S. dollar were all used but none was readily available in 1930—even wage workers on the plantations relied on advances from the plantation *bodegas,* which charged high rates of interest and were called "stranglers"; and almost all rural petty commerce was conducted via barter and pre-harvest advances.[53] Purchase by credit based on personal relations of *confianza* was the norm throughout the economy, and debt was pervasive and crippling; evidence of this was the common practice of "selling one's salary" among public servants, which was one of the few means of credit outside of loans from a family member or *patrón.*[54] And even the elite purchased their clothes *fiado,* or on credit.[55] This culture of indebtedness is nicely encapsulated in the nineteenth-century saying, "If you see at table a white and a black man in his company, either the white man is in debt to the black, or the black is paying for the meal."[56] The resulting economic and social interdependence also made reputation a highly valued and protected form of social currency, giving rise to a vulnerability which made the poor more available to Trujillo's politics of patronage. Accepting gifts from the regime created a moral economy of reciprocity; recipients felt obliged to the state because they could not reciprocate in kind.

Official patronage constituted a form of vernacular politics, since in framing all state disbursements as gifts, Trujillo cast politics in an idiom from everyday life that all Dominicans were deeply familiar with, one that masked domination in a language of friendship and family. Because they express social relationships, gifts have a patina of innocence, yet they conceal a relationship of obligation, one that becomes domination when the gifts are highly assymetrical. As Lancaster says, "The power it [the gift] carries is the power to compel reciprocity."[57] With nothing to offer Trujillo besides loyalty, these gifts indebted one to the regime, creating a sense of moral compulsion because with no other means of materially escaping the debt one had to resort to homage. Compliance under Trujillo translated into abjection, a form of self-loathing one could only escape in one's dreams. This may be reflected in the linguistic split in Dominican Spanish between the *dádiva* of the public sphere, which connotes a coercive gift that binds, as opposed to the truly uninterested gifts or *regalos*, which circulate among friends and family. In Spanish, the notion of trust or confianza embeds friendship within debt relationships, since the word contains *fiar* or loan, but this indexes those for whom no interest is generated.[58]

Official prestation created a heavy burden as those individuals who felt compelled to become complicitous with the regime dealt with that shameful fact. Identity was not a choice but rather a problem since it was close to impossible to cast oneself as an honorable subject resisting Trujillo and his depredations; a political subject was then forced to resort to face-saving strategies when a gaping abyss opened between the self one wished to be and the one he or she had become.[59] For some, this created a kind of split identity, a gap between one's self and person, one's view of oneself and one's public face, one's past and one's present, that took much face work to reconcile.

Identity is a complex affair in Marcio Veloz Maggiolo's novels *Materia Prima* and *Ritos de Cabaret*, which treat everyday life among the *pequeña burguesía* in the 1950s barrio Villa Francisca.[60] Veloz reveals the dark secrets kept by those whose scars and nightmares reveal histories they would rather forget, as he explores how people manage to dissimulate to lovers, sons, and daughters so that they can claim respectability and a modicum of social honor. Here we see individuals struggling to camouflage the fact of having informed for Trujillo's secret police—a stigma one would prefer to keep secret but which inevitably was discovered in the intimate face-to-face society of Santo Domingo—using tactics of subterfuge such as plastic surgery or dark glasses. When all else failed, there was always escapism. Individuals would seek to bracket off their dark secrets and moral compromises by investing their true identity elsewhere, from the satisfaction of their new class status as *hombres decentes*, which they claimed through working for military intelligence in their starched Arrow shirts, their burguesía and Colibrí perfume, and their offices (props that framed them as white-collar professionals); to getting lost in music (bolero, son, or Frank Sinatra, never merengue, which was officialized under Trujillo); to romantic liaisons. Juan Caliente, for example, changed his name to underscore his true identity as an *hombre fatal*; his role as *calié* or regime informer was thus just a day job. Unable to resist frontally, subjects adopted everyday strategies of subversion or *bregar*, a fugitive tactic of dealing with power with roots in colonial Cimarrón society.[61]

Because the perniciousness of the Trujillo regime resided in its vernacular forms of domination, political subjects found it more difficult to step outside the tentacles of state power and resist.[62] I seek to locate Trujillo's forms of rule within deeply embedded assumptions many Dominicans shared about power, authority, and national identity. I hope to uncover how the regime was understood not by the educated denizens of Santo Domingo, many of whom loathed Trujillo and risked their lives to unseat him, but rather the marginal poor, who had far less access to information beyond the seemingly impenetrable surfaces of the official story and, as we shall see, read Trujillo's secrecy and diabolical tendencies as evidence of his sorcery. It is easy to understand why elites despised Trujillo for his unbridled violence and extortion, uncouth narcissism, and gangster style; what is far more difficult to comprehend is why Trujillo made some marginal rural and urban poor feel proud to be Dominican, if at the same time deeply uneasy about who they had become under the Trujillato.

BACKGROUND TO NATIONALISM

Certain features of the Dominican polity and society helped give rise to the preconditions necessary for Trujillo's style of authoritarian populism.[63] Christopher Columbus landed first on Hispaniola (Española), the island shared by Haiti and the Dominican Republic. After the Spanish crown shifted its attention to the more profitable mainland silver mines of Peru and Mexico, however, its Española colony floundered, and a lucrative if illicit contraband economy of smoked meat and tobacco products arose. At first slaves were imported to work in the gold and silver mines and on tobacco and sugar plantations after the indigenous Taíno and Carib populations declined precipitously, but importation was halted early on since colonial planters were too poor to buy new slaves; by the seventeenth century freedmen already outnumbered slaves. Colonial poverty meant that slave ownership was typically intimate and small scale—a couple of slaves engaged in wage labor alongside family labor on small farms. Slaves were rarely purchased outright but were frequently acquired through maritime plunder or theft of French colonial slaves.[64] While neighboring Haiti (ceded to France in 1697), Jamaica, and Cuba were developing sugar plantations staffed by massive slave imports in the eighteenth century, Dominican colonists engaged primarily in a mixed economy of cattle ranching, tobacco production, and fine wood exports, activities producing a more paternalistic style of slavery, a looser regime of social control, and a less hierarchical social order.[65]

Dominican historiography laments the Spanish colony's inability to establish the profitable capital-intensive enterprises of its neighbors, but in large measure this was due to the very success of the itinerant Creole subculture of freed slaves, who hunted wild cattle in the interior and sold smoked meat and tobacco to contrabandists based on neighboring La Tortuga island. Locally termed *monteros*, these protopeasants were the Dominican equivalent of the *jíbaro*, the Puerto Rican backlands highlander.[66] This contraband economy of black "masterless men" was so successful that Spanish authorities had to resort to draconian measures to contain it.[67] In 1606, for example, Governor Osorio torched northern settlements to the ground in a failed effort to curb contraband by forcing rural inhabitants to move closer to Santo Domingo. The fact that many of the wealthiest pirates in this pan-Antillean maritime community were mulattos, such as the highly successful Domingo Sánchez Moreno, probably doubly galled the crown.[68] The mixed economy of cattle ranching, tobacco, and foodstuffs expanded as the neighboring colony of St. Domingue became the jewel in the crown of the French empire and provided a thriving market for Dominican goods until the Haitian revolution (1794–1804). Colonial Santo Domingo thus shaped a far more open social order than elsewhere in the Caribbean and offered more opportunities for upward mobility for former slaves and mulattos; this very fact caused no small amount of consternation among elites since the relative success of the montero subsistence economy made it difficult for elites to recruit labor for their farms and ranches.

The nineteenth century brought protracted military conflict, which resulted in the postponement of the economic recovery and resultant state formation that had begun elsewhere in Latin America by midcentury. Fears of European intervention caused Haiti to invade and occupy colonial Santo Domingo from 1822 to 1844; then the Spanish were called in to help protect Santo Domingo from further incursions from 1861 to 1865, as elites sought a bulwark against Haiti's powerful army. And in 1865 the Dominican Republic narrowly escaped annexation to the United States by one vote. U.S. annexation was solicited in a pragmatic trade-off between the desire for autonomy and the economic realities of micronationhood in the shadow of the United States, at a time when the Dominican Republic, Puerto Rico, and Cuba were all highly reliant on the same major product, sugar, and the same point of sale, the United States.[69] Frequent military incursions provided ample opportunities for a new kind of upward mobility for the poor, who were frequently black or mulatto; they were recruited as infantrymen into the insurrectionary armies and some ascended through the ranks.[70] The liberal strongman General Ulises Heureaux (Lilís) took office in 1882; he remained head of state until 1899.[71]

If the multiple interventions of the nineteenth century strengthened national identity, they did so in a highly fragmented and partisan way, since one of the key divisive issues between the blue and red (Liberal and Conservative) parties was the issue of annexation, the banner of the *rojos*.[72] These parties were regional coalitions based on loyalty to particular caudillos, of whom Buenaventura Baez and Pedro Santana reigned supreme until 1874, when the *azules* took over. The basis of caudillo support was not the hacienda, which was not a feature of Dominican land tenure, but rather the peasants' need for protection from the frequent political strife.[73] Indeed, the pattern of isolated homesteads in the interior was the result of a popular attempt to evade the recurrent bouts of military recruitment.[74] As John Chasteen has argued, *caudillismo* fashioned strongmen as culture heroes who created loyalty among followers by means of patron clientelism, patronage, and "political prestige," becoming collective symbols of masculine values such as bravery and skilled oratory.[75] Their appeal to the masses was based on their humble origins; their leadership was a product of both skill and providence. As the prominent Dominican caudillo General Gregorio Luperón put it, "God in his infinite wisdom has made heroes so that the memory of them might serve the oppressed as a lesson of triumph against their oppressors."[76]

If caudillismo was a byproduct of regionalism and a lack of effective state formation or national integration, this pattern continued into the early twentieth century in the Dominican case due to the absence of national infrastructure. Two mountain ranges divided the country, and rail lines linking the central interior of the Cibao plains with the northern coastal town of Puerto Plata, where most export produce was shipped to Europe, were built only in the 1880s and 1890s; and even these lines, of course, did not link the capital, the administrative center, with the north, the economic center. The high cost of transport by mule train was one major impediment to the development of market agriculture. The country was predominantly rural and underpopulated, with only 638,000 people in 1908, thus providing the peasantry ample access to arable land and giving rise to a majority of subsistence-based small landholders.[77] Much of the land was held not as private property but rather as *terrenos comuneros* or collective plots, access to which was held in common and allocated in shares.[78] Ranching was a mainstay of the economy, so legislation placing the burden of fencing on cultivators also hampered agricultural development.[79]

A distinctive feature of the Dominican rural economy was its predominantly nonmarket character, which lasted much later than that in neighboring Haiti, Cuba, or Puerto Rico.[80] While smallholders close to ports and railroads did grow cash crops such as tobacco, cacao, and coffee, those in the interior remained primarily subsistence farmers.[81] And when the economy shifted to large-scale sugar production, it relied primarily on labor imports from the British West Indies and Haiti, thus impacting the Dominican countryside only indirectly. Rural poverty also inhibited the development of an elite outside of the Cibao, where a small yet affluent tobacco culture flourished.

Liberalism became hegemonic from the 1870s onward, yet with its dictum of "order and progress" it remained socially conservative. The rubric of liberalism embraced an impressively wide spectrum of positions, from the utopic socialist ideas of Pedro Francisco Bonó to the more authoritarian statist vision of Américo Lugo. Bonó had a deep skepticism regarding elite interests and especially development led by foreign investment in sugar plantation agriculture for export; he placed his faith instead in the tobacco smallholding cultivators of the central plains of the Cibao as the true sentinels of a democratic future.[82] His view contrasted sharply with that of Lugo and Eugenio María de Hostos, who argued that the Dominican citizenry were a people but not yet a nation and thus not yet ready for democracy; citizens still needed to be formed by strong state institutions such as public schools, which could help forge a culture of democracy. Influenced by racial determinism emanating from Europe, Lugo held the view that the state must lead because many citizens were at best uneducated and thus ignorant of republican ideals and moral values; at worst, they were seen as degenerate due to racial mixture, a tropical environment, and poor diet.[83] As he stated, the class of workers, day laborers, and peasants (*gente de segunda*), "who can never be governing but rather governed classes[,] have produced high functionaries and even chiefs of state. It's useless even saying that they have been the worst. The city dweller, who is almost as frugal as that of the country, is rash, lazy, sensual, haughty and violent."[84] The prominent liberal Henríquez y Carvajal was even more unforgiving when he wrote that Dominican society is a "chaotic mass of crime and blood . . . most Dominicans are inferior beings, infected by vices or dreams that completely distort their intellectual effort."[85] For all the pessimism of liberals about the state of civic culture, Lugo, for one, held the United States in high esteem as a model of constitutional democracy that the Dominican Republic should eventually follow.[86] Liberals were primarily speaking among themselves, however, since the population was largely illiterate and political parties still did not have deep roots among the popular sectors.[87]

An example of how the conservative potential of liberalism's banner of order and progress could give rise to a highly repressive regime was that of Ulises Heureaux. Lilís came into office as a Liberal, joining the conservative wing once the Liberals split, and held the presidency from 1882 to 1899.[88] Born in 1845 in Puerto Plata, Lilís came from humble origins, the illegitimate child of a civil judge from Haiti, reared by his mother who was from the Lesser Antilles.[89] He entered the army at age sixteen, rising rapidly to general; he was famous for his fearlessness and resilience in battle during the war against the Spanish after reannexation (1861–65), which eventually catapulted him into the presidential seat. Lilís invites many comparisons to Trujillo, from his poor background to his military career, but the most significant may be the way he cultivated U.S. interest and support, using repression to create an image of domestic harmony that he then used to secure financial support in the form of loans. Lilís was responsible for the 1891 reciprocity treaty, which established the United States as the republic's main trading partner. He curried favor via negotiations over leasing Samaná Bay, which the United States wanted for a naval base, to secure loans that he used to buy patronage, dispensed to his supporters in lavish champagne celebrations and sinecures, and to augment the military.[90] Heureaux's emphasis on modernity and progress appealed to liberal elites, who were pleased by his promotion of agricultural development through railroad concessions, fencing laws, monetary reform, and cash crops such as sugar.[91] Like Trujillo, Lilís sought to transform the military into a state organization and to co-opt the opposition through the formation of a national party which drew upon collaborators from a range of regions and factions.[92] Both regimes also shared a deep split between the public theater of power, which deployed the rituals of republicanism, and the reality of patrimonialism and graft behind the scenes.

By the turn of the century, however, the United States began to look less like a savior or ally and more like a threat, as the quest for geopolitical control in the Caribbean encouraged it to gradually expand its influence in the political and economic affairs of the Dominican Republic. After an American firm took over Dominican foreign debt in 1892, the United States assumed control of customs houses in 1905, maintaining fiscal control until 1941.[93] U.S. Marines then invaded and occupied the country from 1916 to 1924. The development of sugar monoculture took off after the Ten Years' War in Cuba, when a new influx of Cubans migrated to the Dominican Republic, alongside Italians, Puerto Ricans, and North Americans; they soon formed part of a growing Creole group of entrepreneurs who, alongside large United States-owned agribusiness corporations, brought the protoindustrial *central* (sugar mill) form of large plantation structure to Dominican sugar. By the 1890s, sugar was the largest source of foreign exchange, creating utopian expectations of affluence. The internationalization of the economy also meant vulnerability to periodic fluctuations, however, as overproduction and competition from beet sugar caused sugar crises in the 1880s and the 1890s. Prices peaked in 1917 and then crashed with the depression.[94]

During this period, sugar became the key symbol of the wrenching effects of modernization wrought by global capitalism, owing to the way this one crop radically transformed the economy and society.[95] Overnight, regional towns such as La Romana and San Pedro de Macoris were transformed from sleepy hamlets to sugar company towns; a transnational community was forged as immigrants from Haiti and the British Antilles were brought in as contract labor, and North Americans, Cubans, and Puerto Ricans formed a new managerial class.[96] Sugar came to stand in for a range of changes brought by market culture, from conspicuous consumption and urbanization to proletarianization and alienation. These changes were even more dramatic because most of the country still remained largely outside the sphere of commodity exchange.

If many Dominican critics lamented the *desnacionalización* of the country via sugar, one can see why. While Dominicans had grown sugar since the colonial period, the new sugar boom was entirely a foreign affair. By 1925, U.S. firms controlled sugar production. The new plantations were far larger and more industrially advanced than the rest of the economy, producing a crop solely for export, largely through immigrant labor paid in *vales* or company store tokens. The minority of Dominicans who left their *conucos* or garden plots to participate as semi-proletarianized day laborers in sugar experienced even a change in diet, as fresh meats were replaced by salted jerky, pork, and dried fish, and local tuber staples were replaced by imported corn meal and flour.[97] Moscoso Puello, in his novel *Cañas y bueyes*, condemned sugar as robbing the country of its essence, by ravenously consuming its land and *monte* (forests), marginalizing traditional agrarian pursuits such as tobacco, and rendering Dominicans strangers in their own land. As one character states, "In no part of the world are people more exploited than here. Peons, workers, grocers, we are all enslaved."[98] If Dominican nationhood was compromised in the nineteenth century by frequent military intervention and occupation, sugar was an even more elusive and intractable enemy. Sugar's evils were a product of U.S. economic expansion, but they were blamed on Haitian labor, a more vulnerable scapegoat, resulting in the massive slaughter of Haitian migrants in 1937.

This contested sovereignty was met with an effort to assert state power by the monopolization of the means of violence, which was the only means left since control of the economy was in U.S. hands and state revenue was drastically reduced. And "pacification" (Lilís's mantra) was requisite to continued U.S. support in economic investment and loans. While this process commenced with the Heureaux regime, it was Ramón Cáceres (1906–11) who formed the first professional national constabulary. A modernizer, Cáceres had deepened dependence on the United States by signing the 1907 Dominican-American Convention, which turned the Dominican state into a "semiprotectorate" of the United States by giving it the power to collect customs receipts directly, a move met with fierce resistance. Yet Cáceres also prioritized state-led economic development on the assumption that agricultural growth would help curb the vices associated with cattle culture on public lands, and his policies brought unprecedented economic growth. His campaign against cattle was also a tool to combat his political enemies; he sought to starve the band of the northeastern caudillo Desiderio Arias, for example, by slaughtering all free-ranging cattle. The formation of the first national army and police force was an effort to pacify resistance to his development program. The 1908 constitution was based on the U.S. model but, on the assumption that the citizenry was not yet ready for democracy, it placed more power in the executive by eliminating the vice presidency and by subordinating the post of civil governor to military governor. Cáceres also added a stipend for cooperative generals as a means of co-opting his opposition.[99]

If the 1907 agreement ceded economic control to the United States, it gained formal political control when it invaded, installing a military government led by U.S. Marines (1916–24) after Cáceres's assassination spun the nation into five years of disruption.[100] The occupation merely "extended and formalized U.S. hegemony there, already made manifest by frequent naval visitors and a 90 per cent share of total Dominican imports."[101] In order to foment economic growth, occupation authorities prioritized public works, for example, constructing the first roads linking the capital with Santiago, the second city where much of the nation's tobacco, cocoa, coffee, and produce were grown. Another major change was the cadastral survey and registry of landed property to enable private acquisition, which was aimed at eliminating the vast expanses of public lands and *terrenos comuneros*, which were seen as an impediment to growth. A process of land grabbing was set in motion that drew much of the peasantry into the market economy, created new stratification among rural proprietors, and dispossessed many without a formal land title. It also enabled U.S. investors to achieve near complete control over the Dominican sugar industry, which more than quadrupled its output between 1916 and 1924 as enormous plantations such as La Romana engulfed whole villages.[102] By 1930, sugar was the principal export, and only one smaller Dominican producer was left.[103]

The U.S. Marines also set out to train and arm a Dominican constabulary to replace the army, navy, and republican guard and thus unify the armed forces for the first time. Their intention was to solve the problem of political stability since the country had experienced intermittent civil war since the death of Cáceres, yet they ended up putting in place a powerful instrument for political domination. While the disbanded servicemen were invited to join, widespread resistance to becoming part of a United States-led force meant that recruiters were forced to enlist what a witness described as "the worst rascals, thieves and assassins in the country."[104] If the military had previously been a means of social ascent for the respectable poor, it now was open to *el montón anónimo*, the anonymous crowd. When the U.S. Marines left the country, they turned over the largest foreign exchange producer to foreign control, flooded the country with duty-free U.S. products that crushed local production, and greatly augmented the national debt.

From his post as *guarda campestre* or security guard at the Boca Chica sugarmill, Rafael Trujillo had joined the national guard in the first class of Creole officers graduating from the Haina military academy. Trujillo advanced rapidly from second lieutenant to captain, notwithstanding allegations of rape and extortion leveled against him during his court-martial.[105] He came from a family with military roots. His paternal grandfather had come from Cuba as a spy with the Spanish troops during the reannexation effort in 1861; his maternal grandmother was an *hija de la calle* (illegitimate child) of a Haitian couple who migrated westward during the Haitian occupation in the 1840s.[106] Trujillo became the political protégé of Horacio Vásquez, who took office after the departure of the marines and placed him in charge of the national police force which Trujillo renamed the Dominican National Army to reflect its new "professional" status. This became Trujillo's power base as he "transformed the force from a surrogate for marine occupation to an agent of Dominican nationalism."[107] In a move characteristic of Trujillo's duplicitous style, in February 1930 he simulated a military uprising with troops marching on the capital from Santiago, replaced army commanders loyal to Vásquez with his own, and thus generated a political crisis that forced Vásquez's resignation.[108] After the coup, Rafael Trujillo and Estrella Ureña supposedly won the elections with 45 percent of the vote, yet no other candidates were offered. A reign of terror followed as Trujillo's hitmen killed his opponents and spread fear throughout the country. The climate of crisis was heightened by the collapse of sugar prices due to the depression and by a cataclysmic hurricane which devastated the capital city just months after the inauguration.

The cumulative result of the highly invasive role the United States played in Dominican politics was similar to what Jorge Domínguez has argued for Cuba; it fragmented political space by weakening the legitimacy of government. As the United States became the ultimate political arbiter, it became the focal point of political activity and discourse among parties who looked to the State Department rather than to the masses for legitimation.[109] It also weakened the formation of a local bourgeoisie, which was poorly developed as a result of colonial poverty and lacked the capital to take advantage of the late-nineteenth-century sugar boom. The economic integration of the country into U.S. markets primarily benefited the predominantly foreign merchant class.[110] Dependent social elites found it harder to establish ideological hegemony and thus were more prone to resort to coercion.[111] The huge gap between legal and effective sovereignty created by U.S. control also created a potent desire for national integrity and agency, what Yael Navaro-Yashin has termed a "fantasy for the state," which Trujillo cleverly used for his own means to power.[112]

BETWEEN TERROR AND RESISTANCE

Analysis of the political and economic rationality of politics under the Trujillato is incomplete without addressing the cultural logic governing statecraft. David Cannadine notes that political analysis, rather than restricting itself to the formal arena, should be cast as the study of power in society, thus as a system of social relations. As he states, "Politics is not confined to the doings of those in authority, and the responses of those who are subordinate, but is . . . the varied means whereby hierarchies of dominance and deference are created, maintained and overturned."[113] Indeed, this is especially so in contexts in which a good part of formal politics operates outside of formal institutions, through traditional face-to-face idioms of exchange such as the circulation of goods through patronage or favors in relations of *confianza* or trust.

By focusing on the apparatus of formal repression, scholars have neglected everyday forms of coercion that were often not necessarily perceived as domination but rather as "legitimate authority."[114] For example, official patronage was not merely a conscious, strategic effort at "co-opting" the populace.[115] Trujillo certainly had strategic objectives, but most Dominicans operated outside the sphere of market exchange in the 1930s and gift exchange was a quotidian means of expressing friendship, which meant that this form of domination worked through the sinews of deeply embedded assumptions about reciprocity that they took for granted. In this context, patronage was an important means of state control, a form of "embedding" the state in the private domain, as well as a technique for coercing consent to the regime.[116] In the public realm, Trujillo gave hand-outs at official ceremonies, offering artificial limbs to the disabled, bags of food to the workers, and bicycles to the children. He was also famous for his monetary gifts while on tour and for offering nuptial trinkets to exemplary newlyweds, such as the "Hollywood Beds" given to couples marrying in 1944, the centennial year of the country's independence. Furthermore, politics within the regime's inner circle revolved around access to honors and perquisites which were defined as gifts from Trujillo, including positions, state monopolies, or land grants. Drawing upon Catholic idioms of paternal authority, gifts from the dictator sought to recast Trujillo's authority in familial terms and to euphemize the violence through which he actually maintained power. Since these gifts incurred debts, state gift giving also drew people into relations of subjection with Trujillo, thus entangling them in a cultural economy of domination.

I examine the cultural economy of a system of domination which was effective because it was able to produce "practical consent" for a terrorist regime.[117] The ideology of the Trujillo regime has been dismissed in part due to its personalism, since it failed to provide a transcendent message. From the outside, it appears to be an absurdly repetitive and farcical effort to dissimulate Trujillo the ruthless racketeer and thug as a dignified modern statesman by constantly associating the developmental progress under Trujillo—the new roads, bridges, treaties—with the man himself. Yet if state ideology was personal, it was by no means insignificant. As under Stalin, the state (i.e., Trujillo) expanded to become an ubiquitous presence in everyday life, since it dispensed jobs, policed speech, owned radio and television, defined the press, provided public entertainment, stole girlfriends, shaped friendships (by, for example, creating strong reasons to curtail relations with enemies of state), and created new social roles, forms of self-presentation, speech, and interaction. The very invasiveness of the state and its multiple roles endowed it with many meanings that transcended Trujillo himself, even if he became the master trope for a new regime of state penetration.

But the power of Trujillo was as much a result of the constant speech of the state, through a barrage of signs, insignia, and icons, as it was a result of its silence. Trujillo both sacralized his inner circle and created generalized fear through tight control over information flows. Since the press served as little more than a calendar of state ceremonial, carrying little or no behind-the-scenes information about politics, selective leaks were used judiciously by Trujillo and his cronies to create impressions.[118] And gossip about insider activities and conflicts became a highly valued currency within the inner circle. Rumors were rife about the true story behind everyday events, especially the fate of those who were tortured and executed.[119] Of course, secrecy itself creates value; like property, secret knowledge can be possessed. The fact of this possession differentiates social groups, creating an insider-outsider distinction. As T. M. Luhrmann states, "[This] difference can create a hierarchy, wherein secrecy cedes social power to those who control the flow of treasured information."[120] Thus, secrecy was an important element of the boundary separating Trujillo's insiders from those outside; and the wall of silence between the plebeians and the small inner circle increased the social distance and thus the sense of intrigue and wonder about the power and secrets of Trujillo and his minions.

Patronage enabled Trujillo to cut a profile as Padre de la patria nueva (Father of the New Homeland), a title which located him within a language of paternalism with deep roots in Dominican liberalism as well as popular culture. Paternalism is a highly ambiguous idiom of authority, however, one rooted in affect as well as relations of power, and thus connoting inclusion and exclusion.[121] This holds true especially in the Dominican Republic, where rural poverty, a history of labor migration, and an insistence on male autonomy combined to forge a pattern of matrifocal families, wherein the mother and child define the family unit, and the absent father who comes and goes is a distant figure often associated more with discipline (*respeto*) than tenderness. In casting himself as father, Trujillo certainly drew upon the liberal idea of the tutelary state that would shape Dominicans into citizens, yet he also diverged from the highly derogatory language about the peasantry that had been a staple of most liberal thought.

Trujillo called on Dominicans to join him in the nation as long as they would agree to become *hombres de trabajo* or men of work; he thus offered them the possibility of redemption, rather than the pathology offered by the liberals. As Espinal argues, he invited them as a "disciplinary father" to join him, an outsider who was not a traditional politician and not a profes-sional.[122] If they respected the law, he promised to transform them from scruffy, shoeless peasants and informal street vendors engaged in *chiripeo* (part-time work) into workers, from faceless rabble into people. In a nation of peasants only partially incorporated into the wage labor economy, many of whom were itinerant monteros, this message of incorporation must have held some initial appeal.[123] Unlike Juan Perón, Trujillo did not find a work-ing class to which he imparted an identity; it did not yet exist. Even the urban poor lived as partial peasants with their conucos or patio garden plots; and in 1930 there was only a minuscule manufacturing sector.[124] His populism was more like that of Haiti's François Duvalier, who drew upon the most marginal of social constituencies—urban shantydwellers—those who lacked any kind of organized occupational identity whatever. Trujillo would impose order on the undisciplined masses through the schools and the military.[125]

While his paternalism did not entail the more radical logic of the sym-bolic equivalence of classical populism, Trujillo's rhetoric did offer the pos-sibility of inclusion within national politics, of transcending a liberal past that had consigned poor Dominicans to the margins of politics in part due to their race.[126] If Perón offered respect to working-class Argentines as fellow men, Trujillo offered something more hierarchical, a subordinate proximity.[127] Perón offered a symbolic equality of common manhood; Trujillo offered a social order based on deference and hierarchy.[128] The relationship was also conditional: Only if you worked—thus joined the market economy—could you be a friend of Trujillo's. Yet this was a markedly different vision than Lugo's negativism: "Our peasants [are] an ignorant race that vegetates without hygiene, prisoners of the most repugnant sicknesses that due to their lack of foresight, their violence and their duplicity, are generally incestuous, gamblers, alcoholics, thieves and murderers."[129]

As frequently in Dominican everyday life, race is an invisible term in Trujillista discourse; when the term appears it is through furthering the interests of *criollos*, that is, the mixed-race browns who form the Dominican ethnos or *nación*. The fact of extensive racial mixing in the Dominican Republic makes everyone a mestizo or *indio*, a transitional category between white and black which conveys racial mixture through that master symbol of autochthony, the figure of the Indian.[130] Creole identity holds the promise that all Dominicans can possibly pass as white, yet it also means that everyone potentially carries the stigma of blackness. Blackness in this context is thus a latent secret. Even if one is phenotypically white with smooth hair and green eyes, for example, one might have a dark mother or brother, or produce a child with kinky hair. This proximity to blackness may also have made poor Dominicans more available to a political language that cast them as capable of civilization, rather than one which othered them as condemned to backwardness, which was the traditional liberal model.[131] Trujillo took the liberals' emphasis on civilization and made it potentially available to all Dominicans, a message conveyed not only linguistically but also through the myriad state functions hosted by the state, which, for example, avoided Creole dishes in favor of European cuisine, and invited even poor Dominicans from the barrios to sit at table at state functions.[132] As Raymundo González has said, Trujillo as farmer, worker, and industrialist promised to create a society with no castes, no gente de segunda, and no blackness—one of only Dominicans united against Haitians.[133] If blackness in this context was a metaphor for social inequality, the Era of Trujillo thus promised to make whiteness available to all Dominicans by incorporating them into the modern nation.[134] Chapters 1–8 explore some of the techniques through which this was achieved.

ONE THE DOMINICAN BELLE ÉPOQUE, 1922

I, as a civilized man and as a citizen of a free country, could not understand as yet, nor can I ever, that a country so advanced and so democratic
and so successful at achieving republican practice, could have invaded a
sovereign country—the Dominican Republic—with troops, and treated us
as though we were Negros from the Congo. We were friends of the United
States. We would have helped them during the war with Germany.
PEDRO A. PÉREZ

Gentlemen, I believe the Dominican people until that moment loved the
people of the United States, and I hope the Dominican people still love
the American people as I love them. All the depredations, the injuries to
the lives of the Dominicans, all the bad actions of the troops, are secondary questions for me. The principal question is that there was no reason at
all, no right at all, to land troops on Dominican territory and to impose on
peaceful people like the Dominicans, who were not at war with the United
States and who loved the United States, a military government for over
five years. That is my principal grievance, and all others are secondary.
FRANCISCO PEYNADO, *INQUIRY INTO OCCUPATION OF HAITI AND
SANTO DOMINGO*

On 21 January 1922, at the height of the United States military occupation
of the Dominican Republic (1916–24), Nuestra Señora de la Altagracia
(Our Lady of Altagracia) was "crowned" amid a groundswell of popular
nationalism that drew some thirty thousand devotees to the capital city of
Santo Domingo, as well as a veritable army of international clerics from
Latin America; considering that the capital population was twenty-one
thousand in 1916, this was a very impressive sum.[1] Aside from the group of
high-ranking Vatican representatives charged with officiating the service,
the delegates resembled a Pan American congress, with representatives
drawn from Venezuela, Haiti, Puerto Rico, and Curaçao, to name but a
sample. The ensuing crowd choked city thoroughfares with carriages and

cars; masses of pilgrims thronged public office buildings, galleries, and parks, camping a full week before the ceremonies began. Dressed in their Sunday best, scores of peasants sang *salves* (religious songs), awaiting the visitation along the roads. Those who missed the festivities in person could see them recreated on the silver screen in the first Dominican film ever made, a fictionalized reconstruction called *La leyenda de Nuestra Señora de Altagracia*, or in a documentary of the event entitled *El milagro de la virgen*.[2] Of course, the real miracle occurred on the day after the coronation, when the U.S. Marines announced the details of their evacuation plan. If the marines were bewildered by these events, the nationalist message of the Virgin of Altagracia's coronation as patron saint of the republic was loud and clear to Dominicans. Santo Domingo was bathed in flags for the occasion, and the Virgin's portrait processed atop a model replicating the twelve provinces. Through its investiture, the Virgin became a synecdoche for the resurrected Dominican nation, one which appealed to a higher, more noble authority than the U.S. Marines. Casting Jorge Washington as a saint, they called upon his guiding spirit to demand justice and rights and to serve as the protector of the weak nations of the world.[3] When he failed them, they invoked the Virgin of Altagracia.

Once a regional symbol of the easternmost province of Higüey, the Virgin was now enshrined as the national numen. The coronation conveyed the message that the United States might control the bureaucracy of the capital city, the bloodless infrastructure of authority, but the Virgin of Altagracia governed the national spirit. At a time when the national body was stripped, bound, and rendered mute by the occupying forces, the Virgin spoke for the Dominican *pueblo*. Indeed, several people even had their speech restored by her holy presence. Her message was feisty—*levántate y camina* (get up and walk)—fight the *Yankis* and reclaim the country.[4] The Virgin had become the avatar of both elite and popular resistance to the marine government, encoding an ardent rejection of the values intrinsic to their secular missionizing impulse and state-building project. The coronation expressed a worldview at odds with the utilitarian pragmatism of the U.S. military, one that privileged morality over money, salvation over progress, and spiritual authority over secular democracy. The Virgin spoke as an instrument of hierarchy and as an affirmation of moral authority.[5] The coronation articulated what Claudio Lomnitz has termed a "peripheral cosmopolitanism," an alternative vision of modernity that patently declared against the path of Anglo Saxon utilitarianism, yet forcefully expressed the power of nationalism in this small island nation which, since the nineteenth century, had had its national autonomy compromised like no other in Latin America.[6]

Woodrow Wilson had landed U.S. Marines on Dominican shores in 1916, ostensibly to put a stop to a series of internecine political struggles that had erupted with the assassination of Ramón Cáceres (1906–11) and were eroding the nation's fiscal stability. Between Ulises Heureaux's departure from office in 1899 and 1916, thirteen presidents had been inaugurated. Outstanding loans to Germany and Great Britain created fears of foreign takeover. The marines were responsible for the formation of the first national constabulary in the country, which they assumed would bring stability to Dominican politics after a period of revolutionary tumult; yet this very force eventually enabled Rafael Trujillo to ascend to the presidency through a disguised military coup. The formation of a national military was not the only reason why a shift in Dominican political life occurred during the occupation, however. The intervention also precipitated a crisis in the liberal project, one that had promised progress and development through free trade and foreign investment. The reigning optimism about national progress and development that had emerged with the sugar boom collapsed with the U.S. military occupation and the 1921 depression, as liberalism and the doctrine of open markets were seen to bring not growth but rather economic and political dependency.

In this chapter I argue that the crisis of liberalism precipitated a crisis of masculinity for Dominican manhood, one that helped usher Trujillo into office as reformers called for a new style of presidentialism to more effectively keep the rabble down and thus the United States out. This model of sovereignty broke with the white, secular, liberal model of propriety of the *doctores*, elegant *prohombres* with their Panama hats; drawing upon the strongman profile of the caudillo, the new form of rule was based on force, and it became far more repressive than that of nineteenth-century caudillo rivalries.[7] Nineteenth-century struggles between the *bolos* and the *rabudos*, or bob-tailed versus long-tailed cocks, were surprisingly bloodless notwithstanding the fact that they were termed revolutions. This changed, however, with the occupation.

United States expansion was in part a project to restore dominance and thus manliness to American foreign policy. As Mary Renda has demonstrated for the case of Haiti, "interventionist paternalism" was a complex tactic of rule, casting the marines as caring fathers who should avail themselves of discipline as needed.[8] From ousting Dominican statesmen from the National Palace, to banning cockfights, to forcibly disarming the rural population, United States occupation policies cut at the core of Dominican male agency. This was not lost on nationalists who descried that "the Dominican people, whose virility and dignity can not be questioned, neither needs nor accepts guardianship."[9] The occupation also brought to the surface certain basic contradictions within liberal thought, since the marines' agenda of statism and tutelary democracy had also been key tenets of Dominican liberalism until Dominicans saw these carried out by bayonet. As press freedoms were curtailed and martial law imposed, Dominicans were able only to voice their objections piecemeal about discrete policies and their failures. They expressed their resistance indirectly, however, by taking issue with key symbols of U.S. penetration, from dance styles to the dollar, and above all with the new modern woman, who became a popular scapegoat for what was seen as the corrosive underside of marine rule.

DOMINICAN NERVOUSNESS

As they became aware that U.S. withdrawal was contingent on the performance of Dominicans as responsible citizens, Dominican elites developed an acute concern with public comportment during the occupation. Yet this new self-consciousness—this new sense of being watched—did not commence in 1916. A growing strategy for ensuring United States hegemony in the Caribbean, which almost rendered the Dominican Republic a U.S. overseas territory in 1865, was followed in the 1890s with large-scale U.S. corporate expansion in sugar for the American market and a bilateral reciprocity treaty.[10] The United States became directly involved in Dominican political life in 1907 when it took over customs revenues, a move that in effect rendered the country a protectorate; it established a presence backed by threat of force in 1912, when it sent its first contingent of marines to the country. As Ada Ferrer has shown for Cuba, liberals felt they needed to persuade the marines of their capacity for republican rule, of their capability for keeping their own house in order.[11] With emancipation in 1822, Dominicans, unlike Cubans, did not have the recent ghost of slavery and "African savagery" to contend with, but they did have a period of tumultuous political strife at the turn of the century which had forged the image in Washington that Dominican leadership was prone to violence and lacked the necessary self-control for effective governance. The assumption at that time, of course, was that "only civilized white men had evolved the advanced intellectual and moral capacity to master their masculine passions."[12] And as a nation of browns, it was not entirely clear which side of the divide Dominican men were on.

In 1906 the first guidebook presenting the Dominican nation to the world declared its intention to show what was propitious to the "development of civilization" there and the *genialidad moral e intelectual* (moral and intellectual genius) of the country; it thus presented photos of elegant Dominican women and Creole waltzes, poetry and essays on social and political thought, as well as descriptions of the provinces, lists of laws, and advertisements.[13] The image is one of Victorian refinement and decorum, a thoroughly Europeanized image of polite society.[14]

The text of a guidebook produced in 1920 indicates that Dominicans still felt they had something to prove:

> The Dominican people are at peace with themselves and with the world, and the men of the country, and more especially the youth, just budding into manhood, who form the backbone of this country, and on whom depend the future government, prosperity, and standing of the country among the nations of the world, are fast learning that greater honor, prestige and personal gain may be won from the work of developing and building up their country than from spending their good time and energy in political broils and revolutions, in order to secure some government position, here today and lost tomorrow, and the American intervention will have been a complete success, if the young men of the Dominican Republic can get this point of view.[15]

The image of the Dominican male presented in this passage is impulsive, violent, and prone to revolution, lacking the self-restraint requisite to respectable manhood. This idea underwrote the necessity of United States tutelage. U.S. Navy Lieutenant Commander Lybrand Smith rejected the Spenglerian position that Dominicans were a young race that could develop its own form of civilization. In his view, miscegenation had tainted Dominican stock such that "if the Dominican nation is to exist it must do so under the guidance of a stronger race."[16] And Dominicans were keenly aware of this view. As one observer noted, "The foreign press considers us a nation of savages" and that assumption had enabled the United States to take on its "absurd exercise as tutors."[17] Like testosterone-ridden adolescents, however, Dominicans were evolving under U.S. rule and developing the force of will necessary for good government. Under the scrutiny of the U.S. Marines, Dominicans urged each other to "overcome, be superior to the environment; that is the way we will progress."[18] In accordance with Gustave Le Bon's crowd theory, Dominican men needed to demonstrate their gentility. They had to show that they were superior to the rural crowd, which was at base rough and irrational, entirely lacking control over its passions, and with a tendency to succumb to a primitive mentality and state of nature, especially given the "racial deficiency" of the country. The innate atavism of crowds required strong leadership for guidance.[19]

The U.S. vision of the Dominican Republic as "democratically illiterate," however, was shared by liberal Dominican elites such as Américo Lugo, whose call for political reform and specifically for a regime of tutelary democracy dated from the turn of the century.[20] The rise of Dominican liberalism and its developmental thrust in the nineteenth century was accompanied by an increasingly disparaging view of the peasantry, as the rural poor became the scapegoat for the nation's lack of progress. In the words of Lugo, "Our peasants [are] an ignorant race that vegetate without hygiene, prisoners of the most repugnant sicknesses, that, due to their lack of foresight, their violence and their duplicity, are generally incestuous, gamblers, alcoholics, thieves and murderers."[21]

The exemplary role of the state changed in accordance with this negative vision of the dangerous classes. As the peasantry came to resemble a force of criminality, the state correspondingly required a more draconian presence. Lugo complained that the Dominican people issued from a Spanish heritage of individualism bordering on anarchism and an African lineage of indolence—a deadly combination that entirely inhibited the formation of a viable national community. And since the people were not yet a nation and were as yet incapable of self-government, the only option left was the formation of a nation through the state. Lugo called for immigration, "tutelary law," and a truly nationalist education to reshape the Dominican citizenry.[22] He invoked an "enlightened minority" (*minoría ilustrada*)—a dictatorship of the intelligentsia—not to govern the masses per se but to shape them through education and eventually prepare them for democracy. Lugo was influenced by the Puerto Rican educational reformer Eugenio María de Hostos, for whom education was the sole avenue of advance toward the civilizing process of which the United States was the emblematic figurehead; as Hostos observed, "To civilize is to make coherent societies that lack cohesion."[23] Lugo invested utopian hopes in education and its transformative powers if it could be truly nationalized. He also argued that civic education was a necessary antidote to and preventive measure against foreign occupation.[24] Pedro Henríquez Ureña also championed the U.S. public education system inspired by John Dewey with its practical emphasis, since education was obligatory yet free of charge.[25]

The role of public schooling in fostering citizenship was but one key element of U.S. liberal thought shared by Dominicans before the occupation; others included federalism, land privatization, and proper fencing laws to encourage settled agriculture over ranching. As the means of articulation between the state and the population, the legal system had a privileged role to play in giving form and moral guidance to the nation. Judicial reform to achieve a stronger, less personalistic state was crucial because of the menacing power of the United States, the small size of the governing elite, and a majority of citizens who were uneducated, mixed-race mulattos; in the words of the writer F. E. Moscoso Puello, mulattos were "intelligent, but lazy, quarrelsome, lacking in foresight, generous and courteous, occasionally valiant, but always ignorant," in sum, "an inferior product."[26] Liberals believed in a strong state that would compensate for the deficiencies of the masses while providing a ballast to the political class, which was "a special caste of men, afflicted by a morbid egoism, devoured by the lowest passions that you could imagine. . . . They are the real calamity of the tropics, along with the mosquitoes and the hurricanes." This view of the caudillo resulted from social prejudice since many hailed from poorer rural backgrounds, yet it also meshed with Le Bon's view that charismatic leadership often emanated from "excitable, half-deranged persons who are bordering on madness."[27]

Yet even as liberals saw the state as an important guiding force for the masses, it was not seen as implying quite the rationalizing project of Max Weber or the disciplinary rationale envisioned by Michel Foucault.[28] There was a near-millenarian set of expectations surrounding the state, that it could enable a certain transcendence of the Creole milieu. José Ramón Lopez wrote that the true *ayuntamiento* or town council must also "cultivate the spiritual realm—the real finality of life." If it did not, it would create "peoples with deficient psychology, peoples who are apathetic and lazy; peoples who have a bestial mentality, peoples with an innate bestial tendency, inferior peoples in a word."[29] Indeed, Dominican liberals included spiritual growth and enrichment in their notion of development, as the state became a locus of utopic possibility in their quest for "progress and civilization." They also held, of course, a sharply hierarchical vision of society. The state's role was not to reflect the *pueblo* but rather to steer it to new heights since, owing to their racial mixture, the masses were seen as potentially degenerate.[30]

POPULAR CULTURE

The acute self-consciousness of Dominicans as they felt their nation and its behavior being "watched and judged" by the United States may help account for the abiding concern with the "unruly" habits of the masses and for the efforts to clean up the public sphere by spatially excluding the popular sectors.[31] Of particular concern were the "bad-mannered" plebes who, through access to money, were able to inhabit public spaces that, as places of "culture," had previously been off-limits to all but the elite. For example, a group of "uncultured, blemished, stupid" spectators in a Santo Domingo movie theater were berated for making "that site of culture into nothing more than a cockfight or a bull ring" by their scandalous behavior as they whistled, made jokes, and chided the orchestra.[32] The great social division was between the benches and the chairs, as those who sat on the benches offered a stream of constant unsolicited commentary on those in the seats, as well as on the acting and the musical accompaniment. Worse still, the newly constituted police did nothing to put an end to this *vagabundería*, although clearly the *gente decente* saw policing public morality and demeanor as part of their duties. In other words, when elites came to the movies, they were welcomed; when the "multitude" came, it was an "invasion."[33]

But one might assume that audience behavior at movie theaters would be particularly unrestrained precisely because cinema was felt to be a "democratic art," the one space of culture truly open to the masses. Thus spectators may have felt particularly entitled to act there as they pleased. However, in the Dominican Republic, film was not initially seen as art for the people; quite the contrary, it was quickly claimed by the upper crust. In 1900 the movie industry made its entry first in Puerto Plata, the seat of the old aristocracy and high society where there was a sizable German community. And the first Dominican cineaste and national photographer, Don Pancho Palau, was also the editor of *Blanco y Negro*, arguably the most important literary magazine of its day. The early sense of cinema as property of the elites, as related to high culture like drama, can be seen in its first appellation in Santiago, "electric theater"; elites hoped that film would some day bring opera into the bourgeois home. Later movie houses came to be called "film salons" (*salones de cine*). In fact, the first Dominican films made in 1923 were divided, like drama, into acts.

Film was expected to share the larger-than-life quality of theater as well. It was intended to provide an idealistic dreamscape, one that transcended rather than reflected society. It was seen as poetry, not journalism. This perspective can be found in the Dominican intelligentsia's response to a local romantic feature film made in 1923, which was rebuffed due to its many quotidian popular scenes: rural washer women in streams, street vendors, and butchers in open-air markets. The film was panned as "a national catastrophe in celluloid" and admonished for representing the country "like a remote African country, completely uncultivated and without traditions."[34] Apparently, the "people" should be neither seen nor heard, particularly not in a medium as public as the silver screen. The upper-class public wanted to see not the *populacho* or rabble but rather images of an idealized topography of "tinted, romantic scenes . . . full of beautiful tropical landscapes" devoid of the poor, a symbolic landscape of their imagination.[35] They wanted, and expected, to "attract spectators that knew how to applaud the good and erase the bad," so as to foment better "contemplation of *true* beauty."[36] This was why the "documentary" *El milagro de la Virgen* (The Miracle of the Virgin), which recreated virgin apparitions and staged miracles somewhat incongruously, was a far greater box office success than this "fictional" romance.[37] Given its preference for seeing the country only in expurgated form, this public ironically had a great thirst for European realist fiction, and Dominican magazines of the 1920s often reprinted excerpts from Emile Zola, Guy de Maupassant, and Miguel de Unamuno alongside the popular visionary Jules Verne.

While by 1915 in Europe and the United States cinema was a spectacle for the lower classes, in the Dominican Republic it was still the terrain of the "distinguidas señoritas y cultos caballeros de la Alta Sociedad" (distinguished ladies and cultivated gentlemen of high society) the upper-middle classes and elites, until open-air showings made their debut in the popular Santo Domingo barrios of San Carlos and Villa Francisca years later.[38] The first films were news shorts (typically European), accompanied by a pianist and a narrator who explained to the audience what was going on and enhanced the action by providing a running dialogue with the actors. But soon theaters started innovating programs that changed daily so as to keep the *damas y caballeros* (men and women) of Santo Domingo society coming throughout the week, including a ladies day, with reduced entry fees for women. Wednesdays were for the men, when they voted in the Concurso de Simpatías y Belleza (Beauty and Congeniality Contest) for their favorite sweetheart; the winner's image would be projected on the silver screen. There were also occasional fundraisers for the poor, and on weekends family activities were held.[39] While in the beginning the films imported were primarily French or Cuban, by 1916 they had become primarily American. The shift was reflected in the style of large graphic advertisements, often in English, that came to dominate the daily newspapers. It was also reflected in the titles, which by 1926 included the *fotodramas Buffalo Bill* and *Son of Tarzan*. The first indication that cinema had become a popular medium was when the U.S. Marines set up a "floating film theater" in a dormant warship in Santo Domingo harbor to show adventure films to poor children.[40] Film was late to catch fire, however, among a reluctant public already accustomed to their *zarzuelas*, concerts, operettas, and traveling circuses.

Correspondingly, there was some dissension among elites over the extent to which the Dominican people could and should be "civilized" through education and artistic exposure; though civilization was a common rallying cry among liberal reformers, the notion was not without its detractors. One critic of the public school system created during the U.S. occupation called it a "white elephant," unduly expensive and a waste of time. What would the popular classes do with such education anyway? For those who believed that the defects of the Dominican people were a result of their race mixture and that "the Dominican social organism" (*el organismo social dominicano*) had "certain organic defects" (*ciertos defectos orgánicos*), it was unclear whether those with mixed blood could advance ethically. In this view, *mestizaje* was an incurable, debilitating condition that resulted in intellectual and physical atrophy and torpor; it was, "a disease inherited and transmitted from generation to generation, like a terrible sediment that creates the total paralysis of collective progress in customs, relations, ideas, and even as far as love and the benevolent inclination to sacrifice for the good of the community is concerned."[41]

This view translated into an interventionist approach to the problem of Dominican healing practices and other "barbarisms." Indeed, during the U.S. occupation, sanitary inspectors commenced round-ups of rural *curanderos* (herbalists), jailing these "malefactors of humanity" on the grounds that they were unhygienic and lacked licenses.[42] Marine efforts at modernization via sanitization became efforts to whiten the nation through the extirpation of syncretic practices associated with blackness, and several Haitians were accused of the evils of sorcery and worse. This served to reassure Dominicans that they were on the right side of the vectors of accusation and thus the Haitian-Dominican divide.[43] Another arena of moral outrage included the bathing areas on the Santo Domingo coast such as Güibia, which came under attack when about thirty plebeian men were discovered bathing there in the nude by a group of women who fled, scandalized. As one observer complained, this "dishonorable, immoral, scandalously censurable" sight called into question the "culture" Dominicans were proud of. And complaints raged about prostitutes "mixing" and offending "public morality" at Andrés Beach at Boca Chica. As in Puerto Rico, plebeian men used United States campaigns to police behavior that was associated with blackness and poverty, hoping to banish it from the national terrain.[44]

A counterview of the Dominican peasantry emerged during the occupation, however, one that defended the peasantry as clever and honorable yet duped by crafty and rapacious Yankees. Editorials began defending the rural poor, claiming that American economic policies were causing prices to rise, not poor production, malingering, or harvest withholding, since "our peasantry knows by heart all the major tenets of political economy even if they can't read."[45] Folkloric treatises celebrating peasant lifeways and customs emerged; one was R. Emilio Jiménéz's classic *Al amor del bohío*, which lovingly described typical rural professions such as water carriers, Creole washer women, and midwives who talk too much, as well as Dominican speech forms for giving one's word, praying, and the divine. The text portrays a courteous, honest, and exceedingly polite peasantry, whose deeply *criollo* virtues were seen as fading away with the encroachment of modernization, urbanization, and, implicitly, the occupation. In the face of its North American detractors, Jiménez defended this fount of Creole culture. Since the peasant is poor, his only defense is his courtesy. "With it, he triumphs in commerce, social life, in games of chance and in love. With it, he resolves conflicts. He speaks poorly but thinks well of what he says. He is ordinary but refined at the same time: ordinary like the land he works, but refined like the fruit that is born from that land."[46]

COMMODITY WARS

From the late nineteenth century to the 1920s, everyday life in Santo Domingo was markedly transformed by the shift from a culture in which

European goods were primarily purchased by the elite to a mass culture of consumption created by an infusion of cheap and accessible products from the United States, products affordable even by emergent middle sectors due to unprecedented prosperity. This shift is clear in the pages of the *portavoz de la cultura nacional* (spokesman of national culture), the journal *Blanco y Negro*, which until the 1920s had restricted its social and cultural universe to Spain, France, or Italy. "Hollywood" arrived with a bang, only slowly becoming chic (first among the youth) as the country began to be flooded with American goods, fashion, and imagery, not to mention the marines in 1916. By the 1920s, the Dominican landscape was already dotted with references to things and places Norteamericano, such as the amusement park called Coney Island, which opened in the heart of the elite Santo Domingo suburb Gazcue. Respectable firms that sold European furniture and other goods had successfully shifted by 1920 to American products such as typewriters, phonographs, bicycles, and automobiles.[47] So it should be no surprise that consumption etiquette became the language through which the Dominican bourgeoisie sought to fashion itself as superior in social and cultural terms in the face of a threat from above, the United States; from the side, nouveau riche immigrant merchants and technicians, and a nascent urban middle class; and from below, the *populacho*.

As Mary Douglas and Baron Isherwood have argued, consumption practices often serve to define social frontiers during moments of flux.[48] In this case, they became markers of both class and national identity. A war against the United States and things American was declared during a moment when the United States came to represent modernity—that is, whiteness and technological superiority—especially in its territorial "backyard." The virulent attack on American commodities expressed anxieties caused by turn-of-the-century socioeconomic change that rendered class boundaries fluid. In part this resulted from the shift toward sugar, which created opportunities for emerging middle sectors providing services to the provincial sugar enclaves.[49] Sugar brought with it an influx of foreigners: Haitians and West Indian immigrants arrived to cut cane, and white immigrants from Spain, Cuba, Syria, Puerto Rico, and Italy formed part of the thriving merchant sector in the marketing and sale of small manufactured goods. The latter were even more of a threat to elites, who sought to restrict their entry to social clubs, and thus second-tier clubs such as La Perla Negra emerged.[50] State infrastructural and urban development by the 1920s had also expanded the *pequeña burguesía* or petty bourgeoisie (also known as *gente de segunda*),

1. Advertisements from *El libro azul*, Santo Domingo, 1920. ARCHIVO
GENERAL DE LA NACIÓN, SANTO DOMINGO.

the term itself expressing the ambiguities of a stratum that was structurally a middle class, yet harbored the identity of a lower tier of the elite stratum. In the 1920s Dominican social space was still perceived as having no middle ground as such; social rank was hierarchical and dichotomous. Society was divided into the caste-like distinctions of *gente de primera* and *gente de segunda*, with the remaining rural *montón anónimo* off the social map altogether.[51] During the U.S. occupation, a sharply vertical cultural taxonomy was carved that left the populacho quite explicitly out. Having lost access to the state, a major source of patronage and class reproduction, and confronted with economic redundancy given the massive infusions of corporate capital investment, the liberal elite had to redefine its raison d'etre. It retreated into an increasingly exclusivist definition of "high culture," one that claimed superiority within the realm of lifestyle, leisure, and consumption habits, even though it had lost whatever effective hegemony it could claim previously.[52]

The U.S. occupation commenced with an unprecedented economic boom, as World War I caused global shortages of raw materials and prices for principal Dominican export crops—tobacco, cacao, coffee, and sugar— hit extraordinary highs. In this historically cash-strapped economy, the boom brought a measure of affluence to all, from cane farmers to merchants. As the price of sugar rose fourfold from 1914 to 1920 during the "dance of the millions," a flood of commodities entered the country as never before. With cash in their pockets, even the provincial working class in sugar boom towns such as San Pedro de Macorís saw an improvement in their standard of living. Due to the Customs Tariff Act of 1919, which eliminated or drastically reduced duties on U.S. manufactured goods, most of the commodities entering the country were from the United States.[53]

Economic transnationalization was accompanied by enormous new flows of immigrants into the country. The economic base of the traditional upper class had previously been their control over regional cattle, tobacco, cacao, coffee, or sugar economies.[54] But from the late nineteenth century on, large expanses of land were taken over by highly capitalized U.S. firms for sugar and timber. Dominicans remained only if they agreed to become intermediaries, such as small cane farmers for U.S. companies that transported, milled, distributed, and sold the final processed sugar to markets overseas.[55] Immigrants from Europe and the Middle East swelled the new merchant class. Indeed, by the 1920s, some reported that a full 50 percent of retail trade was in Syrian hands; their prominence had provoked strong outrage earlier in the century when Arab presence was much less significant.[56] The literature on U.S. influence during this period has focused on its role in monopolizing production, leaving aside a host of important questions about how processes of commodification transformed everyday life and empowered the emerging middle classes, as well as how the specter of consumer culture fueled by U.S. capital and goods was experienced in this bastion of U.S. imperial control.[57]

Dominican liberals in the late nineteenth century had held great expectations for the United States not only as an example of growth and democracy but as a source of foreign capital that they hoped would kick-start the process of capitalist development. U.S. investment would bring roads, and thus "commerce, agriculture, industry, immigration, riches, happiness and well-being."[58] Many looked at the formidable economic growth from the late nineteenth century through World War I and agreed with the assessment of

Otto Schoenrich, who wrote that "Santo Domingo at this moment is a country which has no present, only a past and a future."[59] The new scale of commerce and its insertion into international markets had an impact on the boundaries and markers of social class, however, creating a large amount of anxiety in the face of a tremendous influx of immigrants as well as a new boom-and-bust, export-driven economy. The northern region alone jumped from a population of 90,000 to 250,000 from 1875 to 1908.[60] Foreigners were inordinately represented in retail. All businesses hired traveling salesmen, frequently Syrians, and larger business houses were principally foreign owned: Italian, German, Spanish, Cuban, Puerto Rican, and American. Stores were multilingual, announcing their linguistic command of Arabic, Danish, French, Italian, and German.

A new social constituency of urban professionals had emerged in the early decades of the twentieth century which expanded the ranks of the gente de segunda.[61] Although it shared liberal ideals with its social superiors, this small urban middle sector was still a class in formation, its social insecurity and lack of property causing it to seek to distinguish itself from the rural masses by consumption and comportment, while striving for inclusion in the still primarily white elite.[62] These were what Eileen Findlay has termed "marginal dons," who had a modicum of status due to semi-skilled jobs, but who shared social space with poorer neighbors since they were frequently not formally married, lived in neighborhoods not segregated by class or race, and often had darker-skinned lovers, children, and relatives.[63] The proximity of these "big small men" to signs and practices that signified poverty (hence blackness) created a penchant for claiming respectability whenever possible, either through assertions of moral superiority or through the acquisition of foreign commodities and fashions, thus gaining status in a context in which the foreign is by definition superior.[64] Unlike neighboring Cuba and Haiti, which had plantation economies that forged a clearly stratified social order, Dominican colonial poverty and its mixed smallholder economy formed a relatively homogeneous Creole nation until the end of the nineteenth century, yet it was a nation in which the majority could be liable to the stigma of blackness, and thus were keen to camouflage it via status symbols.[65]

If the flood of U.S. goods and styles was embraced as a means of social climbing by middle sectors, they were anathema to elites facing a novel challenge to their authority. Commodities afforded the principal idiom through which liberals could wage war against the United States as rules governing the use of American products and practices, from dance styles to the dollar, became symbolic weapons against the Yankees.

Even as they found themselves awash in new commodities, Dominicans picked and chose which products they would consume. There was a grammar of appropriation determining which "modernizing goods" would be embraced and which rejected.[66] Small local manufactures also grew in response to increased demand, as Dominican factories sprang up making matches, ice, cigars, rum, straw hats, shoes, and chocolate. But local production was insufficient, and imports of many items expanded rapidly. While many imports were functional—products serving the construction boom, such as reinforced concrete, nails, lumber, barbed wire, and fittings, took off during this period—others were everyday luxuries that enabled the emerging middle classes to engage in a touch of conspicuous consumption. In 1918 some people had enough cash to afford sewing machines and phonographs. Many chose to invest in status accouterments in the home, embellishing the dining table, the centerpiece of sociability, with imported butter, margarine, cheese, spices, crackers, canned vegetables and fish, and various confections.

Some products were available in the country, but the poor transport system made it easier to purchase, for example, powdered or condensed milk, than wait for the next shipment via canoe. Scarcities of basic daily staples such as rice and sugar, which were now key exports, caused a local outcry since the locally produced versions were vastly preferred; some suspected hoarding by traders eager to sell at inflated prices. Sugar shortages caused a particular sting since it had become the country's most important commodity, and critics complained that when available it was sold at inflated wartime prices. It was said that "free trade should not interfere with the health of the people" and life was bitter indeed, it seemed, without sugar.[67]

Of course, concerns about the state of the nation as it became swamped in a sea of commodities date back to the nineteenth century. Some U.S. products such as oleomargarine had seeped into the local diet by the 1860s, causing dismay among liberal critics such as José Ramón López who saw it as a cause of national enervation and worse.[68] Another critic railed that the town council must be the watchdog of public health since "the North American edible products we consume each day are disgusting and criminal adulterations that destroy our organism, deadening our functions."

Adulterated, watered down milk, in particular, was singled out as the most dastardly fraud since it was a mainstay of children and the elderly.[69] Yet by 1920 there was also ample evidence that most Dominicans looked to the United States as an icon of worldliness and sophistication, judging by Santo Domingo replicas such as the Hotel Plaza and the "cosmopolitan" Café and Restaurant New York. And as in Cuba, many Dominican elites were intimately familiar with the United States since they frequently traveled and even sent their children to school there.

Otto Schoenrich, a traveler to Santo Domingo during the occupation, was duly impressed by the popularity of ablutions there. As he said, "If the amount of soap used by a people is really an index of its degree of civilization, then the Dominicans can claim to be far advanced, for the consumption of soap manufactured in the country and imported, is very considerable."[70] A fitting symbol of modernity, soap offered the promise of self-transformation and renewal. And while imported products from France were preferred by those who could afford it, Dominicans clamored for cleansing agents, buying U.S. brands when the less costly Creole versions were sold out. In 1919 soap imports from the U.S. nearly doubled and French imports increased by one-third, Palmolive being a popular brand.[71] Advertisements in apothecaries and pharmacies touting the virtues of salt baths indicate that these were also popular rites of purification.

Many Dominicans also embraced products that helped them cut a more groomed, youthful modern profile. While Dominican men proved reluctant to let go of their beloved moustache, the popularity of Gillette razors indicated that a sharper, less hirsute look was becoming fashionable. Women took to hair dyes to rejuvenate, pomades and powders to refresh, and finally Brownie cameras to capture their new look for posterity.[72] In this small island nation with a history of valorizing the exogenous and exotic, both men and women embraced products such as Tinta Oriental, which could make one look young again; Oriental Drops and Tablets and Red Pills were also very popular.[73] French toiletries and cosmetics were coveted, of course, but because they were costly their use diminished toward the end of the occupation.

Newfound affluence brought respectability within reach of the majority by enabling even the urban poor to purchase footwear and hats. Photos of the period reveal a new public uniform of Panama hats and shoes, which became ubiquitous, if not in everyday life then at least on social occasions such as rallies, strolls, and family outings. At that time, very few rural

2. Male fashion before the U.S. occupation. ARCHIVO GENERAL DE LA NACIÓN, SANTO DOMINGO.

3. The new clean-shaven look for men. ARCHIVO GENERAL DE LA NACIÓN, SANTO DOMINGO.

Dominicans could afford shoes of any kind; peasants wore *soletas* of leather or went barefoot.[74]

Shoes were so scarce that Smedley Butler, a marine who was stationed in both Haiti and the Dominican Republic, read social class through the medium of footwear, describing Haiti as divided into those with bare feet and the "shoe class," those wearing "vici kid shoes with long pointed toes and celluloid collars."[75] If Dominicans were never as flashy, these markers of respectability for the first time trickled down to the middle classes, especially in the urban areas. Shoestores popped up in Santo Domingo, and local firms such as Cintrón y Mañon were staffed by thirty factory operators producing straw hats.[76] Local shoe factories appeared as U.S. imports peaked in 1918 and declined thereafter.[77] And to accompany these fineries, people sought to upgrade their clothing, which increased imports of cotton from the United States and Great Britain, with its reputation for fabrics of the highest quality.

Because this new market society seemed to be a result of U.S. intervention and investment and became manifest via a profusion of cheap consumer goods, it appeared embossed with a U.S. copyright. To add insult to injury, the U.S. dollar became legal tender, rendering Dominican silver and copper pesos mere fractional currency, a fact that seemed to mirror economic and political relations on the island as if Dominicans themselves had been reduced to small change.[78] Since this transformation occurred under a U.S. Marine military government, the consumption of cheap consumer durables from the United States became a charged and vexing issue for some.

One American contraption that met with particular Dominican ire was the gumball machine, which became a key symbol of the wolf-in-sheep's-clothing of American imperialism. First installed in popular barrios of Santo Domingo such as San Carlos, San Miguel, and Villa Francisca, these machines were viewed as stealing all the hard-earned cash of the "naive" peasants, who, it was said, would grow addicted to the lure of gambling and its vices. One writer claimed they were part of a conspiracy to rob the pockets of those without sufficient self-control.[79] The gumball machine was a potent emblem of the surreptitiousness of *Tío Sam* (Uncle Sam)—who called himself your uncle while treating you as his employee—an economic logic quite distinct from the paternalism of traditional Dominican social hierarchy. Yet even if the bourgeoisie seemed to object to the populacho enjoying American commodities, they themselves were not above stooping, on occasion, to such indulgences. It became chic, for example, to import streamers and confetti from New York (even if the champagne had to be French) for the truly great parties of the *sociedad elegante*.[80]

Certain popular cultural forms associated with the United States became highly politicized symbols of Yankee imperialism during the occupation itself. An example was the new fox trot vogue, a U.S. import, which became the rage among the youth during the occupation to the extent that some feared that it would wipe out the elite's "traditional" dance styles, such as the waltz. One writer complained that this latest dance craze was "demoralizing." Much to his chagrin, girls had even taken to practicing the fox trot publicly, in Central Park, in the northern coastal town of Samaná. It was said that Dominican traditions were disappearing owing to the continuous waves of "successive civilizations" arriving at their doorstep, but the fox trot was particularly dangerous because it struck at the "modesty" that gave "splendor" to the Dominican gentler sex. As one author wrote, "We understand that given the contortions, pirouettes, and other voluptuous movements practiced in that Yankee music, our women of the future must distance themselves completely from it and focus strictly on our creole musical forms (the Waltz, *Danza* and *Danzones*, etc.) that in no way affect the delicateness, the decency and the chaste sentiment of the Dominican female."[81]

One wonders here whether it was the Americanness of the dance or the fact of women dancing alone in a space previously reserved for poetry recitals, classical music concerts, and evening strolls that most piqued this observer. Nor were Dominican elites in general nationalistic to the point that they were impervious to outside influences within the realm of dance styles—they just had to emanate from Europe. In fact, the "Apache dance," a Parisian vogue in which the lead male pantomimes a pimp roughing up his prostitute, not only hit Santo Domingo by storm but was actively promoted in journals that printed instructional photos to facilitate learning.[82]

Perhaps the most charged site of all cultural contests, however, were the playing fields, as baseball games between the U.S. Marine team and the Dominican "Stars" became the one arena where Dominicans were allowed to fight back against the occupation authorities, a zone where U.S. and Dominican males put aside their everyday identities and played as equals. Baseball may have become even more significant given the ban on cockfighting, arguably the most popular male leisure pursuit previously.[83] As one anonymous sports reporter proudly reported after one such Dominican victory, "It has now been proven that all the Dominican teams are stronger than any of the Yankee teams that we have met until now. To call a spade a spade, even though it's their national game, the North Americans who visit us have a lot to learn from our players."[84] The Dominican team was especially pleased when the Yankees sought reinforcements from Haiti and Cuba, which made Dominicans by implication the best in the Caribbean, outshining their historically richer and more cosmopolitan neighbors and rivals.[85]

If declaring war on Yankee symbols was one outlet for popular wrath, another was engaging in symbolic resistance to the occupation and the Americanization resulting from free trade by taking refuge in signs of Europe. The Dominican market, thus, seemed to express selective commodity resistance since in certain domains U.S. products made little or no inroads with consumers.[86] Alcoholic beverages constituted one such arena. Neither U.S. liquors nor beer were particularly popular with locals; the many ads for Pabst beer fell on deaf ears. Dominicans preferred local rums with regal names such as Hilo de Oro (Gold Thread), Ron Corona (Crown Rum), or Ponch Imperial (Royal Punch); Creole monikers included Comet Rum and La India. One local manufacturer boasted that Tres Coronas (three crowns) had become "the favorite drink of the foreigner as well as the native Dominican."[87] A restaurant in Santo Domingo even changed its name during this period from a pluralist, welcoming *Ambos Mundos*, or Both Worlds, to an exclusivist *La Europa* (a move which was sharply protested).[88]

Even if certain American forms of recreation, such as cinema, became the vogue among middle-class youths in Santo Domingo, the elite tried to shut its doors against U.S. influence, particularly in the realm of domestic family leisure. In the home, family pursuits remained keyed to European motifs. Of course, by the turn of the century certain activities such as the family picnic (originally French) had become U.S. favorites as well. And *giras campestre* (country outings, as picnics were called) were popular affairs; the entire family including extended kin and friends came out in their Sunday Victorian best, with the requisite millinery and parasol for sun protection, for an abundant meal, fresh air, and exercise. But parlor games, termed *juegos de sociedad* and most likely played after lunch or dinner, were exceedingly fashionable as well; many of these clearly depended upon knowledge of European culture and provided a means of display of such cultural capital. An example was the game *el parelelo*, in which one player chooses a profession and scripts the other related roles, and then calls upon each person to free associate based on the leader's knowledge of high culture. For example, the marketplace is selected, and the assigned roles are fisherman, water seller, soup vendor, fruit vendor, etc. Then the leader asks, "What is the most beautiful task in the opera *Roberto el Diablo* (Robert the Devil)?" "How is the music?" etc., and the players respond accordingly.[89] Thus the game scripts participants into the plots of European theater and opera, providing a telling commentary on the extent to which the Dominican cultural elite actually lived in their own country. Another game called *la metamorfosis* entailed each participant becoming a piece of furniture from the living room (such as the clock); the others were then asked to guess which item they had become.[90] This game reflected the importance of domestic space for the bourgeoisie, since it called upon players to become one with the interior of the great house. Similarly, another game called "the clock" pivoted around that quintessential symbol of modernity.[91] Thus the threat to the bourgeoisie from without was met with an ever-deepening descent into the private realm of domesticity, as the home became a site of refuge as well as a bulwark against a public sphere defined by the United States and a public space increasingly crowded with social outsiders.

Imported luxury goods should best have a European patina. Elites who could afford them selected shoes from France, Cuba, or Spain, and tableware from England or France.[92] For cordials and expensive liquors, Dominicans sought out Spanish muscatel wine and anis and French cognac. Fine toiletries should also come from Europe, and purveyors of fine perfumes, fancy toilet articles, and "high grade candies" tended to have European appellations, such as the Botica Francés. U.S. importers rarely declared themselves as American, generally adopting the Dominican importer's *apellido* or family name. United States values may have been trickling in, but when they did they were camouflaged by a Creole visage. This can be seen in the description of a businessman from Azua. His family was from Syria; he was said to be successful because of his "energy, integrity and straightforward way of doing business," duly U.S. values that were not necessarily reflective of Dominican business culture. Or take the case of Manuel de J. Gómez, who was said to have "transformed the entire character of the Dominican store of this class by making his own store conform with the European and American standards, from ideas and repeated visits made personally with this object in view."[93] His great achievement, it seems, was transforming the Dominican store by adopting features from Europe and the United States.

Liberal critics of the intervention also launched a more frontal offensive, lambasting the United States for its crass materialism and for the social-leveling effects of the newly monetarized economy, in which status came to be associated less with family heritage than access to cash. To further reinforce the antisocial associations of money, of course, not even the monetary unit was Dominican at this time. While the Dominican Republic had issued several local currencies previously, commencing with the late-nineteenth-century dictatorship of Ulises Heureaux, the U.S. dollar became the first truly national currency. Dominican intellectuals such as Pedro Bonó had issued tirades against sugar—now a potent symbol of the United States associated with the newly commodified economy and the culture of the marketplace, a corrosive force that appeared to dissolve social unity—as opposed to the traditional crop, tobacco, which symbolized "Dominicanity" and the old order.[94] The sugar economy and the dollar were also associated with a sudden dependence on the dangerously fluid and unstable global economy, a lesson urban Dominicans learned painfully during the 1929 crash.

The rejection of American values—of secular democracy, Protestantism, and a social system defined by access to money—took shape most dramatically in two phenomena: the popularization of José Enrique Rodó's classic text *Ariel* and the coronation of the Virgin de Altagracia.[95] *Ariel* was first published in Uruguay in 1900, but quickly took Santo Domingo by storm. Indeed, the Santo Domingo edition, reprinted in the *Revista Literaria*, was the first edition outside of Uruguay; it articulated in a powerful way the Dominican elite's vision of the United States and its unsettling effect on the world. Written to the youth of Latin America just after the United States had wrested Cuba, Puerto Rico, and the Philippines from Spain, the book contrasts the vulgar materialism, utilitarianism, and greed of North Americans with the spiritualism and idealism of Latin America. The book calls on Latin Americans to strengthen and renew their "lofty spirit," to counter North American egoism with the power of Latin American collective identity. Stridently antidemocratic, the text asks Latin Americans to look inward, calling for a "strong moral authority" to "ensure the inviolability of high culture."[96] A defense of aristocracy, the text is a messianic admixture of Oswald Spengler, Alexis de Tocqueville, and Friedrich Nietzsche. The book caught fire in Santo Domingo, with a group of *Arielista* intellectuals starting a journal called *Renovación* to keep the spirit alive. *Ariel* inspired the call for a "Gran Unión Latina" (Great Latin Union), a community encompassing all of southern Europe and Latin America, to serve as a counterweight to the U.S. eagle with its "cannons and its money," so as to eliminate the possibility of "absorption of the smaller nationalities."[97] *Ariel* became the sentinel of a crisis of liberalism that came to a crescendo during the occupation of the country in the 1920s.

Complaints about the corrosion of national value, as evidenced by a decline in social values, had begun to appear as early as 1903. In this discourse of degeneration, the penetration of society by the marketplace was seen as sapping the physical strength of men, feminizing the nation, and depleting it of the manly virtue necessary for progress. As in Europe and the United States during this period, the figurative language of social decline drew upon a rhetoric of gendered bodily imagery.[98] Linked to this process was the rise of a "pretentious" and self-interested nouveau riche class, who apparently were so imbued with the spirit of capital, as one observer noted, that "business is the sacred word."[99] Money provided a potent image of the dissolution of hierarchy and the inversion of values associated with a world in which anything could be bought or sold, including people, land, and even nations, one in which there were no limits to the alienability of possessions.[100] Indeed, at times a desire to control through harnessing, naming, and extricating the marketplace resulted in the fetishization of ethnic outsiders as the veritable embodiment of market values. Although in fact the new immigrant merchant class really had no choice but to enter the economy as petty traders, lucre or illicit profit became the predominant ethnic label for one group after another, from the Spaniards and Syrians to the Haitians. For example, a Haitian curandero and diviner who worked with perfumes was accused of charging excessive rates, as well as keeping a mysterious list of wealthy people's names.[101] The Dominican imagination clearly linked money, perceived as a foreign force, and immigrants, who, through cash, were viewed as upsetting the traditional status economy.[102] And a veritable campaign was waged against Arab peddlers, who were said to be ruining national commerce by sucking the value out of the country and sending it overseas.[103]

The disturbing slippage of identities caused by the monetarization of the economy under the U.S. occupation is well expressed in a novel about San Pedro de Macorís in the 1920s, *El hombre alucinado* (The Deceiving Man) by Luis Henríquez Castillo.[104] The novel takes place in one of the southern boom towns most dramatically transformed by the sugar economy. It revolves around a romantic triangle: the narrator, Jacinto, a doctor living in Santo Domingo; his wife, Irene; and her lover, Eduardo (an old friend of Jacinto's), a businessman who works for a mammoth American-owned sugar company significantly called Ingenio Washington (Washington Sugar Mill). The narrative contrasts the cynical but moral Jacinto whose small family is eaten away and finally destroyed by the secret love tryst. Jacinto is a dark film-noir character who is obsessed with the ultimate arbitrariness of social convention; the story is interspersed with his moody ruminations on bourgeois masking and the hypocrisy of society. Nonetheless, Jacinto, as a doctor, embodies the values of the old elite; he is poor but honest, poetic, and struggles to keep his family together.[105] Eduardo is handsome, stylish, and flashy, quintessentially modern, a man both created and polluted by wealth—but not just any wealth. He is el hombre alucinado, fascinating, even hallucinating, and yet ultimately deceiving. He is a creation of the Americans, tainted by a money that generates illusory value, creates hollow masks, and spoils him, friendship, and all the people and families he touches. He is a character both made and broken by his wealth. Irene falls for him when he becomes rich, and he commits suicide when he loses all in the 1929 crash. His bankruptcy, of course, is both financial and moral: in the end, he himself is as devoid of value as his bank account.

The impact of the U.S.-owned and controlled sugar economy is portrayed in stark terms in this novel. The 1920s are described as a "small burlesque of decadent Rome," the canefields as "concentration camps of men and beasts."[106] Jacinto's descent into a tangled cocoon of debt, lies, and escalating obligations commences with a relatively small act of subterfuge but ends up extinguishing his honorable personhood. A thuggish mole he paid for information about his wife's secret liaison blackmails him by threatening to reveal this secret; he then seeks ever-greater payment, eventually demanding his job, and even—the greatest punishment of all—his daughter's hand in marriage. As he rises in status (largely through Jacinto's payments), the reptilian informant seeks to destroy whatever tiny modicum of family and honor remain to Jacinto. Jacinto struggles to resist assimilation into the new social values in which everything has its price, until chided by his wife, "No one is ignoring the fact that honor used to be valuable, but it is now gone, dead, kaput; now it's money that counts."[107] The essence of modernity is dissimulation: to look good and appear moral when you are not. The contrast between the individualizing, corrosive force of the market and the old communalistic honor system is made explicit in a passage in which the narrator defends the Dominican tradition of cross-cousin marriage against its American detractors, claiming that it is integral to maintaining family, community, and implicitly even national ties.[108]

An important theme in the novel is the contrast between class cultures: the old elites, who value honor and family reputation and who sacrifice fast wealth for honest conduct, are pitted against the U.S.-produced bourgeoisie, whose money destroys people, family, and ultimately society through the atomization of individuals, the corrosion of relationships, and the corruption of traditional morality. In a seminal passage, the author contrasts the seemingly real bourgeoisie of Britain with the pretentious manners of the Latin American nouveau riche. Honest poverty (wealth is implicitly produced only through devious means) was an important old elite marker of respectability, as well as a means of defining its members against the moneyed status hierarchy of the United States. In the words of Héctor Incháustegui Cabral, a prominent old elite intellectual and essayist,

> And we don't have money. Money, many say, is made easily . . . [but] it's not easy to make money when one has conduct [una conducta]. The Billini's, too. Uncle Gollito died almost in misery, broke, with his minuscule pension. When you see those family names, that are as much yours as those of your father, you will know that there will be no money, but there will be gentility, poetry, tradition.[109]

In this view, business and respectability, money and morality, were two separate worlds, and should stay that way.[110]

This contrast between cultures of class became manifest as well through a new discourse on social dissimulation. As Karen Haltunnen has argued masterfully in another context, periods of social mobility can result in an upheaval of the criteria by which claims to social status are evaluated and determined. She demonstrates how the figure of the confidence man in nineteenth-century America became a magnet for a range of social anxieties during a period of social flux when the criteria by which to evaluate boundaries of class became increasingly obscured.[111] In the Dominican Republic, similarly, an inability to recognize and define social identity in the context of a new mass society created a similar fascination with, and concomitant revulsion for, the novel social types associated with new wealth and commodities—those that had gained access to the public sphere during the sugar boom—particularly women, blacks, and morenos (mulattos). The link between women and morenos, of course, was the fact that they could move in the social order, passing for a higher status than their origin merited: women, because their personhood was ascribed through their husbands' *apellido* (surname); and mulattos, because of their lack of a fixed racial category. Thus these two groups were more prone to stereotypes of "social posturing."[112]

In part, the new discourse of dissimulation sought to delegitimize the means by which social "inferiors," particularly women, sought to pass as genteel in public settings by means of upscale apparel. Indeed, the elite waged a concerted assault on the forms of status displayed by these *arrivistes*, through fashion articles seeking to educate the public on how to discern the forgeries from the real thing. For example, one article on the new fad for scarves cautions women not to wear those of gauze, for they were "vulgar" because of their use by social frauds. Another chastised the common *abuso de las joyas* (abuse of jewels), the heaping of ever-larger stones and settings. It called for a return to the plainer, simpler, subtler use of adornment, insinuating that both scarves and the ostentatious use of jewelry were favored by hussies and tramps and, therefore, were somehow tarnished.[113] Other pedagogic how-to articles appeared instructing women on how not to wear perfume (excessively) and hats.[114] Like early modern European etiquette manuals, the appearance of these new fashion guidelines coincided with the advent of new social groups which did not know the rules of public decorum and required instruction.[115]

It is clear that the socioeconomic changes produced by foreign capital penetration challenged the traditional grounding of identity for the elite, producing what T. J. Lears has termed the sensation of "weightlessness" or a crisis of cultural authority.[116] Suddenly new middle sectors defined their social position through the consumption of foreign commodities. Like the flâneur, they were constituted in the public sphere and were dependent upon the social gaze, since their legitimacy lay entirely in the eyes of the beholder.[117] Indeed, literature in the 1920s demonstrates a fascination with the danger of encounters with these strangers in the new public sites such as hotels, cafés, streets, and urban promenades. One short story describes an encounter with a lovely blond circus performer in a café, as her desirous admirer (the narrator) repudiates the societal voice that mocks and disdains her as a libertine tart just because she is a public woman. As the author muses, "They saw her as rotten, of perversion and malice, and yet she smiled between the two infinitudes; the death over there, that of the circus;

and that over here, of cowardice and contempt."[118] But it was not only women in public who became signs of identity transmogrification and symbols of social ambiguity and passage. Other new public types, such as the mulatto, evoked an equivalent sense of unease. Another short story encapsulates several linked motifs of social angst: the mulatto, the crowd, and public space. The narrative voyeuristically follows a moreno as he arrives at a hotel, where there are clothes strewn everywhere. But not just any clothes: these are suits of silk, and cufflinks of gold, a scene of unkempt and decadent luxury. Amid this untidy opulence is a red suit, a bullfighter's outfit, which the mulatto cannot restrain himself from pilfering. He steals it and rushes to the ring, where, compelled by the frenzied screams of the crowd, he fights two bulls and ends up lying dead next to one, amid a pool of blood.[119]

This story condenses several images of social danger: first, the power of the crowd, which drove this man to his death; second, the violence, unpredictability, and lack of reason of the mulatto who is governed by impulse and passion. And finally, his uncontrollable lust for lavish costume and sumptuous finery, as well as his need to make a spectacle of himself, his desire for approval. The mulatto is the trickster figure par excellence, one who traverses social worlds, who is both everywhere and nowhere. Ultimately vacuous, without substance, he lives for the gaze of others.

Public women and mulattos were equally frowned upon as profligate poseurs and sybaritic parasites with changeable identities. And in this predominantly mulatto context of historical poverty, morenos with the proper combination of élan and savoir faire (as well as money) could fashion themselves as bourgeois and effectively pass into high society. Both groups were also believed to have a parallel thirst for approbation. Thus women and mulattos shared the hybrid, paradoxically inside-outside social position that represented a threat to the stable, ascribed ideology of social ranking characteristic of the old aristocracy.[120] Public women and mulattos were also troublesome as "phobic mediators between high and low," "sliding signifiers" that horizontally conjoined domains that ought to be kept vertically discrete.[121] Passing, of course, was also disturbing, perhaps because it suggested to the elites the fiction of their own legitimacy as social arbiters.

Yet this crisis of credibility at times blossomed into a more general critique of the hypocrisy and chicanery of this new urban social topos of strangers, as the country was suddenly seen as peopled almost entirely by impostors and fakes. It is no coincidence that the city became the key theater of status display for the new middle service sector, since urbanization had been a by-product of the development of the sugar plantation economy. In the 1920s the social landscape was portrayed as inhabited by characters at once chameleonic, false, and indecipherable. Indeed, the elite obsession with mimicry appears to confirm Homi Bhabha's argument about how doubling threatens authority by revealing the absence of identity behind the mask; this discourse of dissimulation functioned precisely by treading the line between mimicry and mockery.[122] This is apparent in a range of new social types represented in the imagery of the Dominican press. For example, the black gallant with baton, cigar, and tuxedo featured in the *negrito* coffee advertisement has several strands of meaning. In a moment of suffusion in American imagery, this image most certainly draws upon a racial caricature then prevalent in the United States, what Thomas Holt has called the "misplaced urban dandy." Yet even in the complex race-class system of the Dominican Republic, in which race was essentially a metaphor for class and race was euphemized, the black fop functioned in much the same way that Holt has analyzed for the United States. It provided a firm baseline against which Dominicans could fashion their identity, helping assuage the anxieties of race and class slippage in a social order in flux. The Dominican elite knew not what it was, but it now knew what it was not.[123]

Furthermore, the black dandy also challenged the U.S. Marine perception that Dominicans and neighboring Haitians were from the same racial stock. The exaggerated image of the negrito ridiculed the notion that there were black Dominicans during a moment when the United States was blamed for a contract labor policy through which thousands of Haitians and West Indians had been imported since the 1880s to provide a cheap and reliable labor source for the sugar industry. Since the United States had created the "black problem" in the Dominican Republic, it makes sense that Dominicans would portray blacks via a U.S. stereotype. The use of this image seemed to imply that the new black population was not Dominican at all. The black dandy may also have drawn upon a Dominican perception of black and mulatto puffery, ostentation, and frippery among the Haitian urban middle and upper classes. The misplacement of the black fop was that he appeared on Dominican soil at all, where he did not belong.[124] As in Cuba, the figure of the negrito unified Creoles in the face of an intrepid impostor.[125]

But the discourse of social hypocrisy also honed in on Creole social roles

4. *El Negrito* coffee advertisement, *Blanco y Negro*, 30 October 1926, p. 3. ARCHIVO GENERAL DE LA NACIÓN, SANTO DOMINGO.

and stereotypes, seeking to debunk and debase a range of traditional and new figures among the emerging middle classes. The cartoon *Nota cómico-seria de actualidad* (Comic-Serious Note of Nowadays) takes on the floozy (wooed by flattery, driven by cash); the *piccaro* or rogue (charms by seduction, governed by interest); the traditional political sycophant, so full of hot air he floats, awaiting his *botella* (sinecure) or government position; the despotic intellectual (totemized as a snake), who finds fault everywhere; the haughty aristocratic lord who feels above it all, hermetically encased in his shiny car (paid for with "usury and dirty money"); the swank, vain peacock (with knife poised to drop at any time); and finally the worker, a slave without agency. The totem of the snake also appeared in the pushy figure of the *culebrón*, the quintessential party crasher who "hunted" opportunities "to make incursions that raised his social status" by appearing in company higher than that of his own station. As Gómez Alfau put it, "To become a member of good society was not a thing of 'I came, I saw, I conquered'; nationals as well as foreigners had to present credentials and references that testified to the good conduct and lineage of the aspirant."[126]

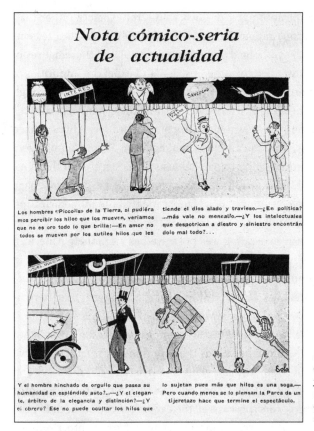

Nota cómico-seria de actualidad

Los hombres «Piccolis» de la Tierra, si pudiéramos percibir los hilos que los mueven, veríamos que no es oro todo lo que brilla:—En amor no todos se mueven por los sutiles hilos que les tiende el dios alado y travieso.—¿En política? ...más vale no menealo.—¿Y los intelectuales que despotrican a diestro y siniestro encontrándolo mal todo?...

Y el hombre hinchado de orgullo que pasea su humanidad en espléndido auto?.—¿Y el elegante, árbitro de la elegancia y distinción?—¿Y el obrero? Ese no puede ocultar los hilos que lo sujetan pues más que hilos es una soga.—Pero cuando menos se lo piensan la Parca de un tijeretazo hace que termine el espectáculo.

5. "Nota cómico-seria de la actualidad." *Blanco y Negro*, 16 January 1926, p. 108. ARCHIVO GENERAL DE LA NACIÓN, SANTO DOMINGO.

Of course, all of the characters in *Nota cómico-seria* are so empty, ephemeral, and ultimately dependent that they could collapse in an instant with a snip to the puppet strings controlling them (held by other people and their money). This cartoon underscores the elites' vision that Dominican society had become a kind of carnivalesque masquerade ball, beautiful yet illusory, tempting yet duplicitous, and potentially gone in a flash. From harlot to gigolo, pompous baron to toady minion, these characters were all dissemblers, and all ultimately both products and signs of a corrupt and venal monetary economy. The U.S.-controlled sugar economy had transformed Dominican society. Moreover, the global marketplace governed by the United States was unnerving because of its unprecedented scale as well as its mysterious abstract logic, unlike the nineteenth-century gentlemen tobacco farmers of the Cibao valley in league with German coastal merchants. The economy of sugar, like usury, represented an unnatural system that seemed to produce cash out of nothing; it drained value from society rather than reinvesting in it and took rather than gave.[127] Through "analogical reasoning," the invention and symbolic damnation (or ridicule) of these figures of social masking were intended to name, restrict, and expel the impurities of this new economic order, which promised to enhance and fulfill through trinkets and goods, but actually seemed to consume society and its values.[128] Through impersonating the new monetary economy in a series of racialized and gendered villains, Dominican elites sought to grasp and humanize a system as distant, abstract, and unimaginable as Wall Street, and thus give form to the intangible. Most of all, these images provided a visual language for expressing the alien feel of the social landscape that the monetarization of the economy had created.[129]

Even though excessive spending was portrayed as a uniquely American phenomenon, this is not to say that Dominican elites failed to engage in conspicuous consumption.[130] Indeed, grandiose displays of wealth were intrinsic to the maintenance of the traditional status hierarchy, and hereditary symbolic capital was often fused with bourgeois economic capital.[131] A prime example of the heights that a truly sumptuous wedding of a Santo Domingo elite family could achieve was the ceremony for the union of two of the most important southern-elite clans in 1919: the Cabral-Baezes and the Pelleranos. After the religious ceremony in the cathedral, the motor cavalcade included forty cars (perhaps all the cars in the capital at that time) and many carriages; nearly every important family from Santo Domingo was represented except the elusive Vicinis, the Italian sugar moguls who were in a class by themselves. The gifts at the reception totaled more than five thousand dollars in silver alone. In addition, the newspaper printed a full list of all guests and their nuptial gifts.[132] However, this kind of ritual excess was perceived as legitimate and fundamentally social, part of a necessary system of redistribution among kin and reproduction of the family name. Prestige spending was also perceived as constitutive of aristocratic status, as it reinforced status boundaries and provided an invisible veil between the gente de primera and outsiders. In essence a kind of anti-market logic, the thrust of this elite spending was to recuperate certain luxury goods from the marketplace and re-monopolize them by taking them out of circulation.[133] Finally, such events reinforced the collective identity of the clan patriarch, who was only as good as the crowd he could summon up at occasions of this kind.

If a critique of monetarization offered one riposte to U.S. rule, another was the revival of Catholicism as evidenced in the coronation of the Virgin of Altagracia. Why would religion become a central idiom of national identity and of alterity to mass consumer culture?[134] It did so in part because Catholicism invoked Spain and *hispanismo*, which were available and legitimate counter-identities. Caribbean nations with multiple colonial legacies have often found it advantageous to play the characteristics of one off another, much as Cuba did when it styled itself as modern, cosmopolitan, and baseball-playing (i.e., American, as opposed to backward and bull-fighting) in an effort to challenge the validity of colonial rule in 1898.[135] However, hispanismo was far from a primordial, never-changing, or generalized aspect of national identity in the Dominican Republic. The construction of the country as eminently Spanish originally dates from colonial rule (1492–1822), but was renewed as an expression of national difference during the Haitian occupation (1822–44), only to quiet down considerably during the later reacquisition of the country by Spain (1861–65), when things Spanish were patently vilified by the majority.[136] The twentieth-century rebirth of hispanismo in the Dominican Republic thus dates from 1907, when customs control was ceded to the United States, not 1865, when independence was stolen at gunpoint from Spain. During this spate of anti-American sentiment, not only was Spanish declared the official language in 1912, but the same year a romantic colonial relic, the Juegos Florales (Floral Games), were resurrected by the select Club Unión, in which bourgeois men competed in poetry contests and women danced around the maypole. And Christopher Columbus became an official icon the same year when Columbus Day became a national holiday, a gigantic Columbus lighthouse project was proposed, and the Teatro Colón was inaugurated.[137] Surprisingly, this revival of popular Catholicism was engineered by liberals, not conservatives. Monseñor Adolfo Nouel, chief organizer of the Virgin of Altagracia's coronation, had initially cooperated with the U.S. Marines but became a critic of the occupation when American authorities imposed censorship and removed the courts from Dominicans' jurisdiction.[138]

UNRULY WOMEN AND MALE VIGOR

The Dominican family was also viewed as hampering both economic and political development and the marines instituted several policies that were perceived as empowering women to the detriment of men. U.S. authorities, horrified by the relative rarity of formal matrimony—particularly in the interior—rewrote marriage laws to facilitate the institution—simplifying the necessary paperwork, abolishing fees, and eliminating the need for a religious ceremony. U.S. policy sought to transform marriage from a luxury to a prerogative. Paternity laws were altered to permit proof of paternity for illegitimate children; the United States also sought abrogation of a civil code article prohibiting paternity inquiries, which thwarted the efforts of wives to legalize their children and claim child support. An executive order was passed requiring parental shelter and support of offspring. Correctional schools were also created to provide for the "thousands of homeless who grow up like wild animals," becoming "vagabonds, bandits and prostitutes."[139] However, in striving to legislate a bourgeois conjugal form in which the family served as a private refuge from public affairs, U.S. intervention actually politicized it as domestic order became an issue of public morality.

Marital reform proposals were intended to encourage greater individual rights within the family. This aspect of legislative change did provide for greater autonomy for women, much to the chagrin of some Dominican men. For example, under previous Dominican law women required their husband's permission to conduct business, but the military governor wanted to give women the freedom to manage their own finances without being hampered by their husbands, and so pushed for equal rights legislation for women. This was particularly important given the custom of serial marriage in the Dominican Republic, which left the majority of older women technically married, but in reality heads of households who required an income to support their children. The surge in marital disputes over women's employment was probably related to the United States–initiated vocational training programs, the Escuelas Vocacionales para Señoritas (Vocational Schools for Girls), which spurred women to find work (another incentive was rising prices for many imported commodities during the Depression). Private trade schools aimed at women, such as the Instituto Comercial founded in 1913, offered training in typing, stenography, and English for men and señoritas. Efforts were also made to facilitate the partition of minors' lands, so that dependents could more easily break away from their parents and become independent wage earners. Previously, excessive legal fees and taxation had inhibited the partition of small property parcels, with the result that family lands were kept intact.[140]

Alongside pro-marital legislation, another major change generated by the U.S. Marines with particular implications for women was prostitution reform. As Donna Guy has argued for Argentina in the 1920s, the two terms limiting the parameters of female citizenship during the U.S. occupation were the wife and the prostitute.[141] Moral reformers championing hygiene as an "emblem of civilization" countered the "prostitutionists," claiming that the liberty of prostitution is the freedom to poison the population.[142] U.S. Marine efforts to identify, segregate, and arrest prostitutes and banish the profession in Santo Domingo were met with concerted resistance by those that did not share the objectified image of the prostitute as a clearly defined entity.[143] Prostitution at the time was practiced along a continuum from professionals to individuals involved in partly commodified long-term relationships; only full-time *mujeres de vida alegre*, or call girls (called "commercial prostitutes" in American parlance), merited the title. U.S. authorities called women involved in extramarital sexual relations "clandestine prostitutes," and many clashes erupted over women involved in long-term concubinage, often with children. The marines set up an emergency hospital on one of the elite thoroughfares of downtown Santo Domingo to isolate, test, and treat potential carriers of syphilis, and isolated prostitution wards were established in provincial hospitals. Rendered outlaws by a clause in the Sanitary Code, prostitutes were perceived as agents of contagion and kept quarantined in solitary confinement. The hospital, however, created an enormous furor as Santo Domingo residents complained, first, about the placement of the hospital on a site of a bourgeois promenade, where prostitutes could be seen by unmarried señoritas who could fall prey to their example, and second, about the possible contagion of neighbors. While the United States felt that these girls should be treated and reformed, middle-class Dominicans, on the other hand, saw them as an irremediable social scourge that should be banished from society. Worse still, the United States sought to place shameful secrets in the public gaze that Dominicans felt should remain concealed.[144] These measures may account for the backlash against public women that was waged in the press.

By the 1920s, women were entering a range of new professions that had emerged with urban growth, from sewing to teaching, and were eager to spend some of their new hard-earned cash on leisure. Cinema gave them a legitimate opportunity to get out of the house, while enabling them to keep an eye on western fashion. However, this pastime, alongside other habits of the new "modern woman," caused considerable consternation among their husbands and male compatriots. One woman complained that her husband wouldn't permit her to go to the movies on her own, even once a week. She found ample support in one *Listín Diario* column, needless to say, which counseled her that too much home stay created "discontented complainers and neurasthenics" (*rengañonas, descontentadizas y neurasténicas*), as well as female bodily and personality disorders caused by excessive enclosure and home entrapment. Not only did the incessant confinement of women create these domestic diseases; it caused divorce.[145] Of course, this was one perspective; conservative men and women saw it altogether differently. As Leonore Davidoff and Catherine Hall have argued, gender is often implicated in class consciousness.[146] The figure of the "modern woman" was beginning to erode the separately demarcated gendered spheres of the past, and women were moving into the public sphere in new ways. In 1913 the first Dominican woman lawyer received her degree, in full expectation that she would pursue a career which would have been unthinkable even one decade previously. Professional women in the nineteenth century were more likely to have careers in teaching and areas associated with children, and in the home, philanthropy, or the arts.[147] Medical advertising for abortions indicates that more women were taking control of their bodies and futures as well.[148]

Nineteenth-century Dominican bourgeois society was highly romantic —even baroque—in style, with women playing a largely ornamental role and representing their families and husbands rather than themselves. For example, presidents were applauded not only for their honor and accomplishment but for their daughters, such as the painter Señorita Celeste Woss y Ricart, who was described as "An artist. A lyric rose. A Cyprian perfume. The sweetest breath" (Una artista. Una rosa lírica. Un perfume de Chipre. Un hálito suavísimo).[149] It was also assumed that men should not bond with, but rather possess, their women.[150] Correspondingly, accomplished *caballeros* (gentlemen) were granted distinction not solely for their achievements, social rank, and decorum, but for the honor of their extended personhood as embodied in their home. Elite diversions often played on male-female erotic desire, hailing women as decorative objects, as in the case of a "flattery contest" in the central theater of Higüey, which tested both the seductive potency of male oratory as well as the magnetic allure of "the delights of our elegant society."[151] And female professionals were inevitably praised not only for their talent (*luz del talento*) but for the "gentle charm of their body and the brilliant expression of their eyes . . . [and] their graceful beauty" (donaire gentil de su cuerpo y de la fúlgida expresión de sus ojos . . . su efímera belleza).[152]

In the 1920s, however, a shrill male outcry picked up steam against the new modern female persona, at times reaching the extreme of veiled threats. Civilization, morality, and even society itself were said to be founded on the "disjunction of the sexes." Women, lured by Hollywood films and American "mercenary women," had become "more imbued with the fatal consequences of the morbid and corrupt relations with the Yankee." One author chastised, "We warn her. . . . Let not woman, by her 'masculinity,' weaken the inviolate case of the entire effective evolution of society. Woman, if she aspires to continue being what she is, must strive to remain separated from man by the divine barriers of sex."[153]

If overturning the respectable gendered division of labor were not bad enough, women became scapegoats for all the evils of the creeping "Americanization" of the country. In a series of chiding reprimands, women were remonstrated for any ventures into appropriately male domains such as assertive sexuality, commerce, positions of authority, and the autonomous pursuit of one's own desires. One author reproached, "Nine things which our women have learned in six years: To show their legs more than they should. To go marketing playing the role of servants. To become typists and neglect the kitchen. To go out riding in automobiles or in airplanes with whom they think best. To become chauffeurs. To marry for business. To cross their legs in public places. To wear excessively low-cut dresses and to dance in cafes and restaurants."[154]

By extension, just as women became the primary index of social and moral degeneration in the Dominican Republic, Dominican travelers to the United States also read the pathology of American society through the status of women. They frequently commented on the world-turned-upside-down of American society, where "the woman is all-powerful" (*la mujer aquí es todopoderosa*), remaining in the streets from dawn to dusk, and where men can even be arrested for public flirtation.[155] A columnist for *Listín Diario* noted with shock and dismay that women in New York are millionaires, obtain divorces, and are able to stroll the streets without the aggressive flirtation and flattery that are such a popular art form in Santo Domingo. Nor are they followed on the streets by men. He recounted in disbelief the story of a woman who called the police on a man who pursued her in the subway and was detained as a result. As he remarked, there "the woman punishes, governs and forgives . . . the woman in New York is an all too absolutely powerful queen."[156] Women in the United States were seen as having too much power.

Further evidence that public women were causing alarm was a baby-stealing trial that shocked and enthralled the *capitaleño* reading public for weeks as it unfolded. The tabloid-style headlines read: "The Criminal Tribunal Rules Against the Cannibals of Guayajayuco," its sparseness indicating that the reading public was already well aware of the contents of the story. In a rural commune of Bánica, a Dominican woman had left her three children home with their grandmother. A Haitian woman had kidnapped the one year old, snatching him from the porch while he was playing with his siblings. It was said that she carried him to the forest, where she slit his throat, hung him from a tree, removed the head, hands, and feet to feed them to a dog, and she and her partner cooked and ate a portion of the remains. She and her daughter were given twenty years of forced labor for cannibalism, although she died in jail before her term was complete.[157] Surely this chilling episode was read as a cautionary tale to working women who were seen to be abandoning their domestic duties, reminding them of the potential hazards implied by such negligence.

The litany of complaints about unruly women may well indicate that the crisis of liberalism was also a crisis of manhood. During the occupation, Dominican men had been deprived of their right to the National Palace, and their control over the home and the street had been compromised. Worse yet, the nation had been violated, penetrated by an occupying force, and thus rendered passive, dependent, emasculated. The U.S. occupation at times targeted men quite explicitly. For example, the Santo Domingo *Blue Book*, which was written under the guidance of U.S. authorities to present the nation to American investors, declared that "the men of the country . . . just budding into manhood" are learning that the key to national success is national development, not making revolution.[158] And one of the "civilizing" features of U.S. rule was mandatory disarmament, which was intended to diminish the inordinate martial prowess of Dominican men. This eliminated the constant adornment of the firearm or knife that Dominican men of all social classes wore previously and not infrequently used.[159] As Teresita Martínez-Vergne has said, national character was cast implicitly as male.[160] Dominican liberals seem to have viewed their displacement from office by uncouth marines as an assault on their manhood, the occupation a symbolic emasculation that rendered them cuckolds.[161]

The extraordinary popularity of blood tonics combating fatigue in the 1920s may also evidence a crisis in masculinity. The press was peppered with advertisements for products such as Ozomulsión, which was particularly aimed at men who had been depleted through excessive work, age, or illness. It could supposedly combat cough, flu, broncular infection, anemia, fever—even the plague. The ad proclaimed, "Male vigor can be maintained!" Ozomulsión promised to "enrich the blood and fortify the nerves, give force, energy and vitality to weak, anemic and nervous people. For general weakness, functional impotency, thin blood, and nervous prostration."[162] The U.S. firm Bristol-Myers sold Sal Hepática, salt baths, to cleanse the body and clarify the mind. Most of these tonics hailed from the United States, but Depurativo Richelet, a blood purifier, was French. Local firms may have tried to gain some market share of this lucrative business, since Ozomulsión and Tonikel appear to have been locally produced. If these potions were not sufficiently restorative, one could always resort to the standard Creole home remedy of a good shot of rum.[163]

These tonics were clearly antidotes for neurasthenia, a disease of the nerves that was particularly rife among elites in the United States and Europe at the time. The malady presumed that the body had a limited supply of energy and could be depleted through excessive mental or sexual exertion. It was a disease of weakness, and thus of feminization, one which required vigorous physical expenditure to cultivate the force of will to overcome. Advertisements for products such as Wampole, which promised to strengthen one's system to resist attacks from the germs of consumption or wasting (but could be absorbed by the liver and be fatal), indicate that concerns over exhaustion reached back to the turn of the century.[164] Yet the frequency and prominence of ads during the 1920s indicate that a new threshold of anxiety had been reached. As Warwick Anderson has noted, male nervousness was considered a failure of character, and thus of manhood.[165] Judging from the variety of available tonics combating "consumption," many Dominican men felt they needed some shoring up of their physical stamina; then too, indolence was considered a national characteristic, particularly among the peasantry.

If neurasthenia was "a racial disease," one caused by the rigors of civilization, its appearance among Dominican liberals may not only have reflected their effeminization by an illegitimate occupation. It may also have served as yet another, albeit backhanded, demonstration of their gentility and refinement, a reminder to the United States that they were not only fit to rule, but so fit that they were infirm. Neurasthenia thus provided a resource for male self-fashioning which cast Dominican men as civilized, and thus white; and if they were weak, they were closer to a French romantic model of selfhood than the sturdier but coarse model of Anglo-American manhood. Neurasthenia proved one's capacity for self-government, a disease which Dominican men combated through melancholia, nostalgia, and poetic introspection rather than embarking upon the strenuous life.[166]

CONCLUSION

In 1920 a *Listín Diario* editorial summed up the Dominican perspective on American rule: "But we Dominicans are, for more than four years, searching for a new Columbus, one that can uproot us from the mysterious shipwreck of which it seems our independence has capsized."[167] The reigning optimism about national progress and development commenced in the late nineteenth century and peaked in 1920, but it collapsed after the years of U.S. military occupation and the depression, as liberalism and open markets became associated with loss of national sovereignty and with national porosity (and thus weakness and feminization); therefore a strong state that could stand up to the United States was seen as the only path of redemption. The depression came at a furious pace as sugar prices collapsed to one-tenth their value over the course of four short months in 1921, with tobacco, cacao, and coffee prices also following this path. Businesses folded overnight, causing a rash of bankruptcies, and buying power evaporated; then, to make matters worse, the U.S. authorities contracted further loans to complete public works projects, thus adding to the heavy national debt.[168]

As a result of this economic and political crisis, conservative nationalists like Joaquín Balaguer called for a Nietzschean superman or "Caesar" who could forge an alternative path to progress rather than the failed liberal model. As he stated, "Progress, in the countries formed by Spain . . . never has been an intellectual creation; it has always been, on the contrary, a product of the evolution imposed by Caesaristic willpower." Balaguer claimed that Trujillo was the *hombre único*—the only man—who could save the nation in 1931. This was a project of saving the nation from itself, as it were, owing to the perceived deficiencies of the masses since in this view the country lacked citizens.[169] The stage was set for a political outsider like Trujillo to bring statist and populist elements together in a new form of rule—one that promised to finally bring true national sovereignty to the republic, one that could at last stand taller than Haiti and stand up to the United States in a nation that lacked the divisions of the past, and one that could curtail the volatility and insecurity of U.S. economic dependence.[170] A history of national intervention in the nineteenth century, coupled with eight years of direct United States rule, rendered Dominicans vulnerable to the idea of a strong nationalist regime that would keep the United States at bay politically and economically by reclaiming key export sectors such as sugar and manufacturing. The Great Depression, combined with the centralization of political authority and the formation of the first national constabulary by the marines, enabled Trujillo to take over the reins of power and stay there; national collective resistance failed to emerge since the U.S. takeover of the economy had weakened elite structures and the peasantry was too autarchic. If the dream of liberalism was crushed by Rafael Trujillo, he co-opted their keyword, *progreso*, as a means of hitching their developmentalist project to his regime, while gutting it of its promise of individual liberty, rationality, and democracy. As we shall see, his greatest "Creole masquerade" was casting liberalism in the service of despotism.[171] Trujillo camouflaged a flagrantly nepotistic regime via a mask of national development, one that "nationalized" United States investment by turning it over to himself and his family.

TWO SAN ZENÓN AND THE MAKING OF CIUDAD TRUJILLO

> In the chords of our past there is an echo with which one falls in love . . .
> it's the walled city with its enchantments and legends . . . the midnight
> moon.
>
> On its solitary streets glide blue spirals of congealed evocations that
> intoxicate the spirit and one is transported very far away, and becomes
> lost in the past . . .
>
> Dream on!
>
> The transformation of Ciudad Trujillo constitutes the most eloquent
> demonstration of the progress Trujillo has promoted.
>
> LEONICIO PIETER, *CIUDAD TRUJILLO*

On 3 September 1930, the capital city of the Dominican Republic, Santo Domingo, was razed by one of the most devastating hurricanes ever to strike Caribbean shores. Fierce winds flattened entire neighborhoods, leveling anything built with wood, which included all but the municipal core of stone Spanish colonial edifices and the few buildings of concrete block erected by the Americans in the 1920s.[1] The event was nightmarish, with the skies turning black at noon and the barometric pressure dipping to almost eighty. The eerie calm at the epicenter of the storm encouraged many to venture forth from basements and bathrooms (those who had them), only to meet their death when its fury returned in the opposite direction. In four hours of devastating winds of 150 miles per hour, which turned metal roofs into flying cutlasses, and torrential rains, which flooded the Ozama River along the eastern city border, an estimated two thousand to three thousand people (4 percent of the city's population) were killed, enough to fill two mass graves with corpses. The next day witnesses described a "Dantesque dawn," as residents awoke to confront what resembled the aftermath of an earthquake: 90 percent of the buildings in the capital were razed; more than fifteen thousand were injured and thirty thousand left homeless; and scores of twisted cadavers were lying in the streets.[2]

With the young Rafael Trujillo just a few weeks in office, the hurricane

6. One of the main streets of Santo Domingo after the devastation of San Zenón. RENÉ
FORTUNATO COLLECTION, BY PERMISSION OF VIDEOCINE PALAU.

became inextricably associated with a regime that seemed like a force of
nature to Dominicans and with a man who appeared superhuman and even
preternatural. Tempest San Zenón quickly seemed to have become San
Rafael. *Huracán* was a Taíno name for a "powerful demon given to periodic
displays of destructive fury," one who stood at the gateway to the pantheon
as principal deity yet was prone to fearsome bouts of rage, requiring constant supplication.[3] Violence and devastation were a sign of the sacred, and
perhaps of divine wrath.

In this view, natural disasters appeared to result from the alchemy of men.
Christopher Columbus's efforts at New World discovery were twice thwarted
by tempests, once keeping him aground in Santo Domingo harbor for a full
week.[4] It is said that he cursed the island in retribution, causing a terrible
cataclysm when he was denied safe shelter by Governor Ovando.[5] Indeed, the
word on the street in 1930 was that the devastating force of the hurricane of
San Zenón signified the return of Columbus's wrath, his fucú, or curse. And
people took note when one of the few structures left standing after the disaster
was Columbus's tomb. Zenón's devastation was clearly a sign that the newly
installed Trujillo was a fierce potentate, a force to be reckoned with.[6] In official
mythology, Trujillo came to represent the restoration of order and the rebuilding of the city after the hurricane. But in popular memory he was remembered,
like the tempest itself, as an agent of seemingly limitless power.[7]

To the elites of Santo Domingo, however, the hurricane held another set
of meanings. Amid the ruins of city edifices, it razed the social hierarchy.

For a society in which social class had been legible in part through its inscription in social space, the hurricane collapsed the boundaries of status through which society had been defined.[8] The colonial city built by Nicolás de Ovando in 1502 had been laid out in a feudal pattern, whereby occupational groups resided in distinct barrios or neighborhoods, each with its own church, plaza, and market area. While this pattern had been modified in the post-1865 Republican period, nonetheless, the city was still characterized by considerable residential segregation by social class. The hurricane erased key status criteria as barrios were leveled and houses were ruined. Apparel had been another important marker of public identity; great care and expense were invested in the public presentation of self in urban Santo Domingo in the 1920s. Yet San Zenón left many urban dwellers in rags, their clothes carried away by wind or ruined by flooding. Without codes of social distinction, Santo Domingo resembled a rag-tag crowd, far from the refined theater of society on parade that flourished during the "dance of the millions," as exports boomed. Indeed, the erasure of the signs through which social identities were represented in the city was as much a part of the terror of the event as the deaths and devastation to property.

In the wake of San Zenón, the bourgeoisie sought to render itself visible once again amid the social chaos. As we shall see, the capital city became the central stage of the elite's project to rearticulate a ranked hierarchy of social class. The hurricane completed a process of social transformation that had taken shape during the U.S. occupation, as visual indices of class such as race, fashion, and the possession of certain commodities changed in meaning because of the expansion of a market economy and the democratization of civic culture through the expansion of the public sphere (see chapter 1).[9] Yet, although the real contest was between the old aristocracy of the colonial zone and the new moneyed class of the suburbs, after Zenón, the bourgeoisie staked its claim as the harbinger of civilization through its project of banishing the peasantry from the urban terrain.

The elite called for state intervention after the storm to put the poor back in their place, away from the urban theater. The "semiotic breakdown" caused by the hurricane was to be rectified by redelineating the boundaries of social class—expelling the urban poor from the city center and placing them in neighborhoods at a distance from the cosmopolitan downtown.[10] The moral fervor of the attack on the urban poor was part of the construction of a new social identity for the bourgeoisie.[11] However, this elite vision was contested from below. And much to the chagrin of the bourgeoisie, the state not only refused to relinquish its newfound centrality after the event, but ended up siding with the crowd. As a moment of social crisis, the hurricane merits close examination because it threw into sharp relief otherwise implicit assumptions about the fault lines of society.[12] It also demonstrated how urban space could become an arena of domination, as well as contestation and resistance, under the Trujillo regime.[13]

The hurricane was a seminal moment since it became, in official propaganda, the founding myth of the Era of Trujillo, as the ever-present chaos of "before" contrasted with the modernity of Trujillo's civilizing mission.[14] In the wake of the coup and the fraudulent elections that catapulted Trujillo into office, San Zenón gave him the perfect opportunity to gain the trust of the nation and the world by demonstrating his skill at handling the crisis. The post-hurricane capital was the tabula rasa on which Trujillo's project to reshape Dominican society was first enacted, becoming a model "modernist city," as well as metonym of the nation and of Trujillo himself.[15] It also was the proscenium where Trujillo cast himself as a resolute man of action who would serve and protect the pueblo in a time of emergency. It was a model of rulership for which Dominicans were ready since the liberal path had resulted in the trauma of U.S. occupation. In symbolic tribute to Trujillo as purported "savior" of the capital, it was even renamed Trujillo City in 1936. Additionally, the story of the devastation and rebuilding of the capital displays the regime's particular combination of populism and authoritarianism, of nationalist communion and statist hierarchy.

THE COUNTRY IN THE CITY

Following the hurricane, the peasantry was defined as a national obstacle, as something to be overcome. The project of national reconstruction after the event was unambiguously urban and modernist in scope and direction. San Zenón was the culmination of a long-term series of efforts to contain the small trickle of rural migrants into the capital at the turn of the century; they came as a result of expanding service sector opportunities as well as land displacement in some provinces when large-scale agrarian enterprises uprooted denizens lacking formal land titles. The trickle became a rivulet during the Great Depression, as migrants fled conditions of poverty. The Dominican "protopeasantry" or backwoods *monteros*—the nomadic hunters and gatherers who did minimal cultivation for domestic subsistence— had come increasingly under fire with the rise of liberal thought in the nineteenth century and had been portrayed in increasingly negative terms.[16]

Liberal reformers such as Américo Lugo and José Ramón López saw the Dominican peasant as the antithesis of their vision of urban development, state formation, and general "progreso." The peasantry was chastised as semi-savage, apathetic, cruel, bloodthirsty, and governed by instinct, conditions emanating from their blood—that is, their putative racial mixture from "degenerate" origins in the backward Spanish and African peoples composing the nation.[17] But in the 1930s, the dangers of the countryside, which represented the antithesis of liberal development and state formation, shifted ground as the displaced peasant in the city became the central figure of social depravity, barbarism, and anxiety. As Raymond Williams argued, the city that presents itself as a symbol of modernity also creates its critical counterpoint, the pastoral countryside.[18] Yet this bucolic image placed peasants on their farms, well distanced from the cosmopolitan city. The negation of the rural positioned the country as modern and indisputably urban.[19]

This image of the uprooted peasant in the urban cityscape and the resultant apprehension that the backward periphery was poised to engulf, and thus overpower, the urban metropolis, constitute a central theme in Andrés Requena's novel, *Los enemigos de la tierra* (The Enemies of the Land, 1936).[20] It focuses on the displaced peasant in the city and the combined effects of both physical and moral dissolution that eventually destroy him. In an organicist vision that posits an essential unity between the peasant and the earth, the rural dweller is restored to wholeness only through returning to the land that sustains him. Here the pathologies of urban life are blamed upon the psychological debilitation caused by dislocated peasants out of their element, where they do not belong. Contrary to other populisms, the figure of the peasant was not idealized in official Trujillista discourse. In a viewpoint aligned with the liberal tradition, the peasant represented an impediment to national growth and development; he was to be transformed by the modernizing state into an "agricultor," a rural laborer or protoproletarian, marching in step with the ongoing progress of the nation.[21] To reveal why the peasant as agent of disorder was so worrisome requires a detour to the urban development of Santo Domingo and the way that status and locality were mapped on the eve of San Zenón.

THE ROMANTIC CITY

In 1930, the Santo Domingo settlement was still confined to the walled boundaries of the colonial city. Like Havana, this was a city defined by its perimeter, a demarcation holding in suspension the primary social divisions of country and city, nature and culture.[22] As the seat of local government and the center of sixteenth-century colonial administration, Santo Domingo was protected and contained by a continuous heavy stone rampart, and until the end of the nineteenth century had its gates locked at nightfall. Originally built in 1506 to protect the town from predatory buccaneers and pirates after the disastrous pillage of Sir Francis Drake, this eight-foot-thick parapet eventually became an encompassing frame providing shape and form to everyday life in the barrios.[23] The spatial partition was indicated architecturally by the stone masonry (*mampostería*) style of home construction inside the walls, as opposed to the mud-and-thatch *bohíos* outside. Being inside the city walls, within the "solid and imposing" stone colonial zone, was to be included in cosmopolitan *capitaleña* culture. By contrast, being outside was to be an agrarian outsider, a rustic denizen of the "semi-clay huts, roofed with palm or straw."[24] The entries and exits of the walled city were more than mere passageways; they were symbolic thresholds separating urban from rural and indicating intraregional distinctions. Coastal commerce in cattle entered through the southern gate; peasants brought vegetables, tobacco, and coffee from the central Cibao plains through the north gate; and popular markets sprang up near the municipal doors. The sense of transition was further accentuated by a moat and drawstring bridge flanking the city wall and rendering it a defensive bastion.[25] Before the nineteenth-century sugar boom, the municipal economy of Santo Domingo depended on a rather limited trade in precious wood and hides. Although it served as the seat of government, it was more a site of administration than commerce, lacking the tourist hotels and ship disembarkations that could have transformed its insularity.[26] For centuries, most trade was oriented west or north, either to Haiti, which consumed Santo Domingo meat and hides, or to Puerto Plata, where tobacco was shipped to Europe.

However, irrespective of the municipal walls that clearly separated the civilization of the city from the barbarism outside it, the lifestyles of the urban poor actually differed little from those of the peasantry. This may have accounted for the small-town feel expressed by Francisco Moscoso Puello when he wrote in the 1890s that Santo Domingo was an *aldea* or village, not a true city. Arranged in an orderly grid-pattern, barrios for the lower classes within the walls were concentrated in San Lázaro, San Miguel, and San Antón, which were built along the northern circumperiphery originally to house the incurably ill, where winds would not retransmit infectious disease into the city. In contrast, San Carlos and Los Mina, technically "communes," were located just outside the city walls, and Villa Duarte was built across the Ozama River. Even in the early twentieth century most residents in these areas maintained a semi-rural lifestyle, working as day labor in adjacent sugar mills, growing food in small patio garden plots for domestic consumption, and keeping chickens in their yards.[27] These popular neighborhoods received and contained new migrants when they arrived in Santo Domingo, housing, in the case of San Miguel, "respectable people of color."[28] For example, Los Mina (San Lorenzo de Los Negros Mina, named for the slave port at El Mina, on the Gold Coast—now Ghana—where they had been purchased) was originally founded by the Spanish in the eighteenth century for slaves from Haiti. San Carlos was populated in the nineteenth century by Canary Island migrants; and across the water, Villa Duarte was the first stop for newcomers from the provinces, since land there was relatively cheap and accessible.[29] The need to keep a domestic *conuco* or garden plot only diminished once improved roads and transport facilitated the provision of subsistence staples to urban dwellers in the 1920s and 1930s.

Colonial Santo Domingo society was organized within a corporatist framework of ranked inclusion; there was not one colonial public sphere as such, but several. The five urban barrios were presumed to be autonomous, with separate municipal authorities governing each neighborhood of curates, slaves, artisans, soldiers, and nobles. Equipped with their own church and plaza, residents were expected to interact only within specifically defined spheres.[30] With its grid-pattern, Santo Domingo was a utopic exemplum of order and efficiency, intended to rectify the disorderly chaos found in Spanish colonial cityscapes. As a contemporary observer noted, "It was laid out with ruler and compass, with all the streets being carefully measured. Because of this, Santo Domingo is better planned than any town I have seen."[31] For reasons of efficiency, salubrity, and surveillance, individual neighborhoods were separated on the basis of status. The ideal of separate spheres was expressed in the fact that the principal thoroughfare was called Calle de la Separación (Separation Street, now el Conde), since it marked the division between both neighborhoods and social ranks. Even the slaughter zones of each occupational group were kept distinct; in the colonial period, there were three. In this context, the central market was the sole public meeting ground where people came together as equals, in contrast to the plaza, where citizens were grouped in terms of their assigned slot in the social hierarchy. Dominican Creole culture first began to take shape in the public marketplace.

For centuries, the great planters and ranchers would not deign to live outside the city center, the colonial downtown area surrounding the Calle de Comercio, next to the Ozama River. This insularity accounts for the fact that the bourgeoisie was often linguistically glossed as those *por allá aden-tro*, meaning those "over there, inside." In the last decade of the nineteenth century, the spatial configuration of Santo Domingo began to change, however. In the 1880s, the sugar boom gave rise to the nouveau riche style of Heureaux's administration, a Francophile court society which called itself "entre nous"; it demonstrated its yearning for things European by sipping champagne at parties and its decadence by tossing fresh American peaches —at the time a rare and expensive novelty item—into the air for amusement.[32] The sugar boom and the newfound access to cash and global products that was its byproduct had created both a "vision of a seemingly unlimited profusion of commodities" as well as a new lexicon of distinction, as elites sought ever scarcer goods with which to mark their difference from the masses.[33] Fostered by a utopic sensibility engendered by fast wealth, this sense of carefree abandon, however, began to recede by 1909, when a recession set in. Sugar proceeds from that point were localized in the sugar boom towns, the vast, "virtually American," foreign-owned estates of La Romana and San Pedro de Macoris.[34]

Santo Domingo had some eighteen thousand inhabitants in 1900, the majority of whom were of mixed race, unlike those of its rival township Santiago, the tobacco capital, which had a pretentious aristocracy claiming descent from the original Spanish *hidalgos* of the conquest. Yet the Santiago elite's claim to racial purity was based more on its possession of the symbols of noble honor—Spanish armor and swords—than exclusive genealogy.[35] The high societies of both Santiago and Santo Domingo were quite mixed in fact, if not in self-perception. As one foreign observer noted, "The vast majority of them give greater or lesser evidence of African graftings on the family tree."[36] As administrative center, though, Santo Domingo received more foreign immigrants, primarily from Spain, Puerto Rico, and Curaçao.[37] The fact that the sugar industry drew many contract laborers from Haiti and the West Indies to the southern coast helps account for the perception of the region as blacker than the rest of the country.

The primary markers of social status in early-twentieth-century Santo

Domingo were the public extensions of self and family, as embodied in neighborhood, home, means of transport, and dress among those who had at least a part-time white-collar occupation and thus were accorded social honor.[38] Indeed, social personhood was heraldic, marked by these external signs of insignia and status.[39] Some of these identity markers were key symbols distinguishing the traditional merchant class from the new sugar bourgeoisie, locality and means of transport in particular. In the colonial zone, the old ruling class, for example, clung to its horse-drawn carriages for errands and outings even after the automobile (a bourgeois symbol) had begun to challenge its hegemony. While large ranchers and state functionaries had their own carriages, others could rely on carriage taxis for both transport and amorous encounters calling for a moment of sanctioned privacy.[40] By contrast, rural caudillos refused the use of carriages to avoid the image of exclusivity, preferring the more populist horse. Carriages "represented the possession of credit and a conspicuous place in Dominican social life."[41] Carriages also became a sign of nostalgic resistance to modernity and to a new social order led by foreign capital and the cash nexus.

Although both the car and the carriage enabled one to circulate and be seen in the period 1895 to 1925, they indexed two variant lifestyles and, thus, types of location in the status economy.[42] Like different currency, they signified two different regimes of social value: the old aristocracy in its slower but more scenic buggies, and the new elite, predominantly foreign engineers, in their faster and more utilitarian cars. While the rising bourgeoisie justified the car's superiority on the basis of its speed, coverage of long distances, and modern style, the formidable potholes in the unpaved streets of Santo Domingo prevented any significant velocity. As one foreign traveler observed, "Ostentation is more important than real use among the two score or more automobiles with wire wheels and luxurious tonneaux that hover about the central plaza."[43] The stubborn resilience of the aristocrats in clinging to the carriage, however, underscores their insularity, since this means of transport was inadequate for leaving the walled city, the circumference of their social universe; thus, by implication, the capital city for them was coincident with the nation.[44] In the eighteenth century, elites had kept small working farms just outside the city walls, where slaves grew cacao and raised pigs. Yet the advent of the automobile enabled the city to expand for the first time horizontally, outside the city walls and into the

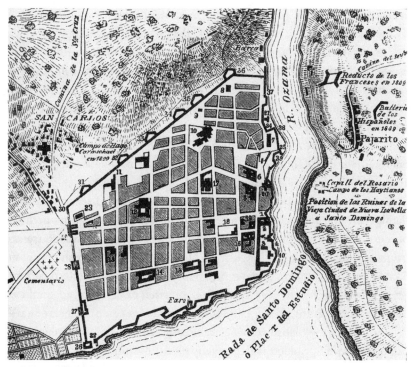

MAP 2 Map of Santo Domingo, 1873 (SAMUEL HAZARD, *SANTO DOMINGO, PAST AND PRESENT*).

metropolitan periphery.[45] By the 1920s, the advent of the automobile had permitted the invention of the Dominican suburb.

Alongside the horse-drawn carriage, another important marker distinguishing the old aristocracy from the nascent elite was the design of their homes and country cottages: the decorative French style versus the sparse simplicity of American modernism. In the nineteenth century, colonial architecture was de rigueur for the bourgeoisie, and was often not unduly costly to obtain. Due to frequent government bankruptcy, state office buildings could often be acquired for a song by moneyed families. These were Spanish colonial structures in austere neobaroque style; however, the most sought after were those adorned with French balconies, which had become the vogue during the Haitian occupation and were added on.[46] When the northern outskirts of the city began to attract a smallholder peasantry, the new elite shifted its attention to the southern coastal periphery. There families like the Alamar, Pou, Ricart, and Vicini clans had established small recreational cottages (*estancias*) for country outings, with chalets, large fruit gardens, and private beach access; they had exclusive English names like "Springtime" and "Our Recreation."[47] By the turn of the century, these established families began to sell these homes to a new class composed of ranchers, merchants, sugar industrialists, and statesmen. With these property transfers arose a new architectural style—ornate gingerbread houses made of wood with richly decorated porticos, iron grating, elaborate yards and gardens, and even English-style lawns. The more grandiose and embellished were pretentiously called "villas" by their owners, such as Villa Gautier-Alfonseca, Villa Gosling, and Villa Vidal-Gautier.[48]

Contrary to the low-key style of the traditional elite, the new class was flamboyant and trendsetting, more willing to break local norms perhaps because it was predominantly foreign and more keyed to stylistic trends overseas. For example, the English aristocrat H. Gosling, British consul in Santo Domingo, was one of the first to build in Gazcue, the western periphery just outside the city walls, an area comprised of dense forest until the building boom in the 1920s. In 1899 Gosling designed an English cottage reminiscent of the British colonial architecture of Jamaica, replete with an expansive lawn sprinkled with bougainvillea, rattan furniture, and a running veranda. Many in this new group were forced to colonize virgin lands since the old elite had refused to break up their plots and sell to the newcomers. Yet the shift toward unpartitioned lands enabled this new social class to purchase far larger plots than had been possible before so close to the capital. For example, the Henríquez property had a garden so large it was said that one could get lost amid its lush shade trees; in 1917, the family even built a hippodrome complete with a one-thousand-meter track.[49]

Another feature of this class was its newfound economic ascendancy, which accorded it an extraordinary bargaining power vis-à-vis the state. As a result, the new bourgeoisie insisted on building willy-nilly, according to personal whims and desires, with no concern for facilitating government road-building efforts as its own houses pushed city expansion westward. The result was a hodgepodge of dead-end streets in the areas of Gazcue and Mis Amores, with almost no connecting thoroughfares, creating a zone perfect for evening strolls but a nightmare for vehicular transit. At times refusal to sell lands to the city government for the construction of roads resulted from hostility to the party in power; another reason for refusal was the desire to hold onto land that was inevitably rising in value. During the 1920s, the city council began for the first time to seriously consider pro-

posals to regulate city growth; it instituted a plan for municipal development largely in reaction to the recalcitrance of the new elite to conform to
public needs. In desperation, the *ayuntamiento* or town hall called for
drastic measures such as land expropriations—anything to enforce a civic
spirit among a group with such a truculent attitude that it preferred its
absolute autonomy, even if that meant sacrificing the construction of
streets and crosswalks, churches, pharmacies, and even an aqueduct.[50] This
almost total lack of public consciousness defined the new elite as radically
at variance with the traditional ruling class, which, it was said, never overlooked its obligation to its political party affiliation, even if it at times
neglected its broader civic duties.

Gosling exemplified the extravagant bourgeois style enabled by the
"Dance of the Millions," the post–World War I surge in primary commodity prices such as sugar, tobacco, cacao, and coffee.[51] By the 1920s, the
carousing parties of his daughter Sherry had become all the rage, her list of
invitees defining the in-crowd of the moment; many followed his lead to the
northern city frontier, seeking neighboring country estates in Gazcue.[52]
This new bourgeoisie redirected the metropolitan facade of Santo Domingo
by building outside the walls and toward the northwest, opening the city up
toward the ocean and the world beyond, unlike the traditional elite which
had remained defensively barricaded within municipal walls and facing
largely inward toward the Ozama River. These new gentleman farms, for
recreation and show rather than for use, blurred the previously rigid divide
between country and city by cultivating little more than flowers and exotic
dessert fruits—passion fruit, cashews, almonds, and mangos—and a lei-
sured upper-class lifestyle. They also contributed to a new spatial segregation by social class that was not nearly as pronounced in the close confines
of the colonial zone, where apart from the tiny elite sector, skilled artisans
lived next to fruit sellers and factory owners next to teachers.[53] Unlike
traditional barrios, which had a range of vernacular architectural styles and
in which a sprawling ranch house might share a block with a thatch-roof
bohío, these new neighborhoods were exclusively modernist in design,
drawing inspiration from the pared-down international style. Previously,
status divisions were not as much based on "locality classifiers" as on a
combination of several other differentiators, including house building material (whether wood, stone masonry, or concrete block, and whether the
roof was of woven reed or zinc), occupation, and social honor. Respectability was not based solely on income, occupation, and apellido, but also on

criteria such as generosity, social honor, and keeping one's "word." These values were implicit in evaluative comments that an individual was sincere or correct, "well thought of by his mates," or that another was "a mason of certain distinction, due to his comportment with his companions, and the good quality of his work."[54] By the 1920s, social position thus had come to be based more on where one lived than on how one lived. The shift was marked by social differentiation based more on wealth and social class than on the gentility and comportment criteria of the virtual caste system of the nineteenth century.[55]

While elite development in the western suburbs was one component of urban expansion, another was the creation of planned middle-class communities in the northern periphery of the city just outside the walls. However, if Gazcue eventually became a new upper-class residential zone of country houses, the northern perimeter was colonized for investment purposes. An unintended side effect of the suburban vogue of Gazcue had been rising land values in the rural environs of Santo Domingo as demand by the nouveau riche increased. Land speculators sought to take advantage of low land values to build affordable middle-class housing just north of the walls after the sugar crash, when these lands were no longer saved for possible plantation expansion. Unlike the situation in other Latin American cities at the turn of the century, then, urban expansion was driven not by rural in-migration but rather by savvy speculation.

Of course, the northern frontier of Santo Domingo was so rough and uneven that only a centrally planned effort could have made it habitable for more than scattered, rough bohíos; it required extensive infrastructural improvement and leveling before construction could commence. The visionary Juan Alejandro Ibarra, who had made a small fortune through keeping the only licensed pawnshop in the capital, purchased a good portion of this land and developed an initial prototype for what later became Villa Francisca. The barrio became one of the most picturesque and salutary of the capital, with a large park (now Enriquillo Park). Ibarra bought some 340,000 cubic meters of terrain and initially constructed twenty-five houses for the project, to be sold off in small individual plots astride a wide central boulevard. Eager to endorse a project that extended the city northward, the municipal government offered free cement for sidewalks. The small bungalows (called chalets) were valued at two thousand dollars each and made of sturdy concrete or wood; they were offered on a credit plan requiring monthly installments of some forty dollars and allowing immediate occupancy—terms highly favorable at a time when mortgages or other forms of credit were not readily available. The final plan included a central station for the rail line linking the capital with the Cibao, although this never came to fruition. Villa Francisca was intended to overcome the most grievous conditions of the colonial zone: "narrow and dusty streets, broken sidewalks, houses lacking ventilation, insufficient water and sorry, poorly-designed parks [which] exercise a direct and sinful influence on the spirit and temperament of the inhabitants." By contrast, Villa Francisca offered sea breezes "and the brisk mountain air that enrichens the blood, dilates the lungs and strengthens the nerves," contributing to a stronger body and spirit.[56] Unfortunately, this nascent dream came to a crashing halt when the project was leveled during San Zenón.

The remapping of public and private space resulting from urban development created no small measure of anxiety for the bourgeoisie, however, as they feared urban development would bring the *chusma* (rabble) into elite neighborhoods. Two magnets of controversy were sidewalks and electric streetlights, which threatened to bring elites under the gaze of society, and perhaps allow the lower classes into their own communities. In 1920, there was an acrid debate in Santo Domingo over the new city council proposal to have electric wires strung from house to house (as in Puerto Rico), rather than on public poles (perhaps to save costs). The principal objection of one *junta* (civic association) was that the new arrangement would bring "unknown" people constantly into people's homes, people who were "of suspicious origins," "dirty and perhaps of bad manners (*de malas costumbres*) creating bother and awkward situations for families."[57] It was said that in "first class cities" such wires would be underground. Others countered that the posts were inhibiting transit and creating public obstacles and dangers.[58] Social mixing clearly was perceived as endangering the very concept of neighborhood that elites were accustomed to.

TRUJILLO TAKES CONTROL

The Brazilian anthropologist Roberto DaMatta has explored the importance of the symbolism of the house and the street in defining a basic cultural opposition in Latin America. As he explains, the house refers to a properly controlled, domesticated universe, a place of rest, leisure, and social rules. In the house, action is governed by the collective concerns of the family. The house, which represents the family, is virtuous due to the reigning governance of the collective over the individual, of culture over nature. This stands in contrast to the street, where individual choice rules and the possibilities for dissimulation are strong because of the variety of social criteria at play; unlike criteria in the family, those in the street are not "naturalized" through ties of blood. According to DaMatta, the "basic rule of the street is deceit, deception and roguery," in contrast to the house where roles are transparent.[59] Given the almost total leveling of housing as a result of the hurricane, however, this spatial map was inverted, as the city seemed to become all street; culture seemed to dissolve in the face of the uncontrollable terrors of nature. In the ruins of the city afterward, the dangers of the street threatened to overcome the domesticated center, the fears of risk to overwhelm the reassurance of family.

Curiously, although the worst destruction occurred in the popular neighborhoods with more flimsy construction, such as Villa Duarte and Villa Francisca, the incessant focus of elite calls for clean-up and recon-struction was Columbus Park (Parque Colón) the civic epicenter of the old city.[60] Secondary cries went out to save Gazcue, where the bourgeoisie of the 1920s had built their country vacation homes just beyond the municipal walls. Overall, elites fared far better during the disaster, because many of their dwellings were constructed from reinforced concrete block, a material that the United States had introduced during the military government. By sharp contrast, the overwhelming majority of urban poor, whose houses were predominantly palm frond, thatch, or wood, were left utterly destitute.

Homeless and in rags, the urban poor became squatters in the first days after the hurricane, establishing campsites virtually anywhere, including city streets, boulevards, and especially parks. Looting and theft of frag-ments of building materials and food became commonplace in the face of starvation as people sought anything they could find to sell. One of Tru-jillo's first moves was declaring martial law because of the state of emer-gency and halting all transit in and out of the city for fear of disease. Food prices skyrocketed, not only because of crop loss and a reduction of food imports into the city, but also because peddlers took advantage of the fact that those with money would buy at any price. Inexpensive food kitchens were established for the poor and a heavy military presence was established to guard food storage facilities. In keeping with Trujillo's training by the U.S. Marine Corps, he appointed Major Thomas Watson, a Marine buddy from the occupation, as food administrator, and called out the entire army to assist in the relief effort. The Department of Sanitation requested that all those leave the city who had the means to do so, so that "sanitation" could be restored, the escalating food crisis relieved, and cadavers properly disposed of through mass burials and incineration. And plenty did, as many as five thousand, including hundreds of foreigners without strong ties to the country. Since public health officials feared mass contagion, a typhoid vaccination campaign was begun. Churches were turned over to the homeless, housing thousands left without shelter. Rapidly, though, this natural disaster became an alibi for several alternative political agendas.

Trujillo used the crisis to legitimate his populist credentials, working closely with public health and rescue teams (Theodore Roosevelt, at the time governor of Puerto Rico, sent a team of doctors) in the most needy areas for nearly two full weeks before resuming his duties in the National Palace. Trujillo's retinue of press sycophants wrote daily of his seemingly "superhuman" efforts, "at all hours, at dawn, in the daytime, at night, untiring, vigilant, energetic," "challenging death face-to-face."[61] This ready chorus of servile griots was prompted to weave these actions into a charismatic narrative of Trujillo's one-to-one identification with the people, a populist mythos in which he was deemed to have an almost thaumaturgical ability to absorb and refract the pain and suffering of his people.[62] As one wrote, "President Trujillo continued today in the Fort, where he is at all hours of the day and night . . . continuously emitting urgent decrees and making arrangements to resolve all problems and situations."[63] Trujillo himself certainly rose to the occasion, using the disaster as an opportunity to bridge the personal hands-on image of the rural caudillo with the less engagé figure of the urban statesman. It also became an occasion to establish his image as an indefatigable worker who was willing to give his all for his fellow countrymen in need. For example, both Trujillo and First Lady Bienvenida Ricardo doggedly walked the streets disbursing handouts of food, utilitarian gifts such as used clothes, and cash. In Trujillo's first public circular to the people, he praised the "virile spirit" of the Dominican people for facing head-on catastrophes such as this one, and portrayed himself as a man of the people. As he remarked, "I have also had to see my family on the street . . . I am, thus, identified with *el pueblo* (people/nation) to suffer with it."[64] During the hurricane he established his charismatic aura, that "mutual mingling of inner selves of leader and follower," or what James Holston has termed the relation of symbolic equivalence characteristic of populist leadership, even if after the fact its authoritarian logic reemerged.[65]

Trujillo's epic salvation of the Dominican pueblo after the hurricane is well dramatized in the Trujillista novel *Gente de portal* (People of the

Gate).[66] "The people of the gate" refers to the national threshold crossed when the Trujillo period began, as the quintessential political figurehead evolved from the traditional strongman on horseback (caudillo) to a modern president; it also refers to how Dominicans passed from a political system based on clientelism and self-interest to one based on a higher calling—a disciplinary state, civic culture, and public works "that speak to and stimulate each and every Dominican . . . to reach his capacity."[67]

In the novel, the tempest of San Zenón has an allegorical component that scripts the people of Santo Domingo into a biblical Adam and Eve scenario and provides the crucial backdrop for Trujillo's heroic salvation. This is staged through the figure of young Jimiano, who discovers both his civic self and his true love in the aftermath of the storm, when he comes across Lizia, naked and quivering with cold and fear on a street corner after the disaster. With her clothes washed away during the storm, she has been reduced to a virginal state: like mother earth, her body is covered only with mud; like Eve, she is in a state of primeval innocence, beyond shame. Here the nation has been reduced to a state of nature, ripe and innocent, like a piece of clay awaiting a strong molding and civilizing hand to form it into a work of art. *El presidente* (i.e., Trujillo) is represented by Jimiano's benevolent and caring touch, as he saves his newly beloved, giving her a protective mantle, food, warmth, and clothes, and thus restoring her humanity. Her personhood is restored by regaining her *pudor*, her modesty, her essential femininity. Lizia represents the feminine and prone nation, emblematically expressed by the city, which is now orphaned and homeless and desperately in need of a divine male protector such as Trujillo. The couple are reborn through their union and newfound civic spirit: first, through a visit to the National Altar (Altar de la Patria), the patriotic shrine which miraculously survived the disaster; and second, through devoting their energies to saving those left destitute by the storm, as they selflessly immerse themselves in their civic duties in the soup kitchens and shelters even before attending to their own relatives' needs.[68] Their romance is the culmination of national destiny, their love of the pueblo that of Trujillo.[69]

HYGIENE AND SOCIAL ORDER

To prevent contagion after the hurricane, a crackdown ensued against a host of public dangers associated with the street, particularly in the poor barrios of the city. Certainly the risks were real ones; there were mountains of corpses to deal with and urgent problems to solve, among them inmates from the asylum running wild in the streets after their shelter lay in ruins. Yet if the governmental response was primarily about health, it was also about social order; and contagion seemed to become a trope for offensive social contact between tiers of society that should best be kept apart.

In part, the overwhelming concern with the popular neighborhoods was because suddenly the barrios were visible; there was no longer a screen demarcating elite and popular urban space and shielding elites from the vices, dangers, and effluvia of the popular sectors. As Mary Douglas has shown, correspondences are common between forms of ritual avoidance, as evidenced in class segregation, and evasion of contagious disease.[70] In the chaotic aftermath of the hurricane, fears of disease ran amuck largely because of the near-total collapse of boundaries separating elite from popular, and thus purity from pollution. In the nineteenth century, the furniture, bedding, and clothes of the fatally infirm had customarily been tossed outside the city walls, where they were burned, a practice that may explain some of the horror expressed at the accumulation of garbage within municipal terrain.[71] An additional belief was that foul smells themselves actually transmitted illness, a vestige of nineteenth-century theories of miasmas and humors. Sanitation brigades were sent to the barrios to test water for "deadly microbes," and mobile vendors of prepared foods were banished from the streets.[72] Complaints raged about "putrid, pestilent" garbage in the popular zones—made especially noxious by body parts decomposing in the tropical heat—that had not been removed by the third week of cleanup. Although the terror of disease loomed over the city for a full two months, the expected epidemic outbreak luckily never occurred.

Ideas about infectious disease can express fears of social boundary crossing and disorder and result in moves to reinstate social authority.[73] Indeed, the possibility of an epidemic provided a ready excuse for elites to urge people to return to the relative privacy of their barrios and, for those who still had them, their homes. Edicts were issued prohibiting practices such as eating food in the street, which had perforce become necessary for the homeless owing to their lack of any protective habitat.[74] Without functioning latrines, complaints surged about people urinating in patios and in the streets. The physical ravaging of the urban landscape had dissolved not only extant plumbing arrangements, however; it had also destroyed the "staging devices" by which "back regions" and posterior functions of the city had been occluded from the public view.[75]

The real reason, however, for the piles of garbage accumulating in the barrios was not the "animal" habits of the poor, as some commentators insinuated. It was a result of intense elite pressure to clean the city center first, so that civic life could return to normal, government could resume work, and "society" could put the hurricane behind it. The barrios were woefully neglected, with some areas, such as Villa Francisca, remaining virtually untouched six weeks after the event. The storm's most severe damage was economic: a major source of employment in the city, the San Luis sugar plantation, was destroyed; virtually all the cattle in the adjacent eastern town of Bayaguana were killed; and the annual plantain, coffee, cacao, and corn crops suffered major losses. With no food to sell and no work to be had, money virtually stopped circulating. Yet surprisingly, the main concern was with reestablishing civility downtown through resegregating urban space, as if culture must be reinstated before economy.

EL PARQUE COLÓN

In the "moral economy of the crowd," though, there was only one way to right the disaster and rectify their world turned upside down.[76] And that was through reconstructing the routines of daily life. Yet the popular sectors chose to do so on the lawn of El Parque Colón (Columbus Park), the jewel of the colonial zone, the quintessential site emblematic of bourgeois respectability and civic virtue. They may simply have sought to publicize their destitute plight as dramatically as possible by appropriating a central zone of bourgeois civility, by violating the unspoken code of class segregation, and by engaging in "filthy rites" on this genteel terrain. Thus, it seems that through the language of parody, they sought to shame elites, who attended to the business of governance without first solving the basic necessities of the poor.[77]

Columbus Park represented the public sphere. It was the central theater of bourgeois sociability and political intrigue, the hub of social and civic activity; "it was the very centre of the city and the natural gathering place for the 'elite' of Santo Domingo. . . . the " 'great white way of town.' "[78] In the words of Eduardo Matos Díaz, it was "the hide-out for intrigues, slander, gossip, of revolutionary schemes and plots, as well as civic mindedness."[79] In the nineteenth century, Columbus Park still retained a utilitarian significance, serving as pasture land for the governor's sheep as well as for a few local goats and fowl. But by the turn of the century, with the installation of an elegant statue of Columbus and gas lights, the meaning of the space changed, becoming more than a scenic proscenium for the municipal offices of the Senate, various governmental ministries, and prison. The arrival

7. Plaza Colón, Santo Domingo, before the hurricane. ARCHIVO GENERAL DE LA NACIÓN, SANTO DOMINGO.

of ornamental street lights inspired the custom of evening strolls, which before then had been near-impossible because of rough, unpaved roads and fears of thieves. In the colonial period, only those with domestic slaves and lanterns would venture forth into the dusk.[80] While illumination of key buildings—the cathedral, National Palace, and central plaza—by lamp for special events was first introduced under Spanish rule, and stores were required to provide light under Haitian leadership, public lighting was not installed until the regime of Ulises Heureaux. And not coincidentally, the first site graced with the sine qua non of modernity and civilization— electric lights—was Columbus Park on Independence Day in 1896.[81]

The central park of the city—flanked by the cathedral, municipal council, and city hall, and adorned with rows of French wrought-iron benches— became the stage for promenades, poetry recitals, and, most important, elegant concerts for which Dominican high society turned out in their best fashion and jewels to see, to be seen, and especially to look for potential romantic partners from the eligible pool of their class. Women turned out for the spectacle; men, particularly poets, journalists, essayists, and intellectuals, came to discuss politics. On Sunday evenings, high-society youths would attend public concerts at the park and afterward go for ice cream at nearby Stanley's Café. Columbus Park was "not a refuge for loafers, ignorance and poor manners (*poca educación*), but rather an oasis where talent, culture, delicacy, gallantry, love and proper etiquette was concentrated."[82] In the highly gender-segregated world of the Dominican bourgeoisie, the park was one of the few arenas where youths could legitimately mingle without family chaperones. It was a space of choreographed ceremony and spectacle, governed by protocol, where the boundaries of society were drawn and the rules of high culture prevailed.[83]

The homeless could not have chosen a more appropriate staging ground for their symbolic riposte than the public parks. Even if they were neglected by the state, they would not allow themselves to be forgotten. Just as the elite were horrified at the idea of using a park for utilitarian purposes, the popular sectors were equally shocked at the state's attention to the cry for the restoration of decorum while many still starved and lacked basic housing and infrastructure. Vandalism became rampant, as people poached pieces of wood, zinc for roofs, clothes, and furniture and built temporary abodes in these civic gardens. As one journalist objected, "In the very center of Columbus Park, the most aristocratic of the city, many families from the *barrios* have installed themselves in this primitive form."[84] In Restoration Park, some squatters erected stands for carpentry and shoe repair and others set up sewing machines, returning to business as usual.[85] Women did their washing, spreading it out on the lawn to dry, and set up provisional kitchens, providing food for the community; families constructed "rustic" lean-to's. Elites were furious at this defilement of patrician sensibility and told their woes to the police, who took no action.[86] Just as the poor seem to have felt that as citizens they deserved more prompt attention from state authorities, this symbolic assault on bourgeois space was perceived by elites as a fundamental violation of what Sylvia Arrom has termed the "social compact" between rich and poor, one that merited unleashing the full scope of persecution available.[87]

Columbus Park was the focal point of elite calls to restore urban order and a modicum of civility from the beginning of the clean-up effort. However, the rationale behind this thrust was far from altruistic. Every day, the press clamored for the return of electricity, not for their homes, nor for the masses, but for the good of the park itself and the morale of elites who used it, and only additionally so that benefit concerts could be staged there, the proceeds of which could be used for the injured. As one observer wrote,

"Light, light, light, light is needed to reduce the misery of Capital evenings,"[88] through restoring drama and shadows to the "romantic city." The restoration of parks, theaters, and public concerts, they argued, was critical to the elevation of civic spirit. As one critic remarked, "If the nights continue like this, those who didn't die from the cyclone will from hypochondria and neurasthenia. . . . These spectacles shouldn't be considered immoral fandangos, but rather means of education and entertainment, completely honest and absolutely necessary. . . . The problem of the city is not one of basements, but rather of men with very strong, large and human hearts."[89] Columbus Park was more than the lungs of the city; it nourished the Dominican national spirit. As the center of civic value, it was a barometer of social equilibrium to elites. Replete with iron benches and lanterns, it should beckon and entice. "Society" would not be restored until the park was rid of social filth, which should be expelled from the heart of the city and banished to its margins. In keeping with this vision of culture as regenerative of citizenship, one of the very first public buildings to be restored was the Teatro Capitolio, or Capital Theater.

By 1930, the urban park was a space of culture, not nature. The meaning of the park had undergone a gradual transformation since the nineteenth century with the sharpening of the public-private divide and the emergence of bounded private property in land. Owing to a deeply entrenched sense of entitlement resulting from a history of abundant public access to state lands and to a separation of land-use rights, parks and even private patios in the past had been considered spaces of nature where anyone had the right of free access to *merodear* (permission to steal fruit). This is demonstrated in the turn-of-the-century memoirs of Santo Domingo, in which rural usufruct rights were commonly extended to urban spaces and where packs of boys frequently collected mangos and bananas freely from both public parks and private gardens. In the 1920s, however, in an effort to redefine the meaning of urban parks, the Santo Domingo city council established a series of ordinances to eliminate unseemly behavior from these public sites, such as picking flowers, stepping on the grass, the presence of loud food sellers, and disorderly conduct.[90] And fees were assessed for the right to collect garden fruit and flowers.

The state of Columbus Park became such a charged issue in part because the hurricane caused far more than physical and economic destruction. It cast doubt upon the very worth of Dominican nationhood as embodied in its architectural glories and colonial past. It called into question whether

Santo Domingo was still the capital without its monuments, chalets, presidential palace, chamber of deputies, court of appeals, or fire department. Moreover, the hurricane not only wrought its own havoc but brought to a boiling point other simmering financial and moral scandals. As Louis Pérez has said, "Hurricanes served at least as much to reveal misfortune as they did to create it."[91] Of particular significance for the elite were the ravages suffered by Club Unión, the central clubhouse of the aristocracy. Money collected to correct the damages was squandered, leaving nothing with which to restore this quintessential symbol of elite prestige.[92] The ensuing scandal left the bourgeoisie with no moral authority whatsoever, as the club ruins seemed to sum up the bankruptcy of elite prestige. San Zenón not only erased the distinctions through which society itself was defined but appeared to reduce the capital city itself to an empty signifier of national value. This may explain in part why elites were so receptive to Trujillo's efforts to resurrect *dominicanidad* by throwing its positive attributes into sharp relief.

URBAN SHANTIES AND SOCIAL DEGENERACY

Only one other issue generated as much vituperative bile from elites as the disorder of Columbus Park: the state of domestic architecture for the poor after the hurricane.[93] Indeed, the central issue in the campaign to restore urban order was the problem of the *ranchito* (or *ranchería, rancherío*), or urban shanty, which some wanted banned from the capital altogether.[94] Unlike the discourse of pathology in European and other Latin American cities, however, the discourse in Santo Domingo did not focus on the slums and rising crime resulting from extensive rural-to-urban migration at the turn of the century.[95] By contrast, the contemptuous term *ranchito* derives from *rancho*, or small farm, indicating that the trouble with this form of abode came from its blurring of boundaries between the country and the city, indexing what the bourgeoisie saw as the "peasantization" of the capital. Indeed, suggestions were made to send those responsible for building these offensive rancherías to the countryside, where, by implication, they belonged.[96] A collective panic, fraught with moral urgency, erupted over housing for the poor. At times the problem was one of offensive lifestyle. As one observer wrote, "These people must abandon the way they are living, in filth and promiscuity. They're human beings and not beasts."[97] Their "embarrassing shacks" are making the city look like a "poor Chinese village."[98] Proposals were made not only to destroy the huts but to burn the materials.

Clarion calls were emitted daily to take action through martial law so that "each case does not become an unending judicial litigation." The writer continued, "With this job, which must be undertaken with authority, urgency and energy, Trujillo's government has a great opportunity to demonstrate its character, and we will support him systematically to defend it from the objections of the small (*los poquitos*), a pest (*plaga*) that abounds here, where everyone only knows how to think about today and the cheap deal (*la pulgada*), without taking into account tomorrow or the long view."[99] Some feared that the squatters, by rebuilding their houses in elite zones, would break down previous urban segregation by social class. As a result, many exhorted that the poor be forced to rebuild where they had lived before.[100] Eventually, the elite got its way, and instructions were given for the police to proceed "drastically" against those who continued to build those "ghastly huts."[101]

There is a longer history of the peasant's shabby rancho being seen as the central sign of its depravity, however. While directing the Santo Domingo municipal census in 1919, the liberal social critic and essayist José Ramón López wrote a very influential tract on social and economic conditions in the capital, which is cited frequently in all subsequent Trujillista regime publications on urban planning. In fact, the 1919 census established an image of urban destitution that, combined with the 1930 hurricane, provided ammunition to urban reformers for decades to come. In fiery muckraker style, López assailed the conditions of urban poverty found in early-twentieth-century Santo Domingo, angrily rebuking the low wages and lack of work that created conditions of starvation and worse. In accord with the late-nineteenth-century notion of degeneration, squalor brought about the permanent physical damage and moral decay of urban indigents, rendering them subjects of irredeemable social pathology if drastic action was not taken. Indeed, Santo Domingo was described as a "vale of tears" for the poor.[102] To his credit, López was more progressive than his contemporaries in his belief that the peasantry should be exposed to the "civilizing process" and was capable of improvement.[103] To achieve this, he called for the establishment of practical agronomy schools in the provinces, where, in addition to instruction about farming methods, the peasantry would be taught to live respectably: to eat well and at regular intervals, to dress properly, to wear shoes, to live in clean houses, and to follow elemental rules of hygiene. However, he was more sympathetic to the plight of the rural poor than to their metropolitan equivalents. Urban vagrants were considered the lowest order of humanity. Society was ranked and divided along strict rural-urban lines, and should stay that way. According to López, a peasant in the city is a "poorly attended exotic flower."[104] One could improve the lot of the peasant, but he must know his place in society and never venture far from it.

Several issues were embedded within the anxieties surrounding the urban shanty blight. One was the potential erosion of land values because of land invasions. After the hurricane, with barrio boundaries blurred and popular areas left in disarray, many urban poor collected wood and zinc fragments and pieced together dwellings on state lands as well as lands along the circumperiphery of the city that had been purchased in the 1920s for investment. While the problem of theft was real, those most victimized were the poor—who could not afford to purchase new building materials without jobs. And speculators emerged who rented out these usurped lands to third parties.[105] These moves could adversely affect elite urban land values and investment opportunities.[106] But these crimes were not the fault of the poor alone. Indeed, many enterprising elites also sought to use the chaos to their own advantage, for example, by securing quick cash through fraudulently selling state property.[107]

A second concern was that popular resettlement would establish communities that could inhibit future urban development at a moment when proposals were circulating to expand the city and thus take advantage of the demolition to improve design and layout. Along these lines, some felt that city renovations should be made in reinforced concrete rather than flimsier materials (the stuff of ranchos), for prevention of future natural disasters as well as for beautifying the city and encouraging investment.[108] The argument was advanced that this was the perfect moment to expand certain principal streets to prolong the main axes of the city in an organized fashion. The expansion of elite housing out of the walled colonial city into the western suburbs of Gazcue had created a desire among many for, if not wholesale urban planning, then at least major east-west and north-south thoroughfares facilitating municipal transport by automobile. Here the tension between reformers, middle-class state bureaucrats, and the new bourgeoisie became apparent. Urban reformers advocated the use of state power to curb elites who lacked community spirit and were only out for themselves, who had built country houses in a helter-skelter fashion with no consideration for the adequate provision of intramunicipal arteries. They insisted that the government purchase tracts of the now-clear terrain for future development, after which the state could embark on the "modern reconstruction" of the city.[109] They regarded the state as a means for checking the cunning of self-interest. Trujillo did respond to calls for urban reconstruction in October 1930, but merely as an expansion of the public works infrastructure essential to economic recovery, that is, ports, bridges, docks, etc., a plan that made sense to him because of his training as a marine. This was not yet a comprehensive project for urban renewal.

THE ASSAULT ON VAGRANTS

But there was clearly something more at stake than transit efficiency in the offensive against the rancho. In this case, urbanism was closely linked to social control.[110] And policy was forged in a rare moment of convergence between Trujillo's interests and those of the elite. The press, for example, called for a campaign to "decongest" the city by forcibly removing the noisome urban crowd from the city limits. Significantly, the clamor to relocate the masses outside the capital was followed by a call to increase the quantity of police garrisons, particularly in the northern (popular) neighborhoods. Three stations had previously served the city, but proposals now called for police in every barrio.[111] Indeed, Trujillo's efforts to house the homeless in churches in the colonial zone was criticized incessantly and countered with proposals—first, to relocate them in "pavilions" or "rural camps" on the outskirts of the city limits, "in a healthy place, and with good wood," attesting that this must be a temporary measure—the presumption being that these indolent peasants would never build their own homes if the state's provisioning was too comfortable.[112] Even the clergy urged the removal of the homeless from churches and their transferral outside the city limits.[113] Later proposals for removal were framed on more utilitarian grounds. Some cautioned that without the forced relocation of labor out of the city and back to the land, there would be severe food shortages.[114] As a result, the police were ordered to conduct roundups and sweeps of beggars and other social "parasites" without employment or known residence, who were to be transported outside the city.[115] Asylums for beggars and vagrants, experimented with in Spain with some success, were studied as possible approaches; these would be sites where, in the terms of Italian criminologist Cesare Lombroso, degenerate criminal types would be sorted out from those who could be rehabilitated.[116] Vagrancy laws applied at the national level later became a key measure of social and economic control under the Trujillato.[117]

While at first the hurricane provided a prime opportunity for Trujillo to demonstrate his credentials as a man of the people who worked hard to provide water, shelter, and food where it was lacking, it ended up revealing the regime's willingness to deploy draconian tactics to reinstate a social order in which the popular sectors knew their place. The destruction wreaked by San Zenón provided the basis for elite and middle-class consent to coercion to reestablish spatial, and by extension social, order in the capital. This was fortuitous timing since the wave of repression that accompanied Trujillo's first months in office had targeted the liberal elites, because they had most forcibly opposed this arriviste; but the hurricane provided an opportunity for Trujillo and the elite to find common ground, at least until the crisis was over. Trujillo shrewdly used the disaster to forge an image of caring paternalism for the popular masses while he simultaneously evinced his capacity for strong-arm discipline to the elites. Louis Pérez has noted how hurricanes insinuate themselves into the "calculus of nation," yet the case of San Zenón demonstrates how they have also figured in shaping expectations of government.[118]

Just as Trujillo was able to effectively use the crisis to craft an image of himself fulfilling expectations of appropriate leadership, he also managed somehow to avoid negative publicity resulting from mistakes. When criticisms of the relief efforts arose, Trujillo himself was never blamed. Rather, local distributors were held responsible and often accused of taking advantage of their position by removing the highest-quality items for themselves, leaving only the leftover refuse for the poor.[119]

Some of the harshest measures were reserved for armed men protecting their homesteads, firing shots that were heard from the northern barrios in the early morning hours. These created a scene described as "a cowboy camp or a far west American ranch," which some feared could lead to foreign intervention.[120] A house-to-house arms search and mandatory disarmament were instituted. One writer called for merciless retaliation, stating that these "disorders should be repressed harshly, with an iron fist, if necessary . . . on the spot . . . the authorities must act with energy, with extreme energy . . . We guarantee that no one will be frightened by the means of repression adopted, no matter how extreme."[121] Others called for "an iron fist," insisting that the destruction of the ranchos must be effected by police—the government, not private lawyers—with the backing of martial law.[122] In the trade-off between rights and repression, the poor lost.

In part a result of these anguished cries for order, the two most despised incursions of the state into the daily lives of individuals were drafted and enacted: the identification card or *cédula*, through which the state policed population mobility, and the "ten *tareas*" law, which required all "unemployed" to have a small cultivated plot. Although vagrancy laws have been remembered as primarily rural forms of social control, the national crackdown on tramps actually commenced in the capital city in the wake of San Zenón. The first efforts were sweeps to arrest people reduced to begging on city streets. These orders authorized the municipal police to collect and remove all "parasites . . . anyone without a known occupation or domicile to be moved to the place of their residence so as to decongest the city," efforts heralded and applauded by city denizens.[123] Yet this escalated into a call also to remove the rural rabble (especially men) that had flocked to the capital because of crop damage and even starvation in nearby blighted rural townships. Emergency measures such as deportations were introduced to forcibly return people to the land so as to preempt any possible food scarcity that might develop as a result, and prison labor gangs were used to collect garbage throughout the city. Only after the initial removals was a census of the urban unemployed suggested.[124] It was felt that charity for the "poor masses" would transform them into "social parasites"; they must be put to work in agriculture. When theft, particularly of building materials, became rampant, these fears were confirmed, and cries erupted against "the wheedling machinations of a stupid and corrupt plebocracy."[125] Those who did have reason to remain should join the ranks of the proletariat or the peasantry: they either should be placed in neighborhoods for workers and the poor outside of the city limits, where daily hygienic inspections would be conducted, or should be forced to cultivate municipal lands.

Plans were drawn up to build a *barrio de obreros* (workers' neighborhood) with funds from international labor organizations, although it was not until 1944 that planned neighborhoods of prefabricated bungalows à la Evanston and Levittown were built, and a Regulatory Office of City Growth was established which prohibited immigration to the capital of anyone not gainfully employed.[126]

The assault on vagrancy had repercussions in the sphere of popular culture, as concerns over idleness blossomed into a full-scale onslaught on leisure time. The near-impossibility of finding work had led to an increase in cockfighting, illicit gambling, and the lottery since people had ample time on their hands. Moreover, games of chance probably reflected a pervasive sense of fatalism in the aftermath of the hurricane, when so many had lost all traces of the everyday grounding of both public and personal identity: their jobs, worldly possessions, and homes. Furthermore, there was a surge in informal pursuits such as distilling bathtub rum (*aguardiente*) and prostitution, since these remained among the few avenues available for gainful employment. In response, elites imbued concerns that the under-privileged were not working to rebuild the city and its economy with a moralist discourse about their "perversions"—a campaign that focused on the cabarets.[127] Critics requested that prostitutes be kept off the streets until after midnight to protect families. Elites proved quite eager to rein-force their stereotype of the poor as indolent loafers, as if hidden inside every destitute urban Dominican was an invisible montero waiting to get out. Even efforts on the part of the indigent to reconstruct housing from building fragments and garbage reinforced the vision of the poor as free-loaders lacking respect for private property, when the poachers could equally have been commended for their efforts at hard work and self-improvement in the face of extreme duress.[128] Food handouts organized by the Red Cross quickly fell into disrepute for supposedly encouraging ten-dencies toward laziness and parasitism. Proposals were made to dispense provisions only to those who could show a coupon representing at least two hours worth of work.[129]

The new vagrancy legislation defining men as the primary wage earners and seeking to reinstall them back on the land through forced removals had a dramatic impact on the gendered nature of public space in the city. The deportations made Santo Domingo a city of women. A range of urban activities that had been shared by both sexes, from popular religious worship to street peddling, became female virtually overnight. Men engaged in any-thing other than work were chastised, penalized, and deported. For example, those discovered participating in processions for the Virgin of Las Mercedes were denounced. As one local official exclaimed, "prayers for women, culti-vation for men!"[130] Orders were given not to provide charity to men but only to women. As a result, the 1930s saw a gradual feminization of the dangers of the streets, as the regulation of daily life increasingly focused on the fre-quently female informal sector, that is, prostitutes, market women, healers (*curanderas*), and food peddlers.

HOMESTEADS AND CITIZENSHIP

Yet the problem of the popular homestead had deeper historical roots. Since the colonial period "the image of the good citizen of the New World was that of a settled peasant, married and working the land." Bartolomé de las Casas even believed that small-scale farming could morally regenerate tramps.[131] In another colonial context, the Comaroffs have described Wesleyan missionary efforts to "domesticate" Africans by placing them in proper homes, which would nurture lawful citizenship and combat vagrancy.[132] And in Spanish, the word for dwelling, *habitación* (from *habitar*), more than the English *house*, implies lifestyle. In addition to the nomadic montero, nineteenth-century liberal reformers made vitriolic attacks on communal lands (*terrenos comuneros*), which were seen as the bane of national development. In this paradigm, civilization was inexorably linked to settlement and enclosure—to agricultural cultivation in nuclear abodes —even for a country which had developed primarily through cattle ranching and wood exports harvested from public lands until the late nineteenth century, and for whom the "family" (generally unmarried, and in serial unions) frequently included domestic slaves in the colonial period and mistresses and their offspring later on.[133]

In the aftermath of the storm, home building became an issue of transcendental significance, one necessary for the well-being of both the citizens and the city. Individual domestic units, it was said, would restore the sense of private property that had been diffused by the provision of state charity, just as it would restore the working spirit, as people returned to the primal nexus of the family, away from the dangerous "mobs" that had clustered in the city.[134] Within a month, on Columbus Day, the state started disbursing public land plots to the poor on the outskirts of the city by lottery, although another decade would elapse before the public housing effort began in earnest.[135]

One legacy of Spanish colonialism was an imaginary social divide between city and country, encoded in the dichotomy between civilization and barbarism as two domains that were opposed and must be kept apart. There was a deep unease about country folk in urban space; their polluting presence generated not only foul smells but dangerous microbes that threatened to bring epidemics.[136] But the common denominator was the street and its transients, which wove a symbolic thread between the dangers of mobility and the discourse of disgust, as the bourgeoisie railed against the the homeless on street corners and the associated perils of microbes, foul smells, shanty towns, dust, flies, prostitutes, peddlars, shoe shiners, armed men, and street urchins. Evidence of the chain of signification linking all forms of public mobility, from odors to insects to monteros, could be seen when presumptuous peasants who pushed their way into the National Palace seeking Trujillo's attention were called *moscones*, or large flies. Apparently the street was by definition collective, anonymous, and permeated by invisible dangers that, like a virus, could engulf the bourgeoisie. As Alain Corbin has argued, there is often a striking congruence between perceptions of social hierarchy and fears of disease.[137]

The city was seen as a body, one that demanded proper circulation and movement. Close concentrations of urban poor created social effluvia, manifestations of social degeneracy such as crime, and thus weakened the city's health. Drawing on this corporal language of urban pathology, one writer explained, "Mendacity is an almost inevitable excretion of social disease and a sad wart on the large accumulations of population."[138] Expelling the poor to the city margins would rid the city of the problem of urban squalor. In a worldview reminiscent of nineteenth-century crowd theory pioneered by Gustave Le Bon, the closeness of the urban poor was foul and morbid, while rural misery in scattered homesteads by contrast was somehow pure. What the peasantry lacked in culture, they made up for in salubrity. Thus, expelling the urban poor from the city margins purified them while it elevated the city.[139]

The social reformers appealing to Trujillo, however, preached a position beyond social distance or disdain; they expressed a class loathing that would accept only the most extreme solutions.[140] At times the link between sanitation and social control was explicit, as in one writer's proposition that the time had come to cede the role of martial law to sanitation; to let the Department of Sanitation, rather than the police, protect public health, which translated as keeping the peasantry and all their trappings out of the city limits.[141] In fact, issues of public health and safety after the hurricane provided a convenient excuse for precisely the kind of state intervention in the private realm which later came to characterize the regime.

One site under particularly caustic attack was the marketplace, where country met city, a place that transgressed the rural-urban divide. Of course, there was likely a sound basis for these fears of contamination. The city was provisioned by the central produce market downtown in the colonial zone La Plaza Vieja, the smaller Plaza Nueva, and la Playita on the banks of the Ozama River, where peasants from Los Mina would bring their vegetables and *casabe* (manioc flat bread) by canoe.[142] Santo Domingo foodstuffs came largely from small producers around the city and from the western town of San Cristóbal until the U.S. occupation, when a road was built from the Cibao, a move which facilitated a broader range of food imports yet also undercut local peasant production and augmented poverty for the rural dwellers of Santo Domingo.[143] After the hurricane, the more popular *hospedaje*, an open-air plaza and lodge outside the city walls, became a place of refuge for many when they lost their homes. The hospedaje was a place of commerce, as well as a site where *marchantas* or market women and peddlers from the countryside (who arrived after six in the evening, when the city walls were shut) would pass the night. With no proper water, sewage, or trash facilities, the hospedaje was typically odoriferous and strewn with rotting vegetable remains and human waste and excrement. It was also a place where prostitutes plied their trade after dark. However, as this transient flow of market sellers turned into a sedentary community of hurricane refugees, cries arose for their removal in the name of public health.[144] The question remained, however, whether the "focus of an infinity of diseases" was the accumulation of decaying garbage or the indigent homeless themselves. The hurricane's devastation provided a convenient excuse to achieve what the Ayuntamiento had been trying to accomplish for some time: crack down on untaxed food sellers to force them into sedentary market stalls where the state could ensure that it received its cut. After the hurricane, a plan was drawn up for the renovation of the municipal markets to be commenced early the following year.[145]

APOCALYPSE NOW

Miguel Matamoros summed up the sense of insecurity produced by the storm in a song, "El trio y el ciclón":

> Each time when I remember the cyclone,
> It makes my heart sick . . .
> Ay, doubtful spiritists,
> There are many of them around.[146]

If recreating an orderly, segregated, and respectable metropolis with a little help from the state was the bourgeois answer to the social problems of the hurricane, things looked quite different from the barrios, where it was understood as an "instrument of divine purpose."[147] First, not only was rebuilding much slower there, but with little effective intervention to mediate conflicts, tensions often erupted into violence. Thus the terrors did not cease as people returned to the work-a-day world. But more important, the hurricane was not understood as a sociospatial problem to be controlled and fixed but rather as a sign of something awry in the moral order.

In the Dominican popular imagination, natural disasters are frequently seen as signs of the demonic, as evidence of a malevolent force that can present itself in various guises, from disease to earthquakes to caudillos. There also seems to be a particular affinity between natural disasters and exceptionally ruthless strongmen, as if political power can have a conjuring effect.[148] For example, the fearsome Ulises Heureaux was welcomed into office by a devastating tropical storm in 1894, which is remembered as the Ciclón de Lilís. Similarly, the Pope's visit to Santo Domingo in 1986, invoking the wrath of God, was said to have engendered Hurricane David. This popular conjoining of human and natural power, however, contains a positive as well as a negative valence, connoting, in the words of Mary Douglas, both purity and danger, simultaneously "controlled and uncontrolled power."[149] For instance, it is said that Columbus planted a miraculous cross that eventually became the sacred site of the Virgin of Las Mercedes, patron saint of the Dominican nation, and not coincidentally protectress from hurricanes.[150]

The hurricane was interpreted by many as a sign of divine retribution and punishment for collective sin, one that demanded penance. The bounds of community had been shattered by a malicious force, requiring channeling, supplication, and appeasement to effect the healing process. After Zenón, rumors were rife that the end of the world was coming. One "extraordinary" spiritist divined a meteor en route to destroy all remaining houses; another claimed that five thousand U.S. troops were poised to disembark to establish a new military government. The press reported apocalyptic hearsay for months after the event, which sent waves of people from the barrios downtown to the perceived safety of the colonial zone in the wee hours of the morning. After learning that the end was in sight, individuals also flocked to church to have candles blessed by priests for protection.[151]

In response to these popular fears, religious pilgrimage became an important medium through which people sought to placate God's wrath and correct the celestial breach. Alongside the official (and several unofficial) masses invoking the Virgin of Altagracia for those who perished in the disaster, the urban poor sought to right their world through scores of other popular religious activities. Processions were commonplace. In Catholic processions, armies of devotees, clothed in rough-hewn burlap or blue denim, carried saint images, walking barefoot or crawling on their knees as they made vows or gifts of personal sacrifice to the saints in exchange for good fortune (in this case, for having survived the hurricane). In Afro-Dominican processions, people carried saint images, rocks, and drums and sang prayers. Municipal authorities organized a parade of thanksgiving and penitence in which firemen rallied alongside worshipers to the drums and bugles of the National Army marching band, an event which drew an impressive six thousand pilgrims. Scores of women "from good society" traveled barefoot to a mass for the Virgin of Carmen.[152] These processions represented a popular reclaiming of public space as devotees used the idiom of the march to impose discipline and order among their rank and file, thus defining themselves against the image of the unruly popular crowd created by the disaster and invoked by the bourgeoisie to justify social control proposals.

Groups of marching worshipers crisscrossed the island. Some three hundred left the central Cibao plains to travel to Higüey, the easternmost tip of the island, just as another group from the barrio of San Carlos walked some fifty kilometers to Bayaguana and back in thanks for being spared death by Zenón. By offering these sacrificial actions to God, the votaries were also asking for divine compensation for their suffering. As fulfillment of a vow, the procession is both a gift as well as a transaction that calls for recompense. Thus, behind the devotional public posture of humility, the pilgrims were also aggressively demanding repayment for the damages of the hurricane's fury.[153]

These saintly processions were what Victor Turner would term group communitas, as well as individual empowerment, as indicated by the woman who defiantly raised her clenched fists upon arriving at the miraculous Christ of Bayaguana.[154] And pilgrims reached for all available religious idioms, from the Catholic saints to the Afro-Dominican water spirits, ancestors, and the most senior Gede, Barón del Cementerio ("the Lord of Life as well as Death")—who were used for magic, witchcraft, and personal protection.[155] Rocks, which were ubiquitous in post-hurricane penitence rites, served as conveyors of sin to be cast off in purification rites in Catholicism, and as nodes of congealed power in Dominican vodú or Haitian vodou.[156] As in Kongo minkisi practice, stones could be invested with medicines and either used as spirit admonishment or animated as charms to improve one's luck; they could also be inhabited by and thus channel the special powers of twins or water spirits.[157]

While the devotees' psalms and saints emulated the revered authority of Catholicism, their invocation of the ancestors drew upon the conjuring powers of "the mysteries" (misterios) or luases, Afro-Dominican deities, to heal the body politic. Processions were intended as a kind of homeopathic purification of the streets, which had been stained by the blood of the dead, blood sacrifice being an integral element of Dominican vodú.[158] On their heads penitents carried rocks which could represent the dangerous lower (*petro*) powers of the ancestors, in an effort to appease them and thus cool their anger so that they would not take surviving relatives as well.[159] Efforts to move the Santo Domingo cemetery from the city center to the periphery after the hurricane may have provoked offerings to the powerful Baron of the Cemetery, chief of the Gede vodú division of gods connoting death and the underworld, to recoup lost wealth and jobs and communicate with dead family members. Cemeteries were focal sites for worship and healing practices and for rites aimed at enabling the dead to find peace. They also represented a space of witchcraft where people in great need solicited the Baron at midnight to obtain extraordinary things, for example, communication with a deceased loved one or acquisition of a *bacá* to protect property, steal from others, or make money.[160] Thus, after San Zenón, people most likely flocked to the Gede as the most powerful group of divinities, seeking divination or spiritual cleansing.[161] They may also have sought to collect ingredients such as bones and dust to be used in recipes for potent *resguardos* for health and protection.[162] Sorcery was a call to divine counter-authorities to accomplish tasks the state seemed powerless to achieve.

Of course, elites saw these religious activities quite differently. Without a clear separation of high and low cultural forms, what had been treated as barrio folklore, distant and quaint, came to be seen as deeply threatening and a comment on dominicanidad more generally. Complaints surged about "one of the many strange things that the hurricane has brought us," these "African scenes" of "ragged peasants carrying saints and stones and singing strange psalms," which were considered inappropriate for the national capital because they undermined the "culture, decency and civilization" of the majority. Under the guise of concern, these overly credulous peasants were taken advantage of by swindlers and conmen, and there was a call to put a stop to the "speculators" who were using religion as a means of tricking the poor and collecting food handouts. Ironically, though, the uncertainties of post-hurricane life encouraged even elites to flock to the occult, with high-society women as the most avid clients of one "world-famous" clairvoyant who set up a practice in the colonial zone. And Espiritista Alan Kardec's books sold like hotcakes to elites in the wake of the disaster.[163]

In sum, popular religion fulfilled a dual function in the aftermath of the hurricane. It provided the connective tissue for communal strength in the face of tremendous individual loss and grief, and thus legitimated a popular community increasingly villainized by the state; yet at the same time it forged a potent counterculture of resistance. Thus, in Turner's terms, these forms of worship were as much antistructure as structure. Unlike other parts of Latin America, where religion provided an important source of legitimacy for the colonial state, the historical weakness of both church and state in the Dominican Republic has meant that religion played a more contradictory—and even ambivalent—role in the culture of state legitimation. While certainly religious practice has commanded many leisure activities of the poor through novenas or week-long patron saint festivals and pilgrimages, for centuries these have been primarily outside the formal auspices of the Catholic Church owing to insufficient clergy.[164] The result has been a deeply popular lay religious culture, in which religion has provided an important "repertoire of contention" as well as an idiom of authority, notwithstanding the official clergy's views that "there was great indifference to religion and that ignorance was appalling."[165]

BUILDING CITIZENSHIP

The city was gradually rebuilt, but the discourse of social disorder remained after San Zenón. The nostalgic voices of the old elite invoking memories of the capital in the 1920s were eventually silenced, with engineers such as Henry Gazón and the Yale-trained architect Guillermo González Sánchez designing avant-garde Dominican Party palaces, luxury hotels, and government buildings for the regime. González's masterpiece was the luxurious Jaragua Hotel on the *malecón* or central boardwalk of the capital city, which was touted by American architectural publications such as *Interiors, The Architectural Forum,* and *Projects and Materials* as one of the first and finest resort hotels in Latin America. Called the "synthesis of an era," his work was both praised by the arbiters of international style for its innovation and slavishly imitated by his minions at the Department of Public Works.[166] Yet American architectural critics found it perplexing that a tourist hotel would devote such a large percentage of space to public areas, which actually dwarfed the space devoted to bedrooms. The ballroom, dining room, and pool overshadowed the living quarters, which totaled a modest sixty-three rooms, few for a hotel of otherwise ostentatious proportions. Clearly, the Jaragua was not primarily intended for tourists. It was

8. The Jaragua Hotel. PHOTO BY THOMSEN ELLIS HUTTON COMPANY.

designed primarily as a stage for Trujillista official events—dinners, dances, and balls—one that would tower above traditional elite venues such as the Club Unión.

In 1944, workers' barrios were created by the state based on the bungalow form, the prefabricated free-standing mass housing then in vogue in the United States. As we have seen, public housing policy was born of a deep mistrust on the part of elites vis-à-vis the poor—first the peasantry and later the urban underclass—because of their presumed rootlessness and nomadism. Trujillista urban reformers argued first that dwellings, apart from being an essential of human life, were "the most clear indication of the level and quality of civilization" of the inhabitant.[167] Thus, shabby housing was more than a sign of poverty; dilapidated dwellings, it was argued, produced bad people. Indeed, not only would the appearance of ramshackle hovels create deficient workers, which damaged the economy, but shack dwellers themselves were predisposed to criminality and social deviance. Lack of sanitation, cleanliness, or organization made for absenteeism and low worker productivity, and even eroded the moral fiber of residents.

The key trope of late-nineteenth-century liberal anxiety was the nomadic montero, which became the rancho or roving shanty during the hurricane of San Zenón; but by the 1940s Trujillista reformers focused on the *turgurio* or hovel, a term that framed the problem of the urban underclass in even more derogatory terms.[168] In part due to shortages of basic housing materials because of World War II, the quality of new low-income residences built by the poor in Santo Domingo declined severely by the 1940s, as the semi-rural style of thatched hut with adjoining kitchen plot or conuco gave way to the shanty pieced together from refuse such as flattened cans. The appearance of "hovels" tucked away in "clandestine" neighborhoods, where there were inadequate plumbing facilities or light, communal kitchens, and insufficient bedroom space, constituted a social danger since such conditions were believed to lead to criminal behavior (such as prostitution). The real problem, of course, was the fact that the liquidation of the terrenos comuneros had forced many rural migrants to migrate to urban centers seeking work. The trickle of migrants became a flood by the late 1930s through the 1950s, as Trujillo fomented the expansion of sugar and small manufacturing around Santo Domingo by forced sales at low prices, dispossessing thousands; they ended up in the barrios marginados surrounding the capital. Indeed, Ciudad Trujillo had growth rates of 7.38 percent in the 1950s, the highest in Latin America, expanding twelve times from 1920 to 1960.[169] And by 1955 it was estimated that 12 percent of the population lived in substandard dwellings.[170]

In the first twenty-five years of Trujillo's rule, the regime spent more than 224 million pesos in buildings and public works, twenty-eight times more than the total of cumulative investment in public building since independence.[171] Indeed, construction insinuated itself into official discourse, becoming a recurrent leitmotif, such as the comment that the Dominican Party was "the only [one] in the Americas . . . which constructs consciences, builds wills . . . and using stone, lime, cement and sidewalks erects civic temples to be used by the people to labor for civilization . . . to rebuild the civic and cultural architecture of the nation."[172] A good part of this investment was spent building workers' housing such as the Barrio de Mejoramiento Social and Ensanche Luperón, which were intended for displaced peasants, although many went to Trujillo's special friends, the high-ranking military.[173] With the purpose of avoiding high-rise units, these housing complexes were built as individual bungalows grouped into clusters of two rows of six homes each. The free-standing houses were intended to elevate the culture of the Dominican family by eliminating the overcrowding typical of the urban underclass and imparting the urban mores that would transform peasant residents into virtuous citizens. For this reason, the planned neighborhoods were built around affordable A-frame units with two or at most three bedrooms and small backyards. The government provided a credit plan through which residents could gradually purchase their units, one intended to give "permanency" to the communities and help consolidate families.[174]

Residents did adapt the design to suit their needs, however. For example, the standardized bungalow design used in Maria Auxiliadora included an enclosed kitchen adjacent to a back entrance, a plan that was anathema to rural Dominicans for whom the kitchen must by definition be located outside the house, so most barrio residents built add-on exterior kitchens.[175] The bungalow design drew on the low-cost prefabricated units of Levittown and on the California mission style which had become popular during the 1920s in Gazcue. A Spanish visitor was suitably impressed: "The [workers'] houses are no different than the good modern dwellings; they are exactly the same as the little country cottages of Hollywood."[176]

The guiding principle of planned neighborhoods built in Ciudad Trujillo in the 1940s was avoidance of irrational mobs with a proclivity to vice and violence by the elimination of overcrowding, both within the house as well as in the greater metropolitan area. As Trujillo stated pedantically at the inauguration of the first planned barrio for "social improvement":

> Conscious workers must avoid "irrationalism," that is to say, the blind acceptance of whatever rash form of behaving, because this leads to an inevitable crisis of values, a demoralization of fatal consequences, and, in the end, makes one float in the middle of the blind and sterile overflow of hatred and passions, in a low-level rebellion of the primary instincts.[177]

When Trujillo stated that the government gift of homes was to bring "stability and love," stability was a code word for wiping out the nomadic montero, as well as its urban equivalent, the informal underclass. "Love" indexed the securing of allegiance through patronage, since apartments were intended to purchase submission to the regime.

If the "dangerous classes" became increasingly feminized during the hurricane, it makes sense that housing, the most potent symbol of the cult of domesticity of the regime, became the fulcrum of urban social policy. For Trujillo, domestic order was the handmaiden of political order, under the notion that good houses would make good citizens. Yet for a culture in which one's home defines one's social person, the gift of shelter was a powerful means of extending the appearance of citizenship, one which encouraged the image of a paternalist state. Unlike other populists whose charisma relied on a union with the masses, Trujillo eventually staked his cult on their containment, their enclosure in nuclear A-frames, and their eventual civilization under state tutelage.

However, the Neighborhoods for Social Improvement were not the most ambitious effort on Trujillo's part to rationalize urban space and residential mobility in Ciudad Trujillo. If, in the 1940s, the state sought to create neighborhoods without crowds, in the 1950s this agenda was expanded to the entire city. The regime first began to design a national urban planning scheme in 1944, when the General Plan of Urbanization and Beautification of Cities was implemented, establishing controls on housing safety and aesthetics.[178] After 1944, all new building plans had to be approved by the Department of Public Works before construction commenced. But the real effort to establish effective urban planning began in 1952, with the founding of the National Commission of Urbanism, blossoming in 1955 into the Office of Growth Regulation of Ciudad Trujillo and the Trujillo Plan of Urban Betterment of the Capital of the Republic. With its concept of the city as an organism, this plan was a comprehensive effort to regulate city growth, including zoning, park development, and the complementary establishment of separate residential and industrial areas. It sought to both differentiate and streamline city functions to permit more orderly growth.[179]

Interestingly, this plan was also an effort on the part of some urban planners critical of the impact of the regime on daily life in the capital to alleviate certain problems: the interiorization of public life, for example, as a result of both the surveillance apparatus, which discouraged people from speaking in public for fear of being overheard, and the elimination of public meeting grounds such as plazas from the new neighborhoods.[180] The style of park permitted by the regime was more monumental than civic, like the Parque Ramfis, lauded for its state-of-the-art children's swing sets and perceived as primarily an expensive gift from the dictator to the people, with the purpose of eliciting gratitude. For example, one admirer described it as "the resplendent enchantment of a pearl, Ramfis Park, pious oasis of the childhood of all social classes."[181] The plan was designed for the rebirth of the spirit of a metropolis which had been crushed by the dictatorship, one which would reestablish the center of social gravity around an expansive park—part recreational site, part educational center—to recreate a public culture. It stood in contrast to the traditional municipal plaza, which, by definition, was an extension of civic society with some governmental functions, primarily for the privileged; the proposed central park would be for the masses, so large that multiple groups could congregate at the same time. Like a green, it would afford privacy in public. In fact, the plan explicitly underscored the need to permit and even encourage the formation of collectivities around "unanticipated activities," as if spontaneous sociability or leisure itself had taken on a sinister and suspect air under the regime. The plan spoke, for example, of policies aimed at conserving the "intimacy" of the barrio by congregating all services in one area, apart from residences, to allow relationships to form outside the state or the market. It also proposed actually widening thoroughfares in residential areas so as to enliven, rather than squelch, street life—a radical proposal given the way in which streets constituted such an important popular realm in the Dominican Republic. Finally, the plan advocated decentralizing the city by allocating services to the barrios so as to make them more autonomous, thus returning some of the vigorous communitarian ethos lost when they became strictly dependent on the municipality for their existence. Proposals such as these could be seen as a revolt against the pervasiveness of public life under the Trujillo regime—the constant rallies, parades, civic rituals, and surveillance. The plan was a reminder that to be alive, barrios needed more than just agents of governmentality; they needed sites of civic society as well, not only schools and police, but parks and coffee houses.[182]

CONCLUSION

The popular support for Trujillo that emerged out of the hurricane was of a particular kind. There was a perceived need for a style of leadership that would combat the image of the Dominican as idle shifter (i.e., montero).[183] Yet as we have seen, this image appeared anew during the hurricane as the collapse of social distinctions uncovered other fears about the relationship between city and country, rich and poor, and leadership and masses. In the end, the tension in state policy under the Trujillato between paternalism and absolutism was resolved in favor of the latter. As one contemporary observer explained, while a certain amount of regime tenderness was necessary in the beginning due to the exceptional circumstances of the hurricane, ultimately "a government must be composed of men, of men of much action, initiative and self-denial."[184] Thus the figure of Trujillo emerged as a strong man, at the helm of a strong state, both crucial to give shape and mass to a shifting, disorderly, and by implication feminine, nation.[185]

This correspondence between leader and people was not the only regime trope fixed during San Zenón. Another element of official rhetoric established during the hurricane, for example, was the need to eliminate political competition and unify around issues of national development, a move intended to stifle dissent. Trujillo's objective was said to be that of "depoliticizing" the country to eliminate the caudillo civil wars of the past. Yet the state of emergency imposed during the hurricane entailed extraordinary powers which were not rescinded after the chaos had subsided. For example, the right to freely travel abroad was withdrawn. For the first time, individuals were required to seek special government permission to travel overseas, on the real or trumped-up charge that merchants who were unable to repay their creditors were fleeing the country and wreaking havoc on national credit.[186] For the next three decades, strict control over access to passports became a key tool with which to police the elite and middle classes. Finally, important social control laws aimed at tying peasants to the land and inhibiting rural-urban migration were initiated as a result of the hurricane, yet continued long after the crisis had passed. In line with the regime's populist face, Trujillo's praise chorus sought to make these policies appear to have broad social appeal. One writer made the following supplication: "Trujillo: the decent people of the country—rich, poor, whites and blacks—(decency doesn't recognize wealth or color) are avid for good government, and these decent people believe that you are prepared for it. Affirm this belief with real acts of government . . . Work, with a strong hand and with justice; weakness doesn't become us."[187]

Trujillo's populist political style finally did engender tension with the elite, which was not accustomed to the intimacy of his appeal to and contact with the masses. A good example of their unease were the complaints registered when, in the aftermath of the hurricane, Trujillo consented to meet the poor face-to-face in the National Palace; as a result, enormous queues of ragged campesinos with bare feet, straw hats, and machetes formed outside the building. This practice violated the rules of respectability as well as respeto. Critics charged that such matters were better resolved outside the palace doors, that "only in our country could a nobody get close to the president" "as if he were mayor of a small town."[188]

The populist rhetoric that emerged during the early consolidation of the Trujillo regime was a contradictory blend of Arielista calls for messianic "renovation" and attacks on clusters of social privilege such as social elites, large landowners, and pretentious pseudo-aristocrats. Spiritual renewal could only be achieved through waging war on the "blue-blooded minorities," "privileged castes," and, as we shall see, foreigners, who continued to monopolize national perks and prerogatives.[189] As one journalist remarked,

> And here is the black [*negrito*] Próspero Diprés, graduated from international schools, Calles, and the mulatto de Artuán, and there are a million more cases like these; that Trujillo and only Trujillo has put the Creole where he belongs, not by closing the door to the foreigner . . . but also not allowing Creole to be passed over when they have real knowledge . . . we must feel Creole, Dominican, and put our birthright first and . . . help the government improve the country.[190]

Yet this movement was not to be led by the masses but rather by a leadership capable of guiding the country out of its state of decadence, mediocrity, and democracy.[191] This was a moment when traditional frameworks were swept aside in favor of new solutions, which drew upon the contradictory languages of liberal reform, fascist revolution, and populism on the one hand, and Arielismo on the other. Certainly the crisis of liberalism was a global phenomenon, which resulted in the emergence of a range of new political phenomena worldwide, from fascism to socialism. Nonetheless each episode had a local component. By the 1920s, liberalism and multiparty democracy in the Dominican Republic had become associated with national fragmentation, U.S. intervention, and the Depression—and thus national humiliation and economic crisis. Trujillo stepped onto the political stage at a moment when a strong state seemed the sole means of righting a world turned upside down. Political parties had tried and failed. And liberal ideologues ultimately lacked confidence in the masses. Indeed, Trujillo's script as Machiavellian prince or Nietzschean superman had already been drafted, to be pastiched on the concept of a "tutelary state" formulated by the conservative liberal Américo Lugo. Later Trujillo would seek to emulate, if only superficially, the übernationalist style of Hitler and the Catholic hispanicism of the Spanish Falange. Demands for "spiritual renovation" were fulfilled through the reconstruction of the national crown jewel, the mirror of state which was named Ciudad Trujillo in 1936.[192]

In 1955, a Free World's Fair of Peace and Confraternity was held in the capital to celebrate the twenty-fifth year of the Trujillo regime. A full year of trade fairs, exhibits, dances, and performances culminated in a "floral promenade" that showcased the dictator's daughter, sixteen-year-old María de los Angeles del Corazón de Jesús Trujillo Martínez, better known as Angelita, who was crowned queen during the central Carnival parade. One-third of the nation's annual budget was spent on this gala affair, a good portion of which was invested in Italian-designed Fontana gowns for chic Angelita and her entourage of 150 princesses. Queen Angelita's white silk satin gown was beyond fantasy proportions: it had a seventy-five-foot train and was decorated with 150 feet of snow-white Russian ermine—the skins of six hundred animals—as well as pearls, rubies, and diamonds. The total cost of the gown was $80,000, a modest fortune at the time. In full regalia, her costume replicated that of Queen Elizabeth I, replete with erect collar and a brooch and scepter that cost another $75,000.[1]

For $1,000, two hairdressers were flown in from New York to set the royal coiffure. A full army of street sweepers scrubbed by hand the central *malecón* (boardwalk) of Ciudad Trujillo, where Angelita's float would process, to protect her majesty's white robe. Her entry was made on a mile of red carpet, in the company of hundreds of courtiers. A new western extension of the city was even built for the fair and became municipal office space after the event. This national extravaganza surpassed all other events of the regime in its excesses of magisterial pomp and spending. The fair framed the dictator's daughter as "a charismatic center" of national value and the numinous totem of the regime, the nation, and even the "free" world (as the name of the fair ironically announced).[2]

As the symbolic climax of the "Year of the Benefactor" dedicated to Trujillo, the fair was intended to highlight the achievements of the regime by placing them on display. And in this nationalist mythology, signs of progress equaled the regime, which equaled the man himself. According to Trujillo, the Free World's Fair of Peace and Confraternity was

9. Angelita at *la Feria*. ARCHIVO GENERAL DE LA NACIÓN, SANTO DOMINGO.

the patriotic achievement of the Era which national gratitude has baptized with my name. There it is, objectively materialized in each one of the exhibitions of this Fair, the period that I have presided over and that I offer today, at the end of twenty-five years, to the judgment of the people who entrusted their destiny to me in 1930 in a gesture of deep faith in my patriotism and in my acts, that rewards my long vigils and my fever for work during these twenty-five years in which was forged this prodigious reality. That work is my only crown and with it I submit myself today to history.[3]

The World's Fair (la Feria), however, was convened not merely to represent the "prodigious reality" of Trujillo's rule. Filtered through Angelita's aura of perfection, it was a particularly grandiloquent manifestation of the larger-than-life ceremonial regime that was the Era of Trujillo. On the cusp of an epoch in which nations were judged by their ability to represent their virtues at trade exhibits and world's fairs,[4] la Feria was proof that a man with a big vision could make even a small country look great. But why did the figure of the dictator not stand in for the regime? Why was the dictator's daughter selected as its emblem and the chosen medium for its consecration?

In this chapter I explore the representation of women in official specta-cles during the Trujillo regime. Like Marie Antoinette, Trujillo had many bodies, which were variously represented through the women of the re-gime.[5] Feminine imagery functioned as a foil for the dictator's multiple masculine identities; each female relationship revealed a different facet of his power. One could say that the display of women was a means of ac-cumulation in Trujillo's drive for symbolic capital, although one that had to be constantly renewed.[6] Trujillo drew upon a traditional genre of mas-culinity in which his self-aggrandizement was based on the sheer number of women, particularly those of high social status, he could lay claim to—those who highlighted his prowess as lover, father, and husband, as well as defender of his extended family. As Roger Lancaster has described it, "ma-chismo produces values and circulates values: the value of men and women. What is ultimately produced . . . is one's social standing."[7]

Trujillo was the quintessential Latin American big man whose authority was based on dramatic acts that drew loyal followers.[8] As elsewhere in Latin America, the good macho expresses the values of activity, dominance, and violence, with metaphorical consumption through the possession of both clients and women.[9] Yet Trujillo's power and charisma were based on the consumption of women (and their status) through sexual conquest as well as the domination of enemies of state, and on the near mythological fear and resultant aura he acquired through eliminating men. Whereas Trujillo's insatiable sexual cupidity brought ignominy, it also brought respect and was a key element in his legitimacy as a caudillo-turned-statesman, respeto being a term which conjoins masculinity, authority, and legitimacy.[10] Thus, in these narratives of sexual conquest, gender served as an allegory of class and race.

THE DICTATOR'S FEMALE BODIES

Scholars exploring the issue of gender representation and politics have focused on the identity of first ladies, female regents, and queens, par-ticularly on how they often become magnets for negative commentary and abuse. In an apparently transnational and transhistorical paradigm, public women from countries as diverse as Argentina (Eva Perón) and Nigeria (Maryam Babangida), and in periods stretching from ancien régime France (Marie Antoinette) to Cold War United States (Nancy Reagan), have borne the brunt of popular disaffection for their husbands. This recurrent nega-tive imagery has been explained in several ways. Historians have argued that the transfer of political life out of regal households and courts, with the growing divergence of public and private domains, banished women from politics. Women then became the focus of loathing and resentment when they ventured onto terrain that was no longer their own.[11] By contrast, Julie Taylor, in her gendered model of power ideologies, has taken an alternative culturalist approach.[12] She seeks to explain the cross-cultural bifurcation of power whereby men inhabit the controlled, ordered, and hierarchical domain, while their female counterparts embody the uncontained, dangerously capricious spiritual power of the feminine. This paradigm stresses the complementarity of feminine and masculine powers and is in line with other theories that explain dualistic gender ideologies in terms of constructions of nature and culture, or power and authority.[13] Taylor demonstrates how this imagery developed into the middle-class myth of Evita as malevolent witch, harboring a deep and secret communion with the irrational masses.

The Trujillo regime did not fit either of these paradigms. The prevalence of feminine iconography did not engender popular loathing of women in the public sphere or an obsessive concern with the sexual exploits of las Trujillo. Rather, stories of hyperactive sexual antics were a stock feature of popular mythmaking concerning all of the Trujillo family, primarily the men but also the women. Even today, books charting the lascivious exploits of Trujillo and his inner court are one of the most popular forms of literature about the regime.[14] In perhaps the most dramatic example, the notorious Trujillista stud Porfirio Rubirosa (see chapter 5) was widely rumored not only to have an exorbitant sexual apparatus but to suffer from a permanent erection, which was "confirmed" by the fact that he never sired children despite his prodigious promiscuity.[15] Stories also abound of Trujillo's abduction of virginal girls during his provincial travels and of beautiful victims spied and romanced during official balls and functions. Indeed, to be chosen as an object of Trujillo's desire elicited a certain forbidden pride as well as fear, even among the sheltered but rebellious adolescent daughters of the elite, who sneaked off to official functions. As a result, parents went to great lengths to prevent their daughters from being noticed by the dictator, since refusing his attentions carried a high price and could even cost a girl's father his job.[16]

Nor was power in the Dominican popular imagination configured in the binary conjugal fashion elaborated by Taylor. Indeed, Trujillo's wives played little or no role in either state iconography or popular mythmaking. His several legal consorts were dowdy and unassuming, taking little or no public role in regime affairs. His first wife, Aminta Ledesma, was of simple peasant stock from Trujillo's provincial hometown; he divorced her to marry "a more socially suitable wife," Bienvenida Ricardo, a "poor blueblood" from a provincial aristocratic family.[17] Although the Dominican Party established a women's branch in 1940, the first lady did not actively participate, outside of an occasional cameo appearance as hostess for party parties—the teas, receptions, cocktails, and balls that were frequently held in her honor.[18] Doña María Martínez, Trujillo's third wife, the daughter of Spanish immigrants, was guarded and reclusive, keeping to a tiny coterie of confidants and insiders. She focused her attention on raising the children and on business affairs; she was less interested in her public profile than in concrete material returns for her efforts. In fact, during her tenure as first lady, Doña María succeeded in amassing one of the largest personal fortunes of the era, in part because her ghostwritten publications were required reading in public schools. Toward the end of the regime, when she began to take an active interest in urban planning and architectural affairs, she did so entirely behind the scenes. In imitation of Evita Perón, whose persona was based on her Social Welfare Foundation and its activities, Doña María commenced a similar organization after 1953. However, she never cultivated an active maternal caregiving role, the hands-on, direct line to the masses that was the basis of Evita's charisma in Argentina. Rather, her reputation was one of cool reserve and sporadic outbursts of impetuous ire that some allege was due to rancor stemming from her earlier social exclusion as Trujillo's mistress.[19] Doña María's most significant venture into the public sphere was as author of an etiquette booklet entitled *Moral Meditations,* a chiding, schoolmarmish mixture of popular philosophy and manners for Dominican mothers. The book disappeared without a ripple.[20]

The Trujillo regime stands out because the dictator's wife did not take center stage in regime iconography. Nor did iconography feature the binomial couple, the basis of the nuclear family—often a privileged metaphor embodying the natural patriarchal authority of nationhood in Latin America.[21] Instead, Trujillo's other women provided erotic imagery for the body politic: most important were his young lover Lina Lovatón, through her participation in the Carnival of 1937, and his two daughters—Angelita, who was queen of the World's Fair of 1955, and Flor de Oro, who served as cultural ambassador in New York, where she became doyenne of the Hollywood jet set by virtue of her one-time marriage to the Dominican playboy Porfirio

Rubirosa.[22] Of course, the intricacy of this imagery in part derived from the complex and contradictory structure of the Dominican family, which is characterized by concubinage, serial unions, female-headed households, de facto polygyny, and a rigid set of unattainable gender-role expectations. For the majority of rural and urban poor, a family headed by a stable male wage earner and subsisting on a single income is an ideal but unreachable goal. For example, although women ideally should not work, most find they have to: either they are the sole wage earners in their family or their husband's income is insufficient. Indeed, some have argued that the economic emasculation of the lower-class urban and rural male has taken its toll on gender roles and driven men to exhibit their masculine prowess, machismo, in alternative arenas of daily life.[23] The Dominican male is expected to be an honorable father to his public *oikos*, which shares his apellido (surname), as well as to secretly maintain his unofficial wives and offspring, his *casa chica* (small house). The Dominican family, then, provides several "triangles of dramatizations" through which "unconscious images of a familial order" are defined, an obvious example being the husband-wife-mistress triangle.[24]

What were some of the ideological effects of this family romance? Stories of the erotic adventures of the Trujillo family brought the regime down to earth by translating the apparently superhuman first family into a vernacular language and mode of expression drawn from daily life. In the genre of popular gossip, official romance offered a medium for sentimental investment in the regime while also providing grist for moral criticism of the excesses of statecraft and male philandering run amok.[25] However, contrary to Doris Sommer's work on national romance, this was a form of legitimation based on lust, not love, since adulation of the daughter and lover did not evoke the promise of "natural" child bearing.[26] Most important, the parading of Trujillo's women involved a performance of masculinity drawing on the figure of the popular antihero from the barrio—the tíguere (per its popular pronunciation; lit. tiger) or quintessential Dominican underdog who gains power, prestige, and social status through a combination of extra-institutional wits, force of will, sartorial style, and *cojones*.[27] The tíguere seduces through impeccable attire, implacable charm, irresistible sexuality, and a touch of violence. His defining feature is a daring willingness to go after whatever he wants—money, commodities, or women, particularly those beyond his social reach. A man of the street, the tíguere operates through cunning, frequently via illicit means.[28]

I wish to examine the 1937 Carnival, which showcased Trujillo's genteel paramour Lina Lovatón as beauty queen, and then analyze the significance of the 1955 World's Fair, in which first daughter Angelita reigned supreme.[29] On one level, the daughters and wives of the state elite created by the Trujillato merely represented their husbands in official pageants, reenacting the exchange of gifts and favors that was part of politics under the regime.[30] But staging affairs of state through a rhetoric of female corporeality had its own effects. First, it constituted a public of voyeurs convened to gaze upon, assess, appreciate, and admire the mythic dimensions of Trujillo's masculinity: as exemplary father, husband, caudillo, patrón, and lover. Second, Trujillo's women as objects of value were crucial tropes of his power; value accrued to the person of the dictator through their evaluation and exchange.[31] Rejected by the traditional white elite as a ruthless mulatto arriviste with Haitian (black) lineage, Trujillo sought out the offspring of the bourgeoisie in his erotic forays. Not only did he seek to defy the aristocracy by stealing their daughters, but, in true tíguere fashion, he also legitimated himself through the acquisition of women of superior status—a logic in which the bigger the woman, the bigger the man. As in the Brazilian social type the *malandro*, the tíguere is an entrepreneurial social climber who uses women to accumulate status; thus it is an idiom of masculinity "constructed on and subsisting from women's subordination."[32] Romantic conquest, then, became a means of both subjugating the bourgeoisie and entering their ranks. Scholars have focused on Trujillo's accumulation of land, commerce, and capital while neglecting an important economy of male personal status in the Dominican Republic.[33]

LINA LOVATÓN: "I, THE QUEEN"

In 1937, Trujillo was taking one of his daily strolls in tree-shaded Gazcue, a scenic neighborhood of Ciudad Trujillo. During his outing on that balmy late afternoon, he came upon the young Lina Lovatón Pittaluga, tall and lithe, who looked ravishing in a dreamy tulle dress. She was the sole daughter of Ramón Lovatón, a prominent lawyer from one of the most exclusive *capitaleña* families, who was known for his elegant attire. Lina, one of the most eligible debutantes at the time, was a contestant for Carnival queen. She was facing stiff competition that year from the beautiful Blanquita Logroño, sister of an esteemed jurist and close ally of Trujillo. But, as the legend goes, Trujillo was smitten and proceeded to arrange things in her favor.[34] And, it seems, Trujillo knew that giving Lina the queenship would create a large debt that would have to be repaid.

Trujillo at this point had recently divorced his second wife, Bienvenida Ricardo, to marry María Martínez. Nonetheless, in 1937 his former spouse was pregnant. Having just married Trujillo, Doña María did not take well to Lina, or to what rapidly became quite a public attack on their marriage. The challenge was multifaceted. First, Lina as a member of the old aristocracy of the capital had social class, something Trujillo craved. She was described as "young, beautiful, cultivated, virtuous, distinguished, aristocratic, while being simple and generous."[35] Stories abound that Trujillo had become vengeful toward the traditional elite when he was denied admittance to a prominent social club. In this context, possessing Lina implied social acceptance; it also signified domination of the new Trujillista state elite over the traditional culture brokers. Lina became the ultimate accouterment and sign of Trujillo's unfulfilled bourgeois ambitions. To make matters worse, Trujillo fell passionately in love with Lina, a secret to which the entire country became privy on her birthday. Trujillo had *Listín Diario*, the preeminent daily paper of the capital, print an eight-by-twelve-inch photo of Lina on the front page, with the following inscription, which people believed had been written by Trujillo himself:

> She was born a queen, not by dynastic right but by the right of beauty, and so when the chords that filled the air during her splendid reign—laughter, music, beauty, fantasy—fell silent, she still reigned with the power of that right—her beauty. There is nothing under the sun comparable to the bewitchment of her eyes—stars for the sky where the nightingale wanders giving voice to the mystery of the night.[36]

Much to Doña María's chagrin, Lina indeed became Carnival queen, and a much-loved one at that. The sole recourse in Doña María's arsenal, it seems, was to pressure the papers into not publishing any further pictures of Lina, and indeed they did not. As a result, 1937 stood out as the year in which no photographs of Carnival festivities appeared in the newspapers.

Although Lina was the centerpiece of the Carnival of 1937, it was clear from the outset that the event was not about her, but about Trujillo, to whom she owed her title. Indeed, entitlement, or empowering individuals to speak in the name of the state, was a common strategy under the regime, which proved useful because it spread responsibility by implicating the citizenry in an otherwise highly centralized political system. But this case was more extreme. The Carnival recreated the state in ritual form through its women, using as a pretext a two-month-long feudal masquerade ball.

Her Majesty Queen Lina stood at the apex, with a court of princesses of her choosing, nearly all of whom were the daughters of state functionaries. Next in line came the ladies of honor and the ambassadors to Lina's court, each of whom represented a province. Each princess also had her own court. The Department of Public Administration, the (official Trujillista) Dominican Party, and social clubs and organizations also sent representatives to Queen Lina. There was even a Princess of Meritorious Firemen. Needless to say, these women were authorized by Trujillo to represent the regime. Lest they forget, they were reminded often. For instance, Queen Lina sent a letter to Lourdes García Trujillo, praising her as the greatest of princesses "because in your veins runs the same blood as the Maximum Hero."[37] The queen also bestowed honorary titles, yet in recognition for efforts made on behalf of Trujillo, not for Lina herself. In the end, she was unquestionably Trujillo's vassal.

Carnival's monarchical theme underscored the "courtly" aspects of the regime. Its simulation of statecraft also extended to the practice of official prestation, a form of ritual tribute and fealty required of insiders during the regime. During her two months in office, Lina not only issued decrees and titles (which constituted, in a sense, symbolic gifts—she named Trujillo's wife and mother "great and unique protectors of her kingdom," probably much to Doña María's consternation). She also participated in the exchange of favors, an important expression of reciprocity and recognition during the regime. She gave a ball for the municipal government; the barrio princesses held a dance for Trujillo; the secretaries of state offered Lina a reception; and Lina gave a champagne toast in gratitude for both the "protectors" of her fiefdom and the allegiance of her vassals. Nor were these activities to be scoffed at by officials. Trujillo arrived at the barrio dance in formal military attire, in a "smoking" jacket (tuxedo) arrayed with a full display of military decorations.[38] If it was not already clear that Lina was but a simulacrum of Trujillo, the true monarch, it became so when she designated "Military Maneuvers of Dajabón" one of the preferred sonnets of her kingdom, just months after the Haitian massacre of border migrants there in 1937.[39] Lina was an elegant feminine mascot for a regime that relied primarily on military iconography. Her Highness even posed for photographs with personnel from the Ministries of the Interior, Police, and War and from the Marines.[40]

Although the 1937 Carnival did invert the social order, its choreography had far more in common with a military parade than with a typical carnival procession.[41] The opening reception took place in the National Palace on

10. Lina Lovatón in military costume. ARCHIVO GENERAL DE LA NACIÓN.

9 January, and Lina received Trujillo as a president would a visiting dignitary. The queen was given symbolic keys to the city to the accompaniment of a twenty-one-gun salute before making her triumphal march; she then proceeded to the principal thoroughfares in a cavalcade. The climax of Carnival thus replicated the form of a presidential rally. The result was an intricate celebration of hierarchy and a dramatization of the glories and pleasures of entitlement.

Even though women were the principal actors, the overall plan of the proceedings made it quite clear that this Carnival was not intended to be a licentious, popular affair, nor was it intended to be touched by a "feminine" perspective. Rather, it was a civic tribute to the manly "populator" Trujillo, "savior of the nation," in Roberto DaMatta's terms, a celebration of hierarchy not verticality.[42] Previously, Dominican Carnival had coincided with the Independence Day celebrations of 27 February, marking the day the country achieved freedom from Haitian rule (1822–44), a commemoration and fête of popular sovereignty. By contrast, in 1937, the central events occurred on 23 February, the anniversary of Trujillo's ascendance to power in 1930. Only a concluding dance remained for Independence Day, since by then the crowning activities were over.

A new event was also scripted into the proceedings that became the culminating moment of the festivities: the unveiling of a forty-meter obelisk. It was intended to pay homage to Trujillo's seemingly miraculous reconstruction of the city after the devastating 1930 hurricane and to mark the name change of the capital city from Santo Domingo to Ciudad Trujillo in 1936, which thus symbolized Trujillo's "sovereign permanence" (see chapter 2).[43] Although Carnival was entrusted to women, they were called upon to sing collective praises to this great phallic token of Trujillo's fecund and promiscuous dominion. If anyone missed the sexual allusion, it was clarified in the inaugural speeches. Jacinto Peynado, head of the Pro-Erection Committee and vice-president, declared the obelisk a fitting tribute to a man "of superior natural gifts." The municipal government chief Virgilio Álvarez Pina remarked, "The allegory of this monument has close similarity with the man it glorifies. Its base firm, its lines severe. . . . This obelisk, a gigantic needle of time in space, will stand out forever."[44] The obelisk, luminescent with marble dust and laced with gold-leaf aphorisms at its base, stood in counterpoint to Queen Lina. Both were symbolic reminders of the force of Trujillo's masculine powers, of the dictator as sexual conquistador, or, in Lina's words, of Trujillo as "inexhaustible sower."[45] Queen Lina and her court were seated at the dignitaries' pavilion on the malecón, where they first viewed the obelisk's inauguration rites, and then Trujillo, Lina, and her courtiers were serenaded by the army band.

Although in 1937 women presided over Carnival, it was by no means a protofeminist affair. The prevailing mood was romantic and highly sentimental. The female image espoused by the regime was ornamental, baroque, and saintly. This aura was enhanced by the fact that Trujillo's wife was invariably accompanied by his mother—she was never alone. Additionally, the patron saint of the Dominican Republic, the Virgin of Altagracia, was championed as the perfect embodiment of the nation so that she even shared the very substance of dominicanidad. Even nonreligious Dominicans were said to feel a "congenital impulse" of reverence and respect toward her.[46] This official version of femininity, however, resonated with middle-class and elite women's values. Bourgeois Dominican women argued for a woman's place in the public sphere, but one sharply delineated from the world of men, which they saw as corrupting.[47] For example, one group, called the Feminine Creed of Culture, argued that male culture—objective and materialist—had reached its decadent zenith and that female culture, embodying subjectivity and the emotions, must be cultivated for renewal. Women would be the sentinels of the spiritual renewal of the West: not to substitute for men but to complement them, to remind humanity of the "correct" path of real human sentiment.[48]

In this sense, the official choreography of the 1937 Carnival accorded with one strand of women's thought that advocated an honor-shame morality and a cult of "good womanhood" and domesticity. This elite vision championed women as representatives of a larger collectivity and stood firmly against a liberal "Americanized" prototype, the "modern woman," which they viewed as antithetical to the values of family and nation. In the 1930s, the image of the "new woman" propagated by Hollywood was received with some ambivalence and not a small measure of fear in the Dominican Republic, a country just emerging from a U.S. military regime and the Depression. Certainly there was coy support for the "modern woman," who need not be merely a good mother or wife but could pursue a career. But there was also anxiety that secretly men were not pleased by this encroachment on their terrain or by the thought of sharing privileges with this "masculinized" woman.[49] However, the debate as articulated was not over whether women could or should aspire to a professional identity; instead, it focused on the politics of self-fashioning, on the right of young women to aspire to a new glamorous image through clothes and adornment.[50] At stake in this debate was whether women should feel free to aspire to a new public identity that recognized them as individuals, not merely as members of their family lineages (and thus as members of a particular race and class). This issue was probably most salient to the new middle sectors of urban professionals, a group resulting from the rapid development of the sugar industry in the 1920s that was still fighting for social space in the 1930s.

The debate over proper womanhood was refracted through a controversy over the pros and cons of makeup, which became a subject of several heated newspaper editorials in 1937. One position was that, contrary to the "professional moralists," it was perfectly natural for women to try to seduce men as they have always sought to do through the use of cosmetics. However, while embellishment was fine, it was not attractive to look "artificial"; Dominican women should not use beauty aids to challenge what nature had given them by whitening their skin or making their lips appear narrower.[51] In other words, pulchritude was one thing, race quite another. Indeed, platinum blond hair had become such a rage in Santo Domingo that clarion calls in the press reminded women that darker-skinned types looked unattractively phony as blonds.[52] In part, this discussion masked anxieties over the bounds of class distinction, as elites (who were primarily white) reacted against new beauty techniques that enabled poorer mulatto women (who were part of an emerging middle class) to partake in a class-and-race-specific female standard that had previously been their monopoly. Thus, elites used the debate over cosmetics to redraw class boundaries that had suddenly blurred, first, as a result of middle-class expansion in the 1920s, and second, as a result of the economic crisis of the Depression and the San Zenón hurricane, which impoverished rich and poor alike. Furthermore, the new availability of cosmetics indexed the onset of consumer capitalism, which had ushered in a mass culture with certain democratizing effects that elites did not appreciate. Relatively inexpensive technologies and products enabled poorer women to partake of the blond, light-skinned paradigm of beauty that had previously been the sole preserve of the rich. As a result, elites who had been championing the "whitening of the race" were forced to eat their words.[53]

Thus the Carnival of 1937, although planned and executed entirely by the regime, articulated with a new reactionary woman's voice that vilified American culture, feminism, modernity, and consumer capitalism in one stroke. Elite tirades against the "new woman" as quintessential emblem of modernity and North American culture (i.e., Hollywood) had commenced in the 1920s but became more uniformly negative in the 1930s. Clearly, many Dominican middle-class women were captivated by the new fashion and hair styles brought to them by the silver screen, as evidenced by the newspaper fashion column "Hollywood Secrets." Articles focused on whether mulatta (trigueña) women's hair would take to the new styles as they came into vogue, such as the gently bobbed "China style" popularized by the film The Good Earth.[54] Nor was this debate relegated to the politics of style; United States norms of etiquette became a highly charged issue as well. Some women complained about the relinquishing of respectful social distance in public that had resulted from North American influence. One writer linked the expanding use of the familiar tú form of address to American influence, a practice which had previously divided honorable from disreputable girls. The loose use of tú by "modern" girls was causing "disequilibrium." As Catalina D'Erzell stated, "A man addressed as '*tú*' feels authorized to solicit. The woman using '*tú*' feels disposed to concede."[55] Concern over adequate social space here clearly indexed a set of class and moral markers that elites felt had disintegrated through a United States-propagated mass culture.

The final message of the Carnival was that Trujillo, the great father, had forged a nation by providing its citizens with an identity. As one editorial writer put it, "Trujillo has taught us who we are and has taught us to be it with satisfaction and dignity."[56] Or, perhaps more accurately, he made *la nación* great by making it masculine—that is, virile, active, and *guapo* or courageous. In the words of Pérez Alfonseca, "We have a president who is a *Repúblico* [male republic]. . . . The *Repúblico* makes a Republic, just as a King makes a Queen."[57] Yet even if Trujillo made the nation great, Lina and others ultimately gave it value.

ANGELITA AT THE FAMILY FAIR

From one of the first major spectacles of the regime, I now turn to one of the last.[58] The "silver jubilee" of La Era Trujillo, the twenty-fifth anniversary of Trujillo's coming to power, was celebrated in 1955.[59] In eight short months, the artists, architects, and urban planners of the Free World's Fair choreographed a year's worth of shows, spectacles, and musical events and built from scratch a new western extension of the capital city, which totaled some eight thousand cubic meters and seventy-one buildings.[60] The event was intended to achieve several objectives. First, it was conceived as a money-making enterprise. Unlike most public entertainments under the regime, tickets were sold. This was only partly an event for the masses; it was also aimed at the expanding bourgeoisie, the new industrial and land-owning class fostered by the growing internal market of the postwar period. But more important, much like the New York World's Fair of 1940, which served as a template for the Dominican version, la Feria was intended to have a strong trade component—the English-language brochures even called it an international trade fair.[61] It was supposed to promote the Dominican Republic as a site for foreign investment and to publicize the country's natural resources, political stability, and national products. However, while the century-of-progress expositions used the fair as a medium for expanding commerce and promoting consumer capitalism, la Feria was essentially what Robert Rydell has called a "theater of power" to legitimate the Trujillo regime.[62] The fair was also intended to render the Dominican Republic a

United States ally by its anticommunist stance. It was a reminder that, even if the United States objected to Trujillo's lack of political liberties at home, the Dominican Republic served as a hemispheric anticommunist bulwark.

A crucial precondition for the fair was the postwar expansion of the Dominican economy. The country embarked on a program of industrialization to produce substitutes for imports during World War II, as global prices for many of the nation's primary commodities soared, especially the price of sugar. Although historians may debate to what extent Trujillo's economic policy was nationalist or not, the net effect of the postwar scarcities was both an expanded production of essential staples and light industrial items and the encouragement of foreign direct investment—as long as investors stayed away from Trujillo's personal fiefdoms. By the mid-1950s, domestic demand had expanded dramatically, as a result of growth in population, per capita income, and urbanization. During the Korean War, Trujillo established highly favorable terms of investment, for example, by eliminating tariffs on raw material imports. In this context, a $25-million-dollar expenditure on a world's fair was only partially lavish showmanship; it also had a strong advertising and public relations component.[63]

One objective of la Feria was to bring the world to the Dominican Republic. Trujillo had tried to encourage tourism from the early days of the regime. In 1937 the first major luxury tourist vessels had arrived from Canada, bringing hundreds of visitors to explore Santo Domingo. In dock, visitors lunched at the exclusive "Country Club." Their arrival caused tremendous excitement, particularly the appearance of one British lord who traveled with an entourage of fifteen servants. One editorial proclaimed that finally Ciudad Trujillo had become "a Mecca of curiosity and universal interest."[64] But it was not until the early 1950s that the regime endeavored to cultivate tourism in earnest, erecting "sparkling and new" beach hotels under American management and persuading Pan-American Airlines to establish direct bargain flights from New York.[65] A highly esteemed historical archaeologist was commissioned to write a walking tour of the colonial city in English for visitors, and pamphlets extolling the virtues of the country were distributed overseas.[66] However, the regime's intended message was not lost on the few visitors who did attend, who enthusiastically commended Trujillo's achievement in transforming the capital from the "dirty, pestilential and unattractive city known as Santo Domingo," "a disease-ridden pest hole . . . loaded with foreign debt and infested with bandits," to the "sophisticated modernity of Ciudad Trujillo."[67] They proclaimed the country "the most modern of all our Latin-American neighbors," "the Switzerland of the tropics," and Dominicans "the Yankees of Latin America"—in sum, an island of familiarity in a sea of difference.[68]

If few foreigners were inspired by la Feria to visit the Dominican Republic, Dominicans were nonetheless thrilled at the exotic global cultures la Feria brought to them. The Trujillo regime had created a virtually closed society, sealing off Dominican access to passports and foreign travel and establishing tight control over the flow of information into the country. The vacuum was partially filled in the 1950s by one of the largest, most technologically advanced state-owned radio and television networks in Latin America.[69] Nonetheless, Dominicans craved news of the outside, particularly the steamy cosmopolitan glamour flourishing in neighboring Cuba and the United States, which they consumed vicariously through Cuban rumba albums and Hollywood films. In this context, by revealing glimpses of faraway dreamscapes and by situating Dominicans as the subjects of the gaze, la Feria provided enticing entertainment to a public starved for high style and things foreign. Each country had its own day at the fair, when its national pavilion was unveiled and its own cultural program and exhibit took center stage. Some of the local favorites were the Chinese pavilion, with its intricately carved porcelain and wooden objects, delicately painted fans, and luxurious silks, and the futuristic Atoms for Peace exhibition, which was later reassembled in Geneva by the United States after its presentation at the fair. France sent a helicopter, and Japan and Mexico sponsored weeklong film festivals. Overall, the Western nations emphasized themes of scientific and industrial progress, while other nations focused on traditional artisanry or culture. And women figured prominently in all of the displays as the quintessential sign of nationhood: from Indonesia, which sent a Javanese woman in traditional batik; to Guatemala, which provided a live display of the country's rich hand-woven textiles. Even Holland (the Dominican Republic's third largest export market) selected tulip and gladiola bulbs with girls in traditional maidens' outfits as conveyors of Dutchness. But Latin American nations more commonly intended their female exhibitors to represent modernity. Such was the case for Venezuela, which flew in the *compatriota* Miss Mundo (Miss World) from London for the occasion; and Mexico, which held a weeklong fashion parade of Mexican designer outfits in honor of Queen Angelita, featuring ballgowns with organza skirts à la haute couture Parisienne. Mexico also courted the ladies,

11. The Dominican woods exhibit at la Feria. ARCHIVO GENERAL DE LA NACIÓN, SANTO DOMINGO.

however, by erecting a tortilla provision stand and handing out free bags of corn flour to housewives.

The national displays provided a means of legitimation on which Trujillo heavily capitalized. Whenever possible, displays were transformed into emblems of commendation and tribute for Trujillo's virtues as a statesman. The letters of praise and thanks from participating countries were reproduced and publicized widely, such as the French delegate's note declaring the progress of the country "miraculous" and that he "felt honored to be Trujillo's friend." Not surprisingly, the most effusive praises came from his fellow strongmen Anastasio Somoza and Francisco Franco, but Japan called Trujillo an "organizational genius" and characterized the Trujillato as "splendorous." Brazilian president Juscelino Kubitschek was the highest-level political figure to attend, and photographs of him embracing Trujillo or standing with Trujillo family members and the regime's inner circle were legion. Somoza even sent a military decoration for Trujillo's elder son Ramfis, the Order of Rubén Darío, in frank recognition that Trujillo, like Somoza, was grooming his son to take over the position of "permanent sentinel of national greatness." The note from the U.S. ambassador strained to praise not Trujillo but the anticommunist significance of the fair, and the "marvelous" energy that went into constructing it in such a short time.[70]

Ultimately the central pedestal of la Feria was reserved for the Trujillo regime. As one visitor observed, "The government itself is the principal exhibitor, displaying evidence of political, economic, social and cultural progress during the past quarter-century—'The Era of Trujillo.'"[71] In fact, most of the pavilions and floats in the central parade were put on by state agencies, ministries, provincial governments, and the central bank, although local and foreign industries and banks participated as well. The ubiquitous image of Trujillo, "El Benefactor," loomed large in all of the government pavilions—here smiling, there bending down or signing a document, such as the all-important Hull-Trujillo treaty of 1940, which canceled the United States administration of customs (since 1907) and established the first national Dominican currency and central bank (and, not coincidentally, also allowed Trujillo closer surveillance over the national coffers). Trujillo's invisible hand lurked behind other exhibits as well, such as the Central Río Haina mill display at the sugar pavilion, where attractive young women handed out sucrose samples to the crowd.[72] Sugar was presented as a technologically advanced major export industry, but this mill also happened to be part of the Trujillo family's real estate portfolio.

The armed forces had a prominent part in la Feria as well, since they were headed at that time by Rafael Trujillo while his brother Héctor "Negro" Trujillo was proxy president. Indeed, this explains the predominance of military iconography at the event, in conjunction with growing opposition to the regime overseas. The armed forces pavilion housed an impressive collection of tanks, jeeps, and advanced artillery, which were also displayed in a military parade that included elegantly uniformed battalions in procession. Over the years, Trujillo had created one of the strongest militaries in Latin America, tripling its size and creating a full-fledged professional air force which he was eager to show off. Needless to say, this amount of military preparedness far exceeded the country's actual defense needs, which were minimal.[73]

The World's Fair presented a family model of state authority in which obedience to the patriarchal father was naturalized.[74] The Carnival parade, which took place on 1 April in tribute to Queen Angelita's birthday, enacted the "family romance" of the regime. This model was laid out in allegorical form, with Trujillo as "Father of the New Fatherland" (*Padre de la Patria Nueva*) at the head of the parade in the form of an enormous bronze bust. In the other floats, however, women figured prominently, as contestants representing provinces and para-statal organizations competed for a ranked series of prizes. Some of the most popular themes were drawn from classical Greece; the display of the Dominican Party, for example, featured a bevy of women representing the muses of Zeus, swathed in Greek togas and adorning a huge lute. In the contribution of the Dominican Electrical Corporation, allegorical women workers dressed in black-and-white men's uniforms waved from the top of an oversized electrical plant; a model of the technically sophisticated Rhadamés bridge was similarly decorated with "professional girls" in the Ministry of Public Works float. Drawing on the iconography of women in World War II cinema, the air force paraded a two-seater airplane amply decorated with uniformed female "pilots." A high school, the Colegio San Luis, featured a boy's choir that sang praises to a queen bee centerpiece amid lush floral garlands.

The folkloric peasantry was another popular theme. Incorporating a bricolage of Mexican peasant dress and Hollywood's Carmen Miranda, this style was represented by young boys in wide-brimmed straw sombreros accompanying ruffled-sleeved and hoop-skirted women with slightly risqué off-the-shoulder Baiana gowns who lacked only the fruit-bowl turbans. The province of Samaná, an isolated Atlantic coastal zone, won first prize for best costume with a group of lithe mermaids crowned by a large conch shell in gentle pastel colors. However, this parade of European queens, folkloric fantasies, and fables was a congeries of imported dreams. The bulk of these costumes were imported from overseas and added to la Feria's otherworldly feel. These imports also drew the ire of local dressmakers, who protested vociferously over the loss of work and questioned just how "nationalist" the fair really was.[75]

While la Feria privileged women in the floats, as symbols they stood in subservient relationship to emblems of manhood, like cattle. In the colonial period free-range ranching had been a backbone of the Dominican economy. Thus, control over women, like that over cattle, represented a "currency of power" expressive of dominion.[76] Both cattle and women were media for extending the male self into the world—for dominating and

12. Rafael Trujillo in equestrian attire. ARCHIVO GENERAL DE LA NACIÓN, SANTO DOMINGO.

mobilizing clients, territory, and familial networks. Cattle also served as currency in the domain of the traditional caudillo, who accumulated cattle, women, and money through which he established ties of patronage and alliance. This was clear in Trujillo's pet project, the International Cattle Fair, which showcased purebred horses, cattle, and pigs from Cuba, the United States, and Puerto Rico. It was a monument to conspicuous consumption, costing three million pesos to build the site alone.[77] La Feria elided cattle, the traditional symbol of national value, with money, the sign of postcolonial nationhood; and the iconography of la Feria linked them both through the person of Trujillo.

Indeed, money was perhaps the most trumpeted symbol at la Feria. Not only were commemorative bronze coins minted for the event, embossed with Trujillo's illustrious stern profile, but the Ministry of Finance set up an entire pavilion with a historical money exhibit, which placed U.S. and Do-

13. A twenty-peso note with Trujillo's image. RENÉ FORTUNATO COLLECTION, BY PERMISSION OF VIDEOCINE PALAU.

minican money side by side, as if rendering commensurable the two na-tions.[78] The Spanish painter José Vela Zanetti also created an allegorical mural in one of the new ministry buildings that depicted sweating futuristic laborers struggling to prop upright an enormous gold coin. This depicted the Hull-Trujillo treaty, which in Trujillista ideology established full fiscal autonomy and, more important, the symbolic sovereignty of the Domini-can nation.[79] Trujillo, then, became the mediator of national conversion: one who transformed cattle into money and colony into nation. At la Feria, he became the principal sign of national sovereignty and value.

More than 250,000 people turned out to see the crowning glory of the fair—Her Majesty Angelita's float, which was named "The Reign of Love." It featured an oversized baroque carriage decorated with gold leaf and adorned with Rubenesque angels floating atop a cloud. The women all wore white, with red hearts on their busts and smaller hearts appliquéd on their expansive skirts. Additionally, Angelita wore a Dominican national emblem on her chest. Cascading from Angelita's pedestal was her court. Her "reign" had actually begun in August, when, at the tender age of sixteen, she was handed the symbolic keys to the city and greeted with the pomp and cir-cumstance afforded a foreign dignitary, with full military observances as combat planes and naval ships came out in her honor. Angelita wore a naval jacket with captain's stripes (perhaps an allusion to her brother Ramfis, who was made an army colonel at age three and brigadier general at age nine) to her *quinceañera* (coming-out party), which was not to be forgotten by her or by the nation.

If the dictator's daughter was supposed to present a lovable face of the regime, however, she was never as successful as Lina. This was in part because of her age; at sixteen she was essentially a tabula rasa, a mute mirror for national fantasy. And in part it was because of Angelita's personality. Distant and reserved, Angelita had grown up as the coddled younger daughter, showered from the first with national attention and sequestered by her jealous father, for whom no suitor was good enough. An unhappy person, she suffered from a strange back malady for which she was frequently hospitalized as a child. Unlike Queen Lina, she was considered by the public neither beautiful nor warm and generous. Nor was she legitimate in class terms. Lina had been born into a traditional aristocratic family; lily-white, she was born to rule. Angelita, on the other hand, lacked either the achieved status of her father or the ascribed social prestige of the Lovatón family. Finally, she was central icon of a festival that lacked the populist trappings or participatory élan of other rituals of state. This event was aimed primarily at impressing the world, not Dominicans, in a context in which a combination of state monopolies and postwar affluence had created unprecedented social distance between the elite and the masses. In the end, la Feria was magnificent, but not inclusive; it inspired reverence, but not love. La Feria reflected what Trujillo wanted his country to be, not what it was. With la Feria, Trujillo stretched too far.[80]

This context may account for the fact that one of the most audacious protests of the regime occurred over the selection of Miss Dominican Republic, the crowning glory of many beauty contests staged for la Feria, which included Miss Ciudad Trujillo, Miss Feria de La Paz, and Miss Universidad de Santo Domingo. The beauty contestants' favorite was overlooked for the daughter of a Trujillista insider (apparently at the behest of First Lady Doña María). When the announcement was made, the contestants (all daughters of public functionaries) angrily threw rum-and-soda bottles and chairs and marched out in disgust.[81] Like all state rituals during the Trujillato, from elections to rallies to civic parades, the fair was choreographed from above; nonetheless, within those confines, state pageants such as this one offered a participatory space, even if only in the realm of symbolic politics. No one objected to the election of Angelita as queen because it was nonnegotiable, but the remaining winners were seen as the choice of the contestants, within the realm of their right to choose. Doña María was perceived as interfering with the populist component of the state rite, which was regarded as outside her jurisdiction. If Angelita represented the state at la Feria, Miss Dominican Republic represented the nation, and the Trujillo family had no claim on who embodied this popular emblem of nationhood.

Angelita symbolized a particular genre of feminine participation in the public realm, however, one based on a vertical as opposed to a lateral principle.[82] Trujillista ideology was highly authoritarian, embodying hierarchy and order. The role of the mystical body of the regime—the ideal, invisible, and immortal "body politic" of Kantorowicz's model—was played by Trujillo's youngest daughter.[83] Authority was ascribed to Angelita, who, like her namesake, came to represent rarefied purity itself—a kind of living embodiment of the Virgin of Altagracia, patron saint of the Dominican Republic. Hierarchy was also expressed by establishing the daughter as the ultimate emblem of the regime, one thoroughly disciplined by the unquestioned authority of her father.

CONCLUSION

This chapter has explored the culture of a particular kind of "theater state" and its impact on the logic of class, gender, and race-marking.[84] As the 1937 Carnival and 1955 World's Fair demonstrate, spectacles of women can exhibit masculinity, and gender representations can convey messages about social class. Indeed, in the Dominican Republic, a nation of predominantly mixed race, where race and class are deeply interwoven, Queen Lina conveyed an important message about social distinction. Trujillo's success in seducing and displaying the crème de la crème of Dominican society demonstrated that it was power and wealth, not race and background, that ultimately counted. In the end, the Trujillo regime did "culturally democratize" the elite to an extent, by transforming the logic of status accumulation of high society.[85] And the coronations of Queen Lina and Queen Angelita had a small part to play in that process. However, such state rituals were effective less as "encapsulations" or even "approximations,"[86] but instead worked through their creation of what Timothy Mitchell has called a "reality effect," in which people come to inhabit the world they see represented.[87]

One conundrum presented by la Feria is how a highly corrupt statesman could fashion himself as a grand patriot. What made credible Trujillo's claim to being a nationalist hero was his positioning of the Dominican Republic on the map, by both extending the country into the world and bringing the world to the Dominican Republic. In part this was achieved by staging his nation as a member of the first world through world-class festivals that were larger than life. The nation's visibility also resulted from its newfound prominence in global tabloids owing to a public relations apparatus that made journalists, congressmen, and other U.S. notables into praise poets for the regime. And when notables refused explicit support, their silent presence in Trujillo's choreographed rites forged a powerful myth of international legitimacy which deferential Dominicans with no other information had little reason to question. As we have seen, an important component of this myth was Trujillo's accumulation of symbolic capital through the seduction and display of women of value who were cast as Americanized—world-class and white—and having transcended the poverty and backwardness of Dominican *creolidad*.

La Feria helped forge a fantasy of national progress that was especially powerful for the participants. Originally a staple of late-nineteenth-century liberal discourse, the very term progreso was both a key word for Trujillo's modernization of the country (deployed frequently in official rhetoric), as well as a popular code word for status and color advancement (and thus whitening). Notwithstanding the *sabor criollo* theme, talent contestants at the Agua y Luz Theater interviewed by the press spoke only of their utopic American fantasies. An accordionist in one of the nationalist floats exclaimed, "Caramba! All my life I have wanted to see Betty Grable and Doris Day. I will learn all the American songs and maybe Charlie you can arrange that Doris sings with me at Club Mocambo." A maraca player said, "Virgin of Altagracia! Who knows if my dreams will become reality! I play maracas, trumpet, piano, drums. . . . If I had more hands I would be a one man orchestra. Maybe Hollywood could contract me for a film."[88] A Miss America beauty contestant at la Feria, Priscilla Magnolia Altagracia Resek Pichardo from Santiago signaled her United States credentials by saying that she spoke English, played ping pong, liked to dress in Christian Dior, and performed pieces by Liszt.[89] La Feria thus championed the image of a modern nation, which was a fantasy that trickled down to the masses through events that blurred the boundaries between spectators and participants, such as talent contests as well as the experience of seeing oneself at the fair in the news.[90]

It is indeed ironic that for Trujillo the opera *Aïda* was a privileged allegory of the family romance of empire, in honor of which he named his two sons. The plot explores the dilemma between patriotism and romantic love through the saga of an Egyptian hero who rejects marriage to a princess (and therefore the legacy of her father's kingdom) for the love of a slave. Set against the lavish and exotic backdrop of the Egyptian empire at the time of the Pharaohs, the story ends in tragedy, as Rhadamés and Aïda die in tandem, the victims of jealousy and patriotism. The story was an ironic nationalist fantasy for Trujillo since it celebrated precisely the opposite dynamic of that revealed by his own family romance. Trujillo himself was not a man to die for reasons of pure romantic fulfillment; he was not one to give up the hand of the king's daughter for the perfect love of an abject slave. Nor was he likely to sacrifice love of nationhood for a love supreme. Yet one strand of *Aïda* does ring true to Trujillo. In the opera, nationhood is defined by fatherhood, and ultimately no one can successfully escape the bonds of family or national allegiance, except through the ultimate exit—death.

It is the centrality of the father-daughter bond in this iconography of state, however, that distinguishes the Trujillo regime from other Latin American family romances. It is the father who ultimately represents the nation, through whom the nation derives its name and lineage and public identity. Yet the father is represented by the daughter. Of course, father-daughter symbolism offers an even more sharply hierarchical relation than the conjugal couple, invoking rankings of age as well as gender. This family romance makes sense given the real Dominican family structure. Outside the Europeanized elite strata, the father tends to have a distant presence and is often absent from the actual raising of children. In the serial marriage system, in which children are raised primarily by their mothers and other female kin, the father figure is problematic and often conjures feelings of resentment and abandonment. So in this context, the daughter analogy presents a more tender and lovable face for the state than the patriarch. Finally, as we have seen, Trujillo's parading of his lover and daughter reverted to a subaltern model of male authority, the tíguere, which is based on virility, fecundity, and control over women. The daughter substituted for the wife, but invoked the mistress.[91] Even as he sought status elevation though the consumption of bourgeois femininity, Trujillo at the same time invoked a barrio style of male self-fashioning—in Pierre Bourdieu's words, "the outcast's aristocratism"—that deliberately broke the rules of elite sexual comportment.[92] The excessive nature of Trujillo's sexual avarice in terms of both quantity and publicity invoked the "hypermasculine pose" of Dominican underclass masculinity, one that challenged the more controlled, respectable self-presentation of the elite.[93]

Unlike other Latin American dictators, Trujillo did not privilege the bourgeois family as a metonym of moral nationhood.[94] In fact, he actually innovated laws aimed at loosening family bonds. For example, he passed one law allowing children to be disinherited and another enabling divorce. Early on, the Dominican Republic had some of the most liberal divorce laws in the Western Hemisphere as a result of Trujillo's maneuvers to accommodate his own tíguere ambitions. A discourse of family values would have resonated with a middle-class and elite audience, for whom marriage was a stable union of social equals. However, Trujillo chose instead an idiom of authority with more mass appeal—one based on social mobility through the conquest of superior women who were more frequently lovers than wives and one that made sense to the rural and urban poor who lived primarily in concubinage, not formal unions. Trujillo was the tíguere, the figure who shares power with no one, especially not his wife.

By the 1950s, however, the tíguere was no longer a focus of elite angst. How did this deeply Dominican genre of underclass *flâneur* eventually achieve respectability? The answer in part lies in the culture of spectacle of the Trujillato. As Walter Benjamin states, "His [the *flâneur's*] leisurely appearance as a personality is his protest against the division of labour which makes people into specialists. It is also his protest against their industriousness. . . . The intoxication to which the *flâneur* surrenders is the intoxication of the commodity around which surges the stream of customers."[95]

However, commodity culture during the Trujillo regime did not enter through the arcade and the department store. Rather, it entered through state pageants that ultimately linked the magic of the commodity to the magic of the regime. This was particularly the case by the 1950s, when the Trujillo family had bought several highly profitable industries and enterprises, and Trujillo himself was one of the richest men in the world. Just as Benjamin called fairs shrines to the commodity fetish, state ceremonies like la Feria and the 1937 Carnival were shrines to the great fetish of state that was Trujillo, in their sensory overload of goods, fashion, women, and money—all of which were ultimately claimed by El Benefactor. These rituals of state were hardly window dressing. Far from it: they were an essential part of making the carnivalesque excess of the Era of Trujillo believable.

Like politics, here gossip (*chismografía*) one could say is the daily bread
and favorite theme of conversations in every social circle.

FIDELIO, *LISTÍN DIARIO, 1903*

Mr. Lucho Nuñez Soriano, the principal member of the tributary services
of this city has disappeared with about $1,500.00 which he received from
numerous people for the renewal of identity cards, licenses, taxes, etc.,
without a stop. . . . The people ask: What kind of office is this, that of tasks
or gangsters?

JUSTO FRANCO, "FORO PÚBLICO," 1958

The case of Central I.D. Office and the situation reigning among the
employees must be resolved in a radical way. . . . [It] must be subject to
removals, transferals or dismissals of certain employees that have created
a deep cancer in a department that in previous times had a great reputation. . . . Of the women, Mrs. Morató is called Her Majesty the Queen of
Gossip because all day long she is antisocial and aspires to be director. . . .
They accept anything in bribes, from money to nail polish. And on top of
it all, they are loose-mouthed and gossips.

JOSÉ LORENZO CASTRO A., "FORO PÚBLICO," 1952

In 1943, Max Rodríguez wrote a letter to the Dominican Party president in
which he enclosed a *décima* (or poem) dedicated to Trujillo from Las
Caobas, a tiny hamlet in Santiago Rodríguez close to the Haitian border, in
honor of the nation's century of independence. A school child recited the
poem in an event celebrating the centennial. He wrote, "In sending you this
composition I wish to indicate not only that I am a poetry aficionado, but
that my love and adhesion to the beloved *Jefe* in his great centennial labor
gave birth to this inspiration." He followed this letter with a twenty-nine-
stanza poem dedicated to the great caudillo who gave the country glory, in
the hopes that it would be published in the national newspaper *La Nación*.[1]
Gifts to Trujillo like this one became a common practice of citizenship

during the regime, even if their "hidden transcript" had little to do with their stated intention.[2]

In this chapter I examine the politics and practice of official discourse during the Trujillo regime, focusing on two official oratorical genres: denunciation and a highly stylized form of panegyric, or praise speech, to Trujillo that became the model for citizens and state officials alike in all public arenas. These speech forms were very important in the capital, Ciudad Trujillo, the central theater of government and Trujillo's dominion, which had expanded dramatically under the regime, giving rise to a new urban middle class by the 1950s.[3] Denunciation and panegyric were institutionalized in the "Foro Público" (Public Forum) column of *El Caribe*, the main organ of the regime. This was not a "Dear Abby" column with a couple of letters. Approximately fifteen letters were published daily, many of which were not individual missives but rather clusters of denunciations and their face-saving responses (eulogy to Trujillo, self-defense, or defense of others). Since each denunciation generated many more letters of apology, *mea culpa*, and self-defense, most letters in the "Foro" were actually defensive, not accusatory. Because the letters do not stand alone, but are in dialogue, one must analyze these letters in clusters, as incidents or "remedial interchanges," to use Erving Goffman's terminology.[4] Some five to fifteen letters of denunciation were published daily from 1948 to 1961; a single accusation might be followed with as many as five letters in defense of the denounced individual, reestablishing one's credentials as a devout Trujillista via an exorbitant encomium to El Jefe. "Foro Público" published a grand total of four thousand such columns, and more than thirty thousand letters in all.[5]

The largest percentage of "Foro Público" letters were written by citizens accusing civil servants of corruption, inefficiency, or improper conduct. This is a surprising discovery given the ironclad control over even trivial forms of dissent during the regime, Trujillo's emphasis on public order and discipline, and the fact that in other cultures of denunciation citizens principally denounced other citizens. In a scan of denunciations during one year and an intensive examination of those during three months (January–March 1958) from *El Caribe*, Brendan Kiley and I found that the greatest percentage were citizen to civil servant accusations (21 percent), with the remainder citizen to citizen (16 percent), citizen to inspector (3 percent), citizen to party (2 percent), and 5 percent miscellaneous. In terms of content, the letters were primarily citizen complaints (31 percent) and accusations of corruption (19 percent).[6] Lipe Collado argues that "reputation death squads" from the official party, the Dominican Party, channeled local grievances collected via intelligence reports into these public missives, although some were authored by Trujillo's cronies or "official *Foristas*" under pseudonyms. Trujillo's son Radamés, for example, wrote under the nom de plume of the Mexican revolutionary general Pancho Villa.[7] At times "Public Forum" accusations originating in private letters of complaint directed to the Dominican Party resulted in the dismissal of public functionaries, as explored later.[8]

Denunciation and panegyric were also pervasive speech genres outside the press, although denunciation was elsewhere generally secret, appearing in private letters to the government concerning third-party infractions or anonymous allegations sent by mail directly to the accused (*pasquines*). Praise, by contrast, was highly public and an ubiquitous feature of the thousands of civic rites and holidays staged in Trujillo's honor. Scholars have portrayed denunciation as evidence of Trujillo's authoritarianism. It should also be seen as a sign of his populism, since even if the accusations were edited or compiled in the National Palace, most originated in local concerns articulated via private letters or in intelligence reports to the Dominican Party, and state officials could be censored or even replaced as a result of such citizens' charges.[9]

The "Foro Público" was populist in another sense as well. It translated into print an oral genre—gossip and backbiting—that was characteristic of the popular sectors in the Dominican Republic; as such it should be seen as another vernacular practice of the regime. Like the mulatto strongman Rafael Trujillo himself, those who had been catapulted into positions of social and political power as a result of the regime held a tenuous grip on their social positions since they lacked the requisite wealth or background necessary for legitimacy. The "Foro" thus mimicked a form of popular speech characteristic of the intense rivalry and status competition among "small big men"—which was normally confined to small talk behind closed doors—and brought it into public view.[10] Trujillo's macabre claim that the "Foro"—as an example of freedom of the press and the responsiveness of government to popular grievances—revealed the democracy of the regime is patently absurd.[11] Nevertheless, it still could have served as a populist technique that lent credence to his claim that his government was "born from the people and maintained by the people," since both the content and the form of the "Foro Público" had deep roots in Dominican popular culture. The use of a vernacular speech form also probably helped combat the cynical "structure of feeling" characteristic of Ciudad Trujillo in the 1950s in the twilight of the regime, perhaps enabling a measure of emotive investment in a state agenda that furthered the regime's hegemony at a time when it was clearly on the wane.[12]

While the practice of denunciation has been seen as evidence of state domination, it was actually a more complex process. Even when the claims of a denunciation were patently false, they nonetheless "operated within a double field of belief and doubt," defiling individuals by the selective revelation of public secrets and by casting aspersion on the public honor of officials.[13] Accusations of public malfeasance could be rebutted. More difficult to contest, however, were charges of amorality, such as those set forth in one accusation that decried "the personal and domestic disasters, the endless orgies, the habitual drunkenness, the welching on gambling debts, the bare-faced passing of bad checks, the broken homes and abandoned homes that this man has left behind him. . . . [He is] a degenerate, a blackmailer, a traitor."[14] Even if the accusations were unfounded, they were painful because of their conspicuity in the national press and because they left little space for what Goffman has termed "the arts of impression management"—individual control over one's self-image.[15] The denunciations examined here represent a boundary where the public and private, the state and civil society, crossed paths.[16]

Denunciation and official praise fulfilled several important functions of state. They enabled citizens to take up certain state roles—such as policing the civil service—either by articulating their gripes, or by merely observing the spectacle of shame that was the "Foro." Indeed, when denunciation became institutionalized in 1948 in the "Foro Público" column of *El Caribe*, civil society was given an important role in this arm of social control in the service of, in the words of the Dominican Party, "rectitude and morality."[17] Trujillo's extension of systematic surveillance outside the police and intelligence apparatus through his creation of Dominican Party "inspectors," or spies, created a panoptical regime in which no one escaped the purview of the state and everyone was implicated. Once intelligence findings were broadcast nationally in the "Foro Público," the entire nation was called upon to judge the crimes and misdemeanors of its citizenry and civil servants.[18] Surveillance also may have fostered a new consciousness of the self as citizens pondered themselves or their acquaintances on the public stage of the print media for the first time.[19]

The effusive recital of accolades to Trujillo, which contrasted with denunciations, had several functions. These ranged from popular use of sycophantic speech as a form of "investiture" to gain recognition and reap rewards such as contracts, jobs, or handouts,[20] to the insinuation of negative criticisms within the very formulaic conventions of praise to the "Benefactor." Within the heavily encoded language of official praise, rich in metaphor and imagery, certain veiled criticisms of Trujillo could be voiced through allusion or even oblique parody. Thus, while both speech forms ultimately fulfilled hegemonic functions for the regime, they did so through the medium of individual agency, and contradictory messages could simmer under the surface.

CULTURES OF TERROR

The literature on authoritarian regimes has assumed a direct correlation between actual violence and what Guillermo O'Donnell has called the "culture of fear."[21] It has thus neglected certain forms of symbolic domination that were very important to the quotidian experience of terror during regimes such as the Trujillato. Most studies of cultures of fear have focused on genocide, ethnocide, civil war, or bureaucratic or authoritarian contexts where disappearances were a daily reality, brutal repression was commonplace, and entire social groups were crushed.[22] Certainly, the dramatic expansion and deprofessionalization of the military and police under Trujillo contributed to unprecedented levels of violent, if sporadic, excess, such as the use of arbitrary incarceration and torture as a preemptive strike against the formation of political opposition. Waves of general repression did occur after the 1949 and 1959 coup attempts and toward the end of the regime, as Trujillo's health and agility declined and his control faltered. Indeed, repressive measures were eventually successful insomuch as they exported all effective antiregime mobilization to exile communities in Havana, New York, Port-au-Prince, and, to a lesser extent, Caracas. Moreover, everyday life during the Trujillato was characterized by pervasive insecurity and atomization as an ever-expanding apparatus of espionage developed, which by the 1950s rivaled the formal political apparatus itself in organizational strength. And in 1957, when Johnny Abbes García was placed at the helm of the newly formed Military Intelligence Service (SIM), a body that centralized and coordinated various intelligence operations that had previously operated in an overlapping honeycomb, the regime sank to unprecedented levels of savagery.[23]

A striking feature of the Trujillato is that while the culture of terror was deep and pervasive, in comparison to other authoritarian regimes relatively few Dominicans were actually killed by state violence until the final years.[24] In part, this was because official assassinations were always reported as mysterious unsolved "accidents" or random crimes in the press. Nonetheless, the middle-class residents of Santo Domingo recall vividly the asphyxiating culture of fear symbolized by the ubiquitous sinister Volkswagen beetles, called *cepillos* (official SIM cars) in popular parlance, in the late 1950s. Unlike Haiti under François Duvalier, for example, the experience of terror was not relegated to a particular class fraction. And unlike Argentina during the Proceso Militar, the state enemy was never clearly defined, and thus no one felt entirely immune from potential repression. The sense of subordination and potential arbitrary punishment was spread throughout society, although it varied in kind from the provincial interior to the urban professional class of the capital. What accounted for the acute and generalized culture of fear under the Trujillo regime? Why did denunciation emerge in the postwar period as a dominant mode of political competition and control? These are the historical questions addressed by this analysis of denunciation.

DENUNCIATION: THE POLITICS OF OFFICIAL PERSONHOOD

Oral narratives of the Trujillo period remember the official use of denunciation and pasquines as pervasive and frightening media of official sanction. For the urban middle class, the culture of terror was arguably more a result of the threat of job loss—as embodied in denunciation as a political practice —than that of random arrests, murder, and torture, although they certainly were mutually reinforcing.[25] And even if one was falsely denounced, simply being *tildado* (called attention to) by the regime caused stigma and social isolation, as others feared their own guilt by association. Denunciation had both material and social costs. It could result in loss of one's job but it also entailed the undoing of social honor. Called in popular parlance "shooting blanks," *denuncias* were a form of symbolic violence that resulted in social death—that is, radical isolation from and rejection by society. Denunciation defiled the public persona, resulting in an aura of sin.[26] Stories abound of prominent intellectuals who, after refusing to collaborate with the regime, were denounced and—it was said—actually died of social disgrace, even when the accusations were clearly false.[27] If social honor was based on a moral hierarchy, denunciation challenged one's social position through claims of inadequate attention to the needs of subordinates. To stand accused was to lose respeto, which in this context was to lose face, to abdicate personhood.[28]

The truth value of the charges was not the most important factor determining whether or not the allegations were believed, since there was no way that the public could easily determine the actual facts. Denunciations were investigated assiduously, albeit in secret, once received by the party in what were termed "discrete investigations," the results only becoming public directly if consequences were apparent, such as when the accused lost his job (although given social networks in a small country, shadowy rumors often emerged as the inquiries proceeded since these involved testimony by many witnesses and parties involved).[29] Moreover, the context was characterized by what Marco Zivkovic has termed a "poetics of opacity."[30] The secrecy surrounding the authorship of accusations probably amplified the fear, as the circulation of rumors echoed and amplified the perceived circuits of power.[31] Not only was Trujillo's inner court shielded by a veil of concealment that created a deep social distance between them and the majority, but the identity of second-tier regime partisans was often masked in ways that tended to augment their perceived potency and influence. An example of this is the bizarre case of José Almoina. While denounced, he wrote a book exalting Trujillo and a play in the name of Trujillo's wife, María Martínez. This created shock waves of gossip about him at a time when he was in exile and officially invisible. Moreover, while in his exile of shame, he received $12,000 for the book, making him the highest-paid griot of the regime.[32]

As Vicente Rafael has said, "Rumors . . . work by separating seeing from believing."[33] Indeed, denunciation wreaked havoc by doing just that: forging ruinous hearsay of unknown provenance and unlikely veracity that was believable only through its everyday style of "equivocal dissimulation."[34] The regime operated less via a system of terror than one of fear generated through insecurity and suspicion. Confidential reports collected gossip, validating it in the process, and sifted through claims and counterclaims of hearsay in an effort to ascertain blame. The Dominican Party president R. Paíno Pichardo cast himself as a virtual judge when he wrote, "Intimated by the general rumor that vituperative and criminal acts had been committed, I wanted to present the official statements, whose deceit was determined by members of said club, who had previously interrogated workers and parts suppliers."[35] Here we see legal language being used to evaluate veracity but without any evidentiary grounding of a court of law. Denunciation gave gossip an official imprimatur. It created the impression that the accused were actually at fault, that there was a responsible agent behind the charges, and finally that there existed a space outside of dissimulation and subjection.[36]

The Trujillo regime invented neither panegyric nor denunciation. Both genres of discourse have deep roots in Caribbean popular oratory as well as in nineteenth-century Dominican regional caudillo politics. Panegyric and denunciation are elaborations of a popular culture of masculine authority and its resultant ritual idioms of deference and defamation, of honorifics and profanation.[37] Public accusation and response was also a staple of nine-teenth-century political discourse, and newspapers from this time are rife with pugnacious reproof of state ineptitude, corruption, and irregularity, or with personal attacks on individual honor often involving unpaid debts, theft, or allegations of influence peddling among politicians and state rep-resentatives. As in the Soviet Union in the 1930s, Nazi Germany in the 1940s, or even China during the Cultural Revolution (via wall graffiti), denunciation was chiefly aimed at local state authorities and their incompe-tence.[38] However, given the stakes involved in leveling accusations against the public honor of prominent local notables in this small, face-to-face society, such allegations were primarily anonymous so as to avoid disrupt-ing the structure of trust undergirding interpersonal relations. The use of pseudonyms in the press was extremely widespread—even when the actual names of certain prolific or popular authors were an open secret—to avoid direct insult or confrontation and thus to conform to a culture of deference that required protecting the public "face" of reputable persons. It was a context in which political positions were inextricably tied to specific indi-viduals and family lineages and to their participation in historical national and regional events.[39]

However, the nineteenth-century Dominican newspaper did not yet hold a monopoly on the formation of public opinion. It competed with other popular fora, such as public poetry—*décimas* or *coplas*—that was typically recited in parks and *colmados* (corner groceries), and sold in single sheets in the marketplace; these poems aired popular or factional com-plaints about official corruption or ineptitude and were also anonymous. Décimas were "popular" insofar as they were memorized, repeated, and adapted by the public at large; yet particular poets did achieve fame for their lyricism, trenchant political satire, or unabashed adulation of politicians, generals, or strongmen. Particular *decimeros* could also become spokesmen for particular parties or politicians. In fact, Ulises Heureaux, the late-nineteenth-century "order and progress" dictator, sponsored the most influential bard of the 1890s, Juan Antonio Alix, to compose verse in his favor as a form of political propaganda. Alix wrote "servile praise" for any person or entity that provided recompense: governors, provisional governments, generals, "friends," Haitian revolutionary leaders, newspapers, even esteemed Dominican gentlemen in New York City.[40] Décimas were considered more effective in swaying public opinion than other printed forms, which were frequently liberal in persuasion and had a small constituency in this highly illiterate society. Nineteenth-century Dominican newspapers were typically blatantly partisan—they depended on state or party subsidies for their existence and were openly acrimonious.[41] Thus, even "anonymous" published denunciations were identified with particular political persuasions.

However, the meaning of the public denunciation changed under Trujillo, since it was widely perceived as emanating from the National Palace and thus as carrying official weight; from a sign of partisanship, denunciation became an insignia of state.[42] If, as Judith Irvine notes, "defamation is fundamentally an audience effect," institutionalizing denunciation in the press brought the entire nation to weigh in on the purported moral improprieties of the accused and thus dramatically increased the scalding impact of the accusations.[43] As it became officialized, denunciation became a key technique of rule during the Trujillato, one that channeled popular grievances against official abuse but kept the civil bureaucracy in check.[44] Yet this form of punishment must be seen as having a complex function, one in which social control was achieved through mechanisms that were intimately linked to repression but not reducible to it.[45] This is why, ironically, it could ultimately become an avenue for resistance as well as hegemony.

Even if Trujillo actually intervened at times in these circuits of accusations, it seems highly unlikely that most were drafted in the National Palace. Sheer numbers aside, the content of many denunciations focused on minor figures in particular hamlets and was simply too local for state invention. Clearly the invisible hand of an editor was at work at least in selecting those to be printed, or at most in actually crafting denunciations from party inspectors' intelligence reports.[46] If the latter scenario was the case, however, such denunciations were compiled from popular sources; they were not drafted freehand in the National Palace, as is the popular impression.[47] Only one genre of denunciations—in which individuals were accused of being communists or political enemies of the regime—seems to have been actually planted by the National Palace, but such denunciations constituted a minority of the total published at some 14 percent.[48] Even if the culture of denunciation ultimately served Trujillo's interests by generating factional strife within the civil bureaucracy that checked the formation of rival political cliques, denunciation derived from the particular political sociology of the regime, not Trujillo himself, even if it was Trujillo who created the structure in the first place. Denunciation thus belies approaches that assume the centrality of the dictator in all areas of policy-making under statist regimes of this kind. In recreating the state bureaucracy, Trujillo forged what Max Weber called "a power instrument of the first order," yet one that could not remain entirely within his control.[49]

THE SHADOW STATE

Trujillo financed an enormous horizontal expansion of government through the creation of the official Dominican Party, a process that did more than merely redistribute political capital in the form of state jobs and enforce the regime's structure of domination. Founded in 1931, the party quickly became the prime nexus of articulation between the state and the political subject, with a mass membership of approximately one-half of the country's population.[50] It provided a mass base to a regime that at the onset did not receive support from the traditional elite. From the perspective of the populace, party membership became synonymous with citizenship itself, since the party card (called the *palmita* for the party's palm tree symbol) was fundamental for access to everything from jobs to bus service, in combination with the *cédula* (official ID) and voter's registration.[51] (These three pieces of identification in tandem were nicknamed *los tres golpes*, "the three blows.") As an extension of Trujillo's person, the party coordinated and planned civic rituals, conducted "civic reviews" (*revistas cívicas*), and dispensed official charity in his name so as to, in its own words, respond to the "urgent need to create a citizen consciousness submissive to the principle of authority."[52] Trujillo also financed a dramatic expansion of the structure of government; by the 1940s he had created seventeen new ministries and other state agencies, resulting in a fourfold expansion of urban professionals as the state came to employ a full 15 percent of the labor force. The number of university graduates had also expanded threefold by the 1950s, thus augmenting the number of middle-sector professionals, especially in the capital city.[53]

State expansion thus not only aided in the consolidation of Trujillo's political control but also formed a new status group of party functionaries, who were middle class in economic terms but had the social capital of a new elite, a form of "state nobility."[54] One Barahona senator described the social structure of his province as effectively divided into two parts: "professionals, businessmen/traders and industrialists" forming an "upper class" that held a "middling economic position, some culture and a certain morality," and a lower-class majority that was composed of workers, day laborers, and so on.[55] This bifurcated vision was in part the legacy of a weak and regionally fragmented bourgeoisie, which became consolidated during Trujillo's rise to power. Note how professionals are accorded a special status as the sole group not defined primarily by socioeconomic position but rather by their access to "culture," as if sufficient culture translated directly into social capital. One indication of the social prestige ascribed to party representatives is the fact that, in 1940, skilled foreigners feigned to be party members.[56] Even a cemetery inspector had not a small measure of status. During the Depression, the vogue of professionalism could be explained as a result of rural poverty and desperation, but after World War II, import substitution meant that Dominican farmers thrived as a result of strong primary commodity prices. Party membership was more than empty status posturing; it was a quest for the protection and political capital to be found under Trujillo's mantle. The creation of a new professional class of party functionaries and civil bureaucrats helped offset the influence of the traditional rural elite (typically white landowners or cattle ranchers) and offered a means of social climbing for mestizos.

With their national affiliation, constituency, and distinction, party functionaries were a novel sort of local intellectual. Indeed, perhaps because much party activity was devoted to disseminating propaganda, local party delegates (*presidentes de sub-juntas del Partido Dominicano*) were called "young intellectuals" in official communiqués, a designation which must have been especially flattering to those from remote provincial hamlets.[57] They represented the "nexus between domination and public discourse." They were brokers whose power appeared to reside in their ability to define the nation to the region and vice versa; however, they drew authority from their social position as state delegates and not from the content of their ideology.[58] Party delegates were exhorted to address the women and men of the urban barrios and rural villages in "clear and simple language" to ensure that they were understood.[59]

Denunciation was a particularly appropriate medium for expressing the

14. Partido Dominicano emblem. ARCHIVO GENERAL DE LA NACIÓN, SANTO DOMINGO.

ambiguities of social position and identity of this interstitial group, since it represented the "intermediate space between the society 'below' and the state or the authorities 'above.'" In this way, as Colin Lucas characterized it, denunciation "lies along the fault line dividing those who find themselves in tension with the state and those who see some of their own identity in the state; it marks the division between a state that is 'externalized' and one that is 'internalized' by the citizens."[60] Trujillo accorded respectability to the expanded middle class of this new party bureaucracy by officializing it with the trappings of professional identity, such as uniforms and responsibilities for official organization and speech making. The basis of traditional forms of clientelism was more limited, since the exchange was based primarily on tangibles—land use for a portion of the harvest and occasional political support or other acts of loyalty rather than the signs of status that Trujillo awarded his bureaucrats for their loyalty. The violence of the Trujillo regime was therefore largely symbolic, inasmuch as its beneficiaries were rewarded with tokens of status and identity and feared the withdrawal of the same.[61] Also, unlike traditional forms of patronage, the social position of these new middle-class bureaucrats was based as much on distinction from the masses as it was on identification with a powerful patrón.

The social category of party functionary built upon previous forms of professional identity, such as the figure of the civil servant that had emerged in the 1920s with state formation and the rise of urban culture. The novel *El hombre de piedra* contrasts the modern state bureaucrat with the traditional caudillo both as forms of rule and styles of political identity.[62] Ricardo Cuesta is a new modern bureaucrat employed by the Department of Public Works who arrives in the town of San Juan de la Maguana as part of a road construction project. While much state activity during the United States military occupation was devoted to road building, this association between the state and roads holds a deeper significance. Ricardo is the quintessential stranger, an alienated nomad who seems to hold no membership in a particular community but rather goes wherever the state sends him: as one character observes, "He is that road"—unknown and unknowable. As the embodiment of the street, he is associated with money (his surname, *Cuesta*, translates as "cost"), which plays on the image of bureaucrats as corrupt and often "bought" through payoffs by whatever party they work for. The street, of course, also invokes social dirt—"matter out of place"—in this case rootless individuals lacking a family lineage. A street person goes against traditional Dominican concepts of status, which must be grounded in a particular region; to "be somebody," you must be from somewhere. The street thus contrasts with home and patriline, and "new bureaucrats" such as Cuesta can be seen as like affines, tied to but not of the bloodline, with all the ambiguities of allegiance this implies.[63]

INTRASTATE CONFLICT AND OCCULT POWERS

The enormous lateral extension of low-level state functionaries created a peculiar political sociology, which helps explain the development of denunciation as an individual phenomenon in the 1940s and its transformation into an officially sanctioned (and even sponsored) practice by the 1950s, when the "Foro Público" column of *El Caribe* newspaper became an institution. In the Trujillato, the bureaucracy did not merely reflect but actively produced a new social order.[64] One aspect of state expansion was the creation of several parallel categories of public functionaries, from inspectors to party heads. This, in part, resulted from Trujillo's desire to institutionalize policing mechanisms that could effectively check potential threats to his base of power. While inspectors (who drew their salaries from the party and were strongly associated with it) were entrusted with surveillance, party delegates were in charge of symbolic mobilization for the regime—choreographing the party functions, civic holidays, and Trujillista rites that proliferated.[65] In contrast to the traditional provincial bureaucracy, these parallel networks' vague set of jurisdictional responsibilities may have created a structural basis for competition with traditional local authorities. Since the invisible hand of the "Foro" was probably a Dominican Party spokesman, one could argue that such party functionaries used the "Foro" and popular gripes to brandish the power of Trujillo's shadow bureaucracy over the civil bureaucracy. Yet these intrabureaucratic tensions had other outcomes as well. Denunciation was also used as a means of resistance against the depredations of Trujillo's cronies, since provincial party secretaries would at times express their resentment against Trujillo by denouncing one of El Jefe's favorites.[66]

The institutionalization of a shadow bureaucracy via the creation of the Dominican Party rearticulated the popular vision of the state. Drawing upon the anthropologist Michael Herzfeld's research on the sociology and culture of bureaucratic organizations, one could say that the traditional civil service came to be seen as the patriline, or male bloodline, of state power and the nation, while the more amorphous, unpredictable, and dangerous party bureaucracy came to be seen as the affines of government.[67] From below, the party was perceived with the same mistrust as in-laws or half siblings, as individuals with conflicting interests and allegiances whose line of access to the top made them capable of great danger. By contrast, the status and position of the traditional municipal staff was more firmly rooted in historic ties of family, blood, and soil. Of course, this perception was reversed at the top. Since Trujillo's control was more firmly established over the party bureaucracy (since the party president was a close personal ally), the party was seen as more reliant on the regime. As Herzfeld has said, "Agnatic kinship clearly provides the moral context for drawing the lines between concern and indifference, in-group humanity and collective inhumanity."[68]

In accord with E. E. Evans-Pritchard's classic work on the subject, denunciatory accusations could thus be classed as witchcraft in two senses: they represented apprehension created by perceived access to extra-institutional, illicit, or occult power, and they were generated by structural conditions similar to those of witchcraft.[69] As Pamela Stewart and Andrew Strathern have said, even "when witchcraft and sorcery ideas are not overtly at work, rumor and gossip may work as a covert form of witchcraft against persons."[70] Finger-pointing resulted from the ambiguous relationship between the state and the party, which was aggravated by structural tensions of dominion and inequality in an atmosphere of extreme suspicion. Conflicts erupted into public view where institutionalized forms of social distance or other social buffers to contain antagonism were lacking. In Mary Douglas's words, "Witchcraft beliefs seem to lie like static electricity activated by incidental friction . . . in a social system permanently harbouring areas of ill-defined relationships."[71] In this framework, accusations served to clarify ambiguous sociopolitical boundaries as well as to express resentment toward Dominican Party arrivistes who had salaries and political clout that exceeded their perceived worth.

In his study of sixteenth-century European witchcraft accusations, the historian Peter Brown found that insecure court officials were chiefly responsible for sorcery charges. Similarly, Dominican Party representatives were thus prime agents of, and at times targets for, admonishment.[72] If by the 1950s the party had acquired a veneer of institutionalization, and thus legitimate authority, the vectors of accusation were a constant reminder that this was merely skin deep and that civilians were willing to put themselves at considerable risk to call the regime to task for its rhetoric of official probity. As Peter Geschiere has argued in his analysis of the circulation of sorcery accusations in Cameroon, the existence of a culture of symbolic infighting indicates above all that "power is an essential problem for these societies." Thus, contrary to the view that denunciation demonstrates Trujillo's ironclad control, it may well be that it also demonstrates quite the obverse: "a profound distrust and impassioned lust for power" on the part of those beneath him. Denunciation could be termed part of the "infrapolitics of the powerless," even if it ultimately served to support the regime's hegemony rather than resist it.[73]

While functionalist explanations help elucidate the phenomenon of denunciation, they cannot explain it in its entirety, since although party-state tensions presumably existed from the 1930s on, it was not until the 1950s that denunciation became institutionalized. Certainly, the very fact that an open forum was created to air grievances across factions was an important causal factor. The creation of the "Foro Público" empowered citizens, since it appeared to include them in a new disciplinary apparatus that gave them the power to judge others, even while their participation in the "Foro" enabled the state to better police them as well. Thus, what may have been experienced as empowering was itself a "technology of power," or "mode of submission," in Michel Foucault's terms.[74]

However, in sketching the fault lines of class and faction that provided the context for denunciation, I do not wish to reduce this complex, multicausal phenomenon to a mechanistic grid. Both functionalist and Foucauldian approaches give short shrift to individual agency, and thus fail to account for the ways in which individual agents deployed denunciation—at times even consciously manipulated it—as a means to their own ends.[75] In approaching denunciation as a structural response, these frameworks also neglect the expressive aspects of the phenomenon—the ways, for example, that the new political sociology was read in the racial imagination of Dominicans.

The symbolic representation of the state-party split as a division between blood kin and affines was reinforced by Dominican racial ideology. While race is an unmarked principle of social classification in the Dominican Republic, and thus is often "unseen," it is intimately bound with social class and serves to reinforce class difference. Indeed, one might say that race is embedded in class and serves as its primary marker.[76] Since the civil service drew more heavily upon traditional provincial elites, who tended to be phenotypically whiter, it was seen as contrasting with the Dominican Party, which, as an avenue of social mobility for the "little man," tended to be darker in hue because of the coincidence of poverty and blackness (or in this case, brownness).[77] Thus, if the state bureaucracy came to represent an endogamous, neatly divided racial "order," the party was the paragon of social "disorder" through race-class mixture. Hence, elites also mistrusted the party owing to latent fears regarding the figure of the mulatto, who was stereotypically perceived as a social outsider harboring resentment and potential violence, a poor man in high places who embodied transgression in his very person. Indeed, this may have been what generated the many stories of Trujillo's ritual humiliation of the upper classes in public. Fears of the shadow bureaucracy were compounded by assumptions of mulatto treachery, just as the mystique of the party as an occult source of power paralleled the mulatto's presumed access to blackness, and thus magic. The party was viewed as highly unpredictable and particularly dangerous because of its potential direct access to Trujillo (a tempestuous mulatto with Haitian family links); it was a reminder of his characteristic rule breaking as opposed to what should be the rule making of state authority. To make matters worse, state-party distrust was further accentuated by the very political structure that positioned the two groups as rivals governing the same terrain, symbiotically interconnected and contiguous, yet simultaneously at odds.[78]

Like illegitimate mulattos, party minions were perceived as only precariously held in check by deferential rules of conduct because of their access to Trujillo. Their power was perceived as outside of the moral economy that circumscribed individual advancement in favor of the group since they could be promoted through intervention by Trujillo or the party president and thus circumvent the rules of bureaucratic advancement.[79] Inspectors may have used public accusation as a means of self-aggrandizement, since as outsiders they were excluded from, and may have felt threatened by, traditional patronage networks. Conversely, denunciation may have been the sole weapon available to most ordinary citizens, who felt threatened by the extraordinary power held by inspectors as confidential informers for the regime. Unlike the case of abuses by a traditional patrón, one could not bring collective networks or social pressure to bear against party inspectors, since they had access to El Jefe.

Yet inspectors piqued the ire of virtually everyone—not just the disenfranchised. Inspectors not only generated fear among the popular classes, they even threatened kingpins in the local government structure, since they could use their links to the party authority structure, and thus to patrons such as the Trujillo-surrogate Paíno Pichardo, to challenge even important regional power brokers such as governors. State officials may have had higher status in the traditional political structure, but they had only their clients behind them. Political networks aside, the fact that party salaries were often more than three times greater than their state equivalents must have also provoked resentment against the Dominican Party on the part of local civil servants.[80] As a result, state magistrates frequently treated local party authorities with deference.

However, even though often villainized in the popular imagination, inspectors could and frequently did provide a check on the corrupt clientelistic redistribution of public resources to friends and family. Thus, at times they could be seen as serving the people's interests. One pharmacist, for example, was denounced by a sanitary inspector for appropriating and redistributing medical supplies to his friends and then fudging the records. He was accused of creating a virtual fiefdom, drawing upon the help of his sister and a nurse to establish his own private medical practice within the hospital in true patron-clientelist fashion.[81] Nor were such denunciations merely symbolic excoriations. This case resulted in the trial and removal of the offender, and he was replaced through a direct appointment by the secretary of state. Ultimately, however, the Dominican Party did become its own avenue of patronage.

These new regional shadow authorities clashed structurally with the clientelistic underpinnings of municipal rule, because they could overrule local hiring decisions and had the power to impose their own personnel on the provincial bureaucracy. This tension could be described as what Herzfeld calls "concealed segmentation," since the party and civil service were ostensibly supposed to work together in "a politics of rapprochement and cordiality," yet in practice were structurally competitive; such competition often meant that the two branches were constantly vying to "embody more perfectly the immanent qualities of the whole."[82] In fact, the Dominican Party president could and did place anyone of his liking within the party bureaucracy, the civil service, and even state hospitals; he was involved with hires ranging from secretaries of state down to the most minuscule of posts, such as ministerial messengers and cleaning staff.[83]

Thus, when the two bureaucratic networks collided, the party or inspector contingent usually won out in the end, since it could appeal to higher authorities closer to Trujillo. For example, in the dispute discussed, the pharmacist contended in his defense that his denouncers were subordinates loyal to the secretary of state for sanitation, an official who may have been in league with sanitary inspectors to take advantage of their position to collect materials for their own benefit under the protection of the shadow bureaucracy. The pharmacist also argued that—as the political Achilles heel of the hospital and without the protection of any powerful doctor—he was frequently scapegoated for ineptitudes elsewhere. He understood that his dismissal resulted from the fact that the pharmacy was a key spoil needed to circulate among the various doctors' subalterns.[84]

Interfactional rivalry ultimately served Trujillo's interests, since it checked the formation of local-level political configurations that could challenge his monopoly on power and thus conformed to the Machiavellian formula *divide ut regnes*. Yet the conflict itself was not entirely his doing, even if the regime was responsible for creating a structure predisposed to infighting rather than harmony. Indeed, in the official ideology of the regime, no intrafactional disputes were tolerated in the administration, and questionnaires that sought to root out personal antagonisms and maintain interdepartmental accord were frequently circulated.[85]

RITUAL POLITICS

The tensions that resulted from "concealed segmentation" help explain denunciations across the party-civil service divide. For example, in 1940, antagonism erupted between the governor and the party in Hato Mayor. Not surprisingly, the power struggle was expressed through the idiom of ritual.[86] The party secretary had organized a major rally for Trujillo without inviting or even notifying the governor. Incensed at being upstaged not by the party junta but rather a minor secretary, which he interpreted as a particularly hostile affront, the governor denounced the party leader to the party president. Worse still, the rally was a disaster, and the governor feared that this poor turnout would reflect badly on him. Thus, his denunciation was partly an effort at preempting potential criticism from above. (Luckily for the governor, the national party president blamed the poor attendance on the *alcaldes pedáneos*, or local magistrates, who were fired because they were deemed ultimately responsible for the presence or absence of bodies at political rallies.) In the end, much to the governor's fury, the Dominican Party president actually sided with the local party chief, who stated that there was no rule requiring party heads to seek approval from anyone other than Trujillo.[87] This case illuminates the extraordinary power of the party bureaucracy and its capacity to surpass that of the traditional civil service. The fact that party personnel had so much clout (owing to their direct line to Trujillo) but little concrete responsibility per se (since they had no formal jurisdiction or job guidelines) caused them at times to lord it over their colleagues in the civil service.

Similar party-civil service tensions emerged in a proposed project to build a bust of Trujillo, yet in this case the two wings of government worked together rather than at loggerheads. Many busts and statues were built in El Jefe's honor during the regime, often as a form of symbolic capital to attract Trujillo's munificence in the form of public investment in a particular provincial municipality. However, for this project the party president tried to conciliate rather than antagonize party-municipal relations. A provincial party head suggested the project directly to the national party president, who sought to preempt authoritarian usurpation of municipal jurisdiction by forestalling further discussion until the governor had been apprised.[88] These two cases demonstrate how within this "theater state," political struggle was frequently expressed through symbolic idioms of rites and monuments; they also demonstrate through their opposite outcomes the lack of equilibrium between the state and party bureaucratic systems.[89]

Thus, the dissension of the party-civil service diarchy enabled Trujillo to retain his sanctimonious air and reinforce his benevolent image through intervention from above.[90] While the subaltern officials were squabbling, Trujillo (either personally or through his Dominican Party surrogates) actually did respond to hundreds of party members' written solicitations for work, cash, or particular items such as artificial limbs, school books, tin roofs, or sewing machines (although key functionaries were graced with prizes such as a Chevrolet DeLuxe sports sedan).[91] As with other forms of state patronage, Trujillo preferred to reward those more likely to become reliable regime dependents. Thus, the more abject the solicitant and the less likely to have a civic identity (such as landless tenant farmers, lumpen street dwellers, disabled or incarcerated individuals, and women), the more likely that a solicitant would be heard and responded to in kind. Thus a party junta leader from a tiny hamlet on the outskirts of the southwestern sugar town of Barahona had his prayer for a hospital berth for his daughter answered; Trujillo ordered her to be interned at one of the best hospitals in the country.[92] It also explained why someone who had been thrown in jail for insulting a policeman—who claimed in a missive to the Grand Benefactor that he had converted to Trujillo's cause—was actually released; as a result, he repaid his debt to Trujillo through voluntary party speeches extolling the virtues of El Jefe.[93] Populist acts such as these recognized by extension even the lowliest of party junta leaders, whose prestige resided in their relationship to the charismatic center of power, Trujillo. The dictator's "calculated arbitrariness" has been noted, but not how the "climate of fear and unpredictability" was paired with an "extravagant generosity which personalizes transactions, rendering them incommensurable."[94]

Finally, denunciation as a political practice followed a logic of social leveling that must have been more significant given the lack of alternatives for channeling popular grievances under the regime. In principle, anyone could bring charges against a high civil servant by public denunciation. Denunciation could be used to fight the sense of entitlement in which authorities, especially those from elite families, felt they had the license to do whatever they wanted. Thus, as with sexual harassment accusations today, it became a populist weapon for airing a whole range of subaltern grievances—from peasant dislocations to multinational company depredations, hidden injuries of class and race, or local histories of abuses by powerful local agents of the state. In one case, a peasant had sold a plot of land to a Haitian, whose payments fell into arrears when he fled during the Haitian massacre of 1937. Yet when the seller approached the mayor for help, the mayor, instead of assisting him, proceeded to steal the land. The mayor then challenged him to sue, which the peasant obviously could not afford. So he denounced the mayor instead.[95] In another case, a young party messenger with a minuscule salary of ten pesos per month was paid only occasionally by his supervisor, until finally he exploded and was beat up and thrown in jail. As he put it, "Ai! So many things are seen by us, the miserable ones, in the interior towns. . . . In the capital, Ciudad Trujillo, there you are, doing what you ought to be, but around here all you see are *caciquillos* [exploitative bosses]!"[96] Such abuses on the part of local authorities against the disenfranchised were legion; for many, denunciation at least provided a possible means of redress. Some charges were highly risky since they called authorities' attention to misdemeanors or felonies that could bring the wrath of authorities accused of malfeasance, such as accusations about shantytown communities that violated immigration, sanitary, building, and housing ordinances.[97]

The fear of denunciation ultimately stemmed from a highly arbitrary, closed system of inquiry that could punish purported abuses with dismissal, whether or not the charges were true. Denunciation also occurred in a context in which Trujillo's firms controlled 80 percent of industrial production and employed 45 percent of the labor force; thus more than half of the population was dependent upon him directly or indirectly.[98] A falling out with Trujillo could leave someone with nowhere else to go or at the very least with a loss of "face." Of course, at times charges were exaggerated or wholly invented. Sometimes fabricated denunciations resulted in nightmarish witch trials for the accused but were also at times perceived as such and dismissed. In one case, a cabal ceased their denunciatory letter-writing campaign, perhaps fearing retribution after hearing through the grapevine that an official inquiry of their charges had begun.[99]

Even if both bureaucratic networks were privileged, bureaucrats paid a high price for their salaries and prestige. In exchange for status, they were subject to an intense regime of social scrutiny and control. Civil servants were constantly in the public gaze, potentially subject to denunciations laterally from the shadow inspectors or party bureaucrats who stood to gain by exposing their faults, or vertically from a disgruntled population below. Their whereabouts, leisure pastimes, and decorum were all scrutinized. One functionary was denounced, for example, for getting drunk and having his wallet stolen, since such behavior was "unbecoming" to his position as representative of the party and state. A deputy was attacked in the "Foro" for wearing a *guayabera*, respectable traditional attire for the tropics, but considered less formal than a suit and tie.[100] Reports might circulate up the party chain if a party hack was observed imbibing excessively or too frequently at a notorious tavern or gambling locale. And even private disagreements or quarrels between public administrators received official notice from higher authorities.[101] Anything deviating from propriety could result in denunciation. Yet if some forms of socializing were sanctioned, others were encouraged. Attendance at official parties was mandatory, and covert anti-Trujillistas had to come up with good excuses to avoid them.[102] Under the regime, both civil and party bureaucracies were considered representative of the executive's person and could face disciplinary action for violations of decent demeanor.

However, social control regulations were frequently out of sync with local realities and required a standard of decorum far exceeding that which Trujillo himself maintained. One example occurred in 1952, when legislation was enacted requiring public employees to reside with their legal families. Requiring a single domicile enabled more effective surveillance of civil servants at the same time that it allowed them to control their constituencies more thoroughly. But this did not square with the everyday life of relatively affluent Dominican men, who were frequently either separated from their legal spouses or married but actually residing with one or more *queridas* (common-law mistresses that were widespread in the Dominican serial family system). The complexity of the Dominican family confounded higher authorities, as lower-level officials sought to explain and exculpate their wide-ranging familial obligations to town wives, rural girlfriends, and the children of both.[103] Of course, restricting the mobility of public officials also expedited the mobilization of local civic rituals, since they were in charge of gathering people for these events. Indeed, officials were branded with a range of labels, such as *indiferente* (a label of shame) for failing to participate actively or "enthusiastically" in public functions.[104] Such accusations could then be passed along to the national party chief and result in further pressure from above. And those who were unable to muster the requisite crowds could be in trouble (woe to those whose events suffered a downpour!), since quarterly reports containing attendance sheets were submitted regularly to the national party chief.[105] During the Trujillato, citizenship required active and public participation by all; there was no place for spectators.

However, this is not to say that the all-too-frequent state rites did not encounter popular resistance. As the historian Detlev Peukert has argued for Nazi Germany, the surface picture of mass popular consent dissolves under more careful scrutiny.[106] Attendance at multiple public festivities was used as an excuse to shirk work responsibilities so frequently that some bureaucrats pleaded that only those functionaries directly recognized by a particular holiday (such as Police Day, Sheriffs' Day, or Teachers' Day—Trujillo established more than a hundred holidays over the course of the regime) take the day off.[107] However, in the interior—where such events took time away from farming or commerce—peasants and traders tended to have poor state ritual attendance, at least at everyday functions. Reports indicated that "morose and apathetic" behavior was commonplace. For example, one *revista cívica* in San Juan de la Maguana, to which some 1,000 were "invited," attracted a "ridiculous" 200 attendees.[108] By 1940, even aldermen, police, and bailiffs were skipping town on days of official acts, much to the chagrin of the local alcaldes, who were accountable for these meager showings.[109] There was also enough resistance to the "voluntary" financial contributions required for major festivals that even this became a topic of denunciation in the press.[110]

Moreover, the moral economy of public mobilization was not always interpreted as intended by higher-level choreographers. If the regime saw the frequent rallies and rites of allegiance to Trujillo as occasions for mobilizing symbolic capital, and also as tools for collecting information on dissent in the interior, the population viewed them otherwise. Participation was interpreted by assistants as an investment in the state that would later yield concrete rewards—be it a position, a raise, or alms to the needy. This was made quite clear in a letter from an aspiring young party member from San José de los Llanos, who complained, "My motive in writing for a position as Assistant Mayor [*Alcalde Pedáneo*] is because I joined the statistical team and I got no assistance. I joined the land-and-cattle census and I still don't; I am staffing the electoral tables, and I would suppose that in the *Alcaldía* I could at least get a certificate."[111]

The Dominican Party needed far more than its local jefes to plan and staff these civic mobilizations. It required dozens of volunteers in many capacities to create and channel symbolic capital for the regime. Indeed, the volunteers and rank-and-file state workers provided an important mobilization base for the party. The party requested many kinds of unpaid work from its regular staff—from manning electoral tables and showing educational films to organizing poetry recitals or taking care of the visiting orchestra for the Restoration (Independence) Day celebrations on 16 August.[112] Speechmaking was a key component of all official acts, and the party recruited locals to participate. Although the content was highly formulaic—the texts were variations on official themes with long quotations, the topics preapproved by party heads—participation in these rituals was hardly empty. Local intellectuals were not only recruited but created by these events, and social hierarchies were established by the order of speakers. In the interior, party functionaries were placed alongside primary schoolteachers as the most prestigious local figures (teachers were frequently young women, while party functionaries were most often men).[113] The choreography of a party event in 1952 displays nicely the new status hierarchy of the regime. The local party head was accorded primacy by opening the event, but the local primary schoolteacher was master of ceremonies. State rituals provided a far wider audience than local notables, especially women, had experienced previously.

By being appointed as authorized spokesmen for the regime, even volunteers were granted a special community recognition at these rituals, where they stood next to the regional governor, the mayor, the local chief of police, the communal party junta leader, and the sanitation inspector. They were accorded a kind of parallel status, even if only for the day. Public speaking was also a channel for advancement through the party hierarchy. For example, Leonicio Pieter, a small-town primary schoolteacher, went on to become a national figure, first through speechmaking and later as a propaganda writer for the regime.[114]

Even if their parents were peasants, in the moment of public appearance these party bureaucrats became instant, if temporary, professionals—*hombres decentes*—distinguished by their neatly pressed, crisp white shirt and tie or guayabera.[115] Thus, party participation provided a mirage, but one that was desperately appealing in this predominantly rural society that greatly valued white-collar work as a status marker. To be a professional was to be cosmopolitan: for example, to shop on the smart downtown street "El Conde," at the "Palm Beach Store" of the German immigrant Ernesto Weisnicht, instead of having one's clothes sewed by a relative or local seamstress. Certainly, the traditional military dressed up as well on these civic occasions, wearing a white twill suit and a Panama hat, but the professional had the added cachet of being *letrado*, with its connotations of urbanity and civilization.[116] But clothes were even more important for the middle class, being de rigueur for notaries and representing "capacity and dignity" for professionals.[117] However, it took considerable sacrifice for professionals to dress as "decently" for their "mission" as they should. In 1940, one official wrote, "I have to go through the horrible ordeal of not being able to dress well—something of indispensable necessity having as I do to be present at official acts as a representative and sometimes to go to the capital."[118] Being a loyal "Trujillista" implied being a paragon of propriety, having *muy buenas costumbres*, as well as dressing in impeccable attire as a civil servant, especially in the frequent official meetings, parades, and celebrations hosted by the party in provincial townships and the capital. Indeed, denunciation, as a practice that exposed the private to the public gaze, may well have helped fashion the "exceptional consciousness" of being observed that made appropriate attire more than desirable—even obligatory—for the public sector during the Trujillato.[119]

The cédula or ID was the most despised symbol of everyday life under the regime; it presumed a unitary notion of personhood or public self.[120] Official identity had not always been fixed in this way, however. Throughout Latin America during the colonial period, cédulas or licenses were routinely used to reclassify individuals from the dishonor of racial mixture to that of "legal whiteness."[121] Indeed, in predominantly mestizo societies such as Colombia or the Dominican Republic, whiteness may be an obligatory, albeit unseen, frame for the presentation of a respectable self, being implicit to notions of propriety. Thus, in this view, race may be based on a metaphor of blood lineage, but it is fundamentally achieved in part by social class and in part by style and manners—rather than by skin color per se. This perspective may have been lurking behind denunciations leveled at—as well as emanating from—the shadow bureaucracy, which tended to be darker in hue, as well as engendering certain forms of uneasiness. As stepchildren of the civil service, party agents may in part have been driven to denounce others because in so doing they could claim a social position of respectability superior to their station in a culture in which race, class, and status were inextricably tied and mutually reinforcing, but also malleable. Thus, denouncing the other situated oneself as superior and enabled transference of the implicit stain that mestizo illegitimacy had in the popular imagination; one passed along the stigma, making possible the fiction of moving up the hierarchy and inhabiting a position of propriety and social ascent. This may explain why the cédula was called in popular parlance the *papel de camino* (the paper of the road) since it enabled movement in social status as well as territorial space.[122] Finally, this may explain some of the fetish-power of the trappings of official identity—uniforms, insignias, and forms of speech—that enabled people to adopt a professional identity under the Trujillo regime, one which scripted poor mulattos into the grand narrative of the nation for the first time.[123] These may have been costumes, but they enabled the *plebe* to wear "white masks," and thus be respectable, if only for a time.[124]

PANEGYRIC AS OFFICIAL SELF-FASHIONING

On 20 January 1940, Governor Cocco of San Juan de la Maguana wrote to the president of the Dominican Party to defend his honor against the shame of a failed public rally:

> The gratitude for having been given personality, honor and benefits cannot be described with mere words, nor with impulsive and grotesque gesticulations that, as insincere and disloyal, are worthy of scoffing and execration by those who due to their patriotism and conviction have entered with all their body and soul into the sublime work of perfecting and pondering the Grandiose and August cause of the Renowned Creator of our nationality. . . . Mr. President, I am a loyal, sincere and unremitting friend of Generalissimo Trujillo . . . enamored with his glory and . . . a decided and fervent admirer of his cooperation.[125]

If denunciation caused shame by creating social distance from the dictator, this was corrected through idioms of praise, which situated the subject as closely allied with Trujillo, as once again a loyal and fervent subaltern. Effusive praise oratory to Trujillo was a stock component of official protocol. Most observers have disregarded the sycophantism required of subordinates as merely a product of Trujillo's megalomania, as a kind of political theater that individuals performed in ways that masked their "true" feelings and intentions.[126] I argue that denunciation and panegyric must be seen in tandem, as forming part of the symbolic economy that bound subjects to the regime.

Moreover, although they are formally opposed speech genres, a skilled orator could make panegyric into a form of denunciation. Thus I wish to consider the logic governing the rhetoric of praise to Trujillo.

As James Scott has stated, "prestige is a relational good."[127] It must be conferred by others. But even if prestige is the public face of domination, to lavish praise upon Trujillo was not necessarily to partake in his hegemonic project. Praise oratory provided an avenue for pursuing individual agendas as well. An example might be a reference to the "Dominican" Party in quotations, since it remained unclear whether the quotes were added by someone who had learned to write in one of the mediocre regime literacy schools, and thus did so out of punctuation ignorance, or whether he actually wished to silently call into question whether indeed this party was of and for the nation, or for Trujillo himself. Such innocent interpretations, however, were not accepted when the caption of a photo of schoolchildren placing bouquets at the unveiling of a bust of Trujillo mistakenly substituted "tomb" for "bust"—an occurrence that cost the editor his job.[128]

Even if declarations of appreciation and obedience for Trujillo were obligatory rituals, excessive praise to Trujillo could be seen as an insult: as cloying, self-serving, and insincere. And the line between appropriate and inappropriate praise was frequently murky, dependent more upon the individual and circumstances than the language itself. One party president who said that "he owed everything to the illustrious Father of the New Fatherland" was called "stupid and braggart" (even though another writer said he served "God and Trujillo" without incurring a backlash in the press).[129] The denouncer of Germán Ornes accused the former editor-in-chief of *El Caribe* of "being incapable of merely writing about Trujillo. He gushed, slavered, postured."[130] Public criticism also did not need to be direct. The rigidity of the formal code was such that even the merest deviation could send a "bifunctional message" to the audience through indirect allusions and substitutions.[131] Some panegyric appears almost tongue-in-cheek in its effusiveness, such as Osorio Lizarazo's comments that "I have known and felt over me the effluvium of [Trujillo's] personality, that extends like an essential atmosphere over the entire country," a comment that could easily describe Trujillo's claustrophobic domination as much as his personal aura.[132]

The "silver-tongued orator" Joaquín Balaguer, one of the regime's most eloquent writers, used substitution as a strategy for indirectly criticizing and satirizing the regime.[133] In a form of ventriloquism, he could voice criticisms of the regime's ruthlessness through foreign commentators; he was safe as long as he did not utter the charges himself. Or Balaguer could say the unmentionable about Trujillo, as long as it was later negated.[134] One of his most imaginative efforts occurred at the coronation of Queen Angelita at the World's Fair of Peace and Confraternity in 1955. This moment invoked the turn-of-the-century tradition of *juegos florales* for May Day, when female beauty contests were coupled with poetry competitions for men in which the poets typically composed love sonnets commending the women for their virtues. Working within this idiom of the fabulous, Balaguer, who was then serving the regime as vice-president, applauded the wonders of Angelita's beauty, her charm, and her magnificent court, but then proceeded to speak in the subjunctive about the "tyranny of her dictatorship," using synecdoche to allude obliquely to Trujillo's authoritarianism. While it would have been inconceivable to describe the regime as tyrannical, referring to Angelita's despotism squarely placed the comment in the realm of the marvelous, since her court was transitory, feminine, and entirely imaginary. It was sarcastic because no one, especially no woman, shared power with Trujillo. Thus his use of the term "tyranny" is striking, but it remained within the official code as a paean of praise to Angelita as beauty queen. Yet it had quite another meaning if Angelita stood in for Trujillo, which some observers understood to be his intention.[135]

Similarly, Balaguer used substitution in other speeches to express his reservations about Trujillo's strongman style of rule and to exculpate himself from the barbaric excesses of the regime. An example from a speech in 1952 described the nineteenth-century caudillo Pedro Santana as a "Judas of the Patria" because he sought to annex the country to the United States for a price, an act demonstrating his "abjection and servitude." He continued: "In the life of these contradictory men, virtue often alternates with crime, patriotism with ambition, honor with perfidy, and abnegation with sin."[136] He then went on to describe Trujillo as establishing an exception to this rule, but nonetheless the allusion through juxtaposition remains. Balaguer's characterization of the nineteenth-century caudillo casts a shadow on Trujillo, since Trujillo was often praised as a great "caudillo." Although Balaguer expressly negates the unfavorable comparison, Trujillo remains linked through a historical genealogy of Dominican leadership with "these contradictory men."

Balaguer's carefully calculated rhetorical strategy was to buy credit by lionizing Trujillo to the highest. He achieved this through a litany of the most patently exorbitant claims about Trujillo's honors—for example, that he belonged among certain immortal men, who, like gods or saints, have "inundated the land with the aroma of their virtues."[137] Sandwiched between exalted tributes, then, Balaguer slipped in a double entendre that made his laudatory aggrandizement resemble a bad joke. Balaguer's central position within the regime, combined with phenomenal rhetorical skills, endowed him with a circumscribed license to play with official discursive codes in a fashion that was both dramatic and unique.

Balaguer also used the technique of separating Trujillo as emblem of the ideal office from a more critical evaluation of his actual performance.[138] In this framework, Trujillo is first praised for making history, as Sparta or Athens did, through his multiple contributions to national development (such as making the country financially independent or building its national infrastructure): in sum, for "rehabilitating the nation."[139] Within this long list of accomplishments as exemplary statesman, Balaguer manages to do the unthinkable, that is, mention the deficiencies of his actual performance. In one example he made perhaps the most critical comment about Trujillo ever recorded in an official speech:

> Trujillo, who has stains, as does the sun, who has his successes and his errors; who is not infallible because infallibility is a gift of gods and gods belong to mythology and not to politics, which is in its essence the domain of the contingent and the possible. Trujillo has created in the Dominican Republic a regime that is in its essence authoritarian. This is a reality that we cannot negate if we wish to be sincere; but also it is true that the police state created by Trujillo has constituted a powerful instrument of economic prosperity, social reconciliation and peaceful coexistence, which surpasses all of those which exist or have existed in the Antilles for the guidance of our countries towards the highest goals of civilized life. . . . We have done much in the last quarter of a century; but that which remains to be done is even more.[140]

After blaming the failures of the Dominican "civic spirit" on the citizenry, not the state (a convention with roots in nineteenth-century liberalism), he then returns to the motif of the ideal office, as symbolized by the founding father of the nation, Juan Pablo Duarte.[141] According to Balaguer, Duarte should serve always as an "outstanding eminence, as the uppermost solitary lodestar [picacho] and as an irreplaceable guide to all Dominicans." In the conclusion, Balaguer unifies these two codes—the ideal and the real, the office and the officeholder—by first substituting another contrast, between the desire of citizens to imitate Duarte as civic model and the impossibility of them ever attaining such a haughty objective. Thus he shifts the burden of fallibility from leader to people and uses substitution to say the impossible about Trujillo.[142] He was arguably the most influential functionary of Trujillo's inner circle, with tremendous longevity, and yet even he suffered a period of disgrace.[143]

Seen in tandem, praise and denunciation established a transcendental image of Trujillo. Trujillo's magnificence as embodiment of formal high office (the object of praise) contrasted semantically with the corruption of his minions (the objects of denunciation), who inevitably appeared debased against his omnipotent perfection. Exalted above the daily (and often dirty) workings of rule, then, the mythic image of Trujillo remained unassailable.[144] Thus, in a sense, denunciation can be seen as a byproduct of the hyperbolic praise to Trujillo, which created a nearly perfect standard of rulership against which lesser bureaucrats could never measure up.[145] It also ironically served as an important safety valve for popular grievances against the state—and against Trujillo—in a context in which others were lacking. The myth of Trujillo as omniscient sovereign was also buttressed by his selective intervention in some denunciations, by which he was able to reinforce his populist image with the masses and against the selfish and sullied bureaucrats who appeared to work for their own gain and against the will of the people.[146]

SEÑOR PRESIDENTE

Structural explanations for the rise of a particular culture of oratory cannot account for the personal motivations impelling individual writers. Use of the "Foro" as a personal platform followed a range of rationales—both expressive and instrumentalist—that cannot be reduced to tensions within the state bureaucracy. First, there were social types that blossomed as a result of the publicity provided by the "Foro Público." For example, Justo Franco was a meddler who wrote six to seven letters a week to the "Foro"— sometimes two a day. Attacking government officials and private citizens alike, his highly literal-minded complaints cited specific infractions of the legal code and provided evidence such as license plate and cédula numbers to make his case. With the voice of a detective or a policeman, "Franco" could well have been a government shill, a mask for official accusations written by someone in the National Palace. Or he could have been a perverse byproduct of the "Foro" itself, a busybody who thrived on the excessive publicity generated by the direct line to the national public and Trujillo. If fame results from the travels of a person's name, then both infamy and fame resulted from frequent appearances in the "Foro."[147]

In a more instrumentalist vein, ordinary citizens also developed strategies of manipulating official codes in order to achieve personal objectives unintended by the regime. In letters to Trujillo seeking favors of various kinds, individuals often used effusive praise to buy credit with Trujillo, especially by employing images of Trujillo as beneficent and magnanimous in order to legitimate their claims to assistance. In one example, a man referred to Trujillo as a fecund and honorable macho, embodying the exemplary qualities of patriarchal father who cares for his wife and children and honorably guards the family bloodline as symbolized by the nontransferable and carefully protected apellido (surname).

Another tactic involved flaunting one's entitlement to attention by displaying a range of status criteria, invoking as many claims to noteworthiness as possible. For example, one man appeals to Trujillo first as a cripple with a mutilated hand, since Trujillo typically privileged the needy in his public charity. However, to underscore his suitability for a white-collar position despite this disability, he says: "I am from the best social centers and belong to a distinguished family, and they say I look completely foreign, I am not the Dominican type."[148] Here both race and physical disability provide status markers signifying entitlement under the regime, albeit according to contradictory principles. Nor was there only an instrumentalist logic at work. In response to an injurious accusation hidden behind a pseudonym, one mode of reply was to brandish as many public markers of identity as possible, striving for the moral high ground through a presentation of absolute transparency. Here one would find reference to family and personal reputation, hometown, cédula number, professional credentials, adhesion to the Trujillista cause, and an appeal to higher authorities to rectify such injustice.[149]

Official codes of masculinity called for expressions of both deference and manliness. One must be a man like Trujillo, but never quite as much a man. Thus, one tension clearly expressed in men's letters was how to represent themselves as active, willful, autonomous men who commanded respect, while at the same time expressing adequate deference. This was particularly sensitive, since masculinity was intrinsically conflictive, requiring a posture of "courage amidst adversity."[150] One party representative found a solution to this discrepancy by coining a slogan that played off Trujillo's official saying, "I will follow on horseback": "A good leader is one who knows how to follow."[151] In losing a post, for example, a man was expected to accept gracefully his fate as defined from above, while simultaneously demonstrating that he was not so devastated as to be undeserving of another position. In one case, a party president who was replaced by the town council secretary wrote, "I am a good collaborator of your government and your cause; neither am I a crushed man, rather I am a man of nerves and only take your orders with my mouth shut like an avocado, because I am not one that leaves the highway for a footpath."[152]

Fatherhood was an important archetype for Trujillo's national authority that was frequently invoked by men seeking his assistance. Some drew upon the regime propaganda of Trujillo as "Father of the Nation" to situate themselves as emulators of his fine example and as men who jealously guard and fight for their patrimony, including wife and children, name, home, and property. In one example, a man uses this device in arguing for a small handout to cover legal fees for his divorce, since his wife had taken up with another man and was procreating under his family name. His note contains the veiled threat that, without assistance, he may have to "do something stupid" (perhaps kill the interloper), which he doesn't want to do but might have to in order to regain his respectable standing.[153] He articulates this potential danger by invoking the bonds of masculine valor and deferring to Trujillo's exemplary patriarchy.

WOMEN AND THE REGIME

With the electoral campaign of 1940, women were officially brought into the party, mobilized by the women's wing (or Rama Femenina) of the Partido Trujillista, a branch of the party. They were given responsibility for social assistance programs, which included providing school breakfasts and uniforms and organizing mothers' clubs for home visitations and didactic talks, yet their quarterly reports testify to their inaction. Additionally, in sharp contrast to the hyperbole of most party reporting of official activities, the women's wing was not ashamed of admitting their poor results, indicating that they were not taken seriously by the regime. While a party official from San Juan de la Maguana proclaimed stridently that thirty-six thousand people came out for a rally and "cheered deliriously the name of our renowned guide GENERALISSIMO TRUJILLO" (surely gross exaggerations), the women's wing frankly confessed to making no social visits, providing no frontier assistance, and offering no simple conversations in poor barrios over the course of a full year, instead padding their reports with achievements such as giving out two pairs of slippers.[154]

Women were not perceived as full and equal participants in the Trujillista project, as evidenced by the fact that women, although frequently denounced, were less frequently penalized than their male compatriots.[155] At times this was a result of nepotism, since the rank and file of the women's wing were often wives and daughters of party hacks and civil servants. A prime example was the case of the Rama Femenina president Dulce Camelia Hirujo, who likely landed her post through her father, party junta president Marcelino Hirujo. She convened a failed rally which no one attended (for which the city council or ayuntamiento president feared that he would ultimately be held accountable); she sent no advance invitations, nor were there plans for music. She then overstepped her authority by threatening to fire a civil servant—the municipal band leader—whom the city council president had called in a final effort to save the event. These violations caused lesser souls to lose their jobs, yet her name was not even mentioned in the first critical report of the incident.[156]

Women were not held to the same standard of official "morality" as their male counterparts either, since their public identity was based on shame, not honor. They were not subjected to the same constraints and pressures that men faced in the definition of their public identity. For example, whereas women could resign from the party, men could not, since such an act could imply betrayal and engender political problems. And much to party officials' chagrin, women were very reluctant to become party members or take out cédulas, perhaps because they were less likely to seek public sector employment and thus had less to gain by doing so.[157]

Women also deployed a different repertoire of "face-work" strategies in appealing to Trujillo than their male counterparts.[158] They tended to present themselves as more unequivocally deferent, since they did not have to maintain public honor in ways that could be interpreted as a challenge to Trujillo's authority. Excessive kowtowing was not dishonorable for women in the way it was for men. One tactic was to frame oneself as dependent upon Trujillo's charity, just as their children were dependent upon them, asking first for houses to maintain their children properly and only secondarily for cash loans or gifts (jobs came in a distant third). Fashioning themselves as women of honor, they requested gifts that reinforced their respectable social identity as domestic and enclosed, and thus protected from the public sphere. They also frequently cast themselves as mothers, invoking their appropriate role as lineage founders and reproducers of good Trujillista citizens, especially young men who were doing their duty in the Guardia Nacional (military service).[159]

Female rhetorical strategies tended toward indirect, passive action. They either positioned themselves as worthy of attention through the actions of their citizen-sons or as devotees of the Virgin of Altagracia. A nationalist symbol, the Virgin of Altagracia conveyed Creole identity, Dominicanidad, and charity. Trujillo promoted devotion to this *matrona* so as to hitch her religious mana to his regime, a move particularly popular among female devotees. Women's letters often drew upon the logic of saint devotion, positing that any gift of charity bestowed to them would also flow to this favored patron saint. Several women wrote that they would ask the Virgin directly, not Trujillo himself, for a house "of little value," and thus since they were devotees, they would receive it in her name. Here the circuit of national value is channeled in, around, and through the national numen; those writing would receive such proceeds fortuitously, by being in the right place at the right time. The use of images of religious and political interpenetration was far more common among female solicitants, who might praise Trujillo as a thaumaturge by saying, for example, that "your helping hand is the balsam that heals all the wounds of all the afflicted who turn to you." They could ask for charity since Trujillo himself was an avatar who had received a divine gift that he could pass on to others. And one may ask honorably for that which will be shared with a higher power such as God.

CONCLUSION

There are a number of conclusions to be drawn from this material on denunciation. In terms of concrete politics, denunciations empowered marginal officials, bureaucrats, and citizens by incriminating higher authorities as they drew attention to themselves. This promotional strategy fed into a structural framework whereby Trujillo benefited by playing factions against each other and by splitting organized assaults against his authority. In discursive terms, this structural dialectic subsumed critical denunciations into the prevailing panegyric of his person.

The denunciation and praise forms of political oratory are historically interesting because they represent in middle-class memory some of the most painful aspects of everyday life during the Era of Trujillo. As the novelist Mario Vargas Llosa wrote in *The Feast of the Goat,* a novel about the daughter of a Trujillista official who was denounced in the "Foro Público":

> Trujillo . . . killed with a method that was slower and more perverse than when he had his prey shot, beaten to death, or fed to the sharks. He had killed him in stages, taking away his decency, his honor, his self-respect, his joy in loving, his hopes and desires, his honor, turning him into a sack of bones tormented by the guilty conscience that had been destroying him gradually for so many years.[160]

Trujillista political speech has been largely dismissed by scholars, either because of its dramaturgical excess or its purported irrelevance to the distribution of the material rewards that were seen as the true basis of state power. Yet denunciation and praise oratory were forms of what Michel-Rolph Trouillot has called "practical consent": political practices that furthered regime hegemony without individuals' conscious choice, blurring the boundaries between the state and civil society by encouraging individuals to act as, and thus see themselves as, state proxies.[161] These speech forms created acquiescence, if not submission, and compliance, if not belief.[162] They worked not through persuasion but by entangling individuals in a political economy of discursive exchange. Like votive offerings, praise to Trujillo was an investment that could convert to other forms of capital—economic, social, or cultural.[163] More broadly, denunciation and praise also demonstrate the inadequacy of models of authoritarianism which categorically oppose the state and civil society, hegemony and resistance, or public and private, because these two genres manifest the bidirectionality, and thus complexity, of the links between them.

The politics of denunciation also underscore the importance of the interstitial middle ground between formal and informal politics—the shadow state and its shadow bureaucracy—in understanding the dialectics of coercion and consent under dictatorships. Scholars have recognized the importance of bringing informal practices such as graft, as well as quasi-official bodies such as intelligence agencies and paramilitary groups, into the analysis of state policy.[164] Indeed, the forms of denunciation explored in this chapter were largely a product of the rise of the official Dominican Party and a web of intelligence-gathering mechanisms that played an important, if at times oblique, role in civic life during the Trujillato. Yet these forms also extend the analysis of politics to a more implicit realm—the structure of expectations regarding rewards, a domain where the material and the moral conjoined.

Thus a focus on the form and deployment of denunciation extends beyond the structural framework of an authoritarian regime and into the less formal arenas of the shadow bureaucracy, which mediated the boundaries between formal and informal politics, between official persons and private selves. Moreover, denunciations not only invoked this shadow state but rhetorically produced it by bringing private transgressions into the public arena and, conversely, bringing public opinion to bear on the private self. It may thus have helped produce the inordinate preoccupation with "looking and being seen" that characterized life in Ciudad Trujillo in the 1950s, especially for the new state elite forged by the regime.[165]

Additionally, a focus on the discursive production of the shadow state helps us rethink the character of formal political arenas by bringing informal networks of social capital into the picture, and, in the Dominican case, helps explain a basic question in Dominican historiography. Why did a regime based on fear endure into the postwar period without serious domestic challenges? The politics of denunciation under Trujillo suggest that the decline in mass repression during much of the 1940s and early 1950s corresponded to the rise of a form of symbolic violence that was the by-product of a new state elite, one whose concerns with honor, reputation, and family secrets became social currencies of, if not life and death, then what was equally important—social life and social death.

APPENDIX

A sample of denunciations from the "Foro Público" column in *El Caribe*, 25 May 1952:

He Says that the "Zero Exam" Is False

24 May 1952

To the Editor-in-chief,

In relation to the public letter of today which was sent the 22nd of this month with the title "Zero in Exam if you Don't Pay Extra," I would like to make the following observation: Those who are examined and are not passed are never in agreement.

The man, Hugo Molina, says that I don't give a license if I am not given 10 or 15 pesos. This is absurd, and I invite Mr. Molina to bring witnesses, people who have given me bribes (*dádivas*) which I accepted to give them a license, since it's very clear that now no one who is not competent as a driver, no matter who it is, can carry the license.

This talk of sold licenses does not exist, because the Executive Power has given me a salary and I am not about to lose the trust that has been deposited in me and in the present commission, the Honorable Present of the Republic, the *Generalísimo* Trujillo.

José Martínez
Public Works Inspector
Cédula No. 34506—Ist
Resident of María de Toledo Street
The Capital

A Silent Organization

Ciudad Trujillo
24 May 1952

To the Editor-in-chief of *El Caribe*,

Sometimes we forget that the Commission of Defense of Sugar and Development of Sugarcane exists, because if it were not for the foreign trips that its most distinguished members take, we would know of no other activity by this silent organization that is so expensive for the state, with all of its luxurious salaries and useless visits.

The legislative project of the tariff and the price of molasses in the country could have been addressed by this commission, but were not; they were only by the initiative of the executive power, one that has no cooperation, since everything must be devised, prepared and directed by the executive, in spite of how well-paid the government functionaries are.

Edwin Pascual Vega

He Says He Was Forced to Sell

Magarín, El Seibo
20 May 1952

Dear Editor-in-chief,

It was more or less five years ago that the ex-chief of the Army, Martínez Arana, forced me to sell 800 *tareas* of land at the absurd price of 50 cents a *tarea* [a local land unit measure]. These lands, which had been sowed with pasture, coconuts, oranges and other fruit trees were worth at that time some DR $10.00 a *tarea*.

I had persistently refused to go through with this sale, but I eventually had to give in due to the fear that this ex-chief exercised in the entire commune since he would just take over whichever lands interested him.

I plead with the authorities in charge to help me recuperate this land, that which enabled me to support my family.

Attentively,
Benito Rodríguez
Note from Editor: Martínez Arana, the man to whom this complaint was directed, has been terminated as Chief of the Army.

30 May 1952

Dear Editor-in-chief,

The case of the Central Office of the Cédula and the situation reigning among the employees must be resolved in a radical way if you want to assure the functioning of this government department, especially given that it is a tax collection agency.

For the Cédula, besides naming a director as was done today, must be subject to removals, transferals or dismissals of certain employees who are those that have created a deep cancer in a department that in previous times had a great reputation.

According to reliable information, the employees are: Andrea Morató Vda. Egea, and Marieta and Margarita. Between the women, Mrs. Morató is called Her Majesty the Queen of Gossip, because all day long she is antisocial and aspires to be Director. No one put in that position will have her cooperation. She feels that her feminist work has not been duly rewarded and lives in constant disagreement.

In terms of Marieta and Margarita, both are professional pilferers (*macuteras*) and incessant demanders (*pedilonas*). When things are slack, they are the ones who run straight for the door to get in with the ones fixing *cédulas* to ask them what's going on. The wrangling (*picoteo*) they have going on every day is like a little customs house. They accept anything [in bribes], from money to nail polish. And on top of it all they are loose-mouthed (*lengueteras*) and gossips.

Among the men we have the case of two that lack protection and constantly live threatening the other employees with denunciations for no reason at all (*guapos*). These employees are a certain Arache, who was a policeman, and Popó Bonetti. These two have terrible references as workers and as people.

Attentively,
José Lorenzo Castro A.

[Note: This last denunciation is of special interest since one of the accused is a Bonetti family member; this family was very close to Trujillo and its political success was entirely due to Trujillo.]

FIVE   CLOTHES MAKE THE MAN

I have a cousin, Baldemiro, and I don't know how to categorize him,

Who now wants to be a Senator,

He can close the game,

He's a tourist, professional,

Surgeon and good actor,

Paid journalist,

Everything he wants and more,

That knows Michael Jordan and is an actor,

That breathes under water and is a painter,

That is a sociologist and a pilot,

That drives backwards, and is a poet and a sculptor,

That cooks without a recipe what he wants and more,

That dresses in wholesale De la Renta,

That is stronger than Sylvester Stallone,

That is a tourist, surgeon, and good singer,

That has climbed Pico Duarte, that is an athlete and a champion,

That dives without a tank, see

That is whatever he wants to be . . .

JUAN LUIS GUERRA, "MI PRIMO" (MY COUSIN)

Verdi's grand opera *Aïda* captures the themes of passion and desire and the seamlessness between the ritual staging of empire and real-political domination exquisitely. And of all the Trujillos, Rafael's first child by his first wife, bad-girl Flor de Oro, and her first husband, the strikingly handsome playboy Porfirio Rubirosa, embodied most vividly the high drama of the regime, even if at times it devolved into a *telenovela* or soap opera. In this chapter I explore the family romance of Flor's relationship with Rubirosa and how in the late 1950s Rubirosa, in tandem with Rafael Trujillo, came to embody a style of masculine self-fashioning and upward mobility called tigueraje, which was an important component of the vernacular politics of the regime, albeit one with contradictory effects.

Trujillo created an image of presidential power that broke with the previous respectable liberal model; it was based instead on an underclass mestizo style of *hombría* or manliness forged through personal risk taking, bravado, and sexual aggression. In the early years of his regime, his commanding leadership in the wake of Hurricane Zenón and his nationalist posturing vis-à-vis the United States were seen as restorative of the country's honor, and thus masculine agency, even if these assets were later effaced by his overblown cult of personality which depleted the collective honor of all Dominican men except himself.[1] While the personalism of the regime was masked by an elaborate theater of modernization, order, and bureaucratic rationality, his surreptitious nickname *el chivo*, the goat, was a reminder of the other face of his rule—his unbridled sexuality, unfettered consumption of women, and raw carnal energy.[2] In chapter 3 I analyzed how Trujillo used spectacles of women to accumulate symbolic capital; here I explore the broader implications of this style of sovereignty: how Trujillo drew upon a vernacular idiom of masculinity which enabled non-white, lower-class men to identify with the regime.[3] Christian Krohn-Hansen has noted how masculinity under Trujillo emerged as a "dominant political discourse" providing a "shared language for constructions of power and legitimacy among Dominicans."[4] As a form of power that is morally ambiguous, tigueraje offers a paradigm of upward mobility for anyone who is cunning and brave, yet it is a form that may involve chicanery and dirty tricks.

The tíguere represents a "hypermasculine pose" characteristic of the mixed-race underclasses in the Dominican Republic; it has a countercultural valence that Trujillo officialized by bringing it into the corridors of power.[5] Like the Brazilian *malandro*, the *tíguere* is a rogue, a trickster who rises from poverty to a position of wealth and power, often through illicit means.[6] Yet the "tíguere is a tíguere," and can be black, mulatto, or white, rich or poor. The tíguere paradoxically emerged as the Dominican "creole figure par excellence" through the audacious and showy subaltern heroes of the *barrios marginados*, or the popular barrios of the colonial zone in the 1950s; consummate *vividores* (gigolos), with their defiant, cool appearance and skill at banter, dancing, and seduction, they were able to command social spaces a cut above the barrio.[7] As Rubirosa recalled, "The only things that interested me were sports, buddies, women, adventure, romance, the lifestyle of the rich; this was, in sum, life."[8] Quintessentially urban, these new flâneurs were a byproduct of the dramatic urban growth of the capital city in the 1940s and

1950s. Staking their claim to the older neighborhoods of San Carlos, Villa Francisca, and Galindo, they chose as their stage urban venues such as parks, cinemas, marketplaces, dance halls, and streets. These new public men styled themselves as popular leaders at a time when only Dominican party hacks and military men could achieve political rank and when the economy offered little more than unskilled factory work or part-time *chiripero* (informal service work) to the lower middle classes.[9] Thus the tíguere as a social type arose alongside a marginalized urban sector of day laborers and unemployed with little education who formed a new subproletariat in the capital city, a group who claimed reputation since respectability was out of their reach.[10] The tíguere took great pleasure in making a spectacle of himself on the new boulevards of Ciudad Trujillo through the mass rites staged there, but he was transgressive because he defiantly called attention to himself and not Trujillo.[11] The popular esteem earned by these "involuntary bohemians," however, made them particularly vulnerable to the iron hand of repression in the late 1950s, since Trujillo did not like to compete with popular heroes.[12] The heights of tigueraje achieved by Trujillo and Rubirosa also forced a reluctant respect on the part of Dominicans, as rendered in a guaracha by the Cuban composer Eduardo Saborit:

> Rubirosa has something
> I don't know what it is
> What could it be, what could it be
> That Rubirosa has.[13]

FLOR AND RUBI: THE PRODIGAL DAUGHTER AND THE DOMINICAN DON JUAN

Flor de Oro was the mirror opposite of the chosen one, the angelic Angelita, the crowned queen of la Feria. She infuriated her father by indulging in the erotic escapades reserved for the men in the family.[14] Like her father, she was sensual, rebellious, and impetuous; playing the role of the mulatta, she was *atrevida* (daring, insolent) as only a man should be. Flor refused to be purely an object of the gaze. Trujillo did his best to control her, but she insisted on playing with the big boys and, in fact, emulating her father. Flor was born while Trujillo was still in the National Guard; as was common during this period among the affluent, she was sent to Paris for schooling and for some culture, and also to help break her defiant spirit. Even at sixteen the tension between Flor and her father was already evident in her letters home from the Collège Féminin de Bouffémont. She was clearly too headstrong for a father bent on total control in the household. With high hopes for her Parisian reacculturation, Trujillo wrote to Flor, "In only one year and a half of absence I can see your favorable change."[15] In Paris she rubbed shoulders with classmates like an Iraqi princess, vacationed in Biarritz and St. Moritz, and became acquainted with the Paris Opera. There she was transformed, in her own words, from a "shy, tropical bumpkin" into "that exotic hybrid, a French-speaking Dominican young lady." However, her acculturation did not rid her of the daring so inappropriate for a "decent" girl.

Upon her return to Santo Domingo, she became infatuated with a young army officer spied at the regal military welcome her father staged for her return. At that time, Rubirosa was Trujillo's aide-de-camp with a vanity rank as army captain. Flor failed to repress her desire as she should have and rashly gazed at him, hence appropriating the masculine position as voyeur. As she recalled, "I noticed one lieutenant instantly—handsome in a Dominican uniform that had a special flair. Even the gold buttons looked real. His name was Porfirio Rubirosa."[16] The first bond between Flor and Porfirio, then, was their shared status as *bichan* (a tíguere subculture of clothes-mongers), with a cult of style and conspicuous sartorial consumption, in which, as Friedman has argued for the Congolese *sapeurs*, "to clothe the self is to define the self."[17] A Haitian newspaper later would proclaim them the "best-dressed, best-educated, most popular couple in town."[18] Rubirosa's elegance later became renowned when he was twice named best-dressed man in Paris, his wardrobe (down to his underwear) custom-made in Paris, Rome, and London.[19]

Porfirio was born of a good but humble family in San Francisco de Macoris. The son of a revolutionary general who lived in Paris after he was named Dominican consul, Porfirio shared with Flor a command of the French language and style since he lived in France from age six to nineteen. When she met Porfirio, Flor described him as "gay, vain, could play the ukelele and do the Apache dance—slim but exotic accomplishments in our simple island society." But clearly there was a *je ne sais quoi* about him. She continues, "In the café on the plaza, I spied Rubi, having his boots shined. (Ignoring Army regulations, he had his elegant boots polished, his uniforms tailored for him and wore his hair long, like a Hollywood movie actor)." She came to watch him perform at the polo games against Nicaragua, a game in which he played valiantly for the Dominican side, which won.[20] She was

15. Porfirio Rubirosa
and Flor Trujillo.
ARCHIVO GENERAL DE
LA NACIÓN, SANTO
DOMINGO.

captivated. They began an illicit courtship that amounted to no more than exchanging a few torrid notes until they were discovered and Trujillo beat the poor letter carrier with a whip. Her stepmother was horrified at the match, calling Rubirosa a "playboy, corrupt, a boy with no future." However, in an about-face to avoid the appearance of impropriety, Trujillo quickly made nuptial arrangements. With their partnership now rendered respectable, Flor and Rubi were showered with gifts, including scores of diamond earrings, a Packard with their initials engraved in gold, and a respectable dowry of $50,000 from dad.[21] Rubi was made undersecretary in the foreign office, basically a "protocol job with no real responsibilities." Besides polo, his great passion, Rubi spent most of his time boxing. But with their "surface *savoir-faire*," they were often asked to host foreign VIPs.

Later Rubi was posted as first secretary to the Dominican legation in Germany in 1937, just as Hitler was consolidating power. Rubi as usual spent his time at fencing lessons and *parrandas*, or marathon parties, and his fame as a lover, athlete, and big spender began to grow in Europe. In Germany, their marriage crumbled as Flor discovered he was cheating on her. But there was another issue at stake as well, which she revealed in a note to her father, "I am not happy here, the secretaries are all leftists, they only invite us to the popular dances. . . . I don't have the chance to meet anyone."[22] Flor found German bourgeois culture impenetrable and was rejected out of hand. She asked daddy for help in finding an escape route, and he came through, inviting her to be his personal representative at the coronation of George VI in London, where Porfirio met the king. Rubi was assigned as chargé d'affaires at the Paris embassy. As Flor wrote, "Moyneaux was then THE great dressmaker of Paris and I had *carte blanche* to spend $3,500 on a coronation dress of pink lamé. At the garden party for the new British King and Queen, I felt that the peasant from San Cristóbal had arrived."[23]

The marriage broke up, nonetheless, and the two parted ways. Although Flor went on to remarry eight times, including a respectable doctor in Santo Domingo, a Brazilian mining baron, her psychiatrist in New York, a French perfumer, a Cuban fashion designer, and eventually a U.S. Air Force pilot, she continued to pine for Rubi. In fact, they had a couple of later trysts that caused friction for their respective spouses. After her third husband died, she decided to become a "career girl" and was named first secretary to the Dominican consul in New York in 1944, and later minister to the American embassy. And she was quite a hit in the American society pages as the first woman ever to hold a position of such stature in the diplomatic corps. She was lauded for her freshness (she was only twenty-six), dynamism, elegance, and sophistication: the country was heralded for its foresight in "recognizing the value of both youth and femininity in high diplomatic circles." It was said that she brought "brilliance . . . [and] dashing soignée to Embassy Row . . . she dresses with an elegance once thought to belong only to Paris. She wears her magnificent jewels and luxurious furs with exquisite taste."[24]

Her image changed somewhat as she sought to accommodate a professional image, though. While at first her photos showcased her extravagant costumes, such as Flor relaxing at home in a nutria coat with yard-long sleeves, in a few months she had shifted to a streamlined, "no frills, no jewels—no dress-up whatever . . . utterly zing-smart" look of gabardine suits and limited accessories.[25] Flor, through her consumption of fashion,

16. Flor Trujillo captures the imagination of the U.S. press. *TIMES-HERALD*, 28 JANUARY 1944.

came to represent a kind of model modern subject, both to American society watchers and Dominicans back at home.[26] And by impeccably following the codes of fashion, a girl with a mulatto background, with a father who was an unseemly dictator, was allowed an entrée into New York society. Although United States columnists puritanically frowned at Flor's intrepidity in housing husband number five under husband number four's roof (even temporarily before their divorce went through), they nonetheless praised her brazen willingness to "go her own romantic way, free and unchecked, regardless of the frowns of her sire," since, as they noted, she may have been the sole individual willing to brave his wrath.[27] But certainly they could find no fault with her style—even if she occasionally skipped town on her monumental Saks Fifth Avenue bills.

Rubirosa also started his rapid ascent up the international status ladder. After a brief period of alienation from Trujillo owing to his mistreatment of Flor and their divorce, he was reinstated in the Dominican foreign service in Belgium and Paris (where he remained during the Vichy government);

later he was assigned to Italy, Argentina, and Cuba. After a run-in with the Gestapo which forced him to go into hiding in Switzerland until the end of the war, he became renowned as a bon vivant and consummate playboy through his marriage to Danielle Darrieux, the French actress and bomb-shell of the 1930s considered at the time the most beautiful woman in the world. His notoriety grew as a jet-set subculture became established in Europe, as the rich looked to *la vie bohème* as a way of forgetting the horrors of the war. The playboy as a social type had been a product of the unemployment and social dislocation of World War I, as upper-class youths without skills suddenly lost everything as a result of war and the Depression. A subcultural style took shape that drew upon lower-class dandyism, the sexual aggressiveness and narcissism of the hipster, and, to a lesser extent, the cult of the Negro, as jazz clubs became favored venues for the idle rich.[28] Paris became the mecca for this sybaritic subculture of hedonists and the rich; they were drawn to the late-night *boites* of Mont-martre, where Latin men-for-hire led women in the tango, thus giving rise to the phenomenon of *vividores*—Latin men such as Rudolph Valentino, the "sloe-eyed seducer" of celluloid, who were "glamorous in a sinister fashion."[29] As Shawn Levy explains, Paris in the 1920s was a golden age for the Latin man, who was seen as the *"ne plus ultra* of male sexual allure." This subspecies of libidinous male came to be known as the Latin Lover, and his "music, manners, dark looks and sultry ways were celebrated in the media."[30] Rubirosa thrived in this context. While much of his career was in Paris, in the 1950s his amorous attentions became tethered to Hollywood and the United States. He had torrid affairs with the actresses Zsa Zsa Gabor and Kim Novak, and later married two American heiresses, both ranked among a handful of the world's richest women: Doris Duke, who inherited an estimated three hundred million dollars in trusts from her father, head of American Tobacco (more than $3.15 billion in 2005 terms); and Barbara Hutton, who inherited the Woolworth fortune. Rubirosa's excessive sexuality was matched only by their excessive wealth.[31]

What was the secret to the "legendary Latin lover," this "boudoir menace of two continents"? For one, Claus von Bülow found him "marvelous."[32] On the eve of his marriage to Barbara Hutton, Zsa Zsa declared him "charming, exciting, volatile," despite wearing a patch to hide a black eye he had given her in a row over his final exit from their relationship. Indeed, the Hungarian actress even exonerated Rubirosa, claiming that "a man only strikes a woman when he loves her intensely."[33] Others said: "The Dominican playboy is not

17. Playboy-diplomat
Porfirio Rubirosa, 1954.
BY PERMISSION OF
CORBIS.

handsome, but has great personal sweetness and physical magnetism." "Rubi was shrewd, manipulative, amusing, self-confident, debonair. He was an easy conversationalist with a continental accent and a sensual voice."[34] Although he was not without detractors (who often called him an impostor, a status-seeking "black"), women generally defended him. As one reporter countered, "The Dominican Don Juan is no shoeless, flop-eared peasant, as has been whispered"; rather, he is "a short, slim-waisted smoothie, swarthy and sophisticated, a veritable Caribbean and Continental Casanova, full of animal vitality."[35] Barbara Hutton, heiress and former wife, declared: "He is the ultimate sorcerer, capable of transforming the most ordinary evening into a night of magic . . . priapic, indefatigable, grotesquely proportioned."[36] By all accounts most people who met him were bewitched. A gossip columnist reported that "a friend says he has the most perfect manners she has ever encountered. He wraps his charm around your shoulders like a Russian sable coat."[37]

While Trujillo censored Rubi for some of his scandals, he also rewarded him by giving him ever higher positions as his conquests became more dramatic. For example, though Rubi was stripped of his credentials after sullying the country's name when he was named in two divorces, he was mysteriously reappointed to Paris after his marriage to Doris Duke. Trujillo's attitude changed a bit, though, as his son Ramfis, the dynastic inheritor, was drawn into the jet-set orbit. Ramfis, who studied at the War College in Fort Leavenworth, Texas, was introduced to Hollywood society by Porfirio, his close friend. Ramfis lacked Rubi's irresistible charm, so he used his dad's line of credit to ingratiate himself with women. He bestowed a Mercedes and a $17,000 chinchilla coat on Zsa Zsa, his procuress; and he bought a lavender Benz, as well as various diamond-encrusted trifles, for the actress Kim Novak, with whom he was completely smitten. His big spending raised enough eyebrows, however, that it launched a congressional investigation into how U.S. military assistance to the Dominican Republic was being spent. As Congressman Hays railed, "Perhaps this federal aid should be paid directly into the bank accounts of Zsa Zsa Gabor and Kim Novak. At least that way we could get taxes on the money."[38] They even became fictive kin, since Rubi married Ramfis's sister, and Ramfis married a close Hungarian friend of Zsa Zsa Gabor's, Lita Milan. Ramfis, who had been treated like a king all his life, could not meet the academic challenge of the military academy and withdrew into *la vida licenciosa* of Hollywood after flunking out.

Trujillo held ambivalent sentiments over the notoriety of Rubi and Ramfis. On the one hand, he was thrilled to have his country represented in the international jet set. As Rhadamés Trujillo once commented, "Porfirio did a hell of a public-relations job for Santo Domingo. Few people had heard of the place until he came along."[39] Trujillo thrived on seeing Dominican personalities in the American gossip columns and society pages, especially during periods of bad press, such as the spate of bad publicity after the assassination of Jesús de Galíndez, a Columbia University lecturer, in a New York subway. Around this time, Trujillo actively courted Walter Winchell, the premier columnist, advocate, and arbiter of the international jet set in the 1950s, by sending him telegrams and even offering him a paid vacation in the Dominican Republic as a guest of the government.[40] He awarded the Order of Trujillo to María Montez, a lovely Dominican actress based in Hollywood, in recognition of her role in fostering good U.S.-Dominican relations through her success in Hollywood.[41] And when he discovered that an attractive and svelte Dominican from a prominent family was modeling Colgate toothpaste in the United States, Trujillo recruited him into the regime and treated him like his own son.[42]

While Trujillo appreciated having his country associated with women, wealth, and high society, he did censor Ramfis's behavior when it crossed the line into debauchery. For example, he wrote him an irate letter, "The fewer Latinos you receive that run around in the '*aventurero*' world, the better."[43] He then silently but disdainfully enclosed a news clipping (written by the Universal Press Syndicate but published in a Dominican paper) about an "elegant" party Zsa Zsa was hosting for Ramfis and other Dominican military men in Hollywood, for which she was preparing champagne and caviar bars.

Porfirio Rubirosa became the son Trujillo wished he had, a far more debonair and successful version of Ramfis. Trujillo used Rubi as an elegant adornment, forcing him to stand behind him at ceremonial occasions in the early days as his presidential guard (a job Porfirio detested). On several occasions, Trujillo protected him by intervening directly into Rubirosa's affairs to help him save face. An example occurred when a group of New York authorities called into question the legality of the Rubirosa-Hutton union, alleging that the couple had not had the requisite blood test. The Dominican government saved the day by declaring Hutton a Dominican citizen, which legalized the marriage (Porfirio also hoped this might enable circumvention of her prenuptial agreement). Needless to say, Dominicans were extremely pleased to welcome the rich and beautiful Hutton to Dominicanidad. Unfortunately, however, the international press often forgot Porfirio's nationality, calling him instead a generic "Latin" or even "Mexican" or "Central American," much to Trujillo's chagrin.[44] Apart from admiring Rubi's female catches, Trujillo most likely revered his lifestyle and coveted his possessions, such as his Parisian West Bank chateau, a three-story, seventeenth-century mansion replete with an army of meticulously uniformed servants, a porcelain collection, and a fully equipped gymnasium, as well as an entire floor of polo equipment and polo, boxing, and car-racing trophies. In this house he had entertained international celebrities from Frank Sinatra to the Kennedys to the Rothschilds to European and even Japanese royalty. He also had a stable of polo ponies and a converted B-25 bomber (refitted with brass, mahogany, a leather-paneled bathroom, and even a bedroom) which he kept for personal excursions. Like James Dean, Rubi died in action. In 1965 he was killed at age fifty-six in his Ferrari in a crash on the Bois de Bologne, as he would have wished.

If Trujillo could not actually be Rubirosa, at least he could profit from him. In a bizarre twist, Trujillo sought to capture and market some of

Rubirosa's sex appeal overseas. In 1956 an article (planted by Trujillo) appeared in an American magazine touting the virtues of a native Dominican vine for erectile dysfunction. Trujillo most likely picked up this popular herbal concoction from Dominican herbalists (*curanderos*), for whom it was a widely prescribed tonic. The government went on to trademark the wild vine (which came from the Haitian border) as an aphrodisiac; Trujillo produced it in his own factory and found a Texas firm to market and distribute *Pega Palo Fortidom* in the United States.[45] Adorned with Rubirosa's portrait and name, this "elixir of virility" created a veritable male craze in the United States, one clearly grounded in Rubirosa's notoriety as a lover; it also created an active black market among National Palace staff, who secretly siphoned liquid from vessels of the elixir for sale; it even inspired drinks, jokes, and merengue refrains.

> Work? It's impossible for me to work.
> I just don't have the time.
> I am and will be a man of pleasure.
> Porfirio Rubirosa

TRUJILLO, THE TÍGUERE

The story of Flor and Porfirio captures more than high drama. As a Trujillista family romance it is also allegorical—a story encapsulating a lesson about the moral boundaries of state power. It is also a narrative that demonstrates the accumulated "symbolic capital" of Trujillo and his family, the part-flâneur, part-tíguere, part-Horatio Alger myth of the regime. Trujillo had little personal charisma to speak of; portly in his later years, he was fiery, enigmatic, and had a notoriously squeaky voice. But he gained prestige in the Dominican Republic through his ability to achieve absolute power and wealth from a socially marginal, mulatto, provincial background.[46] He was "every man," even though he became a member of the global ultra-rich via his monopolization of the economy, which some have proposed reached as high as 60 percent of all arable land and 80 percent of all business.[47] He also refused to play the deferent client of the United States. However, there were limits to Trujillo's achievement. He simply was not chic enough to enter the ranks of the international jet set (nor did he have time). But the second generation clearly could join the jet set, and did.

Flor, Ramfis, and Porfirio embodied the ascendancy of a new class lifestyle, a novel means of distinction, which privileged achieved rather than ascribed criteria.[48] The old aristocracy had marked their superiority through the metaphor of "blood," which indexed filiation with the respectable families of the interior town of Santiago or Santo Domingo, the capital, and expressed an ideal type of phenotypical whiteness or "purity of blood." In this predominantly mulatto society, race and class were inextricably associated and mutually reinforcing. The closed character of the old elite can be seen in the proclivity of the old families for cousin marriage, which was the norm into the 1930s, particularly in the interior. The old elite looked to Paris as cultural beacon; after World War II, this role shifted to the United States.[49] However, even as things American became the vogue, Dominicans chose selectively and reinterpreted the styles, practices, and commodities they consumed. For example, the cultural markers of the new state elite of the Trujillato were not primarily in the realm of domestic consumption, as was the rage among the Yankees. The new Dominican jet set in the 1950s did not buy home appliances, or mow lawns, or spend their leisure time in coffee klatches and barbecues as was the norm in the United States—neither Flor nor Porfirio had stable homes, much less babies.[50] Their success amid the tawdry Hollywood jet set meant so much owing to what Claudio Lomnitz calls "peripheral cosmopolitanism"—a deep sense of inferiority resulting from a history of colonialism and foreign intervention.[51] No one felt this sting more deeply than Trujillo, whose career commenced under the direct tutelage of the United States, at a time when marines sat in the National Palace and collected customs revenues, and the U.S. dollar circulated as currency. Even though Trujillo cast himself as a grand nationalist, pushing foreign firms out of key agro-industries such as rice and sugar (so that he could take them over), his prized gift to his beloved children and key cronies were American cars. He gifted Flor and Rubi with a Packard, his personal favorite, and important Dominican Party hacks received Chevrolets.

Trujillo was the ultimate transgressor of the rules of the game for both race and class. Thus, he fulfilled the dream of the tíguere, the mythic paragon of barrio masculinity who gains power—riches, women, control over others—apparently from nothing (even if he was not technically a tíguere since his operative theater was the state, not the popular underworld; the national palace, not the barrio).[52] Trujillo was particularly proud of his high-status female acquisitions from Santiago, site of the traditional aristocracy, and frequently bragged about them. As he boasted to Paino Pichardo, "You don't know what it is to love, because you haven't loved in Santiago. You don't know what it is to love greatly, because you have loved only one woman."[53] He preferred plump white girls, symbols of affluence in this still rural society.

Like the caudillo, the tíguere is by definition a non-institutionalized form of power. According to Mark Padilla, it "indexes a kind of self-serving opportunism, deception or avarice that is simultaneously disparaged and valorized."[54] It means belonging to the *hampa*, or underworld, the informal sector where work provides cash but not a desirable identity—occupations such as market vendors, part-time haulers, mechanics, dock workers, gigolos, and thieves who prefer to be known for their skill at card games, their ferocity, their good looks.[55] It is intrinsically an urban phenomenon because it expresses marginality and anonymity, even if a true tíguere should be able to seamlessly navigate both the underworld and the world of society.[56] Trujillo was not born to rule; as a mulatto from a poor family with little education he had access to power but not authority.[57] Yet with his penchant for horses, he cut a profile at times too rural for a true tíguere and too *fino* or *elegante* (read white); he was too *pulcro*, too clean, for a true *tíguere callejero*.[58] On the other hand, he could qualify as a *tiguerazo* because of the way he brought criminality into the hallowed corridors of the state.[59]

The tíguere is the classic dissimulator, someone who gains access to a station above his own through dressing for the part, through the appropriate style, but also through being bold, a smooth talker, and having a "predatory masculine" presence.[60] As Antonio de Moya describes it, "*Tigueraje* is a life style and an attitude that combines the extreme traits of masculinity according to the street culture: slyness, courage, aggressiveness, indiscriminate sexual relations. . . . This perspective is associated predominantly with transgressive popular class values and norms . . . the *tíguere* is an ambiguous male, astute, courageous, smart, cunning and convincing."[61]

As Lipe Collado notes, there are several substyles of tigueraje, however.[62] Trujillo gained power through political control and a large dose of violence; his bravery, manliness (*hombría*), athletic build, status as a *mujeriego* or womanizer. and especially his capacity for ruthlessness might have qualified him as a *tíguere gallo* (a tiger-cock). His violence was transgressive, an outsider's means to power that he was forced to resort to owing to his lack of legitimacy. Trujillo brought tigueraje into the National Palace, creating a political culture of Mafioso-style gangsterism and dirty tricks, one steeped in duplicity and delinquency and "Olympic machismo."[63] That said, Trujillo's masculinity was somewhat ambivalent, however, since his use of makeup, penchant for making a spectacle of himself through extravagant costumes, extreme vanity, and rumored male liaisons indicate a certain feminization in the popular imagination.[64]

Porfirio Rubirosa became a legend because he seemed to thrive through his skills as a dramatis persona, especially his ability to deliver an exquisite performance of the hot Latin lover à la Rudolph Valentino.[65] Yet he got his start as a tíguere near San Lázaro church in the colonial zone by putting up boxing matches for two centavos in 1929. Shirtless, he would sit on the sidewalk, whistling and making cat calls to the women passing by, already by age twenty-one a champion in the art of *piropeando*, or verbal flattery.[66] Well before his status as an international playboy he is remembered as a grand poseur who would ostentatiously smoke cigarettes in the park of San Francisco de Macoris even when he could not possibly have paid for them.[67] He hung out with those who frequented the bordellos, prostitutes, and boxers—the lowlife of Santo Domingo—before the U.S. Marines tried to clean them up; he probably would have remained a *barriobajero* were it not for his extraordinary charm and Trujillo's patronage. His magnetic physical attraction, talents as a dissimulator, seductive speech, hyperactive sexuality, and success in conquering women might have qualified him for the epithet *tíguere bimbim* (bimbim is a diminutive for penis), a person of low origins with tremendous sex appeal (*guapetón*) and a touch of narcissism, who gets away with murder (*pendenciero*). As a master of the streets, a partier, boxer, dancer, one who was brave, elegant, educated, attractive, cunning, and ready to show off (*dispuesto a hacerse notar*), he would at least qualify as a *chulo* (hustler).[68] Porfirio surpassed Trujillo in international renown, whereas Trujillo's audience was principally domestic. Yet both were renowned as shameless womanizers and flawless dressers. They were both grand dissimulators, smooth operators, dandies, and *mujeriegos*.[69]

While the tíguere as a mythic figure always appears alone—it is by definition an individual—a larger sociological transformation was at work behind these individual rogue-hero success stories. Trujillo, Porfirio, Flor, and Ramfis expressed a logic of social prestige in which distinction was accorded to those "near the center of things," those in the social gaze.[70] The message of the Trujillista jet set of the 1950s was that "blood" lineage was meaningless; what counted was having style and cash to burn, the ticket of entree to the transnational Hollywood subculture. In this world, social capital was based less on who you were, but on "being there," looking the part, and having a connection to the regime. While access to those spaces of prestige depended on plenty of capital, money, it seems, could also make origin, ethnicity, and even nationality melt away.[71]

HISTORIES OF TIGUERAJE

The historical roots of tigueraje lay in the relatively open social order of the Dominican Republic that was forged largely outside of the agro-industrial sugar plantation. Slave imports were terminated as early as the seventeenth century due to colonial poverty; many former slaves were able to escape the plantations and mines and establish their own *hatos*, or small cattle farms, or live outside the market economy through subsistence agricultural production. In the seventeenth and eighteenth centuries, a thriving contraband economy emerged in which freedmen provided smoked meat and tobacco to buccaneers and pirates, some of the most wealthy and powerful of whom were freedmen themselves. Indeed, the very term *tíguere* appears to first emerge within this lucrative but illegal and hazardous maritime economy (based on La Tortuga island off the coast of Hispaniola), since La Tigre was the name of a French privateer vessel in 1762.[72] The social category of tíguere in the twentieth century was the Creole of the sixteenth, the freed slave of the seventeenth, and the mulatto of the eighteenth—all figures of difference that threatened the social hierarchy through their status as strangers who had more latitude for movement in the social order than everyone else.

Unlike the rigid social order of colonial Haiti or Cuba, the Dominican Republic developed maximal racial mixture and minimal class differentiation because cattle ranching, logging, and coffee and tobacco cultivation, not sugar and plantation slavery, formed the backbone of the economy until the nineteenth century. Slave escape in this context was relatively easy owing to low population density. Indeed, by the eighteenth century, the Dominican peasantry was primarily composed of free blacks and mulattos who subsisted on the margins of social order through shifting cultivation, hunting, and occasional wage labor.[73] By 1780 in the neighboring French colony of Saint Domingue, *mulatto* had shifted from being a racial term to a status marker connoting people of color who were above slaves; thus *mulatto* and *affranchi* (emancipated slave) had become synonymous.[74] The meaning of mixed-race as an emblem of non-servility, as a popular form of distinction, resonated in the Spanish colony where slaves were a minority.

Indeed, the term *tíguere* may have crossed the border with Haitian troops' discovery of the unknown ways of the east. The term first entered the argot of the Haitian troops stationed in Santo Domingo during the Haitian occupation (1822–44). This might account for the curious extended "r" in its colloquial pronunciation as tíguere, since it originated in Haitian Kreyol, which typically slurs that sound. It referred to children of the capital city who roamed in packs and were tough, streetwise survivors.[75] The tíguere as outsider then harbors some of the dangers and secrets associated with Haiti, which until the twentieth century was richer, more cosmopolitan, and stronger in military terms, and associated with slavery, revolution, and the transformative powers of magic and money—all things that its poorer Spanish-speaking neighbor lacked.[76]

In the novel *Eusebio Sapote*, which supposedly takes place in the mid-nineteenth century, Sapote is a traveler who arrives on Dominican shores, a stranger who appears to be concealing secrets.[77] In fact this *tarado*, a precursor to the tíguere, is defined by his powers of dissimulation.[78] Ever the chameleon, he is unknowable, even to himself. Sapote arrives in Santo Domingo in 1859 on a contraband vessel from Curaçao; his gambling skills bring him fast money. When he later becomes a mercenary spy, his political affiliations are infinitely changeable and his allegiance is with anyone who offers him patronage. Preferring the night, he is an expert at forgery; his ability to present a respectable self gives him the ship captain's endorsement, which eventually lands him a room with a society landlady. His association with people of social standing enables him to frame himself as a person of stature, which eventually secures him a wife *de apellido*. As a man who appears white but has some underclass characteristics associated with blackness, Sapote congeals many elite Dominican stereotypes about mestizo identity—through his hidden violence and *rencor* or bitterness (Sapote carries a concealed switchblade), his disguised degeneracy (as a tarado or dolt with sallow skin, anemia, and misshapen cranium) and thus potential as a Lombrosian criminal man, his sterility as a product of race mixture, his agelessness, his hypocrisy, and last but not least, his "potent masculinity," perhaps from his trace of blackness.[79] Located outside of "natural law," he is a monster.[80] He is also passionate, full of animal magnetism, a man-of-words whom women find hypnotically enchanting and irresistible. Sapote conforms to the logic of the tíguere since he inverts colonial rule by scaling the social ladder through the conquest of a woman of a higher social order; through his matrimony to this "flower of the aristocracy," this "gypsy of the wharfs" is transformed and accorded social personhood.[81]

The tíguere figure is transgressive because it crosses borders; as a traveler in social space it conveys the wonder of distant lands or the lure of other social worlds. It thus combines nearness and remoteness in a way that harnesses the power of the foreign, both black and white.[82] It is implicitly racialized, since audacious tígueres can be European but should then be described as white tígueres, such as the notorious admiral Christopher Columbus, who has been called the first *tíguere blanco*.[83] This indicates that the tíguere is Creole, and thus part black. The official tígueres and darlings of the Trujillato such as Porfirio Rubirosa and María Montez radiated duly American images—the Hollywood playboy and the starlet. This subculture drew upon a lifestyle and pattern of consumption that was defined by new money and acquired even more luster from afar. These tígueres fashioned themselves as virtually white through their fashion, parties, and wives, but Eusebio Sapote had a secret—he used sorcery. And the truth hidden behind that secret is that he thus had access to the superior powers of Haitian magic. He may have appeared white, but he could access black magic as a *comprabrujo* who manipulated politicians by scripting counsel for their spiritual advisors. As is typically the case in devil pact narratives, this secret ultimately does Sapote in; it makes him rich, it gets him a wife, but it depletes him in the end.[84] Like the tíguere then, he looks white but actually has a trace of invisible blackness; in true mestizo fashion he is an unstable dual combination. Like the tíguere, he also draws upon the twin sources of power that are near and remote, foreign and domestic, Europe (later the United States) and Haiti.[85]

While the social and economic fluidity of the colonial economy created multiple opportunities for individual achievement, it also generated strong anxieties over the boundaries defining class and racial strata. The other side of the logic of passing in a mestizo culture was anxiety over lineage. Since everyone had a potential claim to whiteness, the white minority struggled to maintain a bulwark against penetration of the racial frontier from below. As a result, the free mulatto in the Dominican Republic became a locus of fear and revulsion representing the antithesis of the civilized colonial order. In 1780, these fears were confirmed by a bandit called "the Unknown Black" (*el Negro Incógnito*) or "the Cannibal" (*el Comegente*), a mulatto who killed, injured, and pillaged, preying almost exclusively on sugar plantations and their property—slaves, harvests, and farm animals. As a result of this wave of terror, colonial authorities suggested an imposed relocation scheme whereby rural blacks and mulattos would be forced to reside within townships.

The objective was to eliminate the black rural subculture that evaded subjection by the colonial state and that stood outside the community of citizens. In the words of one official, "The free blacks are the worst; they cannot be reasoned with . . . they are the cause and origin of all the damage that is committed and that can occur on the Island. These blacks are for the most part wanderers, confused, concubines, drunks and thieves."[86]

It is not coincidental that the dangers of the mulatto were spatialized, seen as deriving from rootlessness and vagrancy, and that the prescribed antidote was forced residence in a township since colonial society was defined by spatial location. The danger of the mulatto lay in its ability to move out of the ranch or *finca* and into the city, and thus across the social hierarchy, and particularly in its ability to pass for white after acquiring capital or adopting elite demeanor. Just as prohibitions emerged against interracial marriage in colonial Cuba when transgressions peaked, colonial injunctions emerged in eighteenth-century Santo Domingo against free blacks who dressed above their rank and wore pearls, gold, or silk, in an effort to circumscribe a love of finery that poor Creole colonists had difficulty matching.[87] Laws prohibited freedmen from professions such as notaries, secretaries, the judiciary, the civil service, and the military; they were a response to the fact that freedmen, by the early years of the eighteenth century, had made such successful inroads in formerly Spanish professions such as teaching and the priesthood.[88] The mid-eighteenth century was also a high point for the founding of *cofradías*, Catholic lay societies that enabled Afro-Dominicans to claim a measure of respectability and thus status in a context in which resident parish priests in rural areas were very rare.[89] This might have been what the late-eighteenth-century traveler Moreau de St. Mery meant by his cryptic remark, "The political construction of the Spanish colony does not allow deference before the civil status of a white and a freedman," or William Walton's shock at the arresting "hauteur and overbearing pride" he encountered among Spanish Creoles, who refused to play their part as grateful former slaves.[90]

Free blacks throughout the colonial Caribbean in general felt little in common with their black brethren and sought every opportunity to proclaim their superiority to slaves. For example, the royal slaves of El Cobre in Cuba developed a sanctuary and eventually a municipality, their pueblo status giving them a kind of legal personhood or virtual citizenship which they cherished as a marker of rank.[91] In colonial Havana, urban *negros curros* expressed their difference through a distinctive appearance that included plaited hair, gold earrings, filed teeth, straw hats, bellbottoms, and even knives crafting a look of "defiant self-possession."[92]

On colonial Hispaniola, freedmen and slaves were worlds apart. Spanish freedmen joined the *maréchaussée*, the militia that hunted runaways, while in Haiti wealthy mulattos owned slaves. By the late eighteenth century in the Spanish colony of Santo Domingo, in sharp contrast to neighboring colonies, mestizos outnumbered slaves by a third, the numbers of both greatly outstripping whites.[93] "Racial drift" from mestizo to white was surely facilitated by the fact that, because of poverty, colonial Santo Domingo had fewer European migrants than neighboring Haiti or Cuba. An observer reported that by 1780 most of the "Spanish" colonists were actually mestizos.[94] Freedman insolence was not merely a result of demographics, however; it may also have been a result of relative affluence since the thriving contraband economy could be quite lucrative. In the freebooting economy of the seventeenth century, Spanish colonial freedmen became very wealthy as corsairs, with mulattos amassing small fortunes in slaves, wax, dye, and cannons.[95]

The same historical openness that created multiple opportunities for individual achievement by the freedman eventually gave rise to the culture of tigueraje, the popular valorization of those who fashioned themselves as "big men" through the accumulation of the comportment and accouterments of status—women, attire, bravado—without the ascribed criteria, the apellido, or family, class, or racial identity. The tíguere wore a uniform and an attitude, which reached out of the hampa and into the cinema, park, and salon with a desire to be seen and a "secret respect for himself."[96] As Rafael Damirón recounts, the tíguere is a charmer who talks his way into places he doesn't belong through "verbosity, charlatanism [and] . . . a false lyricism."[97] The tíguere is not given prestige, he steals it. "Born like rats"[98] in revolt against a bourgeois morality that views them as "matter out of place,"[99] as social filth that should remain at the margins, the tíguere is a man of the public sphere who frequents the cafe, the hotel, the theater. A Cuban cabaret performer of the 1920s through the 1940s remembers the tíguere as one who "dressed in white, with a straw hat, a red ebony cane, silver cuff links, the gift of gab, but tigers." Here the tíguere is associated with the worlds of politics and theater, both zones of dissimulation, where "savages in tuxes" lurked; he is the male equivalent of the "vamp, the rascal, the femme fatale."[100]

The tíguere is without a fixed home or official identity (save to the police); he ridicules the status economy of society, snubbing education or culture as modes of advancement. The tíguere can operate outside the rules of society, because he seeks only the respect and approval of his barrio, of *la gente*, the people. While the mulatto trickster had been popular throughout Dominican history, it was only during the Trujillo period that the figure of the tíguere became generalized—the hero and man of the people, the "typical Dominican character par excellence."[101] This was largely due to the elevation, notoriety, and prestige ascribed to it within the Trujillo regime.

To Dominican elites, the classic tíguere is a dissimulator; he inspires fear as a stranger whose identity resides solely in his appearance. Elites perceive the importance of clothes in tíguere self-fashioning as a ruse, an expression of duplicity, and a threat to conventional standards of masculinity. He constructs himself as a self-conscious object of the gaze, a position only appropriate to women. Thus when the insular aristocracy in the 1930s closed ranks against Trujillo, it was apt that a sartorial metaphor was deployed; as one observer put it, "it was the military dress that was accepted, not the man wearing it."[102] Elite disdain became clear at Trujillo's wedding in 1929 to the patrician Bienvenida Ricardo, from a *familia de primera* (society family). Trujillo is remembered as having an alluring, enigmatic, and disconcerting air about him, with a reputation as a covetous adventurer —a man not averse to taking risks. He was described as elegant, "impeccably dressed, with a sensual mouth and the look of a 'film star more than a military [man].'" At society events girls loved him (nicknamed *las Correa*, the belts, for their attraction to men in uniform), but their parents rejected him as a trickster, with his "incommensurable vanity" and his "false and cunning" airs.

Trujillo's identity as an imposter was unmasked at the wedding in a gesture that became emblematic of his outsider status. Refusing the cake cutter, he used his sword (solid gold) to cut the first slice and inadvertently sent the finely decorated wedding cake, replete with delicate hand-crafted sugar flowers and baroquely adorned with lace, angels, and figurines, crashing down, smashing even the mirror serving as its base.[103] This event embodied to the guests his thinly submerged cruelty and also revealed his status as a stranger to the rules of Dominican high society. Many elites feared that as a poor mulatto who rose from the dregs of society, Trujillo was "resentful" (*resentido*), and they dreaded that he would wage war against the society from which he felt excluded (in popular terms, the revenge of the underdog after his arrival is part of the heroic myth of tigueraje).[104] This saying from Rubirosa's autobiography neatly encapsulates these fears: "It's necessary to be a tíguere to command a group of tígueres."

BLACK MEN IN UNIFORM

Trujillo was notorious for his attention to dress, his penchant for uniforms, and his immaculate grooming; indeed, his passion for medals earned him the sobriquet *chapita* (bottle cap).[105] In 1930, most Dominican poor dressed in humble attire, wearing denim and lacking shoes, yet Trujillo earned the highest marks from the U.S. Marines for his wearing of and caring for uniforms.[106] Indeed, when Trujillo sought to induct Porfirio Rubirosa in his personal guard (*edecan*), he first introduced him to his personal tailor and shoemaker.[107] Trujillo alternated between the uniforms of the army, navy, and air force (while studiously avoiding those of the lowly police).[108] He preferred his photographic portraits and busts to portray him with a chest full of medals, the more foreign and flashier the better. He circulated them carefully so as to array them all; he made their receiving ceremonies highly public photo opportunities, with the photos accompanied by sycophantic articles describing the honors in floral language, often in the name of the Virgin of Altagracia.[109] He both fashioned and signed into law the extraordinary uniform which he wore on solemn occasions: a Napoleonic bicorn hat, with two canes and white gloves. It had real gold trim from hat to shoes and weighed a full twelve kilos (over twenty-six pounds).[110] Previously, members of the military dressed simply in peasant attire and a Panama hat; they rarely wore uniforms and were virtually indistinguishable from the masses.[111] Trujillo's extravagant love for uniforms has been treated as a measure of his psychopathy, yet he drew upon a tradition of black royalism that is an important feature of African American cultures, especially in the Caribbean.

Trujillo's uniform had a historical genealogy indexing a special relationship to the crown during the colonial period, one which provided a basis for the free black militia's sense of itself as unique. This sense of superior status was expressed by dress demonstrating a sense of entitlement as well as by epithets such as "capitán."[112] Royalist iconography appears in many popular religious forms in the Caribbean, which draw upon signs of royalty to consecrate a sense of superiority through coronation rituals and references. Haitian sodalities such as Gagá (known as Rará in Haiti), which emerge during holy week and have mock stick fights over territory in the sugar zones, for example, crown public queens, even if they are secret societies, and Cuban *cabildos* (neo-African associations) incorporate many symbols of monarchy, including thrones and other emblems.[113] Yet the royalism evidenced in Trujillo's costume had a special significance, since it harkens back to the Haitian revolution, which provides a unique iconography of black military heroism. Dressing in the costume of Haitian military generals enabled political leaders to cast themselves as epic warriors who descended from commanding black personages who had successfully defined a nationalist project.[114]

The passion for ornate uniforms in the Dominican Republic has other roots as well. Dandyism seems to have been a feature of the eighteenth-century rural militia, which, as Governor de la Rocha lamented, was "composed of mulatto and cheap people who tend to be attracted by ostentation and vanities, who pay ten thousand *doblones* for a uniform with ample braid and brass, and who ostentatiously insist on the title of *capitán, colonel, maestre de campo*, etc."[115] The popularity of the militia as a means of status marking may help account for the fact that colonial Santo Domingo had a disproportionately large military, with 127 military personnel to each 1,000 inhabitants, four times that of Cuba or Chile.[116] The tiny endogamous white elite, however, tightly restricted access to military privileges, or *fueros*, causing some slaves from the Spanish colony to travel to the neighboring French colony of Saint Domingue, where they could secure titled positions in the colonial free black militia and earn their emancipation after one year of service.[117] The French colonial military leadership also had a penchant for uniforms, alongside weapons and horses—indeed, their swords could include gold hilts.[118] While the two colonial militias were officially enemies, the flourishing intra-island contraband trade in cattle products, which grew throughout the eighteenth century, made them de facto behind-the-scenes collaborators and friends.[119] And members of both militias seem to have viewed participation as a means of facing down the racism and stereotypes of laziness and effeminacy associated with racial mixture. In uniform and on horseback, militia men pronounced their status as valiant and manly and superior to the lowly slave.[120] They protected their status through investing in social capital by creating fictive kin through godparentage as well as by legalizing economic transactions through notarization.[121]

The bicorn hat emerged as a symbol of sovereignty during the Haitian revolution. Toussaint Louverture may have adopted it when he was appointed Bonaparte's commander-in-chief; later, however, he declared for the Spanish and faced down Napoleon's brother-in-law Leclerc, who had been dispatched to Hispaniola to get rid of the "gilded Africans."[122] The hat became part of revolutionary symbolism when it passed to Jean-Jacques Dessalines and Henri Christophe, also veterans, although they removed the tricolor cockade, which represented French colonialism. Coming to power just after the revolution had ended, Christophe embellished his reign with further imperial iconography as an invented means of legitimating the new post-revolutionary northern black elite in the face of pretentious southern mulatto Francophilia. The north became a kingdom, replete with a nobility with court accouterments (including tunics, cloaks, stockings, shoes with gold detailing) and a royal palace in stone called Sans Souci, as Henri Christophe I, first republican king of Haiti, styled himself after George III, his "model monarch."[123] He introduced plumage into his courtly attire, and perhaps into the bicorn, which Dessalines shifted to a vertical rather than horizontal position.[124] Royalism achieved new heights under the regime of Faustin Soulouque, who was crowned emperor in 1849 after a failed effort to reclaim Santo Domingo.[125] The bicorn (worn horizontally) was also part of the uniform of the white Spanish colonial volunteer infantry; the *morenos* (mixed race) wore bowlers. It first appeared in the formal dress of a Dominican head of state with Ulises Heureaux in 1845, who was born during the Haitian occupation and whose father was Haitian.[126]

But what then are we to make of Trujillo's adoption of the bicorn? Trujillo saved his own ostrich-plumed bicorn for very formal occasions, when he dressed in full military regalia. He had a formidable wardrobe, said to be stocked with ten thousand neckties, two thousand suits and uniforms, and five hundred pairs of shoes, inviting comparisons among his supporters to the regal attire of Napoleon.[127] Yet for Trujillo, the bicorn was a unique status marker, an imperial emblem.[128] In this context it was inherently ambiguous since it held associations with black and white sovereignty, slave revolution and European monarchy, power and authority. Yet it was always connected with war and violence, a nation stolen back at the barrel of a gun that resulted in a community founded on bloodshed rather than civitas. Rather than reduce the bicorn to one meaning or another, it would be more appropriate for Dominican racial identity to try to come to terms with it as a composite symbol, a single object with various lines of signification—"internally heterogeneous, contradiction-ridden, and fundamentally polyvalent."[129] Trujillo himself was a complex composite. Although many have noted the racism evidenced by his brutal slaughter of Haitians in cold blood in 1937, Trujillo was also capable of presenting himself as mestizo. One revealing anecdote concerns Lilís's presidential sword, which Trujillo kept

18. Henri Christophe, king of
Haiti, 1811–20, with bicorn in
hand. ARCHIVO GENERAL DE LA
NACIÓN, SANTO DOMINGO.

as a special memento in his office. When showing it to two U.S. Marine
officers, he said, "This sword was used when the Republic was governed by
a black president, not by a mulatto like me."[130]

This story appears paradoxical given Trujillo's elaborate efforts at presenting himself as white. He used pancake makeup and had his photos
retouched to make him appear lighter-skinned; he frequently sought to
frame himself as white by ensuring that the elite military (such as the
Guardia Blanca) surrounding him on presidential visits were white (and
kept their heads covered) and sported crisp uniforms made in Miami.[131]
Since the military was an extension of Trujillo's person, this staging device
helped Trujillo provide the "social front" he desired.[132] Sycophantic minions also developed a fictitious noble Spanish lineage for him. And he often
tried to establish close proximity to things American, from scripting foreign diplomats in elaborate state spectacles to choreographing highly public official visits from U.S. notables, such as senators and the American
press, which conferred a certain whiteness upon him and his country.[133]

19. President Ulises Heureaux in military uniform. ARCHIVO GENERAL DE LA NACIÓN, SANTO DOMINGO.

20. President Rafael Trujillo in military uniform. ARCHIVO GENERAL DE LA NACIÓN, SANTO DOMINGO.

21. Rafael Trujillo in
civilian dress. KURT
SCHNITZER, CON-
RADO COLLECTION,
ARCHIVO GENERAL DE
LA NACIÓN, SANTO
DOMINGO.

Trujillo's obsessive concern with rendering a tableau of whiteness did
not result just from his own racial pathology, however. Trujillo's mother's
side was actually Haitian. His mother came from a wealthy Haitian free
mulâtre family, the Leonidas-Chevalier, who had moved to Santo Domingo
during the Haitian occupation and retained their Haitian nationality. Her
family had not a small measure of status in Haiti and the Dominican Republic. In Port-au-Prince, family members had close ties to the Haitian
governor. They were local notables in San Cristóbal, where they had church
weddings and where Leonidas Saladin Chevalier was president of the communal council; he is mentioned in the late-nineteenth-century social regis-
ter, *La República Dominicana: Directorio y Guía General*.[134] But the family
properties indicate assets that extended well beyond the confines of this
small provincial town, since it owned a two-story building on El Conde in
downtown Santo Domingo worth ten thousand pesos in 1848, as well as a
house facing the monastery in San Francisco, a property in Yaca, and a
substantial farm in San Jerónimo worth thirty-two hundred pesos at the

time.[135] The affranchis of Saint Domingue had been a formidable economic force during the colonial period, owning one third of the slaves and plantation property in the 1780s, and their pretentiousness and sense of superiority only increased after independence.[136] Thus Trujillo may have inherited a sense of entitlement and a resultant thirst for status enhancement from his famous Haitian forebears, who saw themselves as carriers of civilization and thus born to rule.

Trujillo's desire for whitening could also be seen as an exaggerated rendition of a culture of race that is common to mestizo societies, a culture with both instrumental and expressive dimensions. Since Creole society formed outside the plantation economy and slave inputs were minimal after the seventeenth century, the labor force was not characterized by the kind of ethnic segmentation found in colonial Cuba. The free colored (mixed-race) sector became the majority early on, giving rise to a system of status in which socioeconomic position was as important as appearance.[137] Yet even as Creoles formed the majority, they remained an interstitial group in the colonial order, left to distinguish themselves from the Spaniards and the African slaves after the elimination of the indigenous community.[138] Being mestizo could not offer an identity since it was not a social location. It was a pejorative label, a condition to flee, as was blackness, which of course carried the ultimate stigma of bondage and nonpersonhood. As Stuart Schwartz puts it, racial designations such as mestizo and mulatto were legal terms associated with occupation; they "were descriptors of origin but not separate categories of status."[139] This helps explain the extensive "racial drift" in the eighteenth century into the "Spanish" group, which absorbed a good portion of Creoles (especially women) over time for those whose "somatic norm image" enabled them to move for practical considerations.[140] It was not until the 1920s when processes of state formation and nationalism gave new positive connotations to mixed-race terms such as *criollo* and *indio*; under the Trujillo regime these terms came to connote membership in the modern nation state. Dominicans may have been more available to this trade-off between ethnicity and nationalism since the country lacks a heroic indigenous ethnicity to draw upon, because the indigenous groups of Tainos and Caribs did not survive the conquest.[141]

Traces of this culture of mestizaje remain salient today, such as the utilitarian logic of seeking social ascent where possible and the fact that skin color is perceived as just one criterion among several, including apellido or lineage, hair texture, eye color, and social class. Like the Andean figure of the cholo, the partially acculturated Indian, the mestizo is by definition transitional, in between, which is why it tends to split into its composite racial binaries.[142] Its sense of indeterminacy is apparent in the strategic calculation of multiple criteria in race marking, since no single marker is determinant. For example, race is conferred through lineage, but that is not a self-evident issue in a society in which matrifocality prevails and in which siblings can be of various shades. Claims to whiteness may be made in relation to an absent father, even if paternity is unclear or the child is illegitimate, or, for example, through a deceased white grandmother.[143] This explains a seemingly paradoxical comment such as "My parents are Spanish so even though I look like a *mulatta*, I am definitely *blanca*."[144] And individuals who believe they have fathers of some social prominence will go to great lengths to establish legal recognition.[145]

Indeed, notwithstanding the fact that Dominicans perceive themselves as living in a racial democracy in which "black and white are equal," coded markers of blackness such as illegitimacy carry an enormous burden of shame.[146] This is particularly striking since concubinage is so common, particularly in the countryside. A child without a patriline, it seems, is not a social person; being an *hijo natural* is to be not entirely located within society, to be a *don nadie* (mister nobody). Illegitimacy, the condition of lacking a second family name (which confers public identity as Marcel Mauss taught us), seems to invoke the stigma of the nonpersonhood of slavery, since the "doubled surname [is] the classic Iberian signal of legitimate descent."[147] Perhaps this may explain the preference for Greek and Roman names such as Diógenes, César, and Sócrates, which situate Dominicans squarely within a European heritage.

As Brackette Williams has observed, race is a "symbolic representation of status" that becomes manifest in the context of particular interactions.[148] This is particularly true in the case of mestizo identities, which are inherently unstable and thus shift in relation to "interpersonal assessments of status" between subjects, as well as other markers of social rank.[149] In this view, every interaction is a "ritual performance" in which status claims are made according to both individual and collective criteria, notions of moral worth based on face and name, as well as congealed stereotyped notions of region, ethnicity, and religion. Those who are lower in class terms are at a disadvantage in terms of proving their worth and have to work harder to do so.[150] This perspective can help interpret Rafael Trujillo's racial code shifting from white to mulatto in relation to different audiences, and the need to mark his superiority over Lilís when speaking to a higher-status interlocutor. The anecdote pertaining to the U.S. Marines and Lilís's sword is particularly striking since Trujillo was himself a U.S. Marine product and maintained a special relationship to them throughout his life. One means of framing himself as white was to emphasize his association with "Western civilization, modernity, upward mobility . . . the cash market"—which he did in large part via association with things American.[151] This strategy, of course, could not work in relation to an audience of marines. The sword episode is a poignant reminder of the deep humiliation that Trujillo masked but could not hide completely.

CONCLUSION

In a mestizo culture, class can trump race when, for example, brown Dominicans are reclassed as virtually white because they are educated and hold a white-collar job. Additionally, as Kuznesof has argued, in the colonial period the "stickiness" of one's racial identity was also determined by one's gender, since in a patrilineal system women acquired their personhood or public identity through their fathers and then their husbands, and thus could pass in ways that men could not.[152] Indeed, demography rendered women the points of articulation between the rigidly defined ethnic spaces of the colonial order as they shifted from Indians to *doñas* (or wives of Spaniards), and, in lieu of that, at least became mothers of their whitened offspring, a link which gave them access, however partial, to social personhood.[153] Frantz Fanon excoriated Antillean women for precisely this obsession; their fervent desire for what he called "lactification."[154] Men of color lacked these possibilities for social movement; their sole avenue was through class mobility and self-fashioning.

Like the bicorn hat, the tíguere draws upon both Haitian and Dominican ancestry. Yet it is hybrid in another sense as well. The tíguere narrative of upward mobility draws upon two genres that gradually meshed into an intertextual form, a deeply Creole product that combined the pícaro and the trickster genres, from Spain and Africa respectively. The picaresque genre presents a protagonist from lowly and frequently illegitimate origins who rises in status by quick wits and, when necessary, by petty crime. The pícaro is an antihero defined neither by his work, which is transitory, nor by his origins, which are socially marginal, but rather by his ability to make himself out of nothing, to ascend socially through travel and cunning. Deriving from Africa, trickster tales recount the story of an underdog who triumphs over adversaries with natural advantages—either strength, size, or acumen. Both narrative conventions are morally ambiguous, championing the antihero who wins through his talents at dexterous guile. Both genres compel the listener to embrace these imperfect heroes in all their foibles for their ability to achieve against all odds; in the process, these narratives reveal the inequities and moral corruption of the status quo, the world of *los grandes*.[155] Tigueraje thus represented another vernacular practice which served to draw Dominicans into the regime.

Trujillo was a tíguere until he became president; from that time he ruled less through his wits than through the state—the national army and treasury. When he became *jefe* he transferred this tíguere role to the magnetic Porfirio Rubirosa, since neither dynastic first son Rafael (Ramfis) nor second son Leonidas Rhadamés could pull it off. Indeed, Rubirosa—who became an affinal "son," a virtual heir to Trujillo through his marriage to daughter Flor and his close friendship with Trujillo's son Ramfis—became a surrogate for Trujillo, reaching even greater heights of tigueraje than Trujillo himself, for which he was rewarded in diplomatic positions for his unrivaled success in marital conquests.[156] The charming Rubirosa thus served as a Trujillista gigolo and conduit for the symbolic accumulation and display of women—ever more rich, famous, and beautiful—to the regime.

Given the history of United States intervention in the Dominican Republic, Rubirosa's conquest of rich American women represented an underdog tíguere fantasy that Dominican men could only applaud, one that endowed the regime with a particular kind of charisma. Rubirosa was the quintessential impersonator so nicely described by Homi Bhabha; he teetered on the boundary between "mimicry and mockery" by sufficiently learning the rules of bourgeois American style, comportment, and charm to make his way into the boudoirs and gossip columns of Parisian and American high society and thus beat the colonizers at their own game, while earning the respect of Dominican men for his audacity in the bedroom (notwithstanding his own dirty secrets).[157] Rubi's women were also crucial staging devices enabling him to overcome his dark Latin tinge. Langston Hughes, doyen of the Harlem Renaissance, marveled at how effectively Porfirio had succeeded in passing as white.[158] But ultimately it was Trujillo, the greatest tíguere of all, who had the last laugh.

SIX   TRUJILLO'S TWO BODIES

> Most often, human destiny can only be lived through fiction. Although
> in fact, the man of fiction suffers for not himself fulfilling the destiny he
> describes, he suffers because only in his career does he escape fiction. So
> he attempts to bring in the ghosts that haunt him into the real world.
> GEORGES BATAILLE, "THE SORCERER'S APPRENTICE"

> Religion is the basis of the state.
> KARL MARX, RHEINISCHE ZEITUNG

HABEAS CORPUS

On the last day of May 1961, Rafael Trujillo was shot dead on his way
home in an ambushed assault on his car. After months of international
plotting by the Kennedy administration, the CIA, disgruntled Dominican
elites, and a handful of regime-insider defectors, Trujillo's long rule came to
an end in that one instant. Yet while the assassins succeeded in killing their
opponent, the second stage of the military takeover failed. The coup plotters were unable to complete part two of the plan, that of installing themselves in office, because none of the other collaborators could believe that
the dictator had died without actually seeing his corpse and because declaring themselves his successors with Trujillo alive would mean their certain
demise. The dangers of transporting Trujillo's remains, stuffed unceremo-
niously into a Chevrolet trunk, around a city swarming with secret police,
eventually aborted the coup.[1]

The problem of belief in Trujillo's death, I propose, was related to a
larger phenomenon. There was a mystical awe surrounding the dictator, as
if Trujillo's authority transcended corporal limits, endowing him with superhuman status. It was said, for example, that he did not sweat. In the
words of Claude LeFort, he had a "mortal body . . . [yet one] perceived as
invulnerable, which condenses in itself all strengths, all talents, and defies
the laws of nature by his super-male energy."[2] This was a function in part of
Trujillo's ability to apparently enact the impossible. He had survived three

major coup attempts by invasion led by exiles, one with support from Cuba's Fidel Castro and the Venezuelan leader Rómulo Betancourt. Moreover, he had managed to kill his opponents in cities as far away as New York and Caracas. His larger-than-life persona was also a product of the multitude of titles, ranks, decorations, medals, and prizes granted by sycophantic cronies and more than twenty foreign governments and organizations; these ranged from Generalissimo to Benefactor of the Fatherland, from Doctor to Restorer of Financial Independence. Numerous honorifics were bestowed as ritual accompaniments to his visits to the interior and overseas. He even earned the ill-deserved Great Collar of Democracy and Great Medal of Extraordinary Merit (from a Peruvian notable and the government of Lebanon, respectively). His omnipresence was reinforced by the inscription of his person in the national terrain, such as renaming the capital city Ciudad Trujillo, just as many provincial hamlets were renamed after his immediate family members. Additionally, all public works were framed as personal gifts from Trujillo, so that the presidential persona came to be seamlessly identified with the modernization and development of the country.[3] If this was insufficient adulation, an entire year of state spectacle and rites called the Year of the Benefactor celebrated Trujillo and his regime in 1955 (as examined in chapter 3), supplementing dozens of national holidays in his name. Finally, his elaborate array of bedecked costumes and uniforms, including his signature Napoleonic bicorn chapeau, garnered the envy as well as contempt of many.[4]

The popular perception of Trujillo's preternatural omnipotence is clear from the absolute shock when people first heard that he had been assassinated. One version of the event gives the reaction when the body arrived at the home of the plotters: "Everyone froze. It was minutes before anyone found his voice or could take his eyes away from the bloody remains of Trujillo wedged into the back of the trunk. . . . This mangled mess, was this the same person who had such a mania for cleanliness, perfume and well-pressed uniforms? *El Jefe*, who for thirty years had commanded obedience and respect such as few Oriental potentates had known, was now just a mangled corpse."[5] So exalted and seemingly supernatural was his presence, it was hard to believe that he could expire as a mere mortal. A synecdoche for Dominican nationhood itself, the body of Trujillo had become both a repository of individual desire and a vehicle for the transfer of collective forms of value. Trujillo's person became the crux of several overlapping fetishisms. Because of his roles as central owner of national capital and landed property, employer of wage labor, and object of a "theater state," he was a key sign of commodification as well as the embodiment of what Michael Taussig calls maleficium, the modern state as magical power-object.[6] He may also have been subject to a Freudian style of fetishism, in which his lack of class and racial legitimacy (here analogized as insufficient masculinity) was compensated with a demonic phallic substitute. Scholars have sought to deconstruct what Tim Mitchell has called "the state effect": the techniques of governmentality by which the state comes to be seen as an object apart from society.[7] Yet the "myth of the state" produced by the Trujillo regime was distinctive since the state was abstracted in the form of the sovereign himself.[8]

Of course, Trujillo was not the only Latin American leader to have a magical aura around his person, in whole and in part, physical and otherwise. Examples abound, such as the hands of the Argentine revolutionary Che Guevara; after being severed to identify his corpse, they were preserved in formaldehyde, stored in the Palace of the Revolution, and displayed only to the most eminent dignitaries.[9] Others include the infamous amputated leg of Antonio López de Santa Anna, Mexican independence general and president, which was exhibited in a Mexico City shrine for a time and eventually interred in its own mausoleum; Pancho Villa's head, which ended up at Yale's Skull and Bones Society; or Álvaro Obregón's arm, which was pickled for posterity.[10] The popular Catholic traditions of venerating saints' relics and memorializing miracles through iconic signs of grace, such as the tiny legs or hearts called *ex-votos* which provide thanks for healing, probably nourish the custom of sanctifying the limbs of political leaders. Body parts can even become metonymic symbols that transmit larger social currents of meaning, with organs as mundane as the foot at times becoming "central icons of power" refracting general social anxieties of national fragmentation.[11] However, a key difference resides in the fact that after death such relics become representations of the original sacred object, while actual bodily extremities signal a more direct line of contact with the wondrous source.[12] Additionally, Latin American bodies of state are typically masculine and thus do not rely on maternal associations with fertility and reproductive mimesis as do Marian signs.[13]

Yet if not unique, Trujillo was an unlikely candidate for the status of divine rulership. As a mulatto with some Haitian ancestry, he was not considered blessed with extraordinary attractiveness (which would mean whiteness in the Dominican context) or an intrinsically prepossessing presence. He was known for his achieved rather than ascribed demeanor: his love of uniforms, his use of makeup, and his elegance as a dandy. However, with his notoriously squeaky voice and portly stature, he was neither exceptionally statuesque nor a man of words. He relied on cultured regime intellectuals, such as the eloquent poet and speechwriter Joaquín Balaguer, to provide the oratorical presence requisite for a man of stature.[14] Trujillo did not have social honor in a traditional sense, since he was not from an old elite family; nor could he claim status from ancestral participation in historic episodes of nationalist relevance. His reputation for violence earned him "respect," yet this was a byproduct rather than a precondition of his authority.[15]

Nonetheless, in the collective imagination he was accorded several signs as a popular messiah, from his providential role as national protector during the devastating 1930 hurricane to the oral narratives of his occult powers. Memories of Trujillo's charismatic powers are emblematic of a particular cultural understanding of political authority, which derived more from a Dominican conception of power than from any conscious effort on Trujillo's part to fashion himself as a divine king or cosmic oracle; the "social fantasy" of Trujillo thus represented a vernacular myth of the state.[16] This differentiated his otherworldly image, for example, from that of the Haitian leader François Duvalier, who, it is said, consciously styled himself by voice and costume as a fearsome god in the vodou pantheon in order to elicit fear.[17] However, in contrast to Weber's understanding of charisma, Trujillo's was not "revolutionary" since it was perceived as part of the "normality of the extraordinary" and did not exist in contradistinction to the disenchanted world of bureaucratic rationalism. In this context, magic and modernity were not mutually exclusive.[18] Trujillo's charisma was also patently reactionary, his magnificence more a result of elaborate stagecraft than a true transformation of the norm or the redistribution of real economic or political power.

In this chapter I examine the *corpus mysticum* of Trujillo through narratives of the dictator's sorcery.[19] The locus of the leader's charisma in this case resided not in his body but in his alter-corpus, his body double or "superbody," a magical being who enabled Trujillo to extend his person into this world and others.[20] Popular narratives that explained Trujillo's astonishing power in terms of his *muchachito*—which literally means little boy, but can also indicate an economic or political subordinate, a midget, a demon, or a personal guardian angel—have a cultural rationale. Trujillo was also renowned for seeking assistance from a series of female diviners who came and went, but the muchachito had a unique and far closer role in Trujillo's life, as a constant companion, guide, or even appendage of his presidential person.[21] These narratives reveal a vernacular idiom of state fetishism, a cluster of meanings attributed to the state in a context in which sorcery provides a language for conceptualizing absolute power and one in which politics occurred backstage, largely concealed from the public eye. State fetishism is especially pertinent for the urban and rural underclasses during the Trujillato; to them the state appeared to operate according to an inscrutable logic since they lacked the contacts to ascertain the truth behind the "dark secrets" about what was really occurring behind Trujillo's official façade.[22] As Taussig has said, "The real skill of the practitioner lies not in skilled concealment but in the skilled revelation of skilled concealment. Magic is efficacious not despite the trick but on account of its exposure." Itself invisible, the figure of the muchachito was thus a token of Trujillo's inscrutability and evidence of something hidden behind all the theatricality.[23]

When I inquired about the secret of Trujillo's power, I discovered a corpus of stories submerged in life histories of the Trujillo period. My informants traversed rural and urban locales and represented a range of class locations; they included unemployed familial dependents living in Trujillista housing projects in the capital city of Santo Domingo; a family of *minifundista* sharecroppers on the periphery of Trujillo's cattle ranch in the rural hamlet of San Cristóbal (today a satellite of Santo Domingo); and Dominican immigrants residing in Chicago, one of whom works at a used clothing store. Narratives of Trujillo's muchachito form a genre that is thus both unified and widely diffused, as well as covering a broad span of time.[24] Two elements are shared by the authors of these narratives: they lack post-primary education and they are predominantly, but not exclusively, women. Their stories of Trujillo's witchcraft reveal how the state is conceived in the popular imagination from various social locations.[25] Although the general motif of the muchachito as a figure with access to concealed forms of illicit power remains constant in these stories, there are key differences in the interpretation of the phenomena that map onto political sentiment toward the regime.

First, a note on how I am deploying the concept of charisma. In terms of Max Weber's ideal-typical definition of the concept, Trujillo's obsequious minions did cultivate an extraordinary image of him in the press as a person capable of miracles and superhuman feats. However, in contrast to Weber's model, this image continued and arguably even increased during the later, routinized phases of his rule, as his unique longevity in office became one more miracle akin to his special power to combat enemies against all odds. Thus personalism and bureaucracy were not mutually exclusive. Moreover, the Trujillo myth was only partly the result of an explicit effort at propaganda on the part of the regime. While massive state spectacles and public works helped frame Trujillo as the charismatic center of public life, the popular vision of his power was also the result of a particular political cosmology.[26]

TECHNIQUES OF THE BODY POLITIC

One way of understanding Trujillo's "secret," as people referred to his muchachito or embodied other, is as a kind of mimetic slippage.[27] In this view the representational fetish of the muchachito is as much a part of the image of authority as the figure of the dictator himself. Trujillo's absolute authority is thus symbolized by his autocratic control over the fawning underling at his constant call. Indeed, some people saw the gnome as a virtual possession of the dictator, his personal *zonbi* (zombi) that unconsciously enacted his every wish, no matter how capricious. This perspective challenges the assumption of the physical boundedness of personhood.[28] Here, Trujillo's extraordinary authority is glossed by the fact that his physical and metaphysical personhood extended to include his subordinate clients (at times he was even said to have two *seres* or *misterios*—spiritual agents of the vodou-derived pantheon mediating between devotees and God—a male and a female). A vision of power that necessarily includes one's clients defies the modern individualist framework of the bounded, autonomous self. This is a view that privileges collective identity, one in which authority is by definition encompassing, one in which power is defined by the ability to move, control, contain, and claim others.[29] Power in this context is a relationship between people rather than a property or essence.[30] This may explain why the most important caudillos and statesmen in the Dominican Republic are all remembered in tandem with their key subordinates: from the rural frontier strongman Desiderio Arias, who was never seen without his Haitian bandit sidekick Rosilien, to President Joaquín Balaguer, who was said to be guided closely by his spiritist sister Emma Balaguer de Vallejo, a reputed Santera (Santería priestess) of Ochún who was known throughout the capital for her extravagant thanksgiving celebrations. Balaguer was also known for the pair of dwarfs with broomsticks who protected the National Palace from evil eye and disease during his presidency.[31] Even the great healer Olivorio Mateo was said to learn the tricks of his trade from Juan Samuel, who frequently accompanied him when he started his career.

This logic of dualism or diarchy could also be the result of African- and Spanish-derived forms commingling within popular Catholic saint worship.[32] Dominican religious practice is nominally Catholic but has been overlaid by the Afro-Catholic religion of vodou from neighboring Haiti. Thus Trujillo may represent the Spanish Catholic face of saintly authority, while the muchachito corresponds to the potent yet invisible powers of vodou—two spatially distinct domains of religious practice that correspond to different means and ends.[33] While the Dominican Republic (east) and Haiti (west) shared a common history of slavery, freedmen outnumbered slaves during most of the colonial period on the eastern side of the island, which meant that Dominicans usually identified themselves as Spanish Catholics, even if extensive racial mixture indicated that African-derived cultural practices were widely diffused. A constant stream of Haitian immigration to the Dominican Republic from the colonial period onward disseminated Haitian vodou, which today is considered both more powerful and more dangerous than saint worship. This explains why a respectable self-presentation requires a public lineage of Catholic saints, but private practice inevitably combines the saints with Haitian vodou deities.[34] Dominicans thus code shift between religious languages (Catholic saints, Haitian *lwa*) as needed. Both the political and the religious realms are organized not around homogeneous cults of personality but rather around hierarchic clusters of either patrons and clients or saints and their vodou correspondences.[35]

This vision of power also foreshadows a worldview in which it is taken for granted that invisible forces exist and operate beyond one's ability to perceive them. Reality thus includes that which is insensate—invisible forces akin to what Sigmund Freud termed the uncanny. Given the radically democratic ethos of a society based for centuries on foraging and on the hunting of wild cattle and pigs, access to occult forces may provide an explanation of how one person can have much more authority than anyone else when all people are presumed fundamentally equal.[36] In this view, command over spatially distinct and distant realms of esoteric knowledge thus both reflects and helps constitute the mystique of the politically powerful.[37] And through his grandmother Trujillo was known to have Haitian antecedents, which were used to explain his mystical access since Haiti is considered a superior center for "black magic" in the Dominican imagination. If blackness in this world is derogated as demeaned and inferior, in the other world it evokes a more potent genre of witchcraft.[38] In Dominican culture the muchachito is a secret whose very concealment augments Trujillo's potency; it corresponds to the invisible line of maternal lineage.[39]

Additionally, the ability to move between realms seen and unseen can be mapped onto the ability to transgress the boundaries between species. Supernatural power can thus be marked by the ability to shape-shift, as certain people have the power to become spirit animals. For example, Ulises Heureaux (who also had Haitian lineage), the late-nineteenth-century dictator, was said to be a *galipote*, a being capable of transmuting from person to beast.[40] Occult assistance accentuates the power of an authority figure while answering the question why him?

Yet Trujillo's supernatural assistant was more than a quotidian foil that, by proximity and contrast, accentuated the perceived distinction of the central protagonist. He had a far more significant role than, say, Batman's Robin or the Lone Ranger's Tonto. First, Trujillo's muchachito was blessed with powers of divination. He provided Trujillo with secrets about the movements of his close allies and potential enemies, enabling him to portend future events and prepare for eventual tribulations. In this rendition, the muchachito could be a Dominican equivalent of the Haitian *ti anj* or guardian angel, a personal protector. One narrative contends that Trujillo's elf came to him in his sleep, in dreamspace, a common route of access to the supernatural realm. From his nocturnal passageway, the figure would give Trujillo clues about which members of his inner circle could be betraying him, or which business ventures he should go forward with. Although dreamspace provides supernatural access in the Dominican imagination, messages in dreams typically require deciphering from specialists who can translate, for example, the appearance of a particular person into the fact that one should play his birthday or cédula number in the lottery on a given day. Moreover, only people gifted with special powers have constant access to such metaphysical knowledge. Nocturnal visits by a muchachito are thus a sign that one is called by the saints to become a medium and that one therefore must be baptized or suffer dire consequences.

Muchachitos have a liminal status within Dominican vodú, however. They are neither Catholic saints nor seres or misterios (literally "mysteries" or mystical agent) or formal *loas/lwas* (vodú divinities). The muchachito's

lack of a codified place in the pantheon in part explains the varied interpretations of the figure's precise nature. Some believe it was a child. Indeed,
in folk Catholicism as well as animist traditions from Africa, children serve
as a sacred cipher for several divinities. In San Juan de la Maguana, el
Espíritu Santo or the Holy Ghost is represented as a child during cofradía
processions.[41] And Eshu or Elegua (Legba), god of the crossroads in Yoruba
and in new world Orisha worship, often appears as a child. Children are
held to have direct contact with the divine, particularly during the period
preceding their baptism. Insomnia in children is viewed as the result of
nocturnal visitation from the dead, since they are said to "see" occult beings,
substances, and powers which adults cannot. In sharp contrast to adults,
children who die are given joyous funerals characterized by song rather
than prayer. They are called *angelitos*, and their bodies are prepared and
kept amid the living as long as possible as sacred objects. In Africa and
South America, children's close contact with the divine can make them
victims of sorcery accusations. In the Congo, children are seen as particularly vulnerable to evil spirits and thus are held responsible for witchcraft and even cannibalism, resulting in purges, exorcisms, and even abandonment.[42] Among certain Amazonian peoples such as the Arawak, roving
demons are said to teach children witchcraft in their sleep, and cantanker-
ous girls held to be bewitched can be put to death.[43]

The muchachito resonates with several divinities linked to childhood. Of
course, there is always some ambiguity concerning the recognition of the
identity of the misterio or loá because any being can descend in several
puntos (literally points), *nanchon* (Haitian Creole for nations), or forms.
Thus the muchachito could be a representation of El Santo Niño Atocha
(the Divine Heart of Atocha, portrayed in a chromolithograph), a version of
Jesus as a child who is at times glossed as Legba, the messenger of the vodou
pantheon.[44] Legba is the quintessential link between spatially segregated
categories such as life and death, old age and childhood, manhood and
womanhood; he is the loá who arrives first and departs last in any ritual
event. Notwithstanding his appearance as an aged man with a walking stick,
Legba is associated with children as a result of his paradoxical unification of
opposites.[45] The theme of metamorphosis and duality is echoed as well
among other central religious icons of childhood; the twin children, the
Marassa, are held especially dear. They are considered purer, higher beings
than formal divinities and are classed apart. One index of their superior
status is that they rarely descend to possess. As Maya Deren affirms, the

22. A chromolitho-
graph of El Niño
Atocha.

Marassa "are a celebration of man's twinned nature: half matter, half metaphysical; half mortal, half immortal; half human, half divine."[46] Unlike other
divinities, actual twins are worshiped in a manner akin to that of their loa.
Like the muchachito, the twins have special divine powers: they are capable
of bringing or arresting rainfall, healing the infirm, or harming those who
get in their way. As a result they are officiated apart from other divinities—
provided special foods in their own corner of the altar and specially pla-
cated so as to nullify their potential danger.

Yet in vodú, twins seem to represent a deeper dualism that is particularly
fraught with danger in both Dominican and Haitian cosmology. Everything
doubled has an inherent instability. For example, of the two classes of vodú,
the right-handed everyday Rada class and the left-handed Petro or Petwo
class (where "black magic" is executed), those who work with the Petro are
said to "work with both hands," thus marking their exceptional power and
corresponding danger. Indeed, the Petro are often glossed as devilish Haitian spirits.[47] The Petro manifest themselves violently, and while they can

do more than the Rada, they entail far more risk for the practitioner. It is to the Petro, for example, that one must turn for a *bacá*, a man-made misterio that can bring wealth or power to its owner, but usually entails a dear sacrifice, such as the death of a family member.[48] Indeed, Dominicans differentiate their brand of vodú from the Haitian variant by the fact that theirs does not include the motif of doubling. Unlike Haitians, who have two sets of deities, Dominicans say they worship one set of gods only, unlike Haitians who "work with both hands."[49] Moreover, even though each Catholic saint has a corresponding loa identity, a respectable Dominican presentation of self (even for those who "work the mysteries") requires that one deny that one knows the vodú counter-identities of the saints, so as to represent oneself as a good Catholic instead of a questionable practitioner of sorcery.

Indeed, doubling has such an air of potential malevolence that divine twosomes are most frequently cloaked in the more Catholic and respectable Trinitarian logic of three. Twins in a family can inflict terrible witchcraft, attacking the intestines. Dominicans say that the *dosu*, or child born after twins, is superior even to the sacred twins, serving as an invisible third term transforming a devilish double into the holy Trinity.[50] In parallel fashion, Saint Nicholas, the father of the sacred twins, is credited with bringing three children back to life, which makes him sacred by association with three rather than two.[51] And multiples of three are considered holy numbers, especially twenty-one, which is the total number of gods in the pantheon.[52] For example, three people at an accursed witchcraft event can foul it up, producing violence and nullifying its force. Interestingly, the iconographic symbol of the Marassa twins is a kind of trinity, a triad rather than a duo, as is the tripartite jar for their food offering.[53] As Deren confirms, "The twins are not to be separated into competitive, conflicting dualism. In *Vodou* one and one make three."[54]

The image of Trujillo as a double body, individual and collective, private and public, may have derived some symbolic basis from the body of Christ. It shared the medieval notion of the divide between the visible and the invisible, the mortal and the immortal, and even the masculine and feminine.[55] As Caroline Bynum has argued, Christ historically provided a paradigmatic template for bodily regeneration and movement between earthly and celestial domains.[56] But there was not necessarily a Christian genealogy for this idea in the Dominican Republic.

Achille Mbembe argues that the idea of doubling is "charged with dis-

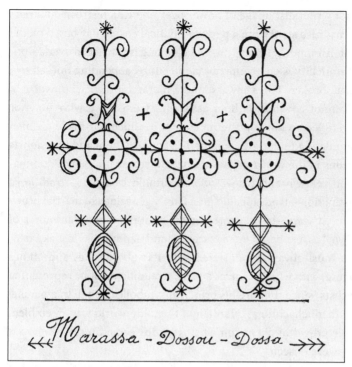

Marassa - Dossou - Dossa.

23. Sacred vèvè or symbol of the twins. FROM ALFRED METRAUX, *VOODOO IN HAITI*, TRANSLATED BY HUGO CHARTERIS (NEW YORK: SCHOCKEN BOOKS, 1972).

turbing powers" in Cameroon because it refers "endlessly, to the multiple and simultaneous functions of life itself."[57] Indeed, in neighboring Cuba and Haiti official Catholicism actively combated African-derived "superstition," but in the Dominican Republic the Church languished after the seat of colonial control was moved to Mexico in the seventeenth century. Many Dominican parishes then had to suffice with irregular and infrequent priest visitations; in fact, some provincial parishes were given their first prelate assignments as late as the 1940s. In this context, official Christianity never quite succeeded in stamping out the marvelous as it did in other contexts, and a popular brand of Catholicism flourished which drew liberally upon Afro-Dominican and Haitian vodou.[58] Not only did a tradition of saint miracles retain its saliency and force, but various malevolent forces traversing the earth were said to roam.[59] Indeed, the endowment of magical powers to both objects and individuals with physical deformities—such as children born with six fingers—indicates this legacy.

If Christ provided one foundational template for body doubling, the preference for a pluralist image of power over one which stressed Christ's uniqueness may also stem from a popular political cosmology based on the patron-clientelist model;[60] in this model belonging is privileged over autonomy, and marginality is overcome not alone but by appending oneself to a more powerful broker. This view assumes a hierarchical social universe in which one cannot advance without assistance from those with superior status. It also reflects a kind of frontier culture in which self-made big men rise by accumulating underlings who both recognize them and function as their extensions in the world.[61] This is a deeply personal mode of domination based on renown and respect. Since Trujillo lacked the traditional means of distinction—land, apellido, or a family genealogy of martial prowess in nationalist wars—he was forced to rely more on sheer numbers of followers as well as fear based on magic as a "fund of power."[62] Just as a truly powerful loa must always be clustered with its subordinates and affines (after its spouse, with which it forms a pair), a caudillo must be represented with his loyalists, since they are his principal symbolic capital. In a parallel logic, Trujillo's muchachito as guardian of the underworld was an emblem of an invisible crowd of client spirit-beings who seemed more numerous because they were unseen.[63]

An extension of this culture of patron-clientelism may be the model of personhood in which exceptional advancement must be seen emanating from outside the subject.[64] In a radically egalitarian framework, power always derives from assistance from either a powerful patron or from the other realm. As Jan Lundius has noted, this paradigm permeates both political and religious forms of charisma; "it is not the man who is worshipped, but the power incarnated in him."[65] The dictator Rafael Trujillo was just a man. However, his personal "muchachito" provided him with the secrets and the sabiduría (wisdom) to gain and hold power. In this view, power by definition is not inherent; it must derive from the invisible, divine realm. It may come from an elfin dwarf, a spirit (el viejo), or a svelte indigenous female (india or ciguapa) who conducts visitations through dreams. Power is also accumulated through spiritual foils or aids which enable one to achieve a position of authority, such as an ouanga (a sorcerer's charm, stone, or coil) that serves as a conduit for sacral energies. One does not seek out a muchachito; it comes in dreams. Spiritual power should be offered to a person without compensation, as a gift, never bought or sought as a commodity.

Most important, such power is a product of one's social matrix of contacts, the web of relations which constitute one's extended identity. This is why the query "do you know who you're talking to?" is an acutely dangerous one, because one's identity is defined not by legible surface criteria but by the range of contacts one can access and invoke—the private, invisible crowd of people one represents.[66] This kind of power presupposes the sociality, and thus the multiplicity, of sources of identity formation as well as its embodied character. The subject, here, is less a transcendent "I" than the nexus—and product—of a particular social field.

In the spirit world, power is less acquired or consumed than accumulated.[67] This agglutinative concept is operative when one is "mounted" (*montado*) or possessed by a misterio, in which the loa is envisioned as crouching on the nape of one's neck, at the top of the spine. Power is achieved through a doubling of self, as the "horse" (*caballo*) becomes the recipient of the identity of a particular *sere*, a force that rises up through the ground, into the spinal column, and eventually into the head.[68] However, while the subject here is conceived as a vehicle through which other identities are channeled, these identities are not seen as ambivalent, since they remain radically distinct and in different spheres. Nonetheless, power in its pure form not only comes from outside but has consequences that can be externalized. Power is "destiny," but it is also *fucú*, an evil charge passed through bodily extensions such as clothing, house, touch, or even the uttering of one's name.[69] Indeed, just as it is taboo to utter the name of Christopher Columbus for the bad luck it carries (which is why he is often referred to as "the Admiral"), it was taboo to name Trujillo during his regime; thus people preferred to call him by myriad official titles (such as el Jefe or el Benefactor) or by his derogatory nickname Chapita.

THE DEVIL AND STATE FETISHISM

Another popular resonance for the muchachito is a class of much-feared man-made spirits. Some allege that Trujillo's muchachito was not found but rather concocted or even purchased by a powerful *bocor* or sorcerer; thus the muchachito only looked like a child but was actually a *bacá*, a being capable of transmogrifying from human to animal to even a machine. Haitian vodou establishes a class of particularly risky "hot" spirits that are bought. As such, the "hot points"—the bacá or the zonbi—stand alone as quintessential strangers, in sharp contrast to the "family" of lwa.[70] Although they are not all technically made (for example, the zonbi is collected from a corpse and bottled), they are defined by their acquisition through purchase, as opposed to more natural means of acquaintance; they are seen as artificial, contrary to nature, and, by extension, God. Their otherness as neighbors but patently not blood kin is also expressed by the fact that ancestral spirits can become lwa and thus reside on the same continuum, but hot spirits, like slaves, are taken forcibly, either by stealing, involuntary capture, or purchase.[71] And like slaves, they often must be bound and chained to the ground and held as captives. Like commodities, of course, they can be appropriated by others and thus must be protected from theft or kidnapping, unlike the lwa, who are personal friends and thus non-transferable.

Unlike kin whose identities are known, the changeability of these hot spirits render them deeply frightening. Often appearing as innocent children or domestic animals such as cats, dogs, or pigs, bacás hide in woods and near county roads and can instantly become cows, crabs, or even enormous monsters defying description. They can also appear as half-dog, half-men. Indeed, their capriciousness extends even to the purported guardian of the being who falls within its control. As Alfred Métraux asserts, "You think you are its master, only to discover you are its slave."[72] The version of the muchachito as bacá makes sense owing to Trujillo's Haitian genealogy through his grandmother. Irrespective of her official portrayal as French, Trujillo's grandmother, Luisa Ercina Chevalier, established a connection to Haiti and thus tapped a vein of its popular associations with blood, sorcery, and commodity exchange.[73] And as Christian Krohn-Hansen argues, the bacá is an emblem of radical alterity with popular nationalist associations.[74] Thus if Trujillo was indeed really Haitian, it makes sense to explain his extraordinary power as a result of a particular genre of devilish spirit that one usually must buy in Haiti, with assistance from a Haitian sorcerer.

Another aspect of the power of the bacá is its involvement with excessive consumption. It is similar to the *kharisiri* in tales of the Andes, which link otherness, money, and blood in gruesome rumors of gringos stealing body parts, blood, and fat to lubricate industrial machinery or to become flesh for sale and consumption in fancy restaurants; it also resembles the goat-blood-sucking kangaroo-vampires called *chupacabras*, which have slaughtered domestic farm animals from Florida to Puerto Rico and Mexico.[75] The bacá not only consumes its victims but sucks their blood dry. This consumption forms part of a circuit of exchange, however, since at great sacrifice, bacás can provide their owners with riches, if only for a short time, because they demand "payment."[76] Consumption in many contexts is a

24. Protestors carry a portrait of Trujillo, altered to give the dictator a satanic appearance, 1961. BY PERMISSION OF CORBIS.

common metaphor for understanding power. Johannes Fabian, for example, has found that the Luba of the Congo see voracious eating as a motif of raw domination, one which invokes a life-and-death struggle.[77] And Birgit Meyer has demonstrated how Ghanaian Pentecostalists view the consumption of foreign goods as satanic, a process which threatens to consume the owner.[78] Those who explained Trujillo's muchachito as a form of man-made bacá, then, are those who saw Trujillo as a ruthless killer, whose power grew at the expense of the lives of many innocent victims; like a leech, he became rich through the blood of others.[79] This model of domination implicitly contrasts the correct social means of ascent by attaching oneself to a more powerful client with a mode in which one grows alone by consuming one's enemies through violence.

Yet there is another way of interpreting the separation of Trujillo's powers in the popular imagination. This is a view of the narratives of Trujillo and his muchachito as the symbolic expression of a political strategy of

Trujillo, by which he sought to remain above the fray of political squabbles and violence so that he could garner all credit for the positive benefits of the regime—for the extensive public housing, the lack of crime, the economic development, the modernization—while remaining disassociated from the daily system of social control. Thus he sought to retain a transcendent image, while his hit men, agents of the SIM or secret police, took the blame for the terror. Thus if the muchachito were a bacá, it might have been an emblem for the daily system of surveillance and violent "excesses" of regime cronies, such as the venal hatchet man Johnny Abbes García. In this "maleficium" model, Trujillo's sacredness remained unsullied by the impure actions of everyday regime assassins, torturers, and spies.[80]

In the muchachito narratives, however, these two modes of power—sacred and beneficent and "black magic" or evil—are contrasted but not in a Manichean moral opposition. Rather, they form a spectrum of possibilities demonstrating a deep ambivalence about particular forms of power abuse, implying that power can level inequalities or lead to excessive accumulation.[81] The tales about Trujillo's secrets express the conviction that ultimately it is not power itself but how it is used which leads to evil. Trujillo's elemental flaw was his lack of confianza, or trust in others, which stemmed from his desire for absolute power. In a story that renders the muchachito a virtual Christ, Trujillo tried to test the muchachito, to make sure that he indeed had powers of clairvoyance: he gave him three pieces of bread, one of which had been poisoned. Of course, the muchachito knew which was which and was not killed. After this insult, the muchachito was so offended that when he divined Trujillo's impending assassination, he refused to inform him, allowing him to die.[82] In another narrative, Trujillo went to Haiti to get a *despojo* (ritual cleansing bath) to protect him from his enemies. After the rite, the Haitian sorcerer said that now Trujillo had nothing to worry about— that only he or God could kill him. Trujillo interpreted this as a veiled threat and murdered the man.[83] Thus, in the end, it was Trujillo's own arrogance, his inability to trust others, that led to his own demise. He attempted to rule alone, a style of authority which, like the bacá, ultimately consumes.

Other tales express the evil that would befall those who tried to interrogate Trujillo's secrets. These take Trujillo's isolation at the top of the political hierarchy for granted; the taboo here lies in ordinary people seeking the secrets of el Presidente. In one version allegedly told by Trujillo's cook, the domestic servants of the household had all been banned from entering a particular room, which was always kept closed and locked. Violating the prohibition, a servant once entered the purported chamber of horrors and instantly went mad as a result, never to recover. The man was able to conduct his daily duties at work like a zonbi, but in the street he spoke only nonsense and was never able to regain any semblance of his private life.[84] In another version of this story, Trujillo's locked room contained an enormous shrine which was so powerful it could kill the uninitiated. In these tales, absolute power clearly exerts a profound fascination but one that should never be indulged. Ultimately, however, in all these narratives the dangers of power are not intrinsic; they are spatially and categorically distinct as well as contingent. One moral emerges: absolute power that is not shared either horizontally or vertically requires a dear sacrifice. For this reason, most witnesses to the inauguration of the Columbus lighthouse (Faro á Colón)—the multimillion dollar monument to Columbus completed by President Joaquín Balaguer in 1992—were not surprised when his sister died days before the event. They said it was the fucú or curse of Columbus, but perhaps it was also Balaguer's conceit in striving to become the Admiral by association that required the sacrifice of his sister (Emma, the Santera). In reaching too far, he lost all.

ALCHEMIES OF STATE

The image of the muchachito condensed more than one idiom of fetishism, just as Trujillo represented more than just state power. On the one hand, Trujillo embodied what Timothy Mitchell has called the "state effect," when the state appears completely severed from civil society;[85] indeed, Trujillo was the personification of the state. His person became the centerpiece of an elaborate theater state which like a hall of mirrors reflected only Trujillo. As in the neon sign deployed by one regime sycophant, only "God and Trujillo" were permitted any form of symbolic elevation, as if Trujillo had built the state single-handedly, which he clearly had not. Trujillo may at times have resembled an *ancien régime* monarch with absolute powers, but in reality he ruled at the apex of a modern bureaucratic state apparatus based on a complex system of social networks of complicity.

However, there is another layer of significance to the fetishism of Trujillo. Trujillo bought virtually all of the major sectors of the economy; by the 1950s he had even taken over the bulk of the formerly foreign-owned sugar sector.[86] And some have estimated that Trujillo and his immediate family controlled as much as 50 to 60 percent of all arable land as well as 80 percent of all business.[87] Not only did he seek to monopolize the most profitable domestic industries, from rice production to cement, but his control of export markets was so complete that when he paid the last installment of the national debt in 1947—in one of the most celebrated nationalist ceremonies of the Era of Trujillo—he wrote a check to U.S. Ambassador Cordell Hull that some say was from his own bank account.[88] As a result of the Hull-Trujillo Treaty, the U.S. dollar, which had been the national currency since the United States customs receivership was installed in 1907, was replaced by the Dominican peso and the first national bank was inaugurated. If the notion of fetish denotes a mirage, then perhaps another term should be deployed because the writing of that check made Trujillo literally the embodiment of national value; this equivalence was deepened when the regime minted solid gold coins with Trujillo's profile to commemorate the twenty-fifth anniversary of his rule. As the peso replaced the dollar, Trujillo replaced the United States as the sovereign sign of national value.[89] As one observer said, "It is impossible to eat, drink, smoke or dress without in some way benefiting *el Benefactor* or his family. The Dominican pays him tribute from birth to death."[90] If he was perceived as the "public authority upon the metal that makes it money," one can see why.[91]

If Trujillo's muchachito were indeed a living werewolf, a demon morphing from animal to human and back, its capacity for metamorphosis was similar to the magic of money as it transforms from generic currency to particular value. Like "a live monster that is fruitful and multiplies," the muchachito resembled a galipote, but with the added horror of being able to transmogrify from wolf to goat to tree branch.[92] By forging the first national currency and paying off the national debt, Trujillo transformed the Dominican Republic from debt colony to nation. During his rule the majority of national labor also shifted from essentially nonmarket nomadic hunting and gathering, swidden agriculture, and cattle ranching on state and communal lands to commodified wage labor on privately held territory, a process which drastically shifted the meaning of money in everyday life.[93] If sorcery is a form of invisible power, Trujillo harnessed the magic of international markets via the regime's sleight of hand. The fetishism of Trujillo not only represented the changes resulting from the development of state capitalism and provided a human face for the new impersonal market; it also personified a new form of material relations.[94] Personalist methods could provide the basis of rule over a face-to-face society of one million, but governing three times that number with a system of rigid social control was quite another thing.

Thus the monstrous quality of the muchachito mimicked that of Trujillo, who had transmogrified from marginal cattle rustler to one of the wealthiest men of the world. He had transgressed the rigid rules of race and class ascent in traditional society, and thus broke all odds not only by obtaining power but by maintaining it for more than three decades. One could argue that Trujillo's apparent fetish power expressed his illegitimacy as a mulatto who violated the patrilineal order. Within a Freudian paradigm one might say that he was feminized in that he represented the counterhegemonic system of matrifocality, that is, the more dominant but illicit family form, the woman-headed household.[95] There is much lore about what might be construed as Trujillo's effeminization—for instance, his pancake makeup, his foppishness, his high-pitched voice. He may have been feminized in popular memory because he was a mulatto outsider who represented "unnatural" social reproduction—from his chaotic extramarital liaisons and offspring to his usurpation of land and property, which was often distributed to his political cronies and fictive kin instead of his patrilineal kin.[96] And yet Trujillo was also deeply masculine—conforming to a gallo or caudillo idiom of masculinity through his passion for horses, his fierce demand for respect, and his womanizing.[97] Thus he may have evoked anxiety owing to his unstable combination of strength and weakness, authority and illegitimacy—an instability resolved through the muchachito, a phallus-substitute which rendered him unequivocally a *macho*. If the muchachito caused horror, it also mitigated it by resolving Trujillo's symbolic castration.[98] If Trujillo had no right to rule, his muchachito provided the requisite authorization.

If the popular classes perceived Trujillo's charisma as deriving from the religious realm, however, they were not entirely to blame. Trujillo's army of regime panegyrists were equally responsible, since they used the language of the miraculous, terms such as *predestination* and *thaumaturgy*, to describe Trujillo's ascent to power in the press and official publications.[99] The sycophant Matos Moya offered a fine example; he drew liberally on scriptural allusions: "Who can ignore that Trujillo—the new Moses—with his thaumaturgical hand has brought forth water to those burning regions where misery and desolation reigned."[100] Indeed, the middle classes were responsible for far greater mystification than the illiterate poor, since they seemed to claim that something intrinsic to Trujillo was responsible for his charisma, as opposed to an alien force like the muchachito. As Julie Taylor has argued for the case of Evita Perón in Argentina, although the middle classes assumed that the irrationality of the rabble had caused the deification of Trujillo, they were actually the chief architects of the symbolic apparatus of rule that rendered Trujillo larger than life—from speeches that compared him to Julius Caesar, to public works and spectacles that framed him as a numinous lodestone of national value, to the name changing of the capital to Trujillo City, as well as numerous provincial streets and townships to the names of his kin.[101] The portentous image of Trujillo was forged through descriptions such as: "The people began to see that they were in the presence of no ordinary man, but of a Hero capable of interpreting their common feelings, often vague and hidden, but alive and throbbing, as an instinct of the Fatherland in the popular mind."[102]

It was the middle classes who constructed the image of Trujillo as conduit for the wild and irrational powers of the masses, one which harnessed their savage energy and channeled it into a state-making project.[103] They wrote of the bleeding of national wealth through foreign investment and the draining of national surplus value invested on Wall Street. In this epic tale, Trujillo arrested this blood-sucking extraction; by proffering his own person, he restored the inalienable value of the nation and thus respeto to the body politic. As he vowed to the banks, " 'If my credit as President of the Republic is not enough . . . I offer my credit as Rafael Leonidas Trujillo." He presented his own value to back a nation with no public credit by replacing the dollar with a Dominican peso, an act that established a powerful "myth of equivalence" between the Dominican Republic and its former colonial patron, an act with a special resonance in a country that had spent eight years under U.S. Marine rule.[104] The magic of Trujillo, then, was ultimately his ability to convert national debt into value by offering no more than the honor of the sovereign—in the end, a conjuring act which would have impressed even Karl Marx.

Trujillo's panegyrists were also responsible for accruing a mystical image of divine redemption around him as embodiment of the nation state. This was achieved through rhetorical flourishes, such as Manuel Peña Battle's speech that "Trujillo was born to satisfy an eminent and imponderable destiny. . . . His work and his personality have begun to be confused with the very roots of the country in its historical and social meaning."[105] Or witness the claim by Antero Cestero, a local functionary, that Trujillo had "saved the nation" due to his great "gift of leadership" that no Dominican statesman before him had achieved.[106] Religious references within Dominican Party discourse were commonplace: Members were called *correligionarios* on a "sacred mission," party visits to interior hamlets were termed *romería* or pilgrimages, and party activists called themselves *servidores* or Trujillo worshipers, the term used for the relationship between a devotee and his venerated saint. Another local functionary praised Trujillo, "with his five stars and his sword, which is like a magic baton that brings progress."[107] Perhaps more important than the metaphors and tropes used to describe his acts were the less immediately identifiable signs which indexed a transcendental destiny to a Dominican audience, such as his miraculous recovery from an infant illness that brought him close to death. Or the concordance of official holidays with Trujillo's saint's day, that of Saint Raphael, who then became an unofficial, masculine patron saint of the nation alongside the traditional patron saint, the Virgin of Altagracia. Or the fact that nationalist celebrations often included a Catholic mass for Trujillo's health and fate.

But while Dominicans may blame the "false consciousness" of the poor for making Trujillo a hero, albeit a sinister one, historians are guilty of another form of state fetishism. Their insistence on seeing Trujillo the man as the sole variable of the regime, as opposed to the network of social relationships through which the regime penetrated civil society and wove the population into a role of complicity with the dictatorship, certainly oversimplifies the problem of agency in a complex modern regime. As José Marti has taught us, reciprocity can be a strategy of power as well. The muchachito narratives demonstrate a form of state fetishism by imputing to Trujillo himself the "secret" of his rule, if only in the sense that he was either lucky or special enough to obtain his own spiritual assistant. Yet at least they cast the problem of authority during the Trujillato as one not reducible simply to the dictator himself, but rather as fundamentally residing in Trujillo's network of relations with his subordinates.[108] The muchachito narratives thus problematize any simple Manichean morality in favor of a complex spectrum of complicity and collusion—one in which Trujillo was to blame for monopolizing excessive power, resources, and wealth in his own hands, just as his underlings were to blame for being seduced by his politics of the gift into providing him with essential support, without which he could never have remained in office for three decades. In this complex moral vision, the right hand can dislike the left but cannot do without it.

CONCLUSION

I have sought to demonstrate that Trujillo's muchachito provides a key to uncoding the cultural logic governing the phenomenology of power in the

Dominican Republic. But this case may also indicate a problem in the literature on state fetishism in the post-colony, which stems from the difficulty of disentangling analytically the phenomena of state and commodity fetishism, at least in contexts in which the state assumes a central role in the economy by means of the dictator and in which the public is kept shielded from the everyday operations of politics. Here, as Bourdieu puts it, the "ministerium appears as a mysterium," and, in the case of Trujillo, eventually becomes a misterio.[109] Ultimately, popular interpretations of the muchachito vary according to the subject's sentiments toward the regime—those who liked Trujillo tended to see his otherworldly assistant as benign, while those critical of the dictatorship saw it as the very incarnation of evil.[110] However, no matter whether people saw the muchachito as the right or the left hand of Trujillo, his private secret or his true public identity, its function was ultimately the same. The muchachito provided mythic confirmation of Trujillo's authority. It was a spiritual manifestation or "political mimesis" of the everyday behind-the-scenes machinations of power, from extortion to juridical manipulation, from graft to assassination, that were the true secrets of Trujillo's longevity in office.[111]

SEVEN

PAPÁ LIBORIO AND THE MORALITY OF RULE

¡Viva Cristo, el rey Mesías!
viva la madre piadosa, viva Liborio Mateo!
esto es todo lo que anhelo
de aquí saldrá un presidente
que domine el mundo entero . . .
El señor Plinio Rodríguez
va para la presidencia
el Cristo lo designó
por ser un hombre de conciencia

Viva Christ, the messiah King!
Viva the devout mother, viva Liborio Mateo!
this is everything I wish for
that a president originating from here
will dominate the entire world . . .
Mr. Plinio Rodríguez
is going to be president
Christ designated him
as a man of conscience

OLIVORISTA LITURGIC STANZA

U pon Trujillo's assassination in 1961, a millenarian movement took shape in the southwestern quadrant of the country, in the mountains over-looking the Haitian-Dominican border. Led by the fictive "twins" Plinio and León Romilio Ventura Rodríguez—along with their brothers Eloy, Manuel, and Hilario—a community in Media Luna (a rural parish of Las Matas de Farfán), was formed and governed by the principles of communal property, cosmic balance, and the Holy Ghost. The twins were said to embody the spirit of "the sorcerer of San Juan," Dios Olivorio Mateo Ledesma (Papá Liborio), a local faith healer, regional hero, and nationalist martyr assassi-nated by marines during the U.S. occupation of the country in 1922.[1] Under the watchful gaze of a living virgin with light skin and blue eyes called *la purísima* (the purest), community members renounced the trappings of modernity—the evils of money, medicine, politics, and even CARE food aid. In its place they created their own form of representation, the Unión Cristiana Mundial (World Christian Union), symbolized by blue and white flags and a blue denim uniform, and founded a utopic community called Palma Sola or single palm. Votes, the medium of political transactions (which are bought and sold like commodities), were supplanted by gifts; thus the *voto* was replaced with its obverse—*ex-votos*, or votive offerings. Local authorities became concerned and asked the federal government to intervene when the group withdrew from the bean harvest and children failed to appear at school. Rumors had spread that the group was engaged in witchcraft, animal sacrifice, and ritual orgies, and that residents had been instructed not to participate in the first democratic elections in decades. Palma Sola was interpreted as an undercover political party, and allegations emerged that it was a front for either an invasion of neo-Trujillistas via Haiti or a communist coup. The result was an assault by the Dominican army that left more than 800 dead, hundreds more injured, and 673 in police custody.[2]

In this chapter I explore the Olivorista community at Palma Sola as a popular "fantasy for the state" in the Dominican imagination and as an idiom of popular commentary on the excesses of official statecraft under the Trujillato.[3] I also trace the origins of this icon of regional autonomy and popular sovereignty. Olivorismo was a complex political product that defied neat dichotomies of coercion and consent or hegemony and resistance. It was a movement of protest, yet also drew on certain Trujillista forms of rule—elaborate hierarchy, an intricate ceremonial use of space, and an imperial style of nationalism. The cult sought to establish a more "balanced" moral economy through the reinvention of both the state and the nation in Palma Sola. My reading of Olivorismo over time reveals a project with a deeply ambivalent conception of authority, which deployed mimicry in the service of transparency and assumed that sanctioned and unsanctioned forms of power by definition operate in tandem.[4]

Why was a marginal religious cult deemed such a threat by the state? One factor was the immediate political context. Tensions ran exceedingly high after Trujillo's death as a multitude of political organizations suddenly sprang to life to take advantage of the political vacuum; exiles returned home, and civic organizations of all kinds pressured the Trujillo family and interim president Joaquín Balaguer to cede power and hold elections. After more than three decades of ironclad authoritarian control and a total absence of civic life, democracy caused much jubilation but also much fear. Rumors abounded of covert plots, particularly regarding the Trujillo family and inner circle, which struggled to maintain power under Ramfis Trujillo's erratic leadership. While the rules of the game of social control were crystal clear under Trujillo, political life was completely opaque, governed by behind-the-scenes political intrigues that became apparent only through rumor; but by the end of the regime, the duplicity of official discourses of "rectitude" became more apparent in the face of grotesque official corruption. Dominicans continued to presume that politics operated according to hidden motives and secret powers or an "occult cosmology," notwithstanding the transition to democracy.[5] In November, a group of military officers forced the Trujillo family and its cronies into exile, yet fears continued that they might take refuge in the Haitian borderlands and launch an invasion. There was gossip that the Liboristas were actually a cover for five thousand peasant guerrillas, armed with contraband weapons from Haiti, who were preparing a revolt.[6] Indeed, the United States consul worried that U.S. napalm would be dropped on religious pilgrims.[7]

Suspicions had also emerged about secret communist organizing. After the 1959 victory of Fidel Castro in neighboring Cuba, the United States was deeply concerned about another revolutionary regime coming to power, with fears compounded by the settlement of hundreds of anticommunist Cuban émigrés on Dominican soil. On 20 December 1962, Juan Bosch of the Partido Revolucionario Dominicano won the presidency by a landslide on a reformist platform that was branded communist by the business community, Cuban exiles, the Catholic Church, and the U.S. embassy.[8] Just eight days after the first democratic elections in more than three decades, a formidable military delegation was sent to Palma Sola, and in a scuffle that remains obscure, the accidental murder of General Miguel Rodríguez Reyes launched a full-scale military assault on the religious pilgrims.

OLIVORISMO AS PATRIA CHICA

The Palma Sola movement has been treated as a local "crisis cult" resulting from the sharpening of class relations and rural impoverishment in the southern border province of San Juan de la Maguana.[9] Olivorismo first emerged in the years 1910–19 when the frontier was transformed into a border as United States officials took over customs houses and cracked down on smuggling, a move with dramatic consequences in a region more tightly linked to Haitian markets than those of Santo Domingo.[10] The civil war of 1912 had created social dislocation, which also probably augmented the pull of the movement. The seeds of its rebirth were laid in the 1950s with the rapid expansion of commercial agriculture as a result of high primary commodity prices on the world market. In this view, proletarianization drove people off the land and into the arms of a subculture preaching a moral economy that inverted the values of an expanding capitalism.[11] Yet this localist model cannot fully explain the multiclass and multiregional component of the community, which became the major site of national pilgrimage in 1961. At the time of the massacre, a 477-page visitor's log recorded 10,000 signatures; some reports claimed that the community had as many as 300,000 pilgrims and 800 sedentary households.[12] Even in Olivorismo's first incarnation, the messianic prophet clearly had a national base of support, and his activities were reported in regional newspapers all over the country, from the eastern tip of Higüey to the central Cibao valley, where this "Dios incarnate" was especially popular.[13]

Furthermore, while the movement certainly offered a critique of the agro-export model of development and its social cost, a socioeconomic analysis cannot account for its nationalist ethos, which is not reducible to its economic determinants. The idea of the Dominican nation originally took shape through networks of pilgrimage to sacred sites associated with indigenous devotion and later with transcendent virgins. Creole identity was forged through the two national patron saints of the country, the Virgin of Altagracia and the Virgin of las Mercedes, who protected protonationalist insurgents in the colonial period by endowing them with her miraculous charisma and later provided the images for a nationalist topos of pilgrimage. As Jacques Lafaye has argued, the national terrain was first sacred; its avatars were not the founding fathers, but rather the twin virgins, whose numinous halos provided the vectors for the regional—and later national— space.[14] Liborismo was part of a long tradition of popular articulations of nationhood rendered through religious idioms.[15]

Nor can materialist or "compensatory" arguments account for the political vision of the Olivorista movement, the utopic recreation of the state in ideal terms.[16] While the increasing marginalization of the rural subproletariat in San Juan province helps elucidate the factors that may have pushed some followers to this sacred communal site, it cannot account for the particular shape and configuration of this community. The twins who were the leaders of the Palma Sola movement derived their legitimacy from selection as the inheritors of the spirit of Dios Olivorio. Certainly both Liborista episodes occurred during periods of profound political and social (not just economic) stress: the first was the result of the imposition of direct U.S. Marine rule and the reconfiguration of local political relations; the second, the result of the death of a dictator who had governed through total personal control, abolishing all parties save the official Dominican Party and allowing wholesale economic monopolization and extortion by an inner circle of cronies and family. When Trujillo was killed in May 1961, the country was quickly overcome by factions battling to take control of the vacant political space, yet there were no legitimate institutions through which to do so. The resulting vacuum was even greater since the regime had suffused civic life with such a dense surfeit of political ritual and pageantry. This regime spent enormous sums to create a symbolic world by saturating the citizenry via enforced participation in everyday rites and by scripting their public personae. In this context, the death of Trujillo was experienced not only as the end of an era but as the end of a social and moral universe as three generations had come to know it.[17]

Olivorismo offers a glimpse into what Michael Taussig has described as the "fantasies of the marginated concerning the secret of the center" during two moments of political transition.[18] In these times of state crisis, popular reinventions of the nation in miniature gained purchase due to the evisceration of official signs of sovereignty. In the early twentieth century, the state lost authority due to growing American imperial control. The 1907 treaty that gave the United States control over customs revenues and rendered trade with Haiti illegal was highly unpopular in the southwestern frontier; it made this region fiercely resistant to state authority until forcibly disarmed by the U.S. Marine constabulary in 1917. Contraband with Haiti had been the mainstay of the San Juan frontier economy and eighteen U.S. customs officials were wounded or killed during the first two years of imposed control.[19] Olivorio Mateo traversed contraband routes in the Cordillera Central mountains and found followers among the Cacos, peasant insurgents who fought U.S. Marines in Haiti; he was also allied with the powerful rancher Wenceslao Ramírez, who had grazing land and political allies across the border.[20] San Juan was a region of extensive ranching and large-scale cacao and wood production; it also had an important peasantry which maintained subsistence *conucos* (garden plots) and engaged in occasional wage labor. Yet during the 1912 civil war, cross-class unity was the norm within San Juan, as rich and poor fought side by side—Olivorio fought for Ramírez, for whom he occasionally did fencing and gardening, and insurgents attacked state symbols, such as the telegraph and telephone office and the office of public works.[21] In this frontier culture accustomed to regional autonomy, Dios Olivorio became a powerful emblem of resistance to the state, especially for the popular sectors.[22]

Although the movement was otherworldly, it was not pure escapism or nostalgia. Olivorismo was insular but also cosmopolitan, and it formed part of a wave of modernist millenarian movements that swept the Caribbean in the early twentieth century. These movements sought to simultaneously embrace and control, adopt and deflect, symbols of modernity at a time when global commerce was bringing a range of new products and practices into the country. In Cuba and Puerto Rico, spiritists married the language of rationalism and science with Afro-Creole syncretic beliefs; Afro-Cuban *babalawos* likewise sought to bring respectability to their neo-African religious practices by standardizing prayers and psalms in printed chapbooks and thus transforming what was pejoratively considered witchcraft into a full-fledged religion by providing it with canonical text.[23]

Olivorismo emerged as part of a global undercurrent of esoteric mystical beliefs that came to a head around the time of Halley's comet in 1910; the comet was interpreted as a sign that the apocalypse was fast approaching since the gaseous tail would bring immediate asphyxiation. Even in New York, rumor had it that the comet's tail would bring death and destruction.[24] Fin-de-siècle Europe had created a vogue for various forms of "white magic" among the rising middle classes, including Hindu beliefs about bodily forces (or *chakra*) and reincarnation which were quickly creolized. The magnetic-spiritual school, popular in Mexico and Argentina, for example, portrayed the body's essence as extending into the world through the voice and aura, which could be read by a medium. The immense popularity of Allan Kardec's books on spiritism among liberal elites in the Hispanic Caribbean also served to legitimate secular spirituality outside of the church; they also may have forged a space for a messianic faith that promised a heaven on earth not through the direct intervention of God but rather through the Holy Ghost.[25]

Olivorismo has been treated as a fringe movement on the border with Haiti, as a phenomenon that stands alone even within the context of Dominican popular religion.[26] Yet the community at Palma Sola invites comparisons with other frontier social movements that exhibited a lack of identification with—and even open hostility to—state projects, owing to the fact that they were constituted within semi-autonomous political spaces.[27] For example, Ana Alonso has written of "the dream of a peasant republic" in the northern border town of Chihuahua during the Mexican revolution, a vision that fueled antistate sentiment to the extent that many actually sided with the United States and against Mexico during the 1916 intervention.[28] The Haitian-Dominican borderlands have had a long history of transnational collaboration, as well as a sense of "moral alienation" from a state that seemed more parasitic than representative. For example, Desiderio Arias, the last regional caudillo to effectively challenge state authority, lived along the frontier; and the coup that ousted Jean-Bertrande Aristide from office in 2004 was launched from the Dominican border town of Dajabón. These frontier phenomena bear some similarity to U.S. militia groups, which cast the state as the nexus of a sinister international cabal that makes war to generate interest and siphons the sweat of hard-working citizens into the coffers of Wall Street. Palma Sola shared this vision, one deploying the power of God against the evils of state.[29] For this reason, Olivorismo presents a privileged site from which to glimpse a vision of the state from below, since the weakness of state control in liminal zones has permitted more space for alternative visions of the nation-state to take shape.[30]

While eventually condemned by some regional elites as a madman, Olivorio was a prophet to his followers, a visionary who exposed the root evils of civil society and showed how to expurgate them.[31] Olivorismo articulated a vision of the demonological excesses of power, especially of the state, and of their rectification. In the Dominican popular imagination, the saints are one's sole protection from the evils of man and nature. The *mellizos*, divine twins and leaders of Palma Sola, served as a bridge between the terrestrial and the metaphysical, the profane and the divine. Because they serve as the origin of the misterios or lwa (gods), twins are the most potent seres (beings, sacred powers) in the pantheon, always greeted and fed first in ceremonial occasions.[32] Only twins had the force to undo the evils of the Trujillista state. Yet the irony is that Palma Sola sought to rectify the sins of the Trujillato through some of the very rituals and symbols used by the regime, thus drawing upon the "magic of mimesis"—a form of sympathetic magic that captures the power of the original through duplication and mimes the power that is being dismantled.[33]

The story commences in 1908, when rumors began to circulate that the *brujo* (witch) of San Juan, Olivorio Mateo, had developed a following in the mountains above Las Matas de Farfán. People said that this *moreno* (mulatto) had established a brotherhood (cofradía) and that he had formed a court of saints and was performing miracles. It was also said that Olivorio disappeared during a severe storm that left San Juan in a shambles for several weeks; he was apparently on an extraterrestrial visitation, transported by an angel on a magnificent white horse. Dios Olivorio seems to have been marked by his association with the storm itself, or with the travel it afforded him, since he was said to be transformed from man into god after nine days.[34] Olivorio returned from his voyage as a diviner and thaumaturge, stating cryptically, "I come from very far away." He returned carrying the gift of healing from God, who set him on a thirty-three-year mission to heal the wounded and cure the sick.[35]

The main sources of Olivorio's spiritual authority were his ability to channel the prestige of the foreign and the tales of his spontaneous healing and miraculous cures.[36] It was said that he learned his skills from a healer who was possibly from Martinique. While there were many popular healers in the country, Dios Olivorio was renowned for his expertise as a supranational shaman who could decipher and invoke other nations' esoteric repertoires; he drew on objects and powers embodying the most geographically distant and thus most potent forces.[37] He also achieved prestige for his otherworldly travels; he visited other celestial universes on horseback and was received as a foreign dignitary by alien gods.[38] Not only did he affect a distant and enigmatic air, but at times he spoke his own opaque language.[39]

While Dominicans are prone to fetishize the powers and products of neighboring Haiti, which seemingly possess extraordinary value and supernatural potency, Olivorio by contrast focused on American commodities, which were just beginning to supplant German and French products at the turn of the century. This may account for his popular appellation as the "modern god."[40] He gained notoriety through his ability to predict and thus in some sense control the fearsome and magisterial U.S. battleships, marine troops, and even the elusive telephone, as well as more common hurricanes, storms, and natural phenomena. For example, Dios Olivorio awaited a massive yacht on which he would travel to heaven. It was said that

25. José Bedia, "El Santo Liborio se fue a la montaña," acrylic on cloth, 74 x 135 cm. COURTESY OF GARY NADER FINE ARTS, CORAL GABLES, FLORIDA.

Olivorio predicted the advent of electricity, as well as the fact that it would bring disaster. He also divined the airplane, the radio, modern women's attire, granulated salt, and a machine through which he would resuscitate the dead; in addition, he could foretell where future roads and canals would be built.[41] On the eve of the U.S. Marines' disembarkation in 1914, a military occupation was beyond Dominicans' wildest imaginings. Nonetheless, even this was no problem for Olivorio; not only did he see the marines coming, he even stalled their arrival. He was rumored to be responsible for the battle cruiser *Memphis* getting stuck on the rocky coast of Santo Domingo.[42] Through the cabalistic science of magic numbers, he could also protect his faithful from American bullets (during certain months they would be consumed by the misterios, leaving their targets unharmed).

As for the commonplace repertoire of Dominican *curanderismo* or popular healing, Olivorio was reported to prophesy natural mysteries as well. He was able to transpose data from one sensory or temporal sphere to another, hearing through seeing or seeing the future. He could "read" a cock's voice, recounting from its sound the bird's color, owner, and distinctive features. He could foretell natural irregularities, such as children born with birth defects (considered "sacred children") in neighboring townships.[43]

Olivorio was a conjurer whose reach went far beyond the everyday hurricane or tempest. As a clairvoyant, he foresaw Halley's comet; some said that he actually felled it, thus preventing an Armageddon. He predicted a storm that obliterated the parish chapel at San Juan de la Maguana. As a channel of God's wrath, Olivorio could punish those who harmed him. After he had a run-in with the police for practicing medicine without a license, an earthquake was unleashed upon his enemies as Olivorio's fucú or divine punishment, with the San Juan River flowing a lacteal white.[44] He even predicted singular phenomena such as a solar eclipse.

THE POWER OF KNOTS

As Jean Comaroff has elaborated, in healing cults the person becomes a semantic as well as somatic landscape upon which to fashion new identities.[45] Thus, in Olivorismo the body became the principal site of historical practice and social transformation, drawing converts from miles away for visits to Olivorio and his sacred sites, to a community in which the world was ritually reconstructed through a regime of healing and corporal purification. Olivorio cured with sacred *salves* (songs), *botellas* (herbal drinks), and his trademark stick, the *palo de piñon*, which he used to identify and extirpate maladies. He pointed the branch at the aggrieved spot, his arm serving as an indexical conduit directing powers channeled through his body. He also drew out malignant forces with his hands, at times using rum or even his own urine as an anointment.[46] He would beat the afflicted body with his branch, muttering in an indiscernible argot with a penetrating gaze and histrionic gestures. He would pace back and forth, tracing sacred *vèvè* drawings near the patient on the ground and reciting "that the bad leaves and the good enters."[47] Dominican popular medicinal theories perceive disease as resulting from an inundation of malignant electromagnetic forces, alien spirits, or the dead; healing involves flushing out these impurities and thus restoring corporal and spiritual balance.[48]

However, the Liborista signature of scarves, and especially cords fastened around the neck or forehead with a series of knots, played a key part in the ritual refashioning of the subject.[49] In one case, Olivorio placed two orange leaves on the patient in a cross and blew on a knotted scarf. Olivorio gave *pabilos* or raveled cotton cords to be tied around the head for especially severe headaches.[50] He requested that visitors to his sacred *calvario* (cross station) wear cords across their chests or heads.[51] He even required the posts of Liborista crosses to be tied together, forbidding the use of nails.[52] Indeed, wound up in these knots were Olivorio's thaumaturgical secrets.

Tying practices in Haiti may be pertinent to the meaning of the knotted cords that formed the core of Olivorio's healing instruments and uniform and that served as the primary markers of his sacral status. As Karen Mc-Carthy Brown has written about Haitian vodou, fastening may symbolize social ties, providing tangible signs of actual or desired emotive or spiritual links; and knotting is a feature of dangerous petwo rites and secret societies and is often used in *ouanga* spells.[53] And in the Dominican popular imagination, health is visualized through the concept of *desenvolvimiento*, the untying of a knot, which includes both physical and financial well-being of the self, ancestors, and kin.[54] Olivorio's cords may have indicated his direct connection to the Holy Ghost, but among his patients, wearing strings may have been signs of their bond to Olivorio, as God's missionary, and to each other, as part of a new community and society.

The significance of binding among the vodou cultures of southern Benin and Togo may also provide some clues. Suzanne Preston Blier has analyzed the centrality of wrapping and knotting with string as expressive visual metaphors of symbolic and physical strength, as well as conveyors of energy and potency.[55] Drawing on her analysis, the cords around the forehead may have symbolized Olivorio's own holy empowerment, forming sutures that directly linked his body like connective tissue to divine energy. In this view, the ties were umbilical cords to higher forces as well as signifying the energy of a stronger authority actively dominating him by strapping him down. The cords indexed a deeply corporeal notion of power, which could refer to the bondage of slavery, to lines of electric current, or both. As Wyatt MacGaffey has argued, binding and knotting are important visual metaphors for the control of hostile forces and are often used as protection against them in Kongo aesthetics.[56] Thus Olivorio was a raw conductor for a pure celestial charge that was barely constrained by the thin threads constricting his body.[57]

Blier's research can help untangle the complex of associations that may have been wound up in the knots and stones suspended in Olivorio's tensile cords. Knotting can be a visual sign of an act of magic or of other meanings sutured into the cord as into a text, marking the presence of supernatural powers.[58] In this sense, the knots and stones may have been fetishes conveying divine energies to Olivorio, or activating charms that empowered him in his godly mission while protecting him from his persecutors. Since Olivorio spent his last years on the run, it is quite likely that these knots were at least additionally protective amulets, as were rocks.[59] In San Juan province, stones are also said to harbor seres, most frequently the class of indio spirits that reside under the water, and among Olivoristas must be kept in a bowl of water in the lower, concealed portion of the altar.[60] Rocks also formed part of penitence rites among the Olivoristas, as members carried stones on their heads and deposited them in predetermined sites, particularly stations of the cross.[61] In this context, stones represented the sinful impurities cast off by officiants.[62] Nor was the fastening of a stone to Olivorio's forehead incidental. The head is the repository of both the self and the divinity during spirit possession; so attaching a stone to the head created a nodal point directly conjoining the material and spiritual domains.[63]

The association between Olivorismo, tying, and bondage was inextricably cemented when, after killing Olivorio Mateo, the U.S. Marines tied him to a stretcher and put his corpse on display in the central plaza of San Juan de la Maguana. Although their intent was desecration, they inadvertently transformed him into a nationalist martyr. This image of Mateo's torso, knotted cords around his neck and bound with rough-hewn sisal rope, is indelibly inscribed in the popular imagination in his contemporary chromolithograph. He was killed but neither vanquished nor forgotten. The Yankees took his body but could not contain his force. Of course, to his devotees, this effigy became proof of Mateo's "crucifixion" by the imperialist Americans, one that virtually guaranteed his eventual resurrection. This image also forever infused the meaning of Olivorio as a Dominican Christ, a sacrificial figure representing a region against the state, as well as a popular nation or pueblo against the imperialist aggressors. Upon his death, Olivorio was collected by a divine emissary on a resplendent white stallion and carried off until his return, when he was reputed to miraculously reappear in the flesh. The stallion invoked the fierce warrior-deity Ogún Balenyó (Saint Santiago), who, like Olivorio, fought and won battles for his people on a white horse with a cross in his right hand; in Haiti this deity was associated with soldiers and politicians, a kind of patron saint of popular nationhood. Indeed, Ogun is the one misterio from vodú included in a Liborista pantheon that also includes Liborio, Jesus Christ, and la Santísima Cruz (the holy cross).[64]

At his death, Olivorio became part of a popular nationalist iconography, which continues to assist and empower Dominicans, providing them with the force to fight venomous politicians, corrupt patrons, and a diabolical state. On his return to earth, Olivorio was said to join the spirits under the water, including *piedras de rayo* (thunder celts); there he worked with Anacaona, a sixteenth-century Indian priestess, and Christopher Columbus.[65] As wife of Caonabo, cacique of Maguana and the most powerful indigenous leader on the island, Anacaona has become a legendary figure representing

26. Death photo of Olivorio Mateo taken by U.S. Marines. ARCHIVO GENERAL DE LA NACIÓN, SANTO DOMINGO.

anticolonial resistance on Hispaniola in the early years of Spanish expansion. She represents an autochthonous nation that was robbed by the Spanish. The trinity of Olivorio, Anacaona, and Columbus today forms a triadic set of popular founding persons that merges political and religious power; it substitutes for the official heraldic trinity of Dominican nationhood in San Juan de la Maguana, one in which the dead live on.[66] According to an Olivorista liturgic song:

Dicen que Liborio ha muerto,
Liborio no ha muerto 'na
Liborio está en la Maguana
comiendo vaca salá.

They say Liborio is dead
Liborio hasn't died at all
Liborio is in Maguana
eating salted beef.

After Olivorio Mateo's death, he was resurrected, as predicted, in the mountains above San Juan de la Maguana. He was first reborn in the figure of one José Popa, who was killed during the first years of the Trujillo regime, after which his spirit continued to circulate more quietly among regional practitioners of the cult. Devotees continued to flock to the holy site at Maguana Arriba, where Mateo's community had been based; it had a sacred waterfall, a rock with an imprint of Olivorio's hand and face, and a shrine in his name where miraculous cures, purification, and protection were sought. Although police records during the Trujillato indicate that the regime kept a vigilant eye on Liborista activities, Mateo continued to be cultivated and worshiped, albeit more privately after 1930, when a more efficient system of social control and surveillance was introduced.[67] Although repression was sporadic and haphazard under the Trujillato, periodic campaigns against popular healers and other religious visionaries with public identities or communities instilled fear among practitioners and encouraged the privatization of religious practices so as to escape state vigilance and possible attacks.[68] Olivorista worship continued in secret, however, and Papá Liborio's fame grew as a popular symbol of both nationhood and regional defiance.

What was it about the community formed by the Ventura Rodríguez brothers at Palma Sola that enabled the second coming of Olivorio? Certainly the principal factor was the "structure of the conjuncture" created by Trujillo's death, which allowed the formation of a community that would have been impossible under the strict social control and surveillance during the regime.[69] The end of the Trujillo era also provoked tremendous popular dread about the future that verged on the apocalyptic for many. Palma Sola was an expression of fears of democracy after three decades of authoritarian rule, but also a popular response to the utopic promise of democratic participation.[70] But what enabled the mellizos to speak with such authority? What authorized them to define a sacred space and political arena in which *el maestro*, Olivorio, was summoned to speak through their voices?[71]

The mellizos were born into a family of nine, with some twenty thousand tareas of land under cultivation, which qualified them as middle peasants in the socioeconomic matrix of San Juan de la Maguana. Notwithstanding their status as *campesinos acomodados* (relatively well-off peasants), they had political problems in 1941, when one of the mellizos, León, was accused in the death of a soldier stationed in their section. As a result, León fled to

Haiti, where he took refuge until Trujillo's death in 1961. There he accumulated symbolic capital from the charismatic aura of being at the center of things divine, the sacred source of vodou, Haiti.[72] But more important, the family had been blessed by twin offspring—it was said that the family had three sets of twins. In fact, León had been born with a twin girl who died. As a mark of distinction, twins cast an aura over the entire family, especially Plinio, who was a dosu, the male child following twins.[73]

Associated with fertility and reproduction, twins are "powerful and dangerous"; they are original doubles, punning on the union of humanity and divinity, of the mundane and the metaphysical, that is mankind.[74] Like Christ, they represent the original birth, the foundational mythology of communities, nations, and races. They are the first children and the first dead; like Gede, or the spirit of death, they stand at the crossroads linking this world with the world of the ancestors.[75] By enabling transformation and change, they offer hope. As mentioned in relation to Trujillo's muchachito, these "spirit doubles" offer access to esoteric knowledge and mystical power; as such they enable the agglutinative "heaping of powers" that is the optimal source of eminence.[76] Twinship enables one to be a crowd. The mellizos are protective against sorcery, but are also associated with it because they can bring wealth.[77]

If mellizos offer one source of passage to alien realms, another portal is accessed through dreams. Dreamspace is everyman's portal to *lo más allá*, the invisible realm. Anyone can receive messages from the other world through dreams, although not everyone can interpret their signs. As in Haiti, prescient dreams can indicate that one is called by the misterios, that the seres want to establish a direct line of access.[78] Dreams can also be predictive, a means through which the seres issue orders. Plinio, the omniscient seer of the two, had a dream in which he was exhorted to visit all the "gates" to the other world; he interpreted them as altars honoring Olivorio, so as to enrich his faith. An old man with flowing white robes—the Holy Ghost—spoke to him in this dream. He was then ordered to establish a shrine to Olivorio. He proceeded to move his entire extended family to a site at Palma Sola, where the community began to take shape. As dosu, Plinio was spiritually charged with forming and maintaining the new branch of the Olivorista cult.[79]

After the death of Trujillo, Plinio began to fulfill his "promise": to establish a calvary of three crosses for Olivorio (today an emblem of the movement). The mission of Plinio and León was to start a *hermandad* or brother-

27. Holy calvary at Palma Sola. PHOTO BY THE AUTHOR.

hood which would do away with evil, sorcery, witches, bacás, and galipotes.[80] It was said that after Trujillo's death an enormous jolt would shake the earth, at which point the "believers" would become ministers of the entire world. Predictions circulated that the end of the world was approaching, that there would be world war, earthquakes, and eternal darkness. Those who lacked faith would not survive. Their mission began with a seven-day pilgrimage through the mountains, where they found invisible springs and hidden tabernacles. Those who wished to be saved were asked to purchase a small candle and a matchbox to be blessed; they were told that the candle would be the sole operative light and that Olivorio would take those with the light to a place called Media Luna, a site discovered during the pilgrimage. Upon the dictator's death, many prophets claiming Olivorio's misterio sprang up, but only Plinio and León succeeded in forming a holy city. While Olivorio's word would travel the world, the seed of his message would be planted there.[81]

One feature that made Palma Sola distinct from the earlier cult of Olivorismo was the spatialization of the community.[82] The new community was forged by establishing a "santo corral" or sacred courtyard, with three crosses inside a stone corral and a simple church.[83] The church had two rooms, one of which served as a bedroom for the mellizos and the "living virgin," who was the Olivorista mascot. There were triadic cross stations, each with different "functions." One of the Ventura brothers, Tulio, was stationed at the Cross of the Oath, where newcomers came to ask God's forgiveness directly and to swear allegiance to Christ and Olivorio; this station was called the interrogatory or the *juramento*;[84] the second was called the Black Cross. The focal point was the third, the calvary, surrounded by a series of concentric stone circles for which a rigorous set of rules applied: visitors must walk in one direction only, firearms were not allowed, no one could enter the interior circle where the crosses stood, and pilgrims must circle three times before entering the holy site. The entire community would process, singing, through this circular maze of crosses. In contrast to a Catholic holy site, there was no altar; there was no need for a gateway to the gods since it was presumed that they were present. The service itself consisted of a series of rites propitiating the crosses.[85]

Palma Sola explicitly modeled itself as a nation in miniature. Drawing upon Haitian terminology, Don León Ventura commonly referred to the misterios as a nación. The movement had a white flag with blue trim (called Christ's Flag), blue for Olivorio and white for the Holy Ghost; in the center was a palm tree and the number one. The flag was intended to be a visual representation of the holy city of Palma Sola (single palm), but it borrowed the palmetto from Olivorio Mateo's original site of worship at El Palmar and perhaps from the official iconography of the Dominican Party. Adepts claimed that the palm was a sign of world freedom and that the number one represented God. The flag's shield had three hearts intertwined, crowned by a cross. Faith, hope, and charity were the group's slogan; the party's name, the World Christian Union. This central flag was raised and lowered meticulously each day.[86]

The overarching objective of the group's ritual life was lustration. Palma Sola offered a utopic withdrawal and rectification of several dangers of the "street," including the unchecked powers of witchcraft.[87] For example, one of the central cult rituals was the "dispatch of the witches" at the Cross of the Oath, where a prayer would be sung that sent all negative spirits upward through a mahogany tree.[88] Trees were cleansing vehicles, enabling the channeling of positive and malevolent spirits into and out of the community. Palma Sola purged worldly evils associated with development and urbanization through the creation of a sanctified urban utopia, a divine blueprint which would become the apotheosis of a new social order. The sacred space was defined by a series of circles, formed with rocks, the stones being spirits incarnate. There was a strict taboo against walking upon, or

RECTITUD
LIBERTAD
TRABAJO
MORALIDAD

DECLARACION DE PRINCIPIOS Y ESTATUTOS DEL
PARTIDO DOMINICANO
15 DE AGOSTO - 1945

28. Dominican Party insignia.
ARCHIVO GENERAL DE LA NACIÓN,
SANTO DOMINGO.

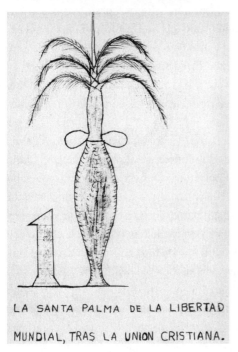

LA SANTA PALMA DE LA LIBERTAD

MUNDIAL, TRAS LA UNION CRISTIANA.

29. Olivorista drawing of sacred palm.
FROM LUSITANIA MARTÍNEZ, *PALMA
SOLA: OPRESIÓN Y ESPERANZA (SU
GEOGRAFÍA MÍTICA Y SOCIAL)* (SANTO
DOMINGO: EDICIONES CEDEE, 1991),
154.

otherwise disturbing, these holy rocks. Bathing in *la agüita*, a sacred pool, and marching in procession through the stone circles purified the missionaries while immersing them in a new moral economy of hygiene. Circling through the stones unlocked the gateway between this world and the other, while at the same time recalling the empowering motifs of containment and bondage in the earlier incarnation of Olivorismo.[89]

The utopic space of Palma Sola was a representation of an ideal world, but was developed from a repertoire of everyday life.[90] The use of terms such as *despacho, función, interrogatorio, juramento,* and *cuenta,* for example, which invoke officialdom and bureaucracy, reveals another feature of Palma Sola: the way in which the magic of the state was called on to expel unwanted impurities. As Holston has argued, bureaucratic power also has its charismatic aspects.[91] The accouterments of office were often used as talismans to define a new social identity.

Palma Sola members drew upon what Taussig has called the "fetish power" of the state to fashion their sacred and sovereign community.[92] From uniforms to civic rites, they relished the trappings of officialdom and deployed them generously in a drive to enchant their own rituals of rule. For example, order and organization were keywords in the formation of a police force, replete with barracks. Protected not by arms but by concentric sacred stone squares decorated with stars, guards were intended to maintain order and to enforce the prohibition against arms or alcohol in the sacred circle.[93] They wore uniforms of blue denim pants (the costume of Olivorio and penitents), with a white shirt and a black tie. Other officials at Palma Sola were given rigid sartorial restrictions. The living virgin, for example, wore a long dress of white and violet, and women were urged not to wear short sleeves or short skirts, pants, brassieres, or shoes. Striped clothes were also prohibited.[94]

The legislative veneer of Palma Sola, in its inadvertent mimicry of the civil apparatus of social control, in effect reproduced the forms of state authority but without their substance. For example, even though few of the faithful were literate among the cult leadership or the pilgrims, upon entering Palma Sola, each person had to inscribe his or her official identity in a large log, including name and cédula number. Moreover, the global vision of the community was deeply marked by the United States cold war ideology, which had become policy in the Dominican Republic as well. In this view, the world consisted of the Americas, the Russians, the Chinese, and Africa.[95] Drawing upon the language of officialdom, Palma Sola sought to

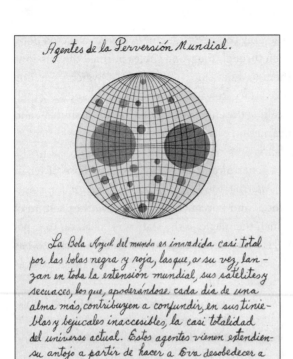

Agentes de la Perversión Mundial.

La Bola Azul del mundo es invadida casi total por las bolas negra y roja, las que, a su vez, lanzan en toda la extensión mundial sus satélites y secuaces, los que, apoderándose cada día de una alma más, contribuyen a confundir, en sus tinieblas y bejucales inaccesibles, la casi totalidad del universo actual. Estos agentes vienen extendiendo su antojo a partir de hacer a Eva desobedecer a Dios, y a Caín exterminar a su hermano Abel, teniendo como consecuencia actual y desde hace millares

30. Olivorista drawing of Agents of World Perversion. "The blue ball of the world is invaded almost entirely by the red and black balls, which extend everywhere their satellites and henchmen, thus contributing to the confusion by taking control day by day of more people, and casting inaccessible darkness and jungle over almost the entirety of the universe. These agents extend their desires after making Eve disobey God, and Cain kill his brother Abel." FROM LUSITANIA MARTÍNEZ, PALMA SOLA, 193.

thoroughly distinguish itself from the ragtag popular healers of the street: this was a community, not a crowd; a political party, not a festive feast.[96]

Over time the persecution of Olivorismo on the basis of its purported *brujería* also gave rise to efforts to theologize it at Palma Sola so as to create a " 'true,' 'modern' religion."[97] These included both intensive ritualization as well as the formation of texts that would become a virtual bible of Olivorismo, which would ratify the authority of the mellizos. As Don León noted, "We have the book of the Union Cristiana Mundial almost written . . . to provide more information about me, my dedication and my intelligence, that is to say, that although I live in the countryside, I am not of the countryside; although I am not a material professional, I am a spiritual professional."[98] Pantheonizing Olivorismo by giving it an emblem and a standardized liturgy also supported its claim to be a real religion, as opposed to saint worship, which might be viewed as coterminous with vodú or brujería practiced informally at home and which had long been associated with criminality and blackness. Olivorismo drew upon elements of Dominican folk Catholicism, yet many Olivorista lay preachers denied that they read the Bible, asserting instead that they received the message directly from Olivorio and the misterios. As Don León stated, "For the Olivoristas, Liborio is Jesus Christ," a statement that seems to locate Olivorismo in a church parallel to and distinct from Catholicism.[99]

In the chiliastic ideology of the cult, numbers were read as divine inscriptions or glyphs, or historical clues. Seven was a key number in Olivorismo. It was the number of trials Olivorio passed through before his sanctification as well as the number of misterios said to be higher than God. There were also seven sacrificial lambs who would die for Olivorismo before the apocalypse. Seven was the number who would be sacrificed before the end of the pact of blood between God and man.[100] Three was also an axial number; indeed, everything divine in Olivorismo broke into clusters of three: three crosses of the central calvary, the Holy Trinity of God, Liborio, and the Holy Ghost (or interchangeably, Father, Son, and Holy Ghost); the three hearts of the flag; the three sets of Rodríguez twins; and the motif faith, hope, and charity.[101] The year 2000 was judgment day, when evildoers would be sent their just dessert.[102] Even the most potent symbol of public identity, the official identification card or cédula that provided the basis of social control and repression under the dictatorship, was integrated into the magic arsenal of the cult—recorded and transformed into a source of magic numbers and divine numerology.[103]

The community at Palma Sola was defined in opposition to the street, a space defined by the seemingly arbitrary criteria of state power and commerce. It was based on neither ascriptive nor achieved criteria but rather on a radically inclusive morality. In the words of the virgin, "All mothers are virgins; all children angels." Anyone could join the movement; anyone who wished was given a plot of land to farm. And most especially, the core purpose of the cult—miraculous healing—was done free.[104] The mellizos healed body and soul through prayer, rum anointment, use of herbs, and the making of crosses on the patient; they were renowned for special adeptness in curing *dolores del misterio*, or maladies sent through witchcraft. But in working the body they were transforming the world; since disease was caused by the Antichrist (Satan) and by the United States, which was the primary agent of global perversion.[105] Don León commonly fabricated *resguardos*, or protective bracelets, from coiled colored threads, which resembled the tensile cords of Olivorio Mateo. Evil was caused by envy and was the result of *malos espíritus* which must be purged.[106] One of the deepest prohibitions of the World Christian Union was against the use of cash, as if commercial exchange itself made strangers out of friends and potential enemies out of family (although ironically twins are often associated with the acquisition of money).[107] The desire for autonomy was expressed through the taboo against the consumption of American foodstuffs, particularly those of the aid organizations CARE and CARITAS. In a vision that conjoined national and bodily boundaries, rejecting United States food implied withdrawal from the imperial economy of commerce and food aid as well as the orbit of the United States.

SORCERY AND THE STATE

Understanding the vampiric vision of the state in peasant ideology, however, requires some consideration of how the state touched the daily lives of individuals during the Trujillato—how it looked from below, particularly in light of the Trujillista politics that defined the state for three decades.[108] Olivorismo clearly vilified the region's hypercommercialization during the 1950s, as commercial agriculture grew enormously. The expansion of export agriculture raised land values, forcing many lower-to-middle peasants off the fertile lands of the San Juan Valley and onto elevated terrain. This migration had commenced during the U.S. occupation, when a new immigrant class arrived and several U.S. lumber firms created agrarian stratification through water diversion, transforming the plains into scrub overnight and thus drastically altering regional topography.[109] The process of land alienation and proletarianization accelerated during the postwar export boom of the early 1950s, as world prices for primary commodities soared. In Palma Sola, however, money was anathema and its use taboo, as the cash nexus was replaced with a moral economy of gift exchange.[110]

On the political front at Palma Sola, the absolute prohibition against betrayal can be seen as a response to the style of government under the Trujillato, with its extensive system of espionage in which informants were rewarded well for denouncing neighbors and kin. During the regime, denunciation became an arbitrary weapon through which those with access to power could eliminate competition for jobs, land, or other resources (see chapter 4).[111] In the popular cosmology of Palma Sola, denunciation was conflated with witchcraft, as succumbing to diabolical temptations. A prominent feature of Palma Sola was a popular tribunal, where individuals could confess their sins and be pardoned by the all-knowing spirit of Olivorio. This tribunal was staffed by guards and handled disputes between pilgrims. Accountability, as well as honesty, were community laws. Palma Sola was founded on a principle of absolute transparency before God. An important aspect of the charismatic authority of Palma Sola was its provision of accountability and the possibility of rehabilitation, both of which were entirely absent from the penal system of the Trujillo regime.[112] Furthermore, the World Christian Union established its own temporal calendar, pulling adults out of the fields and children out of school on Monday, Wednesday, and Friday, when they were summoned to participate in events at Palma Sola. Finally, weaponry was prohibited from the site; devotees believed that their faith would consume bullets and thus provide protection.

On one level, Palma Sola was a recidivist movement that proclaimed society in rebellion against the state, that declared war on modernity. Palma Sola combated the feeling of "weightlessness" that accompanied the crisis of authority on Trujillo's death with a political project based on a new symbolic order; the public culture of the dictatorship was rejected in favor of a holistic community identity based on bodily redemption, renewal, and transcendence.[113] Finally, official markers of the regime—from school, which was the basis of rural civic culture and the public sphere during the Trujillato, to arms—were dispensed with in favor of an inclusive space ruled by celestial government and divine justice. Arms may have been an especially important issue since the penal system had provided an important connection with the state for the Rodríguez family, because León had trained in the army and Tulio's son had been second alcalde or mayor.

However, features of the Trujillista state that had become second nature cropped up inexplicably in Olivorista practice. As Joseph and Nugent have observed, state power can furnish some of the idioms in which subaltern groups frame resistance projects.[114] And indeed the "bureaucratic performative" was an important part of the power of the movement, from the gathering of signatures and cédula numbers in the log to the Dominican Party "palmita," which became the emblem (and visual metaphor) for the Palma Sola community.[115] The ritualized use of space, including twice-weekly processions and parades, recalled in miniature the "theater state" of the Trujillo regime, in which citizenship was marked by participation in a constant round of civic rites, state pageants, official party rallies, rural inspections, nationalist holidays, and patriotic school events. With their autonomous tribunal and uniforms, the Palma Sola guards simulated the secret police of the regime, yet to an antithetical end. Olivoristas drew on the magic power of replication and mimesis to invoke and embody the authority of Trujillista rituals of rule.[116] The power of Olivorista practice lay in its ability to articulate the secrets of state in poetic form.

However, there may be another source for the ritualization of the community at Palma Sola. The historically weak presence of the Catholic Church, especially in the southwestern border zone, enabled parishioners to take religion into their own hands, and it accounts for the very active presence of lay cofradías such as that of Espíritu Santo, one of the largest and oldest in the country.[117] Banned from white confraternities, cofradías or hermandades were the only form of association allowed to nonwhites in the colonial period.[118] Yet the cofradías lacked the external trappings of authority provided by the church and had to rely on their own public rituals, rules, and organizational hierarchy to authenticate their faith. The predominance of lay control may also account for some of the similarities between Olivorismo and evangelical Protestantism, both of which presume a more direct line to God than traditional Catholicism since they involve forms of spirit possession; as such, the mellizos (and other Liborista misioneros) were said to carry the spirit of Dios Olivorio and of Espíritu Santo, the Holy Ghost, the purest manifestation of God.[119]

The Cofradía of San Juan Bautista (the patron saint of San Juan de la Maguana) was the most important Dominican confraternity in the colonial period. Today this brotherhood remains strong in San Juan, and its devotion is linked to Olivorismo, as is the Cofradía of Espíritu Santo, which is based in Las Matas de Farfán.[120] Formed in 1602 by and for Creole freedmen, the Cofradía of San Juan Bautista was located in the Santo Domingo Cathedral and was considered one of the most sumptuous brotherhoods, officially recognized and winning numerous "indulgences" by the Pope.[121] It might have served as a vehicle for marking the status of Creole freedmen, expressing a sense of superiority over the Biafran, Arara, and Mandingo slave cofradías, as did the colonial Cuban cabildo for the Royal Slaves of El Cobre.[122] Less corporate forms of veneration of the Holy Spirit were likely even more commonplace and could serve just as well as a vehicle for claims to ethnic distinction and even political aspiration. For example, in 1781 a Spanish freedman who took the title of Romaine-la-Prophétesse claimed to be possessed by the Holy Spirit, to have a written correspondence with the Virgin Mary, and, according to rumor, wanted to be king of Saint Domingue.[123]

The incipient nationalism of Olivorismo may also be traced to its formation as a hermandad or cofradía. Like the Cabildos de Nación of Cuba, the

31. Olivorista Queen, Doña Reina Alejandro Jimenez, with flags. PHOTO BY THE AUTHOR.

Dominican confraternities borrowed liberally from the heraldic insignia of the state to legitimize their authority—for example, flags, crests, crowns, scepters, medals, and office titles. As David Brown explains, the cabildos were "miniature neo-African monarchies" of the Afro-Cuban communities. He continues: "Such 'borrowed' royal styles constituted, and continue to represent, an African Diaspora lingua franca of authority and elegance" in various forms of public display. And in ritual contexts such as carnival or patron saint festivals, the use of such "tokens of legitimation and empowerment" by marginalized groups could come to represent "alternative structures of authority" for both the communities themselves and the state.[124]

SUBTERRANEAN SECRETS

On 12 October 1992, the five hundredth anniversary of Columbus's arrival in the New World, I traveled to San Juan de la Maguana to speak with Don León Ventura Rodríguez, the surviving mellizo from Palma Sola. I spent some five hours talking to him about Palma Sola, the World Christian Union, and politics. Two themes stood out in this long and often meandering discussion. First, politicians had brought only war, inequity, and division to public life, which is why a divine tribunal was needed to rectify the imbalances created. Society was so off kilter that only the "Lever of Justice," or the Judge of Conscience, could right it. Man had tried and failed, and his experiment had produced only internecine warfare led by political parties and nations. Thus only a direct intervention from the omniscient could rectify the wrongs done by political man. On the day of judgment, there would be a celestial meeting of all twenty-one world presidents, who would become divine ministers for the World Christian Union; they would try the guilty, make them pay for their sins, and free the innocent.

The second message was that *el maestro* Olivorio was still in control, albeit behind the scenes. It was Olivorio who had put Trujillo into office. Trujillo was given the "gift" to stop all the *ñoñería*, the political chaos and infighting. But when he became too big, when he became "the richest man in the world," he became evil. It was then that Olivorio had him ousted from power and killed. Olivorio is a messenger from God, from Christ, from the Holy Ghost, but Don León represents his second coming. León picked up el maestro's spirit in the womb, since he was conceived just days after the Americans slaughtered Olivorio. León wasn't born; he was sent by the misterios. He boasted that he had installed Joaquín Balaguer as president of the Dominican Republic; in exchange he had become an honorary Reformista or member of the PRD.[125] At one point he said, "Today I remember the discovery of America, I remember Columbus, and Diego [son of Columbus, who was first governor of Santo Domingo], I remember all the secrets (misterios), today I have them all piled on top of me . . . I don't have a cent, but I am bigger than all the presidents of the world."

That evening we visited María de Olios, a devout Olivorista, who lives with her mother, husband, sister, and a couple of nieces in a two-room dilapidated home on the outskirts of San Juan de la Maguana. María's husband is a carpenter who accompanied an ailing relative to Palma Sola, where he was cured. She recounted to us the story of Christopher Columbus's arrival on the north coast of what would become the Dominican Republic. She explained that there are two classes of beings, those of the land and those of the water. Olivorio rules the land, and the Indian chief Anacaona the water; they rule together like the left and the right hand. When Columbus arrived, he discovered the land, with the Indians living there mute and in a primitive state. He saw a few on a stone, smoking tobacco, which they offered him. When Columbus sent priests to teach them to speak and read, they fled under the water, giving birth to the land under the water which is the primary source of hidden potency today tapped by curanderos, mystics, and diviners alike. She reported that Indians appear sitting on top of rocks in water pools, most often women with long

32. María de Olios with image of Olivorio Mateo from her altar, Las Matas de Farfán.
PHOTO BY AUTHOR.

33. Closeup of Olivorio image; note how face is worn away because of frequent touching.
PHOTO BY AUTHOR.

34. María de Olios's comadre in front of her altar with images of former presidents Trujillo and Balaguer, Las Matas de Farfán. PHOTO BY AUTHOR.

straight blond hair, although they often disappear on sight. Indians can heal even better than the saints; but they can also take you under the water with them. Once María was abducted for some three days under the water, where she saw the land of gold inhabited by the Indians. They fell in love with her and came to her in a dream: an indio and a moreno; the moreno seduced her and drew her into a cave. Unlike some, she returned and today does spiritual "works" with Anacaona, Columbus, and even Juan Pablo Duarte, founding father of the nation.

The Olivoristas have remapped the nation as a dialectic between two spatialized topoi: that of land, state power, and the rich, and that of an invisible realm of arcane powers under the water, a kind of hidden national space accessed through secret portals such as caves. These two zones are complementary and opposed domains of power and authority. The concealed realm under the water has become an arcane, mysterious, but powerful alternative to the rigid rules and boundaries of official statecraft. As invoked by the Liboristas at Palma Sola, this realm taps the conjuring powers of officialdom—for example, the authoritative discourse of jurisprudence—but displaces it onto a celestial arena—beyond the reach of corrupt politicians and a self-serving government for which there is no accountability, at least from the perspective of the disenfranchised.

I wish to propose that the "dialectical imagery" of Palma Sola which contrasts this world with the occluded world underwater of the indios may be a byproduct of a political ontology that surfaced with the Trujillo regime.[126] In this hermeneutics of suspicion, the world under the water is a visual metaphor of the potent, hidden secrets that were thought to be the true arbiters of the political game under Trujillo at a time when his tentacles were perceived to be behind virtually every act of government. While this cluster of beliefs about Indian water spirits existed in the San Juan area previously, it took on a new significance after Trujillo's death as the nation tried to come to terms with a dark and brutal past, and imagine what a democratic future might look like, or whether it was even safe to take seriously the politicians' claim that democracy had indeed returned to the country. As one manifestation, for example, the press during the Era of Trujillo combined an oversaturation of adulation with a total blackout of critical engagement in ways that may well have helped give rise to a "paranoid style," here envisaged as an invisible domain of hidden agency that bears a similarity to the diarchic model of the muchachito narratives (chapter 6).[127] Further evidence of the paranoia that engulfed the country at that time was the very widespread contention that Palma Sola could not be what it purported to be—an otherworldly religious community—since rumors raged that it was really a cover for ambitious political forces seeking to reclaim the country.[128]

CONCLUSION

Georg Simmel saw the potential for visualizing secrecy as a kind of spatial poetics when he wrote that "the secret offers, so to speak, the possibility of a second world alongside the manifest world; and the latter is decisively influenced by the former."[129] At Palma Sola, a political cosmology was spatialized into discrete, albeit linked, domains.[130] As we see in the Liborista narratives above, the space under the water is marked apart, yet it is in every way attached to this world; it is a space of possibility, of the promise of change, a "moral topography" with the power to recruit through abduction and thus spiritually withdraw those who have seen the light, just as Olivorio (via León) is seen as controlling and ultimately even sanctioning the corrupt through potentially abducting politicians who transgress the bounds of their office.[131] It offers hope since it promises that a higher moral order is invisibly governing, hovering in the shadows, ready to intervene when transgressions occur; thus in true chiliastic form, accountability will arrive with the day of judgement, when the last shall be first. Invisible to mere mortals, this parallel world offers a space of revelation apart from the "opacities of power," and the possibility of political agency for those who most sorely need it.[132]

Olivorismo draws upon the magic of modernity even while rejecting it, and reimagines the architecture of rule in a way that offers a sanctuary beyond the reach of a bloodsucking, kleptocratic state.[133] This view of the state as utterly alien and heteronomous helps explain the urgent need on the part of Olivoristas to fashion a divine democracy. One of the secrets occluded from the public gaze under the Trujillato was the hidden accumulation of wealth behind the official narrative of rectitude, of honesty and righteousness. Yet the Liboristas can see the truth behind this "public secret," that which is known but cannot be articulated, the "spectral radiance of the unsaid"; their tribunal, the juramento, offering the transparency, indemnification and justice sorely lacking in the post-Trujillo polity.[134] Perhaps this is why bondage is such a powerful visual metaphor for the group. It captures the essence of a universe askew for the Olivoristas, how the citizenry has been strangled by a parasitic state, and how God should treat the millionaires who have used legislative power and municipal office to acquire land and riches from no labor of their own. And in this context, divine justice may well be the only way to heal the inequities created by the Trujillato.

CONCLUSION   **CHARISMA AND THE GIFT OF RECOGNITION**

> Dominicans love to receive gifts—this always makes them happier. And
> this is why my father never accepted the gift [from Trujillo]. How do you
> make a gift? It's very simple. He knew that there were people that you
> could not give to. There are those that throw themselves on the floor to
> collect it. There are those that you throw it in the middle of the sea and
> they go in there to find it. Then there are those that ask. The gift is not
> really a gift but rather something else.
>
> INTERVIEW, FRANCISCO ELPIDIO BERAS, APRIL 1992

> "Everything we owe to Trujillo" (Todo se lo debemos a Trujillo)
> TRUJILLISTA SLOGAN

> "The money you pay, will pay you back" (El dinero que pagues, te pagarán)
> CELIA CRUZ, "LA VARA Y LA MONEDA"

What insights does this exploration of the Trujillo regime offer a comparative understanding of Latin American populism? First, that political forms are a product of society, and thus classifications of populism
should be done on the basis of the directionality of their horizontal and
vertical axes, since some populist symbolic politics offer a myth of equivalence based on the leader identifying with the masses, while in other systems leaders seek to elevate the masses. If societies sharply divided along
class hierarchies such as Argentina produced populists whose power resided in their identification with the working class, mestizo societies such
as that in the Dominican Republic, with more homogeneous ideologies of
race and nation, offered an alternative symbolic politics, one based on
providing the illusion of upward mobility.[1]

Herein lies one of the paradoxes of Trujillo's style of populism. In contrast
to Juan Perón, who manifested his connection to the masses via symbolic
forms of social leveling, Trujillo elevated the masses. Perón engaged in
symbolic "blasphemy" by casting himself as a working-class male, whereas
Trujillo brought civilization and high culture to the illiterate underclasses.

Perón stripped off his shirt with the workers in the Plaza de Mayo, rendering himself a "shirtless one" in the very space that defined gentility for the Buenos Aires elite.[2] Trujillo distributed status markers to the population. During the year of the independence centennial in 1944, the Dominican Party allocated "Hollywood beds" as nuptial gifts, held mass marriages, and invited the poor to banquets in the Dominican party palaces where they could eat European cuisine; Trujillo installed television sets in the party branches and shipped pianos to cattle ranchers and sharecroppers in the frontier.[3] He subsidized classical music when the Bellas Artes concert hall was built in 1947, staffing it with exiled Spanish and Jewish musicians who played classical repertoire priced for the masses.[4] He took the rustic campesino music of the Cibao merengue and *se lo vistió de frac*, or made it aristocratic.[5] Given the prevalence of informal unions and the intense stigma of illegitimacy, the regime's pronuptialism must have been seen as a very special gift by those who could not otherwise afford formal wedlock. Trujillo also invested in popular entertainments with a black cast; for example, he provided truckloads of beer (a step up from *kleren* or bathtub rum) for Gagá bands, Haitian sodalities that engage in mock battles in the sugar *bateyes* during holy week, and he elevated an Afro-Dominican cofradía in San Cristóbal by building it a chapel.[6]

In this homogeneous and very poor society, Trujillo distributed the norms and forms signifying whiteness to the mulatto underclasses, making the gente de segunda feel like gente decente by casting its members as white-collar professionals speaking at Dominican Party events, able to eat rice and meat rather than yucca and beans and to drink beer or champagne instead of rum.[7] He was clearly no revolutionary, but allowing poor brown Dominicans into the social spaces of the elite caused enough of a sea change for observers to say that social divisions seemed to disappear under Trujillo, that he "socially democratized" the country.[8] This change was achieved through university education and civil service expansion, which enabled Dominicans to fill occupational niches such as engineering that had previously been occupied by foreigners. The creation and expansion of the Dominican Party also scripted poorer (thus darker-skinned) Dominicans into frequent rites of state that were headlined in the national newspaper and thus placed them in the public eye in a more prominent way than previously, when rules of deference had made them invisible. As one man put it, the overall effect was "that Trujillo has put the Creole where he belongs"; the article was written by a man who fittingly described himself as *canela fina*, or fine cinnamon.[9] The illusion was sustained because of the way this genre of populism accorded with the popular conception of *blanqueamiento*, by which mestizo individuals could advance in status as they advanced socioeconomically.[10] If mestizos were defined as transitioning to white, Trujillo made them feel as if they had arrived. Such practices conveyed a powerful sense of recognition to the masses who had previously not been accorded personhood by the state but had remained a faceless, shoeless, anonymous multitude.[11]

TRUJILLO, EL BENEFACTOR

The secret to unraveling Trujillo's charisma is the politics of patronage under the regime, a feature with both instrumental and expressive dimensions.[12] Trujillo took over the central pillars of the economy and then converted some of the cash he usurped into his own symbolic capital, by investing it in houses and women and by distributing it to his allies and the population at large through gifts. As Pierre Bourdieu has said, "The gift, generosity, conspicuous distribution . . . are operations of social alchemy . . . which tend to bring about the transmutation of economic capital into symbolic capital."[13] Yet this alchemy also transformed the recipients. These gifts became tokens of recognition that fostered a feeling of inclusion, a form of symbolic citizenship as the marginal were acknowledged as members of the nation.[14] This was especially meaningful given a history of a weak state and weak market penetration, especially in the interior.

The growth of the informal sector in the capital city in the 1950s as well as the instability of mestizo identity may have made Dominicans more available to Trujillo's kind of symbolic politics. The fact that Dominicans see themselves as Creoles or mixed-race indios, "both black and white, like dominos," means that everyone potentially carries the invisible stigma of blackness, of nonpersonhood, of anonymity, and harbors a fear of this secret being outed.[15] The other side of the tigueraje fantasy of social climbing is the threat of possible failure, which creates the figure of the *resentido* —someone like Trujillo who dreamed of being rich, loved, and powerful and yet never quite made it, who was ultimately seen by some as an outcast, a foundling, a pariah.[16] Trujillo's vernacular politics played upon a thirst for recognition, which as Frantz Fanon reminds us is a feature of former slave societies; Dominicans in popular parlance call this condition *comparona* (incessantly envious), which is said to be a Creole trait especially among the petit bourgeoisie.[17] Dominicans were also more available to Trujillo's politics of symbolic inclusion because of the nature of economic development under his rule. Notwithstanding the veneer of modernity and urbanity, the percentage of skilled, semi-skilled, or white-collar employment for men did not increase appreciably during the regime, which meant that participating in a Dominican Party rally was one of the very few opportunities to fashion oneself as a "respectable" professional for anyone not lucky enough to secure a job in the bureaucracy.

In Max Weber's classic model, charisma is founded upon recognition; it is expressed via gifts from the population to the leader.[18] Under Trujillo, these vectors were reversed. Thousands of large and small gifts moved from the National Palace into Dominicans' homes as tokens of official recognition that made even poor residents feel part of the national project, as did scripting them into official party events. These exchanges helped forge an illusory bond between them and the president and thus masked a relation of domination in an idiom of *confianza*.[19] Gifts were not an operation of ideological persuasion or interpellation, however; they were an acknowledgment of citizens' personhood as members of the national community as they moved from the periphery to the center—a shift with particular resonance given the individuation of the former peasantry and *chiriperos* (informal sector), who lacked cohesion or identity as a community, and the stains that many Dominicans secretly harbored.[20] The regime also felt more familiar, more criollo, than previous liberal regimes because of the vernacular practices which made this sinister swindler appear to be one of them. Trujillo's biggest gift was offering Dominicans a myth of national *progreso*, one providing the illusion of self-transformation through social mobility, whether through a baptism, a new house, a pair of shoes, or a prosthetic arm. This "authorizing myth" gained legitimacy in part because of Trujillo's personal narrative of conversion from cattle rustler's son to world-class president, a trajectory with both class and racial inflections.[21]

However, there was a dark underside to Trujillo's modernity. The gift of modernization which also resulted in Trujillo's excessive wealth was rumored to be a hex, as examined in chapter 6, a gift produced by sorcery that demanded sacrifice. Sovereignty and sorcery are frequently linked in the Caribbean; "languages of stateness" such as theatricality and secrecy are often assumed to operate within a logic of magic since they draw on a "dialectics of publicity and secrecy, and revelation and concealment."[22]

Trujillo reverted to a traditional mode of power based on providing public works and pleasures to the masses, a logic similar to that of caudillismo.[23] The fact that true authority rested on the national army and police, of course, made this a modern form of rule. Trujillo also merged the logic of the market with that of the gift; he was equally the shrewd capitalist when it came to money making and the clever caudillo when it came to throwing a civic fete. He fashioned a public sphere in an intimate, familial guise, a leadership style modeled more on the patriarch than the president. Sumptuous expenditure became a central reason of state under the Trujillato; it served as a mask of generosity occluding the extortion that was the true logic of the regime.

Patronage was an essential means of control under the Trujillo regime; indeed, it is key to understanding its culture of compliance. All state activities were framed as personal prestations from Trujillo—from public works such as highways, canals, and coastal dredging to antimalarial measures, tax exemptions, library and radio station inaugurations, Christmas bonuses, and mother's day greetings. The bulk of state gifts were public works, although symbolic gestures (e.g., gifts to La Vega prisoners [intended for the Vegano elite] or a gift of gratitude to the president of France) formed one fifth of the total. State gifts increased as the economy improved; in the early years they averaged an annual total of 197, but by 1955, when Trujillo's twenty-five years in office were commemorated, they reached a total of 258, some 40 per month.[24] This accounting merges gifts to the public and private sectors; personal presents ranged from trifles to subsistence payments, from sewing machines, Christmas food handouts, and silver demitasse spoons to more substantial housing, public sector employment, or land.

Tokens from Trujillo extended his name and renown into every household, from the boudoirs of wealthy aristocrats who despised the regime to the rural and urban poor for whom the state seemed a distant locus of dread. They were reminders of his awesome authority, everyday signs that each crack and crevice of the country was Trujillo's immanent domain. They made him appear omnipresent, further instantiating the respeto he had as a result of his brutality.[25] In combination with the frequent and elaborate state rites they also framed Trujillo, as Geertz has put it, as the "charismatic center of social life."[26] These objects appeared to be owned by individuals, yet served as constant reminders of his totalizing possession of the nation; and amid the palpable fear that asphyxiated Ciudad Trujillo, they were also terrifying reminders of the extreme violence that the regime was capable of. Placards saying "In this house, Trujillo is the boss" were displayed in plain view in the foyer during the regime, but personal gifts insinuated Trujillo's presence into private, hidden spaces. The fact that these state fetishes are still guarded and swapped indicates their value as "inalienable possessions," particularly among former Trujillistas and the poor, who were amazed at having such "personal" contact with a person of such awesome power.[27]

The symbolic capital generated by these gifts was intended to translate into social capital or honor—precisely what Trujillo lacked owing to his background as a mulatto underclass arriviste.[28] Thus they formed part of a larger economy of domination in which objects circulated as well as speech forms such as praise and denunciation—one in which praise could buy a post in the Dominican Party or denunciation could cost one's job; one that enmeshed individuals in the tentacles of state power whether they liked it or not.

Trujillo manipulated a complex economy of conversion. The "mysterium tremendum" of his "skilled revelation of skilled concealment" resulted from a slick conversion of graft into gifts.[29] His public face of generosity, such as thousands of crisp hundred dollar bills as baptismal presents to the poor, were funded by backstage sleights of hand—for example, the kickbacks required on all government contracts, revenues from his crop monopolies, and the institutional 10 percent "tax" on all public-sector salaries which went to the Dominican Party, a good portion of which flowed into his private salary (rumored to be hidden in Swiss bank accounts).[30] If Trujillo lacked cultural capital at the onset, he bought it and then converted it to social capital by indebting the citizenry to the state. Although these gifts seemed to be tokens of recognition flattering the recipient, they were actually intended to buy the respect that Trujillo so desperately wanted.[31] They were in fact debts that eventually purchased the charisma of Trujillo by locating him at the apex of an economy of domination.[32]

Official prestations were not merely material plunder, but, in the predominantly nonmarket culture of the Dominican Republic, they were objects conveying moral obligations to the regime. Because commercial agriculture arrived in the late nineteenth century with the development of the sugar industry, and because Trujillo and his inner circle monopolized the most important sectors of the domestic and export economy during the regime, capitalism not only came late to the Dominican Republic but was relegated in large part to a bounded enclave—first the sugar economy, then Trujillo's honeycomb of properties. This helps explain the apparent contradiction that Trujillo could combine state formation and economic modernization with rule through asymmetrical prestation; he co-opted his would-be opponents through calculated beneficence, an idiom of power more characteristic of monarchs than depression dictators. Indeed, under the guise of generosity, a gift was degraded by creating indebtedness if it had such excessive value that the recipient could not match it. As Frederick Bailey has noted, "the overgenerous gift, so big that it cannot be returned, becomes a humiliation," or as Jean-Paul Sartre put it, "to give is to enslave."[33]

Scholars have focused attention on the more dramatic forms of repression of the regime—for example, the arbitary police reprisals when one interfered with the plans and desires of Trujillo and his cronies, the use of arbitrary torture and imprisonment, and the assassination of political enemies. All of these certainly created a generalized culture of fear, especially when this arbitrary system eventually picked on everyone—even the inner circle was not exempt. The most dangerous aspect of this means of domination, or "symbolic violence," was its "collective misrecognition"—that these forms of compulsion appeared to be altruistic gifts, not tokens of extortion binding people to the regime by force. According to Pierre Bourdieu, "The most successful ideological effects are those which have no need for words, and ask no more than complicitous silence."[34]

The crux of Trujillo's hegemony thus lay in the political economy of symbolic exchange that provided the infrastructure of domination. In recompense for gifts from the dictator, party representatives paid tribute to Trujillo. Thus praise and denunciation became forms of oratorical currency binding citizens and officeholders to the regime in a transactional web of exchanges; over time people became trapped in circuits of favors. Denunciation caused one to lose symbolic credit with Trujillo; one then needed to gain currency by engaging in panegyric and thus creating symbolic power for the dictator, either verbally or via a gesture honoring him such as a title, a bust, or a rally.

These forms of political oratory also helped forge an official identity and are important in explaining how Trujillo was able to maintain power for so long: how everyday forms of domination and terror became normalized over three decades and how individuals daily experienced a regime that has been described as totalitarian because of the state's invasiveness.[35] As Michael Herzfeld has said, "Rhetoric is not simply an epiphenomenon of other sources of power." It is key to the social production of indifference in nation-state bureaucracies.[36] It may also be one of the keys to the production of consent under an authoritarian regime. The genres of praise and denunciation also help explain how a regime that thrust aside the traditional elite was able to forge a social base. Official speech protocols drew political subjects into the regime, even if they forced them to perform according to a set of scripts not of their own accord and often against their will.

Nor was there much effective distinction between the material and the symbolic in these circuits of speech. The threat of denunciation was terrifying, since it could mean not only the stain of public dishonor and stigma but the loss of one's job. Enforced panegyric, on the other hand, was humiliating because it constructed Trujillo as superhuman and therefore reduced the speaking subject to groveling mendicant. Indeed, this was its intent. Unlike other forms of exchange under the regime, the gift of praise to Trujillo was uniquely one-sided, since no one else could be the object of commendation, and certainly Trujillo paid tribute to no one.

GIFTS INTO DEBTS

While this symbolic economy ultimately forged Trujillo's charisma since it located him at the center, its complex series of conversions was ultimately underwritten by lies hidden by a veil of "magnificent deceit."[37] Trujillo appeared to bestow social honor by casting working-class members as professionals at Dominican Party rallies, but this masked what was in fact a regime of humiliation, because as soon as they eulogized him, they risked denunciation in the Foro Público. Trujillo's state-owned enterprises paid a pittance for wages and then converted some of the surplus value into gifts that he generously distributed to the population; these in turn bought him the social stature he lacked. The culture of official gift giving appeared to be beneficent, but it was actually generating debt, since asymmetrical prestation flowing from Trujillo to the people rendered the Dominican citizenry into a nation of beggars. Indeed, it is tragically revealing that one of Trujillo's most popular forms of patronage was the installation of Dominican Party pawn shops in the barrios marginados. The sociologist Peter Blau has also suggested, "Overwhelming others with benefactions serves to achieve superiority over them."[38]

As Marcel Mauss reminds us, the term *gift* has a double meaning—present and poison.[39] This may explain the curious fact that in eighteenth-century Dominican Spanish, the term for flatter, *dar jabón*, was a colloquialism for conquer, as if subjection were inextricably tied to accepting prestation and its resultant indebtedness.[40] If Trujillo's prestation practices produced an "extraordinary quality," it was not about love; it was, in Max

Weber's words, "a devotion born of distress and enthusiasm," "fear and hope."[41] The distress generated by this police state is easy to comprehend, but getting inside the enthusiasm is more challenging. What I have described is the cultural economy that bound Dominicans to the regime, that ultimately left them obliged but not necessarily beholden. The most forceful vernacular practice deployed by Trujillo was the one he found when he arrived in 1930—the peasant culture of reciprocity. It provided the matrix within which his gifts became debts, in which cash purchases were disguised as friendship, as ñapa or calculated gifts. When he twisted the logic of the gift—which should be an expression of friendship among equals—into a vehicle for producing deep inequality, it should not be surprising that such a gift was viewed as the work of the devil.[42]

Mauss offered another insight into the gift that is relevant to this discussion. Gifts resemble secrets. They are inherently duplicitous, apparently disinterested and voluntary, but in fact interested and binding.[43] In a reflection of the paranoid culture of the Trujillato in which the true logic of politics was constantly occluded from public view, Liboristas in 1961 were accused of being communists in spite of their claim to be religious pilgrims. Yet Olivorismo offered rituals of unmasking that enabled the faithful to see behind official lies, just as muchachito narratives exposed the inscrutable machinations of Trujillo's power. Like Olivorio's neck bound by tensile cords, Liboristas were bound by Trujillo's gifts, but their clairvoyant powers enabled them to see behind the subterfuge of Trujillo's double-dealing and dirty tricks. Their divine tribunal offered the possibility of a polity no longer governed by occult forces and the capricious hand of avaricious politicians, but rather by the utopic dream of a total transparency before God, a dream that completely broke the link between the state and predation.[44]

Ever the virile statesman because he purportedly protected la nación from the Haitian "hordes" in the 1937 massacre and because he seemingly broke off its colonial dependence upon the United States, Trujillo also morally castrated el pueblo dominicano by creating a public culture that even his most illustrious cortesano Joaquín Balaguer described as "abjection."[45] Even as he claimed to rescue Dominicanidad from these outside forces, he surreptitiously drew on forms of the foreign—in particular the United States—as a source of prestige, value, and authority.[46]

The real secret of the Trujillo regime was its profound ambivalence, its peculiar combination of populism and terrorism. Thomas Mann in *Death in Venice* visualizes the secret as a crouching tiger, an elegant and cunning animal whose physical magnificence masks its savagery.[47] The union of opposites helps explain the ambiguity of Trujillo's power, his dual roles as hero and trickster, his magic and his necromancy.[48] If Creole identity in the Dominican Republic is a composite of reputation and respectability, black and white, private self and public person, these terms are not coequal. The concept of personhood originated in the idea of masking. Just as Dominicans need to present a white, respectable face to the world, they are also bound by the secret that they may be "black behind the ears." Because of the dynamic amalgam of these facets of identity, Dominicans navigate between two styles of comportment, one that is lower class and coded as brown, and another that is elite and coded white. This contradiction, forged within colonialism where miscegenation was prohibited yet a fact of everyday life, continued in the post-independence period in the Creole family form of serial polygyny, in which men were poised between their whiter esposas in the city and their darker mistresses in the campo.[49]

The mestizo, the bicorn, and the tíguere navigate between these two ideologically distinct yet coterminous domains. Trujillo's tigueraje, then, struck a chord because he made official a style of comportment that should reside on the streets, not in the National Palace, thus revealing a public secret by valorizing precisely that which Dominicans had previously felt ashamed of. Dominicans were given permission to embrace an aspect of their identity which for centuries they had been condemned for, their "exaggerated consciousness of self importance"—that as freedmen they acted like whites when in the eyes of Europe they were *really* black.[50] As Taussig has said, "Magic is efficacious not despite the trick but on account of its exposure."[51] And the illusionist who conjures in broad daylight is the greatest trickster of all.

NOTES

PREFACE

1. Blanchot, "Everyday Speech," 12–20, esp. 15.
2. Javier Garcia, *Mis 20 años*, 140, for example, mentions Trujillo's private *brujo* (sorcerer) and that he protected witchcraft from bad press or any form of anti-superstitious campaign, as the Catholic church had enacted several times in Haiti. I did hear of sporadic waves of persecution against *curanderos*, although I did not find evidence of it myself.

INTRODUCTION

A preliminary draft of this chapter was presented at the meetings of the American Anthropological Association and benefited greatly from comments by Ana Maria Alonso and Fernando Coronil. Special thanks to Mir Yarfitz and Victor Rodríguez, who helped collect some of the research presented here.

1. Said, *Culture and Imperialism*, 111.
2. Osorio Lizarazo, *Portrait of Trujillo*, 12.
3. Ramfis and Rhadamés. As did Ramfis, who named his daughter Aída, and his son, Ramses, after the king of Egypt.
4. Zaglul, " 'El Gancho,' " *Apuntes*, 27–30.
5. For more on the militarization of the nation under Trujillo, see Peguero's excellent study, *The Militarization of Culture*, 147.
6. For more on the Haitian massacre, see Derby, "Haitians, Magic and Money," 488–26; and Turits, "A World Destroyed," 589–635.
7. Bustamante [pseud.], *Una satrapía.* For more on repression under the regime, see Wiarda, *Dictatorship, Development and Disintegration*, vols. 1–3; Cassá, *Capitalismo y dictadura*; Vega, *Unos desafectos*; Vega, *Control y represión*, 9; Vega, *La vida cotidiana.* A fine general history of the Trujillo period is Crassweller, *Trujillo.*
8. This was quite a commendation, since during Trujillo's rule authoritarianism was rampant in Latin America, so he had stiff competition for this title. Moya Pons, "The Dominican Republic," 536; Hartlyn, "The Trujillo Regime," 85–112. Both Peguero and Wiarda use the term *totalitarian* to describe Trujillo, although it is implied by many others; see Peguero, *The Militarization of Culture*; and Wiarda, *Dictatorship, Development and Disintegration.*

9. The former military intelligence chief Arturo R. Espaillat describes Trujillo's covert operations in detail in *The Last Caesar*.

10. Examples include Gabriel García Márquez's classic, *The Autumn of the Patriarch*, and more recent accounts by Mario Vargas Llosa, *The Feast of the Goat*, and Julia Alvarez, *In the Time of the Butterflies*, as well as numerous rich accounts of the life and times of the regime by the Dominican novelist Marcio Veloz Maggiolo, such as *Trujillo, Villa Francisca*. For more on literary representations of Trujillo, see López-Calvo, *"God and Trujillo."*

11. The estimate is twenty thousand if one includes the Haitian massacre, which should be accounted for since (1) many of the so-called ethnic Haitians were actually Dominican because they were born on Dominican territory, and (2) one rationale of the massacre was to terrorize Dominicans, a goal certainly achieved, at least in the border regions where most of the killing occurred. However, since there were no mass graves and many bodies were thrown to the sharks, it is impossible to establish an accurate body count for those killed.

12. Evans, "Predatory, Developmental and other Apparatuses," 561–87. On "bossism," see Sidel, *Capital, Coercion and Crime*.

13. Trujillo's system of monopolies and properties are listed in Bustamante, *Una satrapía*, chapter 8; and Cordero Michel, *Análisis de la Era de Trujillo*. Vedovato examines how corruption affected policymaking under the regime, see his *Politics*.

14. Peguero, *The Militarization of Culture*, 77, 120.

15. Catherine LeGrand treats the sugar industry under the Trujillo regime in her article, "Informal Resistance on a Dominican Sugar Plantation," 555–96.

16. Moya Pons, *The Dominican Republic*, 359; Inoa, *Estado y campesinos*, 66.

17. A key difference, of course, is that Trujillo worked through the state and the Mafiosi by definition were extralegal. See Blok, *The Mafia of a Sicilian Village*; and Hess, *Mafia and Mafiosi*. Hailing from one of the three wealthiest families in the country, Rafael Espaillat, head of military intelligence, was one of the few top officers of the regime not related to Trujillo. Peguero includes a fascinating discussion of the political infighting among Trujillo's brothers in *The Militarization of Culture*.

18. See Linz, *Sultanistic Regimes*; Vedovato, *Politics*; Wiarda, *Nation in Transition*; Wiarda and Kryzanek, *A Caribbean Crucible*; Wiarda and Kryzanek, *The Politics of External Influence*; and Hartlyn, *The Struggle for Democratic Politics*.

19. Espinal, *Autoritarismo y democracia*, 64; Campillo-Pérez, *Historia Electoral Dominicana*, 69.

20. West and Sanders, Introduction, *Transparency and Conspiracy*, 1–37; Taussig, *Shamanism, Colonialism*; and Palmié, *Wizards and Scientists*, 222.

21. Paul Christopher Johnson, *Secrets, Gossip and Gods*, 23; and Paul Christopher Johnson, "Apotheosis of Duvalier," 420–45.

22. Espaillat, *The Last Caesar*, 37, 40; and Jean and John Comaroff, "Occult Economies," 283.

23. Ornes, *Little Caesar*, 228. The statue of Chiang Kai-shek in Taipei, Taiwan, may top this dimension.

24. Galíndez, *The Era of Trujillo*, 181–85.

25. Mosse, "Political Liturgy of Nationalism," 39–54.

26. Peguero, *The Militarization of Culture*, 3. These are not the only invisible mementos of the Trujillo era, however; El Presidente beer is still the national beer, although the current generation may not know which president is referred to (or it may think the name refers to Balaguer, who also spent many years as head of state).

27. Geertz, *Negara*. Richard Turits first called this to my attention.

28. H. E. Chehabi and Juan J. Linz say that "loyalty to the ruler is motivated not by his embodying or articulating an ideology . . . nor by any charismatic qualities, but by a mixture of fear and rewards to his collaborators"; see "A Theory of Sultanism," in *Sultanistic Regimes*, 7, also 14, 23. For a psychological approach to Trujillo that locates his inferiority complex at the core of his problems, see Gómez, *Trujillo visto por un psiquiatra*. The debate over whether or not the symbolics of power make a difference is not new; it has been waged in the field of rites of rule among European and non-Western monarchies; see Cannadine, "Introduction: Divine Rites of Kings," 1–19.

29. Peguero, *The Militarization of Culture*, chapter 8, esp. 146.

30. Ibid., 175, 186.

31. Turits, *Foundations of Despotism*.

32. For more on this theme, see Eric Roorda's rich and original analysis of relations between the United States and the Dominican Republic in *The Dictator Next Door*.

33. Espaillat, *The Last Caesar*, 169.

34. Roorda, *The Dictator Next Door*, 118.

35. This trope popped up in many interviews I conducted about the Trujillo era.

36. Mbembe, *On the Postcolony*, 102–42; James C. Scott, *Domination and the Arts of Resistance*. I am indebted to Lisa Wedeen's insightful work, *The Ambiguities of Domination*, and her distinction between compliance and consent (6). Scholars who have sought to bring cultural analysis to statist regimes from kingship to fascism include Hunt, *Politics, Culture and Class*; Fitzpatrick, *Everyday Stalinism*, and her edited volume *Stalinism: New Directions*; Peukert, *Inside Nazi Germany*; and Berezin, *Making the Fascist Self*. Scholars who have incorporated culture into the study of politics in Latin America include Joseph and Nugent, *Everyday Forms*; Joseph, *Reclaiming the Political*; Roorda, *The Dictator Next Door*; Coronil, *The Magical State*; Lomnitz, *Deep Mexico, Silent Mexico*; James, *Resistance and Integration*; Stern, *Remembering Pinochet's Chile*; and Alonso, *Thread of Blood*.

37. The term *vernacular* is used in a slightly different sense by Hansen and Stepputat, Introduction, *States of Imagination*, 10, 12; and Comaroff and Comaroff, "Transparent Fictions."

38. See Claudio Lomnitz's wonderful essay, "The Personification of Mexican National Sovereignty," 119–38; and Van Young's magnum opus, *The Other Rebellion*, chapter 18, 454, for a fascinating discussion of "monarchist messianism" in Mexico.

39. Hunt, *Politics, Culture and Class*, 55.

40. Balaguer, *Memorias de un cortesano*. Of course, this type of language contains an element of whitewash, since the author is also trying to put a more legitimate European face on Trujillo's form of absolute power, which was highly arbitrary and venal.

41. Elias, *The Court Society*, 93. See also Elias, *The History of Manners*, vol. 1; and Espaillat, *The Last Caesar*, 40.

42. Javier García, *Mis 20 anos*, vol. 1, 307–10.

43. Balaguer, *Memorias de un cortesano*.

44. Wedeen, *Ambiguities of Domination*, 6.

45. Abrams, "Difficulty of Studying the State," 58–89.

46. This concept of charisma as relational is developed in Lindholm, *Charisma*; James C. Scott, *Domination and the Arts of Resistance*; Chasteen, *Heroes on Horseback*; Fuente, *Children of Facundo*. On trickery, concealment, and public secrets, see Taussig, "Viscerality, Faith and Skepticism," 272–306.

47. Coronil, *The Magical State*; Stanley, *The Protection Racket State*; Heyman, *States and Illegal Practices*; and Roldán, *Blood and Fire*.

48. Knight, "Populism and Neo-Populism," 223–48.

49. Wedeen, *Ambiguities of Domination*, 6. The notion of "command performances" is from James C. Scott, *Domination and the Arts of Resistance*, 29.

50. The generation of political pragmatism may be a feature of longevity rather than political tendency, since this kind of pragmatism is apparent among many Cubans today as well.

51. See the essays in Carrithers, *The Category of the Person*.

52. See Mahmood's *Politics of Piety*, chapter 1, esp. 25.

53. del Castillo, "The Formation of the Dominican Sugar Industry"; and Schoenrich, *A Country with a Future*, 239. The *bodega* credit system is also treated in Ramón Marrero Aristy's novel *Over*.

54. The Partido Dominicano documents treat this issue frequently until finally the regime moved to forbid the practice. See, for example, Damián Silva, Presidente de la Junta Comunal de Barahona, to Virgilio Álvarez Pina, Presidente de la Junta Superior Directiva, 11 Dec. 1943, Partido Dominicano (PD), Junta Central Directiva (JCD), Corres. 11–20 Dec. 1943. These archival documents are housed in the Archivo General Nacional (AGN), Santo Domingo.

55. Matos Díaz, *Santo Domingo de Ayer*, 131–32. For legal evidence of petty theft

that drove people to the courts to reclaim their goods and for a discussion of the loan culture that was commonplace before Trujillo, see Martínez-Vergne, *Nation and Citizen*, 152–54.

56. Hoetink, *The Dominican People*, 192.

57. Lancaster, *Life Is Hard*, 57.

58. This idea is derived from Todd Ochoa, "Debt and Trust: 19th Century Influences on Contemporary Cuban-Kongo Healing," paper presented at the Cuba and the Caribbean Working Group, UCLA, 11 May 2007.

59. The concept of "face saving strategy" is from Goffman, "On Face-Work," in *Interaction Ritual*, 5–46.

60. This theme of identity is also very important in Edwidge Danticat's fascinating novel *The Dew Breaker*, which treats the Duvalier regime in Haiti, one with many similarities to that of Trujillo. An important distinction to keep in mind, however, is that the subjects in Veloz Maggiolo's novels are middle class, and thus their humiliation reflects a different form of subjectivity from that of the poor, who take deference for granted.

61. Díaz Quiñones, *El arte de bregar*, 54.

62. James C. Scott, *Domination and the Arts of Resistance*, 33. He describes this phenomenon as a "division of the self, in which the self observes, perhaps cynically and approvingly, the performance of the other self."

63. This concept is from Dix, "Populism," although this regime was significantly more repressive than the cases he mentions. I am grateful to Mark Sawyer for this citation.

64. See Deive's classic work, *La esclavitud*, vols. 1 and 2.

65. I treat the peculiarities of colonial Santo Domingo in more detail in my essay "National Identity and the Idea of Value." For more on ranching and slavery, see Silié's important book, *Economía, esclavitud y población*. For more on the colonial economy and society, see Cassá, *História social y económica*. The argument that patterns of social hierarchy derive from plantation structures has been explored by Sidney Mintz in *Caribbean Transformations*.

66. The term *protopeasant* is from Mintz and describes the newly reconstituted peasantry which emerged after the abolition of slavery; see *Caribbean Transformations*. For more on the montero, see González, "Ideología del progreso."

67. Beier, *Masterless Men*.

68. Sánchez Valverde, *La idea del valor*, 142.

69. For more on the annexation question and the predominance of conservatism in the nineteenth century Hispanic Caribbean, see Martínez-Vergne, "Politics and Society," 185–202.

70. As in other parts of Latin America, militia participation enabled upward mobility and thus a form of social whitening through enhanced status and recognition; see Andrews, *The Afro-Argentines*.

71. For more on nineteenth-century militarization, see Peguero, *The Militarization of Culture*, chapter 1.

72. Peguero feels that the second Spanish intervention was especially important in this regard (*The Militarization of Culture*, 16).

73. This is in contrast to the pattern elsewhere in Latin America. See the classic argument made by Wolf and Hansen, "Caudillo Politics," 168–79.

74. Eugenio María de Hostos, cited in Peguero, *The Militarization of Culture*, 21.

75. Chasteen, *Heroes on Horseback*. "Political prestige" is from Chasteen's "Making Sense of Caudillos," 39.

76. Hoetink, *The Dominican People*, 123.

77. Veeser, *A World Safe for Capitalism*, 44.

78. For more on *terrenos comuneros*, see Turits, *Foundations of Despotism*; San Miguel, *Los Campesinos del Cibao*; Inoa, *Estado y campesinos*; and Julie Franks, "Transforming Property: Landholding and Political Rights in the Dominican Sugar Region, 1880–1930" (Ph.D. diss., State University of New York, Stonybrook, 1997).

79. In *A World Safe for Capitalism*, chapter 4, Veeser describes Lilis's struggle to impose fencing laws, which resulted in a ranchers' revolt.

80. While there is some debate over the scale of peasant participation in market agriculture in the Dominican countryside, the question is not one of scale but of form, since peasants can grow cash crops according to a nonmarket logic, as Juan Guisti-Cordero demonstrates effectively in his thorough and original thesis. See Guisti-Cordero, "Labor, Ecology and History in a Caribbean Sugar Plantation Region: Piñones (Loíza), Puerto Rico 1770–1950" (Ph.D. diss., State University of New York, Binghamton, 1994). For more on Dominican agriculture, see Clausner, *Rural Santo Domingo*. On land in the nineteenth century and the impact of sugar, see the essays in Fraginals et al., *Between Slavery and Free Labor*.

81. See Michiel Baud's rich study, *Peasants and Tobacco*.

82. González, *Bonó*.

83. His argument was by no means a racial determinist one, however. He saw race as one factor among many producing a generally unfavorable climate for democratic preparedness. As he wrote, "Planta exotica, la libertad, en nuestra tierra, en donde todas las condiciones biológicas parecen serle adversas, clima, medio social, tradiciones, leyenda, raza, confusión de elementos étnicos, educación incipiente o violada, desarrollo individual exiguo, desenvolviemiento mental reducido . . ." (N. A. Francisco Henríquez y Carvajal, *El Liberal*, 26 Oct. 1900, quoted in Américo Lugo, "El estado dominicano ante el derecho público," *Obras escogidas I*, 384).

84. See Lugo, "El estado dominicano," 384.

85. N. A. Francisco Henríquez y Carvajal, *El Liberal*, 24 Oct. 1900, quoted in Lugo, "El Estado Dominicano," 384.

86. See Américo Lugo's thesis, "El estado dominicano," 388. For more on Dominican liberal thought, see the excellent edited volume by Raymundo González et al., *Política, identidad y pensamiento social*.

87. Espinal, *Autoritarismo y democracia*, 34.

88. Betances, *State and Society*.

89. Monclús, *El caudillismo*, 85.

90. Veeser, *A World Safe for Capitalism*, chapter 2, treats the reciprocity treaty in detail, and chapter 4 correlates the cultivation of United States support with increased domestic repression. For more on Lilís, see Mu-Kien Sang's classic work, *Ulises Heureaux*. Peguero, *The Militarization of Culture*, also notes the similarities between Heureaux and Trujillo (21–23), as does Luis F. Mejia, who juxtaposes their photos in uniform on the cover of his book, *De Lilís a Trujillo*. Benjamin Orlove notes that many Latin American regimes of the late nineteenth century used foreign goods as a vehicle of legitimation, which in the long run racked up dangerously high levels of debt; see his introduction to *The Allure of the Foreign*.

91. Baud, *Historia de un sueño*. Lilís negotiated adopting the gold standard but eventually dropped it because of formidable opposition at home, as noted by Veeser, *A World Safe for Capitalism*.

92. Hoetink, *The Dominican People*, 116.

93. Veeser, *A World Safe for Capitalism*; and Roorda, *The Dictator Next Door*, 14.

94. By this time the sugar companies had both surpassed the tobacco industry in earnings and had become a key source of credit to the government during the dictatorship of Ulises Heureaux (1886–99) in a period of escalating indebtedness; see Moya Pons, *The Dominican Republic*, 275–76. For more on sugar in the Hispanic Caribbean, see Ayala, *American Sugar Kingdom*; and Moreno Fraginals et al., eds., *Between Slavery and Free Labor*.

95. LeGrand, "Informal Resistance." See also Derby, "Gringo Chickens with Worms," 451–93.

96. Louis Pérez describes these company towns very nicely in his book *On Becoming Cuban*; indeed, some of the same firms he discusses, such as the United Fruit Company, also came to the Dominican Republic.

97. Castillo, "The Formation of the Dominican Sugar Industry," 230.

98. Moscoso Puello, *Cañas y bueyes*, 178.

99. See Betances, *State and Society*, for a more critical view of Cáceres; and Moya Pons for a more positive evaluation, in *The Dominican Republic*.

100. Unlike for example in Haiti, where the elite agreed to serve under U.S. rule. The classic work on the U.S. occupation is Bruce Calder's rigorous and penetrating study, *The Impact of Intervention*.

101. Roorda, *The Dictator Next Door*, 17. He notes that U.S. Navy vessels visited Dominican shores "on dozens of occasions between 1911 and 1916 . . . to 'protect American lives and property,'" thus making the distinction between the Platt Amendment of Cuba and the Dominican Republic one of name only.

102. Ayala, *American Sugar Kingdom*, 101–4. For more on the impact of land privatization on rural class relations in the eastern provinces, see Franks, "Dominican Sugar Zone."

103. Santiago Michelena; the Vicini family was originally Italian, yet by 1930 controlled 9 percent of the nation's sugar output (Ayala, *American Sugar Kingdom*, 107).

104. Franck, *Roaming through the West Indies* (1920), cited in Betances, *State and Society*, 235.

105. Vega, *Trujillo ante una corte marcial*.

106. Collado, *Anécdotas y crueldades*.

107. Roorda, *The Dictator Next Door*, 22.

108. Betances, *State and Society*, 97. The "Revolution of 1930" is treated in detail in Roorda, chapter 2; Malek, "The Rise of a Caribbean Dictator"; Moya Pons, *The Dominican Republic*, chapter 17; and Galíndez, *The Era of Trujillo*.

109. Domínguez, *Order and Revolution*, 13.

110. Although much of this group had intermarried with Dominican elites by the early twentieth century.

111. Alfred Stepan, *The Military in Politics*, 23.

112. Navaro Yashin, *Faces of the State*, 5.

113. Cannadine, Introduction, *Rituals of Royalty*, 2. He also calls for an investigation of secrecy, or, as he states, how "important issues and options are kept off the agenda or public discourse altogether."

114. Bourdieu calls this phenomenon "misrecognition," when "overt domination" is taken for legitimate authority; see Bourdieu, *Outline of a Theory of Practice*, 192. Contrast this to Nora Hamilton's treatment of patronage in Mexico as conscious and highly strategic "cooptation" in her *Limits of State Autonomy*.

115. My discussion here focuses on the symbolic economy of patronage, but of course the exchange of land for political consent and the meaning of citizenship this implied was a major component of rural political support; see Turits, *Foundation of Despotism*, and San Miguel, *Los Campesinos del Cibao*.

116. The notion of "embedding" is originally from Peter Evans, "Predatory, Developmental and other Apparatuses," but the concept is used by Alan Smart, "Predatory Rule and Illegal Economic Practices," 117.

117. Trouillot, *State Against Nation*. Other works that challenge a rigid coercion-and-consent dichotomy include Stone, *The Patron State*; de Grazia, *The Culture of Consent* and *How Fascism Ruled Women*.

118. Trujillo's gradual acquisition of the newspapers is well described in Bustamante, *Una satrapía*; and Ornes, *Little Caesar*.

119. This explains the high level of prurient interest in ex post facto texts that reveal the fates of the disappeared, such as Ferreras, *Cuando la era*.

120. Luhrmann, "The Magic of Secrecy," 137.

121. Renda, *Taking Haiti*.

122. Espinal, *Autoritarianismo y democracia*, chapter 2. On the language of friendship and citizenship under Trujillo, see also San Miguel, "La ciudanía de Calibán," 269–90.

123. The message of incorporation had some appeal, although the peasantry still ardently resisted incorporation in the norms and forms of capitalism, as witnessed in their refusal to contemplate a daily wage; they preferred piece work. See Castillo, "The Formation of the Dominican Sugar Industry," 229.

124. The incipient textile industry is described in Guerrero Villalba, *Tras las huellas*.

125. Trujillo, *Discursos, Mensajes, Proclamas*, vol. 1, 66, cited in Espinal, *Autoritarismo y democracia*, 63. Trujillo thus built upon the school as a medium of "tutelary democracy," a concept found in Lugo's writings. As Espinal notes, however, while this discourse was effective in the early years, it became a repetitive litany over time, and with little ideological innovation and continuing repression, it lost its appeal. For more on the ideology of the Trujillo regime, see Mateo's original study, *Mito y cultura*.

126. For more on Perón's far more radical populism, see James's masterful study, *Resistance and Integration*. For more on race and politics in the Dominican Republic, see Sagás, *Race and Politics*.

127. Goffman uses the concept "subordinate intimacy" in *The Presentation of Self*, 193.

128. *Respeto* was clearly a key word during the Trujillo Era, as in Rafaela Candelaria's comment that "la gente dice que Trujillo era bueno, porque se respetaba" (see Mujeres en Desarrollo Dominicano [MUDE], *La Era de Trujillo*, 33); but as Lauria notes, *respeto* in this sense "is a basic prop of the deference game" ("Respeto," 57). Lauria is drawing upon Goffman, "The Nature of Deference and Demeanor," *Interaction Ritual*, 47–96.

129. Lugo, "El estado dominicano," 33.

130. In popular parlance, however, indio refers merely to a *café con leche* color and does not invoke *indigenismo* or any reference to an autochthonous Indian past.

131. On the stigma of blackness, see Mir, *Tres leyendas de colores*. I wish to thank Ginetta Candelaria for bringing this text to my attention. This "latent secret" helps account for what Dominicans call "el gran pesimismo dominicano," or the devaluation of *lo nacional*; see Zaglul, "La sub-estimación de lo nuestro," *Apuntes*, 31–38. This discourse commenced with the arrival of scientific racist thought from Europe and coincided with the deepening of market ties to Europe in the late nineteenth century.

132. For the liberals' emphasis on civilization, see Eugenio María de Hostos, "¡Civilización o muerte!," *Obras Completas*.

133. González, *Bonó*, 152.

134. This notion of race is developed in Roediger, *Towards the Abolition of Blackness*, cited in Mary Weismantel, *Cholas and Pishtacos*, 184. Claudio Lomnitz-Adler discusses the effect of "brokering modernity through the presidential office," as opposed to previous racialist images of the presidency; see his innovative collection of essays, *Deep Mexico, Silent Mexico*, 109.

1. THE DOMINICAN BELLE ÉPOQUE

1. Calder, *Impact of Intervention*, xxiv.
2. Saez, *Sueño importado*, 49 and 52.
3. "Editorial: Jorgé Washington," *Listín Diaro* (hereafter LD), 23 Feb. 1920.
4. F. Mortimer Dalman, "Un milagro de la coronada Virgen de la Altagracia," LD, 4 Sept. 1922; "Crónicas: Un milagro de la Virgen," *Boletín Eclesiastico* (hereafter BE), Aug. 1916, 144. For a description of the coronation ceremony, see BE, Aug. and Sept., 1922, as well as the articles in BE during the month of August 1922 and in the newspaper LD; also Eliseo Pérez and Félix M. Pérez S., *Album de la canónica*, entry of 15 Aug. 1922. For more on the history of the Virgin of Altagracia worship, see Utrera, *Ntra. Sra de Altagracia*; Pepen, *Donde floreció el naranjo*; and Polanco Brito, *Exvotos y "milagros."*
5. William Beezley, "Dining with Diaz and Crowning the Virgin: Forging Images of Mexico's New Society," paper presented at the Latin American History Workshop, University of Chicago, 26 Jan. 1995.
6. The forging of an alternative cosmopolitanism via Catholicism was pursued by Hidalgo as well during the Mexican war of independence; see Lomnitz, "Passion and Banality," 242–43; González, Introducción, *Política, Identidad y pensamiento social*, 22.
7. Damirón, *De soslayo*, 20. *Caudillismo* was a form of political factionalism born of a weak state and strong regional formation that was characteristic of the nineteenth century, a pattern that disappeared once export revenues improved and allowed the state to wield more effective hegemony.
8. Renda, *Taking Haiti*.
9. Unión Nacional Dominicana, 24 Dec. 1920, Record Group (hereafter RG) 45, Box 756, WA 7, United States National Archives (hereafter USNA). The classic work on the United States occupation of the Dominican Republic is Calder, *The Impact of Intervention*.
10. The geopolitical component of relations between the United States and the Caribbean is well treated in Langley, *The United States and the Caribbean*. For more on 1865, see Nelson, *Almost a Territory*.
11. Ferrer, *Insurgent Cuba*, 200.
12. Bederman, *Manliness and Civilization*, 85.
13. Deschamps, *La República Dominicana*, 12, 308. The first guidebook produced to present the country to the world for investment purposes is Abad, *La República Dominicana*.
14. For more on gender roles and respectability, see Martínez-Vergne, *Nation and Citizen*, chapter 4.
15. *Libro azul*, 14.
16. Lybrand Smith, Report on Memorandum of Dr. Henríquez y Carvajal, 29 Sept. 1920, Sec. de Est. de San. Y Ben., Corres., 1922, Leg. 517, Archivo

General de la Nación (hereafter AGN). Smith cites J. P. Widney's *Race Life*, vol. 2, 205.

17. "La elección II," *LD*, 14 Sept. 1922.

18. Luis Magin, "Avanza!," *LD*, 3 Mar. 1920.

19. See "El interés personal y la muchedumbre: El valor de un testamento colectivo, según la psicología de Gustave Le Bon," *LD*, 22 Mar. 1920; Pick, *Faces of Degeneration*, 90–96; and Le Bon's highly influential book, *The Crowd*.

20. Quote from Campillo Pérez, *Historia electoral dominicana*, 161. For Américo Lugo's perspective on Dominican political culture, see "El estado dominicano ante el derecho público" (his 1916 doctoral thesis in law), in *Obras escogidas I*, and "Sobre política" (in Alfau Duran, *Américo Lugo*, 29–42), in which he applies Hostos's views on education as a "moralizing" and "civilizing" force to the nation-state. See also Lugo, *A punto largo*, 7–30.

21. Lugo, "El estado dominicano," 33. This argument is developed by Raymundo González in his important essay "Ideologia del progreso y campesinado en el siglo XIX," 25–44. The same image is present in Lugo's "Sobre política," in which he describes "el pueblo dominicano [como] . . . semi-salvaje por un lado, ilustrado por otro, en general apático, belicoso, cruel, desinteresado" (22). However, he goes to great lengths to argue that, nonetheless, the Dominican people are not "degenerate" and can be reformed through "instrucción." He also links the need for obligatory public education directly to the formation of citizens (29). For more on Dominican liberal thought, see Hoetink, *The Dominican People*, 112–37; and González et al., *Política, identidad y pensamiento social*.

22. The term *tutelary law* is from Lugo, "El estado dominicano," 389.

23. Hostos, "Falsa alarma, crisis agrícola," cited in González, "Hostos y la conciencia moderna en República Dominicana," in *Política, identidad y pensamiento social*, 101.

24. Lugo, "El estado dominicano," 41–42; "La educación del pueblo" (in *Antologia*, vol. 2, 187–92). In "La educación del pueblo" he argues that political parties should be seen as a form of "public education," which apparently was synonymous with civic training. The phrase "dictatorship of the intelligentsia" is from Roberto Cassá, "Teoria de la nación y proyecto político en Américo Lugo," unpublished ms., 1992. For more on Hostos, see Gordon K. Lewis, *Main Currents*, 271–76.

25. Pedro Henríquez Ureña, "La instrucción pública en los Estado Unidos juzgada por un dominicano," *LD*, 28 Feb. 1920.

26. Moscoso Puello, *Cartas a Evelina*, 89–90. For more on statist liberalism in Dominican thought, see González, "Hostos y la conciencia moderna en República Dominicana"; and Roberto Cassá, "Nación y estado en el pensamiento de Américo Lugo," in González et al., *Política, Identidad y pensamiento social*, 95–130.

27. Moscoso Puello, *Cartas a Evelina*, 45; Le Bon, *The Crowd*, 119. For more on liberals and the national project, see Martínez-Vergne, *Nation and Citizen*, introduction and chapter 1.
28. Max Weber, *The Protestant Ethic*; Foucault, *Discipline and Punish*.
29. José Ramón Lopez, "Los Ayuntamientos II," *LD*, 15 Nov. 1919. For more on liberalism as a utopic ideology, see Baud, *Historia de un sueño*.
30. For more on the reception of scientific racial thought from Europe in Latin America, see the essays in Graham, *The Idea of Race*.
31. Ferrer, *Insurgent Cuba*, 188. I am using the concept of public sphere not in the sense of Habermas's work, but rather that of Mary Ryan; see her "The American Parade," 131–53.
32. "Cinematógrafo," *LD*, 27 Aug. 1903. Of course, American audiences in the nineteenth century, before they were disciplined, were prone to the same style of behavior; see Levine, *Highbrow/Lowbrow*, 169–242. For more on the history of cinema in the Dominican Republic, see Saez, *Sueño importado*.
33. "Estreno de la película nacional: 'La leyenda de Nuestra Señora de la Altagracia,'" *LD*, 17 Feb. 1923, 1.
34. *Panfilia*, 15 Sept. 1923, 11–12, quoted in Saez, *Sueño importado*, 57.
35. "Estreno de la película nacional," 1.
36. Saez, *Sueño importado*, 168; my emphasis.
37. As Saez sardonically puts it, "Y, aun en ese caso, se recurre a la ficción, en vez de acercarnos más a nuestra realidad a través del documental" (Saez, *Sueño importado*, 71). Although an authentically "Dominican" cinema did not develop during the 1920s, a few Dominican playwrights were writing and staging plays drawing upon national themes; Rafael Damirón's *Alma criolla*, performed in 1916, was one example.
38. Saez, *Sueño importado*, 20, 37–38, and 41.
39. Ibid., 40–41.
40. Ibid., 45. U.S. marine government records also mention that the marines showed traveling educational films in the interior, especially on topics of sanitation and hygiene.
41. "Civismo en acción II," *LD*, 2 Sept. 1922. However, liberal reformers had been debating this issue since the nineteenth century; individuals such as José Ramón López (1866–1922) sought to debunk racialist theories of degeneration by claiming that diet and environment accounted for Dominican laziness, not racial mixture. See his "La alimentación y la raza" (republished in *Ensayos y Artículos*, 11–61), which presents the plantain as the bane of the peasantry. His view contrasts starkly with the more authoritarian strand of liberalism found in the work of Américo Lugo, for instance in "La educación del pueblo." For a rich exploration of the reception of European racialist thought in Brazil and the range of responses it generated

in a parallel predominantly mulatto society, see Skidmore, *Black into White*, 38–68, 145–69.

42. "El oficial del distrito . . . ," *LD*, 20 Nov. 1919.

43. *LD*, 14 Sept. 1922; see also "Hallazgo macabre," *LD*, 14 Oct. 1920. Eileen Findlay demonstrates a similar response to U.S.-imposed public health measures in Puerto Rico, where middling Puerto Ricans supported the anti-prostitution campaign as a means of social climbing; see her thoughtful and penetrating account in *Imposing Decency*.

44. "Espectáculo afrentoso: Se pone en tela de duda la cultura de que hacemos gala," *LD*, 30 Aug. 1922; "Mujeres de conducta sospechosa se refugian en Boca Chica," *LD*, 25 June 1923. On Puerto Rican prostitution and U.S. policy, see Findlay, *Imposing Decency*.

45. "Dos cuestiones del momento," *LD*, 28 Nov. 1919.

46. Jiménez, *Al amor del bohío*, 34.

47. See, for example, the write-up for Evangelista Cornelio, La Vega, in *Libro azul*, 156.

48. Douglas and Isherwood, *The World of Goods*, 67. For more on the theoretical and methodological concerns related to consumption in the European theater, see de Grazia, "Introduction: Changing Consumption Regimes," 1–24.

49. The nature of this new broker class—which, for example, in the eastern province of Seybo, took advantage of U.S. legislative efforts to privatize land to accumulate land for *colono* (small cane-farming) production—has been well documented in Julie Franks's groundbreaking dissertation entitled "Transforming Property: Landholding and Political Rights in the Dominican Sugar Region, 1880–1930" (Ph.D. diss., State University of New York, Stonybrook, 1997). See also "Forging National Institutions in the Dominican Sugar Zone, 1880–1924," paper presented at the Conference on Rethinking the Post-Colonial Encounter, Yale University, 1995.

50. Betances, *State and Society*, 42. A hundred thousand Haitians arrived yearly for the sugar harvest, one tenth of the total population of the country (Landolfi, "El desarrollo cultural," 347). Gómez Alfau mentions La Perla Negra in his *Ayer*.

51. Gómez Alfau, *Ayer*, 125. See also Hoetink, "The Dominican Republic in the Nineteenth Century" and *The Dominican People*. D. S. Parker demonstrates the remarkable resilience of a similar bifurcated vision in *The Idea of the Middle Class*, 66.

52. Max Weber argued that status groups are defined through lifestyle and consumption; see his essay "On Class," 31–40, esp. 39.

53. Moya Pons, *The Dominican Republic*, 324–26.

54. Baud, "The Struggle for Autonomy," 120–40.

55. Dominican products were sold internationally in the nineteenth century, but

the scale and form of international economic penetration was very different. By 1907, 62 percent of foreign capital in sugar was invested by Americans or by Cubans residing in the United States; see José del Castillo and Walter Cordero, "La economia dominicana," 87–125, esp. 98. For more on the development of the American owned and controlled sugar economy, see the essays on the Dominican Republic in Moreno Fraginals et al., *Between Slavery and Free Labor*; and Ayala, *American Sugar Kingdom*.

56. Schoenrich, *Santo Domingo*, 238. See *LD*, 1903, for many articles berating the Syrians, accusing them of hoarding to inflate prices. For more on Arab immigration, see Inoa, *Azúcar*.

57. An important exception, of course, is Mintz, *Sweetness and Power*. See Gilbert Joseph's call for research on consumption issues in "Close Encounters," 19. Recent research on consumption in Latin America includes Arnold J. Bauer, *Goods, Power, History*; and Orlove, *The Allure of the Foreign*.

58. From an 1875 article in *El Orden* (Santiago), cited in Baud, *Historia de un sueño*, 15. Part of this sense of imminent prosperity had to do with the notion that the opening of the Panama Canal would make the Dominican Bay of Samaná (which the United States had nearly annexed in the 1870s) strategically essential, and thus would bind the futures of the two nations; in the words of José Leopoldo Hungria, "Most Dominicans think it funny that soon the future of the colonial imperium of the United States will depend upon the bay of Samaná" (*LD*, 12 Oct. 1903).

59. Schoenrich, *Santo Domingo*, vi.

60. Baud, *Historia de un sueño*, 8.

61. Hoetink, *The Dominican People*, 165–66, 176–81.

62. Bauer, *Goods, Power, History*, 133–37. He is describing this group in the nineteenth century in more central parts of Latin America, but in the Dominican Republic this process was delayed.

63. See Findlay's insightful and rich discussion of this phenomenon in *Imposing Decency*, 37. See Baud, *Peasants and Tobacco*, 121, on the prevalence of extramarital unions among the tobacco elite of the Cibao, which forged links across lines of race and class.

64. Williams, *Stains on My Name, War in My Veins*, 81. See also Wilson, *Crab Antics*.

65. Lancaster here draws upon the work of Erving Goffman in a discussion of the stigma of homosexuality; see *Life Is Hard*, 243.

66. Bauer, *Goods, Power, History*, chapter 5.

67. "Dos cuestiones del momento," *LD*, 28 Nov. 1919.

68. José Ramón López, "La alimentación y las razas."

69. J. O., "Urgente," *LD*, 9 Oct. 1903.

70. Schoenrich, *Santo Domingo*, 241.

71. United States Senate, Hearings before a Select Committee on Haiti and Santo Domingo, *Inquiry into the Occupation*, vol. 2, 1036.

72. These are all products advertised in the *LD*.

73. *LD*, 14 Sept. 1922; *Libro azul*, 87. The advertisement mentions that it's good for hair and beards, indicating that it was intended for both sexes. For more on the importance of imports, see Orlove, *The Allure of the Foreign*.

74. Gómez Alfau, *Ayer*, 67.

75. United States Senate, Hearings, *Inquiry into the Occupation*, vol. 1, 517. The shoe class also wore "cut away coats, brass-head canes, stove-pipe hats 3 inches in diameter, and did everything they could to make themselves conspicuous." The Dominican elite was not as showy, though.

76. *Libro azul*, 58.

77. United States Senate, Hearings, *Inquiry into the Occupation*, vol. 2, 1030.

78. Schoenrich, *Santo Domingo*, 383–84.

79. "Ruletas y chewing gum," *LD*, 22 Oct. 1919.

80. "Notas de la semana," *Blanco y Negro*, 23 Jan. 1926.

81. [Anonymous observer], "La vida en provinces: Samaná," *LD*, 15 Sept. 1922.

82. "Crónica," *Blanco y Negro*, 15 Jan. 1911. The Apache Dance commenced between 1910 and 1919, but it didn't really become a craze until the 1920s. For example, Flor Trujillo mentions in her memoirs that Porfirio Rubirosa was accomplished at it; for more on this, see chapter 7.

83. Baud, *Peasants and Tobacco*, 169. As Baud notes, efforts to inhibit cockfighting in the end were futile.

84. Un Tal Big Ben, "Gran triunfo de las Estrellas Dominicanas," *LD*, 6 Sept. 1922. For more on Dominican baseball, see Klein, *Sugarball*. For more on how colonial relationships are mediated through sports contests, see C. L. R. James, *Beyond a Boundary*. On sports and politics in Mexico, see Beezley, *Judas at the Jockey Club*.

85. "Crónica de baseball," *LD*, 31 Aug. 1922.

86. Appadurai, "Introduction: Commodities and the Politics of Value," *The Social Life of Things*, 30.

87. *Libro azul*, 76.

88. *LD*, 28 Aug. 1903.

89. "Juego de sociedad," *Blanco y Negro*, 22 June 1913.

90. "Juego de sociedad," *Blanco y Negro* 5, no. 245 (n.d.) (the sole copy in the National Archives was damaged).

91. "Juego de sociedad," *Blanco y Negro* 6, no. 266 (1914).

92. United States Senate, Hearings, *Inquiry into the Occupation*, vol. 2, 1030.

93. *Libro azul*, 77, 81, 93.

94. Bonó's work predates Fernando Ortiz's classic text, *Cuban Counterpoint*, which draws upon the same symbolism of tobacco and sugar to express a contemporaneous process in Cuba. For more on Bonó, see González, "Notas sobre el pensamiento socio-político dominicano," *Estudios Sociales*, 20, no. 67 (1987). On Dominicans' rejection of the sugar industry, see Ciriaco Landolfi,

"El desarrollo cultural del pais en el primer cuarto del siglo XX," in Mejia-Ricart, *Sociedad Dominicana*, 328.

95. Rodó, *Ariel*. I would like to thank Bernardo Vega for bringing this text to my attention.

96. Rodó, *Ariel*, 59.

97. "Editorial: La gran unión latina," *LD*, 10 March 1920; "Editorial: La futura gran unión," *LD*, 19 Feb. 1920.

98. Pick, *Faces of Degeneration*, 6; and Lutz, *American Nervousness*.

99. Mariano Cestero, "Simple ojeada," *LD*, 28 Aug. 1903. There is a corresponding discourse on inflation as well.

100. See Weiner, *Inalienable Possessions*.

101. "Supercherias de un Haitiano," *LD*, 28 Aug. 1903.

102. The association between status outsiders and money can be found in the labels, epithets, and accusations leveled at immigrant groups such as Italians, Sephardic Jews, "Turcos" or Syrian immigrants, and Spanish; see Hoetink, *The Dominican People*, and also the debate over Arab immigration in *LD*, Sept. and Oct. 1903. Haitians had a unique association with money and magic. For a discussion of anti-Haitianism and popular associations between Haitians and money, see Derby, "Haitians, Magic and Money," 488–526. In sharp contrast to the Dominicans, Argentine elites during this period worshipped fast wealth, and extravagant consumption was a legitimate means to acquire status. See Johns, "The Antinomies of Ruling Class Culture," 74–101.

103. See, for example, "Comercio Arabe," *LD*, 7 Oct. 1903.

104. Henríquez Castillo, *El hombre alucinado*.

105. The doctor is the prototypical profession of the old elite. Another doctor embodying the values of the old aristocracy is Doctor Augusto Lima, a character in Federico Perez's *La ciudad herida*. As I discuss in chapter 2, he is the one who cares for all the wounded during the 1930 hurricane and is the symbolic "savior" of the city of Santo Domingo (then Ciudad Trujillo). The real "savior," of course, is Trujillo. Doctor Augusto Lima's role as a sign of the old aristocracy and tradition is reflected in his old colonial house and the horse and buggy he refuses to relinquish, even when everyone else is driving cars.

106. Henríquez, *El hombre alucinado*, 106 and 109.

107. Ibid., 63.

108. Ibid., 103.

109. Incháustegui Cabral, *El pozo muerto*, 14.

110. There were complaints during the occupation that patron saint festivals had become opportunities for "business" and had lost their previous spark; thus interest in money seemed to sap interest in "culture": see "Barahoneras," *LD*, 13 Oct. 1920.

111. Haltunnen, *Confidence Men and Painted Women.*
112. See D. S. Parker, *The Idea of the Middle Class*, 30–31. On "racial drift" in the colonial period in Latin America more generally and the role of gender in enabling this process, see Kuznesof's "Ethnic and Gender Influences" in relation to Stuart Schwartz's "Colonial Identities."
113. "Para las damas: Echarpes y salida de teatro" and "Las prendas," *Blanco y Negro*, 14 April 1912.
114. "Para las damas: El perfume de la casa," *Blanco y Negro*, 24 Mar. 1912; and "Para las damas: Higiene de la cabeza," *Blanco y Negro*, 7 April 1912.
115. Elias, *The Civilizing Process.*
116. Lears, *No Place of Grace.* See also Friedman, "Narcissism, Roots and Postmodernity," 331–66.
117. The link between the middle class and dissimulation was also apparent in Peru; see D. S. Parker, *The Idea of the Middle Class*, 30–31.
118. "La pobre muchacha rubia," *Blanco y Negro*, 23 Jan. 1926.
119. Ramón Hurtado, untitled article, *Blanco y Negro* 15 Feb. 1914. Although this story may not have been written by a Dominican, it seems to reflect local concerns and it also seems designed for a prestigious journal. The mulatto as man of the crowd is clearly a variation on a theme; see Kasson, *Rudeness and Civility*, 82–86.
120. I stress that this was more ideology than reality since in fact the Dominican elite was quite porous because of a colonial history of poverty, an absence of plantation agriculture, maximal racial mixture, and minimal class differentiation.
121. Stallybrass and White, *Politics and Poetics*, 144–46.
122. Bhabha, "Of Mimicry and Man," 86–88.
123. Raymond T. Smith, "Race and Class," 93–119; and Holt, "Marking."
124. The triangulation of identity based on the inextricable linking of Americans and Haitians in the Dominican imagination is well expressed in *Trementina, Clerén y Bongo*, the novel by González Herrera. Michiel Baud notes the way in which anti-imperialism and anti-Haitianism become mutually constitutive and reinforcing as a result of Haitian labor imports during this period; see Michiel Baud, "'Constitutionally White,'" 121–51.
125. Lane, *Blackface Cuba.*
126. *Blanco y Negro*, 16 Jan. 1926; Gómez Alfau, *Ayer*, 123.
127. I was inspired here by a talk by Jud Newborn entitled "The Jew, the Devil, and Commodity Fetishism: The Symbolic Transformation of Antisemitic Practice from the Early Modern Period to Nazi Genocide," University of Chicago Seminar on Forbidden Practices, 2 Dec. 1995. Sugar was also portrayed as villainous in the work of the Dominican essayist Pedro Bonó, as well as in *Cuban Counterpoint*, by the Cuban ethnologist Fernando Ortiz.
128. Taussig, *The Devil and Commodity Fetishism.*

129. See Derby, "Haitians, Magic and Money," for an exploration of the cultural effects of monetarization on racial and national taxonomies in the border during the same period.

130. In "La carestia de la vida: Nuevos puntos de vista," *LD*, 20 October 1919, the author implies that the Depression was caused by the nouveau riche of the West and their excessive spending in the 1920s.

131. For more on this relationship among Japanese elites, see Lebra, *Above the Clouds*.

132. See the front-page article (the father of the bride was editor of the paper) entitled "Aristocráticas y suntuosas nupcias," *LD*, 20 Oct. 1920.

133. Levine describes this logic as "the constant attempt to hinder the free development of the market; to withhold certain goods from free exchange through monopolization, 'which may be effected either legally or conventionally'" (*Highbrow/Lowbrow*, 230). See also Weiner, *Inalienable Possessions*.

134. In this case, religion was a means of resistance. However, virgins frequently carry highly conservative messages. For an example of a virgin becoming a symbol of conformity and counterrevolutionary resistance, see Becker, "Torching La Purísima," 247–64.

135. Louis Pérez, "Between Baseball and Bullfighting"; Pérez, "The Invention of Identity: A Century of the Cuban-North American Encounter," unpublished manuscript, 1995; see Hall, "Negotiating Caribbean Identities," for another take on Caribbean multiple identities.

136. On the waxing and waning of Hispanismo, see Michiel Baud, "The Problem of National Identity in the Dominican Republic," paper presented at the Latin American History Workshop, University of Chicago, 9 Nov. 1995.

137. While in the rest of Latin America, Columbus Day is called "el Dia de la Raza," Dominicans preferred to call it "el Dia de Colón" since their country was "la tierra del amor a Colón"—the site where Columbus first landed; where Diego Colón, the admiral's nephew, had been governor; and where Columbus's reliquary was housed (although this was later disputed by Italy, which also claimed his remains). On the Faro a Colón, see "Faro de Colón, En Cuba," *LD*, 18 Sept. 1922. William Pulliam, an American in charge of Dominican customs collections, originally proposed that it be funded by pooling monies from North America and South America. See also the Pan American Union, *Memorial Lighthouse Competition*. In 1914, a colonial column was also donated to Spain in commemoration of the discovery of America.

138. In his masterful account, Calder explains the liberal reaction in rich detail; see *Impact of Intervention*, chapter 8.

139. "Report on Public Instruction," 1 Feb. 1920, Gobierno Militar (hereafter GM), Leg. 16, p. 18, AGN. For more on U.S. Marine impressions, see U.S. Marine Government, *Santo Domingo*.

140. Richard U. Strong, Legal Advisor to Military Governor, 13 Nov. 1920, and Thomas Snowden, Military Governor, 9 Dec. 1920, both in Corres., Sec. de Ben., Fom. y Com., GM, Leg. 51, AGN. The U.S. government in the end decided not to alter the laws surrounding married women's legal status because of the radical nature of the proposal; however, means were sought to circumvent the legislation to permit women to have autonomous commerce. For more on the politics of land tenure under U.S. rule, see Julie Franks, "American Intervention, Local Proprietors, and the Transformation of Private Property in the Dominican Sugar Zone, 1916–1930," unpublished manuscript, 1995. Gael Graham, in her essay "Exercising Control," discusses similar American efforts to transform gender roles in China.

141. Guy, " 'White Slavery.' "

142. Aguiles Rodríguez, "De la vida moderna: Higiene y sanidad," *LD*, 10 March 1920.

143. Sander L. Gilman, "Plague in Germany."

144. "Asuntos Varios. Hospital de Emergencia," 25 Jan. 1921, and Sanitary Officer, 24 May 1921, Corres., Secr. de San. y Ben., GM, 1921, p. 11, AGN. If prostitution arrests are a valid indicator, it appears that most prostitution was in San Pedro de Macorís, where perhaps it catered to the many male contract laborers without families (see "Cuadro demonstrativo de arrestos," Guardia Nac. Dom., Record Group 38, Box 40, U.S. National Archives [hereafter USNA]).

145. "Del hogar y sociedad: Correo de Dorothy Dix," *LD*, 19 Dec. 1922.

146. Davidoff and Hall, *Family Fortunes*, 13.

147. "Crónica," *Blanco y Negro*, 9 Feb. 1913. Women were also moving into fields such as the sciences and pharmacy.

148. See *LD*, 24 March 1920, announcement re. Dr. Celio Estruch, who conducted abortions and *raspados uterinos*; and the advertisement for Dr. Abel González, a surgeon specializing in gynecology.

149. "Crónica," *Blanco y Negro*, 19 June 1913.

150. In the words of one author speaking of his love, "Somos dueños de su alma, de su sér entero. Somos los árbitros adorados de todos sus pasos y hasta de sus pensamientos más íntimos" (from "Tardes del Paladion," *Blanco y Negro*, 16 Jan. 1926).

151. "Las delicias de nuestra sociedad elegante," *LD*, 12 Oct. 1920.

152. "Homenaje al talento," *Blanco y Negro*, 18 May 1912. For more on this topic, see Martínez-Vergne, *Nation and Citizen*, chapter 4.

153. "La mujer" (translated from *El Dogal* of Santiago, 27 Aug. 1921), found in Record Group 38, Box 48, Records of the Chief of Military Operations, Military Government of Santo Domingo, 1917–24, Gen. Corres. 1922, USNA. The author of this article blames moving pictures for "perhaps unconsciously" providing a channel of moral corruption and American values.

154. "9 Cosas," *El Indice* (Santiago), 1 Sept. 1921.

155. "Desde el Hudson," *LD*, 5 March 1920.

156. L. Fran, "Desde el Hudson," *LD*, 5 March 1920.

157. *LD*, 14 Sept. 1922. This case bears some similarity to an event in Cuba, when a white disemboweled girl was said to be mined for wizardry potions; see Stephan Palmié's discussion of the "niña Zoila" case in his *Wizards and Scientists*, chapter 2. Special thanks to Dennis Hidalgo and Eddy Jaquez for providing me with data on this case. I will write about the anti-Haitian implications of this story elsewhere.

158. *Libro azul*, 14.

159. The op-ed states, "Sufrimos a pesadumbre de una casta . . . una avalancha de gente sin principios, sin moral, sin responsibilidad, a caza de aventuras y de señalar constancia de que eran varones fuertes y a quienes se les importaba un ardite suprimir una o mas vidas útiles a la familia y a la sociedad" ("El porte de armas," *LD*, 6 Sept. 1922). By contrast, in 1903 the crisis of values and anomie was articulated as a lack of public virility; see "Simple ojeada," *LD*, 28 Aug. 1903. Outside of urban liberal sectors, however, disarmament was considered one of the most shameful policies enacted by the marines.

160. Martínez-Vergne, *Nation and Citizen*, 24.

161. I am drawing here upon E. Antonio de Moya's innovative exploration of masculinity and political legitimacy in Dominican sexual and political culture; see "Power Games and Totalitarian Masculinity," 105–46.

162. *LD*, 28 Feb. 1920, 10 March 1920; quote from *LD*, 24 March 1920.

163. *Libro azul*, 76. The ad proclaimed, "If you feel sick and want a quick remedy, just ask for a 'Ron Tres Coronas.'"

164. *LD*, 22 Oct. 1903.

165. Warwick Anderson, "The Trespass Speaks," 1343–70. Yet during the U.S. occupation of the Philippines, neurasthenia was a disease of U.S. servicemen, not the Filipinos.

166. Bederman, *Manliness and Civilization*.

167. "Editorial: 12 October 1920," *LD*, 12 Oct. 1920.

168. Moya Pons, *A National History*, 331–32.

169. Joaquín Balaguer, "El principio de la alternabilidad en la historia dominicana," cited in González, *Bonó*, 151; Balaguer, "El hombre único," *La Opinión,* 29 Jan. 1931; and Balaguer, "El ejecutivo y la crisis municipal de Santiago," *La Opinión*, 7 Oct. 1930.

170. Peña Battle, *Política de Trujillo*, 95–96; González, "Notas sobre el pensamiento socio-político dominicano."

171. Scarano, "The *Jíbaro* Masquerade."

2. SAN ZENÓN AND CIUDAD TRUJILLO

1. Nueva Villa, Duarte, and San Carlos were completely wiped out and almost all the civic buildings of the capital were destroyed (except the colonial structures); at the airport, only the terminal remained.

2. For information on the hurricane of San Zenón, I have drawn upon the article series "Diversas informaciones sobre el huracán" and "Otras Informaciones sobre el catástrofe del dia 3" in *La Opinión*, 13 and 14 Sept. 1930 (earlier dates were unavailable in the Archivo General de la Nación, Santo Domingo. See also "Santo Domingo Wrecked by Hurricane," *New York Times*, 5 Sept. 1930; and "Hurricane Toll Now 1,200," *New York Times*, 6 Sept. 1930. The first Dominican estimates of death hovered around two thousand, the Puerto Rican Press reported three thousand, Miami five thousand, and Roorda six thousand; see Roorda, *The Dictator Next Door*. Roorda discusses how Trujillo used the hurricane to cement ties with the U.S. Marines since he faced opposition from the State Department (55–59).

3. Louis Pérez, *Winds of Change*, 17–18. For data on pre-Columbian mythology, Pérez draws upon Ortiz, *El huracán*.

4. "Una breve reseña de los huracanes del Caribe," *La Opinión*, 30 Sept. 1930. Palm reports that the arrival of Diego Colón, the governor of Santo Domingo who arrived in 1509, was also met with a cyclone. See Palm, *Los monumentos arquitectónicos*, vol. 1, 82.

5. "No creemos en maldiciones ni supersticiones," *La Opinión*, 17 Sept. 1930.

6. "No creemos en maldiciones."

7. For more on Trujillo's reconstruction of the city and its role in official regime mythology, see Mateo, *Mito y cultura*.

8. Here I use the term *social space* in terms of social domains—the mapping of social groups in urban space—not in the purely figurative sense of social position used by Pierre Bourdieu in his "Social Space and Symbolic Power," in *In Other Words*, 123–39. For more on social space, see Ryan, *Women in Public*.

9. The state was previously so weak and insignificant, the cities so small, that it is questionable whether a true public sphere existed, in Habermas's sense of a "sphere mediating between state and society," with a corresponding "principle of publicness." For more on the public sphere, see Habermas, "The Public Sphere," 398–404, esp. 399.

10. Kasson, *Rudeness and Civility*, 70. This is similar to what Pamela Voekel, drawing on Patricia Seed's work, argues for the period of the Bourbon reforms in Mexico City. See her illuminating essay, "Peeing on the Palace."

11. Darnton, "A Bourgeois Puts His World in Order," in *The Great Cat Massacre*, 127. Other comparative examples include White, "Bodily Fluids and Usufruct," 418–38; and Corbin, *The Foul and the Fragrant*.

12. Stuart Schwartz, "The Hurricane of San Ciriaco," esp. 307; Charles Walker, "The Upper Classes and Their Upper Stories"; and Louis Pérez, *Winds of Change*, 21.

13. Certeau, "Spatial Practices," in *The Practice of Everyday Life*, 91–130.

14. Mateo, *Mito y cultura*, 108.

15. Holston, *The Modernist City*.

16. On the Caribbean "protopeasant," see Mintz, "From Plantations to Peasantries," 127–54, esp. 134.

17. For more on liberalism and the increasingly deprecating image of the Dominican peasantry over the course of the nineteenth century, see González, "Ideología del progreso," and González, "Notas sobre el pensamiento," 1–22. On Lugo's vision of the peasantry, see "Sobre política," in *A punto largo*, 22–23.

18. Raymond Williams, *The Country and the City*; Roseberry, "Images of the Peasant," 55–79, esp. 70; and Skurski and Coronil, "Country and City."

19. This argument, and the notion of "phantasm," is derived from Ivy's fascinating *Discourses of the Vanishing*, 4–5. On the peasant as "internal other" and how this image has changed over time, see San Miguel, *La guerra silenciosa*. I am referring only to official rhetoric since indeed the country remained predominantly rural and the Trujillo regime gained much rural support by providing land grants and implements to the peasantry; this topic is treated in Turits, *Foundations of Despotism*; and Inoa, *Estado y campesinos*. The history of the peasantry is covered by Baud, *Peasants and Tobacco*; and San Miguel, *Los campesinos del Cibao*.

20. Andrés Requena, *Los enemigos de la tierra*. I wish to thank Neici Zeller for bringing this text to my attention.

21. Fabian, *Time and the Other*; and Roseberry, "Images of the Peasant." Of course, Trujillo also initiated pro-peasant policies, using patronage and price supports as a means of soliciting peasant support. This topic receives excellent attention in Turits, *Foundations of Despotism*; San Miguel, *Los campesinos del Cibao*; and Inoa, *Estado y campesinos*.

22. Raymond Williams, *The Country and the City*. On the walled perimeter of Havana, see Segre et al., *Havana*, 26–27.

23. This can be seen in the prominence given the walls and their named portals in anecdotal literature of the city, such as Veloz Maggiolo's *La Misericordia*. La Misericordia is the name of one of the colonial city wall entrances.

24. Hazard, *Santo Domingo*, 220.

25. M. de J. Mañón Arredondo, "Viejos nombres de lugares y terrenos del distrito nacional: El Rastrillo," *Suplemento Listín Diario*, 21 June 1986.

26. The sleepiness of Santo Domingo made Hazard question whether "St. Domingo city, under any circumstances, will ever become a great business place" (*Santo Domingo*, 222).

27. M. de J. Mañón Arredondo, "Crónicas de la ciudad primada: Perfil y crecimiento urbano de Santo Domingo en tiempos del Gobernador Azlor (1762)," *Suplemento Listín Diario*, 21 Nov. 1981. Villa Duarte was originally called Los Pajaritos. Samuel Hazard describes San Carlos as a separate "town," indicating that it was not yet a dependency of the capital in 1873. See Hazard, *Santo Domingo*. For more on animal husbandry and butchery in Santo Domingo, see Martínez-Vergne's rich account, *Nation and Citizen*, 129.

28. Matos Díaz, *Santo Domingo de ayer*, 13.

29. The history of Los Minas can be found in Martínez, *Actitudes femeninas*.

30. Erwin Cott, architect, interview, March 1993. Colonial Santo Domingo thus exhibited a form of class segregation similar to the ethnic segregation of Mexico City, where Indian communities were established *extramuros*, or outside the city walls. See R. Douglas Cope, "Muddle in the Marketplace: Commerce and Conflict in Mexico City's Plaza Mayor, 1680–1780" (paper presented at the Mexican Studies Workshop, University of Chicago, Feb. 1996), 6. For more on colonial Santo Domingo, see Palm, *Los monumentos arquitectónicos*, vols. 1 and 2; and Palm, *Los orígenes del urbanismo*.

31. Gonzalo Fernández de Oviedo y Valdés, quoted in Low, "Cultural Meaning of the Plaza," 88. For more on the grid-pattern debate, see Stanislawski, "Town Planning in the New World," 94–120; and Stanislawski, "The Origin and Spread of the Grid-Pattern Town," 105–20.

32. M. de J. Mañón Arredondo, "Crónicas de la ciudad primada: La primera iluminación eléctrica de la capital," *Suplemento Listín Diario*, 14 May 1983.

33. Rosalind Williams, *Dream Worlds*, 3.

34. Franck, *Roaming through the West Indies*, 254. I would like to thank Eric Roorda for bringing this text to my attention.

35. In *Peasants and Tobacco*, Baud discusses the common practice of taking mistresses out of wedlock with social inferiors who were typically darker in hue, a pattern which resulted in substantial racial mixture.

36. Franck, *Roaming through the West Indies*, 199.

37. M. de J. Mañón Arredondo, "Crónicas de la ciudad primada: Imagen de la capital en los comienzos del siglo XX (1905–1910)," *Suplemento Listín Diario*, 28 Nov. 1981.

38. The notion of status as social honor is from Max Weber; see Gerth and Mills, *From Max Weber*, 405.

39. Turner, *The Body and Society*, 108–9.

40. See M. de J. Mañón Arredondo, "Crónicas de la ciudad primada: Imagen de la capital," *Suplemento Listín Diario*, 28 Nov. 1981, for more on Santo Domingo transport in the early twentieth century.

41. M. de J. Mañón Arredondo, "Crónicas de la ciudad primada: La extinción de coches y caleseros de la capital," *Suplemento Listín Diario*, 10 July 1982.

42. On lifestyles as markers of status and social location, I have been guided by

Brackette F. Williams's brilliant analysis in *Stains on My Name, War in My Veins*, esp. chapter 3. This contrast in groups is intended to reveal some of the associations surrounding the car as a symbol; clearly, the small size of the two groups did not allow for a firm boundary between the groups as social constituencies.

43. Franck, *Roaming through the West Indies*, 252.
44. Mañón Arredondo, "La extinción de coches y caleseros de la capital." The capital had also been equated with the nation in the previous period, as evidenced in Martínez-Vergne's account, *Nation and Citizen*.
45. Hazard, *Santo Domingo*, 236.
46. M. de J. Mañón Arredondo, "Viejos nombres de terrenos y lugares del distrito nacional: Calle La Chancleta," *Suplemento Listín Diario*, 3 Sept. 1984; Matos Díaz, *Santo Domingo de ayer*, 15; José Enrique Delmonte Soñé, Ricardo José Rodríguez Marchena, and Martin Mercedes Fernández, "La época republicana en la arquitectura ciudad intramuros, 1844–1930" (B.A. thesis, School of Architecture and Urbanism, Universidad Nacional Pedro Henríquez Ureña, 1988), 126–27.
47. M. de J. Mañón Arredondo, "Viejos nombres de terrenos y lugares del distrito nacional: Las estancias," *Suplemento Listín Diario*, 12 Nov. 1983.
48. Ibid.
49. M. de J. Mañón Arredondo, "Viejos nombres de terrenos y lugares del distrito nacional: La Primavera," *Suplemento Listín Diario*, 31 March 1984.
50. M. de J. Mañón Arredondo, "Crónicas de la ciudad primada: Los nuevos ensanches de la capital y su predominio individualista," *Suplemento Listín Diario*, 6 Oct. 1984.
51. See Baud, "Appendix: Export Figures and Prices of Dominican Tobacco," *Peasants and Tobacco*, 223.
52. M. de J. Mañón Arredondo, "Viejos nombres de lugares y terrenos del distrito nacional: Villa Gosling," *Suplemento Listín Diario*, 13 June 1987.
53. This is demonstrated nicely in Veloz Maggiolo's fabulous memoir, *La misericordia*.
54. Descriptions such as "Hombre correcto y de buenos modales entre sus compañeros," "Don José Café como todos le decían, era un hombre sano, correcto, y estimado por todos los vecinos," and "que era un oficial de albañil de cierta distinción, por su comportamiento con los compañeros y la buena ejecución de los trabajos que se le encomendaban" also imply moral categorization (Veloz Maggiolo, *La Misericordia*, 43, 82, 38). The value placed on generosity here bears some resemblance to the distinction between "givers" and "takers" and to the importance of egalitarianism that Brackette Williams elaborates for Guyana in *Stains on My Name, War in My Veins*.
55. For more on this shift, as well as the "aristocratic" social ideology which continued to define the old elite, see Hoetink, *The Dominican People*, 165–92.

56. "Urbanización de Villa Francisca," *Blanco y Negro*, 31 March 1912. I wish to thank Julie Franks for providing me with this citation.

57. "Editorial: Junta de propietarios," LD *(Listín Diario)*, 13 Oct. 1920; and "Junta de propietarios. Postes sobre las casas. Exposición al Gobierno. Reunión importante," LD, 12 Oct. 1920.

58. S. Valdés, "El contratista de la planta y el asunto de los postes sobre las casas," LD, 14 Oct. 1920.

59. DaMatta, *Carnivals, Rogues and Heroes*, 64; Lauderdale Graham, *House and Street*.

60. Jesús Galíndez notes that the mansions of the colonial zone, which were primarily stone, emerged from the hurricane unscathed; the lion's share of damage occurred to the wooden and thatch residences of the poor and to the country houses in the western extension of the capital. See *La Era de Trujillo*, 23.

61. "Diversas informaciones," *La Opinión*, 10 Sept. 1930; Tulio H. Pina, "El Presidente Truillo desafió a la muerte y la venció," *La Opinión*, 30 Sept. 1930.

62. Antonio Calderón, "Extracto," *La Opinión*, 15 Sept. 1930.

63. "Diversas informaciones," *La Opinión*, 10 Sept. 1930.

64. Circular público, *La Opinión*, 15 Sept. 1930.

65. Lindholm, *Charisma*, 7; Holston, *The Modernist City*, 215. However, the Trujillo regime's approximation of populism was more a stylistic correspondence than anything else, since the regime was not reformist and did not rule with a broad-based coalition or labor support. For more on the populist regime type, see Conniff, "Urban Populism," 97–102.

66. Miguel Alberto Román, *Gente de portal*.

67. Ibid., 237.

68. Ibid., 186.

69. For more on Latin American national romances, see the innovative work of Sommer, *Foundational Fictions* and *One Master for Another*.

70. Douglas, *Purity and Danger*, 29.

71. Moscoso Puello, *Navarijo*, 20.

72. "Malos olores," *La Opinión*, 15 Sept. 1930.

73. Lauderdale Graham, *House and Street*, 108–36. Another example of fears of boundary transgression being displaced from one realm to another were proposals to create a special border police force, since the press provided no evidence of increased Haitian immigration or border contraband ("Se establecerá un servicio especial de policía militar en la frontera," *La Opinión*, 19 Sept. 1930).

74. "Colección de boletines lanzados al público por la Oficina de Sanidad del Distrito Núm. 1," *La Opinión*, 15 Sept. 1930.

75. Goffman, *The Presentation of Self*, 123.

76. E. P. Thompson, "The Moral Economy of the English Crowd," 71–136.

77. Stephen Greenblatt, "Filthy Rites," in *Learning to Curse*, 59. I follow James C. Scott's argument here about how practices of domination create counterhegemonic, "hidden transcripts"; see his *Domination and the Arts of Resistance*, 27.
78. *Libro azul*, 49.
79. Eduardo Matos Díaz, *Santo Domingo de ayer*, 21–22; and Ricard, "La plaza mayor en España y en América Española," 321–27.
80. M. de J. Mañón Arredondo, "Crónicas de la ciudad primada: El primer alumbrado público de la capital," *Suplemento Listín Diario*, 20 March 1982. This article documents considerable protest from shop owners and elites about the expense of providing street candles and paying the new illumination tax.
81. M. de J. Mañón Arredondo, "Crónicas de la ciudad primada: La primera iluminación eléctrica de la capital," *Suplemento Listín Diario*, 14 May 1983.
82. Matos Díaz, *Santo Domingo de ayer*, 24; Damirón, *Cronicones de antaño*, 37–39.
83. Scobey, "Anatomy of the Promenade," 204–27. The search for privacy in public is also discussed in Chauncey, *Gay New York*, 201–2.
84. Photo caption, *La Opinión*, 18 Sept. 1930.
85. Luis A. Peguero, "Ambiente popular," *La Opinión*, 17 Sept. 1930.
86. Cooking and washing in Parque Colón were considered particularly shameful; see "Informaciones sobre el ciclón," *La Opinión*, 24 Sept. 1930.
87. Arrom, "Introduction: Rethinking Urban Politics in Latin America," 5–6.
88. "El servicio de luz eléctrica," *La Opinión*, 18 Sept. 1930; "Illuminación del Parque Colón," *La Opinión*, 22 Sept. 1930.
89. "Hay que empezar a tomar disposiciones para que los barrios no se conviertan en vergonzosas rancherias," *La Opinión*, 18 Sept. 1930; "El gobierno debe prohibir por un decreto la construcción de nuevas rancherias," *La Opinión*, 20 Sept. 1930.
90. Alfredo Ricart Olives and Dr. Ramón Baez, *Anales del Municipio* (Santo Domingo: Imprenta de J. R. Vda. Garcia, 1927), Annex 16, AGN.
91. Louis Pérez, *Winds of Change*, 110.
92. "La situación lamentable del Club Unión," *La Opinión*, 4 Oct. 1930.
93. Zenón was the fifth deadliest Atlantic hurricane on record, and official reports describe it as either a cyclone or a hurricane.
94. "Despues de la catástrofe," *La Opinión*, 30 Sept. 1930.
95. Szuchman, "The City as Vision," 17–18.
96. "Hay que empezar a tomar disposiciones para que los barrios no se convierten en vergonzosas rancherías," *La Opinión*, 18 Sept. 1930. The term is significant since there were plenty of other terms such as *choza*, which were not used.
97. *La Opinión*, 2 Oct. 1930.
98. *La Opinión*, 18 Sept. 1930.

99. *La Opinión*, 19 Sept. 1930.

100. "Rapidas actuaciones del Mayor Watson, Jefe de alimentos y Hospitales," *La Opinión*, 20 Sept. 1930.

101. "Sigue en pie, grave y amenazante, la ocupación de solares ajenos," *La Opinión*, 24 Sept. 1930; and "Interesantes gráficos alrededor del ciclón," *La Opinión*, 22 Sept. 1930. Wooden houses—i.e., "ranchos"—were also prohibited from being built on block corners, a pet peeve of the elite.

102. José Ramón López, *Censo 1919*, quoted in Bonnelly, "El desarrollo de las ciudades," in *Las obras públicas en la era de Trujillo*, vol. 1, 140.

103. Elias, *The History of Manners*, vol. 1.

104. Ramón López, "Alimentación y la raza," in *Ensayos y articulos*, 46. For more on López and the context of Dominican social and political thought at the turn of the century, see González, "Notas"; Baud, "Ideología y campesinado," 63–81; and González et al., *Política, identidad y pensamiento social en la República Dominicana (Siglos XIX y XX)*.

105. "Aumentan las quejas contra la ocupación de solares ajenos," *La Opinión*, 27 Sept. 1930.

106. While many complained about peasant squatters, others defended them, arguing that "the right [*derecho*] of property has had to pay the debt [*deber*; also duty] of humanity" ("Como se vive en los barrios," *La Opinión*, 17 Sept. 1930).

107. "Santiago," *La Opinión*, 20 Sept. 1930.

108. "El cuadro pavoroso creado por el ciclón se va despojando lenta, pero gradualmente," *La Opinión*, 15 Sept. 1930. Although indeed even many homes of reinforced concrete in Gazcue did not survive this storm.

109. López Peña was an instrumental figure in the plan for the extension of key axes. See "Hay que empezar" and his authoritative book *Por qué Santo Domingo es así*.

110. Rabinow, *French Modern*.

111. "Continuan las informaciones sobre el ciclón," *La Opinión*, 22 Sept. 1930. Since Trujillo had called out the entire army, I would suspect that this particular measure was part of his project of militarization.

112. "El reestablecimiento de la instrucción pública," *La Opinión*, 15 Sept. 1930. Major Thomas Watson of the U.S. Marines was dispatched to help organize the relief effort (he was Chief of Food and Hospitals) and by the third week of the campaign had already built four hundred large houses and fifteen small ones (*La Opinión*, 20 Sept. 1930).

113. "Una buena idea del Padre Pérez," *La Opinión*, 15 Sept. 1930.

114. "Revista de la prensa," *La Opinión*, 18 Sept. 1930. "Revista de la prensa," *La Opinión*, 19 Sept. 1930, declared that "inactive" hands in the city should be removed to the countryside, and that there would be a food shortage without an increase in production. See also "Sigue en pie, grave y amenazante, la ocupación de solares ajenos," *La Opinión*, 23 Sept. 1930.

115. "Continuan las informaciones sobre el ciclón," *La Opinión*, 19 Sept 1930.

116. Juan Sánchez Azcona, "La industria de la mendicidad," *La Opinión*, 1 Oct. 1930; León Ichaso, "Actualidad: Ley contra los vagos," *LD*, 6 July 1933.

117. Most authors presume that Trujillo's resurrection of vagrancy legislation had a purely rural genealogy, but this evidence indicates that vagrancy laws had another source—the social disorder created by the hurricane in the capital.

118. Louis Pérez, *Winds of Change*, 140.

119. "Elementos menesterosas que protestan," *La Opinión*, 20 Sept. 1930.

120. "Campaña de la reconstrucción," *La Opinión*, 19 Sept. 1930.

121. "Las salvas de tiros de anoche en los barrios de la ciudad," *La Opinión*, 24 Sept. 1930. One fear was that the United States could use social banditry in the barrios as an excuse to invade again, and indeed there were several bouts of rumors that U.S. troops had already landed.

122. "El gobierno debe prohibir por un decreto la construcción de nuevas rancherias," *La Opinión*, 20 Sept. 1930; "Las salvas de tiros de anoche en los barrios de la ciudad," *La Opinión*, 23 Sept. 1930; "La occupación de solares ajenos," *La Opinión*, 1 Oct. 1930.

123. "Continuan las informaciones sobre el ciclón: Una buena medida contra los vagos," *La Opinión*, 19 Sept. 1930; "Revista de la prensa," *La Opinión*, 22 Sept. 1930.

124. "Censo de los sin trabajo," *La Opinión*, 1 Oct. 1930.The assault on idleness commenced around 1901 with the drafting of vagrancy legislation; see Martínez-Vergne, *Nation and Citizen*, 38.

125. Rafael Morel, "El concurso a Trujillo," *La Opinión*, 22 Sept. 1930.

126. "Revista de la prensa," *La Opinión*, 3 Oct. 1930. On the Barrio de Obreros, see "La sesión de ayer tarde de la Camera de Diputados," *La Opinión*, 3 Oct. 1930; and "El diputado Medrano propone la creación de un barrio obrero," *La Opinión*, 6 Oct. 1930. For proposals to enforce legislation establishing ten *tareas* within the city limits, see "Sugerencias," *La Opinión*, 1 Oct. 1930.

127. "Juegos de azar sorprendidos," *La Opinión*, 20 Sept. 1930; "Prosíguese la campaña contra los alcoleros clandestinos," *La Opinión*, 3 Oct. 1930; "Sobre prostitución," *La Opinión*, 1 Oct. 1930; "Una reunión de oficiales de la Policia," *La Opinión*, 2 Oct. 1930. Although critics cloaked their commentary in moralist language, evidence suggests that the state sought to combat these practices because they were untaxed; see "Impuesto al juego de azar," *La Opinión*, 30 Sept. 1930.

128. "Una llamada a la policía," *La Opinión*, 20 Sept. 1930.

129. "La cuestión alimenticia reclama ya una reforma hacia la normalidad," *La Opinión*, 20 Sept. 1930.

130. "Informe semanal de provincias," *La Opinión*, 23 Sept. 1930.

131. Baretta and Markoff, "Civilization and Barbarism," 594.

132. Jean and John Comaroff, "Homemade Hegemony," in their *Ethnography and the Historical Imagination*, 265–96.
133. Raymond T. Smith, "Hierarchy and the Dual Marriage System," 163–96.
134. "Revista de la prensa," *La Opinión*, 23 Sept. 1930.
135. "Nuevas y acertadas disposiciones del Mayor Watson, Jefe de Alimentos y Hospitales," *La Opinión*, 24 Sept. 1930.
136. See Raymond Williams, *The Country and the City*.
137. Corbin, *The Foul and the Fragrant*, 226.
138. Sánchez, "La industria de la mendicidad."
139. A good example of the antinomies of imagery depicting the rural and urban poor in terms of hygiene and defilement can be found in *Memoria de la gobernación provincial de Santo Domingo 1924* (Santo Domingo: Imp. J. R. Vda. Garcia, 1925), 48–49. Le Bon's classic work is *The Crowd*.
140. See "Revista de la prensa," *La Opinión*, 22 Sept. 1930, for a good example of the horror at the "hundreds of peasants transplanted to the city that must be *forcibly* returned to the countryside to work the land . . . when this exodus to the cities began we denounced it with honorable conviction indicating the dangers of this kind of anomaly" (original emphasis).
141. "Nuevas e interesantes informaciones de la catástrofe que abatió la capital," *La Opinión*, 18 Sept. 1930. The Department of Sanitation had a broad role in social control measures during the U.S. occupation period as well, since some force was necessary to create a red light district and effect vaccination campaigns, measures that the public feared and did not adequately understand.
142. Matos Díaz, *Santo Domingo de ayer*, 10.
143. Ibid., 9, 11.
144. "Por la salud pública," *La Opinión*, 18 Sept. 1930.
145. "Los planes de los mercados tocan a su fin," *La Opinión*, 29 Sept. 1930.
146. In Spanish: "Cada vez que me acuerdo del ciclón, Se me enferma el corazón . . . Ay, espiritistas inciertos, Que muchos hay por allí." Miguel Matamoros, of the famous Cuban Son band Trio Matamoros, was visiting Santo Domingo during the hurricane and composed this song as a memento. I am grateful to Raul Fernandez for alerting me to these lyrics.
147. Louis Pérez, *Winds of Change*, 140. This subheading borrows its title from the Francis Ford Coppola film released in 1979.
148. The causality is reciprocal, however, since, for example, comets are also perceived as causing epidemics (Moscoso Puello, *Navarijo*, 85). For more on power and conjuring, see Benedict Anderson, "The Idea of Power," in *Language and Power*, 17–77. As we shall see in chapter 7, natural disasters are also associated with power that is not demonic, as in Dios Olivorio's relationship to the storm that was said to bestow extraordinary powers upon him.

149. Douglas, *Purity and Danger*, 98.

150. M. de J. Mañón Arredondo, "Crónicas de la ciudad primada: El culto a los milagros en el pasado de los dominicanos," *Suplemento Listín Diario*, 28 March 1981.

151. "Hubo anoche una gran alarma en los barrios," *La Opinión*, 2 Oct. 1930. For an example of rumors that San Zenón was divine punishment, see "Revista de la Prensa," *La Opinión*, 20 Sept. 1930; and U. Heureaux, hijo, "Las propagandas de los enemigos del Gobierno," *La Opinión*, 1 Oct. 1930, in which the author calls a spiritist-diviner an enemy of the regime and asks for government intervention to silence him. Hurricanes have also been interpreted this way in Cuba and Puerto Rico; see Stuart Schwartz, "The Hurricane of San Ciriaco," 317; and Louis Pérez, *Winds of Change*, 140.

152. "El piadoso acto religioso de ayer tarde," *La Opinión*, 22 Sept. 1922; "Ecos del Pasado Temporal," *La Opinión*, 1 Oct. 1930.

153. "La coronada imagen de la Altagracia será traida de esta capital en visita de consuelo" and "Romeria de penitencia," *La Opinión*, 27 Sept. 1930. For more on the logic of the "promise" in pilgrimage and the notion of "communitas," see Victor Turner, "Pilgrimages as Social Processes," in *Dramas, Fields, and Metaphors*, 166–230.

154. Victor Turner, *The Ritual Process*.

155. Quote about Gede from Cosentino, "Envoi," 403. Data on religious pilgrimages as penance for the damnation of San Zenón are culled from "Noticias relativas a los damnificados por el ciclón del dia 3," *La Opinión*, 18 Sept. 1930; and "Romeros agradecidos del cura de Bayaguana," *La Opinión*, 6 Oct. 1930. For more on the Christ of Bayaguana and pilgrimage in the context of Afro-Dominican Catholicism, see Martha Ellen Davis, "La devoción al Santo Cristo," 4–7.

156. Stones were also an important part of Dios Olivorio Mateo's repertoire, as examined in chapter 7.

157. Thompson and Cornet, *The Four Moments of the Sun*, 37; MacGaffey, "Twins, Simbi Spirits and Lwas," 213. Thanks to Judith Bettelheim for bringing this text to my attention.

158. Of course, sacrifice is a part of Christianity as well but in more symbolic terms since feast days for the saints in Dominican *vodú* require offerings of goats, pigs or chickens.

159. I say lower because in Dominican altars the surface of the table frequently holds the *rada* (saint) chromolithographs, while images of the Petro, such as Santa Marta, are often underneath the table alongside stones, dishes of water, and food offerings.

160. While the Barón is considered Dominican, he works through his lieutenants, Tebú Tecacho (a great Haitian *bocor* or sorcerer) and El Rey de la Encabezó (a Haitian Indian).

161. These practices are commonplace today, and nocturnal cemetery visits are frequently denounced as evidence of witchcraft that must be routed out by authorities. I am using the terms witchcraft and sorcery here because Dominicans differentiate agentive magic from everyday religious practices (brujería vs. curanderismo), and see the former as more dangerous; on the other hand practitioners do not see the two branches as necessarily morally opposed.

162. For a later example, see "Varias mujeres sustraen huesos del cementerio de Mao" (*La Tribuna*, 17 Mar. 1937). Bones are an essential component of Palo Monte, a form of sorcery and divination in Cuba based on Kongo influences from Central Africa, and are also important in Haitian and Dominican *vodú*. For more on this form, see Bettelheim, "Palo Monte Mayombe," 36–49, 95–96. MacGaffey mentions the use of bone shards and cemetery dirt in Kongo *minkisi*, man-made vessels that contain ancestral spirits (*Kongo Political Culture*, 79).

163. On efforts to close the cemetery, one observer exclaimed, "La higiene, la estetica, la conveniencia, piden ya a gritos la clausura" ("El momento es oportuno para la construcción de un nuevo cementerio," *La Opinión*, 19 Sept. 1930). See also "Esas ceremonias africanizantes deben terminar," *La Opinión*, 27 Sept. 1930; "Propagandistas que merecen castigo," *La Opinión*, 29 Sept. 1930. On elite mysticism, see "Del mundo social," *La Opinión*, 26 Sept. 1930; "Muy visitada," *La Opinión*, 30 Sept. 1930; and the advertisement for Libreria Nueva in the colonial zone, *La Opinión*, 1 Oct. 1930. For more on Kardec and espiritismo, see Bettelheim, "Caribbean Espiritismo."

164. For contrast, see Arrom, Introduction, *Riots in the Cities*, 7 and note 22.

165. Dominican Archbishop Nouel, quoted in Inman, *Through Santo Domingo and Haiti*, 8. See Tilly, "Contentious Repertoires," 253.

166. Rancier, "Documentos: La arquitectura de Guillermo González Sánchez," 2. The entire issue of *Arquivox* was dedicated to González Sánchez. See also Pérez Montás, "Guillermo González," 29–41; and Moré Guaschino, "Notas sobre forma e identidad," 3–11.

167. O. Herrera Bornia, *Construcción de viviendas*, 7.

168. Other derogatory terms employed in the literature were *casuchas* and *ranchetas*.

169. Moya Pons, "Dominican Republic," 188–214; and Lattes, "Población urbana y urbanización," 70.

170. Ibid., 31–32.

171. *La Era de Trujillo*, vol. 12, 445. I would like to thank Gustavo Moré and Ramón Vargas Mera, who were extremely knowledgeable guides to architecture and urbanism during the Trujillo regime.

172. Bonnelly, "Un partido que construye: El Partido Dominicano," *Las obras públicas*, vol. 1, 298–99.

173. Called the Plan Trujillo de Urbanización, the barrios included La Fuente,

Agua Dulce, Maria Auxiliadora, Barrio Benefactor "Villa Duarte," Ensanche "Radhamés," Villa Consuelo, La Fe, La Caridad, Villas Agrícolas, Ensanchito, Barrio Obrero, and Capotillo. They were built on state lands along the periphery of the city, close to the burgeoning manufacturing zone. Planned barrios, based on the Mejoramiento Social model, were also built in some of the provinces, such as San Cristóbal, Santiago, San Pedro de Macoris, Puerto Plata, and Monte Cristi. Some towns received isolated housing units ("chalets"), particularly in the frontier. When I interviewed residents in Luperón, some said they had received their houses through a public lottery.

174. Bonnelly, *Las obras públicas*, vol. 1, 23.

175. This insight is based on a series of extended interviews with residents of Maria Auxiliadora who received apartments during the Trujillo period.

176. Pepper and Rincón-Calcano de Pepper, *Realidades Dominicanas*, 222.

177. Rafael Trujillo, inaugural speech at first opening of Barrio de Mejoramiento Social, 21 April 1947; reprinted in Herrera Bornia, *Construcción de Viviendas*, 150.

178. El plan general de urbanización y embellecimiento de las ciudades de la República, Ley #675, 31 Aug. 1944.

179. One implicit justification for zoning apparent in the plan is to avoid 'functional heterogeneity which might prejudice land values.' This language could have been intended to persuade Trujillo and his cronies of the plan, by reminding them of the threat that the appearance of shanties could be to their property values.

180. Ramón Vargas Mera, interview, November 1993.

181. Álvarez Sánchez, *La reconstrucción de la capital*, 21.

182. Vargas Mera, *Evolución urbanística de Ciudad Trujillo*, 43–53.

183. As "discolor, indocile y levantisco"; see San Miguel, *La guerra silenciosa*, 19.

184. "Funcionarios eficaces," *La Opinión*, 22 Sept. 1930.

185. On the relationship between ideas of leadership and ideas of the people, see the innovative work by Julie Skurski, "The Ambiguities of Authenticity in Latin America," 605–42; and by Coronil and Skurski, "Dismembering and Remembering the Nation," 288–337.

186. For the technocratic vision of the state, see "El diario de la mañana," *La Opinión*, 22 Sept. 1922; and the ad for the Unión Nacional de San Pedro de Macorís, *La Opinión*, 4 Oct. 1930. On permission to travel overseas, see "Una oportuna medida del Sr. Presidente," *La Opinión*, 22 Sept. 1922.

187. Ulises Heureaux, hijo, "Carta abierta al Pte. Trujillo," *La Opinión*, 22 Sept. 1930.

188. "El Presidente necesita urgentemente su tiempo," *La Opinión*, 22 Sept. 1930.

189. "La America Latina esta convulsa," *La Opinión*, 7 Oct. 1930.

190. Caton, "Canela Fina," *La Tribuna*, 17 March 1937.

191. While clearly not an avid reader, Trujillo was said to be an enthusiastic

follower of José Ortega y Gasset, and occasionally was seen prominently carrying *The Revolt of the Masses.*

192. "La herencia del Maquiavelo," *La Opinión,* 7 Oct. 1930; "En la brecha," *La Opinión,* 25 Sept. 1930; Bernardo Vega, "Peña Battle, Nietzsche y Trujillo: El enigma de una claudicación," *LD,* 3 Feb. 1930.

3. THE MASTER OF CEREMONIES

1. Crassweller, *Trujillo,* 294; Ferreras, *Trujillo y sus mujeres,* 80; Ornes, *Little Caesar of the Caribbean,* 219. Thanks to Linda A. Curcio-Nagy and Bill Beezley for their comments on this essay.
2. Geertz, "Centers, Kings, and Charisma," 150–71.
3. Crassweller, *Trujillo,* 296.
4. For more on world's fairs, see Rydell, *All the World's a Fair* and *World of Fairs.* Trujillo apparently visited the World's Fair in New York in 1939 and was duly impressed; this experience inspired him to mount such an event on Dominican soil.
5. Hunt, "The Many Bodies of Marie Antoinette," 108–30. For more on national identity as represented through spectacles of women, see Ballerino Cohen et al., *Beauty Queens on the Global Stage;* and Deford, *There She Is.*
6. I am drawing here upon the work of Christopher Waterman, who discussed performance as a means of accumulation in a talk entitled "The Production of Celebrity in Yoruba Music Videos," Department of Anthropology, University of Chicago, Nov. 1994.
7. Lancaster, *Life Is Hard,* 236.
8. Sahlins, "Poor Man, Rich Man," 287–303.
9. Richard Parker, *Bodies, Pleasures and Passions,* 43; Stern, *The Secret History of Gender,* chapter 7.
10. For more on the semantics of respeto, see James, *Resistance and Integration;* on tigueraje, see Krohn-Hansen, "Masculinity and the Political," 128. Krohn-Hansen stresses the ambiguous valence of the legitimacy of the tíguere, which is very appropriate for Trujillo.
11. Maza, *Private Lives and Public Affairs;* Landes, *Women and the Public Sphere;* Ryan, *Women in Public.*
12. J. M. Taylor, *Eva Perón.* For a fascinating treatment of Imelda Marcos and her image, see Rafael, "Patronage and Pornography," 282–304.
13. Ortner, "Is Female to Male as Nature Is to Culture?," 67–87. In his *Black Critics and Kings,* Andrew Apter has theorized gendered notions of authority (male) and power (female) as contextually unstable and reversible.
14. See works by Ferreras such as *Trujillo y sus mujeres* and *Cuando la era,* vols. 1–4. Rueda's *Bienvenida y la noche* covers Trujillo's second marriage. Enriquillo Sánchez's *Musiquito* is a thinly veiled fictional account of a lascivious dictator fond of deflowering virgins that is clearly based on Trujillo;

de la Rosa's *Petán* includes a chapter on Trujillo's brother's sexual antics; and Veloz Maggiolo's *Ritos de cabaret* explores Villa Francisca, the underworld barrio of pimps and prostitutes that Trujillo liked to visit. René Fortunato's documentary film *Trujillo: El poder del Jefe II* (1995) also treats Trujillo's love life.

15. Moats, *The Million Dollar Studs*. Moats reports that very tall pepper mills in the 1950s were called "Rubirosas" and that Porfirio's valet even sold cut squares of his used silk underpants (203–6).

16. There was a certain pride in being chosen, although there was definitely shame in consummation. During interviews in 1992 I heard many stories from elite women in Santo Domingo about being noticed by Trujillo, as well as how parents often withdrew their girls from the public arena (i.e., ballet classes, society balls, etc.) so as to avoid possible deflowering by Trujillo.

17. Flor Trujillo, as told to Laura Berquist, "My Tormented Life as Trujillo's Daughter," *Look*, 15 June 1965, 44–66, esp. 52. The scandal among the Dominican provincial elite in Monte Cristi and Santiago as a result of Bienvenida Ricardo's downwardly mobile marriage to Trujillo is the main theme in Rueda's *Bienvenida y la noche*.

18. See Tancer, "La Quisqueyana," on official feminism during the Trujillo regime. For more on the fate of women during the Trujillo regime, see Zeller, "El régimen de Trujillo," 429–45. For more on the Dominican Party, see Ornes, *Trujillo*; and Crassweller, *Trujillo*.

19. Joaquín Balaguer, *Memorias de un cortesano*, 197–98. Doña María also drew a sizable income from her military laundry monopoly and hardware store. Her architectural role was mentioned in interviews with the engineer-architect Margot Taulé and the urban planner Ramón Vargas Mera, both of whom worked for the Ministry of Public Works.

20. Maria Martínez, *Moral Meditations*.

21. Unlike the Gómez regime in Venezuela; see Skurski, "The Ambiguities of Authenticity," 605–43, esp. 614. In other areas of official policy, however, pro-family ideology was important. For example, the Dominican Party rewarded young married party couples with living-room sets and even organized group marriages in 1944.

22. Hunt, Introduction, *Eroticism and the Body Politic*, 1. See also Andrew Parker et al., *Nationalisms and Sexualities*; and Mosse, *Nationalism and Sexuality*.

23. Tancer, "La Quisqueyana," 215; and Ferrán, "La familia nuclear de la subcultura," 137–85, esp. 163–65. For more on Dominican gender identity, see Peter Grant Simonson, "Masculinity and Femininity in the Dominican Republic: Historical Change and Contradiction in Notions of Self" (Ph.D. diss., University of Michigan, 1994).

24. DaMatta, *Carnivals, Rogues and Heroes*, esp. 204–6 and 207–9; Hunt, *The Family Romance*, xiii. For a historical discussion of the development of the

dual marriage system in the Caribbean, see Raymond T. Smith, "Hierarchy and the Dual Marriage System," 163–96.

25. Sommer, *Foundational Fictions*; Sommer, "Irresistible Romance," 71–98, esp. 76; and Sommer, *One Master for Another.*

26. See Gallop, "The Father's Seduction," 56–79, for an exploration of the Electra complex and father and daughter desire.

27. I am drawing upon DaMatta's discussion of the hero figure in Brazil; see his *Carnivals, Rogues and Heroes*, 204–6. Although the malandro resembles the tíguere, the tíguere has been embraced in the Dominican Republic as the embodiment of national character but rejected in Brazil. There is now quite a debate over the essence of tigueraje and whether Trujillo fits the mold. For a critical view, see Marcio Veloz Maggiolo, "Trujillo, la garra del 'Tigre,'" *Listín Diario* (hereafter *LD*), 3 Aug. 1997. Other positions include those of Collado, *El tíguere dominicano*; Collado, *La impresionante vida*; de Moya, "Power Games," 105–46; and Krohn-Hansen, "Masculinity and the Political."

28. *Cunning* is a key term in Krohn-Hansen's "Masculinity and the Political."

29. While Flor was Trujillo's real first daughter, Angelita assumed this role for the regime because of Flor's defiance of traditional gender-role expectations.

30. The literature on public ritual is now extensive. Some important texts include DaMatta, *Carnivals, Rogues and Heroes*; Beezley et al., *Rituals of Rule, Rituals of Resistance*; Hobsbawm and Ranger, *The Invention of Tradition*; Wilentz, *Rites of Power*; Tickner, *The Spectacle of Women*; and Ozouf, *Festivals and the French Revolution.*

31. The classic article on the production of masculine prowess through the exchange of women is Rubin, "The Traffic in Women," 157–210.

32. Webb, "Masculinities at the Margins," 257–58.

33. Ortner, "Gender and Sexuality in Hierarchical Societies," in Ortner and Whitehead, *Sexual Meanings*, 358–409.

34. Trujillo's relationship with Lina Lovatón is mentioned in Alvarez, *In the Time of the Butterflies*, 22. However, in "My Tormented Life as Trujillo's Daughter," 15, Flor notes that Trujillo first met Lina as one of Flor's adolescent friends.

35. "Editorial: El gran carnaval de 1937," *LD*, 9 Jan. 1937.

36. Cited in Crassweller, *Trujillo*, 134. My discussion of Trujillo's relationship with Lina draws from Crassweller's account (133–35), as well as from Ferreras, *Trujillo y sus mujeres* (83–88).

37. "Ecos del Gran Carnaval," *LD*, 12 Jan. 1937. See also "Imponente fué la presentación de las princesas a S.M. La Reina del Carnaval de 1937," *LD*, 12 Jan. 1937.

38. See Roorda, "Gold Braids and Striped Pants," in *The Dictator Next Door*, 149–91.

39. "Maniobras militares de Dajabón" in "Ecos del Gran Carnaval," *LD*, 12 Jan. 1937. The choice of this poem had special significance since the Haitian

massacre was drawing to a close in January 1937 and most of the killing had taken place in the Dajabón area. By selecting this poem Lina is commending Trujillo's patriotic border reinstatement and ethnic "cleansing" of the country.

40. True to his origins in the National Guard, Trujillo made developing the military a top priority; see Peguero, *Militarization of Culture*.

41. I am referring to the distinction made by DaMatta in his classic essay, "Carnivals, Military Parades, and Processions," in *Carnivals, Rogues and Heroes*, 26–60.

42. Trujillo is called *el poblador* in Sánchez's *Musiquito*, a sobriquet which plays on his official title as founder (as in cities and architecture) and his fecundity (to people, to populate). DaMatta, *Carnival, Rogues and Heroes*.

43. Bataille, "The Obelisk," 215.

44. "Esplendida conmemoración," *LD*, 12 Jan. 1937.

45. Letter from La Reina, *LD*, 9 Jan. 1937.

46. "Editorial: Nuestra Señora de Altagracia," *LD*, 21 Jan. 1937.

47. As Koontz argues in her "Competition for a Women's Lebensraum," 199–236.

48. "Credo feminino de cultura," *LD*, 22 Feb. 1937.

49. "La mujer nueva," *LD*, 21 Feb. 1937.

50. For parallels in turn-of-century New York, see Peiss, *Cheap Amusements*, 63–67.

51. "Editorial: El embellecimiento del rostro," *LD*, 21 Feb. 1937.

52. "Editorial: Madame le brun," *LD*, 28 Feb. 1937.

53. Additionally, facial powder was used for its whitening effect from at least the turn of the century and probably earlier. As one observer noted in 1919, "The heat of the climate makes necessary the use of powders and frequently the darker the shade of her skin, the more powder is used. The result is an ash-grey shade on many blacks that strikes the traveler as being a little ridiculous" (from Inman, "A través de Santo Domingo y Haití," 172). After the Haitian massacre in 1937, the regime adopted an official white supremacist policy in which immigration was fomented to "whiten the race." Jewish and Spanish colonists arrived in the 1940s. As one booklet stated, "The question of the racial improvement of our population by means of crossing or by the establishment of white people, is urgent" (*Capacity of the Dominican Republic to Absorb Refugees*, 43). For more on European immigration after the massacre and the official whitening policy, see Roorda, *The Dictator Next Door*.

54. "Secretos de Hollywood," *LD*, 28 Feb. 1937.

55. Catalina D'Erzell, "Digo yo como mujer," *LD*, 28 Feb. 1937. D'Erzell's column most likely originated in Argentina or Mexico and was reprinted in many Latin American newspapers. Nonetheless, it articulated Dominican concerns and sparked controversies. I wish to thank Katherine Bliss for bringing this

issue to my attention. For another criticism of modern female style (particularly the shorter skirt), see Damirón, "De Modas," in *De soslayo*, 118–20.

56. "Editorial: El 'Duchess of Richmond' en Ciudad Trujillo," *LD*, 21 Feb. 1937.

57. Ricardo Pérez Alfonseca, "El repúblico," *LD*, 27 Feb. 1937.

58. The Carnival of 1937 was the first major pageant to be officially staged and choreographed. The first state spectacle of the regime occurred in 1932, when Trujillo paraded the entire military arsenal through the provinces.

59. The data for this discussion have been culled from the *Album de oro*.

60. While this is the official version, it was confirmed by the architects William Reid Cabral and Margot Taulé, both of whom worked in the World's Fair. Taulé recounted working on site often past midnight to make the deadline (interviews, October 1992).

61. "10 Reasons Why You Should Discover the Dominican Republic," Dominican Republic Tourist Office advertisement, *American Magazine*, April 1955, 106.

62. Rydell, *World of Fairs*, 11.

63. This paragraph draws upon Moya Pons, *Empresarios en conflicto*, 23–72. By contrast, Vedovato focuses on the economic distortions caused by Trujillo's nationalist economic policymaking; see his *Politics, Foreign Trade and Economic Development*.

64. "Editorial: El 'Duchess of Richmond'" and "Llegaron en el transatlántico Inglés 'Duchess of Richmond' numerosos turistas ingleses," *LD*, 20 Feb. 1937. A positive portrayal of the pre-Feria touristic experience can be found in Cooper, *Sambumbia*.

65. Jack Long, "Columbus Landed Here!," *American Magazine*, April 1955, 104–8.

66. Palm, *Pocket Guide to Ciudad Trujillo*. For negative and positive views of the Dominican Republic as a tourist site, see "La Feria de la Paz será la mayor atracción invierno en naciones mundo libre," *La Nación*, 28 Nov. 1955; "Rediscovery," *New Yorker*, 7 Jan. 1956, 14–15; and "El Benefactor Wants to See You," *Harper's*, Dec. 1955, 83–84.

67. Long, "Columbus Landed Here!," 107–8.

68. Ibid. The modernity of the Dominican Republic is also praised in "Mademoiselle Says Let's Go Caribbean Island-Hopping—to the Dominican Republic," *Mademoiselle*, Dec. 1956, 6.

69. In 1952, the Dominican Republic became the fourth country in Latin America to have national television. See Arístides Incháustegui and Blanca Delgado Malagón, "En el cincuentenario de La Voz Dominicana," *Isla Abierta*, 1 Aug. 1992, 1–20, for a brief history of radio and television in the Dominican Republic.

70. The letters of international praise are collected in the section entitled "Salutatión de bienvenida a los pueblos libres del mundo"; the U.S. ambassador's letter is reprinted in the *Album de oro*, 147.

71. "Mademoiselle Says Let's Go," 6.
72. A fascinating essay that blends memories of a childhood visit to la Feria with analysis is Cordero and Zeller, "El desfile trujillista," 113–74.
73. On Trujillo's expansion of the army, see Peguero, *Militarization of Culture*; and Crassweller, *Trujillo*, 263–66. Crassweller treats the Hull-Trujillo treaty on pages 182–83. On the impact of the invasions, see Vega, *Trujillo y las fuerzas armadas*. Of course, equally important to the heavy military presence at la Feria were two attempted exile invasions in 1947 and 1949 and the growing climate of hostility to the regime from abroad, including the formation of the pro-democratic Caribbean Legion and organized anti-Trujillista forces in Haiti and Cuba.
74. Hunt, "The Family Model of Politics," in *The Family Romance*, 1–16. Schatzberg has also explored paternalistic ideology in Mobuto's Zaire; see "The State as Family," 71–98.
75. Raymundo González, personal communication, March 1992.
76. Comaroff and Comaroff, "Goodly Beasts, Beastly Goods," 205. I also treat the symbolics of cattle, money, and gender in "Haitians, Money and Magic."
77. Ferreras, "Feria Ganadera costará alrededor de tres milliones," *El Caribe*, 18 May 1956.
78. I believe that Trujillo, in minting a special Feria commemorative coin, was copying the one for the New York World's Fair. Andrés L. Mateo discusses this "myth of equivalence" in *Mito y cultura*, 124. For more on the logic of icons and sovereignty, see Marin, *Portrait of the King*.
79. The Dominican display at the Pan American Exposition in 1901 had a painting of the first coinage mint on the continent as its centerpiece (University of Chicago Library, Department of Special Collections, Frederick Starr Collection, Box 29, Pan American Exposition Notebook, 1–8 Sept. 1901). My thanks to Bill Beezley, who provided me with this citation. Vela Zanetti developed a series of murals that adorned all new government buildings built for the fair; he also painted many other murals in several parts of the country during the twenty years he resided there. In 1953 he made a mural for the United Nations General Assembly in New York. See Elias Ruiz Matuk, "Remodelación de Palacio Consistorial mutiló en parte mural de Vela Zanetti," *Hoy*, 9 Jan. 1999.
80. Another important factor was Trujillo's loss of control after 1955, as evidenced in a wave of domestic repression attacking targets previously considered out of bounds, such as women and the elite.
81. This incident was recounted to me by Divina Beras, who participated in Queen Angelita's court at la Feria (interview, December 1992).
82. Outram, *The Body and the French Revolution*, 3.
83. Kantorowicz, *The King's Two Bodies*, 409.
84. Geertz, *Negara*.

85. Berezin, "Created Constituencies," 142–63.

86. The notion of "encapsulation" is from Beezley, "The Porfirian Smart Set," and that of "approximation" from Van Young, "The State as Vampire," 173–90 and 343–69.

87. Mitchell, "Egypt at the Exhibition," in *Colonizing Egypt*, 1–33.

88. Charlie See, "Conjunto de merengues firma para competir en el Agua-Luz Angelita," *La Nación*, 20 May 1956.

89. "Torneo modas Miss América atrae atención jóvenes país," *El Caribe*, 23 May 1956.

90. Cordero and Zeller, "El desfile trujillista," 118.

91. The substitution of the First Lady by the First Daughter has also taken root in Peru and Argentina; see Calvin Sims, "El Presidente's New First Lady: Take Your Daughter to Work," *New York Times*, 23 April 1995.

92. Bourdieu, "Appendix: Did You Say Popular?," in *Language and Symbolic Power*, 90–102, esp. 96.

93. Lewis, "Fieldnotes on Masculinity Research," 57–68. For another take on underclass masculinity that evaluates masculine style in relation to working-class status, see Limón, "Carne, Carnales, and the Carnivalesque," in *Dancing with the Devil*, 123–40.

94. Family values such as pronatalism were promoted, for example, during the 1944 centenary celebrations when prizes were given to families with many children.

95. Benjamin, *Charles Baudelaire*, 54–55.

4. COMPATRIOTAS! EL JEFE CALLS

1. Max Rodríguez to Pres. de la Junta del PD, 16 Dec. 1943, Partido Dominicano (hereafter PD), Junta Central Directiva (hereafter JCD), Corres. 11–20 Dec. 1943. The title of this chapter is from a stanza in the poem. All PD archival documents are from the AGN, Santo Domingo (hereafter AGN).

2. James C. Scott, "Domination, Acting, Fantasy," 55–84.

3. Betances, *State and Society*, 100. This emergent urban middle class still constituted a minority at this time, when most of the country was rural and illiterate, but it grew considerably during the Trujillo regime as a result of urban development, the growth of manufacturing, and state expansion.

4. Goffman, "On Face-Work," *Interaction Ritual*, 19; and Goffman, *Relations in Public*, 120.

5. Collado, *El Foro Público*, 49. The column ran from five to seven days a week. I am greatly indebted to Collado's pathbreaking reading of denunciation during the regime.

6. Ibid., 37, 47. I would like to thank José Antinoe Fiallo for sharing his collection of denunciations; Brendan Kiley and I used these as a sample for this statistical portrait. I am grateful to Brendan Kiley for providing a

statistical analysis of the material. Denunciation as a feature of the Dominican political landscape was apparent both before and after the appearance of the "Foro Público": see, for example, the *Unión Cívica*, a paper that emerged in the wake of Trujillo's death in 1961 that is chock full of denunciations. But the apex of its social and political import occurred during the 1950s. For a comparative perspective on denunciation, see Fitzpatrick and Gellately, "Introduction to the Practices of Denunciation," 763.

7. Collado claims that Luis Álvarez Pina, Paíno Pichardo, and Max Uribe were important writers, compilers, and editors of the "Foro Público"; they were also chief Dominican Party functionaries (*El Foro Público*, 47). Since the identity of those operating behind the scenes at the Foro was a highly guarded secret, there is no way of corroborating this.

8. I discovered several caches of intelligence case files in the Dominican Party papers in the Archivo General de la Nación in Santo Domingo, and was able to follow up a few cases in the "Foro Público"; see the PD, JCD, Informes Confidentiales, Informes Presidentes de Juntas, and Correspondencias for the years 1946, 1947, 1950, 1951, and 1952. Special thanks to Eddy Jáquez for his assistance in locating these materials. I examined more than one year's worth of denunciations from the "Foro Público," and four groups of Dominican Party confidential reports from 1942 and 1952 (as well as more that I discovered elsewhere in the Dominican Party papers). I am thus analyzing in tandem two very different sources and thus different forms of denunciation. However, these two streams were actually part of an even broader phenomenon that included *pasquines* (private anonymous denunciatory letters received in the mail), anonymous books published by the government that denounced individuals (for example, see *Germán Ornes: A Self Portrait*), as well as oral forms, such as Trujillo's infamous tirades against cronies in his inner court. An interesting subset of denunciation and praise was written by Trujillo's "pens for hire," who wrote praise and denunciation under their own names as well as pseudonyms. For panegyric, see Ariza, *The Man and His Country*; and Osorio Lizarazo, *Así es Trujillo*. Even U.S. senators and congressmen could be drawn into Trujillo's whirlwind of praise and excoriation; for example, they made favorable speeches about him and the country, as in McCormack's "25 Years of Peace and Prosperity." Americans could be denounced as well; see Pepper, *I Accuse Braden/Yo Acuso a Braden*; the use of English demonstrates that this book was not intended for a Dominican audience. For a fascinating analysis of the behind-the-scenes career of José Almoina Mateos, one of Trujillo's best-known paid sycophants, see Vega, *Almoina, Galíndez*.

9. Collado is the only author I have found who contends that this may be the case, on the basis that 15 percent of the letters were from citizens to civil servants (21 percent in my data) (*El Foro Público*, 36). In a classification based on accusation content, fully one-third were citizen complaints about the

government (the rest concerned corruption, political issues, class, sex, morals, and sorcery).

10. See Brackette F. Williams's masterful account of status competition in Guyana, *Stains on My Name, War in My Veins*; Peter J. Wilson's classic account, *Crab Antics*; also Abrahams, "A Performance-Centered Approach to Gossip," in *The Man-of-Words*, 77–87. I am using the term *populism* here to describe a particular political style; see Knight, "Populism and Neo-Populism," 223–48.

11. I draw on Collado's provocative and fascinating analysis in *El Foro Público* for his argument about the "Foro Público" as a "monument of gossip"; see denunciations reproduced on page 66 and a cover of *El Caribe* reproduced on the back cover, from Rafael Trujillo and his brother Héctor. See Wiarda, *Dictatorship and Development*, 118, for the quote on Trujillo's democracy.

12. I am borrowing here from Navaro-Yashin, *Faces of the State*, 5.

13. Nancy Zemon Davis, *Fiction in the Archives*, 65; Taussig, *Defacement*.

14. Ornes, *Germán Ornes: A Self Portrait*.

15. Goffman, *Stigma*, 130.

16. While the literature on early modern Europe has considerably problematized the relation between public and private domains (see Brewer, "This, That and the Other," in Castigione and Sharpe, eds., *Shifting the Boundaries*, 1–21, for example), the literature on modern authoritarianism tends to turn on a hard boundary between the public and private, one that may be inaccurate for highly personalistic regimes such as that of Trujillo, Ferdinand Marcos in the Philippines, or Saddam Hussein in Iraq; see, for example, the study by Berezin, *Making the Fascist Self*. The nuanced treatment of the culture of complicity in Syria by Wedeen, *Ambiguities of Domination*, depends on a sharp divide between the state and civil society. For more on the "sultanistic" dictatorships such as that of the Trujillato, see Chehabi and Linz, *Sultanistic Regimes*.

17. While I propose here that most denunciations were initiated by private citizens, Trujillo did found *El Caribe* newspaper and owned it from 1948 to 1954 (during this time he required public servants to subscribe), which is why the "Foro Público" has been attributed exclusively to Trujillo himself; it is said that it was designed to "bludgeon Trujillo's friends and foes alike, with anonymous slanderous missives written at the National Palace" (Ornes, *Little Caesar of the Caribbean*, 195). See also Diederich, *The Death of the Goat*; and Balaguer, *La palabra encadenada*. "Rectitude and morality" were part of the motto of the Dominican Party.

18. Clearly, the "Foro Público" did instantiate a new "technology of power"; see Foucault, *Discipline and Punish*, 23. My argument corroborates that of Jonathan Hartlyn's work on the structure of repression of the regime; see *The Struggle for Democratic Politics*, 52–58.

19. Brewer, "This, That and the Other." See also Bourdieu, "The Biographical Illusion."
20. Bourdieu, "Political Representation: Elements for a Theory of the Political Field," in *Language and Symbolic Power*, 195. See also Claudio Lomnitz, "Corruption," in *Deep Mexico, Silent Mexico*, 162–64.
21. Juan E. Corradi et al., Introduction, *Fear at the Edge*, 3.
22. A few examples of this literature include Feldman, *Formations of Violence*; Daniel, *Charred Lullabies*; and Taylor, *Disappearing Acts*.
23. Crassweller, *Trujillo*, 331–33. In the 1950s, of course, the rise of the SIM (secret police) also occurred; yet scholars have focused on the SIM to the exclusion of denunciation and the rise of lower-level forms of policing through the "inspectors," which were a more quotidian and intimate means of social control that may have had a deeper impact via policing behavior. For more on formal structures of repression, see Wiarda, *Dictatorship and Development*.
24. Aside from the atrocious Haitian massacre in 1937, there were relatively low levels of Dominican deaths by official repression. (Tragically and ironically, Galíndez was abducted by Trujillo's henchmen in a New York subway, and thus is remembered as the victim of one of the most audacious and cruel acts of state violence by Trujillo.) Yet the terror engendered by the massacre was by no means confined to Haitians. First, the massacre affected a population that was ethnically Haitian, but actually Dominican by nationality, since the majority had been born on Dominican territory. Second, it was carried out by machete over a period of months, so it created panic among many Dominicans who feared they would be next. In an interview with Richard Turits and me (Guadeloupe, 1988), Father Robert, who was parish priest in Ouanaminthe, Haiti, at the time, estimated that fifteen thousand ethnic Haitians were slaughtered. For more on the massacre, see Derby and Turits, "Historias de terror y los terrores de la historia," 65–76; and Turits, "A World Destroyed," 589–635; Vega, *Trujillo y Haití (1937–1938)*, vol. 2; and Cuello, *Documentos del conflicto*.
25. Galíndez, *The Era of Trujillo*, 138. Wiarda also privileges "thought control" in the "totalitarian excesses" of the regime, claiming that the Trujillato was "one of the tightest dictatorships the world had ever seen." See Wiarda and Kryzanek, *A Caribbean Crucible*, 36–37. As Hartlyn notes, labor was a focus of repression after the strikes of 1942 and 1947, when the regime sought to root out political opposition and banned the Communist Party; see *The Struggle for Democratic Politics*, chapter 2.
26. On the colonial origins of honor as public identity, see Johnson and Lipsett-Rivera, Introduction, *The Faces of Honor*, 15.
27. The case of Américo Lugo belongs in this category, although certainly there are stories of intellectuals who were murdered after being denounced; Ramón

Marrero Aristy, for example, was killed in the wave of repression after the coup attempt in 1959; see Vega, *Unos desafectos y otros en desgracia*, 248. Marrero Aristy, who was a frontier cultural agent, was denounced by Pedro L. Vergés Vidal, Presidente de la Junta Comunal del PD, for "ridiculing the community," for being an "ingrate," and for creating "collective indignation." These were code words for his antipathy to Trujillo, although the denunciation appends a list of purported names of people from Neiba who testified to the "sad truth" of his improper conduct (13 Dec. 1943, PD, JCD, Corres. 11–20 Dec. 1943). Vergés Vidal himself had been denounced on 9 December for absconding with public funds, however, so it is possible his accusation of Marrero Aristy was retributory (V. Álvarez Pina, Presidente de la Junta Superior Directiva, to R. Paíno Pichardo, Directiva del PD, PD, JCD, Corres. 11–20 Dec. 1943). For a personal account of denunciation written by a prominent *forista* and owner of *El Caribe*, see Ornes, *Little Caesar of the Caribbean*, 194–200 (although Ornes had the personal resources to emigrate to the United States after his "fall from grace" and thus did not suffer the full force of social ignominy).

28. Abu-Lughod, *Veiled Sentiments*, 85. On *respeto*, see Lauria, " 'Respeto,' 'Relajo,' " 53–67.
29. V. Álvarez Pina to Carlos Sención Féliz, Confidencial, 2 Dec. 1943, PD, JCD, Corres. 11–20 Dec. 1943. Take, for example, the incident involving Camelia Hirujo Dulce, the Partido Trujillista Rama Feminina president, discussed below. The incident was reported anonymously to the Dominican Party president, who wrote to the provincial governor for clarification; he then expressed his grievances to the Rama Feminina president in a letter directly to her; the president of the ayuntamiento next filed a report on the incident to the Secretary of State of the Interior and Police. Each of these reports channeled hearsay from various sources since the highest authorities were not direct witnesses to the altercation.
30. Marco Zivkovic, "Garbled Genres: Conspiracy Theories, Everyday Life and the Opacity of the Social World in Milosevic's Serbia," unpublished manuscript, 2001.
31. Vicente L. Rafael highlights other effects of rumors in the Philippines under Japanese rule in his essay "Anticipating Nationhood," 67–82. A main feature binding together the inner circle was their shared knowledge of "dark" and "entrusted" secrets; see Goffman, *The Presentation of Self*, 142–43.
32. Vega, *Almoina, Galíndez*, 30–31. The book was called *Yo fuí secretario de Trujillo*. José Almoina Mateo was from Spain.
33. Rafael, "Anticipating Nationhood," 76. Other stimulating essays on rumor include S. A. Smith, "Talking Toads and Chinless Ghosts," 405–27; and Perice, "Rumors and Politics in Haiti," 1–10. Nancy Munn describes witchcraft as an "open secret" in *The Fame of Gawa*, 215. On secrecy and

social distance, see Simmel, "The Secret Society," in *The Sociology of George Simmel*, 345.

34. Blanchot, "Everyday Speech," 15.
35. R. Paíno Pichardo to Presidente de la Junta Superior Directiva del Partido Dominicano, 8 Dec. 1943, PD, JCD, Corres. 11–20 1943.
36. In his "Everyday Metaphors of Power," 573, Timothy Mitchell develops a powerful critique of models of domination that assume a split between "physical coercion and ideological persuasion."
37. Lauria, "'Respeto,' 'Relajo,'" 63; see also Mañach, *Indagación del Choteo*. Thanks to Guillermo Giucci for bringing the Mañach text to my attention. On gossip and the quest for reputation in the Caribbean, see the classic accounts in Wilson, *Crab Antics;* and Abrahams, *Man-of-Words*, esp. chapter 5.
38. Fitzpatrick, "Signals from Below"; and Connelly, "The Uses of *Volksgemeinschaft*," 831–66 and 899–930. However, the convention of denunciation in the newspaper disappeared during the U.S. occupation.
39. The prevalence of pseudonyms is evidenced in Emilio Rodríguez Demorizi's 280-page book listing the true authors of the multitudes of anonymous Dominican editorialists; see *Seudónimos dominicanos*. On deference, see Goffman, "The Nature of Deference," in *Interaction Ritual*, 47–96.
40. Many volumes of Alix's poetry have been subsequently published. See, for example, Juan Antonio Alix, *Décimas políticas*, 7. On the use of popular poetry as a form of political propaganda, see Miguel Tejada, "El folklore como mecanismo de control político," 19–39.
41. Hoetink, *The Dominican People*, 148.
42. See Wiarda, "Dictatorship, Development and Disintegration," 1096–97.
43. Irvine, "Insult and Responsibility," 111.
44. Koslov, "Denunciation and Its Function in Soviet Governance," 867–98.
45. Foucault, *Discipline and Punish*, 23.
46. Collado, *Foro Público*, 31. Denunciations involving graft which diminished state coffers and resulted in confidential case files could be sent to Trujillo, but these were a distinct minority of the total; see V. Álvarez Pina to Trujillo, 11 Dec. 1942, PD, JCD, Corres. 11–20 Dec. 1943.
47. Wiarda argues that the letters in the "Foro" originated in the National Palace and served to justify the demotion of public officials for other reasons; see *Dictatorship and Development*, 73 and 127. Francisco Rodríguez de León, *Balaguer y Trujillo*, 202, describes the "Foro" as an "escape valve."
48. Not only the nature of local grievances but the sheer volume of material would have been very challenging for someone to invent. The group of denunciations that I assume were least likely to be planted by the regime were citizen-to-civil-servant accusations regarding inefficiency or corruption, frequently from isolated rural hamlets. The group most likely to be planted by the regime would be political accusations—for example, being unfaithful to

Trujillo's cause, being "indifferent" to the regime, or being a communist (i.e., a person who traveled frequently to Russia or Cuba—which was virtually impossible during the Trujillato, as travel outside the country was strictly controlled and passports were difficult to obtain). For more on denunciation and political crimes under the regime, see Vega, *La vida cotidiana*, 13; Vega, *Unos desafectos;* and Vega, *Control y represión.* Having scanned denunciations from 1954 on, my impression is that the percentage of political denunciations—accusations of communism or lack of loyalty to Trujillo—does increase at the end of the regime, which may be why many argue backward that this was the case for the entire decade of the "Foro." Since I only observed the outcome of denunciation cases in the confidential Dominican Party papers (a small percentage of the total surveyed), I cannot guess what percentage of denunciations Trujillo actually intervened in. I can say, however, that his pattern of intervention followed no reason I could discern and that he clearly delighted in surprise—which may be why the poor and abject most frequently lucked out, not the rich and famous. Dominican Party papers indicate that the complaints were channeled up the chain of command, from the local level to the junta presidents to the party president— who, being a close crony of Trujillo, most likely provided the dictator with a selection of cases. The best study of the fate of denunciation cases is by Vega, *Unos desafectos*, but he focuses on individuals with name recognition— individuals who collaborated or opposed the regime, intellectuals, and people from prominent families. Thus his sample is not representative of Dominican society or of most denunciations.

49. Gerth and Mills, eds., *From Max Weber*, 228.
50. This estimate is from 1950; see Galíndez, *Trujillo*, 151–52. For more on the expansion of governmental and party bureaucracy under Trujillo, see Betances, *State and Society*, 100.
51. To the extent that citizenship existed at all under the regime. In his *Populist Seduction*, xi, Carlos de la Torre reminds us that citizenship is not strong even under democratic regimes in Latin America.
52. Uribe, *El Partido Dominicano*, vol. 1, 58.
53. Moya Pons, *The Dominican Republic*, 365 and 378.
54. Bourdieu, *The State Nobility*.
55. Francisco Barón González, Senator Barahona, "Report on Provincial Conditions," 23 June 1939, PD, JCD, Corres., exp. 13. The lack of convergence between the economic and social boundaries of class is noted in Hoetink, *The Dominican People*, chapter 8.
56. Manuel A. Goyco, hijo, to Paíno Pichardo, Presidente de la Junta Comunal del PD, 5 Feb. 1940, PD, JCD, Corres., exp. 5. Of course, this also indicates that the party was a crucial gatekeeper during the regime.
57. See Javier Herasme Díaz, Presidente de la Junta del Partido Dominicano,

Bahoruco, to Virgilio Álvarez Pina, 13 Dec. 1943, PD, JCD, Corres. 11–20 Dec. 1943.

58. They were not unlike the colonial *letrados* so wonderfully described in Angel Rama's *The Lettered City*, with the important caveat that they were not true elites and had no property; they had nothing besides their title and social position as party delegates. For more on interstitial brokers in other contexts, see Feierman, *Peasant Intellectuals*, 5; and Claudio Lomnitz, "Provincial Intellectuals," in *Deep Mexico*, 263–86.

59. Máximo Acosta, Presidente de la Junta Comunal del PD, to Álvarez Pina, Cabrera, 13 Dec. 1943, PD, JCD, Corres. 11–20 Dec. 1943.

60. Fitzpatrick and Gellately, "Introduction to the Practices of Denunciation," 751; and Colin Lucas, paraphrased in Fitzpatrick and Gellately, "Introduction to the Practices of Denunciation," 763.

61. Bourdieu, "The Production and Reproduction of Legitimate Language," in *Language and Symbolic Power*, 52. But I do not mean to be opposing here the material and symbolic components of these exchanges; see de la Torre, *Populist Seduction*, xi.

62. Lacay Polanco, *El hombre de piedra*; this is a Trujillo-era look at the civil servant of the 1920s and is inflected with a 1950s cynicism that would not be characteristic of the time.

63. Brackette F. Williams, *Stains on My Name, War in My Veins*, 92–126; Douglas, *Purity and Danger*; and DaMatta, *Carnivals, Rogues, and Heroes*, 63–67.

64. Handelman, "The Idea of Bureaucratic Organization," 17. See Stuart Schwartz, "State and Society," 4–35, for a call for the study of the norms and values of bureaucracy.

65. Wiarda, *Dictatorship and Development*, 79.

66. Señor Delima, interview, Jan. 1993.

67. Herzfeld, *Social Production of Indifference*, 29–30.

68. Ibid., 75. This contrast resembles what Larissa Lomnitz and others describe as a dynamic between system men and president's men for the PRI regime in Mexico ("The Function of the Form," 361).

69. Niehaus, Mohlala, and Shokane develop the notion of witchcraft as mystical or occult power in the book *Witchcraft, Power and Politics*.

70. Stewart and Strathern, Foreword, *Witchcraft, Sorcery, Rumors, and Gossip*, ix.

71. See Mary Douglas, "Introduction: Thirty Years after *Witchcraft, Oracles and Magic*"; and Robert Brain, "Child Witches," xvii–xviii and 161–82. While it is true that party functionaries were better paid (and highly taxed), this was compensated by their lack of clear authority in relation to civil servants. Another functionalist explanation of denunciations—that they strengthened the community in the face of deviants—makes sense for denunciations that made explicitly political accusations against communists.

72. Peter Brown, "Sorcery, Demons and the Rise of Christianity," 17–56.

73. Geschiere, *The Modernity of Witchcraft*, 43; and James C. Scott, *Arts of Resistance*, xiii.

74. Foucault, *Discipline and Punish*, esp. 22–24.

75. In formulating this point, I am indebted to a critique by Jonathan Barry of Keith Thomas's *Religion and the Decline of Magic*, in "Introduction: Keith Thomas and the Problem of Witchcraft," 1–49.

76. Stuart Hall, "Race, Articulation and Societies," 340.

77. For parallels with the Nazi party (upward mobility albeit without the racial valence), see Peukert, *Inside Nazi Germany*.

78. Bailey, "Gifts and Poison," 1–26, esp. 18. Taussig also discusses how in the borderlands, where the "official and the 'extra-official' " meet and overlap, the "mystery" of this "strategic confusion" is dramatically magnified; see *The Magic of the State*, 18.

79. Goffman, "The Nature of Deference and Demeanor," in *Interaction Ritual*, 47–96.

80. For example, a Dominican Party secretary earned sixty pesos per month, while a secretary for the ayuntamiento made only eighteen pesos.

81. A: Señor Secretario de Estado de la Presidencia, Ciudad Trujillo, Asunto: Denuncia de irregularidades cometidas por el Encargado de la Farmacia del Hospital Padre Billini y expediente formulado, 21 June 1939, PD, JCD, Corres., exp. 13.

82. Herzfeld, *Social Production of Indifference*, 102–4.

83. Paíno Pichardo to Secretario de Estado de la Presidencia, Asunto: Solicitud de nombramientos, 2 Feb. 1940, PD, JCD, Corres., exp. 5.

84. Interogatorio al St. Victorino Baez Vargas, Farmaceutico del Hospital "Padre Billini," 21 June 1939, PD, JCD, Corres., exp. 13.

85. This is clear in the questionnaire structure, which asked whether there was any "antagonism between Party members," to which respondents were prompted to answer in the negative, perhaps because factionalism might indicate someone had "political aspirations" (see the 1940s reports, for example). It is important to stress that this factionalism was apparent only at the lower echelons of civil and party bureaucratic structure, since at the top Trujillo was in control; as Moya Pons notes, once Trujillo's approval was secured, the party even "elected" senators and deputies (*The Dominican Republic*, 375).

86. See Cordero and Zeller, "El desfile trujillista," 113–74.

87. Paíno Pichardo to Salvador A. Cocco, 27 Jan. 1940, PD, JCD, Corres., exp. 5. The full *expediente* with further responses from Pichardo and Cocco elucidates the event in detail: Pichardo to Enrique Apolito, Presidente de la Junta Communal del PD, Sánchez, 30 Jan. 1940, PD, JCD, Corres., exp. 5.

88. PD, JCD, Corres., exp. 5.

89. Geertz, *Negara*. Geertz's concept of the "theater state" derives power and

authority from ritual and cosmology, rather than the other way around. Although somewhat reductive (reducing politics to ritual), the concept applies to historical kingdoms that have highly developed courtly ritual. Its relevance to other forms of government and political hierarchy is an issue of lively debate. See his conclusion "Bali and Political Theory" for the wider implications of his model. For a rich collection of essays on ritual and the state in Latin America, see Beezley et al., *Rituals of Rule, Rituals of Resistance*. State rituals under Trujillo frequently scripted the army into these events but denunciations never emerged between these tiers of the state, surely because this constituency was so privileged by Trujillo that it was viewed as untouchable.

90. For more on the logic of diarchy in other contexts, see Valeri, "Diarchy and History," 45–80. Thanks to Martha Feldman for suggesting to me the literature on diarchy.

91. The gift of the Chevy sedan was authorized by Trujillo himself to Isabel Mayer, senator from Monte Cristi, and was paid for with a party check in 1940.

92. Paíno Pichardo to Dr. M. Guerrero Hijo, Director del Hospital Padre Billini, 23 Jun. 1939, PD, JCD, Corres., exp. 13.

93. Elpidio Eladio Mercedes to Trujillo. Of course, Trujillo's divine intervention didn't solve all problems, as witnessed by one man who had been framed by local authorities and later released by Trujillo. He still had to face the wrath of the local politicians upon his release; see José A. Lara Ricardo to Trujillo, 22 Jan. 1940, PD, JCD, Corres.

94. As Paul Sant Cassia has argued in another context; see "Banditry, Myth and Terror," 773–95, esp. 786.

95. José Ramirez, Neyba, to Trujillo, n.d., Feb. 1940, PD, JCD, Corres. There are a surprising number of denunciations against the Grenada Company and complaints of peasant evictions in the "Foro Público," grievances that must have taken not a small amount of courage to articulate in the press; see, for example, *El Caribe*, April 1958.

96. Julio A. Fela to Paíno Pichardo, Seybo, 3 Feb. 1940, PD, JCD, Corres.

97. See "Barriada clandestina," Raymundo Bid, "Foro Público," *El Caribe*, 26 April 1958.

98. Moya Pons, *The Dominican Republic*, 365.

99. Francisco A. Read, Junta Comunal Jefe, Las Matas de Farfán, to Paíno Pichardo, Junta Central Directiva, CT, 24 June 1939, PD, JCD, Corres., exp. 13.

100. Collado, *El Foro Público*, 64–65.

101. José O. Rosado, PD, JCD, Constanza, to Paíno Pichardo, 21 June 1939, PD, JCD, Corres., exp. 13.

102. See notes from Luis Alemar and R. Emilio Jiménez excusing themselves from Trujillo's banquet at the Hotel Francés, 30 Jan. 1940, PD, JCD, Corres., exp. 5.

103. "Al Señor Modesto Diaz, Pres JCD, Ref. Su Carta Confidential de fecha 7 del

Corriente, Asunto: Residencia de Empleados Públicos, Esperanza, PDC, 14 Feb. 1952." There was a wave of denunciations due to public-sector employees' matrimonial infidelity. See, for example, "Foro Público: Empleados burlan disposiciones," *El Caribe*, 13 May 1952. For more on the West Indian serial family, see the classic essays by Raymond T. Smith in *The Matrifocal Family*.

104. For more on the official categories of opprobrium, see Vega, *La vida cotidiana*, 13; and Vega, *Unos desafectos*.

105. There are many examples in the party correspondence of this kind of letter, which is not threatening in tone but remarkably polite. See, for example, the letter from Paíno Pichardo, PD, JCD, to Rodríguez Toribio, 20 June 1939, PD, JCD, Corres., exp. 13.

106. Peukert, *Inside Nazi Germany*, esp. chapter 3.

107. Julio Santaclia, "Foro Público: Deben limitarse," *El Caribe*, 26 April 1958.

108. José del Carmen Rodríguez, Diputado, San Juan de la Maguana, to Pichardo, 26 Jan. 1940, PD, JCD, Corres., exp. 5.

109. Hernán Cabral, Juez Alcalde, Villa Julia Molina, to Pichardo, 31 Jan. 1940, PD, JCD, Corres., exp. 5.

110. In an extraordinarily frank complaint about official corruption ("Foro Público: Planes en detrimento de la política de Trujillo," *El Caribe*, 12 May 1952) it is alleged that a 15 percent informal tax was raised from everyone in Santiago to pay for a luxurious fete, which the governor and the president of the junta of the Dominican Party hoped would result in a $5,000 kickback to each from El Generalísimo himself. Even minor rites such as the frequent "agropolitical meetings" were apparently subject to informal taxation at exorbitant levels, in this account as high as $150 a person.

111. Maximiliano Martínez to Paíno Pichardo, 5 Feb. 1940. Lomnitz argues that the assumption of reciprocity in ritual makes corruption a natural correlate; see his chapter, "Ritual, Rumor and Corruption," *Deep Mexico, Silent Mexico*, 162–63.

112. A celebration of the Dia del Benefactor (Trujillo's birthday) on 24 Oct. 1952 in Enriquillo, for example, included talks such as "La educación y la cultura" and "Las creencias y las supersticiones," as well as short films such as "El maní y su cultivo," "El cuidado del niño," and "Protejases contra la sífilis."

113. This changed, however, with the formation of the women's wing of the Dominican Party in 1942. Schoolteachers were especially important in the provincial status economy, because in rural parts of the Dominican Republic the church was weak and understaffed, unlike the situation in countries such as Mexico where teachers competed with priests.

114. See, for example, Pieter, *Ciudad Trujillo*.

115. One novelist underscores the importance of this uniform to the *hombre decente*; see Veloz Maggiolo, *Ritos de Cabaret*, 13.

116. On the significance of clothing for the military, see Roorda, *The Dictator Next Door*. For a description of a mulatto general dressed to the nines, see Román, *Gente de Portal*, 8. For the colonial significance of being *letrado*, see Ramos, *The Lettered City*.

117. Moscoso Puello, *Cartas*, 204. The importance of attire for civil servants is evidenced in denunciations for improprieties such as "dancing in shirt-sleeves in cafés of ill repute" or even in complaints that lottery ticket sellers were ragtag and shoeless and thus "an embarrassment for the state and society" ("Foro Público: Fiscal parrandero" and "Se defiende la lotería," *El Caribe*, 13 May 1952).

118. Pablo Rodríguez Tavárez, Secretario de Junta Comunal del Partido Dominicano and Pres. del Hon. Ayuntamiento, to Pres. Trujillo, 28 Jan. 1940, PD, JCD, Corres., exp. 5.

119. I am drawing here upon Brewer's "This, That and the Other," 15.

120. "Otra vez la cédula," in *La era de Trujillo*, 17.

121. Wade, *Blackness and Race Mixture*, 9.

122. *La era de Trujillo*, 7. For a critique of the notion of essentialized identity, see Handler, "Is 'Identity' a Useful Cross-Cultural Concept?," 27–40.

123. Somers, "Narrativity, Narrative Identity, and Social Action," 591–630. I am suggesting a parallel, then, between the role that the Ton Ton Macoutes played in forging a space of citizenship for the lumpen class of Port-au-Prince under Duvalier and role of the Dominican Party under Trujillo; see Laguerre, *The Military and Society in Haiti*.

124. Fanon, *Black Skin, White Masks*.

125. Cocco to Pichardo, 20 Jan. 1940, PD, JCD, Corres., exp. 5.

126. Crassweller, *Trujillo*, 5. The novelist and cultural critic Marcio Veloz Maggiolo has also scoffed at these rites of subordination during the Trujillato as "formas de la ridiculez"; see his "Trujillo, la garra del 'Tigre,'" *Listín Diario*, 3 Aug. 1997.

127. James C. Scott, "Prestige as the Public Discourse of Domination," 145–66.

128. Ornes, *Trujillo*, 197.

129. Dr. Apolinar A. Montás G., "Foro Público: Presidente JPD rectifica," *El Caribe*, 23 April 1958; and Francisco Montero, "Foro Público: Una respuesta infortunada," *El Caribe*, 23 April 1958. Montero continued in his friend's defense, stating that he invoked "the name of the Father of the New Fatherland merely to shield himself against judgement of his own work as a public functionary, not how those affiliated with the Dominican Party must justify their actions and clarify their conduct." Tragically, "Serving God and Trujillo" was written by Manuel Tavárez in a desperate effort at defending the honor of his wife, the anti-Trujillista martyr and heroine Minerva Mirabal de Tavárez, albeit to no effect, since both were later assassinated (Dr. Manuel Aurelio Tavárez, "Foro Público: Desmiente acusaciones," *El Caribe*, 29 April

1958). For more on the Mirabal case, see Cassá, *Minerva Mirabal*; and Julia Alvarez, *In the Time of the Butterflies*.

130. *Germán Ornes: A Self Portrait*, 136.

131. For more on the subtleties of symbolic resistance in another authoritarian context, see Wedeen, *Ambiguities of Domination*. The concepts of bifunctionality and substitution are from Andrew Apter, "In Praise of High Office," 149–68.

132. Osorio Lizarazo, *Así es Trujillo*, 8.

133. Balaguer's rhetorical skills are described under the thinly camouflaged character of Dr. Mario Ramos in Sención, *They Forged the Signature of God*, 61. I wish to thank René Fortunato, who in his film *El Poder del Jefe III* inserts a telling excerpt from Balaguer's speech to Angelita at the 1955 Free World's Fair, which demonstrates his use of heteroglossia. I also owe thanks to Julio César Santana, who brought to my attention this and other speeches by Balaguer that included critical commentary about the regime. Interestingly, this speech to Angelita was not included anywhere in the press during 1955, nor did it appear in the many volumes of Balaguer's speeches published during his ten years as president.

134. A bold example occurred when Balaguer described the "black legend" of Trujillo in the Puerto Rican press: "They painted him as a despot with hands red with crime and black with exiles. They called his government a regime of force, an oppressor of the most basic rights, and they accused his methods of imposing decency, and keeping suspicions of public fraud and temptation of embezzlement out of the state treasury, dictatorial" (Balaguer, *Trujillo y su obra*, 36). He could get away with this because he later noted how the journalist in question, after a visit to the Dominican Republic, recanted her views in a cable, stating that Trujillo "was a gentleman, a prince, and a nobleman" (ibid., 37). Foreigners were used to voice denunciations, and they also were not exempt from them. The U.S. ambassador in Havana was accused of fomenting communism in the hemisphere, contrary to the interests of Juan Perón, Trujillo's ally (Pepper, *I Accuse Braden*).

135. Fortunato, *El Poder del Jefe III*.

136. Balaguer, "La obra de Trujillo," *La palabra encadenada*, 41.

137. Ibid., 40.

138. John Comaroff, "Talking Politics," 141–60; and Apter, "In Praise of High Office," 150.

139. Balaguer, "Al cabo de un cuarto de siglo," *La palabra encadenada*, 185.

140. Ibid., 187.

141. Goffman would term this "derisive collusion" since it involves a "secret derogation of the audience" (Goffman, *The Presentation of Self*, 187).

142. Balaguer, *La palabra encadenada*, 188. Of course, this split is quite reminiscent of Kantorowicz's argument in *The King's Two Bodies*.

143. Collado, *El Foro Público*, 269–71.

144. As Gilbert Joseph suggested to me, this structure bears a striking family resemblance to the colonial distinction between the idealized if distant Spanish monarch and his lowly and corrupt minions. I am reluctant, however, to propose that this was a historical legacy, since the colonial regime of La Española (as the Spanish side of the island was known at that time) was notoriously weak. For a rich treatment of this type of dualism in colonial Mexico, see Van Young, "The Raw and the Cooked," 75–102. It is possible that the form of diarchy or dual government described here could have resembled the uneasy relationship between bureaucrats and the letrados (the new elite of lawyers and judges), particularly after offices were sold by the crown; letrados also frequently drew corruption complaints.

145. This structural correspondence was suggested to me by Andrew Apter; see "In Dispraise of the King," 521–34; "In Praise of High Office"; and "Discourse and Its Disclosures," 68–97.

146. Thus the popular notion among Dominicans that Trujillo (or one of his right-hand men) read, wrote, and responded to every letter in the "Foro Público" is an aspect of the "social fantasy" of his godlike omnipotence (Vargas Llosa, *The Feast of the Goat*, 114). On this form of state mythologizing, see Hansen and Stepputat, Introduction, 18–19. This is similar to Hitler's mythic image, although without his initial popular groundswell; see Kershaw, *The Hitler Myth*. For other aspects of Trujillo's charisma, see chapter 6.

147. I am indebted to Brendan Kiley for bringing this individual, as well as this reading of his behavior, to my attention. See Munn, *The Fame of Gawa*, 105.

148. Ceha Baez Castillo to Pichardo, La Romana, 29 Jan. 1940, PD, JCD, Corres., exp. 5.

149. Dr. Manuel Aurelio Tavárez Justo, "Foro Público: Desmiente Acusaciones," *El Caribe*, 29 Apr. 1958. On identity markers and their display under Stalin, see Fitzpatrick, "Lives under Fire," 225–41; see also Bourdieu, "Biographical Illusion."

150. Steve J. Stern, *The Secret History of Gender*, 177. Autonomy is also a key component of Bedouin notions of honorable manhood; see Abu-Lughod, *Veiled Sentiments*, 87.

151. Ulises Montas, Presidente, 1940, PD, JCD, Corres., exp. 5.

152. Response to *Manifiesto de la expulsión del Partido por deslealtad*, no. 92, 31 Jan. 1940, PD, JCD, Corres., exp. 5. In the words of de Moya we see men fashioning themselves as subordinate masculinities in relation to Trujillo's "totalitarian masculinity"; see "Power Games and Totalitarian Masculinity," *Caribbean Masculinities*, 105–46.

153. Baudilio Perdomo to Trujillo, San Pedro, 27 Jan. 1940.

154. Alba Ercilia P. de Samboys, Pda. JCPT, "Datos acerca de la labor de asistencia social realizada durante el año de 1943," Pedernales, 16 Dec. 1943, and P.

Plutarco Caamaño, PJC, PD, 13 Dec. 1943, both in PD, JCD, Corres. 11–20 Dec. 1943; also Mercedes Franco Vda. Molina, Presidenta Rama Femenina, Jimaní, to Carmita Landestoy, Head, Sección Femenina del Partido Trujillista, 13 Dec. 1943, PD, JCD, Corres. 11–20 Dec. 1943.

155. For a more thorough treatment of women during the Trujillo regime, see Zeller, "El régimen de Trujillo y la fuerza laboral femenina"; and Ferreras, *Historia del feminismo*. Beth Hanley and Ginetta Candelaria have important work in progress on this subject. Some of the most prominent women in the regime were suspect because of rumored sexual relations with Trujillo. Carmita Landestoy was one; see her response to allegations about her improprieties, *Mis relaciones*.

156. See Aristide Peguero, Confidential, to Álvarez Pina, Monte Plata, 21 Dec. 1943, and Peguero to Secretario de Estado de lo Interior y Policia, 16 Dec. 1943; both in PD, JCD, Corres. 11–20 Dec. 1943. The governor stepped in to lay the blame where it was due, denouncing Srta. Hirujo to the party president Álvarez Pina and characterizing the Rama as a "fickle and apolitical organization."

157. For an example of a woman's renunciation, see Aliada Cary Espinosa to President Trujillo, Cabral, 1 April 1946, PD, JCD, Corres. They even rescinded the tax to encourage women to take out cédulas (making it free) but women still refused. See *Asunto: Cooperación de los organismos del Partido en favor de la recaudación de la cédula para mujeres*, Circular no. 286, 18 Aug. 1942, PD, Informes Confidentiales, segunda quincena, 1941–42.

158. Goffman, "On Face-Work," *Interaction Ritual*, 5–46.

159. I am drawing upon Boddy's association between enclosure and fertility in another context; see her *Wombs and Alien Spirits*, 58. On the political meanings of motherhood in fascist Italy, see Berezin, "Political Belonging," 355–77.

160. Vargas Llosa, *The Feast of the Goat*, 90.

161. Trouillot, *Haiti State against Nation*, 189. Although Trouillot focuses on the meanings associated with regime participation through graft and patronage, I am applying his notion more broadly. Two important exceptions to this statement are in Collado, *El Foro Público*; and Vega, *Unos desafectos*. The pathbreaking work of Sheila Fitzpatrick on denunciation in the Soviet Union has been indispensable in guiding my understanding of the social and political significance of the phenomenon. See Fitzpatrick and Gellately, "Introduction to the Practices of Denunciation," and especially Fitzpatrick, "Signals from Below" and "Supplicants and Citizens," 106–24.

162. This distinction corresponds to that between learning and believing in Plato's *Gorgias*; see Plato, *Gorgias and Phaedrus*, 36. Thanks to Bernard Bate for bringing this citation to my attention. See Goffman, "Performances," in *The Presentation of Self*, 17–77.

163. Barber, "How Man Makes God in West Africa," 724–45; and Bourdieu, "The Forms of Capital," 241–58.

164. David Nugent also uses the term *shadow state*, but with a slightly different meaning. He refers to an alternative rival clan in provincial Peru in the early twentieth century that mirrored official functions and alternated in power with the municipal bureaucracy; see "State and Shadow State," 63–98. Pakistani intelligence agencies have a strong structural similarity to the behind-the-scenes role of the Dominican Party; see Verkaaik, "The Captive State," 345–65. Other parallels might be the paramilitary groups of El Salvador in the 1980s or in Colombia today. Studies seeking to extend the analysis of statecraft beyond the domain of formal politics include Heyman, *States and Illegal Practices*, as well as Claudio Lomnitz, *Vicios públicos, virtudes privadas*. Alpers, "'A Family of the State,'" 122–38, demonstrates what he describes as class struggle within the bureaucratic apparatus in Mozambique.

165. I take inspiration from John Brewer's argument ("This, That and the Other," 15).

5. CLOTHES MAKE THE MAN

Epigraph selection is from Juan Luis Guerra's album *Ni es lo mismo, ni es igual* (Santo Domingo: Karen, 1998). Thanks to Dennis Hidalgo, who brought this text to my attention, and to Adrian López-Denis, who assisted me in its translation. Special thanks also to Mir Yarfitz, who provided research assistance for this chapter.

1. As de Moya argues in "Power Games": "Every dyadic relationship seems to be 'gendered' or rank ordered" in the Dominican Republic (139); he also notes the eventual emasculation of Dominican men under Trujillo (117). For more on masculinity, see Gutmann, *Changing Men and Masculinities*.

2. As Blok argues, the goat "symbolizes sexuality out of place and out of control" ("Mediterranean Totemism," *Honour and Violence*, 177). All of the literature on Trujillo notes his unbridled thirst for sleeping with young damsels, which he demanded; some people created elaborate schemes for hiding daughters so that they might avoid Trujillo's clutches, while those currying favor were said to bring their fair offspring to him (see, for example, Javier García, *Mis 20 años*, vol. 2, 56–58). However, I wonder if some of these excesses may have been a result of what George Chauncey describes as "sexual panic," a popular form of vilification expressing Trujillo's monstrosity in the eyes of Dominicans; one might compare it with the rumors about sexual abuse in daycare centers in the United States in the 1980s. For more on the latter, see Kyle Zirpolo as told to Debbie Nathan, "I Lied," *Los Angeles Times*, 30 Oct. 2005; and Nathan and Snedecker, *Satan's Silence*.

3. Alonso, "Sovereignty, Politics of Security, and Gender," 42.

4. Krohn-Hansen, "'The Dominican Tiger,'" 108. See also de Moya, "Power Games." My thinking about tigueraje has greatly benefited from these deeply insightful essays, as well as from Lipe Collado's innovative books, *El tíguere dominicano* and *La impresionante vida*.

5. Linden Lewis, "Fieldnotes on Masculinity Research," 65. De Moya ("Power Games") notes the "hegemonic masculinity," by which he means the "compulsory heterosexuality" of the regime (139).

6. DaMatta, "Pedro Malasartes," 204. Or, as Dominicans say, "aprovechandose de otros," the contemporary tíguere is synonymous with *delincuente*; on this, see Mark B. Padilla, "Looking For Life: Male Sex Work, HIV/AIDS, and the Political Economy of Gay Sex Tourism in the Dominican Republic" (Ph.D. diss., Emory University, 2003), 190. I wish to thank Amalia Cabezas for bringing this study to my attention.

7. Collado, *El tíguere dominicano*, 24 and 35. As a subset of Creole identity, it approximates what Cubans describe as their *Cubanía*, what Raul A. Fernandez defines as "a mixture of hustle, showmanship, and ability" among Cuban musicians; see *From Afro-Cuban Rhythms to Latin Jazz*, 46.

8. Rubirosa, *Mis memorias*, 19.

9. The *flâneur* is from Benjamin, *Charles Baudelaire*.

10. Moya Pons, *A National History*, 379. Reputation and respectability form a contrastive pair of values in Peter J. Wilson's account, *Crab Antics*.

11. Vanessa R. Schwartz, *Spectacular Realities*.

12. Balaguer, *La palabra encadenada*, 207. The tíguere as a figure of resistance is stressed in Collado, *El tíguere dominicano*, 32; and in Krohn-Hansen, "Masculinity and the Political," 127. De Moya, in "Power Games," 117, notes the emasculation of Dominican men via Trujillo's symbolic politics, for example, requiring domestic signs such as "En esta casa Trujillo es el jefe." But the crackdown on urban street life of the 1950s must also have contributed to a sense of powerlessness which was experienced as emasculation. For another relationship between Trujillismo and tigueraje, see Torres-Saillant, *El tigueraje intellectual*. For an interesting argument about emasculation, policing, and unemployment in another context, see Bourgois, *In Search of Respect*.

13. Lyrics from "Qué es la Tuyo Rubirosa," by Eduardo Saborit. The original is: "Rubirosa tiene una cosa, Que yo no sé qué será, Qué será, qué será, Lo que tiene," from Collado, *La impresionante vida*, 11.

14. At one point Trujillo, infuriated with Flor's "emancipated" ways, banished her from Paris and New York high society, and brought her home to live in shame with her mother. She so enraged him that he passed a law allowing a father to disavow and disinherit his children and then made her the first test case. See Ornes, *Trujillo*, 220.

15. Vega, *Los Trujillo se escriben*, 64. Incidentally, Vega gives a fairly favorable portrayal of the "cultured" Flor, who bravely stood up to her domineering

father (although he reprimands her for her "vida desordenada," her wild ways).

16. My emphasis. Flor Trujillo with Laura Berquist, "My Tormented Life as Trujillo's Daughter," *Look*, 15 June 1965, 52. For a treatment of gender, scopic desire, and the gaze in another context, see Hansen, "Pleasure, Ambivalence, Identification," 6–32.

17. Friedman, "Consuming Desires," 154–63, esp. 157.

18. Levy, *The Last Playboy*, 50.

19. Javier García, *Mis 20 años*, 275. Rubi also counseled his wives in tasteful attire, as his last wife Odile Rodin noted in his memoirs (Rubirosa, *Mis memorias*, 194).

20. Rosendo Álvarez Jr., "Rubirosa: Vida y amores de un dominicano," *Ahora!* 11 Sept. 1972, 34–36. For more on Rubirosa, see Levy, *The Last Playboy*; Collado, *La impresionante vida*; Peña Rivera, *El playboy Porfirio Rubirosa*; and Clase, *El primer playboy del mundo*. However, the American public has also proved to be enthusiastic consumers of Rubirosa lore. Alongside the tabloid press articles, he is a major character in the following biographies of his wives: Frank, *Zsa Zsa Gabor: My Story*; Mansfield, *Richest Girl in the World*; Valentine and Mahn, *Daddy's Dutchess*; Heymann, *Poor Little Rich Girl*; and Moats, *Million Dollar Studs*.

21. Their divorce agreement also reveals some very substantial loans to Rubirosa from Trujillo; see "Anexo: Divorcio Rubirosa-Trujillo," in Rubirosa, *Mis memorias*, 199–218. Rubirosa claims that their marriage cast a measure of respectability on Trujillo, enabling him to enter and even become president of the Club Union, from which he had previously been rebuffed (Rubirosa, *Mis memorias*, 74).

22. Vega, *Los Trujillo se escriben*, 69.

23. Flor Trujillo (with Laura Berquist), "My Tormented Life," 52.

24. Betty Hynes, "Society: Dynamic Sénora Flor Trujillo First Woman to Become Minister of the Dominican Embassy," *Times-Herald*, 28 Jan. 1944, 20; Frances Lide, "Dominican Embassy's First Secretary: Diplomatic Appointment Thrills Senora Trujillo," *Washington Star*, n.d. The bibliographic information for some of these articles is incomplete because they were clipped and filed as part of a personal collection related to Flor Trujillo's personal life in the United States, and their owner wishes to remain anonymous.

25. *Town and Country*, Sept. 1943; "No Hat," *Washington Post*, 11 Jan. 1944.

26. Holland, "Fashioning Cuba," 147–56.

27. "The Rich Good Neighbor Lends her No. 5-to-be the Guest Room!," *Sunday Mirror Magazine*, 16 Dec. 1945; "Diplomatic Career Girl," *New York Post*, *Daily Magazine and Comic Section*, 26 April 1944.

28. Clase, *El Primer playboy del mundo*, 11; Hebdige, *Subculture*, 47–48, esp. 83.

29. Levy, *The Last Playboy*, 119, 120.

30. Ibid., 118.

31. Ibid., 107. In 1958 he was made Dominican ambassador to Cuba, until the revolutionary government expelled him in 1959; his last ambassadorial appointment was to Belgium. His association with Paris was cemented by the fame of his fine polo team Cibao-La Pampa and its success in Parisian tournaments; it won the Paris Open three times between 1953 and 1965 (its last success in 1965 would have guaranteed a fourth win were it not for his untimely death).

32. "Doris Duke's Final Mystery," *Vanity Fair*, March 1994, 170.

33. Rosendo Álvarez Jr., "Rubirosa." Rubirosa and Zsa Zsa carried on a highly public affair during his relationship with Hutton and after their divorce.

34. "Men who Fascinate Women," *Look*, 12 July 1956, 86; David C. Heymann, *Poor Little Rich Girl*, 257.

35. Irene Corbally Kuhn, "Rubi's Back and Zsa Zsa's Got Him," *American Mercury*, August 1954, 7–11. An exception is Moats, *The Million Dollar Studs*, who is extremely critical of Rubirosa.

36. Heymann, *Poor Little Rich Girl*, 259.

37. Levy, *The Last Playboy*, 125.

38. Ibid., 254. The chapter entitled "The Student Prince in Hollywood" provides full disclosure on Ramfis's notorious adventures in the United States alongside Rubirosa; see also "Ramfis' Conquests," *Time*, 19 May 1958.

39. Moats, *Million Dollar Studs*, 207.

40. Ibid., 93.

41. Vicens de Morales, *María Montez*, 42. Montez starred in a number of exotic roles in the Hollywood B movie set in the 1940s, after Hollywood opened its doors to Latin American actresses because of the Good Neighbor policy. See Fein, "Everyday Forms of Transnational Collaboration," 400–450.

42. Balaguer, *Memorias de un cortesano*, 241–43.

43. Vega, *Los Trujillo se escriben*, 80.

44. Ibid., 7.

45. Espaillat, *The Last Caesar*, 48; and Javier García, *Mis 20 años*, 242. Trujillo himself was fond of aphrodisiacs and partook of them on a regular basis. He was said to eat bull testicles three times a day to increase his virility (Javier García, *Mis 20 años*, 332).

46. I am homing in on one aspect of Dominican sentiments toward Trujillo. As should be clear by now, he was also despised for his ruthless killing, his monopolistic hold on the economy, his iron-clad control, his megalomania, the total absence of civil liberties during the regime, the requisite deference toward him, and the frequent rituals of submission by the bourgeoisie that he particularly relished. Dominican memories of the Trujillo regime are complex and volatile; in this chapter I focus on only one aspect of the popular mythology of the man and his thirty-year rule. In his *Heroes on Horseback*,

103, Chasteen uses the term *prestige* to convey a relationship of obvious hierarchy and a cluster of sentiments that include fear and admiration. One must also keep in mind that the term *respeto* in Spanish connotes a measure of fear and awe, not just admiration or love.

47. Wiarda, *Nation in Transition*, 40.

48. I am drawing here on the work of Bourdieu: "Social Space and the Genesis of 'Classes,'" in *Language and Symbolic Power*, 229–51; and *Distinction*.

49. This shift can be seen even within Trujillo's own family. In 1930 Flor de Oro was sent to an all-girls school in Paris, while in 1941 Ramfis was sent to Browning Academy, an elite boys school in Manhattan.

50. American leisure culture in the 1950s is well described in May, "The Commodity Gap," 162–82.

51. See Lomnitz's original essay, "Passion and Banality in Mexican History," 81–109. In her magnificent study, *Insurgent Cuba*, 188, Ada Ferrer has a penetrating discussion of the effects wrought by black combatants' sense of being observed and scrutinized during the Cuban independence war.

52. This seems to be the reason for Veloz Maggiolo's discomfort with my use of this term for Trujillo, since he sees tígueraje as a deeply barrio or local phenomenon; see Veloz Maggiolo, "Trujillo, la garra del 'Tíguere,'" *Listín Diario (LD)*, 3 Aug. 1997. Rubirosa described him as a tíguere, "more cruel than other *tígueres* known in Santo Domingo until then. This *tíguere* was . . . more crafty than a sly fox" (*Mis memorias*, 47). As someone defined the tíguere to me, the tíguere "works without sweating" (Bánica, Oct. 2008).

53. Javier García, *Mis 20 años*, 56–58.

54. Padilla, "Looking for Life."

55. Patín Maceo, *Dominicanismos*, defines the tíguere as a *muchacho del hampa*, a guy from the underworld, a word that connotes blackness, as Fernando Ortiz reminds us; see Ortiz, *Hampa Afrocubana*. Veloz Maggiolo, "Trujillo, la Garra del 'Tíguere,'" offers several interesting anecdotes about three tígueres he remembers from the central marketplace (Mercado Modelo) in the downtown Santo Domingo of his youth. The link between tigueraje and the informal work sector is also made by Padilla in "Looking for Life."

56. Veloz Maggiolo, "Trujillo, la garra del 'Tíguere,'" notes marginality as a criterion.

57. This distinction is derived from Apter, *Black Critics and Kings*.

58. These points are made by Veloz Maggiolo in "Trujillo, la garra del 'Tíguere.'" Trujillo's preference for staging himself alongside his beloved purebred heifers is noted in Javier García, *Mis 20 años*, 51. However, Rubirosa describes his father, a revolutionary general, as a tíguere before his appointment to Paris (*Mis memorias*, 17).

59. This point is made by Collado, in *La impresionante vida*, 161. The Collado–Veloz Maggiolo debate hinges on whether the tíguere must be a barrio figure

(Veloz Maggiolo) or whether its definition depends on the success of the tíguere in a theater outside the barrio. Collado claims that tígueres who cut a profile only in the *submundo* of the barrio would be deemed *fracasados*, as "pariguayos barriobajeros que simulan ser tígueres gallos" (*La impresionante vida*, 161).

60. Gregory, *The Devil Behind the Mirror*, 41. Edelman found predatory sexuality a feature of devil pact narratives in Costa Rica; see his "Landlords and the Devil," 73.

61. De Moya, "Power Games," 114, n. 7. Collado also mentions transgression of social, moral, and political rules in his discussion (*La impresionante vida*, 165).

62. Collado, *El tíguere dominicano*.

63. This is Collado's argument laid out in *La impresionante vida*, 159.

64. This point is made by de Moya in "Power Games," 121; he cites Bustamante, *Una satrapía en el Caribe*, 69, who elaborates on Trujillo's infamous vanity. Alternatively, his ambivalent masculinity could be read as rule breaking since vanity is a female characteristic. However, though Trujillo possessed an uncanny femininity and came from a poor brown background, he ended up far wealthier than he should be; his masculinity thus merits comparison to the secret masculinity of the Andean Cholo, who, as Weismantel reminds us, is part white and wealthier than she should be as a woman (*Cholas and Pishtacos*, chapter 6).

65. See Hansen, "Pleasure, Ambivalence, Identification."

66. Rubirosa, *Mis memorias*, 36–37, describes his participation in the verbal arts of flattery in Santo Domingo. Also see Crassweller, *Life and Times of a Caribbean Dictator*, 51.

67. Veloz Maggiolo, "Trujillo, la Garra del 'Tíguere,'" recounts this story.

68. A roughly translated paraphrase from Collado, *La impresionante vida*, 163.

69. Collado, *La impresionante vida*, 165. As Collado notes, they were closely associated in the popular imagination.

70. Geertz, "Centers, Kings and Charisma," 150–71.

71. The fact that machismo was officialized during the Trujillato may account for the virulent assault on it by the prominent Dominican sociologist Tirso Mejia-Ricart, since hypermasculinity became another nefarious feature of the regime that needed to be rooted out afterward; see "Observaciones sobre el machismo," 351–64. See also the forceful critique by Ramírez, in *What It Means to Be a Man*, chapter 1.

72. Peabody, *Merchant Venturers of Old Salem*, 15.

73. Torres Saillant, "Creoleness or Blackness?"

74. Moreau de Saint-Méry, *Description topographique*.

75. Collado, *El tíguere dominicano*, 23. Since the capital was still small at that time, I suspect that these street urchins were not orphans or homeless, as

might be the case today, but rather young boys working and left to fend for themselves while their mothers were otherwise occupied (perhaps in trading or street food sales, which are common occupations for Haitian women); they probably trained as *guapos* in the ways of the street, which was part of the socialization in appropriate masculinity, especially for those from poor families.

76. For more on these associations, see Derby, "Haitians, Magic and Money." The tiger epithet is linked to Haiti as well in Penson's short story about the Virgins of Galindo, who were said to be killed by Haitians during the Haitian occupation in 1822; see *Cosas Añejas,* 326. The Haitian killers were called *tígueres.*

77. See Simmel on secrecy and the stranger in *The Sociology of Georg Simmel,* 330–44, 402–8.

78. Aguiar, *Eusebio Sapote.* Many thanks to Mir Yarfitz for his reading of this novel.

79. Ibid., 226.

80. Ibid., 133.

81. They have a loveless marriage, but in the novel the fact of marriage itself seems to accord him as much rank as his upscale companion. According to Kuznesof, the colonial rule is that women absorb the social personhood of their husbands, so ethnic wives "pass" through marrying up; here it is the reverse. Ibid., 213.

82. Simmel, "The Stranger," *The Sociology of Georg Simmel,* 402–408.

83. Francisco Comarazamy, Introduction to Collado, *El tíguere dominicano,* 6.

84. *Comprabrujos* are a class of Haitian sorcerers (Aguiar, *Sapote,* 238–39).Today Dominicans might describe this as a Haitian bacá. I use the term *sorcery* since it involves the use of supernatural power over others through the assistance of spirits and since Dominicans class Haitian magic as more dangerous and powerful than their own, although it is not necessarily malicious as the term might imply. For more on Dominican views of Haitian magic, see Derby, "Haitians, Magic and Money." The classic work on Latin American devil-pact narratives is of course Taussig, *The Devil and Commodity Fetishism.*

85. In Sapote, he is creolized by marrying a local but he originally was Danish.

86. González, "Hay tres clases de gentes en la campaña . . . ," *El Caribe,* 23 Nov. 1991, 18. For more on the Comegente phenomenon, see González's fascinating work on the subject: "El Comegente," in *Homenaje a Emilio Cordero Michel,* 175–234; " 'Comegente': Tradición, literatura e historia," *El Caribe,* 28 Sept. 1991, 18; "El 'Comegente' atacaba personas y propiedades cerca de las poblaciones," *El Caribe,* 5 Oct. 1991, 18; "Para capturar al 'Comegente' comisionó la Real Audiencia a uno de sus oidores," *El Caribe,* 12 Oct. 1991, 18; and "Agitación rural y rebelión esclava a finales del siglo XVIII dominicano," *El Caribe,* 19 Oct. 1991, 18.

87. On Cuba, see Stolcke, *Marriage, Class and Colour*. As Stuart Schwartz tells us, as Creole identity formed, the social categories of free black and mestizo (mixed race) merged; see "Spaniards, *Pardos*, and the Missing Mestizos," 5–21.
88. Hoetink, *The Dominican People*, 183.
89. See Rodríguez Demorizi, *Sociedades, y otros corporaciones dominicanas*.
90. Moreau de Saint Méry, *Descripción*, 94; Walton, *Present State of the Spanish Colonies*, 380. As much as I would like to claim this as a feature unique to the Dominican Republic, the evidence suggests otherwise, as witnessed by Bryan Edwards's aghast reaction to the exaggerated "consciousness of self importance" of Jamaican Creoles; see his *History of the British Colonies in the West Indies*, vol. 3, 9.
91. Díaz, *Royal Slaves of El Cobre*.
92. Fernando Ortiz, *Los Negros Curros*; David H. Brown, *Santería Enthroned*; Palmié, *Wizards and Scientists*, 152–53; and Díaz, *Royal Slaves of El Cobre*.
93. Hoetink, *The Dominican People*, 183.
94. Moreau de Saint-Méry, *Descripción de la parte española*.
95. See Derby, "National Identity and the Idea of Value," 5–37.
96. Hoetink, *The Dominican People*, 170.
97. García Godoy, *El derrumbe*, 72.
98. Damirón, "El Tíguere," in *De soslayo*, 106.
99. Mary Douglas quoted in Stallybrass and White, *The Politics and Poetics of Transgression*, 23.
100. Barnet, *Rachel's Song*, 96 and 92.
101. Collado, *El tíguere dominicano*, 24. Other examples of Dominican popular heros before the ascendence of the urban tíguere include the mountain peasant, Enrique Blanco, killed by Trujillo's army in 1936; and Olivorio Mateo or Dios Olivorio (see chapter 7). Both Blanco and Olivorio became popular martyrs in part through their struggle against the state. For more on Blanco, see Arzeno Rodríguez, *Cuentos de Enrique Blanco*. Lewis Hyde stresses the adversarial role of the trickster in his *Trickster Makes This World*.
102. Ornes, *Trujillo*, 41. The idea of dissimulation is also part of the earlier social climber figure, the *culebrón* (see chapter 1).
103. The elites' perception of Trujillo is well described in Ornes, *Trujillo*, 41; and Rueda, *Bienvenida y la Noche*, 22–25, 79, and 149–50. Special thanks to César (Jochy) Herrera who brought this text to my attention.
104. This is true also in Brazil; see DaMatta, *Carnivals, Rogues and Heroes*, 206.
105. Arzeno Rodríguez, "Orígen de un apodo," *Chapita no – Trujillo!*, 11.
106. Roorda, *The Dictator Next Door*, 164.
107. Rubirosa, *Mis memorias*, 55.
108. Javier García, *Mis 20 años*, 363.
109. Rafael Herrera, then editor in chief of *El Caribe*, called them "publicity glutons"; see Javier García, *Mis 20 años*, 386. Of course, many regimes seeking

to establish a strong break with established tradition resort to "insignomania"; see Wrigley, *The Politics of Appearances*, 61. Thanks to Lynn Hunt for bringing this source to my attention.

110. Bustamante, *Una satrapía en el Caribe*, 47–48.

111. Moscoso Puello, *Cartas a Evelina*, 25.

112. See Díaz, *Royal Slaves of El Cobre*, chapter 2.

113. See David H. Brown's rigorous and nuanced, *Santería Enthroned*; and Rosenberg, *El Gagá*.

114. In *Wizards and Scientists*, 133, see Palmié's brilliant analysis of Haitian revolutionary drawings found in the *Libro de pinturas* of the free black mason Aponte.

115. Gascón, "The Military of Santo Domingo," 451.

116. Ibid., 432. The country also had an inordinate amount of foreign intervention.

117. King, *Blue Coat or Powdered Wig*, 73.

118. Ibid., 248 and 239.

119. Baud, "Una frontera de refugio"; Gascón, "Military of Santo Domingo"; and King, *Blue Coat or Powdered Wig*. King notes the prevalence of the Spanish horse and cattle trader in the notarial archives of Saint Domingue (64).

120. Nancy Leys Stepan, *"The Hour of Eugenics,"* discusses how degeneration was seen as producing effeminacy. The key primary text rendering such accusations was Cornelius de Pauw, *Recherches scientifiques sur les Américains* (Berlin: [n.p.], 1777), and eighteenth-century Dominican texts energetically took issue with his portrayal; see Sánchez Valverde, *La idea del valor en la isla española*.

121. King, *Blue Coat or Powdered Wig*, chapter 11.

122. Leclerc also wore the bicorn, but vertically and without feathers. Robert Debs Heinl and Nancy Gordon Heinl, *Written in Blood*, 101.

123. Cole, *King of Haiti*, 64. Trouillot asserts that Christophe did over time succeed in generating a new black northern aristocracy, some of whom eventually intermarried with prominent southern mulatto families. See *Haiti: State Against Nation*, 121–22.

124. From his portraits, however, it appears that Christophe wore the bicorn horizontally, in Napoleonic style.

125. The first Haitian emperor, however, was Dessalines. For more on Soulouque, see D'Alaux, *L'Empereur Soulouque et Son Empire*. For more on Christophe, see Cole, *Christophe*. For more on the Haitian revolution, see Dubois, *Avengers of the New World*.

126. Lilis wore it vertically, however. Veeser notes the royalism of Lilis's political rituals; see his excellent account, *A World Safe for Capitalism*, 59. For more on Lilis, see Sang, *Ulises Heureaux*.

127. Bolívar Belliard S., speech, 22 Feb. 1943, PD #44, JCD, PD, Corres. 20–27 Dec. 1943. Trujillo's fascination with the bicorn is central to the historical novel by Ubiñas Renville, *El niño y el bicornio*.

128. Crassweller, *Trujillo*, 78. Jamaican founder of the Black Star Line, Marcus Garvey also incorporated the bicorn into his ceremonial uniform. I am grateful to Robert Hill for his insights on Black royalism in the Caribbean.

129. Palmié, *Wizards and Scientists*, 116. The term hybridity was used by Freyre to describe racial mixture in *The Masters and the Slaves*.

130. Vega, *Trujillo y las fuerzas armadas*, 228; cited in Valentina Peguero, *The Militarization of Culture*, 131. This chapter includes a lengthy discussion of the politics of race within the various branches of the military under the Trujillo regime.

131. To protect their "bad hair" (a marker of blackness) from view; see Javier García, *Mis 20 años*, 375.

132. "Social front" is from Goffman, *The Presentation of Self*, 29.

133. This topic receives excellent treatment in Roorda, *The Dictator Next Door*, chapter 4.

134. Deschamps, *La República Dominicana*.

135. Julio G. Campillo Pérez, "La parenté haïtienne de Trujillo," *La Revue de la Société Haïtienne d'Histoire et de Géographie d'Haiti*, Dec. 2000. I wish to thank Kevin Yelvington who brought this piece to my attention.

136. These figures are from King, *Blue Coat or Powdered Wig*, 84; and Fick, *The Making of Haiti*, 20. Evidence that their sense of superiority increased after independence is from Jonathan Brown who described the mulattos as a "caste"; see Nicholls's classic account, *From Dessalines to Duvalier*, 72.

137. Duany, "Ethnicity in the Spanish Caribbean," 106. For comparisons with similar cultures of race in Cuba and Colombia, see de la Fuente, "Race and Inequality in Cuba," 131–68; and Wade, *Blackness and Race Mixture*.

138. Stuart Schwartz, "Spaniards, *Pardos*, and the Missing Mestizos."

139. Stuart Schwartz, "Identities and Racial Categories," 12.

140. The concept of somatic norm image is from Hoetink, *Caribbean Race Relations*.

141. Baud, "Constitutionally White"; and Stutzman, *"El Mestizaje,"* 45–94. *Indio* emerges as a fictive trope of mestizaje, a synonym for mixed-race Creole which at least today has no connotation of indigenous blood. Under Trujillo it became the official code word for mixed-race Creoles used in identity cards. See Sommer, *One Master for Another*.

142. Weismantel, *Cholas and Pishtacos*, 90.

143. Fanon, *Black Skin, White Masks*, 46. Passing through ancestral claims is also treated in Virginia R. Domínguez's extraordinary study, *White by Definition*, chapter 7.

144. David Howard, "Colouring the Nation: Race and Ethnicity in the Dominican Republic" (D.Phil. thesis, Oxford University), 197, 76.

145. And there is little financial rationale behind these actions, since Dominican courts rarely enforce alimony claims.

146. Rubirosa, *Mis memorias,* 90. For more on illegitimacy, see Twinam's fine study *Public Lives, Private Secrets.*

147. Marcel Mauss's famous essay on the person can be found in Carrithers et al., *The Category of the Person,* 1–26. Quote from Rebecca J. Scott, "The Provincial Archive," 161; also see Zeuske, "Hidden Markers, Open Secrets," 211–42. Interestingly, one name for elites is *aristocracia del apellido,* a term which underscores the close link between naming, personhood, and social status in this context (Balaguer, *Memorias,* 93). Ramfis was illegitimate and this stigma haunted him throughout his life, as is demonstrated by his frequent efforts to deny it; see León Estévez, "¡Que bárbaro, ni siquera aquí descansa!" in *Yo, Ramfis Trujillo,* 26–31. On stigma and self-fashioning, see Goffman, *Stigma.*

148. Brackette F. Williams, *Stains on My Name, War in My Veins,* 29, 74. Williams's analysis draws on the work of Goffman, such as *Interaction Ritual.* Although her book is based on research in Guyana, a plural society, I think this approach has applicability for the Dominican Republic, even though it has a more homogeneous mestizo culture.

149. The interweaving of race and class is demonstrated in Stutzman, *"El Mestizaje,"* as well as in Hall, "Race, Articulation and Societies."

150. This is apparent in Findlay's account, *Imposing Decency,* 38.

151. Weismantel, *Cholos and Pishtacos,* 90.

152. See the provocative and intriguing debate between Kuznesof, "Ethnic and Gender Influences on 'Spanish' Creole Society" (153–76), and Stuart Schwartz, "Colonial Identities and the *Sociedad de Castas*" (185–95). I wish to thank Stuart Schwartz for bringing these essays to my attention.

153. Linda Gordon's elegant book discusses the adoption of children as enabling claims to whiteness in nineteenth-century California; see *The Great Arizona Orphan Abduction,* 148.

154. See chapter 2, "Women of Color and the White Man," in Fanon, *Black Skins, White Masks.*

155. See Austen, "Social and Historical Analysis of African Trickster Tales," 135–48; Congreso Internacional sobre la Picaresca, *La Picaresca*; and James C. Scott, *Domination and the Arts of Resistance,* 162–66. The trickster genre in Haiti is represented by the tales of *Ti bouki.* I wish to thank Tamar Herzog for suggesting the *tígueres'* link to the *pícaro.*

156. Although he was attractive—good-looking and a strapping six feet tall— Ramfis is typically remembered as a disagreeable person. Ornes described Ramfis as "hot-tempered, brash and rude . . . a spoiled brat . . . at official functions he remains apart, aloof" (Ornes, *Trujillo,* 217). The theme of a handsome and charming Porfirio substituting for the more timid and alienated Ramfis appears in the novel *Galíndez* by Manuel Vásquez Montalbán, esp. 221–22. In the novel (based on real life), not only do Ramfis

and Rubirosa share women (Zsa Zsa Gabor and Kim Novak), but Trujillo forces Porfirio to take over Ramfis's lover, Zsa Zsa, since Trujillo did not want his princely son associating with Hollywood low life. In an emotional moment, Trujillo also makes the revealing lament that no one in his family could ever have Rubirosa's elegance in polo, evidence of his longing for a son like Rubi.

157. These included the coverup of Chichi's (his cousin Luis) murder of Sergio Bencosme in New York in 1936, illegal jewel smuggling and theft, and the sale of visas to Jewish immigrants hoping to emigrate to the Dominican Republic (Levy, *The Last Playboy*, 59, 74, 79). See Bhabha, "Of Mimicry and Man," in *Location of Culture*, 85–92, esp. 86. For more on state fetishism and the carnivalesque, see Mbembe, "The Banality of Power," 1–30.

158. Langston Hughes, "Playboys," *New York Post*, 9 July 1965, cited in Levy, *The Last Playboy*, 320. Candelario also posits the Dominican culture of whitening as a mode of resistance to U.S. racial norms; see her insightful essay, "On Whiteness and Other Absurdities," 89–118.

6. TRUJILLO'S TWO BODIES

1. See Diederich, *The Death of the Goat*, for a full description of the assassination.
2. LeFort, *Political Forms*, 300.
3. Lomnitz, "Passion and Banality in Mexican History," in *Deep Mexico, Silent Mexico*, 104.
4. Roorda, *The Dictator Next Door*, 149–191.
5. Diederich, *The Death of the Goat*, 154.
6. Karl Marx from *The Grundrisse*, in Robert C. Tucker, *The Marx-Engels Reader*, 244; Taussig, "*Maleficium*"; Taussig, *The Magic of the State*; and Geertz, *Negara*.
7. Mitchell, "The Limits of the State," 77–96; although a critical approach to the state was pioneered by Michel Foucault; see his essay "Governmentality." Also see Corrigan and Sayer, *The Great Arch*; Cohn, *An Anthropologist among the Historians*; and the work of Bourdieu.
8. Hansen and Stepputat, "States of Imagination," 18. The particular fixation on the presidential body in Latin American notions of sovereignty was highlighted for me by Ana M. Alonso; see her essay "Sovereignty, Politics of Security, and Gender"; and Krohn-Hansen, "Negotiated Dictatorship," 27–54, 96–122. The link between processes of commodification, state fetishism and the figure of the sovereign are explored in Coronil, *The Magical State*, esp. "The Nation's Two Bodies," 67–120.
9. Larry Rohter, "Cuba Buries Che, the Man, but Keeps the Myth Alive," *New York Times*, 18 Oct. 1997.
10. Lomnitz, "Passion and Banality," 90, 104. There is also the mystery of

Christopher Columbus's bones, which are said to be in the possession of Spain, Italy, and the Dominican Republic; see Krohn-Hansen, "A Tomb for Columbus," 165–92. For more on Latin American body politics, see Lyman L. Johnson, *Death, Dismemberment and Memory*.

11. Stallybrass, "Footnotes," 313–26.
12. Taussig, *Mimesis and Alterity*, 21.
13. An important exception was the numinous afterlife of Evita Perón's remains and her cultic following; see Tomás Eloy Martínez, *Santa Evita: A Novel*; Taussig, *Mimesis and Alterity*, 35.
14. See Abrahams, *The Man-of-Words in the West Indies*.
15. Lauria, " 'Respeto,' 'Relajo' and Interpersonal Relations," 53–67.
16. Anderson, *Language and Power*, 17–77; Hansen and Stepputat, "States of Imagination," 18.
17. Rotberg, "*Vodun* and the Politics of Haiti," 342–65; Laguerre, *Voodoo and Politics in Haiti*; Cosentino, "Envoi," 399–415. I will use the Kreyol spelling *vodou* and *lwa* in reference to the Haitian religious system, and the Spanish spelling *vodú* and *loa* in reference to the Dominican variant.
18. Anderson, *Language and Power*, 81. For further rethinking of the opposition between magic and rationality in Max Weber's theory of charisma, see Meyer and Pels, *Magic and Modernity*, esp. the introduction; and Lindholm, *Charisma*.
19. Sorcery here means use of supernatural power over others with the assistance of spirits. The use of a *muchachito* might be defined as *brujeria* (witchcraft) if someone else has one, but not if the speaking subject does.
20. Kantorowicz, *The King's Two Bodies*, 13.
21. Interestingly, Trujillo's female diviners, such as Mama Iné, are named, but his muchachito is not.
22. Goffman, *The Presentation of Self*, 141–42. Taussig discusses "public secrets" in his essay "Viscerality, Faith and Skepticism," 272–306.
23. Taussig, "Viscerality, Faith and Skepticism," 272 and 287.
24. There is also a wide temporal range for these stories, since the muchachito emerged in life-history interviews during my dissertation fieldwork in 1992, and in interviews with Dominicans living in Chicago in 1997–98.
25. Joseph and Daniel Nugent, eds., *Everyday Forms of State Formation*.
26. Geertz, "Centers, Kings, and Charisma," 150–71.
27. Taussig, *Mimesis and Alterity*, 115–16.
28. Handler, "Is 'Identity' a Useful Cross-Cultural Concept?" 32.
29. Dumont, *Homo Hierarchus*; Sahlins, "Rich Man, Poor Man," 287–303.
30. Handler, "Is 'Identity' a Useful Cross-Cultural Concept?," 37.
31. Ubaldo Guzmán Molina, "La casa de Balaguer, escenario de historias," *Hoy*, 11 July 2002. Thanks to Andrew Shrank for providing me with this citation.
32. On the concept of diarchy, see Valeri, "Diarchy and History," 45–80.
33. I want to stress that these two domains of religious practice are not mixed as

in the model of religious syncretism, but rather are seen as two distinct systems. The distinction between front stage and backstage behavior is from Goffman, "Regions and Region Behavior," 106–40. For a critical rethinking of the syncretic paradigm, see Stewart and Shaw, "Problematizing Syncretism, 1–26.

34. Martha Ellen Davis, *La otra ciencia*, describes "dominican vodú as an eastern variety of Haitian vodou" (58); also see Deive, *Vodú y magia en Santo Domingo*. Not all misterios are putatively Haitian; many are considered Dominican spirits. In fact, the entire Petwo line of Haitian deities in Haiti is attributed to a Dominican sorcerer—Sr. Don Pedro—who is said to have fashioned a "point" (*pwen*) in Haiti. I take no sides in these genealogical debates, but cite their relevance to negotiating categories of spiritual powers. On "points," see Larose, "The Meaning of Africa in Haitian Vodou," 85–116; and Martha Ellen Davis, *La otra ciencia*.

35. Apter, "Herskovits's Heritage," 235–260, esp. 249; and Apter, *Black Critics and Kings*, 149–64. Additionally, elites replace the dualistic structure of Trujillo and his muchachito with Trujillo and his key subordinate Joaquín Balaguer, at times gendering Balaguer as the female term of the pair since he never married and lived with his sister.

36. Williams, *Stains on My Name, War in My Veins*, 92–106.

37. Helms, *Ulysses' Sail*, 5.

38. Krohn-Hansen, "Haitians, Money and Alterity," 129–46; and Wade, *Blackness and Race Mixture*, 23.

39. Barber, "How Man Makes God in West Africa," 740.

40. Deive, *Vodú y magia*, 192.

41. Lundius and Lundahl, *Peasants and Religion*, 351.

42. "They Say I Ate My Father. But I Didn't," *Los Angeles Times*, 29 Aug. 2006, 1, 8.

43. Santos-Granero, "The Enemy Within," 272–305.

44. In this chapter I refer to *vodú* when a phenomenon is more typical of Dominican popular religious practice, and *vodou* when it is more Haitian. However, there is a porous boundary between the religious cultures of the two nations.

45. Deive, *Vodú y magia*, 136; Deren, *Divine Horsemen*, 97.

46. Deren, *Divine Horsemen*, 38. See also MacGaffey, "Twins, Simbi Spirits."

47. Martha Ellen Davis, *La otra ciencia*, 136–37; Brodwin, *Medicine and Morality in Haiti*. Scholars now spell the Haitian term *Petwo* with a "w" to reflect its actual pronunciation; however, Dominicans pronounce it with an "r," unless they are spirit possessed, in which case they might imitate Haitian pronunciation; I have thus left it as *Petro* here. I am explaining a popular Dominican view of the Petro spirits and Haitian magic.

48. These are the rumors surrounding the phenomenon. The bacá thus conforms to the classic devil-pact narratives treated in Taussig, *The Devil and Commodity Fetishism*.

49. Martha Ellen Davis, *La otra ciencia*, 112. Although this is the public, respectable self-presentation, I have met many Dominican *servidores* who actually do have double altars.

50. See Houlberg, "Magique Marasa," 267–86. This was the case with the powerful twin cult which formed at Palma Sola (see chapter 7). The Ventura Rodríguez brothers who led the movement, although called twins in popular parlance, actually had an invisible third term—another sister who died.

51. Métraux, *Voodoo in Haiti*, 146.

52. Martha Ellen Davis, *La otra ciencia*, 125.

53. Métraux, *Voodoo in Haiti*, 148 and 151.

54. Deren, *Divine Horsemen*, 41.

55. LeFort, *Political Forms*, 306; Kantorowicz, *The King's Two Bodies*.

56. Bynum, *Fragmentation and Redemption*.

57. Mbembe, "The Thing and Its Doubles," 146.

58. Deive, *La esclavitud del negro, 1492–1844*, vols. 1 and 2. Hürbon also makes the point that Catholicism throughout the Caribbean is perceived as continuous with Afro-Caribbean spiritism. He argues that this explains why some people convert to Protestantism, since it is seen as offering superior protection from the dangers of the *loa*, especially if one is being "called" to be baptized as a "*servitor*." See Hürbon, "New Religious Movements in the Caribbean," 146–176; and McGaffey, "Twins, Simbi Spirits," 212.

59. Le Goff, *The Medieval Imagination*.

60. Barber, "How Man Makes God in West Africa," 724–45; Peter Brown, *The Cult of the Saints*, 61.

61. Barber, "How Man Makes God in West Africa," 724.

62. Sahlins, "Rich Man, Poor Man," 292.

63. Canetti, *Crowds and Power*, 42–47.

64. I am referring here to inexplicable or socially illegitimate advancement, not to hegemonic forms of social distinction such as class authority.

65. Lundius, *The Great Power of God*, 370 and 269; contrast with Edelman, "Landlords and the Devil," 74–75.

66. DaMatta, *Carnivals, Rogues and Heros*, 137–97.

67. Anderson, *Language and Power*, 23; Fabian, *Power and Performance*. This accords with the Kongo *nkisi* concept of bundling or containment; see MacGaffey, *Kongo Political Culture*, 82.

68. Gilroy, *The Black Atlantic*; Lambertus, "Aspectos históricos y psicológicos del culto," 171–82.

69. Jiménez, *Savia dominicana*, 65–68; Deive, "Fukú."

70. Métraux, *Voodoo in Haiti*, 288; Brodwin, *Medicine and Morality*, 142.

71. Martha Ellen Davis, *La otra ciencia*, 112–13.

72. Métraux, *Voodoo in Haiti*, 130.

73. Derby, "Haitians, Magic and Money."

74. Krohn-Hansen, "Haitians, Money and Alterity."

75. Wachtel, *Gods and Vampires*, 82–83.

76. Martha Ellen Davis, *La otra ciencia*, 111.

77. Fabian, *Power and Performance*; Geschiere, *The Modernity of Witchcraft*; Mbembe, "The Banality of Power," 1–30; Bayart, *The State in Africa*.

78. Meyer, "Commodities and the Power of Prayer," 19.

79. In this version, the *muchachito* resembles the *bakuu* or demons of Surinamese maroons who are represented as killers and "money machines." See Bonno Thoden van Velzen, "Priests, Spirit Mediums, and Guerrillas in Suriname," 209–28; and Thoden van Velzen, "Dramatization," 173–88.

80. Taussig, "*Maleficium*"; Leiris, "The Sacred in Everyday Life," 24–31.

81. Geschiere, *Modernity of Witchcraft*.

82. Interview, Corporan family, San Cristóbal, March 1992.

83. Interview, Daniel Parede, Chicago, Jan. 1997.

84. Interview, Miguelina Ramírez, Chicago, Nov. 1997.

85. Mitchell, *Colonizing Egypt*.

86. LeGrand, "Informal Resistance on a Dominican Sugar Plantation."

87. Wiarda, *The Dominican Republic*, 40; and Vedovato, *Politics, Foreign Trade and Economic Development*.

88. Roorda, *The Dictator Next Door*, 192–230.

89. Galíndez, *The Era of Trujillo*, 183–93.

90. Wiarda, *The Dominican Republic*, 41.

91. Karl Marx, *Capital*, vol. 1, chap. 3, 145 n. 1.

92. On the metamorphosis of money, see Marx, *Capital*, vol. 1, chap. 7, 217. For a rich exposition of narratives of shape-shifting creatures, see Bynum, *Metamorphosis and Identity*. See also Labourt, *Sana, sana, culito de rana*, 189. The morphing metaphor may have some illustrative validity as well since in Haiti, bacás can become machines as well as animals (fieldwork in Ouanaminthe, Haiti, 1988).

93. Turits, *Foundations of Despotism*; and San Miguel, *Los campesinos del Cibao*.

94. Karl Marx, *Capital*, vol. 1, 165; Pietz, "Fetishism and Materialism," 148.

95. Raymond T. Smith, *The Matrifocal Family*.

96. Simpson, "Response," 194–96.

97. Peter Grant Simonson, "Masculinity and Femininity in the Dominican Republic: Historical Change and Contradiction in Notions of Self" (Ph.D. diss., University of Michigan, Ann Arbor, 1994), chapter 4.

98. Hertz, *The End of the Line*; Sigmund Freud, *Sexuality and the Psychology of Love*, 202–9. I wish to thank Danilyn Rutherford for suggesting these citations to me.

99. Osorio Lizarazo, *Portrait of Trujillo*, 73 and 131.

100. M. A. Matos Mena, "Al César lo que es del César," *Listín Diario*, 14 Jan. 1937.

101. Taylor, *Eva Perón*.

102. Osorio Lizarazo, *Portrait of Trujillo*, 97.

103. Coronil and Skurski, "Dismembering and Remembering the Nation."

104. Mateo, *Mito y cultura*, 124–26. While I am borrowing Mateo's argument about myths of equivalence, he is discussing how Trujillo became equivalent to the nationalist founding father Juan Pablo Duarte by paying off the national debt, and thus "making the idea [of nationhood] a reality."

105. Peña Battle, cited in Cassá, *Capitalismo y dictadura*, 773.

106. Antero Cestero, Dominican Party speech, Guayubín, 12 Dec. 1943, PD, JCD #44, Corres. 20–27 Dec. 1943.

107. Bolívar Belliard S., n.d., PD, JCD #44, Corres. 20–27 Dec. 1943. See also Pantoy Samboys Castillo, Pres. de la Junta Comunal, to Virgilio Álvarez Pina, Pres. de la Junta Superior, Pedernales, 13 Dec. 1943, PD, JCD, Corres. 11–20 Dec. 1943.

108. This argument about authority was inspired by Webb Keane's talk "Words and Agency," Department of Anthropology, University of Chicago, 20 Oct. 1997. The point is also stressed in the film directed by René Fortunato, *El Poder del Jefe I* (1991).

109. Indeed, this feature might also qualify this form of fetishism as residing within the general criteria laid out by Arjun Appadurai in "Commodities and The Politics of Value," 54, namely, one developing in contexts in which "there are sharp discontinuities in the distribution of knowledge concerning [the] trajectories of circulation," such as enclaves. This form of fetishism is also similar to Pierre Bourdieu's argument about political fetishism in "Delegation and Political Fetishism," *Language and Symbolic Power*, 204.

110. This broad characterization, however, camouflages the fact that more women portrayed the muchachito in positive terms, which may be because more women than men are active saint/loá devotees and thus more women have muchachitos themselves.

111. Fischlin, "'Counterfeiting God,'" 6; Bourdieu, *Language and Symbolic Power*, 182.

7. PAPÁ LIBORIO

1. Dominican Spanish renders "v" and "b" virtually indistinguishable, which accounts for the variable spellings of Olivorio and Liborio; my spelling follows that of local orthography.

2. The classic works on the movement include Martínez, *Palma Sola*; Martínez, "Palma Sola," 9–20; and García, *La masacre de Palma Sola*. The most comprehensive treatment of the movement, commencing with its origins in the years 1910–19, is in Lundius, *The Great Power of God*; also see the impressive and exhaustively researched Lundius and Lundahl, *Peasants and Religion*. An important volume with testimonial material from many believers and witnesses is Martha Ellen Davis, *La ruta hacia Liborio*. See also Lundahl and Lundius, "Foundations of a Messianic Cult," 201–38; de Mota, "Palma Sola: 1962," 197–223; Espín, "Hacia una 'teología' de Palma Sola," 53–68; and

Deive, "El Olivorismo," 30–52. García and Martínez claim that eight hundred died in the Palma Sola slaughter; the contemporary press reported only forty ("En Guerra Contra Liborio," *La Nación*, 11 Jan. 1963). Thomas Reilly, the bishop of San Juan de la Maguana (a Catholic priest from Boston), also raised the alarm over Palma Sola which he saw as *vodúistic* witchcraft.

3. Navaro-Yashin, *Faces of the State*, 5.

4. Lewis, *Hall of Mirrors*.

5. The term *occult cosmology* is from Sanders and West, "Power Revealed and Concealed," 6; the term is inspired by Comaroff and Comaroff, "Notes from the South African Postcolony." Lomnitz, *Deep Mexico, Silent Mexico*, 82, discusses split perceptions of the state in Mexico.

6. The delegation included fifty antiriot police and forty-two army soldiers in full combat gear. Rodríguez Reyes's death occurred when the site was clouded in a fog of tear gas, which accounts for some of the controversy over who was responsible.

7. Martin, *Overtaken by Events*, 304. The CIA was actively albeit surreptitiously involved in the Dominican Republic during this period, from Trujillo's assassination until U.S. Marines intervened for the second time in 1965. Martin was then ambassador to the Dominican Republic.

8. He was ousted by a coup d'etat in 1963 lead by military and police still loyal to Trujillo.

9. See Lundius, *Great Power of God*; and Lundius and Lundahl, *Peasants and Religion*.

10. The transformation of the frontier into a border is a concept from Katz, *The Secret War in Mexico*.

11. For an extremely well-researched analysis of the socioeconomic changes that transformed San Juan de la Maguana, see Angel Moreta, "Desarrollo de relaciones capitalistas en la agricultura del Suroeste (SJM): Capitalismo y campesinado" (master's thesis, CLACSO, Santo Domingo, 1986).

12. Félix A. Gómez, "Revelan Liboristas eran partidarios del tirano, *El Caribe*, 1 Jan. 1963; Orlando Espín, "Hacia una teología," 58. On some days as many as three thousand visitors traveled to the cult site (José Rafael Sosa and Alonso Rosario, "Palma Sola Hoy no es Lo que Antes Fue . . . ," *¡Ahora!*, 12 Aug. 1982, 11.

13. Rodríguez Demorizi, "Liborio," *Seudónimos dominicanos*, 167–76.

14. Lafaye, *The Formation of Mexican National Consciousness*.

15. The conflation of religious and national identity in Latin America is considered by Claudio Lomnitz, "Nationalism as a Practical System," in *Deep Mexico, Silent Mexico*, 21.

16. See James Holston's lucid critique of "compensatory" explanations of millenarian phenomena in his essay "Alternative Modernities," 605–31.

17. This was patently clear in the effusive spectacle of grief at Trujillo's wake where eighteen thousand mourners appeared and thousands were turned

away. Mourners appeared shattered and hysterical; men wept and women shrieked and beat their heads on the ground. See "One of Trujillo's Assassins Reported Slain, 3 seized: Crowds Turn Out in Farewell to Trujillo in the Dominican Capital," *New York Times*, 3 June 1961, 2.

18. Taussig, *"Maleficium,"* 132.

19. Clausner, *Rural Santo Domingo*, 142; for more on border contraband, see Baud, "A Border of Refuge."

20. Lundius, *Great Power of God*, 103–12. Lundius notes that after the death of the prominent Caco leader Charlemagne Peralte a prayer very popular among Liboristas was found printed in Higüey, one of their pilgrimage sites (108). See also "Operations of a Detachment of the 9th Company, G.D.D.," From: The Comandante, G.N.D., To: Dept. of Interior and Police, National Palace, Ministerio de lo Interior y Policia #379, 23 Jan. 1919, in AGN, Santo Domingo.

21. See letters signed "habitantes, propietarios, comerciantes, funcionarios públicos, artesanos y braceros en general," including scions of the Ramírez family and many illiterates (who clearly signed via a notary), San Juan, Feb. 1915; also Dir. Gen. de Telégrafos y Teléfonos del Estado, 13 Sept. 1915, both in Diversas Correspondencias del Secretaría de Fomento y Comunicaciones 1915, Leg. A, AGN, Santo Domingo.

22. Although Ramírez eventually turned Olivorio over to marine authorities during the occupation. On the transformation in micropolitical relations as a result of the U.S. occupation, see the articles by Franks, "The *Gavilleros* of the East," 158–81; and Lundahl and Lundius, "Olivorismo." Lusitania Martínez acknowledges Olivorio as a nationalist symbol (*Palma Sola*, 81). Roberto Cassá describes the movement as a "countersociety" in "Problemas del culto Olivorista," in Martha Ellen Davis, *La ruta hacia Liborio*, 13; see also Cassá, "Algunas claves del Olivorismo," 3–15.

23. See Reinaldo L. Román's fascinating book *Governing Spirits*, esp. chapters 1 and 2; and David H. Brown's landmark study, *Santería Enthroned*, chapter 3.

24. For Dominican reactions, see Pedro Mir, "El mundo termina en año Nuevo," *¡Ahora!*, 27 Aug. 1973; "La noche del cometa," *La voz del sur*, [n.d.] Jan. 1910; and Díaz Matos, *Santo Domingo de Ayer*, 142–43. For New York, see "Queries from the Curious and Answers to Them," *New York Times*, 30 Jan. 1910. The portentousness of the comet in New York made it both an evil and a blessed occurrence, however, as wines from the comet year were also said to be of exceptional vintage.

25. See Lears, *No Place of Grace*, for a discussion of anti-rationalism in the United States. See Hodges, *Intellectual Foundations of the Nicaraguan Revolution*, 24–58, for a discussion of anti-rationalist thought in Nicaragua and its influence on the anti-U.S. guerrilla leader Augusto César Sandino. See Hess, "The Many Rooms of Spiritism in Brazil," 15–34, for a discussion of spiritism in Brazil. Skurski examines the reception of European mystical thought on

Venezuelan elites in her essay "The Ambiguities of Authenticity," 605–42. The popularity of Kardecism in Puerto Rico is also treated in Romberg, *Witchcraft and Welfare*.

26. Writers that characterize the phenomenon as Haitian vodou are guilty of this kind of othering, which presumes that vodou has no Dominican practitioners, and Haitian and Dominican practices are absolutely divided. Liborismo appears to have been highly syncretic—a mixture of elements of Haitian vodou and popular Catholicism. De Mota, "Palma Sola: 1962," characterizes it as vodou; Espin, "Hacia una teologia," calls it essentially Catholic; and Martha Ellen Davis describes it as part of Dominican folk Catholicism although fundamentally a healing cult in "La religiosidad popular del sureoeste," *La ruta hacia Liborio*, 102–3.

27. Koreck, "Space and Revolution in Northeastern Chihuahua," 127–49.

28. Alonso, "Popular Ideology in the Chihuahuan Sierra," 210.

29. Poole, "Landscapes of Power," 367–98. On the history of the Haitian-Dominican frontier, see Baud, "A Border of Refuge," and his "A Border to Cross."

30. Kearney, "Borders and Boundaries," 52–74, esp. 69–70; and Baud and van Schendel, "Towards a Historical Analysis of Borderlands" (paper presented at Social Science History Association meeting, Chicago, 9 Nov. 1995).

31. Comaroff and Comaroff, "The Madman and the Migrant," 191–208.

32. Deren, *Divine Horsemen*, 39. In the Dominican vodú pantheon, gods are called *misterios* or *seres*; they are called *lwa* in Haiti (there is terminological overlap in the Haitian-Dominican frontier, however). For more on the powers of twinship, see Houlberg, "Magique Marasa," 267–86.

33. Taussig, *Mimesis and Alterity*, 13, although he is primarily concerned with visual representations, rather than ritual practices, in this account; Sanders and West, "Power Revealed and Concealed," 17.

34. Jackie Conde, "Olivorio: Un escape de la leyenda hacia la superstición," *La Tarde Alegre*, 3 Aug. 1984.

35. E. O. Garrido Puello, *Olivorio*, 8; Deive, "Olivorismo," 37; Víctor Garrido Puello, "Común de San Juan," 223–33, esp. 232. The association with the white horse is why some viewed him as an apparition of San Antonio, who rides a white stallion in his chromolithograph.

36. Rutherford, *Raiding the Land of the Foreigners*.

37. Helms, *Ulysses' Sail*.

38. Rodríguez Demorizi, "Liborio," *Seudónimos dominicanos*, 174, reprinted from *Panfilia*, 30 Sept. 1925.

39. Mejía, "Si me permiten hablar, 11, refers to "el sabio's" voice as indecipherable because it came from "under the waters." So Olivorio's travels were celestial as well as subterranean. The idea that the spirits reside in Guinea or under the water is also a feature of Haitian vodou.

40. Rodríguez Demorizi, "Liborio," 167 (quoting from *Blanco y Negro*, 4 July

1909). For example, while spirit possessed, Dominicans frequently speak in Haitian Kreyol.

41. Ibid., 170 (reprinted from *El Imparcial* [Higüey], 21 Feb. 1914); Lundius, *Great Power of God*, 75–76; and Lusitania Martínez, *Palma Sola*, 77.

42. George Marvin, "Watchful Acting in Santo Domingo," *The World's Work*, June 1917, 205–18, esp. 214.

43. E. O. Garrido Puello, *Olivorio*, 16. On "sacred children," see Houlberg, "Magique Marasa," 270.

44. Flérida de Nolasco, in E. O. Garrido Puello, *Olivorio*, Appendix No. 1, 56; Lundius, *Great Power of God*, 52; "En 1910 cuando apareció el cometa 'Halley' el rumor mezcló esto con la existencia milagrera de Olivorio," *Hoy*, 13 March 1986.

45. Jean Comaroff, "Bodily Reform as Historical Practice," 541–67, esp. 551; Jean Comaroff, *Body of Power, Spirit of Resistance*; and Taussig, "Folk Healing," 217–78. Deive also links healing and salvation in Olivorismo ("Olivorismo," 42).

46. Lundius, *Great Power of God*, 62; Lusitania Martínez, *Palma Sola*, 76–77; Vetilio J. Alfau Durán, "El Santo Liborio en Higüey," *La Nación*, 22 June 1940.

47. This is practically verbatim to what Metraux heard in healing rites in Haiti; see *Voodoo in Haiti*, 277.

48. Martha Ellen Davis, *La otra ciencia*; Juan Salazar Díaz, "El 'poder' oculto de la medicina popular," *¡Ahora!*, 20 March 1978, 34–36. This balance is often expressed through the metaphor of temperature and clarity. For example, disease can be said to produce a "cold cloud" in the urine.

49. Deive, "Olivorismo," 44, claims the group used twelve knots; Víctor Garrido Puello mentions Olivorio's knot in "Común de San Juan," 223–33, esp. 232. See E. O. Garrido Puello, *Olivorio*, 56 and 19, for healing accounts.

50. Interview by Roberto Cassá, cited in Lundius, *Peasants and Religion*, 64.

51. E. O. Garrido Puello, *Olivorio*, 24.

52. Lundius and Lundahl, *Peasants and Religion*, 183.

53. Karen McCarthy Brown, *Mama Lola*, 398. Craige describes the *ounga-mort* in *Black Bagdad*, 28 and 60, and mentions in his account many knotted and braided charms.

54. Ana Teresa Ortiz, "No Peace for the Dead: The Persecution of an Afro-Dominican Healing Community," in "Healers in the Storm: Dominican Health Practitioners Confront the Debt Crisis" (Ph.D. diss., Harvard University, 1994), 238–75, esp. 250.

55. Blier, *African Vodun*, 31.

56. MacGaffey, *Kongo Political Culture*, 82. And of course Haitian Petwo rites have a strong Kongo component. Thanks to Judith Bettelheim for bringing this to my attention.

57. Ibid., 74–76, 80, and 201. Ana Teresa Ortiz mentions that the gift of being a *caballo*, or having a personal relationship with a misterio (the ability to

become possessed), is expressed in terms of electrical imagery, namely, having a *corriente* or *luz*. See her "Healers in the Storm," 288. On tying as a motif of slavery, see Karen McCarthy Brown, "Serving the Spirits," 220.

58. Blier, *African Vodun*, 82–83.

59. The popular bandit Enrique Blanco wore a string around his waist with seven knots and carried chains as protection; see Arzeno Rodríguez, *Enrique Blanco, héroe o foragido?*, 33–34.

60. Martha Ellen Davis, *La otra ciencia*, 232. Twins are also water spirits and can inhabit rocks and *minkisi* or "power objects" (MacGaffey, "Twins, Simbi Spirits," 212).

61. Lundius, *Great Power of God*, 74; E. O. Garrido Puello, *Olivorio*, 24. On pages 86–88 Lundius discusses Olivorista dress and the use of cords, which he interprets as signs of belonging to the *hermandad*.

62. This reading would conform to the logic of flow and blockage described by Christopher Taylor in *Milk, Money and Honey*, esp. 9–12.

63. E. O. Garrido Puello, *Olivorio*, 24. For more on Kardacist theories of existential planes, see Greenfield, "The Return of Dr. Fritz," 1095–108.

64. Karen McCarthy Brown, "Systematic Remembering, Systematic Forgetting," 65–89. Ogun's name appears prominently several times in a Liborista drawing reprinted in Lusitania Martínez, *Palma Sola*, 98. In our interview on 12 Oct. 1992 Don León Ventura Rodríguez described this foursome as the "four powers," saying that this particular Ogun (there are several manifestations) was Ogun Balenyo, also known as San Santiago, "uno de los que batalló en aquella época." In explaining the pantheon he continued, "estas son ordenanzas y se firmó en la cruz, ese es el emblema del movimiento."

65. For more on the indignuous (Taíno) component of Dominican popular religion, see Lundius, *Great Power of God*, 129–44. Lundius links *piedras de rayo* with Taino (Amerindian) culture (131), although in Cuban Santería and among the West African Yoruba people they are also venerated, representing Shango, the god of thunder. Interview, Maria de Olios, San Juan de la Maguana, 4 Oct. 1992.

66. For more on Anacaona and the Jaragua cacicazgo, see Victor Garrido Puello, *Espigas historicas*, 329. Lundius also discusses the merging of political and religious charisma (*Great Power of God*, 370). Called "los Trinitarios," the Dominican founding fathers Juan Pablo Duarte, Francisco del Rosario Sánchez, and Ramón Mella created the underground movement that brought Dominican independence from Haiti in 1844. Note the more inclusive ethnic coding of this trinity, with a mulatto, an Indian, and a Spaniard (the official trinity is represented as quite Caucasian). Olivoristas have actually incorporated Duarte in their popular pantheon as well; they are also mounted or possessed by him as well as by Christopher Columbus (interview, Maria de Olios, 4 Oct. 1992).

67. Vega, *La vida cotidiana*, 131; Vega, "La muerte de Liborio: Una nueva versión," *Isla Abierta*, 7 Dec. 1991. Vega mentions complaints from a parish priest in 1938 that many Olivoristas were practicing unseemly rites in Las Matas de Farfán.

68. For the repression of Liboristas during the Trujillato, see Lundius and Lundahl, *Peasants and Religion*, 154–55, 167–68. As in Brazil under the Vargas regime, repression under Trujillo was haphazard and probably had less to do with official policy against African-based religious practices than with the whims of parish priests disgusted by paganism and sorcery or with regional police fearful of "some kind of outbreak of disguised communism" (ibid). While there were certainly sweeps of curanderos and diviners, particularly in Santo Domingo in the 1940s, I would argue that this was more because of state dislike of public groupings (which could become a focus of anti-Trujillista sentiment) than official dislike of things African. The highly syncretic nature of popular Catholicism in the Dominican Republic has often made it difficult to sort out the Spanish-Catholic from the African-and-Haitian-derived; it has led to some interesting inconsistencies, such as Trujillo's officialization of a syncretic religious brotherhood (devotees of the Holy Spirit [Espíritu Santo], for which he built a church), merely because the group was based in San Cristóbal, Trujillo's birthplace. For more on umbanda and spiritism under the Vargas regime, see Diane Brown, *Umbanda*. I wish to thank Emilio Cordero Michel for bringing Trujillista repression against curanderos to my attention.

69. Sahlins, *Islands of History*.

70. As the Trujillo-era stereotype of the peasantry as obedient and submissive gave way to the previous image of it as rebellious and violent; see San Miguel, *La guerra silenciosa*, 19.

71. Lincoln, *Authority*.

72. Geertz, "Centers, Kings, and Charisma," 150–71.

73. *Soquete* is the term used by Don León (interview, Don León Ventura Rodríguez, 12 Oct. 1992).

74. Houlberg, "Magique Marasa," 268.

75. For more on the Gede spirits, see Cosentino, "Envoi," 399–415, and "Exit Laughing," 239–260.

76. Blier, *African Vodun*. Elsewhere she refers to this Fon tactic as "agglomeration" or "uniting"; see Blier, "Vodun," 75.

77. Deren, *Divine Horsemen*, 279, 38–39; Andrew Apter, "The Saints Go Marching On . . . ," text for exhibit "The Saints," University of Chicago, Aug. 1995. On foreign powers, see Helms, *Ulysses' Sail*, 131–35. Evidence that the cult of twinship was widespread was the Dominican cofradía to Cosme and Damián, the Catholic "twin" saints, founded by "Negros Ararás" in 1702 (Rodríguez Demorizi, *Sociedades, cofradías, escuelas*, 154).

78. Karen McCarthy Brown, *Mama Lola*, 295–304.

79. Don León told us that this vision was the Holy Ghost and that he and Plinio had the same dream simultaneously, which is why they both arrived at the site.

80. Interview, Don León Ventura Rodríguez, 12 Oct. 1992. I wonder whether this is a post-Palma Sola rendition, since the massacre was executed on the basis of the purported witchcraft of the Liboristas; this event may have encouraged members to stress the benevolent Christianity of the cult and its opposition to "Haitian" black magic in the aftermath. For example, while Don León told us that they had been sent to eliminate "mounting" (*los montados*) or spirit possession, we were told that this was commonplace in the early days of the cult. The term *hermandad* was used by Tulio Rodríguez's son (interview, Las Matas de Farfán, Dec. 1992).

81. Mejía, "Si me permiten hablar," 3–68, esp. 6–21.

82. This was impossible in the earlier incarnation since Olivorio's persecution meant that he was on the run for much of his career as a living saint.

83. Lusitania Martínez refers to this as a "mythic geography" in *Palma Sola*.

84. These were the terms used by Tulio Rodríguez's son (interview, Dec. 1992).

85. This implicit combining of symbols of twinship (the *mellizos*) and the holy trinity with all the Calvaries is similar to the conjoining of twins and triples discussed in chapter 6. Houlberg discusses this phenomenon in "Sacred Children: Why Two Equals Three," in "Magique Marasa," 270–71.

86. Several flags were in use, although the one described here was the one intended to symbolize the movement as a whole. The other flags seem to have drawn on the cluster of saints/misterios accompanying Olivorio, such as the Holy Ghost, etc. (with the colors violet, red, etc.) See Lusitania Martínez, *Palma Sola*, 211.

87. In "New Religious Movements," 146–76, Hürbon argues that the popularity of Seventh Day Adventism in Martinique is related to its perceived ability to check witchcraft; see also DaMatta, *Carnivals, Rogues and Heroes*.

88. Lusitania Martínez, *Palma Sola*, 142. Trees have this significance in Cuban Santería as well, and the Ciguaraya and the Ceiba are sacred; similarly, in Haitian vodou, spirits rise and descend via the *poto mitan* or central column in the ritual space.

89. Víctor Garrido Puello, "Común de San Juan," 230.

90. Marin, *Utopics*; Taussig, "La magia del estado," 489–518.

91. Holston, "Alternative Modernities," 626. The term *cuenta* is from Ney Rodríguez's testimony in Martha Ellen Davis, *La ruta hasta Liborio*, 254.

92. Michael Taussig, "*Maleficium*," 237.

93. José Rafael Sosa and Alonso Rosario, "Palma Sola hoy no es lo que antes fue . . . ," *¡Ahora!* 12 Aug. 1982, 9. The guards had a square of stones, with another square inside decorated with stars. I found this detail in a description in this article; Sosa and Rosario, however, provide an extremely deprecating

picture of Palma Sola, and they recapitulate official claims at the time of the massacre that the cult was a cover for a paramilitary force, which is false.

94. Lusitania Martínez, *Palma Sola*, 147; Sosa and Rosario, "Palma Sola," 10.

95. Espín, "Hacia una teología," 60.

96. Today the authoritative veneer of Olivorismo has adopted a new idiom—that of a nonprofit organization—and it has now formed a foundation; see Martha Ellen Davis, *La ruta hacia Liborio*.

97. As David H. Brown describes for Santería, *Santería Enthroned*, 128.

98. Interview, Don León Ventura Rodríguez, 12 Oct. 1992.

99. "Para ellos (Los Liboristas), Liborio es el Jesucristo de los católicos," in Lundius and Lundahl, *Peasants and Religion*, 177 n. 3; Martha Ellen Davis, *La ruta hacia Liborio*, 247. Although they say they have not read the Bible, they then claim that they are quoting from it, thus providing another miracle authenticating their faith and mission. The relationship between Liboristas and Catholicism is complex since they felt deeply betrayed by church support for the massacre at Palma Sola. At the same time, Don León stressed to me that "siempre hemos sido Católicos, siempre, siempre, todo el tiempo, y lo somos y lo seguiremos siendo" (interview, Don León Ventura Rodríguez, 12 Oct. 1992).

100. Seven was also the number of the *misterios purales*.

101. Don León told us that his mother had had three sets of twins. As he said, "después de tres partos mellizos, es decir que ya esa era una herencia de misterio, de San Cosme, San Damian, los mellizos de agua dulce . . ." (interview, Don León Ventura Rodríguez, 12 Oct. 1992).

102. For information about numerology and Palma Sola, see Lusitania Martínez, *Palma Sola*, 206–7.

103. Numerology is a very important aspect of popular religious practice and divination in the Dominican Republic and is not confined to Olivorista beliefs. Dreams are a popular source of magic numbers, which can be bought, sold, or given as gifts, for use in the lottery. Dream signs can also be translated into numbers. For example, a friend once recounted to me that a water spirit, an indio, visited him on the day his father died. When he dreamed of his father's house, this was a signal that he should have played one of the numbers corresponding to his father's identity in the lottery: either his address, age, or cédula number. Small booklets are sold that translate symbols in dreams into numbers for use in the lottery; an example is "El Libro Supremo de la Suerte: Los Sueños y sus números," n.p., n.d. Ortiz also discusses passports and magic numbers in "Healers in the Storm."

104. Of course, all *curanderismo* in the Dominican Republic purports to be free, and all payment for services rendered must be cast as a gift.

105. The global struggle was mapped into a war between red and black, which were threatening to overcome blue (Olivorismo). This color scheme may

represent the Cold War representation of communism (red), with black invoking the Haitian menace of *Trujillista* anti-Haitian propaganda.

106. Don León and other Olivoristas we spoke with argued that the Palma Sola massacre was the result of *celos* or jealousy; as Don León stated, "Entonces ya eran la mayoria en el pueblo dominicano, entonces ya de ese movimiento ya hemos llegado a un malestar que ha venido por envidia de poderes, del poder personal, poder gubernamental" (interview, Don León Ventura Rodríguez, 12 Oct. 1992). This view demonstrates how political analysis can be understood through the popular discourse of the evil eye.

107. Apter, "The Saints go Marching on . . ." None of the officials at Palma Sola were allowed to accept money for services rendered (only gifts were permitted as recompense), and shopkeepers were forced to keep their stands outside the sacred community limits. On the doubling of moral economies in Brazil, see DaMatta, "The Ethic of Umbanda, 239–264. Víctor Garrido mentions that San Juaneros commonly bury their money in the ground (Garrido, "Común de San Juan," 226).

108. I am stealing the notion of the state as vampire from Van Young, "The State as Vampire," 343–69.

109. Moreta, "Proletarianización rural"; and Moreta, "Desarrollo de relaciones capitalistas."

110. On the prohibition against money, see Espín, "Hacia una teología," 58.

111. As one Liborista adherent put it, " . . . decía que había que respetar la justicia. Tenía enemigos en el pueblo. Esos enemigos eran los grandes del pueblo que informaban arriba para hacer daño" (from Raymundo González's interview with Maria Dolores Medrano, Duvergé, 1991; unpublished manuscript).

112. As Holston argues in "Alternative Modernities," 626–27.

113. Berman, *All That Is Solid Melts into Air.*

114. Joseph and Nugent, "Popular Culture and State Formation," 13.

115. "Bureaucratic performative" is from Holston, "Alternative Modernities," 622.

116. Taussig, *Mimesis and Alterity*; and Holston, "Alternative Modernities."

117. See Lundius and Lundahl, *Peasants and Religion*, 350–53.

118. Martha Ellen Davis, *La otra ciencia*, 54.

119. Another similarity is that both forms perceive the world as corrupt. Of course, not all evangelical Protestantism is subject to lay control; I have in mind certain Creole churches in Puerto Rico; see Mintz, *Worker in the Cane.*

120. Today the cofradía of Espíritu Santo is the largest in the country according to Martha Ellen Davis, *La otra ciencia*, 100; and it shares with Olivorismo devotion to the cross. Today Olivoristas carry their flag, as well as the flags of the San Juan bautista cofradía and the nation.

121. Rodríguez Demorizi, *Sociedades, Cofradía del Espíritu Santo*, 152–53.

122. Díaz, *Royal Slaves of El Cobre.*

123. Fick, *The Making of Haiti*, 127–28.

124. David H. Brown, *Santería Enthroned*, 27, 43, and 45. The chapter entitled "Black Royalty" has a fascinating discussion of the origins of royalist iconography on pages 25–61. Such borrowings formed part of a wider political imaginary in Latin America that adopted royal symbolism for its own means and ends; see Van Young, *The Other Rebellion*, chapter 18.

125. Don León has a framed photograph in his house of himself with former president Joaquín Balaguer. Then as now, Balaguer's party—the Partido Reformista Social Cristiano—has cultivated the Liboristas as a source of votes in the southwestern provinces. Many politicians over the years have sought the support of Olivorio and the Liborista community, from Eladio Victoria to Rafael Trujillo; see "Al santón Olivorio Mateo llegaron a consultar algunos políticos de la época," *Hoy*, 22 Oct. 1985, 8A; Mario Bobea Billini, "Fué Trujillo devoto del 'Dios' Liborio?," *¡Ahora!*, 25 Jan. 1963, 9–10; and Juan Daniel Balcácer, "Fue Olivorio un 'Dios' anti-imperialista?" *El Nuevo Diario*, 24 June 1981.

126. I am stealing this term from Michael Taussig, who in turn poached it from Walter Benjamin; see Taussig, "History as Sorcery," in *Shamanism*, 369.

127. George Marcus, as cited by Caroline Humphrey, "Stalin and the Blue Elephant," in Sanders and West, *Transparency and Conspiracy*, 183.

128. The 1961 press was full of such accusations, for example, that the community was harboring guns smuggled from Haiti, or that it was being used by the Unión Cívica Nacional. As one writer said, "The Liborista cult was taken advantage of for apparently hidden objectives by clever minds that were after far more than what a peasant might be after" (Reginaldo Atinay, "Palma Sola: Víctima de la ignorancia," *La Nación*, 31 Dec. 1962, 3). See also Santiago Estrella Veloz, "Dato Pagan afirma tergiversan historia sobre Liborio Mateo," *La Nación*, 4 Jan. 1963, 11.

129. Simmel, *The Sociology of Georg Simmel*, part IV, chapter 3.

130. For an argument about spatial figuration as expressing forms of alienation in another millenarian context, see Lattas, *Cultures of Secrecy*, chapter 3.

131. "Moral topography" is from Taussig, *Shamanism*, chapter 18. Laura Lewis provides a fascinating discussion of the co-dependence of sanctioned and unsanctioned domains in colonial Mexico in her *Hall of Mirrors*.

132. Sanders and West, "Power Revealed and Concealed," 16.

133. This view of Olivorismo as a critique of the state is echoed by several Dominicans: in an interview with Maria Dolores Medrano, who complains about the "grandes del pueblo" (Raymundo González, unpublished manuscript, 1991); by Blanco Fombona, "El marino rubio," who states that Olivorio "no era enemigo de un Gobierno determinado, sino de todos los gobiernos"; and by Don León, who blames the government with good reason for the slaughter at Palma Sola.

134. Taussig, *Defacement*, 5–6.

CONCLUSION

1. This contrast between mestizo societies and more homogeneous class-based social hierarchies bears some comparison to Bruce Kapferer's contrast between egalitarian and hierarchical nationalisms in Australia and Sri Lanka respectively; see his masterful account, *Legends of People, Myths of State*.

2. See Daniel James's rich analysis of Perón's symbolic politics in *Resistance and Integration*, chapter 1.

3. "Veinticinco pianos serán enviados a la región," *La Nación*, 6 Jan. 1944.

4. Arístides Incháustegui, an opera singer at Bellas Artes in the 1950s, asserts that this practice ruined the market for classical music since even today Dominicans refuse to pay for it (personal communication, Jan. 1993).

5. Paul Austerlitz, *Merengue*; and Pacini Hernandez, "Merengue."

6. The classic account of Dominican Gagá is by Rosenberg, *El Gagá*.

7. Weismantel, *Cholas and Pishtacos*, discusses race marking through food; and Matos Díaz, *Santo Domingo de ayer*, mentions that "el ron era bebida de gente de más o menos y de borrachones" (69).

8. Balaguer, *Memorias de un cortesano*, 93. Hoetink also notes the increase in prestige and income accorded the gente de segunda under the regime; see "The Dominican Republic in the Twentieth Century," 216. The perceived whitening of the population is reflected in the shift between the 1935 and 1950 censuses, for which the percentage of urban whites increased from 22 percent to 35 percent, with the rural percentage more than doubled (from 10 percent to nearly 26 percent); this shift is only partly accounted for by immigration (*Tercero Censo Nacional de Población* [Santo Domingo: Dirección General de Estadistica, Oficina Nacional de Censo, 1950], xxvi).

9. Caton, "Canela fina," *La Tribuna*, 17 March 1937.

10. Whitten and Torres, "General Introduction," in Whitten and Torres, *Blackness in Latin America and the Caribbean*, vol. 1, 3–34. Dominicans do not use the term *mestizo* but rather *indio* or *creole* instead, but either term means mixed race.

11. In selecting the term *recognition* here I am purposefully avoiding the concept of interpellation, which connotes a deeper identity transformation. The form of hegemony I describe here worked on the surfaces of the body—it entrapped, it provided a mirror, but it was not ultimately transformative, perhaps because it was not accompanied by genuine citizenship expansion. See Laclau's seminal work on populist interpellation, *Politics and Ideology in Marxist Theory*, and his *On Populist Reason*.

12. Turits, *Foundations of Despotism*; and Krohn-Hansen, "Negotiated Dictatorship," 96–122.

13. Bourdieu, *Outline of a Theory of Practice*, 192.

14. This underscores the parallels between the racialized nationalist inclusion of

François Duvalier and Trujillo; see Trouillot, *Haiti: State Against Nation*, 191. Virginia Domínguez, *White by Definition*, 10, makes the argument that social identities are imparted only through social affirmation.

15. Mir, *Tres leyendas de colores*, 168 and 199. I wish to thank Ginetta Candelario for bringing this text to my attention. Alexander, in "Jamaican Images of the Family," 147–80, an article on the middle class in Jamaica, describes this as a "belief in its own dishonor"; on other invisible markers of blackness or open secrets of race in Cuba, see Zeuske, "Hidden Markers, Open Secrets," 211–42.

16. Balaguer actually characterizes Trujillo as a *"grand resentido"* in *La palabra encadenada*, 282.

17. Fanon, *Black Skin, White Masks*, chapter 7.

18. Max Weber, *Economy and Society*, 242–45. That said, people did bring plenty of gifts to Trujillo and his family, but not nearly as many as Trujillo stated. His brother Negro received piles of shoes, for example. See Javier García, *Mis 20 años*, 125.

19. Eisenstadt and Roniger, *Patrons, Clients and Friends*.

20. Laclau, "Towards a Theory of Populism," in *Politics and Ideology in Marxist Theory*, 143–99. Stutzman develops an argument about national space which I draw upon here; see *"El Mestizaje,"* 45–93. The concept of "stains" is from Brackette Williams, *Stains on My Name, War in My Veins*.

21. Sørenson and Stepputat, "Narrations of Authority and Mobility," 337. This essay examines how migration—movement in real space—confers authority on individuals in diasporas such as those involving the Dominican Republic and Guatemala; their argument can be nicely applied to narratives of social mobility as well. There is a good measure of nostalgia in elderly narratives of the Trujillo period, which may result from the more generalized terror of the subsequent Balaguer period of "los doce años," when residents of the *barrios marginados* were frontally targeted. For more on Balaguer's regime, see Cassá, *Los doce años*. For nostalgic as well as critical popular narratives of the Trujillo period, see Mujeres en Desarrollo Dominicano (MUDE), *La era de Trujillo*.

22. Hansen and Stepputat, "Introduction: States of Imagination," 5; Pels, Introduction to *Magic and Modernity*, 31; Jean and John Comaroff, "Transparent Fictions," 294.

23. Which Veyne has termed "euergeticism"; see his *Bread and Circuses*.

24. Special thanks to Mir Yarfitz, who tabulated this data for me. The material is culled from the compendia of official prestation, Archivo General de la Nación, *Obras de Trujillo*. These were official prestations; however, a small percentage did indicate when Trujillo gave from his personal funds. Not included, of course, were many more named gifts to family, lovers, and friends, some of which were allocated by the Dominican Party; the cash gifts

he made to peasants during his rural tours, or outright bribes, were, of course, under the table.

25. For more on respeto and personhood in other corners of the Hispanic Caribbean, see Lauria's essay " 'Respeto,' 'Relajo' and Interpersonal Relations in Puerto Rico," 53–67. See also Bourgois, *In Search of Respect.*
26. Geertz, "Centers, Kings and Charisma"; and Geertz, *Negara.*
27. Former Trujillistas still meet and swap their memorabilia from La Trujillo Era, some of which now trickles into the Internet via eBay; they also get together to celebrate mass on Trujillo's birthday in Santo Domingo. The concept of "inalienable possessions" is from Weiner, *Inalienable Possessions.*
28. Bourdieu discusses "conversion rates" between different forms of capital—social, cultural, symbolic, and economic—in "The Forms of Capital," 242–58.
29. Taussig, "Viscerality, Faith and Skepticism," 300.
30. Espaillat, *The Last Caesar,* 54.
31. Mauss, *The Gift,* 39–45. On conversion, see Bourdieu, "The Forms of Capital."
32. Bourdieu, *Outline of a Theory of Practice,* 190–92.
33. Bailey, "Gifts and Poison," 24; Sartre, *Being and Nothingness,* quoted in Berking, *Sociology of Giving,* 137.
34. Ibid., 188; "Misrecognition" is discussed on page 192. See also Eisenstadt and Roniger, *Patrons, Clients and Friends.*
35. Mbembe, "The Banality of Power," 1–30; and Mbembe, "Prosaics of Servitude," 123–48. See Dain Borges on the application of Mbembe's argument to Latin America, in "Machiavellian, Rabelaisian, Bureaucratic?," 109–12. Trujillo certainly fits his model of the "spectacular vulgarity" of Latin American dictatorship, circa 1930–60, although the small size of the Dominican Republic did lend a feel of "monolithic intimacy" more akin to Zaire than Brazil. Gilbert Joseph has called for approaches to the state in Latin America that take into account how bureaucracy was experienced in everyday life; see "Reclaiming 'the Political,' " in Joseph and Nugent, *Everyday Forms of State Formation,* 3–16.
36. Herzfeld, *The Social Production of Indifference,* 81. For a study of networks and the transactionalist basis of modern state power in Latin America, see Lomnitz-Adler, *Exits from the Labyrinth.*
37. Taussig, "*Maleficium*," 240.
35. Blau, *Exchange and Power in Social Life,* 111.
39. Mauss, *The Gift,* 62.
40. Lescallier, "Itinerario de un viaje," 114.
41. Lindholm, *Charisma,* 25; Max Weber quote is from Taussig, "*Maleficium*," 222. See also Allahar, *Caribbean Charisma.*
42. The classic work on devil-pact narratives in Latin America is Taussig, *The*

Devil and Commodity Fetishism. For a more recent take on the phenomenon, see Crain, "Poetics and Politics in the Ecuadorean Andes," 67–89.

43. This is Mauss via Michael Taussig, *Defacement*, 62.

44. West, "Who Rules Us Now?," 115.

45. Balaguer, *Memorias de un cortesano*, 108, 100. For more on abjection, see Cruz-Malavé, "What a Tangled Web!," 132–51.

46. I am drawing from Rutherford's study, *Raiding the Land of the Foreigners*, 4; and from Helms, *Ulysses' Sail*. With his interest in vodú, Trujillo also drew on blackness, and thus Haiti, as well.

47. Mann, *Death in Venice*, cited in Taussig, *Defacement*, 82.

48. Krohn-Hansen, "Masculinity and the Political," 109. "Magic and necromancy" is from Karl Marx's discussion of the duel form of the commodity; see Tucker, *The Marx-Engels Reader*, 324.

49. Walker, "Power Structure and Patronage," 496; Baud, *Peasants and Tobacco*, 120–23.

50. Edwards, *History, Civil and Commercial, of the British Colonies*, vol. 3, 9.

51. Taussig, "Viscerality, Faith and Skepticism," 273. I am drawing here on Mauss's essay in Carrithers et al., *The Category of the Person*, 1–26; and on Herzfeld's concept of "cultural intimacy," which he defines as the secret spaces of nationhood (see his fascinating collection of essays *Social Poetics in the Nation-State*).

BIBLIOGRAPHY

ARCHIVES

Archivo General de la Nación, Santo Domingo, Dominican Republic (AGN)
United States National Archives, Washington (USNA)
University of Chicago Library, Department of Special Collections, Frederick Starr
Collection

PERIODICALS

¡Ahora!, 1963, 1972, 1973, 1982
American Magazine, 1955
American Mercury, 1954
Blanco y Negro, 1912, 1913, 1914, 1926
Boletín Eclesiástico (BE), 1916
El Caribe, 1956, 1958, 1963, 1991
Harpers, 1955
Hoy, 1985, 1986, 1999, 2002
El Índice, 1921
Isla Abierta, 1991, 1992
Listín Diario (LD), 1903, 1919, 1920, 1922, 1923, 1930, 1933, 1937, 1997
Look, 1956, 1965
Los Angeles Times, 2005, 2006
Mademoiselle, 1956
La Nación, 1940, 1944, 1955, 1956, 1962, 1963
New York Post, 1965
New York Post Daily Magazine and Comic Selection, 1944
New York Times, 1910, 1930, 1961, 1995, 1997
New Yorker, 1966
Nuevo Dia, 1981
La Opinión, 1922, 1930, 1931
Sunday Mirror Magazine, 1945
Suplemento Listín Diario, 1981–84, 1986–87
La Tarde Alegre, 1984
Time, 1958
Times-Herald, 1944

Town and Country, 1943
La Tribuna, 1937
Vanity Fair, 1994
La Voz del Sur, 1910
Washington Post, 1944
World's Work, 1917

PUBLISHED SOURCES

Abad, José Ramón. *La República Dominicana: Reseña general geográfico-estadística, redactada por José Ramón Abad; de orden del señor ministro de fomento y obras publicas ciudadano Pedro T. Garrido.* Santo Domingo: Banco Central de la República Dominicana, 1973.

Abrahams, Roger D. *The Man-of-Words in the West Indies: Performance and the Emergence of Creole Culture.* Baltimore: Johns Hopkins University Press, 1983.

Abrams, Philip. "Notes on the Difficulty of Studying the State." *Journal of Historical Sociology* 1, no. 1 (1988): 58–89.

Abu-Lughod, Lila. *Veiled Sentiments: Honor and Poetry in a Bedouin Society.* Berkeley: University of California Press, 1985.

Aguiar, Enrique. *Eusebio Sapote: La historia y la novela de un tarado.* Bogotá: Editorial Selecta, 1938.

Album de oro de la Feria de la Paz y Confraternidad del Mundo Libre. Ciudad Trujillo: n.p., 1956.

Alexander, Jack. "Love, Race, Slavery, and Sexuality in Jamaican Images of the Family." In *Kinship, Ideology and Practice in Latin America*, edited by Raymond Smith, 147–80. Chapel Hill: University of North Carolina Press, 1984.

Alfau, Luis E. Gómez. *Ayer, o el Santo Domingo de hace 50 años.* Ciudad Trujillo: n.p., 1944.

Alfau Duran, Vetilio, ed. *Américo Lugo: Antologia.* Ciudad Trujillo: Librería Dominicana, 1949.

Alix, Juan Antonio. *Décimas políticas.* Santo Domingo: Editora de Santo Domingo, 1977.

Allahar, Anton, ed. *Caribbean Charisma: Reflections on Leadership, Legitimacy, and Populist Politics.* Boulder, Colo.: Lynne Rienner Publishers, 2001.

Almoina, José. *Yo fuí secretario de Trujillo.* Buenos Aires: Editora y Distribuidora del Plata, 1950.

Alonso, Ana María. "Sovereignty, the Spatial Politics of Security, and Gender: Looking North and South from the U.S.-Mexico Border." In *State Formation: Anthropological Perspectives*, edited by Christian Krohn-Hansen and Knut G. Nustad. London: Pluto Press, 2005.

——. *Thread of Blood: Colonialism, Revolution and Gender on Mexico's Northern Frontier.* Tucson: University of Arizona Press, 1995.

——. "U.S. Military Intervention, Revolutionary Mobilization, and Popular

Ideology in the Chihuahuan Sierra, 1916–1917." In *Rural Revolt in Mexico and U.S. Intervention*, edited by Daniel Nugent, 207–32. Center for U.S.-Mexican Studies, University of California, San Diego, 1988.

Alpers, Edward A. "'A Family of the State': Bureaucratic Impediments to Democratic Reform in Mozambique." In *African Democracy in the Era of Globalization*, edited by Jonathan Hyslop, 122–38. Witwatersrand, South Africa: Witwatersrand University Press, 1999.

Alvarez, Julia. *In the Time of the Butterflies*. New York: Penguin Books, 1995.

Álvarez, Rosendo, Jr. "Rubirosa: Vida y amores de un dominicano." *¡Ahora!*, 11 Sept. 1972, 34–36, and 18 Sept. 1972, 66–72.

Álvarez Sánchez, Virgilio. *La reconstrucción de la capital de la república, obra exclusiva del genio de Trujillo* (speech given in Dominican Party headquarters, 23 Aug. 1940). Ciudad Trujillo: Editora Listín Diario, 1940.

Anderson, Benedict. *Language and Power: Exploring Political Cultures in Indonesia*. Ithaca: Cornell University Press, 1990.

Anderson, Warwick. "The Trespass Speaks: White Masculinity and Colonial Breakdown." *American Historical Review* 102, no. 5 (1997): 1343–70.

Andrews, George Reid. *The Afro-Argentines of Buenos Aires, 1800 to 1900*. Madison: University of Wisconsin Press, 1980.

Appadurai, Arjun, "Introduction: Commodities and The Politics of Value." In *The Social Life of Things*, edited by Arjun Appadurai, 3–63. New York: Cambridge University Press, 1986.

Apter, Andrew. *Black Critics and Kings: The Hermeneutics of Power in Yoruba Society*. Chicago: University of Chicago Press, 1992.

———. "Discourse and Its Disclosures: Yoruba Women and the Sanctity of Abuse." *Africa* 68, no. 1 (1998): 68–97.

———. "Herskovits's Heritage: Rethinking Syncretism in the African Diaspora." *Diaspora* 1, no. 3 (1991): 235–60.

———. "In Dispraise of the King: Rituals 'Against' Rebellion in South-East Africa." *Man,* n.s., 18, no. 3 (1983): 521–34.

———. "In Praise of High Office: The Politics of Panegyric among Three Southern Bantu Tribes." *Anthropos* 78 (1983): 149–68.

Archivo General de la Nación. *Obras de Trujillo*. Ciudad Trujillo: Editora Montalvo, 1956.

Ariza, Sander. *Trujillo: The Man and His Country*. New York: Orlin Tremaine, 1939.

Arrom, Silvia Marina. "Introduction: Rethinking Urban Politics in Latin America before the Populist Era." In *Popular Politics and the Urban Poor in Latin America, 1765–1910*, edited by Silvia M. Arrom and Servando Ortoll. Wilmington, Del.: Scholarly Resources, 1996.

Arzeno Rodríguez, Luis. *Cuentos de Enrique Blanco*. Santo Domingo: Expansion Editorial, 1985.

———. *Enrique Blanco, héroe o foragido?* Santo Domingo: Publicaciones América, 1980.

———. "Orígen de un apodo." *Chapita no – Trujillo!* Santo Domingo: n.p., 1980.

Austen, Ralph. "Social and Historical Analysis of African Trickster Tales: Some Preliminary Reflections." *Plantation Society in the Americas* 2, no. 2 (1986): 135–48.

Austerlitz, Paul. *Merengue: Dominican Music and Dominican Identity.* Philadelphia: Temple University Press, 1996.

Ayala, César J. *American Sugar Kingdom: The Plantation Economy of the Spanish Caribbean, 1898–1934.* Chapel Hill: University of North Carolina Press, 1999.

Bailey, F. G. "Gifts and Poison." In *Gifts and Poison: The Politics of Reputation*, edited by F. G. Bailey, 1–26. New York: Schocken Books, 1971.

Balaguer, Joaquín. *Memorias de un cortesano en la "Era de Trujillo."* Santo Domingo: Editora Corripio, 1989.

———. *La palabra encadenada.* Santo Domingo: Editora Taller, 1985.

———. *Trujillo y su obra: Apuntes sobre la vida y la obra política de un jefe de estado.* Madrid: Sáez Hermanos, 1934.

Ballerino Cohen, Colleen, Richard Wilk, and Beverly Stoeltje, eds. *Beauty Queens on the Global Stage: Gender, Contests, and Power.* New York: Routledge, 1996.

Barber, Karin. "How Man Makes God in West Africa: Yoruba Attitudes toward the Orisa." *Africa* 5, no. 3 (1981): 724–45.

Baretta, Silvio R. Duncan and John Markoff. "Civilization and Barbarism: Cattle Frontiers in Latin America." *Comparative Studies in Society and History* 20, no. 4 (1978): 587–620.

Barnet, Miguel. *Rachel's Song: A Novel.* Translated by W. Nick Hill. Willimantic, Conn.: Curbstone Press, 1991.

Barry, Jonathan. "Introduction: Keith Thomas and the Problem of Witchcraft." In *Witchcraft in Early Modern Europe: Studies in Culture and Belief*, edited by Jonathan Barry, Marianne Hester and Gareth Roberts, 1–49. New York: Cambridge University Press, 1996.

Bataille, George. *Visions of Excess: Selected Writings, 1927–1939.* Edited by Allan Stoekl. Minneapolis: University of Minneapolis Press, 1985.

Baud, Michiel. "A Border of Refuge: Dominicans and Haitians against the State, 1870–1930." *Centre of Border Studies.* Occasional Paper 2. Erasmus University, Rotterdam, 1992.

———. "A Border to Cross: Rural Society across the Dominican-Haitian Border, 1870–1930." *Centre of Border Studies.* Occasional Paper 3. Erasmus University, Rotterdam, 1994.

———. " 'Constitutionally White': The Forging of a National Identity in the Dominican Republic." In *Ethnicity in the Caribbean: Essays in Honor of Harry Hoetink*, edited by Gert Oostindie, 121–51. London: Macmillan, 1996.

———. *Historia de un sueño: Los ferrocarriles públicos en la República Dominicana, 1880–1930.* Santo Domingo: Fundación Cultural Dominicana, 1993.

———. "Ideología y campesinado: El pensamiento social de José Ramón López." *Estudios Sociales* 19, no. 64 (1986): 63–81.

———. *Peasants and Tobacco in the Dominican Republic, 1870–1930.* Knoxville: University of Tennessee Press, 1995.

———. "The Struggle for Autonomy: Peasant Resistance to Capitalism in the Dominican Republic: 1870–1924." In *Labor in the Caribbean: From Emancipation to Independence*, edited by Malcolm Cross and Gad Heuman, 120–40. London: Macmillan Caribbean, 1988.

Bauer, Arnold J. *Goods, Power, History: Latin America's Material Culture.* New York: Cambridge University Press, 2001.

Bayart, Jean-François. *The State in Africa: The Politics of the Belly.* New York: Longman Group, 1993.

Becker, Margaret. "Torching *la purísima*, Dancing at the Altar: The Construction of Revolutionary Hegemony in Michoacán, 1934–1940." In *Everyday Forms of State Formation: Revolution and the Negotiation of Rule in Modern Mexico*, edited by Gilbert M. Joseph and Daniel Nugent. Durham: Duke University Press, 1994.

Bederman, Gail. *Manliness and Civilization: A Cultural History of Gender and Race in the United States, 1880–1917.* Chicago: University of Chicago Press, 1995.

Beezley, William H. *Judas at the Jockey Club and Other Episodes of Porfirian Mexico.* Lincoln: University of Nebraska Press, 1987.

———. "The Porfirian Smart Set Anticipates Thorstein Veblen in Guadalajara." In *Rituals of Rule, Rituals of Resistance: Public Celebrations and Popular Culture in Mexico*, edited by William H. Beezley, Cheryl English Martin, and William E. French, 173–90. Wilmington, Del.: Scholarly Resources, 1994.

Beezley, William H., Cheryl English Martin, and William E. French, eds. *Rituals of Rule, Rituals of Resistance: Public Celebrations and Popular Culture in Mexico.* Wilmington, Del.: Scholarly Resources, 1994.

Beier, A. L. *Masterless Men: The Vagrancy Problem in England, 1560–1640.* London: Methuen, 1985.

Benjamin, Walter. *Charles Baudelaire: A Lyric Poet in the Era of High Capitalism.* London: Verso, 1983.

Berezin, Mabel. "Created Constituencies: The Italian Middle Classes and Fascism." In *Splintered Classes: Politics and the Lower Middle Classes in Interwar Europe*, edited by Rudy Koshar, 142–63. New York: Holmes and Meier, 1990.

———. "Political Belonging: Emotion, Nation, and Identity in Fascist Italy." In *State/Culture: State Formation after the Cultural Turn*, edited by George Steinmetz, 355–77. Ithaca: Cornell University Press, 1999.

Berezin, Mabel. *Making the Fascist Self: The Political Culture of Interwar Italy.* Ithaca: Cornell University Press, 1997.

Berking, Helmuth. *Sociology of Giving.* Translated by Patrick Camiller. Thousand Oaks, Calif.: Sage, 1999.

Berman, Marshall. *All That Is Solid Melts into Air: The Experience of Modernity.* New York: Penguin Books, 1988.

Betances, Emelio. *State and Society in the Dominican Republic,* Latin American Perspectives Series, no. 15. Boulder, Colo.: Westview Press, 1995.

Bettelheim, Judith. "Caribbean Espiritismo (Spiritist) Altars: The Indian and the Congo." *Art Bulletin* 87 (June 2005): 312–30.

——. "Palo Monte Mayombe and Its Influence on Cuban Contemporary Art." *African Arts* 34 (summer 2001): 36–49, 95–96.

Bhabha, Homi. *The Location of Culture.* New York: Routledge, 1994.

Blanchot, Maurice. "Everyday Speech." *Yale French Studies,* no. 73 (1987): 12–20.

Blau, Peter M. *Exchange and Power in Social Life.* New Brunswick, N.J.: Transaction Publishers, 1996.

Blier, Suzanne Preston. *African Vodun: Art, Psychology and Power.* Chicago: University of Chicago Press, 1995.

——. "Vodun: West African Roots of Vodou." In *Sacred Arts of Haitian Vodou,* edited by Donald J. Cosentino, 61–87. Los Angeles: Fowler Museum of Cultural History, 1995.

Blok, Anton. *Honour and Violence.* Cambridge, England: Polity, 2001.

——. *The Mafia of a Sicilian Village, 1860–1960.* London: William Clowes, 1974.

Boddy, Janice. *Wombs and Alien Spirits: Women, Men and the Zar Cult in Northern Sudan.* Madison: University of Wisconsin Press, 1989.

Bonnelly, Juan Ulises García. *Las obras públicas en la era de Trujillo.* 2 vols. Ciudad Trujillo: Impresora Dominicana, 1955.

Borges, Dain. "Machiavellian, Rabelaisian, Bureaucratic?" *Public Culture* 5, no. 1 (1992): 109–12.

Bornia, O. Herrera. *Construcción de viviendas en la República Dominicana.* Ciudad Trujillo: Editora del Caribe, 1958.

Bourdieu, Pierre. "The Biographical Illusion." *Working Papers and Proceedings of the Center for Psychosocial Studies* 14, no. 4 (1987).

——. *Distinction: A Social Critique of the Judgement of Taste.* Translated by Richard Nice. Cambridge: Harvard University Press, 1984.

——. "The Forms of Capital." In *Handbook of Theory and Research for the Sociology of Education,* edited by John G. Richardson, 241–58. New York: Greenwood, 1986.

——. *In Other Words: Essays Towards a Reflexive Sociology,* 123–139. London: Basil Blackwell, 1990.

——. *Language and Symbolic Power.* Edited by John B. Thompson. Translated by Gino Raymond and Matthew Adamson. Cambridge: Harvard University Press, 1991.

——. *Outline of a Theory of Practice.* New York: Cambridge University Press, 1977.

Bourdieu, Pierre, and Monique de Saint Martin. *The State Nobility: Elite Schools in the Field of Power.* Translated by Lauretta C. Clough. Stanford: Stanford University Press, 1989.

Bourgois, Philippe. *In Search of Respect: Selling Crack in El Barrio*. New York: Cambridge University Press, 1996.

Brain, Robert. "Child Witches." In *Witchcraft Confessions and Accusations*, edited by Mary Douglas, 161–82. London: Tavistock, 1970.

Brewer, John. "This, That and the Other: Public, Social and Private in the Seventeenth and Eighteenth Centuries." In *Shifting the Boundaries: Transformation of the Languages of Public and Private in the Eighteenth Century*, edited by Dario Castigione and Lesley Sharpe, 1–21. Exeter: University of Exeter Press, 1995.

Brodwin, Paul. *Medicine and Morality in Haiti: The Contest for Healing Power*. New York: Cambridge University Press, 1996.

Brown, David H. *Santería Enthroned: Art, Ritual, and Innovation in an Afro-Cuban Religion*. Chicago: University of Chicago Press, 2003.

Brown, Diane. *Umbanda: Religion and Politics in Urban Brazil*. Studies in Cultural Anthropology no. 7. Ann Arbor, Mich.: UMI Research Press, 1986.

Brown, Karen McCarthy. *Mama Lola: A Vodou Priestess in Brooklyn*. Berkeley: University of California Press, 1991.

——. "Serving the Spirits: The Ritual Economy of Haitian Vodou." In *Sacred Arts of Haitian Vodou*, edited by Donald J. Cosentino, 205–25. Los Angeles: Fowler Museum of Cultural History, 1995.

——. "Systematic Remembering, Systematic Forgetting: Ogou in Haiti." In *Africa's Ogou: Old World and New*, edited by Sandra T. Barnes, 65–89. Bloomington: Indiana University Press, 1989.

Brown, Peter. *The Cult of the Saints: Its Rise and Function in Latin Christianity*. Chicago: University of Chicago Press, 1981.

——. "Sorcery, Demons and the Rise of Christianity from Late Antiquity into the Middle Ages. In *Witchcraft Confessions and Accusations*, edited by Mary Douglas, 17–56. London: Tavistock, 1970.

Bustamante, Gregorio R. [pseud.] *Una satrapía en el Caribe: Sus curas y sus guardias. Historia puntual de la mala vida del despota Rafael Leonidas Trujillo*, Santo Domingo: Central del Libro, n.d.

Bynum, Caroline Walker. *Fragmentation and Redemption: Essays in Gender and the Human Body in Medieval Religion*. New York: Zone Books, 1992.

——. *Metamorphosis and Identity*. New York: Zone Books, 2001.

Calder, Bruce. *The Impact of Intervention: The Dominican Republic during the U.S. Occupation of 1916–1924*. Austin: University of Texas Press, 1984.

Campillo-Pérez, Julio G. *Historia electoral dominicana, 1848–1986*. Santo Domingo: Editora Corripio, 1986.

——. "Trujillo y su parentela de origen haitiano." *Clio: Organo de la Academia Dominicana de la Historia*, no. 157 (1997): 81–86.

Candelario, Ginetta E. B. "On Whiteness and Other Absurdities: Preliminary Thoughts on Dominican Racial Identity in the United States." In *La República*

Dominicana en el umbral del siglo XXI: Cultura, política y cambio social, 89–112. Santo Domingo: PUCMM, 1999.

Canetti, Elias. *Crowds and Power*. New York: Farrar, Straus and Giroux, 1962.

Cannadine, David. "Introduction: Divine Rites of Kings." In *Rituals of Royalty: Power and Ceremonial in Traditional Societies*, edited by David Cannadine and Simon Price, 1–19. Cambridge University Press, 1987.

Capacity of the Dominican Republic to Absorb Refugees. Ciudad Trujillo: Editora Montalvo, 1945.

Carrithers, Michael, Steven Collins, and Steven Lukes. *The Category of the Person: Anthropology, Philosophy, History*. New York: Cambridge University Press, 1985.

Cassá, Roberto. "Algunas claves del Olivorismo." *Vetas: de la cultura dominicana y el Caribe*, 3, no. 19 (1996): 3–15.

———. *Capitalismo y dictadura*. Santo Domingo: Editora de la Universidad Autónoma de Santo Domingo, 1982.

———. *História social y económica de la república*. Santo Domingo: Editora Alfa y Omega, 1978.

———. *Los doce años: Contrarevolución y desarrollismo*. Santo Domingo: Alfa y Omega, 1986.

———. *Minerva Mirabal: La revolucionaria*. Santo Domingo: Tobogan, 2000.

———. "Problemas del culto olivorista." In *La ruta hacia Liborio: Mesianismo en el sur profundo dominicano*, edited by Martha Ellen Davis, 3–44. Santo Domingo: Secretaria de Estado de Cultura and UNESCO, Editorial Manatí, 2004.

Cassia, Paul Sant. "Banditry, Myth and Terror in Cyprus and Other Mediterranean Societies." *Comparative Studies in Society and History* 35, no. 4 (1993): 773–95.

Castillo, José del. "The Formation of the Dominican Sugar Industry." In *Between Slavery and Free Labor: The Spanish-Speaking Caribbean in the Nineteenth Century*, edited by Stanley Engerman, Manuel Moreno Fraginals, and Frank Moya Pons, 215–34. Baltimore: Johns Hopkins University Press, 1985.

Castillo, José del, and Walter Cordero. "La economía dominicana durante el primer cuarto del siglo XX." In *La sociedad dominicana durante la segunda república, 1865–1924*, edited by Tirso Mejía Ricart G., 87–125. Santo Domingo: Editora de la Universidad Autónoma de Santo Domingo, 1982.

Chasteen, John Charles. *Heroes on Horseback: A Life and Times of the Last Gaucho Caudillos*. Albuquerque: University of New Mexico Press, 1995.

———. "Making Sense of Caudillos and 'Revolutions.'" In *Problems in Modern Latin American History: A Reader*, edited by John Charles Chasteen and Joseph S. Tulchin, 37–41. Wilmington, Del.: Scholarly Resources, 1994.

Chauncey, George. *Gay New York: Gender, Culture and the Making of the Gay Male World, 1890–1940*. New York: Basic Books, 1994.

Chehabi, H. E., and Juan J. Linz, eds. *Sultanistic Regimes*. Baltimore: Johns Hopkins University Press, 1988.

———. "A Theory of Sultanism: A Type of Nondemocratic Rule." In *Sultanistic Regimes,* edited by Chehabi and Linz, 3–25. Baltimore: Johns Hopkins University Press, 1998.

Clase, Pablo, hijo, *Porfirio Rubirosa: El primer playboy del mundo.* Santo Domingo: Editora Taller, 1986.

Clausner, Marlin David. *Rural Santo Domingo. Settled, Unsettled and Resettled.* Philadelphia: Temple University Press, 1973.

Cohn, Bernard S. *An Anthropologist among the Historians and Other Essays.* Delhi: Oxford University Press, 1987.

Cole, Hubert. *Christophe: King of Haiti.* London: Eyre and Spottiswoode, 1967.

Collado, Lipe. *Anécdotas y crueldades de Trujillo.* Santo Domingo: Editora Collado, 2002.

———. *El Foro Público en la era de Trujillo: De cómo el chisme fue elevado a la categoría de asunto de estado.* Santo Domingo: Editora Collado, 2000.

———. *La impresionante vida de un seductor: Porfirio Rubirosa, de cómo un Dominicano se convirtió en chulo del jetset internacional.* Santo Domingo: Editora Collado, 2001.

———. *El tíguere dominicano.* Santo Domingo: El Mundo, 1992.

Comarazamy, Francisco. "Ponderaciones sobre el ensayo." In Lipe Collado, *El Tíguere dominicano,* 177–83. Santo Domingo: Editora Collado, 2004.

Comaroff, Jean. "Bodily Reform as Historical Practice: The Semantics of Resistance in Modern South Africa." *International Journal of Psychiatry* 20 (1985): 541–67.

———. *Body of Power, Spirit of Resistance: The Culture and History of a South African People.* Chicago: University of Chicago Press, 1985.

Comaroff, Jean, and John L. Comaroff. *Ethnography and the Historical Imagination.* Boulder, Colo.: Westview Press, 1992.

———. "Goodly Beasts, Beastly Goods: Cattle and Commodities in a South African Context." *American Ethnologist,* 17, no. 2 (1990): 195–216.

———. "The Madman and the Migrant: Work and Labor in the Historical Consciousness of a South African People." *American Ethnologist* 14, no. 2 (1987): 191–208.

———. "Occult Economies and the Violence of Abstraction: Notes from the South African Postcolony." *American Ethnologist* 26, no. 2 (1999): 279–303.

———. "Transparent Fictions; or, The Conspiracies of a Liberal Imagination: An Afterword." In *Transparency and Conspiracy: Ethnographies of Suspicion in the New World Order,* edited by Harry G. West and Todd Sanders, 287–300. Durham, N.C.: Duke University Press, 2003.

Comaroff, John. "Talking Politics: Oratory and Authority in a Tswana Chiefdom." In *Political Language and Oratory in Traditional Society,* edited by Maurice Bloch. New York: Academic Press, 1975.

Congreso Internacional sobre La Picaresca. *La Picaresca: Orígenes, textos y estructuras.* Madrid: Fundación Universitaria Española, 1979.

Connelly, John. "The Uses of *Volksgemeinschaft:* Letters to the NSDAP Kreisleitung Eisenach, 1939–1940." *Journal of Modern History* 68, no. 4 (1996): 899–930.

Conniff, Michael L. "Urban Populism in Twentieth-Century Peru." In *Problems in Modern Latin American History: A Reader,* edited by John Charles Chasteen and Joseph S. Tulchin, 97–102. Wilmington, Del.: Scholarly Resources, 1994.

Cooper, Page. *Sambumbia: A Discovery of the Dominican Republic, the Modern Hispañiola.* New York: Caribbean Library, 1947.

Corbin, Alain. *The Foul and the Fragrant: Odor and the French Social Imagination.* Cambridge: Harvard University Press, 1986.

Cordero, Walter J. and Neici M. Zeller, "El desfile trujillista: Despotismo y complicidad." In *Homenaje a Emilio Cordero Michel,* 113–74. Santo Domingo: Collección Academia Dominicana de la Historia, 2004.

Cordero Michel, José. *Análisis de la Era de Trujillo: Informe sobre la República Dominicana.* Santo Domingo: Publicaciones de la Universidad Autónoma de Santo Domingo, 1970.

Coronil, Fernando. *The Magical State: Nature, Money and Modernity in Venezuela.* Chicago: University of Chicago Press, 1997.

Coronil, Fernando, and Julie Skurski. "Dismembering and Remembering the Nation: The Semantics of Political Violence in Venezuela." *Comparative Studies in Society and History* 33, no. 2 (April 1991): 288–337.

Corradi, Juan E., et al. "Introduction. Fear: A Cultural and Political Construct." In *Fear at the Edge: State Terror and Resistance in Latin America,* edited by Juan E. Corradi et al. Berkeley: University of California Press, 1994.

Corrigan, Philip, and Derek Sayre. *The Great Arch: English State Formation as Cultural Revolution.* Cambridge, Mass.: Blackwell, 1985.

Cosentino, Donald J. "Envoi: The Gedes and Bawon Samdi." In *Sacred Arts of Haitian Vodou,* edited by Donald J. Cosentino, 399–415. Los Angeles: Fowler Museum of Cultural History, 1995.

——. "Exit Laughing: Death and Laughter in Los Angeles and Port-au-Prince." In *Of Corpse: Death and Humor in Folklore and Popular Culture,* edited by Peter Narváez, 239–60. Logan, Utah: Utah State University Press, 2002.

Craig, John Houston. *Black Bagdad.* New York: Minton, Balch and Compnay, 1933.

Crain, Mary. "Poetics and Politics in the Ecuadorean Andes: Women's Narratives of Death and Devil Possession." *American Ethnologist* 18, no. 1 (1991): 67–89.

Crassweller, Robert D. *Trujillo: The Life and Times of a Caribbean Dictator.* New York: Macmillan, 1966.

Cruz-Malavé, Arnaldo. "What a Tangled Web! Masculinity, Abjection, and the Foundations of Puerto Rican Literature in the United States." *Differences: A Journal of Feminist Cultural Studies,* no. 8 (1996): 132–51.

Cuello, José Israel, ed. *Documentos del conflicto dominicano-haitiano de 1937.* Santo Domingo: Ed. Taller, 1985.

D'Alaux, Gustave. *L'Empereur Soulouque et son empire*. Port-au-Prince: Les Editions Fardin, 1988 [1856].

DaMatta, Roberto. *Carnivals, Rogues and Heroes: An Interpretation of the Brazilian Dilemma*. Translated by John Drury. Notre Dame, Ind.: University of Notre Dame Press, 1991.

———. "The Ethic of Umbanda and the Spirit of Messianism: Reflections on the Brazilian Model." In *Authoritarian Capitalism: Brazil's Contemporary Economic and Political Development*, edited by Thomas C. Bruneau and Philippe Faucher. Boulder, Colo.: Westview Press, 1981.

Damirón, Rafael. *Cronicones de antaño*. Ciudad Trujillo: Impresora Dominicana, 1949.

———. *De soslayo*. Santo Domingo: Ed. Alfa y Omega, 1983 [1948].

Daniel, E. Valentine. *Charred Lullabies: Chapters in an Anthropology of Violence*. Princeton: Princeton University Press, 1996.

Danticat, Edwidge. *The Dew Breaker*. New York: Alfred A. Knopf, 2004.

Darnton, Robert. *The Great Cat Massacre and Other Episodes in French Cultural History*. New York: Vintage, 1985.

Davidoff, Leonore, and Catherine Hall. *Family Fortunes: Men and Women of the English Middle Class, 1780–1850*. Chicago: University of Chicago Press, 1987.

Davis, Martha Ellen. "La devoción al Santo Cristo de los milagros de Bayaguana." *El Cristo de Bayaguana: Exposición fotográfica de Camilo Yaryura*. Santo Domingo: Museo del Hombre Dominicano, 1981.

———. *La otra ciencia: El vodú como religión y medicina populares*. Santo Domingo: Editora Universitaria-UASD, 1987.

———, ed. *La ruta hacia Liborio: Mesianismo en el sur profundo dominicano*. Santo Domingo: Secretaría de Estado de Cultura; UNESCO, Editorial Manatí, 2004.

Davis, Natalie Zemon. *Fiction in the Archives: Pardon Tales and Their Tellers in Sixteenth Century France*. Stanford: Stanford University Press, 1987.

Davis, Wade. *The Serpent and the Rainbow*. New York: Warner Books, 1985.

de Certeau, Michel de. *The Practice of Everyday Life*. Translated by Steven Rendell. Berkeley: University of California Press, 1984.

Deford, Frank. *There She Is: The Life and Times of Miss America*. New York: Viking, 1971.

de Grazia, Victoria. *The Culture of Consent: The Mass Organization of Leisure*. Cambridge: Cambridge University Press, 1981.

———. *How Fascism Ruled Women*. Berkeley: University of California Press, 1992.

———. Introduction. In *The Sex of Things: Gender and Consumption in Historical Perspective*, edited by Victoria de Grazia, 1–24. Berkeley: University of California Press, 1996.

de la Fuente, Alejandro. "Race and Inequality in Cuba, 1899–1981." *Journal of Contemporary History* 30 (1995): 131–68.

de la Fuente, Ariel. *Children of Facundo: Caudillo and Gaucho Insurgency During the Argentine State-Formation Process (La Rioja, 1853–1870)*. Durham, N.C.: Duke University Press, 2000.

de la Torre, Carlos. *Populist Seduction in Latin America: The Ecuadorian Experience*, Ohio University Center for International Studies, Latin America Series no. 32. Athens, Ohio: Ohio University Press, 2000.

de Moya, E. Antonio. "Power Games and Totalitarian Masculinity in the Dominican Republic." In *Caribbean Masculinities: Working Papers*, edited by Rafael L. Ramírez, Víctor I. García-Toro, and Ineke Cunningham, 105–46. San Juan, Puerto Rico: HIV/AIDS Research and Education Center, University of Puerto Rico, 2002.

de Pauw, Cornelius. *Recherches scientifiques sur les Américains*. Berlin, 1777.

Deive, Carlos Esteban. *La esclavitud del negro, 1492–1844*. 2 vols. Santo Domingo: Musco del Hombre Dominicano, 1980.

——. "Fukú: Del negro boruco a Evtushenko." *Fukú*, by Yevgeni Yevtushenko. Santo Domingo: Fundación Cultural Dominicana, 1988.

——. "El Olivorismo: Estudio de un movimento mesiánico." *Aula* 2, no. 4 (1973): 30–52.

——. *Vodú y magia en Santo Domingo*. Santo Domingo: Fundación Cultural Dominicana, 1988.

Derby, Lauren. "Gringo Chickens with Worms: Food and Nationalism in the Dominican Republic." In *Close Encounters of Empire: Writing the Cultural History of U.S.-Latin American Relations*, edited by Gilbert M. Joseph, Catherine C. LeGrand, and Ricardo D. Salvatore, 451–93. Durham, N.C.: Duke University Press, 1998.

——. "Haitians, Magic and Money: *Raza* and Society in the Haitian-Dominican Borderlands, 1900 to 1937." *Comparative Studies in Society and History* 36, no. 3 (1994): 487–526.

——. "National Identity and the Idea of Value in the Dominican Republic." In *Blacks, Coloreds and National Identity in Nineteenth-Century Latin America*, edited by Nancy Naro, 5–37. London: Institute of Latin American Studies, 2003.

Derby, Robin L. H., and Richard Turits. "Historias de terror y los terrores de la historia: La masacre haitiana de 1937 en la República Dominicana." *Estudios Sociales* 26, no. 92 (1993): 65–76.

Deren, Maya. *Divine Horsemen: The Living Gods of Haiti*. New York: McPherson, 1953.

Deschamps, Enrique. *La República Dominicana: Directorio y guía general*. Barcelona: Litografía y encuadernación de la Vda. de J. Cunill, 1906.

Díaz, María Elena. *The Virgin, The King, and the Royal Slaves of El Cobre: Negotiating Freedom in Colonial Cuba*. Stanford: Stanford University Press, 2000.

Díaz Quiñones, Arcadio. *El arte de bregar: Ensayos*. San Juan: Callejón, 2000.

Diederich, Bernard. *Trujillo: The Death of the Goat.* Boston: Little, Brown, 1978.

Dix, Robert H. "Populism: Authoritarian and Democratic." *Latin American Research Review* 20, no. 2 (1985): 29–52.

Domínguez, Jorge I. *Cuba: Order and Revolution.* Cambridge: Belknap Press of Harvard University Press, 1978.

Domínguez, Virginia R. *White by Definition: Social Classification in Creole Louisiana.* New Brunswick, N.J.: Rutgers University Press, 1986.

Douglas, Mary. "Introduction: Thirty Years after *Witchcraft, Oracles and Magic.*" In *Witchcraft Confessions and Accusations,* edited by Mary Douglas, xvii–xviii. London: Tavistock, 1970.

———. *Purity and Danger: An Analysis of the Concepts of Pollution and Taboo.* New York: ARK Paperbacks, 1988.

Douglas, Mary, and Baron Isherwood. *The World of Goods.* New York: Basic Books, 1979.

Duany, Jorge. "Ethnicity in the Spanish Caribbean: Notes on the Consolidation of Creole Identity in Cuba and Puerto Rico, 1762–1868." *Ethnic Groups* 6 (1985): 106.

Dubois, Laurent. *Avengers of the New World: The Story of the Haitian Revolution.* Cambridge: Belknap Press of Harvard University Press, 2004.

Dumont, Louis. *Homo Hierarchicus: The Caste System and Its Implications.* Chicago: University of Chicago Press, 1980.

Edelman, Marc. "Landlords and the Devil: Class, Ethnic, and Gender Dimensions of Central American Peasant Narratives." *Cultural Anthropology* 9, no. 1 (1994): 58–93.

Edwards, Bryan. *The History, Civil and Commercial, of the British Colonies in the West Indies.* Vol. 3. London: Printed for John Stockdale, 1807.

Eisenstadt, S. N., and L. Roniger. *Patrons, Clients and Friends: Interpersonal Relations and the Structure of Trust in Society.* New York: Cambridge University Press, 1984.

Elias, Norbert. *The Court Society.* Translated by Edmund Jephcott. London: Basil Blackwell, 1983.

———. *The History of Manners: The Civilizing Process.* Translated by Edmund Jephcott. Vol. 1. New York: Pantheon Books, 1978 [1939].

Espaillat, Arturo R. *Trujillo: The Last Caesar.* Chicago: Henry Regnery, 1963.

Espín, Orlando. "Hacia una 'teología' de Palma Sola." *Estudios Sociales* 13, no. 50 (1980): 53–68.

Espinal, Rosario. *Autoritarismo y democracia en la política dominicana.* Costa Rica: Ediciones CAPEL, 1987.

Evans, Peter. "Predatory, Developmental and other Apparatuses: A Comparative Political Economy Perspective on the Third World State." *Sociological Forum* 4, no. 4 (1989): 561–87.

Fabian, Johannes. *Power and Performance: Ethnographic Explorations Through*

Proverbial Wisdom and Theater in Shaba, Zaire. Madison: University of Wisconsin Press, 1990.

———. *Time and the Other: How Anthropology Makes Its Object.* New York: Columbia University Press, 1983.

Fanon, Frantz. *Black Skin, White Masks.* New York: Grove Press, 1967.

Feierman, Steven. *Peasant Intellectuals: Anthropology and History in Tanzania.* Madison: University of Wisconsin Press, 1990.

Fein, Seth. "Everyday Forms of Transnational Collaboration: U.S. Film Propaganda in Cold War Mexico." In *Close Encounters of Empire: Writing the Cultural History of U.S.-Latin American Relations,* edited by Gilbert M. Joseph, Catherine C. LeGrand, and Ricardo D. Salvatore, 400–450. Durham, N.C.: Duke University Press, 1998.

Feldman, Allen. *Formations of Violence: The Narrative of the Body and Political Terror in Northern Ireland.* Chicago: University of Chicago Press, 1991.

Fernandez, Raul A. *From Afro-Cuban Rhythms to Latin Jazz.* Berkeley: University of California Press, 2006.

Ferrán, Fernándo. "La familia nuclear de la subcultura de la pobreza dominicana: Notas introductorias." *Estudios Sociales* 27, no. 3 (1974): 137–85.

Ferrer, Ada. *Insurgent Cuba: Race, Nation and Revolution, 1868–1898.* Chapel Hill: University of North Carolina Press, 1999.

Ferreras, Ramón Alberto. *Cuando la era era era.* Vols. 1–4. Santo Domingo: Editorial del Nordeste, 1991.

———. *Historia del feminismo en la República Dominicana: Su origen y proyección social.* Santo Domingo: Editora Cosmos, 1976.

———. *Trujillo y sus mujeres.* Santo Domingo: Editorial de Nordeste, 1990.

Fick, Caroline E. *The Making of Haiti: The Revolution of Saint Domingue from Below.* Knoxville: University of Tennessee Press, 1990.

Findlay, Eileen. *Imposing Decency: The Politics of Sexuality and Race in Puerto Rico, 1870–1920.* Durham, N.C.: Duke University Press, 1999.

Fischlin, Daniel. " 'Counterfeiting God': James VI (I) and the Politics of Daemonologue (1597)." *The Journal of Narrative Technique* 26, no. 1 (1996): 1–30.

Fitzpatrick, Sheila. *Everyday Stalinism: Ordinary Life in Extraordinary Times: Soviet Russia in the 1930s.* Oxford: Oxford University Press, 1999.

———. "Lives under Fire: Autobiographical Narratives and Their Challenges in Stalin's Russia." In *De Russie et d'ailleurs: Feux croisés sur l'histoire,* edited by Martine Godet, 225–41. Paris: Institut d'Études Slaves, 1995.

———. "Signals From Below: Soviet Letters of Denunciation of the 1930s." *Journal of Modern History* 68, no. 4 (1996): 831–66.

———, ed. *Stalinism: New Directions.* New York: Routledge, 2000.

———. "Supplicants and Citizens: Public Letter-Writing in Soviet Russia in the 1930s." *Slavic Review* 55, no. 1 (1996): 106–24.

Fitzpatrick, Sheila, and Robert Gellately, eds. "Introduction to the Practices of Denunciation in Modern European History, 1789–1989." Special issue. *The Journal of Modern History* 68, no. 4 (1996): 747–67.

Fortunato, René. *El Poder del Jefe I.* Santo Domingo: Videocine Palau, 1991.

———. *El Poder del Jefe III.* Santo Domingo: Videocine Palau, 1996.

Foucault, Michel. *Discipline and Punish: The Birth of the Prison.* Translated by Alan Sheridan. New York: Vintage, 1979.

———. "Governmentality." In *The Foucault Effect: Studies in Governmentality,* edited by Graham Burchell, Colin Gordon, and Peter Miller. Chicago: University of Chicago Press, 1991.

Franck, Harry A. *Roaming Through the West Indies.* New York: Century Company, 1921.

Frank, Gerold. *Zsa Zsa Gabor: My Story.* New York: World Publishing, 1960.

Franks, Julie. "The *Gavilleros* of the East: Social Banditry as Political Practice in the Dominican Sugar-Growing Region, 1900–1924." *Journal of Historical Sociology* 8, no. 2 (1995): 158–81.

———. "Property Rights and the Commercialization of Land in the Dominican Sugar Zone." *Latin American Perspectives* 26, no. 1 (1999): 106–28.

Freud, Sigmund. *Sexuality and the Psychology of Love.* Edited by Philip Pieff. New York: Touchstone Books, 1992 [1922].

Freyre, Gilberto. *The Masters and the Slaves: A Study in the Development of Brazilian Civilization.* Berkeley: University of California Press, 1986.

Friedman, Jonathan. "Consuming Desires: Strategies of Selfhood and Appropriation." *Cultural Anthropology* 6, no. 2 (May, 1991): 154–163.

———. "Narcissism, Roots and Postmodernity: The Constitution of Selfhood in the Global Crisis." In *Modernity and Identity,* edited by Scott Lash and Jonathan Friedman, 331–66. Cambridge, Mass.: Basil Blackwell, 1982.

Galíndez, Jesús de. *La Era de Trujillo.* Santo Domingo: Editora Taller, 1984.

———. *The Era of Trujillo: Dominican Dictator.* Tucson: University of Arizona Press, 1973.

Gallop, Jane. "The Father's Seduction." In *The Daughter's Seduction: Feminism and Psychoanalysis.* Ithaca: Cornell University Press, 1982.

García, Juan Manuel. *La masacre de Palma Sola: Partidos, lucha política y el asesinato del general, 1961–1963.* Santo Domingo: Editora Alfa y Omega, 1986.

García Godoy, Federico. *El Derrumbe.* Santo Domingo: Editora del Caribe, 1975 [1916].

García Márquez, Gabriel. *The Autumn of the Patriarch.* Translated by Gregory Rabassa. New York: Harper and Row, 1976.

Garrido Puello, E. O. *Olivorio: Ensayo histórico: nuevas narraciones.* Santo Domingo: Librería Dominicana, 1963.

Garrido Puello, Víctor. "Común de San Juan: datos acerca de la situación." In *Lengua y folklore de Santo Domingo,* edited by Emilio Rodríguez Demorizi. Santiago: Universidad Católica Madre y Maestra, 1975.

———. *En la ruta de mi vida, 1886–1966*. Santo Domingo: Impresora "Arte y Cine," 1970.

———. *Espigas históricas*. Santo Domingo: Impresora "Arte y Cine," 1971.

Gascón, Margarita. "The Military of Santo Domingo, 1720–1764." *Hispanic American Historical Review* 73, no. 3 (1993): 431–52.

Geertz, Clifford. "Centers, Kings, and Charisma: Reflections on the Symbolics of Power." In *Culture and Its Creators: Essays in Honor of Edward Shils*, edited by Joseph Ben-David and Terry Nichols Clark, 150–71. Chicago: University of Chicago Press, 1977.

———. *Negara: The Theatre State in Nineteenth-Century Bali*. Princeton: Princeton University Press, 1980.

Gerth, H. H., and C. Wright Mills, eds. *From Max Weber: Essays in Sociology*. New York: Oxford University Press, 1946.

Geschiere, Peter. *The Modernity of Witchcraft: Politics and the Occult in Postcolonial Africa*. Charlottesville: University of Virginia Press, 1997.

Gilman, Sander L.. "Plague in Germany, 1939/1989: Cultural Images of Race, Space and Disease." In *Nationalisms and Sexualities*, edited by Andrew Parker, Mary Russo, Doris Sommer, and Patricia Yaeger. New York: Routledge, 1992.

Gilroy, Paul. *The Black Atlantic: Modernity and Double Consciousness*. Cambridge: Harvard University Press, 1993.

Goffman, Erving. *Interaction Ritual: Essays on Face-to-Face Behavior*. New York: Pantheon Books, 1967.

———. *The Presentation of Self in Everyday Life*. New York: Doubleday, 1959.

———. *Relations in Public*. New York: Harper Torchbooks, 1971.

———. *Stigma: Notes on the Management of Spoiled Identity*. New York: Simon and Schuster, 1963.

Gómez, José Miguel. *Trujillo visto por un psiquiatra*. Santo Domingo: Editora Búho, 2003.

González, Raymundo. *Bonó, un intelectual de los pobres*. Santo Domingo: Centro de Estudios Sociales Padre Juna Montalvo SJ, 1994.

———. "El Comegente, una rebelión campesina al final del periodo colonial." In *Homenaje a Emilio Cordero Michel*, 175–234. Santo Domingo: Academia Dominicana de Historia, Colleción Estudios I, 2004.

———. "Ideologia del progreso y campesinado en el siglo XIX." *Ecos* 1, no. 2 (1993): 25–44.

———. Introducción. In *Política, identidad y pensamiento social en la República Dominicana (Siglos XI y XX)*, edited by Raymundo González et al. Santo Madrid: Ediciones Doce Calles, 1999.

———. "Notas sobre el pensamiento socio-político dominicano." *Estudios Sociales* 20, no. 67 (1987).

González, Raymundo, Roberto Cassá, Pedro L. San Miguel, and Michel Baud, eds. *Política, identidad y pensamiento social en la República Dominicana (Siglos XIX y XX)*. Madrid: Ediciones Doce Calles, 1999.

Gordon, Linda. *The Great Arizona Orphan Abduction*. Cambridge: Harvard University Press, 1999.

Graham, Gael. "Exercizing Control: Sports and Physical Education in American Protestant Mission Schools in China, 1880–1930." *Signs* 20, no. 1 (1994): 23–48.

Graham, Richard, ed. *The Idea of Race in Latin America, 1870–1940*. Austin: University of Texas Press, 1990.

Greenblatt, Stephen. *Learning to Curse: Essays in Early Modern Culture*. New York: Routledge, 1990.

Greenfield, Sidney M. "The Return of Dr. Fritz: Spiritist Healing and Patronage Networks in Urban, Industrial Brazil." *Social Science and Medicine* 24, no. 12 (1987): 1095–108.

Gregory, Steven. *The Devil Behind the Mirror: Globalization and Politics in the Dominican Republic*. Berkeley: University of California Press, 2007.

Guerrero Villalba, María Angustias. *Tras las huellas . . . La mujer dominicana en el mundo de trabajo, 1900–1950*. Santo Domingo: CIPAF, 1991.

Gutmann, Matthew C. *Changing Men and Masculinities in Latin America*. Durham, N.C.: Duke University Press, 2003.

Guy, Donna. " 'White Slavery,' Citizenship and Nationality in Argentina." In *Nationalisms and Sexualities*, edited by Andrew Parker et al., 201–17. New York: Routledge, 1992.

Habermas, Jürgen. "The Public Sphere." In *Rethinking Popular Culture: Contemporary Perspectives in Cultural Studies*, edited by Chandra and Michael Schudson Mukerji, 398–404. Berkeley: University of California Press, 1991.

Hall, Stuart. "Negotiating Caribbean Identities." *New Left Review* 209 (1995): 3–14.

——. "Race, Articulation and Societies Structured in Dominance." In *Sociological Theories: Race and Colonialism*, edited by UNESCO. Paris: UNESCO, 1980.

Haltunnen, Karen. *Confidence Men and Painted Women: A Study of Middle-Class Culture in America*. New Haven: Yale University Press, 1982.

Hamilton, Nora. *The Limits of State Autonomy: Post-Revolutionary Mexico*. Princeton, N.J.: Princeton University Press, 1982.

Handelman, Don. "The Idea of Bureaucratic Organization." *Social Analysis* 9 (Dec. 1981): 5–23.

Handler, Richard. "Is 'Identity' a Useful Cross-Cultural Concept?" In *Commemorations: The Politics of National Identity*, edited by John R. Gillis. Princeton: Princeton University Press, 1994.

Hansen, Miriam. "Pleasure, Ambivalence, Identification: Valentino and Female Spectatorship." *Cinema Journal* 25, no. 4 (1986): 6–32.

Hansen, Thomas Blom, and Finn Stepputat. "Introduction: On Empire and Sovereignty." In *Sovereign Bodies: Citizens, Migrants, and States in the Postcolonial World*, edited by Hansen and Stepputat, 1–38. Princeton: Princeton University Press, 2005.

———. "Introduction: States of Imagination." In *States of Imagination: Ethnographic Explorations of the Postcolonial State*, edited by Hansen and Stepputat, 1–40. Durham, N.C.: Duke University Press, 2001.

Hartlyn, Jonathan. *The Struggle For Democratic Politics in the Dominican Republic.* Chapel Hill: University of North Carolina Press, 1998.

———. "The Trujillo Regime in the Dominican Republic." In *Sultanistic Regimes,* edited by H. E. Chehabi and Juan J. Linz, 85–112. Baltimore: Johns Hopkins University Press, 1998.

Hazard, Samuel. *Santo Domingo, Past and Present; with a Glance at Hayti.* Santo Domingo: Editora de Santo Domingo, Sociedad Dominicana de Bibliofilos, Colección Cultura Dominicana, 1974 [1873].

Hebdige, Dick. *Subculture: The Meaning of Style.* New York: Routledge, 1988.

Heinl, Robert Debs, and Nancy Gordon Heinl. *Written in Blood: The Story of the Haitian People, 1492–1971.* Boston: Houghton Mifflin, 1978.

Helms, Mary W. *Ulysses' Sail: An Ethnographic Odyssey of Power, Knowledge, and Geographical Distance.* Princeton: Princeton University Press, 1988.

Henríquez Castillo, Luis. *El hombre alucinado.* Ciudad Trujillo: Editora Listín Diario, 1938.

Herrera, Julio González. *Trementina, clerén y bongo.* Santo Domingo: Taller, 1985 [1943].

Hertz, Neil. *The End of the Line: Essays on Psychoanalysis and the Sublime.* New York: Columbia University Press, 1985.

Herzfeld, Michael. *Cultural Intimacy: Social Poetics in the Nation-State.* Routledge: New York: 1997.

———. *The Social Production of Indifference: Exploring the Symbolic Roots of Western Bureaucracy.* Chicago: University of Chicago Press, 1992.

Hess, David. "The Many Rooms of Spiritism in Brazil." *Luso-Brazilian Review* 24, no. 2 (1987): 15–34.

Hess, Henner. *Mafia and Mafiosi: The Structure of Power.* Lexington, Mass.: Lexington Books, 1973.

Heyman, Josiah M. *States and Illegal Practices.* New York: Berg, 1999.

Heymann, David C. *Poor Little Rich Girl: The Life and Legend of Barbara Hutton.* New York: Pocket Books, 1984.

Hobsbawm, Eric, and Terence Ranger, eds. *The Invention of Tradition.* New York: Cambridge University Press, 1983.

Hodges, Donald C. *Intellectual Foundations of the Nicaraguan Revolution.* Austin: University of Texas Press, 1986.

Hoetink, Harry. *Caribbean Race Relations: A Study of Two Variants.* London: Oxford University Press, 1967.

———. *The Dominican People, 1850–1900. Notes for a Historical Sociology.* Translated by Stephen K. Ault. Baltimore: Johns Hopkins University Press, 1982.

———. "The Dominican Republic in the Nineteenth Century: Some Notes on Stratification, Immigration, and Race." In *Race and Class in Latin America*, edited by Magnus Mörner, 96–121. New York: Columbia University Press, 1970.

———. "The Dominican Republic in the Twentieth Century: Notes on Mobility and Stratification." *New West Indian Guide* 74, nos. 3 and 4 (2000): 209–33.

Holland, Norman S. "Fashioning Cuba." In *Nationalisms and Sexualities*, edited by Andrew Parker et al., 147–56. New York: Routledge, 1992.

Holston, James. "Alternative Modernities: Statecraft and Religious Imagination in the Valley of the Dawn." *American Ethnologist* 26, no. 3 (1999): 605–31.

———. *The Modernist City: An Anthropological Critique of Brazília*. Chicago: University of Chicago Press, 1989.

Holt, Thomas. "Marking: Race, Race-Making, and the Writing of History." *American Historical Review* 100, no. 1 (1995): 1–20.

Hostos, Eugenio María de. *Obras completas: Cuna de América*. San Juan: Instituto de Cultura Puertorriqueña, 1969.

Houlberg, Marilyn. "Magique Marasa: The Ritual Cosmos of Twins and Other Sacred Children." In *Sacred Arts of Haitian Vodou*, edited by Donald J. Cosentino, 267–86. Los Angeles: Fowler Museum of Cultural History, 1995.

Humphrey, Caroline. "Stalin and the Blue Elephant: Paranoia and Complicity in Post-Communist Metahistories." In *Transparency and Conspiracy: Ethnographies of Suspicion in the New World Order*, edited by Harry G. West and Todd Sanders, 175–203. Durham, N.C.: Duke University Press, 2003.

Hunt, Lynn, *The Family Romance of the French Revolution*. Berkeley: University of California Press, 1992.

———. Introduction. In *Eroticism and the Body Politic*, edited by Lynn Hunt. Baltimore: Johns Hopkins University Press, 1991.

———. "The Many Bodies of Marie Antoinette: Political Pornography and the Problem of the Feminine in the French Revolution." In *Eroticism and the Body Politic*, edited by Lynn Hunt. Baltimore: Johns Hopkins University Press, 1991.

———, ed. *The New Cultural History*. Berkeley: University of California Press, 1989.

———. *Politics, Culture and Class in the French Revolution*. Berkeley: University of California Press, 1984.

Hürbon, Laennec. "New Religious Movements in the Caribbean." In *New Religious Movements and Rapid Social Change*, edited by James A. Beckford, 146–76. London: Sage, 1986.

Hyde, Lewis. *Trickster Makes This World: Mischief, Myth and Art*. New York: Farrar, Straus and Giroux, 1998.

Incháustegui, Arístides, and Blanca Delgado Malagón. "En el cincuentenario de La Voz Dominicana." *Isla Abierta* 11, no. 572 (1992): 1–20.

Incháustegui Cabral, Héctor. *El pozo muerto*. Santiago: Universidad Católica Madre y Maestra, 1980.

Inman, Samuel Guy. *Through Santo Domingo and Haiti: A Cruise with the Marines*. New York: Committee on Co-operation in Latin America, 1919.

———. "A través de Santo Domingo y Haití" (Spanish translation). In *Los primeros turistas en Santo Domingo*, edited by Bernardo Vega, 155–84. Santo Domingo: Fundación Cultural Dominicana, 1991.

Inoa, Orlando. *Azúcar: Árabes, cocolos y haitianos*. Santo Domingo: Cole and FLACSO, 1999.

———. *Estado y campesinos al início de la Era de Trujillo*. Santo Domingo: Libreria la Trinitaria, 1994.

Irvine, Judith T. "Insult and Responsibility: Verbal Abuse in a Wolof Village." In *Responsibility and Evidence in Oral Discourse*, edited by Jane T. Hill and Judith T. Irvine. New York: Cambridge University Press, 1992.

Ivy, Marilyn. *Discourses of the Vanishing: Modernity, Phantasm, Japan*. Chicago: University of Chicago Press, 1995.

James, C. L. R. *Beyond a Boundary*. New York: Pantheon Books, 1983.

James, Daniel. *Resistance and Integration: Peronism and the Argentine Working Class, 1946–1976*. Cambridge: Cambridge University Press, 1988.

Javier García, Manuel de Jesús. *Mis 20 años en el Palacio Nacional junto a Trujillo y otros gobernantes dominicanos*. Vols. 1–2. Santo Domingo: Taller, 1986.

Jiménez, Ramón Emilio. *Al amor del bohío*. Santo Domingo: Virgilio Montalvo, 1927.

———. *Savia dominicana*. Santo Domingo: Publicaciones ONAP, 1981 [1946].

Johns, Michael. "The Antinomies of Ruling Class Culture: The Buenos Aires Elite, 1880–1910." *Journal of Historical Sociology* 6, no. 1 (1993): 74–101.

Johnson, Lyman L., ed. *Death, Dismemberment and Memory: Body Politics in Latin America*. Albuquerque: University of New Mexico Press, 2004.

Johnson, Lyman L., and Sonya Lipsett-Rivera. Introduction. In *The Faces of Honor: Sex, Shame and Violence in Colonial Latin America*, edited by Lyman L. Johnson and Sonya Lipsett-Rivera, 1–17. Albuquerque: University of New Mexico Press, 1998.

Johnson, Paul Christopher. *Secrets, Gossip and Gods: The Transformation of Brazilian Candomblé*. New York: Oxford, 2002.

———. "Secretism and the Apotheosis of Duvalier." *Journal of the American Academy of Religion* 74, no. 2 (2006): 420–45.

Joseph, Gilbert M. "Close Encounters: Toward a New Cultural History of U.S.-Latin American Relations." In *Close Encounters of Empire: Writing the Cultural History of U.S.-Latin American Relations*, edited by Gilbert M. Joseph, Catherine C. LeGrand, and Ricardo D. Salvatore, 3–46. Durham, N.C.: Duke University Press, 1998.

———. "Reclaiming 'the Political' at the Turn of the Millennium." In *Reclaiming the Political in Latin American History: Essays from the North*, edited by Joseph, 3–16. Durham, N.C.: Duke University Press, 2002.

———, ed. *Reclaiming the Political in Latin American History: Essays from the North*. Durham, N.C.: Duke University Press, 2001.

Joseph, Gilbert M., and Daniel Nugent Joseph, eds. *Everyday Forms of State Formation: Revolution and the Negotiation of Rule in Modern Mexico*. Durham, N.C.: Duke University Press, 1994.

Julia, Julio Jaime, ed. *Antología de Américo Lugo*. Vols. 1–2. Santo Domingo: Taller, 1977.

Kantorowicz, Ernst H. *The King's Two Bodies: A Study in Mediaeval Political Theology*. Princeton: Princeton University Press, 1957.

Kapferer, Bruce. *Legends of People, Myths of State: Violence, Intolerance and Political Culture in Sri Lanka and Australia*. Washington: Smithsonian Institution Press, 1988.

Kasson, John H. *Rudeness and Civility: Manners in Nineteenth-Century Urban America*. New York: Noonday Press, 1990.

Katz, Friedrich. *The Secret War in Mexico: Europe, The United States and the Mexican Revolution*. Chicago: University of Chicago Press, 1981.

Kearney, Michael. "Borders and Boundaries of State and Self at the End of Empire." *Journal of Historical Sociology* 4, no. 1 (1991): 52–74.

Kershaw, Ian. *The 'Hitler Myth': Image and Reality in the Third Reich*. New York: Oxford University Press, 1989.

King, Stewart R. *Blue Coat or Powdered Wig: Free People of Color in Pre-revolutionary Saint Domingue*. Athens: University of Georgia Press, 2001.

Klein, Alan. *Sugarball: The American Game, the Dominican Dream*. New Haven: Yale University Press, 1991.

Knight, Alan. "Populism and Neo-Populism in Latin America, Especially Mexico." *Journal of Latin American Studies* 30 (1998): 223–48.

Koontz, Claudia. "The Competition for a Women's Lebensraum, 1928–1934." In *When Biology Became Destiny: Women in Weimar and Nazi Germany,* edited by Renate Bridenthal, Atina Grossmann, and Marion Kaplan, 199–236. New York: Monthly Review Press, 1984.

Koreck, María Teresa. "Space and Revolution in Northeastern Chihuahua." In *Rural Revolt in Mexico and U.S. Intervention*, edited by Daniel Nugent, 127–49. Center for U.S. Mexican Studies, University of California, San Diego, 1988.

Koslov, Vladimir A. "Denunciation and Its Function in Soviet Governance: A Study of Denunciations and Their Bureaucratic Handling from Soviet Police Archives, 1944–1953." *Journal of Modern History* 68, no. 4 (1996): 867–98.

Krohn-Hansen, Christian. "Haitians, Money and Alterity Among Dominicans." *Social Anthropology* 3, no. 2 (1995): 129–46.

———. "Masculinity and the Political among Dominicans: 'The Dominican Tiger.' " In *Machos, Mistresses, Madonnas: Contesting the Power of Latin American Gender Imagery*, edited by Marit Melhuus and Kristi Anne Stølen Melhuus. New York: Verso, 1996.

———. "Negotiated Dictatorship: The Building of the Trujillo State in the Southwestern Dominican Republic." In *State Formation: Anthropological Perspectives*, edited by Christian Krohn-Hansen and Knut G. Nustad, 96–122. London: Pluto Press, 2005.

———. "A Tomb for Columbus in Santo Domingo. Political Cosmology, Population and Racial Frontiers." *Social Anthropology* 9, no. 2 (2001): 165–92.

Kuznesof, Elizabeth Anne. "Ethnic and Gender Influences on 'Spanish' Creole Society in Colonial Spanish America." *Colonial Latin American Review* 4, no. 1 (1995): 153–76.

Labourt, José. *Sana, sana, culita de rana*. Santo Domingo: Taller, 1982.

Lacay Polanco, Ramón. *El hombre de piedra*. Ciudad Trujillo: n.p., 1959.

Laclau, Ernesto. *On Populist Reason*. London: Verso, 2005.

———. *Politics and Ideology in Marxist Theory: Capitalism, Fascism, Populism*. London: Verso, 1979.

Lafaye, Jacques. *Quetzalcóatl and Guadalupe: The Formation of Mexican National Consciousness, 1531–1813*. Chicago: University of Chicago Press, 1976.

Laguerre, Michel S. *The Military and Society in Haiti*. Knoxville: University of Tennessee Press, 1993.

———. *Voodoo and Politics in Haiti*. London: MacMillan, 1989.

Lambertus, Abelardo Jiménez. "Aspectos históricos y psicológicos del culto a los luases en República Dominicana." *Boletín del Museo del Hombre Dominicano* 9, 15 (1980): 171–82.

Lancaster, Roger N. *Life Is Hard: Machismo, Danger, and the Intimacy of Power in Nicaragua*. Berkeley: University of California Press, 1992.

Landes, Joan. *Women and the Public Sphere in the Age of the French Revolution*, Ithaca: Cornell University Press, 1988.

Landestoy, Carmita. *Mis relaciones con el Presidente Trujillo*. Ciudad Trujillo: n.p., 1945.

Landolfi, Ciriaco, "El desarrollo cultural del pais en el primer cuarto del siglo XX." In *La sociedad dominicana durante el primero cuarto del siglo XX*, edited by Tirso Mejía-Ricart, 317–56. Santo Domingo: Editora de la Universidad Autónoma de Santo Domingo, 1982.

Lane, Jill. *Blackface Cuba, 1840–1885*. Philadelphia: University of Pennsylvania Press, 2005.

Langley, Lester D. *The United States and the Caribbean in the Twentieth Century*. Athens: University of Georgia Press, 1989.

Larose, Serge. "The Meaning of Africa in Haitian Vodou." In *Symbols and Sentiments: Cross-Cultural Studies in Symbolism*, edited by Ioan Lewis. London: Academic Publishers, 1977.

Lattas, Andrew. *Cultures of Secrecy: Reinventing Race in Bush Kaliai Cargo Cults*. Madison: University of Wisconsin Press, 1998.

Lattes, Alfredo E. "Población urbana y urbanización en América Latina." In *La*

Ciudad Construida: Urbanismo en América Latina, edited by Fernando
Carrión, 49–76. Quito, Ecuador: FLACSO, 2001.

Lauderdale Graham, Sandra. *House and Street: The Domestic World of Servants
and Masters in Nineteenth-Century Rio de Janeiro.* New York: Cambridge
University Press, 1988.

Lauria, Anthony. "Respeto, 'Relajo' and Interpersonal Relations in Puerto Rico."
Anthropological Quarterly 37, no. 2 (1964): 53–67.

Leach, Edmund. *Claude Lévi-Strauss.* New York: Viking, 1970.

Lears, T. J. Jackson. *No Place of Grace: Antimodernism and the Transformation of
American Culture, 1880–1920.* Chicago: University of Chicago Press, 1981.

Le Bon, Gustav. *The Crowd: A Study of the Popular Mind.* Atlanta: Cherokee
Publishing Company, 1982.

Lebra, Takie Sugikama. *Above the Clouds: Status Culture of the Modern Japanese
Nobility.* Berkeley: University of California Press, 1993.

Le Fort, Claude. *The Political Forms of Modern Society: Bureaucracy, Democracy,
Totalitarianism.* Cambridge: MIT Press, 1986.

Le Goff, Jacques. *The Medieval Imagination.* Chicago: University of Chicago Press,
1988.

LeGrand, Catherine. "Informal Resistance on a Dominican Sugar Plantation
During the Trujillo Dictatorship." *Hispanic American Historical Review* 75, no.
4 (1995): 555–96.

Leiris, Michel. "The Sacred in Everyday Life." In *The College of Sociology (1937–
39),* edited by Denis Hollier. Minneapolis: University of Minnesota Press, 1988.

León Estévez, Luis José. *Yo, Ramfis Trujillo.* Santo Domingo: Editorial Letra
Gráfica, 2002.

Lescallier, Daniel. "Itinerario de un viaje por la parte española de la isla de Santo
Domingo en 1764." In *Relaciones geográficas de Santo Domingo,* edited by
Rodríguez Demorizi, 113–42. Santo Domingo: Editora del Caribe, 1970.

Levine, Lawrence. *Highbrow/Lowbrow: The Emergence of Cultural Hierarchy in
America.* Cambridge: Harvard University Press, 1988.

Levy, Shawn. *The Last Playboy: The High Life of Porfirio Rubirosa.* New York:
Harper Collins, 2005.

Lewis, Gordon. *Main Currents in Caribbean Thought: The Historical Evolution of
Caribbean Society in Its Ideological Aspects, 1492–1900.* Baltimore: Johns
Hopkins University Press, 1983.

Lewis, Laura A. *Hall of Mirrors: Power, Witchcraft, and Caste in Colonial Mexico.*
Durham, N.C.: Duke University Press, 2003.

Lewis, Linden. "Fieldnotes on Masculinity Research in the Caribbean." In
Caribbean Masculinities: Working Papers, edited by Rafael L. Ramírez, Víctor I.
García-Toro, and Ineke Cunningham, 57–68. San Juan, Puerto Rico: HIV/AIDS
Research and Education Center, University of Puerto Rico, 2002.

El libro azul. Santo Domingo: Editora de la Universidad Autónoma de Santo
Domingo, 1976 [1920].

"El libro supremo de la suerte: Los sueños y sus números." N.p., n.d.

Limón, José E. *Dancing with the Devil: Society and Cultural Poetics in Mexican-American South Texas*. Madison: University of Wisconsin Press, 1994.

Lincoln, Bruce. *Authority: Construction and Corrosion*. Chicago: University of Chicago Press, 1994.

Lindholm, Charles. *Charisma*. Cambridge, Mass.: Basil Blackwell, 1990.

Lomnitz, Claudio. *Deep Mexico, Silent Mexico: Interpretations of the Sentiments of the Nation*. Minneapolis: University of Minnesota Press, 2001.

——. *Exits from the Labyrinth: Culture and Ideology in the Mexican National Space*. Berkeley: University of California Press, 1992.

——. "The Personification of Mexican National Sovereignty." In *The Empire of Things: Regimes of Value and Material Culture*, edited by Fred R. Myers, 119–38. Santa Fe, N.M.: School of American Research Press, 2001.

——. *Vicios públicos, virtudes privadas: La corrupción en México*. Mexico City: CIESAS and M. A. Porrúa, 2000.

Lomnitz, Larissa, Claudio Lomnitz-Adler, and Ilya Adler. "The Function of the Form: Power Play and Ritual in the 1988 Mexican Presidential Campaign." In *Constructing Culture and Power in Latin America*, edited by Daniel H. Levine, 357–428. Ann Arbor: University of Michigan Press, 1993.

López, José Ramón. *Ensayos y artículos*. Santo Domingo: Ediciones de la Fundación Corripio, 1991.

López-Calvo, Ignacio. *"God and Trujillo": Literary and Cultural Representations of the Dominican Dictator*. Gainesville: University Press of Florida, 2005.

López Peña, José Ramón Baez. *Por qué Santo Domingo es así*. Santo Domingo: Colección Banco Nacional de la Vivienda, 1992.

Low, Setha M. "Cultural Meaning of the Plaza: The History of the Spanish-American Gridplan-Plaza Urban Design." In *The Cultural Meaning of Urban Space*, edited by Robert Rotenberg and Gary McDonogh. Westport, Conn.: Bergin and Garvey, 1993.

Lugo, Américo. *A punto largo*. Santo Domingo: Impresora la Cuna de América, 1901.

——. *Obras escogidas I*. Santo Domingo: Ediciones de la Fundación Corripio, 1993.

Luhrmann, T. M. "The Magic of Secrecy." *Ethos* 17, no. 2 (1989): 131–65.

Lundahl, Mats, and Jan Lundius. "Socioeconomic Foundations of a Messianic Cult: Olivorismo in the Dominican Republic." In *Agrarian Society in History: Essays in Honor of Magnus Mörner*, edited by Mats Lundahl and Thommy Svensson. London: Routledge, 1990.

Lundius, Jan. *The Great Power of God in the San Juan Valley: Syncretism and Messianism in the Dominican Republic*. Lund: Lund Studies in History of Religions, 1995.

Lundius, Jan, and Mats Lundahl. *Peasants and Religion: A Socioeconomic Study of Dios Olivorio and the Palma Sola Movement in the Dominican Republic*. London: Routledge, 2000.

Lutz, Tom. *American Nervousness, 1903: An Anecdotal History*. Ithaca: Cornell University Press, 1991.

MacGaffey, Wyatt. *Kongo Political Culture: The Conceptual Challenge of the Particular*, Bloomington: Indiana University Press, 2000.

———, "Twins, Simbi Spirits, and Lwas in Kongo and Haiti." In *Central Africans and Cultural Transformations in the American Diaspora*, edited by Linda M. Heywood, 211–27. New York: Cambridge University Press, 2002.

Mahmood, Saba. *Politics of Piety: The Islamic Revival and the Feminist Subject*. Princeton: Princeton University Press, 2005.

Mañach, Jorge. *Indagación del choteo*. Habana: Ediciones Revista-Avance, 1928.

Mansfield, Stephanie. *The Richest Girl in the World: The Extravagant Life and Fast Times of Doris Duke*. New York: G. P. Putnam's Sons, 1992.

Marin, Louis. *Portrait of the King*. Translated by Martha M. Houle. Minneapolis: University of Minnesota Press, 1988.

———. *Utopics: The Semiological Play of Textual Spaces*. Atlantic Highlands, N.J.: Humanities Press International, 1990.

Marrero Aristy, Ramón. *Over*. Santo Domingo: Librería Dominicana, 1963.

Martin, John Bartlow. *Overtaken by Events: The Dominican Crisis from the Fall of Trujillo to the Civil War*. New York: Doubleday, 1966.

Martínez, Lusitania. *Actitudes femeninas hacia los oficios no tradicionales*. Santo Domingo: Editora Palma, 1994.

———. *Palma Sola: Opresión y esperanza (su geografía mítica y social)*. Santo Domingo: Ediciones CEDEE, 1991.

———. "Palma Sola: Un caso de movimiento social campesino con características mesiánicas." *Revista Estudios Dominicanos* 2, no. 4 (1985): 9–20.

Martínez, Maria. *Moral Meditations*. New York: Caribbean Library, 1954.

Martínez, Tomás Eloy. *Santa Evita: A Novel*. Translated by Helen Lane. New York: Alfred A. Knopf, 1996.

Martínez-Vergne, Teresita. *Nation and Citizen in the Dominican Republic, 1880–1916*. Chapel Hill: University of North Carolina Press, 2005.

———. "Politics and Society in the Spanish Caribbean during the Nineteenth Century." In *The Modern Caribbean*, edited by Franklin W. Knight and Colin A. Palmer, 185–202. Chapel Hill: University of North Carolina Press, 1989.

Marx, Karl. *Capital: A Critique of Political Economy*. New York: Modern Library, 1906.

———. *Grundrisse: Foundations of the Critique of Political Economy*. Translated by Martin Nicolaus. New York: Monthly Review Press, 1973.

Mateo, Andrés L. *Mito y cultura en la Era de Trujillo*. Santo Domingo: Libreria la Trinitaria, 1993.

Matos Díaz, Eduardo. *Santo Domingo de ayer: Vida, costumbres y acontecimientos*. Santo Domingo: Taller, 1985.

Mauss, Marcel. "A Category of the Human Mind: The Notion of Person, the

Notion of Self." In *The Category of the Person: Anthropology, Philosophy, History,* edited by Michael Carrithers, Steven Collins, and Steven Lukes, 1–26. Cambridge: Cambridge University Press, 1985.

———. *The Gift: Forms and Functions of Exchange in Archaic Societies.* New York: W. W. Norton, 1967.

May, Elaine Tyler. *Homeward Bound: American Families in the Cold War Era.* New York: Basic Books, 1988.

Maza, Sarah. *Private Lives and Public Affairs: The Causes Célèbres of Prerevolutionary France.* Berkeley: University of California Press, 1993.

Mbembe, Achille. "The Banality of Power and the Aesthetics of Vulgarity in the Postcolony." *Public Culture* 4, no. 2 (1992): 1–30.

———. *On the Postcolony.* Berkeley: University of California Press, 2001.

———. "Prosaics of Servitude and Authoritarian Civilities." *Public Culture* 5, no. 1 (1992): 123–48.

McCormack, John W. "The Dominican Republic: 25 Years of Peace and Prosperity." Trujillo City: Editora del Caribe, 1955.

Mejía, Domingo Antonio Bautista. "Si me permiten hablar. La historia de Palma Sola." *Estudios Sociales* 11, no. 74 (1988): 3–68.

Mejia, Luis F. *De Lilís a Trujillo. Historia contemporánea de la República Dominicana.* Santo Domingo: Editora de Santo Domingo, 1976.

Mejia-Ricart, Tirso. "Observaciones sobre el machismo en la América Latina." *Revista de Ciencias Sociales* 19, no. 3 (1975): 351–64.

Métraux, Alfred. *Voodoo in Haiti.* Translated by Hugo Charteris. New York: Schocken Books, 1972 [1959].

Meyer, Birgit. "Commodities and the Power of Prayer. Pentecostalist Attitudes Towards Consumption in Contemporary Ghana." *WOTRO Research Program on Globalization and the Construction of Communal Identities, Working Paper No. 1.* The Hague: WOTRO, 1997.

Meyer, Birgit, and Peter Pels, eds. *Magic and Modernity: Interfaces of Revelation and Concealment.* Stanford: Stanford University Press, 2003.

Mintz, Sidney W. *Caribbean Transformations.* Baltimore: Johns Hopkins University Press, 1984.

———. "From Plantations to Peasantries in the Caribbean." In *Caribbean Contours,* edited by Sidney W. Mintz and Sally Price. Baltimore: Johns Hopkins University Press, 1985.

———. *Sweetness and Power: The Place of Sugar in Modern History.* New York: Viking Penguin Books, 1985.

———. *Worker in the Cane, a Puerto Rican Life History.* New Haven: Yale University Press, 1960.

Mir, Pedro. *Tres leyendas de colores.* Santo Domingo: Editora Taller, 1984.

Mitchell, Timothy. *Colonizing Egypt.* New York: Cambridge University Press, 1988.

———. "Everyday Metaphors of Power." *Theory and Society* 19 (1990): 545–77.

————. "The Limits of the State: Beyond Statist Approaches and their Critics." *American Political Science Review* 85, no. 1 (1991): 77–96.

Moats, Aline-Leone. *The Million Dollar Studs*. London: Hale, 1978.

Monclús, Miguel Ángel. *El caudillismo en la República Dominicana*. Santo Domingo: Publicaciones CETEC, 1983.

Moreau de Saint-Méry, M. L. E. *Description topographique, physique, civile, politique et historique de la partie française de l'île Saint Domingue*. Paris: Société de l'histoire des colonies françaises, 1958.

————. *Descripción de la parte española de Santo Domingo*. Translated by Armando Rodríguez. Ciudad Trujillo: Editora Montalvo, 1944.

Moré Guaschino, Gustavo Luis. "Notas sobre forma e identidad en la arquitectura de la 'Era de Trujillo.'" *Arquivox* 1, no. 1 (1984): 3–11.

Moreno Fraginals, Manuel, et al., eds. *Between Slavery and Free Labor: The Spanish Speaking Caribbean in the Nineteenth Century*. Baltimore: Johns Hopkins University Press, 1985.

Moreta, Angel. "Proletarianización rural, capitalismo y clases sociales en el suroeste (San Juan de la Maguana) (Tendencias e hipótesis)." *Revista de Antropologia de la Universidad Autónoma de Santo Domingo*, nos. 23–26 (1982–83): 125–79.

Moscoso Puello, F. E. *Cañas y bueyes*. Santo Domingo: Asociación Serie 23, 1975 [1935].

————. *Cartas a Evelina*. Ciudad Trujillo: Editora Cosmos, 1974.

————. *Navarijo*. Santo Domingo: Editora Cosmos, 1978 [1956].

Mosse, George L. "Mass Politics and the Political Liturgy of Nationalism." In *Nationalism: The Nature and Evolution of an Idea*, edited by Eugene Kamenka, 39–54. New York: St. Martin's Press, 1976.

————. *Nationalism and Sexuality: Middle-Class Morality and Sexual Norms in Modern Europe*. Madison: University of Wisconsin Press, 1985.

Mota, Ana Maritza de la. "Palma Sola: 1962." *Revista del Museo del Hombre Dominicano* 9, no. 14 (1980): 53–68.

Moya Pons, Frank. "Dominican Republic." In *Latin American Urbanization: Historical Profiles of Major Cities*, edited by Gerald Michael Greenfield, 188–214. Westport, Conn.: Greenwood Press, 1994.

————. *The Dominican Republic: A National History*. Princeton, N.J.: Marcus Weiner Publishers, 1998.

————. "The Dominican Republic since 1930." In *The Cambridge History of Latin America*, edited by Leslie Bethell, vol. 7, 509–44. New York: Cambridge University Press, 1984.

————. *Empresarios en conflicto: Políticas de industrialización y sustitución de importaciones en la República Dominicana*. Santo Domingo: Fondo Para el Avance de las Ciencias Sociales, 1992.

Mujeres en Desarrollo Dominicano (MUDE). *La era de Trujillo: Décimas, relatos, y testimonios campesinos*. Santo Domingo: Mujeres en Desarrollo Dominicana, 1989.

Munn, Nancy. *The Fame of Gawa: A Symbolic Study of Value Transformation in a Massim (Papua New Guinea) Society*. Durham, N.C.: Duke University Press, 1986.

Nathan, Debbie, and Michael Snedecker. *Satan's Silence: Ritual Abuse and the Making of a Modern American Witch Hunt*. New York: Basic Books, 1995.

Navaro-Yashin, Yael. *Faces of the State: Secularism and Public Life in Turkey*. Princeton: Princeton University Press, 2002.

Nelson, William Javier. *Almost a Territory: America's Attempt to Annex the Dominican Republic*. Newark: University of Delaware Press, 1990.

Nicholls, David. *From Dessalines to Duvalier: Race, Colour and National Independence in Haiti*. Cambridge: Cambridge University Press, 1979.

Niehaus, Isak, Eliazaar Mohlala, and Kally Shokane. *Witchcraft, Power and Politics: Exploring the Occult in the South African Lowveld*. London: Pluto Press, 2001.

Nugent, David. "State and Shadow State in Northern Peru *circa* 1900: Illegal Political Networks and the Problem of State Boundaries." In *States and Illegal Practices*, edited by Josiah McC. Heyman, 63–98. New York: Berg, 1999.

Nyberg, Sørenson, Ninna Nyberg, and Finn Stepputat. "Narrations of Authority and Mobility." *Identities* 8, no. 3 (2001): 314–42.

Orlove, Benjamin, ed. *The Allure of the Foreign: Imported Goods in Postcolonial Latin America*. Ann Arbor: University of Michigan Press, 1997.

Ornes, Germán. *Trujillo: Little Caesar of the Caribbean*. New York: Thomas Nelson, 1958.

——. *Germán Ornes: A Self Portrait*. Trujillo City: Dominican Press Society, 1958.

Ortega y Gasset, José. *The Revolt of the Masses*. New York: W. W. Norton, 1957 [1930].

Ortiz, Fernando. *Cuban Counterpoint: Tobacco and Sugar*. Durham, N.C.: Duke University Press, 1995 [1947].

——. *Hampa Afrocubana, Los negro brujos (apuntes para un estudio del etnologia criminal)*. Madrid: Editoral-América, 1917.

——. *El huracán, su mítología y sus símbolos*. Mexico City: Fondo de Cultura Económica, 1947.

——. *Los negros curros*. Havana: Editorial de Ciencias Sociales, 1986.

Ortner, Sherry B. "Gender and Sexuality in Hierarchical Societies: The Case of Polynesia and Some Comparative Implications." In *Sexual Meanings: The Cultural Construction of Gender and Sexuality*, edited by Sherry B. Ortner and Harriet Whitehead. Cambridge: Cambridge University Press, 1981.

——. "Is Female to Male as Nature Is to Culture?" In *Women, Culture and Society*, edited by M. Z. Rosaldo and L. Lamphere. Stanford: Stanford University Press, 1974.

Osorio Lizarazo, J. A. *Así es Trujillo*. Buenos Aires: Artes Gráficas, 1958.

———. *Portrait of Trujillo.* N.p., 1958.

Outram, Dorinda. *The Body and the French Revolution: Sex, Class and Political Culture.* New Haven: Yale University Press, 1989.

Ozouf, Mona. *Festivals and the French Revolution.* Translated by Alan Sheridan. Cambridge: Harvard University Press, 1988.

Pacini Hernández, Deborah. "The Merengue: Race, Class, Tradition and Identity." In *Americas: An Anthology,* edited by A. Douglas Kincaid, Mark Rosenberg, and Kathleen Logan. New York: Oxford University Press, 1992.

Palm, Erwin Walter. *Los monumentos arquitectónicos de la Española.* 2 vols. Ciudad Trujillo: Industria Gráficas Seix y Barral Hnos., 1955.

———. *Los orígenes del urbanismo imperial en América.* Mexico City: Instituto Panamericano de Geografía e Historia, Comisión de Historia, 1951.

———. *The Pocket Guide to Ciudad Trujillo and Its Historical Sites.* Ciudad Trujillo: Impresora Dominicana, 1951.

Palmié, Stephan. *Wizards and Scientists: Explorations in Afro-Cuban Modernity and Tradition.* Durham, N.C.: Duke University Press, 2002.

Pan American Union. *The Christopher Columbus Memorial Lighthouse Competition.* Washington: Pan American Union, 1930.

Parker, Andrew, et al., eds. *Nationalisms and Sexualities.* New York: Routledge, 1992.

Parker, D. S. *The Idea of the Middle Class: White Collar Workers and Peruvian Society, 1900–1950.* University Park: Pennsylvania State University Press, 1998.

Parker, Richard G. *Bodies, Pleasures and Passions: Sexual Culture in Contemporary Brazil.* Boston: Beacon Press, 1991.

Patín Maceo, Manuel A. *Dominicanismos.* Ciudad Trujillo: Librería Dominicana, 1947.

Peabody, Robert E. *Merchant Venturers of Old Salem.* Boston: Houghton Mifflin, 1912.

Peguero, Valentina. *The Militarization of Culture in the Dominican Republic, from the Captains General to General Trujillo.* Lincoln: University of Nebraska Press, 2004.

Peiss, Kathy. *Cheap Amusements: Working Women and Leisure in Turn-of-the-Century New York.* Philadelphia: Temple University Press, 1986.

Pels, Peter. Introduction. In *Magic and Modernity: Interfaces of Revelation and Concealment,* edited by Birgit Meyer and Peter Pels, 1–38. Stanford: Stanford University Press, 2003.

Peña Battle, Manuel Arturo. *Política de Trujillo.* Ciudad Trujillo: Impresora Dominicana, 1965.

Peña Rivera, Victor A. *El playboy Porfirio Rubirosa: Su vida y sus tiempos.* Miami: Victoria Press, 1991.

Penson, César Nicolás. *Cosas Añejas.* Santo Domingo: Taller, 1972.

Pepen, Juan F. *Donde floreció el naranjo: La altagracia: Orígen y significado de su culto.* Santo Domingo: Amigo del Hogar, 1984.

Pepper, José Vicente. *I Accuse Braden/Yo Acuso a Braden*. Trujillo City: Editora Montalvo, 1947.

Pepper, José Vicente, and Graciela Rincón-Calcaño de Pepper. *Realidades dominicanas*. Ciudad Trujillo: Editora Montalvo, 1947.

Pérez, Carlos Federico. *La Ciudad Herida*. Santo Domingo: Universidad Nacional Pedro Henríquez Ureña, 1977.

Pérez, Eliseo, and Félix M. Pérez S., eds. *Album de la canónica coronación de la venerada imagen de Nuestra Señora de la Altagracia*. Santo Domingo: Rafael V. Montalvo ed., 1922.

Pérez, Louis. "Between Baseball and Bullfighting: The Quest for Nationality in Cuba, 1868–1898." *The Journal of American History* 81, no. 2 (1994).

———. *On Becoming Cuban: Identity, Nationality and Culture*. Chapel Hill: University of North Carolina Press, 1999.

———. *Winds of Change: Hurricanes and Transformation of Nineteenth-Century Cuba*. Chapel Hill: University of North Carolina Press, 2001.

Pérez Montás, Eugenio. "Guillermo González y el movimiento moderno en Santo Domingo." *CODIA* no. 23 (1970): 29–41.

Perice. Glen A. "Rumors and Politics in Haiti." *Anthropological Quarterly*. 70, no. 1 (1997): 1–10.

Peukert, Detlev. *Inside Nazi Germany: Conformity, Opposition, and Racism in Everyday Life*. Translated by Richard Deveson. New Haven, CT: Yale University Press, 1987.

Pick, Daniel. *Faces of Degeneration: A European Disorder c. 1848–c. 1918*. New York: Cambridge University Press, 1989.

Pieter, Leonicio. *Ciudad Trujillo: Transformación urbanística, social y política de la capital de la República Dominicana durante la gloriosa Era de Trujillo*. Ciudad Trujillo: Impresora Arte y Cine, 1958.

Pietz, William. "Fetishism and Materialism: The Limits of Theory in Marx." In *Fetishism as Cultural Discourse*, edited by Emily Apter and William Pietz, 119–51. Ithaca: Cornell University Press, 1993.

Plato, *Gorgias and Phaedrus*. Translated by James H. Nicholas. Ithaca: Cornell University Press, 1998.

Polanco Brito, Hugo E. *Exvotos y milagros del Santuario de Higüey*. Santo Domingo: Ediciones Banco Central, 1984.

Poole, Deborah. "Landscapes of Power in a Cattle-Rustling Culture of Southern Andean Peru." *Dialectical Anthropology* 12 (1988): 367–98.

Rabinow, Paul. *French Modern: Norms and Forms of the Social Environment*. Cambridge: MIT Press, 1989.

Rafael, Vicente L. "Anticipating Nationhood: Collaboration and Rumor in the Japanese Occupation of Manila." *Diaspora* 1, no. 1 (1991): 67–82.

———. "Patronage and Pornography: Ideology and Spectatorship in the Early

Marcos Years." *Comparative Studies in Society and History* 32, no. 2 (1990): 282–303.

Rama, Angel. *The Lettered City*. Translated and edited by John Charles Chasteen. Durham: Duke University Press, 1996.

Ramírez, Rafael L. *What It Means to Be a Man: Reflections on Puerto Rican Masculinity*. Translated by Rosa E. Casper. New Brunswick: Rutgers University Press, 1999.

Rancier, Omar. "Documentos: La arquitectura de Guillermo González Sánchez." *Arquivox* 3–4 (Dec.-May 1984–85): 3–25.

Renda, Mary A. *Taking Haiti: Military Occupation and the Culture of U.S. Imperialism, 1915–1940*. Chapel Hill: University of North Carolina Press, 2001.

Requena, Andrés. *Los enemigos de la tierra*. Ciudad Trujillo: Editorial La Nación, 1936.

Ricard, Robert. "La plaza mayor en España y en America Española." *Estudios Geográficos*, 38, no. 11 (1950): 321–27.

Rodó, José Enrique. *Ariel*. Translated by Margaret Sayers Peden. Austin: University of Texas Press, 1988 [1900].

Rodríguez de León, Francisco. *Balaguer y Trujillo: Entre la espada y la palabra*. Santo Domingo: F. Rodríguez de León, 1996.

Rodríguez Demorizi, Emilio. *Seudónimos dominicanos*. Ciudad Trujillo: Montalvo, 1956.

———. *Sociedades, cofradías, escuelas, gremios, y otras corporaciones dominicanas*. Santo Domingo: Editora Educativa Dominicana, 1975.

Roldán, Mary. *Blood and Fire: La Violencia in Antioquia, Colombia, 1946–1953*. Durham: Duke University Press, 2002.

Román, Miguel Alberto. *Gente de portal*. Ciudad Trujillo: Impresora Dominicana, 1954.

Román, Reinaldo L. *Governing Spirits: Religion, Miracles, and Spectacles in Cuba and Puerto Rico, 1898–1956*. Chapel Hill: University of North Carolina Press, 2007.

Romberg, Raquel. *Witchcraft and Welfare: Spiritual Capital and the Business of Magic in Modern Puerto Rico*. Austin: University of Texas Press, 2003.

Roorda, Eric Paul. *The Dictator Next Door: The Good Neighbor Policy and the Trujillo Regime in the Dominican Republic, 1930–1945*. Durham, N.C.: Duke University Press, 1998.

Rosa, Gilberto de la, *Petán: Un cacique en la Era de Trujillo*. Santiago: Universidad Católica Madre y Maestra, n.d.

Roseberry, William. "Images of the Peasant in the Consciousness of the Venezuelan Proletariat." In *Anthropologies and Histories: Essays in Culture, History and Political Economy*, 55–79. New Brunswick, N.J.: Rutgers University Press, 1989.

Rosenberg, June. *El Gagá: Religión y sociedad de un culto dominicano*. Santo
Domingo: Publicaciones de la Universidad Autónoma de Santo Domingo, 1979.

Rotberg, Robert I. "Vodun and the Politics of Haiti." In *African Diaspora*, edited by
Robert I. Rotberg, 342–65. Cambridge: Harvard University Press, 1976.

Rubin, Gayle. "The Traffic in Women: Notes on the Political Economy of Sex." In
Toward an Anthropology of Women, edited by Rayna R. Reiter, 157–210. New
York: Monthly Review Press, 1975.

Rubirosa, Porfirio. *Mis Memorias*. Santo Domingo: Letra Gráfica, 2000.

Rueda, Manuel. *Bienvenida y la noche*. Santo Domingo: Fundación Cultural
Dominicana, 1994.

Rutherford, Danilyn. *Raiding the Land of the Foreigners*. Princeton: Princeton
University Press, 2003.

Ryan, Mary P. "The American Parade: Representations of the Nineteen-Century
Social Order." In *The New Cultural History*, edited by Lynn Hunt, 131–53.
Berkeley: University of California Press, 1989.

———. *Women in Public: Between Banners and Ballots, 1825–1880*. Baltimore:
Johns Hopkins University Press, 1990.

Rydell, Robert W. *All the World's a Fair: Visions of Empire at American
International Expositions, 1876–1916*. Chicago: University of Chicago Press,
1984.

———. *World of Fairs: The Century of Progress Expositions*. Chicago: University of
Chicago Press, 1993.

Saez, José Luis. *Historia de un sueño importado: Ensayos sobre el cine en Santo
Domingo*. Santo Domingo: Ediciones Siboney, 1983.

Sagás, Ernesto. *Race and Politics in the Dominican Republic*. Gainesville:
University Press of Florida, 2000.

Sahlins, Marshall. *Islands of History*. Chicago: University of Chicago Press, 1985.

———. "Rich Man, Poor Man, Big Man, Chief: Political Types in Melanesia and
Polynesia." *Comparative Studies in Society and History* 5, no. 1 (1962): 287–303.

Said, Edward W. *Culture and Imperialism*. New York: Vintage Books, 1994.

Sánchez, Enriquillo. *Musiquito: Anales de un déspota y de un bolerista*. Santo
Domingo: Editora Taller, 1993.

Sánchez Valverde, Antonio. *La idea del valor en la isla española*. Ciudad Trujillo:
Editora Montalvo, 1947.

Sanders, Todd, and Harry G. West. "Introduction: Power Revealed and Concealed
in the New World Order." In *Transparency and Conspiracy: Ethnographies of
Suspicion in the New World Order*, edited by West and Sanders, 1–37. Durham,
N.C.: Duke University Press, 2003.

Sang, Mu Kien A. *Ulises Heureaux: Biografía de un dictador*. Santo Domingo:
INTEC, 1987.

San Miguel, Pedro L. "La ciudanía de Calibán: Poder y discursiva campesinista en
la era de Trujillo." In *Política, identidad y pensamiento social en la República*

Dominicana (Siglos XI y XX), edited by Raymundo González et al., 269–90. Madrid: Ediciones Doce Calles, 1999.

———. *Los campesinos del Cibao: Economía del Mercado y transformación agraria en la República Dominicana, 1880–1960*. San Juan: Editorial de la Universidad de Puerto Rico, 1997.

———. *La Guerra Silenciosa: Las luchas sociales en la ruralía dominicana*. Mexico City: Instituto Mora, 2005.

Santos-Granero, Fernando. "The Enemy Within: Child Sorcery, Revolution, and the Evils of Modernization in Eastern Peru." In *Darkness and Secrecy: The Anthropology of Assault Sorcery and Witchcraft in Amazonia*, edited by Neil Whitehead and Robin White, 272–305. Durham: Duke University Press, 2004.

Scarano, Francisco. "The *Jíbaro* Masquerade and the Subaltern Politics of Creole Identity Formation in Puerto Rico, 1745–1823." *American Historical Review* 101, no. 5 (1996): 1398–1431.

Schatzberg, Michael G. "The State as Family: Mobuto as Father." In *The Dialectics of Oppression in Zaire*, 71–98. Bloomington: Indiana University Press, 1988.

Schoenrich, Otto. *Santo Domingo: A Country with a Future*. New York: Macmillan Company, 1918.

Schwartz, Stuart B. "Colonial Identities and the *Sociedad de Castas*." *Colonial Latin American Review* 4, no. 1 (1995): 185–201.

———. "The Hurricane of San Ciriaco: Disaster, Politics and Society in Puerto Rico, 1899–1902." *Hispanic American Historical Review* 72, no. 3 (1992): 303–34.

———. "Spaniards, *Pardos*, and the Missing Mestizos: Identities and Racial Categories in the Early Hispanic Caribbean." *New West Indian Guide* 17, nos. 1 and 2 (1997): 5–21.

———. "State and Society in Colonial Spanish America: An Opportunity for Prosopography." In *New Approaches to Latin American History*, edited by Richard Graham and Peter H. Smith, 4–35. Austin: University of Texas Press, 1974.

Schwartz, Vanessa R. *Spectacular Realities: Early Mass Culture in Fin-de-siècle Paris*. Berkeley: University of California Press, 1998.

Scobey, David. "Anatomy of the Promenade: The Politics of Bourgeois Sociability in Nineteenth-Century New York." *Social History* 17, no. 2 (1992): 204–227.

Scott, James C. "Domination, Acting, Fantasy." In *The Paths to Domination, Resistance and Terror*, edited by Carolyn Nordstrom and JoAnn Martin, 55–84. Berkeley: University of California Press, 1992.

———. *Domination and the Arts of Resistance: Hidden Transcripts*. New Haven, Conn.: Yale University Press, 1990.

———. "Prestige as the Public Discourse of Domination." *Cultural Critique* 12 (spring 1989): 145–66.

Scott, Rebecca J. "The Provincial Archive as a Place of Memory: Confronting Oral and Written Sources on the Role of Former Slaves in the Cuban War of

Independence (1895–98)." *New West Indian Guide* 76, nos. 3 and 4 (2002): 191–210.

Segre, Roberto, Mario Coyula, and Joseph L. Scarpaci. *Havana: Two Faces of the Antillean Metropolis.* New York: John Wiley, 1997.

Sención, Viriato. *They Forged the Signature of God.* Translated by Asa Zatz. Willimantic, Conn.: Curbstone Press, 1996.

Sidel, John T. *Capital, Coercion and Crime: Bossism in the Philippines.* Stanford: Stanford University Press, 1999.

Silié, Rubén. *Economía, esclavitud y población: ensayos de interpretación histórica del Santo Domingo espanol en el siglo XVIII.* Santo Domingo: Universidad Autónoma de Santo Domingo, 1976.

Simmel, Georg. *The Sociology of Georg Simmel.* Translated by Kurt H. Wolff. New York: Free Press, 1950.

Simpson, Catherine. "Response." In *The End of the Line: Essays on Psychoanalysis and the Sublime,* by Neil Hertz, 194–96. New York: Columbia University Press, 1985.

Skidmore, Thomas E. *Black into White: Race and Nationality in Brazilian Thought.* Durham, N.C.: Duke University Press, 1993.

Skurski, Julie. "The Ambiguities of Authenticity in Latin America: *Doña Barbara* and the Construction of National Identity." *Poetics Today* 15, no. 4 (1994): 605–42.

Skurski, Julie, and Fernando Coronil. "Country and City in a Postcolonial Landscape: Double Discourse and the Geo-Politics of Truth in Latin America." In *Views Beyond the Border Country: Raymond Williams and Cultural Politics,* edited by Dennis Dworkin and Leslie Roman, 231–59. New York: Routledge, 1993.

Smart, Alan. "Predatory Rule and Illegal Economic Practices." In *States and Illegal Practices,* edited by Josiah McC. Heyman, 99–128. New York: Oxford University Press, 1999.

Smith, Raymond T. "Hierarchy and the Dual Marriage System in West Indian Society." In *Gender and Kinship: Essays Toward a Unified Analysis,* edited by Jane Collier Fishburne and Sylvia Junko Yanagisako, 163–96. Stanford: Stanford University Press, 1987.

———. *The Matrifocal Family: Power, Pluralism and Politics.* New York: Routledge, 1996.

———. "Race and Class in the Post-Emancipation Caribbean." In *Racism and Colonialism: Essays on Ideology and Social Structure,* edited by Robert Ross, 93–119. The Hague: Martinus Nijhoff, 1982.

Smith, S. A. "Talking Toads and Chinless Ghosts: The Politics of 'Superstitious' Rumors in the People's Republic of China, 1961–1965." *American Historical Review* 111, no. 2 (2006): 405–427.

Somers, Margaret. "Narrativity, Narrative Identity, and Social Action: Rethinking

English Working-Class Formation." *Social Science History* 16, no. 4 (winter 1992): 591–630.

Sommer, Doris. *Foundational Fictions: The National Romances of Latin America.* Berkeley: University of California Press, 1991.

———. "Irresistible Romance: The Foundational Fictions of Latin America." In *Nation and Narration,* edited by Homi K. Bhabha. New York: Routledge, 1990.

———. *One Master for Another: Populism as Patriarchal Rhetoric in Dominican Novels.* Lanham, Md.: University Press of America, 1983.

Stallybrass, Peter. "Footnotes." In *The Body in Parts: Fantasies of Corporeality in Early Modern Europe,* edited by David Hillman and Carla Mazzio. New York: Routledge, 1997.

Stallybrass, Peter, and Allon White. *The Politics and Poetics of Transgression.* Ithaca: Cornell University Press, 1986.

Stanislawski, Dan. "Early Spanish Town Planning in the New World." *Geographical Review* 37, no. 1 (1947): 94–120.

———. "The Origin and Spread of the Grid-Pattern Town." *The Geographical Review* 36, no. 1 (Jan. 1946): 105–20.

Stanley, William Deane. *The Protection Racket State: Elite Politics, Military Extortion and Civil War in El Salvador.* Philadephia: Temple University Press, 1996.

Stepan, Alfred. *The Military in Politics: Peru in Comparative Perspective.* Princeton: Princeton University Press, 1988.

Stepan, Nancy Leys. *"The Hour of Eugenics": Race, Gender, and Nation in Latin America.* Ithaca: Cornell University Press, 1991.

Stern, Steve J. *Remembering Pinochet's Chile: On the Eve of London, 1998.* Durham, N.C.: Duke University Press, 2004.

———. *The Secret History of Gender: Women, Men and Power in Late Colonial Mexico.* Chapel Hill: University of North Carolina Press, 1995.

Stewart, Charles, and Rosalind Shaw. "Introduction: Problematizing Syncretism." In *Syncretism/Anti-Syncretism: The Politics of Religious Synthesis,* edited by Charles Stewart and Rosalind Shaw, 1–26. London: Routledge, 1994.

Stewart, Pamela J., and Andrew Strathern. *Witchcraft, Sorcery, Rumors, and Gossip.* Cambridge: Cambridge University Press, 2004.

Stolcke, Verena. *Marriage, Class and Colour in Nineteenth Century Cuba: A Study of Racial Attitudes and Sexual Values in a Slave Society.* Ann Arbor: University of Michigan Press, 1989.

Stone, Marla Susan. *The Patron State: Culture and Politics in Fascist Italy.* Princeton: Princeton University Press, 1998.

Stutzman, Ronald. "El Mestizaje: An All-Inclusive Ideology of Exclusion." In *Cultural Transformations and Ethnicity in Modern Ecuador,* edited by Norman E. Whitten Jr., 45–94. Urbana: University of Illinois Press, 1981.

Szuchman, Mark D. "The City as Vision—the Development of Urban Culture in

Latin America." In *I Saw a City Invincible: Urban Portraits of Latin America*, edited by Gilbert M. Joseph and Mark D. Szuchman. Wilmington, Del.: Scholarly Resources, 1996.

Tancer, Shoshana B. "La Quisqueyana: The Dominican Woman, 1940–1970." In *Female and Male in Latin America*, edited by Ann Pescatello. Pittsburgh: University of Pittsburgh Press, 1973.

Taussig, Michael. *The Devil and Commodity Fetishism in Latin America*. Chapel Hill: University of North Carolina Press, 1980.

——. *Defacement: Public Secrecy and the Labor of the Negative*. Stanford: Stanford University Press, 1999.

——. "Folk Healing and the Structure of Conquest in Southwest Colombia. *Journal of Latin American Lore* 6, no. 2 (1980): 217–78.

——. "La magia del estado: María Lionsa y Simón Bolivar en la Venezuela contemporanea." In *De palabra y obra en el nuevo mundo. 2 Encuentros interétnicos, Interpretaciones contemporáneas*, edited by Manuel Guitierrez Estevez. Mexico City: Siglo Veintiuno, 1992.

——. *The Magic of the State*. New York: Routledge, 1997.

——. "*Maleficium*: State Fetishism." In *Fetishism as Cultural Discourse*, edited by Emily Apter and William Pietz, 217–47. Ithaca: Cornell University Press, 1993.

——. *Mimesis and Alterity: A Particular History of the Senses*. New York: Routledge, 1993.

——. *Shamanism, Colonialism and the Wild Man: A Study in Terror and Healing*. Chicago: University of Chicago Press, 1987.

——. "Viscerality, Faith and Skepticism: Another Theory of Magic." In *Magic and Modernity: Interfaces of Revelation and Concealment*, edited by Birgit Meyer and Peter Pels, 272–306. Stanford: Stanford University Press, 2003.

Taylor, Christopher. *Milk, Money and Honey: Changing Concepts in Rwandan Healing*. Washington: Smithsonian Institution Press, 1992.

Taylor, Diana. *Disappearing Acts: Spectacles of Gender and Nationalism in Argentina's Dirty War*. Durham, N.C.: Duke University Press, 1997.

Taylor, J. M. *Eva Perón: The Myths of a Woman*. Chicago: University of Chicago Press, 1979.

Miguel Tejada, Adriano. "El folklore como mecanismo de control político en Heureaux y Trujillo." *Eme Eme: Estudios Dominicanos* 6, no. 34 (1978): 19–39.

Thoden van Velzen, Bonno. "Priests, Spirit Mediums, and Guerrillas in Suriname." In *Transactions: Essays in Honor of Jeremy F. Boissevain*, edited by Jojada Verrips, 209–28. Amsterdam: Hev Shinhuis, 1994.

Thoden van Velzen, H. U. E. "Dramatization: How Dream Work Shapes Culture." *Psychoanalytic Review* 84, no. 2 (1997): 173–88.

Thompson, E. P. "The Moral Economy of the English Crowd in the Eighteenth Century." *Past and Present* 50 (1971): 71–136.

Thompson, Robert Farris, and Joseph Cornet. *The Four Moments of the Sun: Kongo Art in Two Worlds*. Washington: National Gallery of Art, 1981.

Tickner, Lisa. *The Spectacle of Women: Imagery of the Suffrage Campaign, 1907–1914*. Chicago: University of Chicago Press, 1988.

Tilly, Charles. "Contentious Repertoires in Great Britain, 1758–1834." *Social Science History* 17, no. 2 (1993): 253–78.

Torres-Saillant, Silvio. "Creoleness or Blackness? A Dominican Dilemma." *Plantation Society in the Americas*, 5, no. 1 (1998).

———. *El tigueraje intellectual*. Santo Domingo: Editora Manatí, 2002.

Trouillot, Michel-Rolph. *Haiti: State Against Nation. The Origins and Legacy of Duvalierism*. New York: Monthly Review Press, 1990.

Trujillo, Flor (with Laura Berquist). "My Tormented Life as Trujillo's Daughter." *Look*, 15 June 1965, 44–66.

Tucker, Robert C. *The Marx-Engels Reader*. New York: W. W. Norton, 1978.

Turits, Richard. *Foundations of Despotism: Peasants, The Trujillo Regime and Modernity in Dominican History*. Stanford: Stanford University Press, 2002.

———. "A World Destroyed, A Nation Imposed: The 1937 Haitian Massacre in the Dominican Republic." *Hispanic American Historical Review* 82, no. 3 (2002): 589–635.

Turner, Bryan S. *The Body and Society*. New York: Basil Blackwell, 1984.

Turner, Victor. *Dramas, Fields, and Metaphors: Symbolic Action in Human Society*. Ithaca: Cornell University Press, 1974.

———. *The Ritual Process: Structure and Antistructure*. Chicago, Ill.: Aldine, 1969.

Twinam, Ann. *Public Lives, Private Secrets: Gender, Honor, Sexuality and Illegitimacy in Colonial Spanish America*. Stanford: Stanford University Press, 1999.

Ubiñas Renville, Guaroa. *El niño y el bicornio. La infancia del dictador Trujillo: Novela histórica*. Santo Domingo: Editora Búho, 2007.

United States Marine Government. *Santo Domingo: Its Past and Present Condition*. Santo Domingo: U.S. Marine Government Printing House, 1920.

United States Senate. Hearings before a Select Committee on Haiti and Santo Domingo. *Inquiry into the Occupation of Haiti and Santo Domingo*. Vol. 1. Washington: Government Printing Office, 1922.

Uribe, Max. *El Partido Dominicano*. Vol. 1. Ciudad Trujillo: Impresora Dominicana, 1959.

Utrera, Fray Cipriano de. *Ntra. Sra. de Altagracia: Historia documentada de su culto y su santuario de Higüey*. Santo Domingo: Padres Franciscanos Capuchinos, 1933.

Valentine, Tom, and Patrick Mahn. *Daddy's Dutchess: The Unauthorized Biography of Doris Duke*. Secaucus, N.J.: Lyle Stewart, 1987.

Valeri, Valerio. "Diarchy and History in Hawaii and Tonga." In *Culture and History in the Pacific*, edited by Jukka Siikala, 45–80. Finnish Anthropological Society Transactions No. 27. Helsinki: Suomen Antropologinen Seura, 1990.

Van Young, Eric. "Conclusion: The State as Vampire—Hegemonic Projects, Public Ritual, and Popular Culture in Mexico, 1600–1990." In *Rituals of Rule, Rituals of Resistance: Public Celebrations and Popular Culture in Mexico*, edited by William H. Beezley, Cheryl English Martin and William E. French. Wilmington, Del.: Scholarly Resources, 1994.

——. *The Other Rebellion: Popular Violence, Ideology, and the Mexican Struggle for Independence, 1810–1821*. Stanford: Stanford University Press, 2001.

——. "The Raw and the Cooked: Elite and Popular Ideology in Mexico, 1800–1821." In *Values and Attitudes in the 17th-19th Centuries*, edited by Mark D. Szuchman, 75–102. Boulder: Lynne Rienner, 1989.

Vargas Llosa, Mario. *The Feast of the Goat*. Translated by Edith Grossman. New York: Farrar, Straus and Giroux, 2001.

Vargas Mera, Ramón. *Evolución urbanística de Ciudad Trujillo*. Ciudad Trujillo: Consejo Administrativo del Distrito Nacional, República Dominicana, 1956.

Vásquez Montalbán, Manuel. *Galíndez*. Madrid: Seix Barral, 1991.

Vedovato, Claudio. *Politics, Foreign Trade and Economic Development in the Dominican Republic*. Lund: Lund Economic Studies No. 32, 1984.

Veeser, Cyrus. *A World Safe for Capitalism: Dollar Diplomacy and America's Rise to Global Power*. New York: Columbia University Press, 2002.

Vega, Bernardo. *Almoina, Galíndez y otros crímenes de Trujillo en el extranjero*. Santo Domingo: Fundación Cultural Dominicana, 2001.

——. *Control y represión en la dictadura Trujillista*. Santo Domingo: Fundación Cultural Dominicana, 1986.

——, ed. *Trujillo ante una corte marcial por violación y extorsión en 1920*. Santo Domingo: Fundación Cultural Dominicana, 1995.

——, ed. *Los trujillo se escriben*. Santo Domingo: Fundación Cultural Dominicana, 1987.

——. *Trujillo y Haití (1937–1938)*, vol. 2. Santo Domingo: Fundación Cultural Dominicana, 1995.

——. *Trujillo y las fuerzas armadas norteamericanas*. Santo Domingo: Fundación Cultural Dominicana, 1992.

——, ed. *Unos desafectos y otros en desgracia: Sufrimentos en la dictadura de Trujillo*. Santo Domingo: Fundación Cultural Dominicana, 1986.

——, ed. *La vida cotidiana a través del archivo particular del generalísimo*. Santo Domingo: Fundación Cultural Dominicana, 1986.

Veloz Maggiolo, Francisco. *La Misericordia y sus contornos, 1884–1916: Narración de la vida y costumbres de la vieja ciudad de Santo Domingo de Guzmán*. Santo Domingo: Editorial Arte y Cine, 1967.

Veloz Maggiolo, Marcio. *Materia Prima: Protonovela*. Santo Domingo: Fundación Cultural Dominicana, 1988.

——. *Ritos de cabaret (novela rítmica)*. Santo Domingo: Fundación Cultural Dominicana, 1991.

———. *Trujillo, Villa Francisca y otros fantasmas.* Santo Domingo: Colección Banreservas, 1996.

Verkaaik, Oskar. "The Captive State: Corruption, Intelligence Agencies, and Ethnicity in Pakistan." In *States of Imagination: Ethnographic Explorations of the Postcolonial State*, edited by Thomas Blom Hansen and Finn Stepputat, 345–65. Durham, N.C.: Duke University Press, 2001.

Veyne, Paul. *Bread and Circuses: Historical Sociology and Political Pluralism.* Translated by Brian Pearce. New York: Penguin Press, 1990.

Vicens de Morales, Margarita. *María Montez: Su vida.* Santo Domingo: Editora Corripio, 1992.

Voekel, Pamela. "Peeing on the Palace: Bodily Resistance to Bourbon Reforms in Mexico City." *Journal of Historical Sociology* 5, no. 2 (1992): 183–208.

Wachtel, Nathan. *Gods and Vampires: Return to Chipaya.* Translated by Carol Volk. Chicago: University of Chicago Press, 1994.

Wade, Peter. *Blackness and Race Mixture: The Dynamics of Racial Identity in Colombia.* Baltimore: Johns Hopkins University Press, 1993.

———. *Race and Ethnicity in Latin America.* London: Pluto Press, 1997.

Walker, Charles. "The Upper Classes and their Upper Stories: Architecture and the Aftermath of the Lima Earthquake of 1746." *Hispanic American Historical Review* 83, no. 1 (2003): 53–83.

Walker, Malcolm T. "Power Structure and Patronage in a Community of the Dominican Republic." *Journal of Inter-American Affairs* 12, no. 4 (1970): 485–504.

Walton, William. *Present State of the Spanish Colonies, including a particular report of Hispañola, or the Spanish Part of Santo Domingo.* London: Longman, Hurst, Orme and Brown, 1810.

Webb, Simon. "Masculinities at the Margins: Representations of the *Malandro* and the *Pachuco*." In *Imagination Beyond Nation: Latin American Popular Culture*, edited by Eva P. Bueno and Terry Caesar, 257–58. Pittsburgh: University of Pittsburgh Press, 1998.

Weber, Eugen. *Peasants into Frenchmen: The Modernization of Rural France, 1870–1914.* Stanford: Stanford University Press, 1976.

Weber, Max. *Economy and Society: An Outline of Interpretive Sociology.* Vol. 1, edited by Guenther Roth and Claus Wittich. Berkeley: University of California Press, 1978.

———. "On Class: The Distribution of Power: Class, Status, Party." In *Class*, edited by Patrick Joyce. Oxford: Oxford University Press, 1995.

———. *The Protestant Ethic and the Spirit of Capitalism.* New York: Routledge, 1930.

Wedeen, Lisa. *Ambiguities of Domination: Politics, Rhetoric, and Symbols in Contemporary Syria.* Chicago: University of Chicago Press, 1999.

Weiner, Annette B. *Inalienable Possessions: The Paradox of Keeping-While-Giving.* Berkeley: University of California Press, 1992.

Weismantel, Mary. *Cholas and Pishtacos: Stories of Race and Sex in the Andes.* Chicago: Chicago University Press, 2001.

West, Harry G. "Who Rules Us Now? Identity Tokens, Sorcery, and Other Metaphors in the 1994 Mozambican Elections." In *Transparency and Conspiracy: Ethnographies of Suspicion in the New World Order,* edited by Harry G. West and Todd Sanders, 92–124. Durham, N.C.: Duke University Press, 2003.

White, Luise. "Bodily Fluids and Usufruct: Controlling Property in Nairobi, 1919–39." *Canadian Journal of African Studies* 24, no. 3 (1990): 418–38.

Wiarda, Howard J. *Dictatorship and Development: The Methods of Control in Trujillo's Dominican Republic.* Gainesville: University of Florida Press, 1968.

———. *Dictatorship, Development and Disintegration: Politics and Social Change in the Dominican Republic.* Vols. 1–3. Ann Arbor, Mich.: Xerox University Microfilms, 1975.

———. *The Dominican Republic: Nation in Transition.* New York: Praeger, 1969.

Wiarda, Howard J., and Michael J. Kryzanek. *The Dominican Republic: A Caribbean Crucible.* Boulder, Colo.: Westview Press, 1982.

———. *The Politics of External Influence in the Dominican Republic.* New York: Praeger, 1988.

Widney, J. P. *Race Life of the Aryan Peoples.* Vol. 2. New York: Funk and Wagnalls, 1907.

Wilentz, Sean, ed. *Rites of Power: Symbolism, Ritual, and Politics since the Middle Ages,* Philadelphia: University of Pennsylvania Press, 1985.

Williams, Brackette F. *Stains on My Name, War in My Veins: Guyana and the Politics of Cultural Struggle.* Durham, N.C.: Duke University Press, 1991.

Williams, Raymond. *The Country and the City.* New York: Oxford University Press, 1973.

Williams, Rosalind H. *Dream Worlds: Mass Consumption in Late Nineteenth-Century France.* Berkeley: University of California Press, 1982.

Wilson, Peter J. *Crab Antics: The Anthropology of English-Speaking Negro Societies of the Caribbean.* New Haven: Yale University Press, 1973.

Wolf, Eric R., and Edward Hansen. "Caudillo Politics: A Structural Analysis." *Comparative Studies in Society and History* 9 (1967): 168–79.

Wrigley, Richard. *The Politics of Appearances: Representations of Dress in Revolutionary France.* Oxford: Berg, 2002.

Zaglul, Antonio. *Apuntes.* Santo Domingo: Editora Taller, 1982.

Zeller, Neici. "El régimen de Trujillo y la fuerza laboral femenina en la República Dominicana, 1945–1951." In *La República Dominicana en el umbral del siglo XXI: Cultura, política y cambio social,* edited by Ramonina Brea, Rosario Espinal, and Fernando Valerio Holguín, 429–45. Santo Domingo: Pontificia Universidad Católica Madre y Maestra, 2000.

Zeuske, Michael. "Hidden Markers, Open Secrets: On Naming, Race-Marking, and Race-Making in Cuba." *New West Indian Guide* 76, nos. 3 and 4 (2002): 211–42.

INDEX

Authority: ambiguity in Dominican
Party, 149, 313 n. 71; of Angelita,
131; crisis of cultural, 51; elites' loss
of, 37, 39–40; legitimate, 21, 274
n. 114; love versus, 131; "misrecognition" of, 274 n. 114; Olivorio Mateo's
spiritual, 234–36, 340 n. 39; of party
president, 152; paternalism and,
165–66; Trujillo's loss of, 130, 305
n. 80. *See also* Power
Azules, 14

Bacá (man-made misterio), 214, 218–
19, 220, 336 n. 92
Baez, Buenaventura, 14
Balaguer, Joaquín, 8, 64, 270 n. 40, 300
n. 19, 322 n. 12, 346 n. 125; pan-
egyric by, 161–63, 207, 317 n. 133,
317 n. 134; power aided by, 209–10;
regime of, 349 n. 21; as sent by mis-
terios, 252
Barón del Cementerio, 99, 100
Barrio de Mejoramiento Social, 103
Barrios, 71, 174; autonomy for, 106; po-
lice in all, 91; tíguere and, 174, 185,
193; traditional versus new, 77;
worker, 93, 102, 103–4
Baseball, 44–45
Batista, Fulgencio, 3
Beauty contests, 114–15, 130
Bedia, José, 235
Beer, 45
Benefactor, El, 109, 134, 139, 205, 222,
259–64
Benjamin, Walter, 134
Bhabha, Homi, 53, 203
Bicorn hat, 194, 195–96, 197
Black dandy, 53
"Black legend," 317 n. 134
Black magic, 213
Blackness, 99–100; poverty associated
with, 24, 35, 39, 52; stereotypes of,

189; stigma of, 39, 200, 259; tíguere
and, 189, 190
Blanco, Enrique, assassination of, 2–3
Blanco y Negro (magazine), 32, 36, 54,
283 n. 119
Blau, Peter, 263
Blier, Suzanne Preston, 237
Body: alter-corpus (double), 207, 214–
16; mortal and superhuman, 204–5.
See also Muchachito
Body doubling, 207, 214–16
Body parts of leaders, 206
Body politic, techniques of, 209–17
Bondage, visual metaphor of, 256
Bonó, Pedro Francisco, 15, 47
Bosch, Juan, 229
Bourdieu, Pierre, 133, 226, 259, 263
Brazil, 125–26
Bribery, 7
Bristol-Myers, 63
Brotherhoods, 250, 258
Brown, David, 251
Brown, Karen McCarthy, 237
Brown, Peter, 149
Bureaucracy. *See* Civil service/servants
Bust, 153, 161
Butler, Smedley, 43
Bynum, Caroline, 214

Cáceres, Ramón, 18–19, 27
"calculus of nation," 92
Calvary rituals, 242, 243, 245, 247
Campillo-Pérez, Julio, 4
Cañas y bueyes (Moscoso Puello), 18
Cannadine, David, 21
Cannibalism, 62
Capitalism, 38–40
"Capitán," 5
Caribe, El, 136, 147, 161
Carnival: la Feria, 109, 110, 122–31; in
1937, 114, 115–22
Cars: advent of, 74–75; carriages versus,
74; of SIM, 140

Commemorative coin, 129, 304 n. 78

Commodity: culture, 134; economy of, 226

Commodity wars: caused by U.S. occupation, 35–43; Yankee symbolism in, 44–46

Communism, 143–44

Concealed segmentation, 152

Concentration camps, 2

Concubinage, 134, 201

Confianza, 260

Constitution of 1908, 18–19

Construction, 103, 105; boom, 40; of la Feria, 122, 303 n. 60; of Santo Domingo, 68, 71, 72, 101–2, 289 n. 23, 289 n. 30

Consumption: conspicuous, 40, 56, 128; cosmetics and, 121; fashion and, 178–79; mass culture of, 35–46; power of bacá and, 218–19; respectability through, 41–42; social class defined by, 51; violence and, 219, 335 n. 79

Conuco (garden plot), 72

Corbin, Alain, 96

Coronation: of Angelita, 110, 161; of Virgin of Altagracia, 25–26, 47, 57

Corruption: denunciation of civil service, 157, 315 n. 110; of leader, 318 n. 144

Cosmetics, 120–21, 197, 223, 302 n. 53

Cotton, 43

Coup by Trujillo, 20, 27

Cousins, marriage of, 50, 185

Credit, 10, 78–79, 224

Creole, 53–54; culture of, 35, 39; identity, 24, 230, 266; image of, 46, 54, 55; society of, 200; tíguere as, 174, 190

"Crucifixion" of Olivorio Mateo, 238

Cuba, 28, 36, 124, 215, 232

Cuisine, European, 24

Cultural economy, 22

Cultural taxonomy, middle-class, 38

Culture: commodity, 134; consumption as creating, 35–46; Creole, 35, 39; crisis of cultural authority, 51; dance styles and, 44; of deference, 142; housing as means to elevate, 103; of indebtedness, 10; mestizaje, 200–201, 202, 330 n. 141; nature and, gender represented by, 112; peasantry cultural practices, 34–35; rumor and, 4, 141; of terror, 7, 9, 139–40, 151, 155; tigueraje, 134, 192. See also Popular culture

Culture of reciprocity, of peasantry, 265

Curanderos (herbalists), 34

Currency: cattle as, 128; commemorative coin, 129, 304 n. 78; national, 222; social, 10; U.S. dollar, 43, 47

Customs Tariff Act of 1919, 38

DaMatta, Roberto, 79–80, 118, 301 n. 27

Damirón, Rafael, 192

Dance, 44

Dance of the Millions, 77

Darrieux, Danielle, 180

Daughters, 130; Angelita, 109, 110, 115, 122–31, 161, 175, 299 n. 4; families hiding of, 321 n. 2; Flor de Oro, 113, 173, 175–78, 182, 183, 184, 300 n. 17; pursuit of elite, 115

Davidoff, Leonore, 60

Death, 3, 308 n. 24; culture of fear versus actual, 139–40; death squads, 136–37; method of inflicting, 168; of Olivorio Mateo, 238–39; social, 140–44; of Trujillo, 204–5, 229, 231, 338 n. 17. See also Assassination

Death in Venice (Mann), 265–66

Deceiving Man, The (El hombre allucinado) (Henríquez Castillo), 48–50

Décimas (poems), citizenship practice through gifting, 135–36

Delegates, of Dominican Party, 147

Democracy, 9, 47, 240; divine, 256; tutelary, 275 n. 125

Denunciation, 262, 313 n. 71, 317 n. 134; agency of individual through, 149–50; attire and, 158–59; civil service corruption and, 157, 315 n. 110; of communists, 143–44; Dominican Party context for, 145–46, 169; of favorites, 148; fear of, 155; inquiry into charges, 155; institutionalizing of, 136, 147, 149; local versus state source of, 143–44; main targets of, 142; of mayor, 154, 315 n. 95; Palma Sola alternative to, 248–49; panegyric and, 135–39, 142–43, 160–64, 168, 263; party attendance and, 315 n. 105; party-civil service conflict and, 147–59; peasant grievances vented through, 154–55, 315 n. 95; personal motivations behind, 164–66; polite tone of, 315 n. 105; politics of personhood in, 140–44, 169; practice of, 138; pseudonyms used in, 310 n. 39; questionnaire structure and, 152, 314 n. 85; race or mulatto stigma and, 159; Rama Femenina president and, 166–67, 309 n. 29; repression and, 143, 309 n. 25; rumors and, 141; sample letters of, 135, 170–72; sanctioning of, 147; social status and, 159; truth of accusations in, 141, 155; as witchcraft, 148–49; of women, 166–68; writers of, 136–37

De Olios, María, interview with, 252–54

Deportations, of unemployed, 93

Deren, Maya, 212–13

D'Erzell, Catalina, 122

Dessalines, Jean-Jacques, 196

Development (progress): capitalist, 38–40; dissent stifled by focus on, 106–7; fantasy of, 132; la Feria intended as reflection of, 124; Hurricane Zenón thwarting of, 79; liberal vision of, 31–32; male image and, 62; nouveau riche and, 76–77; occupation and, 30, 62, 277 n. 21; peasantry blamed for lack of, 30, 277 n. 21; Trujillo's use of ideology and, 22, 65

Dewey, John, 31

Diarchy, 210

Diet, 18, 24, 40–41

Disability, 165

Disarmament, mandatory, 92

Disease: "racial disease," 63–64; segregation caused by fear of, 83, 292 n. 73

Dissent, 106–7, 157

Dissimulator, tíguere as, 186–88, 189

Divine intervention, 154, 314 n. 93

Diviners, women, 207–8, 333 n. 21

Divorce, 116, 134; of Rubirosa, 179, 182

Domination, 96, 245–46; confianza mask of, 260; dramaturgical character of, 2; patron-clientelist model for, 216; social class and, 12. *See also* Coercion; Denunciation; Gifts: as means of domination; Repression

Domínguez, Jorge, 20

Dominican National Army, 20

Dominican Party, 9, 113, 154, 301 n. 21; ambiguity in authority of, 149, 313 n. 71; conflict between civil service and, 147–59; denunciation in context of, 145–46, 169; emblem of, 146; factionalism in, 152, 314 n. 85; formation of, 144; inspectors in, 147, 151, 308 n. 23; parties and festivals and, 156–58, 315 n. 105; professionals and party functionaries, 145–47; religious discourses in, 224–25;

Dominican Party (*cont.*)
  sacred palm insignia of, 244; salaries
  of inspectors in, 147, 151, 313 n. 80; as
  shadow state, 144–47, 148, 159, 169,
  320 n. 164; social class and, 144, 145–
  47, 312 n. 58; women in, 166, 167
Dominicans, self-consciousness of, 28–
  32, 193
Doubling, body, 207, 214–16
Douglas, Mary, 36, 83
Drake, Francis, 71
Dreams, 216, 241
Duarte, Juan Pablo, 163
Duke, Doris, 180
Duvalier, François, 23, 207

Economy: census in 1919, 89; colonial,
  200; commodity, 226; construction
  boom and, 40; cultural, 22; freedmen
  and contraband, 188; market, 68;
  monetarization of, 47–57; peasantry
  entering market, 19, 275 n. 125; pre-
  sugar, 71; pre-Trujillo, 13, 15; purchase of all sectors of, 221–22;
  ranching, 15; U.S. occupation influence on, 38, 68
Education, 30–31, 278 n. 24
"Effect of power," 8
Effeminacy, 195, 328 n. 120
Effeminization, 63
Egyptian empire, 132–33
Elias, Norbert, 8
Elites, liberal: cinema taste of, 33, 45;
  diet criticized by, 40–41; hurricane
  meanings for, 67–68; loss of authority, 37, 39–40; luxury goods re-
  monopolized by, 56; mulattos
  viewed by, 31; parlor games of, 45–
  46; popular culture as property of,
  32–34, 45; public presentation of,
  28–32, 193; traditional versus
  nouveau riche, 76

Elites/bourgeoisie, traditional (white):
  consent to coercion by, 92; daughters of, pursuit of, 115; Dominican
  Party and, 144, 145; humiliation of,
  150; Hurricane Zenón and, 76–80,
  84, 86–87, 88; nouveau riche versus,
  76–80; peasantry and poor housing
  viewed by, 88–91; rituals viewed by,
  100; Trujillo viewed by, 193; urban
  development feared by, 79; ven-
  geance toward, 116; women's place
  viewed by, 119–20
Elizabeth I, 109
Employment: Hurricane Zenón abolishing, 93–94; social status and, 158;
  state, 144; threatened loss of, 140,
  262; white-collar, 260
Enemigos de la tierra, Los (The Enemies
  of the Land) (Requena), 70
Ensanche Luperón, 103
Epithets, 5; El Benefactor, 109, 134, 139,
  205, 222, 259–64; feudal, 8; the goat,
  1, 168, 174, 321 n. 2; paternal, 23,
  165–66; populator, 118, 302 n. 42
Equal rights legislation, 58, 285 n. 140
Espinal, Rosario, 4, 23
Espíritu Santo, 25
Ethnic segregation, 200
Etiquette, 8
Europe, immigrants from, 38
Eusebio Sapote, 189
Evans-Pritchard, E. E., 148
Everyday life, 139–40; denunciation and
  panegyric aspects of, 168; meaning
  of money in, 222; most despised
  symbol of, 159
Exile of Trujillo family, 228–29

Fabian, Johannes, 219
Factionalism, 152, 231, 314 n. 85
Family, 23, 113, 300 n. 21, 301 n. 21;
  contradiction of, 114; daughters hid-

Hispanismo/Spanish, 57; imposter and, 193; markers of, 68, 74; of men of work, 23; Mestizo, 189, 196–97, 257–59, 326 n. 81; monetization and, 48–49; mulatto, 52, 159; peasantry and masses given new, 23–24; professional, 146, 159; race and, 24, 159, 272 n. 83, 275 n. 131; slaves' non-identity 201; social class and, 11–12, 23–24, 51, 159, 271 n. 60; U.S. egoism versus Latin American collective, 47. *See also* Image

Illegitimacy, 258, 330 n. 147; mulatto, 223

Image: Creole, 46, 54, 55; Europeanized, 29; gender and, 48, 51–52; of good citizen, 94-95; individual and collective, 214; Liberals' concern with, 28–32; machismo, 111; male, 29, 62, 114; of modern woman, 60; of Olivorio Mateo, 253; of paternalism, 27–28; of public women, 51–52, 94; somatic norm and, 200; sovereign, 164, 205, 318 n. 146; of tíguere, 114–15, 133, 134, 174, 175, 322 n. 12; of women, 44, 51–52, 57–64, 60, 111, 119–20, 130–31. *See also* Identity; Muchachito

Image of Trujillo, 7-8; Hurricane Zenón and, 92; party-civil service conflict and, 153–59; paternal, 23, 165–66; pervasive inscriptions of, 5; popular versus state, 209; satanic, 219; as strong man, 106; as superhuman or transcendent, 204–26; as worker, 81

Immigrants: Haitian, 53; merchant/middle class created by, 36–37, 38

Immigration: sugar industry supported by, 36, 37, 53, 280 n. 50; whitening purpose of, 302 n. 53. *See also* Occupation, U.S.

Imports: cotton, 43; of la Feria costumes, 127; of luxury goods, 46; U.S., 41, 43, 46

Impression, management of, 138

Inauguration of Trujillo, 5–6

Incháustegui Cabral, Héctor, 50

Indebtedness, from gifts, 264–66

Industries. *See* Sugar industry

Infectious disease, fear of, 83

Informants, life histories of, 208

Inquiries into denunciation charges, 155

Inspectors, Dominican Party, 308 n. 23; fear generated by, 151; salaries of, 147, 151, 313 n. 80

Interiors, 101

Interviews of Olivoristas, 208, 251–54, 346 n. 125

Irvine, Judith, 143

Isherwood, Baron, 36

Italy, 36

Jaragua Hotel, 101–2

Jefe, El, 136, 148, 154

Jet set, 1950s, 176, 182, 185, 187–88, 322 n. 20

Jiménez, Ramón Emilio, 35

Joseph, Gilbert, 318 n. 144

Kardec, Alan, 100, 232

Kennedy administration, 204

Kidnapping, 62

Kiley, Brendan, 136

Knots, power of, Olivorio Mateo and, 236–39

Korean War, 123

Krohn-Hansen, Christian, 218

Kubitschek, Juscelino (Brazilian president), 125

Kuznesof, Elizabeth Anne, 202

"La Cuarenta" prison, 2

Lafaye, Jacques, 230

Lancaster, Roger, 111

Land: displacement of, 69; nouveau riche purchase of, 76; partitioning of, 58, 76, 285 n. 140; state disbursement of, 95; U.S. takeover of, 38; unemployed returned to, 93

Land grabbing, 19

Landholders, 15

Las Casas, Bartolomé de, 94–95

Latin America: collective identity of, 47; other authoritarian regimes in, 3; urbanization in cities of, 78

Law: disarmament, 92; divorce, 134; freedmen, 191; marriage, 57–58; martial, 80, 91, 92; paternity, 58; vagrancy, 91, 93, 94

Lears, T. J., 51

Le Bon, Gustave, 30, 96

Ledesma, Aminta, 113

LeFort, Claude, 204

"Legal fantasy," 4

"Legalitus," 4

Legba, 212

Letters of denunciation, 136; response to, 164, 318 n. 146; sample of, 135, 170–72

Levittown, 104

Liberalism, Dominican, 23; crisis of, 47–48, 108; hierarchy vision in, 31–32. See also Elites, liberal

Liborismo/Liboristas. See Olivorio Mateo

Life histories in Trujillo period, 208

Lilís. See Heureaux, Ulises

Lineage of Rubirosa, 176

Listín Diario, 64

Lomnitz, Claudio, 26, 185

López, José Ramón, 31, 40, 89; on peasants in city, 89–90

Los Mina, 71–72

Louverture, Toussaint, 195

Lovatón, Lina (Trujillo's mistress): Angelita versus, 115, 130; as beauty queen, 114–15; carnival of 1937 display of, 114, 115–22; in military costume, 118

Lovatón, Ramón (Lina's father), 115

Love: authority versus, 131; Reign of Love float, 129–30

Lugo, Américo, 15, 16, 30, 70, 108, 309 n. 27

Luhrmann, T. M., 22

Lundius, Jan, 216

Luperón, Gregorio, 14

Luxury goods, import of, 46; elites' remonopolizing of, 56

MacGaffey, Wyatt, 237

Machismo, 111, 186–87

Mafia, 4, 268 n. 17

Magic, 99, 208, 266; black, 213; Haitian, 190, 211, 327 n. 84; of mimesis, 233; modernity and, 207. See also Muchachito

Maguana Arriba (pilgrimage site), 240

Mahmood, Saba, 10

Make-up, 197, 223

Male image, 29, 62, 114

Mann, Thomas, 265–66

Mansions in colonial zone, 291 n. 60

Marassa (twins), 214

Marketplace, 96–97, 97

Marriage, 57–58, 193; cross-cousin, 50, 185; of Rubirosa, 178, 180; serial, 58. See also Rubirosa, Porfirio

Marti, José, 225

Martial law, 80, 91, 92

Martínez, María (Trujillo's third wife), 3, 113, 116, 130

Martínez-Vergne, Teresita, 62

Masculinity: ambivalent, 186–87, 325 n. 64; crisis of, 27–28, 62–63; deference balanced with, 165–66; hypermasculinity, 133–34; official codes of, 165–66; panegyric or denunciation and, 142; subordinate, 165, 319 n. 152; women used to portray, 115. *See also* Tíguere

Massacre: Haitian, 2, 18, 117, 268 n. 11, 308 n. 24; of Olivorismo community, 228–29, 230, 242, 337 n. 6, 338 n. 8, 345 n. 106

Matamoros, Miguel, 97

Mateo, Olivorio. *See* Olivorio Mateo

Materia Prima (Veloz Maggiolo), 11, 271 n. 60

Matos Díaz, Eduardo, 84

Matrifocality, 223

Mauss, Marcel, 264

Mbembe, Achille, 7, 214–15

Medals, 194

Media Luna, 242

Mellizos. *See* Twins

Men: fashion among, 41–42; food handouts denied to, 94; male image, 29, 62, 114; neurasthenia in, 63–64; public, 174–75; women addressing, 122; of work, 23. *See also* Masculinity

Merchant class, 74

Mestizaje culture, 200–201, 330 n. 141

Mestizo identity, 196–97; gift of whiteness to, 257–59; as tíguere, 189, 326 n. 81; transitional nature of, 201

Metamorphosis, 212

Metamorphosis, La (game), 46

Métraux, Alfred, 218

Mexico, 124–25

Meyer, Birgit, 219

Middle class, 136, 306 n. 3; consent to coercion by, 92; cultural taxonomy of, 38; denunciation impact on, 140; Dominican Party membership of, 144, 146; fear of employment loss, 140, 262; immigrants creating, 36–37, 38; lower, 175; panegyric or denunciation and, 168; petty traders as, 48; public women in, 51–52; sugar industry and, 53; womanhood and, 120

Middle East, immigrants from, 38

Migration, 248

Milagro de la Virgen, El (The Miracle of the Virgin), 33

Milan, Lita, 182

Military: barrios given to high-ranking, 103; in colonial period, 195–96; costume of Lovatón, 118; coup, 20, 27, 204-5; expansion of, 2, 3, 6, 126; Heureaux's use of, 16; social status through, 195–96; uniforms, 118, 158, 194, 195–96

Military Intelligence Service (SIM), 139, 140

"Million man march," 6

Mimesis, magic of, 233

Mirabal de Tavárez, Minerva, 317 n. 129

Miracle of the Virgin (*El milagro de la Virgen*), 33

"Misrecognition," 274 n. 114

Misterios: bacá as man-made, 214, 218–19, 220, 336 n. 92; Balaguer as sent by, 252

Mistress, 113, 114–15, 134, 201; Carnival display of, 114, 115–22; common-law, 156; inferior social class of, 289 n. 35; serial family system and, 156, 315 n. 103; virginal, 112, 300 n. 16. *See also* Lovatón, Lina

Mitchell, Timothy, 131, 221

Mobility: of civil servants, 156–57; social, 134, 194–202, 347 n. 1; state control of, 93

Modernity, 123, 249, 260; la Feria as, 124; games as symbols of, 46; magic and, 207; U.S. occupation and, 36

Monetarization: cartoons depicting, 54; literary representations of, 48–50

Slaves, 12–13, 191–92, 218, 250; noni-
dentity of, 201; tigueraje history and,
188–89; Trujillo's family ownership
of, 199–200. *See also* Freedmen
Smith, Lybrand, 29
Social capital, 145
Social class: architecture and, 75–76;
cinema and, 32–34, 278 n. 37; city-
country divide of, 95; of Creoles, 53–
54; "dangerous classes," 30, 104, 191;
denunciation practice and, 154; dissimulator of, 186–88; Dominican
Party and, 144, 145–47, 312 n. 58;
fear of disease and, 83; gender and,
50–51, 111; marketplace and, 96–
97; of mistresses, 289 n. 35; monetarization blurring boundaries of,
47, 50–51; of new public men, 174–
75; nouveau riche, 48, 50, 73, 76–80;
race and, 111, 159, 184–88, 190–91;
segregation of, 68, 72–73, 77, 83,
89–90, 289 n. 30, 292 n. 73; social
mixing of, 79; street life and, 94–97;
sugar industry transformation of,
48–50, 55–56, 73; Trujillo and, 116;
U.S. occupation and, 30, 32–34, 39,
43, 47, 48, 50–51, 53–54, 271 n. 60,
278 n. 37; of wives, 113. *See also*
Identity
Social control, 96, 245–46. *See also*
Domination
Social disgrace, denunciation causing,
140–44
Social disorder, discourse of, 101–6
Social honor, illusion of, 264
Social mobility, 134, 194–202, 347 n. 1
Social relations, 21
Social space, 68, 79–80, 287 n. 8
Social status: attire and, 158–59, 316
n. 117; comparison of in eighteenth
century and nineteenth century, 77–
78; denunciation and, 140–44, 159;

distributing markers of, 258; employment and, 158; mulatto as
marker of, 188; outsider status of
Trujillo, 193; socioeconomic basis of,
200; style versus race basis of, 187–
88, 201
Social Welfare Foundation, 113
Society, high: American, 178; jet set,
184–88; Rubirosa lifestyle in, 176,
322 n. 20; tíguere and, 184–88, 324
n. 46, 324 n. 49, 324 n. 52
Somatic norm, 200
Sommer, Doris, 114
Somoza, Anastasio, 4, 125, 126
Sons: affinal, 203; elder, 1–2, 126, 182,
183, 201, 229, 330 n. 147, 331 n. 156
Sorcery, 12, 207, 241, 248–51, 333 n. 19;
Catholicism and, 214; of peasantry,
34–35
Soviet Union, 142
Spatial segregation, 77–78
Speculation, urbanization driven by, 78
Speeches: vernacular, 138; voluntary,
154; writer of Trujillo's, 207
Spirits, 217–21, 237–39, 254
Squatters, post-hurricane, 80, 86, 87,
88–94
Stalin, Joseph, 22
State: alchemies of, 221–25; crisis of,
231; employment by, 144; fetishisms,
205, 208, 217-21, 226, 336 n. 109;
post-Trujillo, 228–29; shadow, 144–
47, 148, 159, 169, 320 n. 164; theater,
5–6, 153, 206, 221–25, 249, 314
n. 89
State control: expansion of, 147; forms
of, 92–93; mobility under, 93; parties
and festivals under, 156–58; public
health under, 94–97; travel under,
93, 124
Statecraft, 21, 117
Statist approach, 7

15; General (el Generalissimo), 2–12; grandmother, 218; Heureaux compared to, 16; Hurricane Zenón response by, 79–82, 91; loss of authority by, 130, 305 n. 80; military career of, 20; Olivorio as installing, 252; omniscience of, 164, 205, 318 n. 146; Order of Trujillo award, 182, 324 n. 41; Perón compared to, 257–58; prestige, basis of, 184–85; Rubirosa's treatment by, 181–82; social class craved by, 116; two bodies of, 204–26; wedding of, 193; women's relations with, 319 n. 155. *See also* Epithets; *specific topics about*

Trujillo, Ramfis (elder son), 1–2, 126, 182, 183, 201, 203, 330 n. 147, 331 n. 156; leadership of, 229

Trujillo family, exile of, 228–29

Tú, use of, 122

Turgurio (hovel), 102–3

Turits, Richard, 6

Turner, Victor, 99, 101

Tutelary democracy, 275 n. 125

Twins (mellizos), 213, 214, 215, 334 n. 50. *See also* Ventura Rodríguez, Plinio and León

Unemployed, deported to land plots, 93

United States, 6, 7, 182, 229–30; ally of Dominican Republic, 122–23; annexation of Dominican Republic fails, 14; bribing of, 7; dollar, 43, 47, 222; Dominican self-consciousness and, 28–32; egoism of, 47; la Feria and, 124, 132; fiscal control by, 17; imitation of, 132; imports from, 41, 43, 46; invasive role of, 20; Palma Sola rejection of, 248; pre-Trujillo influence of, 19–20; rejection of, 265; sugar controlled by, 17–18, 19,

20, 38; support by, 6, 7; tutelage of, 185. *See also* Occupation, U.S.

Uprisings, 2–3

Urbanization, 52–53, 89–90, 174–75; in Dominican Republic, comparison with Latin American cities, 78; elites' fear of, 79; Hurricane Zenón and, 69, 91; in nineteenth-century, 77–78; speculation as basis of, 78; zoning plan for, 105, 298 n. 179

Urban poor, 71, 102–3

Urban shanties (*ranchito*), 88–91

Ureña, Estrella, 20

U.S. Marines, 28, 34, 185, 224, 231; Olivorio Mateo and, 235, 238; paternal image of, 27–28

Utilitarianism, 26–27

Vagrancy laws, 91, 93, 94

Valentino, Rudolph, 180, 187

Vargas Llosa, Mario, 168

Vásquez, Horacio, 20

Veloz Maggiolo, Marcio: *Materia Prima*, 11, 271 n. 60; *Ritos de Cabaret*, 11, 271 n. 60

Venezuela, 124

Ventura Rodríguez, Plinio and León (twins), 227, 230–31, 240–41, 243; interview with surviving, 251–52, 346 n. 125

Verdi, Giuseppe, 1, 2, 132–33, 173

Vernacular politics, 1–24, 7, 173, 259

Vernacular speech, in Foro Público, 138

Villa Duarte, 72

Villa Francisca, 78–79

Violence: consumption and, 219, 335 n. 79; fear correlated with, 139; gift giving related to, 21–22; savage nature of, 139, 308 n. 23; symbolic, 140, 146; theater of, 2–3

Virgin, 33; abduction of, 112, 300 n. 16

Portions of chapter 3 appeared in "The Dictator's Seduction: Gender and State Spectacle during the Trujillo Regime," in *Latin American Cultural Studies: A Reader*, edited by William Beezley and Linda Curcio-Nagy (Wilmington, Del.: Scholarly Resources, 2000), 213–39; in *Callaloo* 23, no. 3 (2000) 1112–46; and in *La República Dominicana en el umbral del siglo XXI*, edited by Ramonina Brea, Rosario Espinal, and Fernando Valerio-Holguín, 195–214 (Santo Domingo: Centro Universitario de Estudios Políticos y Sociales, Pontificia Universidad Católica Madre y Maestra, 1999); reprinted with permission by Scholarly Resources, Callaloo, and Centro Universitario de Estudios Políticos y Sociales respectively.

An earlier version of chapter 4 appeared as "In the Shadow of the State: The Politics of Denunciation and Panegyric during the Trujillo Regime in the Dominican Republic," *Hispanic American Historical Review* 83, no. 2 (2003): 295–344; reprinted with permission from Duke University Press.

Chapter 6 appeared previously as "The Dictator's Two Bodies: Hidden Powers of State in the Dominican Republic," *Etnofoor* 12, no. 2 (1999): 92–117; reprinted with permission by *Etnofoor*.

Lauren Derby is an associate professor of history at the University of California, Los Angeles.

Library of Congress Cataloging-in-Publication Data
Derby, Lauren Hutchinson.
The dictator's seduction : politics and the popular
imagination in the era of Trujillo / Lauren Derby.
p. cm. — (American encounters/global interactions)
Includes bibliographical references and index.
ISBN 978-0-8223-4486-5 (cloth : alk. paper)
ISBN 978-0-8223-4482-7 (pbk. : alk. paper)
1. Trujillo Molina, Rafael Leónidas, 1891–1961.
2. Dominican Republic-Social conditions.
3. Dominican Republic—Politics and government—1930–1961.
4. Dominican Republic—History—1930–1961. I. Title.
II. Series: American encounters/global interactions.
F1938.5.D463 2009
972.9305'3—dc22 2009010567